Microsoft®

Windows®

7

Faithe Wempen
Lisa Bucki

Paradigm
PUBLISHING
St. Paul • Los Angeles • Indianapolis

Developmental Editor: Spencer Cotkin
Director of Production: Deanna Quinn
Cover and Text Designer: Leslie Anderson
Production Specialists: Jack Ross, Petrina Nyhan
Proofreaders: Lindsay Ryan, Susan Capecchi, Tanya Brown
Indexer: Susan Capecchi
Copy Editor: Lianna Wlasiuk, the aubergine word LLC

Care has been taken to verify the accuracy of information presented in this book. However, the authors, editors, and publisher cannot accept responsibility for Web, e-mail, newsgroup, or chat room subject matter or content, or for consequences from application of the information in this book, and make no warranty, expressed or implied, with respect to its content.

Trademarks: Some of the product names and company names included in this book have been used for identification purposes only and may be trademarks or registered trade names of their respective manufacturers and sellers. The authors, editors, and publisher disclaim any affiliation, association, or connection with, or sponsorship or endorsement by, such owners.

We have made every effort to trace the ownership of all copyrighted material and to secure permission from copyright holders. In the event of any question arising as to the use of any material, we will be pleased to make the necessary corrections in future printings.

ISBN 978-0-76383-732-7

© 2011 by Paradigm Publishing, Inc.
875 Montreal Way
St. Paul, MN 55102
E-mail: educate@emcp.com
Web site: www.emcp.com

Printed in the United States of America

18 17 16 15 14 13 12 11 10 09   1 2 3 4 5 6 7 8 9 10

Brief Contents

Contents

Chapter 15: Securing and Monitoring Your System   475

Chapter 16: Sharing Information On and Off the Road   501

Preface

Windows 7 will help students learn how to operate a computer equipped with the powerful new Windows® 7 operating system. This text presents the essential conceptual information and procedures for students who want to learn how to manage files, secure and customize a computer, and more. Students can use the book without prior knowledge of computer operating systems and become proficient computer users. After successfully completing a course using this textbook, students will be able to:

- Start the system, and log on and off
- Manage disks, folders, and files
- Run applications
- Add and remove hardware and software
- Customize the desktop
- Browse the Web and use e-mail
- Work with several media features
- Work with networking features
- Perform basic security and maintenance tasks

Microsoft® created several editions of the Windows 7 operating system. *Windows 7* covers the Windows 7 Ultimate edition, which offers the broadest feature set of all the editions. Users of any of the other Windows 7 editions can still work with this book, but their edition may not include all of the features covered.

Chapter Features: A Visual Walk-Through

Windows 7 was designed from the ground up to help novice students minimize frustration and maximize successful learning. The book presents concepts and skills in student-friendly language and provides clear steps for using the features of this new operating system from Microsoft.

Page Elements

Chapter pages are designed and formatted with special elements to make it easy for students to find specific types of information. These elements are highlighted below.

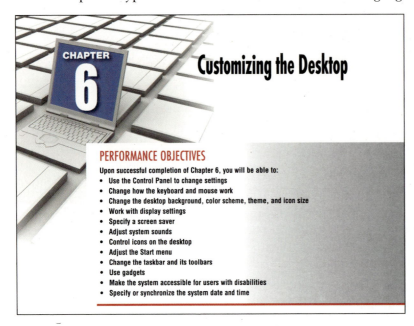

CHAPTER OPENERS present Performance Objectives that students should aim to achieve.

Exercise 5

Working with Gadgets

EXERCISES provide the opportunity for hands-on practice and instructor evaluation.

1. Right-click the desktop and click *Gadgets* to display the Gadget Gallery window.
2. Double-click the Feed Headlines gadget. If your classroom does not have a live Internet connection, choose an alternate gadget if indicated by your instructor.
3. Click the Gadget Gallery window's Close (X) button to close the window.
4. Click *View headlines* in the gadget to start the feed, if necessary.
5. Right-click the Feeds gadget and click *Options*.
6. Open the *Display this feed* drop-down list, and review the available feeds.
7. Press Esc to close the list of feeds and the gadget options.
8. Move the mouse pointer over the upper-right corner of the gadget, so its toolbar appears.
9. Capture a screen shot, paste it into Paint, and save the file as **C06E05S09**.
10. Display the Feeds gadget toolbar, and click the Larger size button.
11. Capture a screen shot, paste it into Paint, and save the file as **C06E05S11**.
12. Right-click the Feeds gadget, and click *Close gadget*.
13. E-mail your screen shots to your instructor or submit them on your USB flash drive, as required.

Align icons to grid: A feature that snaps an icon into alignment with a desktop grid when you move the icon

DEFINITIONS call out key terms in the text.

Auto arrange icons: A feature that arranges desktop icons to fill the desktop grid slots in order

HERE'S HOW steps make it easy to find and review key procedures.

Here's How

To change window color and appearance in Control Panel:

1. Right-click the desktop, and click *Personalize*.
2. Click *Window Color* near the bottom of the window.
3. Click another color at the top of the Window Color and Appearance window.
4. Drag the *Color intensity* slider to make the color more or less intense, as desired.
5. To customize the color, click *Show color mixer*; drag the *Hue, Saturation,* and *Brightness* sliders that appear to adjust the color; and then click *Hide color mixer*.
6. To work with transparency, click the *Enable transparency* check box to turn on (check) or turn off (uncheck) transparency.

7. Click Save changes to apply the new color settings.
8. Click the Close (X) button for the Control Panel window.

A Locked Taskbar
If you can't drag the taskbar, that means it is locked. Right-click the taskbar, and then click *Lock the taskbar* to unlock it. Repeat the process to relock the taskbar after you have dragged it to the desired location.

QUICK FIXES identify common problems encountered by users and provide fast solutions.

NOTES and TIPS present details and shortcuts to enhance understanding and proficiency with Windows 7.

Note: *Because the available gadgets will change over time, you may see different offerings if you click the Fun and games category than the ones shown in Figure 6.21.*

Tip: To remove a gadget that you have downloaded, right-click the gadget in the Gadget Gallery window and click *Uninstall*.

Chapter Review Activities

Each chapter concludes with materials that review key concepts and reinforce newly learned skills.

CHAPTER Summary

- The Control Panel provides a central location for accessing system settings.
- Click Start and then click *Control Panel* to open Control Panel. Click a category icon or link to find lower-level categories of actions, and then click the task to perform. You also can click a category or task in the list at the left side of Control Panel.
- You can adjust such settings as the keyboard repeat rate, the mouse double-click speed, or the functions of the mouse buttons.
- Right-click the desktop and click *Personalize* to find settings for customizing the desktop.
- You can change window colors and transparency, the picture or background on the desktop, screen saver, theme, and system sounds. You also can choose the right resolution and refresh rate for the display (monitor).

CHAPTER SUMMARY recaps vital concepts, commands, and tools presented in the chapter.

CONCEPTS Check

Completion: Answer the following questions on a blank sheet of paper.

Part

1

MULTIPLE CHOICE

1. To change system settings, use the _____ .
   a. Start menu
   b. taskbar
   c. Control Panel
   d. desktop

2. Click the _____ command on the Start menu to access system settings.
   a. Start menu
   b. taskbar
   c. Control Panel
   d. desktop

CONCEPTS CHECK questions assess knowledge recall in both multiple choice and short answer formats.

SKILLS Check

Save all solution files to the default Documents folder, or any alternate folder specified by your instructor.

Guided Check

Assessment

1

SLOW DOWN THE MOUSE AND DISPLAY MOUSE TRAILS

1. Start Control Panel.
   a. Click Start.
   b. Click *Control Panel*.
2. Find Mouse Settings.
   a. Click *Hardware and Sound*.
   b. Click *Mouse* under Devices and Printers.

SKILLS CHECK assessments test skill proficiency, prompting students to complete a variety of tasks using multiple Windows 7 features.

CHALLENGE Project

As a special education teacher, you will be teaching a computer class to high-school students who have a variety of disabilities. You need to prepare specific computers in the computer lab for each student based on his or her unique capabilities.

1. Open WordPad and create a new file named **Student Setup Needs**.

   Imagine that you have three students. Jane cannot see at all. Tim has a disability that makes it difficult for him to use his hands. And Sam has both limited hearing and some trouble using his hands. Type each student's name into the WordPad file.

The final activity, a chapter **CHALLENGE PROJECT**, invites students to apply their skills in completing a project based on a real-world computing scenario.

Student Resources: Internet Resource Center

For some exercises in *Windows 7*, students will need to download files. These Student Data Files can be accessed on the Internet Resource Center for this book, located at www.emcp.net/windows7. In addition to downloading data files for exercises, students will also find study aids, Web links, and tips for using computers effectively in academic and workplace settings.

Instructor Resources

Windows 7 offers a number of resources to help instructors enhance student learning, including an Instructor Resources CD with an **EXAM**VIEW® Assessment Suite, a password-protected Internet Resource Center at www.emcp.net/windows7, and, for distance-learning or hybrid courses, Blackboard coursepaks.

Instructor Resources CD

This CD includes planning resources such as teaching hints and sample course syllabi; PowerPoint slide shows and handouts; assessment resources, including an overview of assessment venues and PDF model answers for intrachapter projects and end-of-chapter exercises; and the **EXAM**VIEW® Assessment Suite with chapter item banks. Most of the content on the Instructor Resources CD is also available on the password-protected instructor side of the Internet Resource Center for this title at www.emcp.net/windows7.

Blackboard Course Content

Blackboard files provide course content, self-quizzes, and study aids and facilitate communication among students and instructors via e-mail and e-discussion.

Acknowledgements

The authors and Paradigm staff would like to thank Lynn Bowen of Valdosta Technical College, Valdosta, GA, and Rob Neilly of the Humber College Institute of Technology & Advanced Learning and the Seneca College of Applied Arts and Technology, both in Toronto, Ontario, for testing the exercises in this book.

System Requirements

This text is designed for the student to complete projects and assessments on a computer running a standard installation of Windows 7 Ultimate. To effectively run this operating system, your computer should be outfitted with the following:

- 1 GHz 32-bit (x86) or 64-bit (x64) processor
- 1 GB of system memory
- 16 GB available hard disk space (32-bit) or 20 GB (64-bit)
- DirectX 9 graphics device with WDDM 1.0 or higher driver

In addition, the following are required to access certain features:

- Internet access (fees may apply)
- Depending on resolution, video playback may require additional memory and advanced graphics hardware
- HomeGroup networking requires a network with at least two PCs running Windows 7
- DVD/CD authoring requires a compatible optical drive
- Music and sound require audio output

Note: *Screen captures in this book were created using 1024 × 768 resolution; screens with higher or lower resolution may look different. The desktop background shown also is not the default for Windows 7 but was selected to provide better images.*

About the Authors

Faithe Wempen, M.A., is an A+ certified PC technician, an adjunct instructor of Computer Technology at Indiana University/Purdue University at Indianapolis, and the author of more than 100 books on computer hardware and software, including *PC Maintenance: Preparing for A+ Certification* (EMC/Paradigm). She writes and teaches online courses in Office applications for clients including HP and Sony, and her articles about Microsoft Office have appeared in *Microsoft OfficePRO* and *Microsoft Office Solutions* magazines.

Lisa A. Bucki is an author, trainer, and publishing consultant, and has been writing and teaching about computers and software for more than 19 years. She has written or contributed to dozens of books and multimedia tutorials covering a variety of software and technology topics including Photoshop, FileMaker Pro and Keynote for the Mac, iPhoto, Fireworks and Flash from Macromedia, Microsoft Office applications, and digital photography. In her consultant and trainer role, Ms. Bucki primarily provides training in the use of Microsoft Project, but has also conducted Word and Excel training courses.

Part 1

Windows® 7

➤ Working with the Windows 7 Desktop

➤ Working with Disks and Other Removable Media

➤ Learning about Files, Folders, and Libraries

➤ Organizing and Protecting Information

➤ Using Windows 7 Programs

➤ Customizing the Desktop

1

Working with the Windows 7 Desktop

PERFORMANCE OBJECTIVES

Upon successful completion of Chapter 1, you will be able to:

- Understand what an operating system does
- Refresh your knowledge of using a mouse or touchpad
- Start Windows 7 and log on to your user account
- Work with essential Windows 7 tools like the Start menu, taskbar, and desktop icons
- Explore new features like Snap, Shake, Aero Peek, and Aero Flip 3D
- Use menus, dialog boxes, and windows
- Create, edit, and remove standard user accounts
- Pause a work session and save power with sleep mode
- Protect information by locking the system when you are away
- Switch users without shutting down
- Restart or shut down the computer
- Browse and search for help or more information

Every time you start your computer, the Windows 7 desktop will greet you. The desktop serves as the gateway for accessing programs and files, viewing e-mail or information on the Internet, and working on a network. Once you have started Windows 7, handy tools such as folder windows make it easy to work with your programs and files. With Windows 7, you can create an account for each user of the computer to better organize and secure information, as well as to enable each person to customize the desktop to his or her own taste. You can take advantage of features that enable you to walk away from your computer and leave it in a secure and power-conserving state, and restart and shut down the system as needed. Finally, Windows 7 Help is there when you need it.

Introducing Your Computer's Operating System: Windows 7

Hardware: Physical computer parts

For most users, what goes on inside a computer system is a mystery. Although you might envision that your computer is stuffed with primitive switches or vacuum tubes or a Rube Goldberg-style system of hamster wheels and sprockets, what you would really see inside the case is a relatively inert collection of system boards and silicon chips with tiny transistors. These physical parts within the computer case are called its *hardware*.

On its own, hardware cannot do much. It needs instructions and information to perform a task. Those instructions and information come in the form of *software* or *programs*. Every computer has to have at least one type of program installed: the operating system (OS). The **operating system** software runs the computer system overall and enables the hardware to work with programs that have more specific purposes, such as word processing programs.

The various versions of Windows operating systems run more computers than any other operating system today. This book teaches you how to use the latest version of the Windows operating system, Windows 7, to work with your computer.

Reviewing Mouse and Touchpad Skills

Even during the process of starting your computer and Windows 7, you will need to know how to use your system's *mouse* or *touchpad* to select and manage items you see on-screen. While you can accomplish some tasks using the keyboard and still others—like typing text—may require keyboard use, a mouse or touchpad provides the easiest, most natural way to accomplish tasks in Windows 7.

A *mouse* is a plastic device that you roll on your desk using your hand. A ball housed in the bottom of a traditional mouse enables you to move the mouse smoothly and with precision. Using a mouse pad under the mouse helps the ball work more reliably than it would if rolled on a smooth surface. Alternate mouse types such as an optical mouse (wireless or wired) or trackball eliminate the need for a mouse pad. Further, a wireless mouse requires no cable connected to the computer.

As you move the mouse, a graphical *mouse pointer* moves on-screen in the corresponding direction and distance. When the pointer arrives over an object that you want to select or work with, you can use one of the buttons on the mouse to accomplish the action you want.

Mobile computers also typically include a pointing device called a *touchpad*. The touchpad appears as a rectangular inset below the keyboard. Dragging your finger on the touchpad moves the mouse pointer. When you have the pointer in position over an object, you can press a button below the touchpad or tap your finger on the touchpad to choose an action.

Windows 7 and programs running in Windows 7 typically all enable the same type of mouse actions. The rest of this book assumes you can perform the following basic actions with a mouse or touchpad:

- **Point.** Drag the mouse or drag your finger on the touchpad until the mouse pointer is over the button, command, or other object you want to select or manipulate. Often when you point to an icon or button, a pop-up description of the item appears. (Some applications call these ScreenTips or ToolTips.)

- **Click.** After pointing to an item on-screen, press and release the left mouse or left touchpad button once, or tap once on the touchpad with your finger. You typically click to select a command from a menu or a choice in a dialog box. In some cases, you also click to select an object on-screen.

- **Double-click.** After pointing to an item on-screen, press and release the left mouse or touchpad button twice quickly. You also can tap twice on the touchpad or press and release the left touchpad button once. Double-clicking typically opens an item; for example, double-clicking an icon might start a program.

- **Right-click.** After pointing to an item on-screen, press and release the right mouse button or right touchpad button once. Some touchpads offer a special "hotspot" area, typically located in a corner, where you can tap to right-click. Right-clicking often displays a shortcut menu like the one that appears in Figure 1.1.

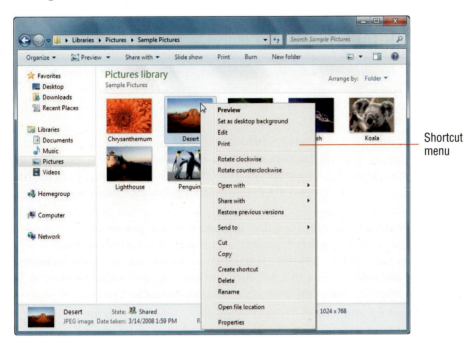

Shortcut menu

Figure 1.1 One of the basic mouse actions, right-clicking, displays a shortcut menu as shown here.

- **Drag.** You often drag to move or resize an on-screen item. With a mouse, point to the item, press and hold the left mouse button, move the mouse until the on-screen item reaches the desired destination or size, and then release the mouse button. A touchpad makes dragging a bit trickier. Typically, you point to the item, double-tap but hold your finger on the pad at the end of the second tap (tap-hold), drag your finger until the item reaches the desired destination, and then lift your finger off the touchpad.

- **Scroll.** Windows and lists often include scroll bars at the right and bottom to help you move additional window or list contents into view. Typically, you scroll by clicking the scroll arrows at either end of the scroll bar on-screen or by dragging the large scroll box in the middle area of the scroll bar. Some mouse models include a scroll wheel between the mouse buttons; with this type of mouse, you can scroll by pointing anywhere on the scroll bar and then rolling the wheel away from you to scroll up or towards you to scroll down. (You cannot use the wheel to scroll left and right.) Some touchpads enable you to scroll by pointing to the on-screen scroll bar, and then dragging your finger along the right edge of the touchpad.

When you point to certain items on-screen or choose a particular tool, the mouse pointer may change shapes. For example, the mouse pointer may change to a double-headed resizing pointer when over a window border or a crosshair (plus sign) after you have selected a drawing tool. The pointer changes shape in this way to indicate that Windows 7 or the program you are working with is ready for your next action.

Touchpad Alternatives
If you don't like using the touchpad on a notebook computer, you can plug in a regular mouse or use a wireless mouse instead. Also, the software that runs the touchpad may offer an option for disabling the touchpad.

Note: *Another type of computer called a tablet PC enables you to work using a pen or stylus rather than a mouse. You can tap and drag with the pen to execute actions like clicking and dragging. You also can use special strokes called flicks to perform navigational and editing tasks. Attaching a graphics tablet device to a desktop or notebook PC enables you to use some pen-based input for mouse tasks and drawing.*

Starting Windows 7

Windows 7 is the *operating system* for your computer. The operating system software enables you to give commands to both the system hardware and other software programs installed on the system. Without an operating system installed, a computer cannot operate.

Because a computer is a relatively expensive piece of equipment that often takes up a lot of space, multiple users may share a single computer. For example, a number of students might share a computer in a school lab, family members might share a computer at home, or coworkers with different schedules might share a computer on the job.

Windows 7 enables you to create a **user account** for each person using a particular computer. When a user logs onto a user account, he or she can customize settings such as the desktop appearance without changing those settings for other users of the system. The user account settings also govern certain activities such as whether a user can edit certain files or install software.

When you start up your computer and Windows 7, you have to log on under your user name. If your user name includes a password, you must enter it as well.

Note: *If your computer connects with a large corporate or campus network, Windows 7 might also prompt you to enter network domain information when you log on. The network administrator can provide the proper domain log on information.*

Logging On

The process for logging on begins with starting or restarting the computer system. Windows 7 displays an introductory screen that shows an **icon** for each user account on the system. You choose the icon for the account to use to log on. After you successfully log on, your Windows 7 desktop appears. Note that when only one user is set up on the system and that user has no password, the desktop will appear immediately.

Logging On with a Password

If you start a system that has a single user with a password or if you click the icon for a user account that has a password assigned at the introductory screen, Windows 7 prompts you to enter the password in the text box below your user name. Because the text box is automatically ready for your user input (a blinking insertion point appears in the text box), type the password. A black dot appears to represent each character you type in the text box. When you log on successfully, your Windows 7 desktop appears.

Here's How ▶ To log on to your Windows 7 user account:

1. Power up the computer. (You also can restart it, if needed, as described later in this chapter.)
2. Click the icon for your user account on the introductory screen.

QUICK FIX

Logon Misstep
Clicking the Switch User button takes you back to the introductory screen rather than continuing the log on process. If you accidentally click this button, restart the process from Step 2, above.

Passwords in Windows 7 are case-sensitive, meaning that you must type the password exactly as it was typed when originally created, including using capital letters for characters originally entered as capitals. If you type the wrong password or make a mistake when you type the password, Windows 7 redisplays the screen with the password prompt, and displays your Password Hint below the text box. Retype your password, and then click the blue right arrow button again to finish logging on.

 ## Exercise 1

Logging On and Working with the Mouse

1. Power on the system.
2. If the introductory screen appears, click the icon for your user name.
3. If you are prompted to enter a password, type your password, and then press Enter or click the blue right arrow button to finish logging on.
4. Move the mouse around or drag your finger around on the touchpad. Notice how the default mouse pointer (an arrow) moves around on-screen in sync with the direction you move the mouse or your finger.
5. Look for an icon named *Recycle Bin* on the screen. Move the mouse pointer over the icon. Note how a lighter highlight appears behind the icon.
6. Right-click on the *Recycle Bin* icon. A shortcut menu appears.
7. Move the mouse pointer away from the *Recycle Bin* icon, and click. The shortcut menu closes.
8. Point to the *Recycle Bin* icon, and drag it down and to the right. A picture of the icon appears behind the mouse pointer as you drag. (Remember, on a touchpad you have to double-tap and hold your finger on the touchpad at the end of the second tap to begin dragging.)
9. Release the mouse button, and the *Recycle Bin* icon appears in its new position.
10. Drag the *Recycle Bin* icon back to its original location.

QUICK FIX

Cannot Move Icon
If you can't move the icon as described in Steps 9 and 10, right-click away from the icon, point to *View* in the shortcut menu, and then click *Auto arrange icons* to uncheck it.

Using the Windows 7 Interface

All the work you do in Windows 7 begins from the Windows 7 **desktop**: working with files, using programs, searching for information, browsing the Web, customizing your system, and so on. Just as you can have multiple file folders for

Desktop: The starting point for activities in Windows 7, where you also can view and organize information

in-process projects lying on your physical desktop, Windows 7 enables you to **multitask** and have multiple activities underway on your computer desktop. For example, you can have two programs open and switch back and forth between them, print from one of the programs, and then view information from the Internet—all without needing to close any of the open programs.

Figure 1.2 shows the Windows 7 desktop and the most important elements that appear there by default. Your desktop might look slightly different than the one pictured in Figure 1.2. For example, your system might have an image displayed on the desktop, or you might have different icons resulting from a previous Windows installation. Despite such minor differences, the steps you use to work with the Windows 7 desktop remain consistent, and the rest of this section teaches you the essential steps you need to learn to work in Windows 7, starting with using the Start button and Start menu.

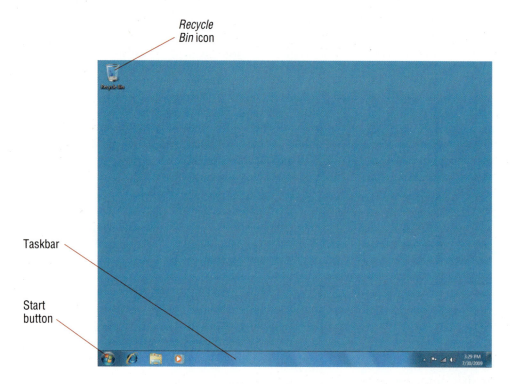

Figure 1.2 Start all of your activities in Windows 7 from the desktop.

Using the Start Menu

As its name implies, the Start menu enables you to start up or launch programs (applications) installed on Windows 7. In addition, Windows 7's Start menu enables you to access system settings, get Windows 7 help, open folders to view files, shut down the system or put it in a power-conserving state, and log off or switch users. In addition, the Windows 7 Start menu enables you to search for files and programs.

Figure 1.3 shows the Windows 7 Start menu, which you can open by clicking the Start button in the lower left corner of the desktop or by pressing the Windows logo button on your computer's keyboard. The menu is divided into several areas offering different types of selections, while the area near the bottom of the menu offers additional controls for performing specific operations.

Figure 1.3 **The Start menu enables you to launch programs, access Windows 7 system features, and perform other operations like shutting down the system.**

The name of the user currently logged on to the system appears at the top of the darker right portion of the menu. You can click that user name to display your personal folder. The three items listed below—Documents, Pictures, and Music— are the user's *libraries*, designated to manage *files* created or obtained by that user only. The two sections below the user's libraries (set off by divider lines) offer links to other features and settings in Windows 7. For example, the *Help and Support* choice opens a window where you can browse for or search for help. Clicking a choice in any of the areas on the right side of the menu immediately opens that area, such as the Games folder.

The left side of the menu offers three overall features. First is a list of programs. The programs you see initially may vary depending on how your computer was set up. By default, the list is dynamic and changes to reflect the programs that you use most frequently. Clicking a program in the list starts the program. One way that you can control which programs appear on the list is to *pin* a program to the Start menu. You will learn how to pin a program to the Start menu in Chapter 3.

Use the *All Programs* choice to browse and select a program or Windows feature to start. When you click *All Programs*, the Start menu changes (see Figure 1.4) to show commonly used Windows 7 applications, as well as folders where you can find additional programs and features. The folders you see on your system will vary depending on the programs installed. For example, Figure 1.4 shows a folder for Microsoft Office, which holds the programs that are part of the Microsoft Office software suite. (The folder name is in a highlighted color because the programs were just installed.) Clicking a folder displays the choices held in the folder. Clicking any listed program launches the program.

Library: A location for working with a particular type of file; each library may monitor a number of storage locations to identify and track a particular type of file such as a digital picture

File or document: Digital information that you create and save with a name for later retrieval; a file may include programming instructions, an image, text, or any other type of content

Pin: Designating an item such as a program or file to appear in the left column of the Start menu, for easy access

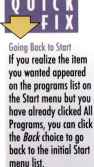

QUICK FIX

Going Back to Start
If you realize the item you wanted appeared on the programs list on the Start menu but you have already clicked All Programs, you can click the *Back* choice to go back to the initial Start menu list.

Figure 1.4: After you click *All Programs*, the Start menu lists additional programs and features that you can click to start.

Here's How ▶ To start a program from the Start menu:

1. Click the **Start** button on the desktop or press the Windows logo key on the computer keyboard.
2. If the program appears in the listing of frequently used programs at the left side of the Start menu, click the program name. If the program does not appear, click *All Programs*.
3. If needed, click the folder that holds the program or Windows 7 feature to start. The programs in that folder appear in the Start menu list.
4. Click the program name.

If you know the name of the program you want to start, a file you want to open, or a Windows 7 feature that you want to work with, you do not even have to use the efficient Start menu to find it. The convenient search box enables you to search for programs and files directly from the Start menu. When the Search finishes and the program or file name appears in the Start menu, you can open it from there.

To search for and open a program, feature, or file from the Start menu:

1. Click Start or press the Windows logo key on the keyboard.
2. Type the name of the program or file to search for. The menu lists matching programs and files as you type.
3. Click the program or file to open.

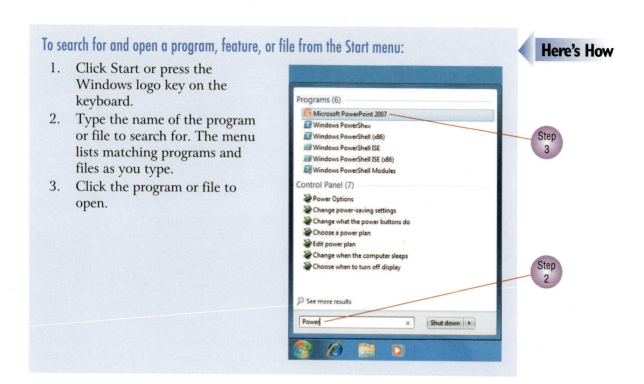

Step 3

Step 2

Note: *You will learn more details about exiting an open program in a later chapter. For now, if you need to close a program, you can press Alt+F4 or click the Close (X) button in the upper right corner of the program window.*

You can use the Shut down button and its accompanying arrow button to put the system in a power-conserving state, change the current user, and more. The later section called "Pausing or Finishing Your Work Session" covers these buttons in greater detail.

Capturing a Screen Picture to Complete an Assignment

This book includes both exercises within the text and assessments at the end of each chapter. Your instructor may require you to demonstrate that you have successfully completed an exercise or assessment by capturing a picture of your Windows 7 screen, and then e-mailing and/or printing the picture or providing it on a USB flash drive (also called a thumb drive). You might want to flag this page in the book with a sticky note so that you can refer to these steps whenever you need to provide a screen shot to your instructor.

To capture, save, and print a picture of the computer screen:

1. Complete the steps required to come to the point in the exercise or assessment where you need to shoot a picture of the screen.
2. Press the Print Screen key, which is commonly found to the right of the F12 key at the top of the keyboard. This key might have an abbreviated name, like PrtSc. Some systems may require you to press the Shift key along with Print Screen (Shift+Print Screen). If you are using a mobile computer, you will typically have to press a function (fn) key along with Print Screen (fn+Print Screen).
3. Click Start.

Here's How

Making Printouts a Single Page

If the Paint printout is more than one page, click the Paint menu button, point to *Print*, and click *Page setup*. Under Scaling, click the Fit to option button, specify that the printout should be *1 by 1 pages*, and click OK. Then reprint.

4. Type Paint in the *Search* text box.
5. Click *Paint* in the list of programs that appears.
6. Press Ctrl+V. This shortcut pastes the image into the Paint application.
7. Press Ctrl+S. The Save As dialog box opens.
8. Type the file name specified by the exercise or assessment. It will appear in the *File name* text box. Choose PNG or JPEG as the *Save as type*, and navigate to the folder location specified by your instructor.
9. Click Save. This saves the file. If your instructor wants you to submit the file by e-mail, ask the instructor for instructions about how to do so.
10. Press Ctrl+P.
11. Click the printer to use (as indicated by your instructor) in the *Select Printer* area, and then click Print. Label and submit the hard copy to your instructor as directed.
12. Press Alt+F4 to exit Paint. Always exit Paint after saving and printing a screen shot unless instructed to do otherwise in the steps in this book.

Note: *Windows 7 includes a new program called the Snipping Tool that you also can use to take a screen shot of some or all of what you see on the desktop. You will learn about using the Snipping Tool in Chapter 5. You can use the Snipping Tool in place of the above instructions if you are comfortable with it and your instructor approves of that technique.*

Using the Taskbar

Taskbar: A bar at the bottom of the desktop that you use to manage active tasks

The **taskbar** appears along the bottom of the desktop by default. You can use the tools on this bar (shown in Figure 1.5) to start tasks (programs and files) and manage active tasks. You saw earlier that the Start button appears at the far left end of the taskbar.

Pinned items   Buttons for active tasks   Notification area   Show desktop button

Figure 1.5 The taskbar includes icons for launching programs and a button for each active task.

The other tools that reside or appear on the taskbar include the following:

*   **Pinned items.** A group of icons appears on the taskbar immediately to the right of the Start button. Clicking an icon here starts the associated program, such as the Internet Explorer Web browser. Clicking the second icon, with the file folder on it, opens a window that shows you the Libraries window. Libraries are discussed more later in this chapter. You can pin and unpin programs to the taskbar as necessary.
*   **Task buttons.** When you start a program or open a document, a task button for the program or document appears on the taskbar. You can click a button to open the window for a particular task. See the later section, "Moving Between Windows," to learn more.
*   **Show desktop button.** The new Aero Peek features include the ability to display a temporary preview of the desktop, temporarily hiding open windows.

Click the Show desktop button at the right end of the taskbar to hide open windows, and click the button again to redisplay them. Holding the mouse pointer over the Show desktop button makes open windows transparent, and moving the pointer off the button returns the windows to their normal appearance.

- **Notification area.** Also sometimes called the system tray, this area at the far right end of the taskbar provides icons that you can use to show the status of certain system functions, like a network connection or battery power, as well as icons that you can use to manage certain programs and Windows 7 features, like Action Center Alerts. The Show hidden icons button appears to the left of the icons. Click that button to display hidden icons. Right-click any icon in the notification area to see a shortcut menu for working with that program or feature.

Note: *The taskbar appears on-screen by default. Chapter 6 will explain how you can hide the taskbar if you prefer.*

Note: *Aero Peek is part of the Aero desktop experience available in all but the Starter edition of Windows 7. Aero includes other features such as glass, or transparency, in some parts of windows.*

The icons for Windows 7 features often give the status of system functions, such as a network connection. To view the status of a function, point at the function's icon with the mouse. A pop-up tip like the one shown in Figure 1.6 appears, giving the status information. If you click such a function icon, an enlarged window like the one in Figure 1.7 appears. This window includes the status information as well as one or more links that you can click to display and change settings for that system function.

Note: *The icons that appear in the notification area will vary depending on the software, hardware, and active Windows 7 features on your system, so the icons you see on your desktop may be different than those that appear in Figures 1.6 and 1.7.*

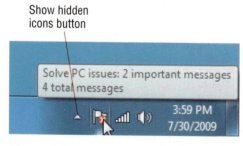

Show hidden icons button

Figure 1.6 **Pointing to one of the icons in the notification area provides status information.**

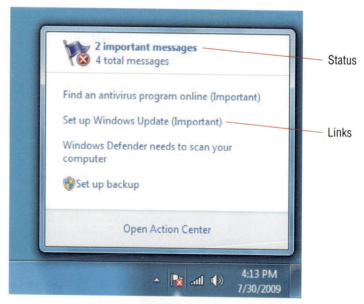

Status

Links

Figure 1.7 **Clicking one of the icons in the notification area provides status information, plus one or more links that you can use to change settings.**

When you right-click an icon in the notification area, a shortcut menu displays choices for working with the program or feature. The shortcut menu for a program in the left grouping (see the top of Figure 1.8) typically includes choices for opening the program in a window or exiting the program. The shortcut menu for a feature in the right grouping (at the bottom in Figure 1.8) may include choices for changing program settings or choices for working with Windows features and hardware.

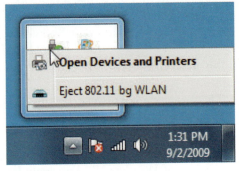

Figure 1.8 Right-clicking a notification area icon displays a shortcut menu.

Here's How

QUICK FIX

Closing a Shortcut Menu
Press Esc to close a shortcut menu if you decide not to click a command in it.

To work with a program or feature in the notification area:

- Point to an icon to see a pop-up status window.
- Click a system function icon to see a window that includes status information and links you can click to display and change settings for that function.
- Right-click the feature's icon in the notification area. Or, click the Show hidden icons button, and then right-click an icon. Click a command in the shortcut menu that appears, such as the *Exit* choice to exit a program or a choice for changing a feature setting or starting a feature.

Notification: A message that pops up in the notification area to warn you about a situation that may require action or a settings change

In addition to the icons that appear in the notification area, at times an actual ***notification*** like the one shown in the top of Figure 1.9 will pop up. Click in the notification message to open a window where you can learn more or change settings related to the notification. These notifications deal with issues such as security settings; later chapters of the book teach you how to work with settings like these. As the right image in Figure 1.9 illustrates, in some cases, an icon will change in appearance to let you know there's a problem. For example, a yellow starburst appears on the icon for networking if the connection is not working properly.

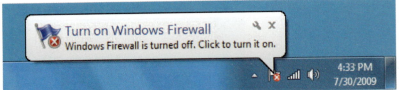

Figure 1.9 A notification can be a pop-up balloon in the notification area. Icon appearance also can change to communicate a problem.

Using a Jump List Windows 7 includes a new feature called *Jump Lists*. A Jump List for a program shows you documents that you have opened recently and, in some cases, common commands. The contents of a Jump List will vary depending on what you do with a program or what features the program offers. You can open a Jump List from either the taskbar or Start menu. Right-click a taskbar icon to see its Jump List, or click the right arrow to the right of a program's name on the Start menu. Once the Jump List is open, click a file to open it or a command to execute it. Figure 1.10 illustrates taskbar and Start menu Jump Lists.

Jump List: A menu of frequently used documents and commands that you can access for a program via the taskbar or Start menu

Jump List

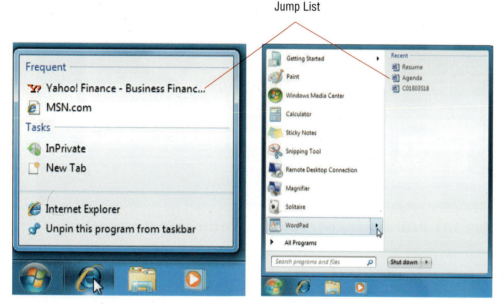

Figure 1.10 Jump Lists provide quick access to favorite files or commands.

To use a Jump List:

- On the taskbar, right-click an icon, and then click the desired document or command in the Jump List that appears above the icon.
- In the Start menu, click the arrow button that appears to the right of the program name, and then click the desired document or command in the Jump List that appears to the right.

Here's How

Using Aero Peek to Preview an Open Item Aero Peek also enables you to take a look at the contents of open folders or open documents for a program without closing the window that you are currently working in. To start, move the mouse pointer over the program's icon in the taskbar. As shown in Figure 1.11, large thumbnails for the open items appear above the taskbar icon. You can then move the mouse pointer over one of the thumbnails to preview it in its larger window, or click a thumbnail to switch to that document.

Figure 1.11 **Hover the mouse over a taskbar icon to take a peek at open windows.**

Here's How

To preview an open document from the taskbar:

1. Move the mouse pointer over the program icon on the taskbar.
2. Move the mouse pointer over a thumbnail in the preview to preview the document's fully opened window.
3. Click a thumbnail to switch to that document, or move the mouse pointer off the thumbnail, back over the desktop or another document window, to close the preview.

Selecting Icons, Buttons, and Other Items

The mouse provides the most quick and convenient way to make selections in Windows 7 and most programs that run in Windows 7. Whether you are working on the desktop, in a window, or in an application, selection techniques remain consistent:

Selected icon

Figure 1.12 **Click an icon to select it.**

- To select an icon, click it once with the mouse. A highlight appears around the icon, as shown in Figure 1.12. You also can drag over multiple icons to select them.

- To open a file or application, double-click its icon. Opening a file starts the application in which it was created and opens the file in that application.

- To select text in a document, Web page, or Help window for copying or editing, drag over the text. A highlight appears behind the text, as shown in Figure 1.13.

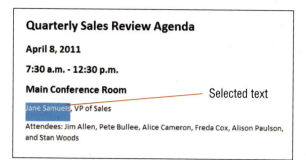

Quarterly Sales Review Agenda

April 8, 2011

7:30 a.m. - 12:30 p.m.

Main Conference Room ——————— Selected text

Jane Samuels, VP of Sales

Attendees: Jim Allen, Pete Bullee, Alice Cameron, Freda Cox, Alison Paulson, and Stan Woods

Button toggled on

Figure 1.13 Drag over text to select it.

Figure 1.14 Click a toolbar button to select it.

- To select a button on a toolbar in Windows 7 or in an application, click the button. Note that some buttons *toggle* a feature on and off (that is, turn the feature on and off). When you click the button to turn the feature on, it will take on a pressed in or colored appearance, like the example in Figure 1.14, to show you that the feature is active. Click the button again to toggle the feature off.

Toggle: A command or feature that can remain in an "on" (toggled on) or "off" (toggled off) state

 Exercise 2

Using the Start Menu and Taskbar

1. Power on the system and log on, if the system is not still on from the last exercise.
2. Click Start, and then click *All Programs*.
3. Leaving the Start menu open, use the Print Screen function as described earlier to take a screen shot. Use Paint as described earlier to save the file as **C01E02S03**. Submit the file to your instructor as a printout or e-mail attachment or on a thumb drive, and close Paint. Consult your instructor if you have any questions about saving, printing, or e-mailing the file.
4. Click Start, click *All Programs*, click *Accessories*, and then click *WordPad*. The WordPad application starts, displaying a blank document.
5. Click Start, and then click *Documents*. A window holding your Documents library appears. There may or may not be folder and file icons in the Documents folder.
6. Click Start. Type Internet in the *Search* text box, and then click *Internet Explorer* in the Programs list that appears. If Internet Explorer is not the default browser, click Yes or No when prompted.
7. Click the tab that appears to the right of the tab for the home page that opened. This displays a new tab with the address box text selected.
8. Type smithsonian.org in the box, and then press the Enter key.
9. After the page loads, click the *WordPad* icon on the taskbar.
10. Move the mouse pointer over the *Internet Explorer* icon on the taskbar and leave it there.
11. Use the Print Screen function to take a screen shot. Use Paint as described earlier to save the file as **C01E02S11**. Submit the file to your instructor as a printout or e-mail attachment, or on a thumb drive and close Paint. Consult your instructor if you have any questions about saving, printing, or e-mailing the file.
12. Right-click the *Internet Explorer* icon on the taskbar, and then click *Close window* in the Jump List.
13. Click the Close all tabs button in the message box that appears.
14. Leave the Documents library and WordPad windows open for a later exercise.

Working with Other Menus

So far, you have seen and worked with both the Start menu and shortcut menus. In Windows 7 and in other applications, you will encounter other types of *menus*. Some menus open when you click a menu name on a menu bar. Others open when you click a button on a toolbar or command bar.

Menu: A list of commands

Clicking one of the ***commands*** listed on a menu tells Windows 7 or the application to perform that command. You can tell whether the command will be performed directly or whether you have to take further action based on the command's appearance on the menu:

- **Command name only.** When the command name appears by itself on the menu, clicking the command in the menu executes the command immediately.

- **Command with a right arrow (triangle) beside it.** As shown in Figure 1.15, pointing to or clicking a command with a right arrow to the right of the command name displays a submenu. Click a command in the submenu to execute it.

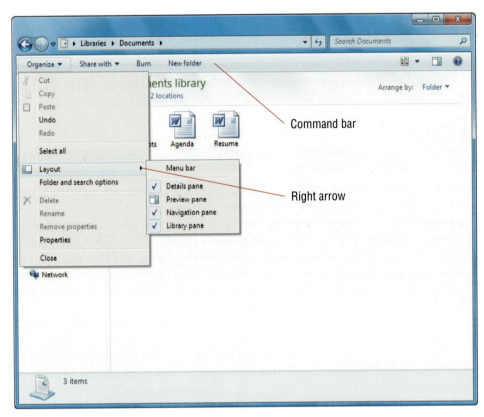

Figure 1.15 **A triangle beside a command indicates that a submenu will appear when you click or point to the command.**

- **Command with an ellipsis (...) beside it.** Figure 1.16 illustrates a Notepad menu with an ellipsis beside several of the commands. Clicking a command with an ellipsis opens a dialog box. Use the dialog box choices (described in the later section, "Working with Dialog Boxes") to provide more details about how Windows 7 or the program should complete the command.

> **Tip:** Figure 1.16 shows that some commands have a keyboard combination such as Ctrl+P beside the command name. You can press that combination, often called a keyboard shortcut, to execute the command directly without using the menu. For example, you can press Ctrl+P to open the Print dialog box in many applications.

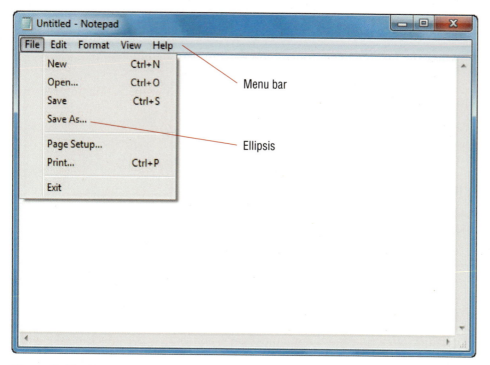

Figure 1.16 Clicking a command with an ellipsis opens a dialog box.

- **Command with a check mark.** When a command has a check mark to the left of the command name, that command toggles on and off when you click it. Clicking the command when it is checked removes the check and toggles the command off, while clicking the command when it is unchecked rechecks it and toggles the command on. As shown in Figure 1.17, many commands that control window features toggle on and off.

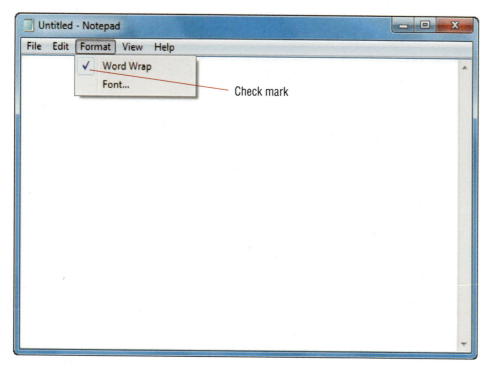

Figure 1.17 A check mark indicates that a command toggles on and off when you click it.

To choose a menu command:

1. Click the menu name or button on a menu bar or command bar.
2. Click the desired command.
3. If a submenu appears, click the desired command in the submenu.
   If a dialog box appears, make choices in the dialog box to refine the command's behavior as desired, and then click OK.

Working with a Ribbon

Ribbon: An enhanced tabbed toolbar, where each tab offers commands for a particular overall activity and groups commands for more specific activities

Dialog box launcher: A button found in the lower-right corner of a group on a Ribbon tab that you click to open a dialog box

Some applications—notably the WordPad and Paint applications in Windows 7 and the applications in the recent version of the Microsoft Office suite—use a newer type of interface called a **Ribbon**. The Ribbon replaces the menu bar, and organizes related commands on tabs. Each tab further collects related commands in various groups. Figure 1.18 shows the Ribbon in WordPad. To display the commands on one of the tabs, click the tab. The far left "tab" in Figure 1.18 actually is called the WordPad menu button, and clicking it opens commands for working with files; this arrangement where the first tab opens a file menu is also found in Paint. Note that the "commands" on each of the other tabs can take a variety of formats; in addition to buttons, there are other types of tools like those found in dialog boxes, which you will learn about next. Some buttons are even divided into two parts, where clicking the upper part gives the command, while clicking the lower part (usually labeled with a down arrow) opens a list or menu with additional choices. The lower-right corner of some groups also offers a small button called a **Dialog box launcher**. Clicking a Dialog box launcher opens a dialog box with more detailed settings for a particular activity. Finally, the Quick Access Toolbar above the Ribbon offers buttons for the most commonly used commands, such as saving the file.

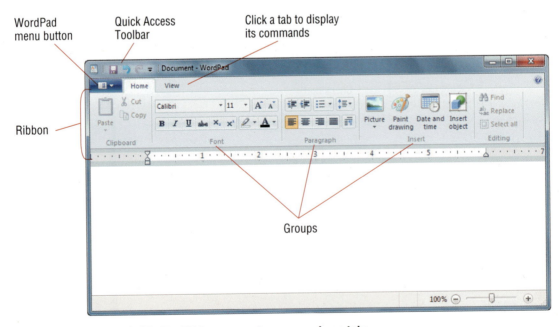

Figure 1.18 The Ribbon presents commands on tabs.

Here's How

QUICK FIX

Can't See a Ribbon Choice
The items visible on a Ribbon tab will vary depending on the window size. If you can't see a Ribbon choice that you need, maximize the window as described later in the chapter to ensure the choices are visible. If that doesn't work, increase your screen resolution, as described in Chapter 6.

Tip: You can hide the Ribbon to open up more space on-screen for working with the current file. To hide the Ribbon in an application, press Ctrl+F1. Press Ctrl+F1 again to redisplay it.

Working with Dialog Boxes

Dialog boxes in Windows 7 and Windows 7 applications use fairly standardized *controls* to enable you to provide specific details about how a command should execute. For example, if you are working with text in a document and you have chosen a command for formatting that text, a Format dialog box might appear. That dialog box might have a list of fonts (letter styles) that you can apply, a list of styles like italics that you can apply, a box where you can type a new size for the text, other controls for applying special effects, or an area where you can choose a color for the text. A dialog box might arrange similar choices in a named group, or might include tabs or sheets that group information.

After you make your choices in a dialog box, click the OK button to apply your changes. If you decide not to follow through with the changes, click Cancel. Here is a review of the most common dialog box controls and how to use them.

Figures 1.19 and 1.20 show how many of these controls look in a dialog box.

- **Tab**. Click a tab or sheet to display its group of controls in the dialog box.
- **Drop-down list or palette.** Click the drop-down list arrow (right arrow) to open the list, and then click a choice in the list. Rather than a drop-down arrow, the dialog box may offer a Palette button that you click. If the list is lengthy, it may include a scroll bar, and you can click the scroll arrows on the scroll bar to see additional choices. If clicking opens a drop-down palette of choices, such as color choices, click the desired choice in the palette.

Controls: The various types of selection mechanisms in a dialog box

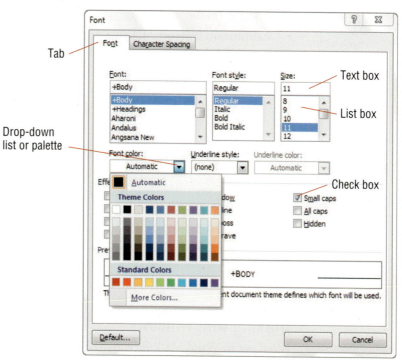

Figure 1.19 **Formatting dialog boxes often include a variety of controls.**

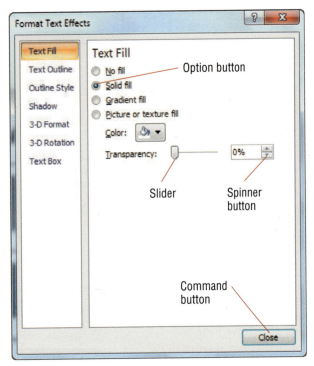

Figure 1.20 **The available controls vary depending on the dialog box purpose.**

- **Check box**. When a check mark appears in a check box, that control is active or selected. You can click any check box to check or uncheck (deselect) it as needed. When multiple check boxes appear in a dialog box, each one operates independently, and they can be checked or unchecked in any combination.

- **List box**. A list box includes a scroll bar at the right. Click the scroll arrows on the scroll bar to see additional choices, and then click the desired choice. As shown in Figure 1.19, a list box (or a drop-down list) may include a text box where you can type in an entry rather than choosing from the list.

- **Text box**. You type a value or other entry such as a file name into a text box. If the text box contains a previous entry, drag over it to select it, and then type a replacement entry. If the text box has an accompanying list, choosing one of the list items automatically fills in the text box.

- **Spinner buttons**. You can click the small up or down arrow button to change the value in the accompanying text box. If you prefer, you can instead drag over the value to select it, and then type a new value to replace it.

- **Option buttons**. Option buttons are mutually exclusive. Only one option button in a group can be selected or active at a time. Click an option button to select it (make it active).

- **Command buttons**. Click a command button to continue or apply it immediately. In many dialog boxes, for example, you must click an OK button to apply the changes you have made in the dialog box and close the dialog box.

- **Slider**. Some dialog boxes include a slider control than enables you to set a value or the intensity of a change. Drag the thumb or handle on the slider to change the value.

Here's How To use a dialog box:
1. Click the tab that holds the settings to change, if needed.
2. Make changes to the desired control settings.
3. Repeat Steps 1 and 2 to make changes on other tabs.
4. Click OK to apply your choices. Or, click Cancel to close the dialog box without applying the command.

Working with Windows

Window: An independent frame that holds a program, document, or folder contents

Windows in Windows 7 provide the capability to multitask. You can have a letter open in a word processing program in one window, a digital photo open in an image editing program in another, and a Web page open in a browser in another. You can switch between the windows at will, and you can adjust the size and position of any window as needed to enable you to work most efficiently. When you finish working with the contents of a window, you can close it to clear it off your desktop.

Minimizing and Redisplaying a Window

Minimizing a window reduces it to a button on the taskbar. The program in the window continues to run, and any file open in the window remains active, too. In this way, minimizing enables you to set a program or file aside temporarily while you work on other tasks. When you need to revisit the minimized program or file, you can open it more quickly from the taskbar than opening it from scratch from the Start menu or a folder window.

Minimize: Reduce a window to a taskbar icon to clear it from the desktop temporarily

> Tip: If you are working in some applications, you can open multiple files in the application and minimize each file within the application window as well.

You can use one of a variety of techniques to minimize a window. One of the most common techniques is clicking the Minimize button at the right end of the *title bar* at the top of the window (see Figure 1.21). You also can use shortcut menus to both minimize and redisplay a window. Windows 7 also includes a new feature called *Shake* that you can use to minimize all open windows except the one you want to focus on. Move the mouse pointer over the window that you want to focus on, and then drag back and forth quickly to simulate a shaking motion. Any other windows that are open will be minimized.

Title bar: The bar at the top of a window that lists the program name, as well as the name of any open file, and has controls for working with the window

Shake: A feature that enables you to minimize several open windows at once by dragging the title bar for the window you want to keep open side to side at a rapid pace

Title bar   Minimize button

Minimized file

Figure 1.21 **Click the Minimize button on the window title bar to minimize a window, or use a shortcut menu.**

To minimize a window:

- Click the Minimize button at the right end of the title bar.

OR

- Right-click the window title bar, and then click *Minimize*.

OR

- Right-click the window's taskbar button, and then click *Minimize*.

OR

- Drag the title bar for a window that you want to leave open from side to side quickly, which minimizes all other open windows.

To redisplay a window:

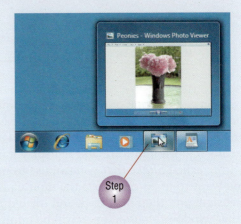

1. Point to the taskbar button for the minimized window. An *Aero Peek thumbnail* appears so that you can preview the window contents to verify that you are redisplaying the correct window.
2. Click the taskbar button to redisplay the window. Or, if multiple thumbnails appear, click the thumbnail for the window that you want to redisplay.

Step 1

Aero Peek thumbnail: A thumbnail image of a file that pops up when you point to the minimized file's taskbar button

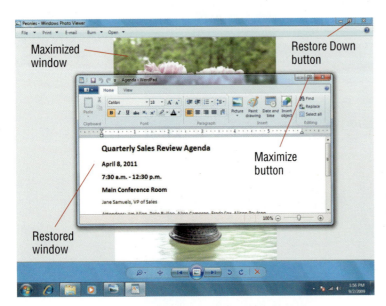

Figure 1.22 Maximize a window to have it fill the screen. Restore a window to return it to its prior (less-than-maximized) size.

Maximize: To increase a window to full-screen size

Restore: To return a window to its size before it was maximized

You learned earlier about the Show desktop button at the far right end of the taskbar. Showing the desktop temporarily minimizes all open windows to taskbar buttons. Use this handy new feature when you want to go directly to the desktop without the need to minimize open windows one by one.

Maximizing and Restoring a Window

When you really need to focus on the contents of the file that you are working on, or when you need to see as much of a program or file on-screen as possible, you should *maximize* the window that contains that file or program. As the name suggests, maximizing increases the window to fill the full area available on-screen, as illustrated in Figure 1.22. When you want to return the window to a smaller size so that you can see other information on-screen in addition to the window, you can *restore* the window.

Just as each window title bar includes a Minimize button, Maximize and Restore Down buttons appear as well so that you can perform those tasks on the window. You also can use shortcut menus to maximize and restore files. A new feature called

Snap also enables you to maximize a window by dragging it toward the top of the desktop. Move the mouse pointer over the window's title bar, drag up until a preview outline of the full-sized window appears, and then release the mouse button.

Here's How

To maximize a window:

- Click the Maximize button on the window title bar.

OR

- Right-click the window title bar, and then click *Maximize*. Or, point to the taskbar button, and then right-click the window's preview thumbnail and click *Maximize*.

OR

- Drag the window by its title bar to the top of the screen, and release the mouse button when the full-screen-sized preview outline appears.

Snap: A feature that enables you to maximize or resize a window automatically by dragging the window to the edges of the screen

Tip: When a single document is open for an application, you can minimize and maximize its window simply by clicking its taskbar button.

Here's How

To restore a window:

- Click the Restore Down button on the window title bar.

OR

- Right-click the window title bar or the taskbar button for the window, and then click *Restore*.

Tip: A maximized window has the Restore Down button on the title bar, and a restored window has the Maximize button on the title bar.

Resizing a Window

Windows 7 does not limit window sizing to the size that you see when you restore a window. You can resize any window that is not maximized by dragging the window border. When you move the mouse pointer over a window border, it changes to a resizing pointer (two-headed arrow). When you point to the left or right window border, the mouse pointer becomes a horizontal two-headed arrow, and you can drag left or right to resize the window. When you point to the bottom window

Window border   Resizing pointer

Figure 1.23 **Drag a window border to resize the window.**

border, the mouse pointer becomes a vertical two-headed arrow, and you can drag up or down to resize the window. When you point to the lower corner of the window, the mouse pointer becomes a diagonal two-headed arrow (Figure 1.23), and you can drag diagonally to resize the window width and height simultaneously.

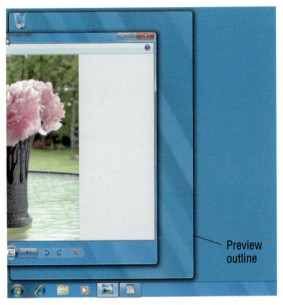

Preview outline

Note: *Figure 1.23 illustrates that the window border may take on a slightly different appearance depending on the application's design. Many applications have a narrower, plain border around the window rather than the one for the application shown in Figure 1.23. No matter what the border's appearance is, the edge of the window constitutes the window border.*

The Snap feature mentioned earlier also enables you to resize windows so that they'll fit side-by-side on-screen. This time, you drag the window by its title bar until it is about halfway off the left or right side of the screen. When a preview outline appears, as shown in Figure 1.24, release the mouse button, and the window will snap to the previewed size.

Figure 1.24 Drag a window halfway off the screen to snap it to a side-by-side size.

Here's How

To resize a window:

- Point to the left or right window border, and drag horizontally.

OR

- Point to the bottom window border, and drag vertically.

OR

- Point to a lower corner of the window (typically the lower right corner), and drag horizontally.

OR

- Drag the window to the left or right by its title bar until it is halfway off screen. When you see the preview outline, release the mouse button.

Can't Resize a Window
If you are not able to resize a window, it may be maximized. Check to see if a Restore button appears on the title bar, and click it. You may then be able to resize the window.

Moving a Window

You can move any window that is not maximized to another position on your desktop. This is another technique that you can use to set up the desktop in any way that makes your current computing work more convenient. Moving the window is a simple matter of dragging.

Here's How

To move a window:

1. Point to the window title bar.
2. Drag the window to the desired location.

Windows 7 provides shortcuts for rearranging windows on-screen, as well. You can right-click a blank area of the taskbar (that is, not on a taskbar button), and then click *Cascade windows* to arrange the windows in a pile on-screen. Because this action sizes the windows at a less-than-full-screen size, you can see a bit of each window in the pile. If you right-click the taskbar and then click *Show windows side by side*, Windows 7 arranges the open windows to fill the screen, so you see the maximum amount of each window. The shortcut menu also includes a *Show windows stacked* command, which maximizes all the windows and shows the most recently used one on top. You also can use the *Show the desktop* command on the shortcut menu to minimize all open windows.

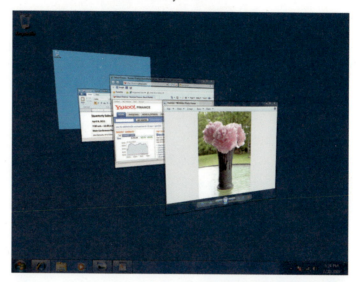

Note: *The cascade and side-by-side arrangements work only on windows that are not minimized.*

Moving between Windows

The Aero Flip 3D feature gives you visual guidance when you want to switch to the file or program in another open window. Pressing Ctrl+Windows logo key+Tab overlaps all the open windows and the desktop in a 3-D preview stack, as shown in Figure 1.25. Click on a window to open it. Or, after opening the stack, press Tab to cycle the windows through the stack, and press Enter when the window that you want to open appears on the top of the stack.

Figure 1.25 After you display the open windows with Aero Flip 3D, you can click to select which window to go to.

Active (current) window: The working window on-screen, where you can make selections and perform other actions

You also can use one of several other methods involving the taskbar or a window itself to switch to another window. Switching to another window makes it the *active (current) window*.

To switch between open windows (program or document):

Here's How

- Click the task's button on the taskbar. If there are multiple windows open, move the mouse pointer over the taskbar button, and then click the thumbnail for the desired window.

OR

- If you can see part of the window on the desktop, click the visible part of the window.

OR

- Press Ctrl+Windows logo key+Tab, and then click the window to go to.

OR

- Press and hold Alt+Tab. Press an arrow key or repeatedly tab the Tab key to highlight the desired window in the task-switching window that appears, and then release all keyboard keys.

Agenda - WordPad

QUICK FIX

Sizing Situations
When you redisplay a window, it appears at its previous size. So if the open windows were stacked or arranged in a particular way, your window may not appear to be selected at all. In such a case, you'll need to maximize or resize the window as needed.

Close button

Figure 1.26 Click a button, close a window.

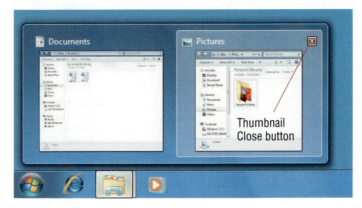

Thumbnail
Close button

Figure 1.27 Click the thumbnail Close button to close the window.

Closing a Window

Closing a program window shuts down the program and file (if any) within the window, freeing up system resources and potentially space on the desktop. You should close program windows before shutting down your system, in particular because the application will prompt you to save any unsaved changes you have made to the file in the window. As for other window activities, every window includes a Close (X) button that you can click to close the window (Figure 1.26). You also can use the taskbar to close a window. One way is to right-click the taskbar icon and click *Close window* in its Jump List. You also can move the mouse pointer over the taskbar icon, move the mouse pointer over the thumbnail for the window to close, and then click the smaller close (X) button that appears in the thumbnail, as illustrated in Figure 1.27.

Tip: The buttons on a title bar can help you tell the difference between a window and a dialog box. A dialog box typically lacks Minimize and Maximize buttons. A dialog box will have only the Close button, and perhaps an additional button you can click to get Help.

Here's How ▶ To close a window:

- Click the Close button on the window title bar.

OR

- Right-click the window's taskbar button, and click *Close window*.

OR

- Move the mouse pointer over the taskbar icon, move the mouse pointer over the thumbnail for the window to close, and then click the smaller close (X) button that appears in the thumbnail.

OR

- Press Alt+F4.

Exercise 3

1. Click Organize on the command bar of the Documents library window.
2. Point to the *Layout* choice. A submenu appears.
3. Move your mouse pointer over the details pane choice, but do not click it.
4. Use the Print Screen function as described earlier to take a screen shot. Use Paint as described earlier to save the file as **C01E03S04**. Submit the file to your instructor as a printout or e-mail attachment or on a USB flash drive, and close Paint. Consult your instructor if you have any questions about saving, printing, or e-mailing the file.
5. Switch to the WordPad window by clicking its taskbar button (labeled Document – WordPad).
6. In the Insert group on the Home tab of the Ribbon, click the Date and time button.
7. In the Date and Time dialog box that appears, click the *DD Month, YYYY* format (which will show the current date as in *15 July, 2009*) in the Available formats list, and then click OK. (If the specified format is not available, your instructor will tell you which format to select.) That inserts the date at the top of the WordPad file.
8. Drag over the newly inserted date to select it.
9. Click the *Font size* drop-down list arrow in the Font group of the Home tab, and then click *14* in the list to increase the text size.
10. Click the *Text color* drop-down list arrow in the Font group of the Home tab, and then click *Vibrant blue* (the second from last swatch in the second column).
11. Press the right arrow key, and then press Enter. Type your name.
12. Observe the ruler above the document text. Click the View tab on the Ribbon, and then click the *Ruler* check box in the Show or Hide Group. Observe how the ruler disappears. Click the *Ruler* check box again to redisplay the ruler.
13. Click the Home tab on the Ribbon to redisplay its commands.
14. Drag over the two lines of text in the file.
15. In the Paragraph group on the Home tab of the Ribbon, click the Center button.
16. Click the WordPad window Close button. In the message box that asks whether you want to save changes to the file, click Save.
17. Type C01E03S17 into the *File name* text box to name the file. If needed, change the save location as indicated by your instructor. Click Save. Print out or e-mail the file to your instructor or provide it on a USB flash drive as directed after the file window closes.
18. Maximize the Documents library window by dragging it up to the top of the screen.
19. Minimize the Documents library window using the method of your choice.
20. Maximize the Documents library window by moving the mouse pointer over its taskbar button and then clicking the thumbnail.
21. Click the Restore Down button on the Documents library window to return the window to a smaller size.
22. Click the Internet Explorer button on the taskbar, and then resize the window to less-than-full-screen size using the method of your choice, if necessary.
23. Use the Snap feature (dragging the window partway off the side of the screen) to position the Internet Explorer window at the left and the WordPad window at the right.
24. Use the Print Screen function as described earlier to take a screen shot. Use Paint as described earlier to save the file as **C01E03S24**. Submit the file to your instructor as a printout or e-mail attachment or provide it on a USB flash drive, and close Paint. Consult your instructor if you have any questions about saving, printing, or e-mailing the file.
25. Using the method of your choice, such as pressing Alt+F4 or clicking the window Close button, close each of the open windows.

Understanding User Accounts

When you install and set up Windows 7 for the first time, it prompts you to enter the user name for the first user account. You can add more user accounts as needed to enable others to work with the system. In addition to enabling each user to customize his or her desktop, the user account controls the permissions and restrictions governing what the user can do when working with the system.

User accounts help enhance security and reliability. A user account can be set up to require the user to enter a password to log on to Windows 7. In addition, user accounts work with the *User Account Control (UAC)*, the Windows 7 feature that helps control changes to the desktop, including unauthorized changes made by a user or by malicious software.

User Account Control (UAC): The overall Windows 7 security component that works with user accounts to prevent unauthorized system changes

Note: *A User Account Control prompt may appear when you attempt to make changes to the system, such as adding a user account. In some cases, you must supply an administrator password to continue working.*

Further, Windows 7 creates a set of libraries for each user account. When you log on to your account, you can only access and use the files and folders in your account—not those of other users. This approach ensures that each user's data remains confidential and secure.

Windows 7 provides three different types of user accounts: standard, administrator, and guest. A standard user account enables the user to work with the software and hardware installed on the system, but the user is mostly prevented from making system changes that might affect other users, such as changing security settings. (However, standard account users can make some changes by supplying an administrator password when prompted.) An administrator user account enables the user to make changes to system hardware and software, settings that affect other users, and files not accessible to standard user account users. By default, the first account established when Windows 7 is set up is an administrator account. A guest account enables a user to work with programs installed on the system, but the guest user may not make any system changes or access personal files.

Adding a Standard User Account with Password

As a rule, most user accounts you create should be standard user accounts. Ensuring that the system remains free from unstable or potentially damaging malicious software provides the best insurance for system reliability and safety. Because the standard user account prevents software installation (unless the user can provide an administrator password when prompted), this account type prevents the user from introducing potentially damaging software or making other changes that might have unwanted consequences.

Password: A secret series of characters that must be entered to access an account or make changes

Control Panel: The central location where you can change system preferences and settings, from the desktop appearance to programs installed

Including a *password* as part of a standard user account's setup also protects the security of that user's folders and files. Anyone who wants to make changes to a standard user's folders and files must have the password to log on to that user's account. No other standard account holder without the user's password can gain unauthorized access to his or her files.

You use the *Control Panel* in Windows 7 (Figure 1.28) to work with user accounts, among other settings. Creating a user account with a password provides you a good first opportunity to work in Control Panel.

Both administrator and standard users may create a new standard user account. However, a standard user will need to obtain and enter an administrator password to add an account.

Figure 1.28 The Control Panel enables you to change settings in Windows 7.

Here's How

To add a user account with a password:

1. Obtain an administrator password from an administrator of the computer system you use or from the IT (Information Technology) department in your organization, if you do not have an administrator account.
2. Click Start, and then click *Control Panel*.
3. Click the *Add or Remove User Accounts* link below the User Accounts and Family Safety category.
4. If a User Account Control dialog box appears and prompts you for a password, enter the password for the listed administrator user (as provided by your instructor) in the *Password* text box, and then click Yes.
5. Click the Create a new account link below the listing of available accounts.
6. Type the new user account name in the *New account name* text box near the top of the window.
7. Leave the Standard user option button selected, and click Create Account.

Control Panel Views
If Category is not selected from the View by drop-down list in the upper-right corner of Control Panel, you need to open that drop-down list and click Category so that you will be able to follow the steps in this book.

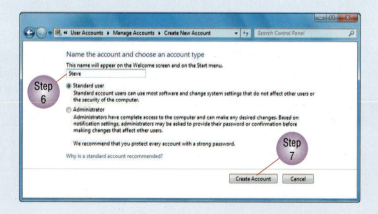

8. Click the new standard user account in the *Choose the account you would like to change* list.

9. Click the Create a password link in the list at the left.

10. Type the password in the *New password* text box, press Tab, and then type the password again in the *Confirm new password* text box.

11. Click the *Type a password hint* text box, and then type a hint that Windows 7 can display to help you remember the password, when needed.

12. Click Create password.

13. Click the Close (X) button to close the Control Panel window.

> **Tip:** To create what is known as a *strong password*, make it at least eight characters long and include a combination of uppercase and lowercase letters, numbers, and symbols, including spaces. Don't use complete words, but do use memorable acronyms or abbreviations, alternate spellings, or substitute numbers for entire words (*2* to stand for *to*). Also avoid using any easily-recognizable personal information like your name, birth date, and so on. So, *P@yattenzion2Me* would be a stronger password than *PayAttentionToMe*. As always, keep a written record of the password in a separate, but easy-to-access location like a locked file cabinet.

Creating a Password Reset Disk

You may have noticed the warning Control Panel presents when you assign a password to a new user account: If you do this, [User Name] will lose all EFS-encrypted files, personal certificates and stored passwords for Web sites or network resources. The same warning appears if an administrator tries to change a user's password. When a standard user account's password is added or changed by an administrator account, then the standard user will no longer be able to access encrypted files or e-mail messages. Stored Web site and network passwords also will be lost. To avoid this potential data loss, every standard user should create a *password reset disk* for his or her account. "Disk" is really a misnomer, because in addition to being able to save the password information to a floppy disk if your system is equipped with a floppy disk drive, you also can save the information to a USB flash drive or a flash drive in another format if your computer is equipped with the right reader (drive). You'll learn more about the various types of removable media in Chapter 2. You also use Control Panel to create the password reset disk. Chapter 15 explains how to use a password reset disk. If your book does not have Chapter 15, you are using a condensed-version book and you can search Help for "password reset" to learn how to reset your password. The last sections of this chapter explain how to get help.

Password reset disk:
Data stored on a floppy disk or USB or other flash drive that enables you to reset your user account password if you forget it

To create a password reset disk for the current user:

Here's How

1. Insert your media (plug the USB into the USB port, insert another form of flash media into the appropriate slot, or insert the floppy disk into the floppy disk drive.) If any AutoPlay windows open, close them.
2. Click Start, and then click *Control Panel*.
3. Click the *User Accounts and Family Safety* link.
4. Click the *User Accounts* link. The Make changes to your user account choices appear in Control Panel.
5. In the list at the left, click the *Create a password reset disk* link. The first Forgotten Password Wizard dialog box appears.
6. Click Next to advance to the next wizard dialog box. Choose the removable disk drive corresponding to the drive where you inserted your media in Step 1 from the *I want to create a password key disk in the following drive* drop-down list.

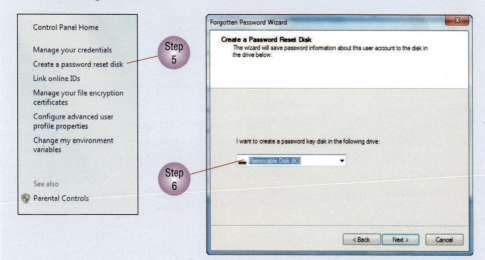

Here's How

7. Click Next. Enter the current account password in the *Current user account password* text box.
8. Click Next. The wizard informs you of the operation progress.
9. When the Forgotten Password wizard displays the message Progress: 100% complete, click Next, and then click Finish.
10. Remove your media from the drive, and store it in a safe location.
11. Click the Close (X) button to close the Control Panel window.

QUICK FIX

Avoiding Drive Damage
Most removable flash media can be removed immediately, but that's not a safe practice. To find out how to safely remove or eject removable media, see Chapter 2.

Settings a Standard User Can Change

If you have a standard user account, you can make three different changes to your account setup. A standard user can:

*   Change your account password.
*   Remove your account password.
*   Change your account picture.

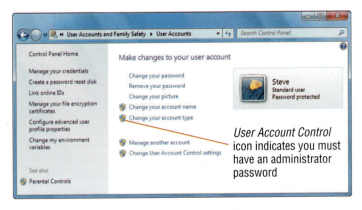

User Account Control icon indicates you must have an administrator password

Figure 1.29 The Control Panel shows the settings you can change for your user account.

Just as you use the Control Panel to create a user account, you use the Control Panel to make changes to your standard user account. In the Control Panel window, you click the *User Accounts and Family Safety* link, and then click the *User Accounts* link next. The Control Panel then presents the choices for editing your account, as shown in Figure 1.29. Notice that a special *User Account Control* icon appears beside the other settings not mentioned above. This icon means that you must have an administrator password to change those settings, such as the user name for the account, so they will not be covered here.

Here's How

To change a standard user account password and picture:

1. Click Start, and then click *Control Panel*.
2. Click the *User Accounts and Family Safety* link.
3. Click the *User Accounts* link. The Make changes to your user account choices appear in Control Panel.
4. Click *Change your password*. The Change your password choices appear.
5. Type your current password into the *Current password* text box.
6. Press Tab, and then type the new password into the *New password* text box. Press Tab again, and type the new password a second time in the *Confirm new password* text box.
7. Click the *Type a password hint* text box, and then type a hint that Windows 7 can display to help you remember the password, when needed.
8. Click Change Password.

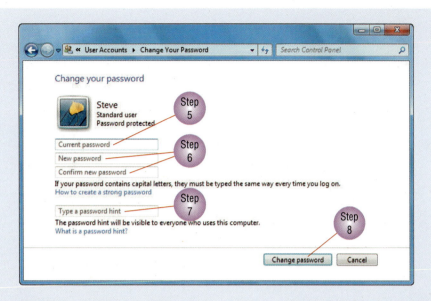

9. Back at the Make changes to your user account choices screen in Control Panel, click *Change your picture*.

10. Click another picture in the Choose a new picture for your account screen. (Use Browse for more pictures to display and use the Open dialog box to select a picture other than those included with Windows.)

11. Click Change Picture.

12. Click the Close (X) button to close the Control Panel window.

QUICK FIX

Catching Incorrect Entries
If you make a typo when entering the new password in Step 6, Windows 7 will display a message box telling you that your entries do not match, so that you can try again.

Tip: Your user account picture also appears on the Start menu when you are logged on.

To remove a standard user account's password:

1. Click Start, and then click *Control Panel*.
2. Click the *User Accounts and Family Safety* link.
3. Click the *User Accounts* link. The Make changes to your user account choices appear in Control Panel.
4. Click *Remove Your Password*.
5. Type the password to remove in the *Current password* text box.
6. Click Remove Password.

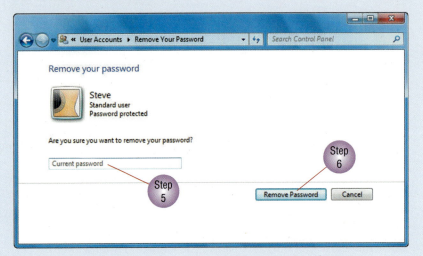

7. Click the Close (X) button to close the Control Panel window.

QUICK FIX

Reapplying a Password
Windows 7 deletes the password immediately, without any warning message. If you realize you want to reapply a password to your standard user account, follow Steps 1–3, and then click the *Create a password for your account* choice under Make changes to your user account to display the controls for recreating a password.

Deleting a Standard User Account

Deleting a user account is an activity that requires an administrator password under the Windows 7 security scheme. Nevertheless, it is an activity that a user with a standard account may need to complete from time to time. For example, if you have decided that you want to start with a cleaner slate in terms of your desktop settings, you may decide that you want to delete your current standard user account and create a new account.

During the process of deleting the account, Windows 7 gives you the option of saving files in the personal folders for the accounts. Note that any e-mail messages or settings for the account will not be saved.

To remove a standard user account:

1. Obtain an administrator password from an administrator of the computer system you use or from the IT (Information Technology) department in your organization, if you do not have an administrator account. Start windows, and log on to an account other than the account you want to delete.
2. Click Start, and then click *Control Panel*.
3. Click the *Add or remove user accounts* link.
4. If the User Account Control dialog box appears to prompt you for a password, enter the password for the listed administrator user in the *Password* text box, and click Yes.

5. Click the account to delete in the Choose the account you would like to change list.
6. Click *Delete the account*.

7. Click Delete Files or Keep Files, depending on whether or not you want to keep a copy of the user's personal libraries and folder contents or not.
8. Click Delete Account to confirm that you want to continue with the account deletion.
9. Click the Close (X) button to close the Control Panel window.

 ## Exercise 4
Creating and Deleting a Password-Protected User Account

1. Obtain an administrator password and account name from your instructor for use with this exercise. Start windows, and log on to the administrator account.
2. Click Start, and then click *Control Panel*.
3. Click the *Add or remove user accounts* link.
4. If the User Account Control dialog box appears to prompt you for a password, enter the password for the listed administrator user in the *Password* text box, and click Yes.
5. Click the *Create a new account* link below the listing of available accounts.
6. Type **01 Ex4 Account** in the *New account name* text box near the top of the window.

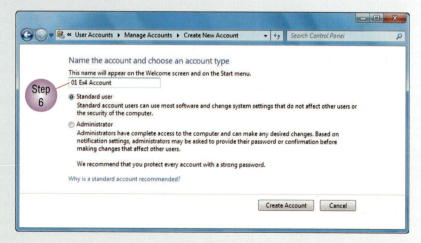

7. Leave the Standard user option button selected, and then click Create Account.
8. Use the Print Screen function as described earlier to take a screen shot of the list of user accounts. Use Paint as described earlier to save the file as **C01E04S08**. Submit the file to your instructor as a printout or e-mail attachment, or on a USB flash drive, and close Paint. Consult your instructor if you have any questions about saving, printing, or e-mailing the file.
9. Click the new standard user account in the *Choose the account you would like to change* list.
10. Click the Create a Password link in the list at the left.
11. Type $PracticeEx4@ in the *New password* text box, press Tab, and then type the password again in the *Confirm new password* text box.
12. Click the *Type a password hint* text box, and then type Exercise.
13. Click Create Password.
14. Click the Close (X) button to close the Control Panel window.
15. Click Start, and then click *Control Panel*.
16. Click the Add or Remove User Accounts link.
17. If the User Account Control dialog box appears to prompt you for a password, enter the password for the listed administrator user in the *Password* text box, and click Yes.
18. Click the account to delete in the Choose the account you would like to change list.
19. Click Delete the Account.
20. Click Delete Files.
21. Click Delete Account to confirm that you want to continue with the account deletion. (Do not turn on the guest account if prompted.)
22. Click the Close (X) button to close the Control Panel window.

Pausing or Finishing Your Work Session

Most people do not spend hour after hour working nonstop on the computer. Even if someone did, it would be unhealthy. Most users work for shorter periods of time, with phone calls, meetings, and other types of distractions in between.

Windows 7 provides a variety of ways that you can put a work session on hold rather than shutting down your computer altogether. These features can provide security for your work, conserve power, or both.

Using Sleep or Hibernate

Sleep: A power-saving state that preserves your work in memory and on the hard disk so that you can resume working quickly

If you want to walk away from your computer for a while and want to save power without having to close all your files and shut down the system, you can take advantage of the *sleep* feature in Windows 7. When you choose to put the system to sleep, Windows 7 saves your files and information about which programs are open both in system memory and on the computer's hard disk (or just system memory for a mobile computer); then it puts the computer in a lower-power state. (It does not shut the computer down.) When you wake the system up, your programs and files reappear on the desktop in a brief time, as little as several seconds.

The sleep state can save significant power. A desktop system will use about one tenth the power when asleep, and a mobile computer will consume only 1–2% of the power it consumes normally. Plus, sleep can give you peace of mind that your in-progress work remains secure. By default, if your account is password-protected, you must enter the password when you wake up the system. So, unauthorized users cannot wake up your computer and pry. You also can set up the system to go to sleep after a particular time frame, so that if you leave the computer unattended, it will save and secure your work automatically, plus save power.

Note: *If you are using Windows 7 on a mobile computer (or any type of mobile PC), sleep has a few extra functions. If you leave the system in sleep mode for three hours and the battery power gets too low, sleep will make sure all your work is saved to the hard disk and then will shut down the system. Also, by default you can put the system to sleep by shutting the computer's lid and wake it back up.*

Here's How

To put a computer to sleep and wake it up:

1. Click Start, click the arrow button to the right of the Shut down button, and then click *Sleep*. The computer goes to sleep. The computer's power and disk lights may remain on, and the hardware power button might blink slowly or change colors.

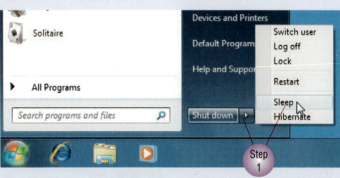

2. To wake the computer back up, press the hardware power button quickly. On some systems, you may have to press and hold it for a moment before releasing the button.

3. If a logon screen prompts you to enter your account password, type your password in the *Password* text box, and then press Enter or click the blue right arrow button to the right of the *Password* text box. If you see your account icon with a message that the system is locked, click the icon. Within several seconds, the desktop should reappear.

Note: *If the Power button on the Start menu changes so that the vertical dash is completely within the circle, clicking the button shuts down the computer.*

Some systems, particularly mobile computers, also offer a hibernate state. *Hibernate* saves the work session but shuts down the computer. Restarting opens your files and programs back on the desktop; however, this process works more slowly than the sleep state. To hibernate the system, click Start and then point to the arrow button to the right of the Shut down button, and click *Hibernate* in the pop-up menu that appears. When you want to resume work, restart the system by pressing the hardware Power button.

Note: *Sleep and hibernate settings work with power plans in Windows 7. The BIOS (basic input/output system) for the computer must support sleep or hibernate for those modes to be available.*

Windows 7 offers a new state for desktop computers called *hybrid sleep*. As with regular sleep, hybrid sleep puts the computer into a power-saving state when you choose to put the computer to sleep. But before it does so, it saves information about open files and programs to the hard disk. Then, if a problem occurs,

Hibernate: A more advanced shutdown state that saves your work and shuts the system down; your in-process work reappears on the desktop when you restart your system

Hybrid Sleep: A power-saving mode for a desktop computer where open documents and programs are saved to the hard disk before the computer enters the low-power state

Windows can still quickly retrieve data from the hard disk and make it available for your work. By default, hybrid sleep is turned on (assuming the hardware of your computer supports it) so that you don't have to do anything but put your desktop computer to sleep to take advantage of it. (If hybrid sleep is enabled, typically the Hibernate option will not be available.) However, you can turn off the hybrid sleep feature if desired. The setting for turning hybrid sleep resides with the other power plan settings, which are described in Chapter 12.

Locking the System

Lock: A state that hides the desktop without shutting down the system or changing its power consumption

Locking the system hides the desktop, but does not shut the system down or conserve power. As with the sleep mode, if your user account is password-protected, you will need to enter the password to unlock the system and redisplay the desktop. You might lock the computer rather than putting it to sleep when you intend to be away from the system for a very brief time.

Here's How   To lock and unlock the computer:

1. Click Start, click the arrow button to the right of the Shut down button, and then click *Lock.* The computer goes to a screen resembling the Windows 7 introductory logon screen appears, but it displays only your user account icon, along with the word *Locked.*

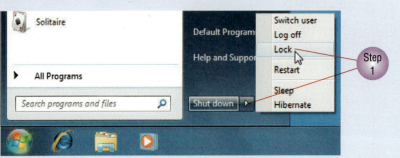

2. To unlock the computer, click the icon for your user account.
3. Type your password in the *Password* text box and then press Enter or click the blue right arrow button to the right of the *Password* text box.

Switching Users (Fast User Switching)

If you are working in a hectic environment where many users need to log on to and off from a system repeatedly throughout the day, shutting down and starting up the system or repeatedly logging all the way on and off would take too much time. Instead, you can switch to your user account from the desktop without forcing the current user to log off or shut down.

Fast User Switching: Changing between user accounts without shutting down files or programs for any logged on user

This capability takes advantage of a Windows 7 feature known as **Fast User Switching**. Fast User Switching keeps each logged-on user's programs running and files open, so when a user switches back to his or her account, his or her files appear immediately on the desktop.

Note: *Because switching users does not automatically save your work, be sure to save any open files frequently to prevent losing data.*

To switch users:

1. Click Start, click the arrow to the right of the Shut down button, and then click *Switch user*.
2. Click the icon for your user account.
3. If needed, type your password in the text box and then press Enter or click the blue right arrow button to the right of the text box.

Logging Off

Logging off from the system shuts down your applications and open files, making more system resources available to other users logged on to the system. Logging off also provides added security, because it prevents any other user from accessing your files when your system is connected to a network. It is a good practice to save and close your files before logging off to ensure that you do not lose any work.

Log off: To exit your user account and desktop without shutting down the system

To log off:

1. Click Start, point to the arrow to the right of the Lock button, and then click *Log Off*.
2. If you have any unsaved files open, a dialog box will prompt you to save changes. Click Yes or Save (depending on the program in which you are saving), and repeat the process for every prompt that appears. If you pause too long before completing this step, Windows 7 will display a black screen asking you to verify whether to log off. You can click Log Off Now to continue or Cancel to stop the log off. Windows 7 then displays its introductory screen with an icon for each user account, where another user could log on.
3. If you later decide to shut down from this screen, click the red Shut down button in the lower right corner.

Restarting

You may need to restart the system after performing certain operations like installing new hardware or software. Sometimes, an install process will display a dialog box asking if you want to restart the system now, and then restarting becomes a simple matter of clicking Yes in that dialog box. In other cases, you may need to restart the system manually. To do so, you can again use a choice on the Start menu.

To restart the system from the Start menu:

1. Click Start, click the arrow to the right of the Shut down button, and then click *Restart*.
2. If you have any unsaved files open, a dialog box will prompt you to save changes. Click Yes or Save (depending on the program in which you are saving), and repeat the process for every prompt that appears.
3. At the Windows 7 introductory screen, click your user account icon and enter your password as you normally would.

Restarting When the Computer Hangs

While computers have dramatically increased in performance and reliability over the years, writing an operating system that works with thousands of possible internal and external hardware models remains a monumental task. For that reason, you still may encounter situations where the computer *hangs*—appears to stop working altogether, also known as being locked up—or has another problem like a display that appears differently. Situations like this force you to restart the system.

Restarting by using the Start menu as just described is called a **soft reboot** or **restart**. This means that the process restarts the system without turning off its power, which is technically gentler on the internal and external components of the computer. However, if a computer is truly hung, it may not respond when you try to open the Start menu.

In such a case, you can try a keyboard combination that will also perform a soft reboot, or you can try a **hard reboot** by powering the system all the way off and then back on.

Here's How

To restart a hung system:

- Press Ctrl+Alt+Delete. A screen with choices for locking the computer, switching users, and so on appears. Click the red Shut down button in the lower right corner of this screen. If the mouse does not respond when you try to click the button, use the hard reboot technique described next.

OR

- To hard reboot or restart the system, press any restart button on the system's case. (In some cases, the button will be a small, recessed button that you must press with a pen tip or other small object like the extended end of a paper clip.) If there is no restart button, press and hold the Power button until you hear the system beginning to shut down. When you hear the drives stop whirring and all the system lights go dark, press the Power button again to restart the system as usual.

Shutting Down Completely

At the end of the workday, you should shut down your system. Saving your work and shutting down your system ensures that your work—even properly saved work—is much less likely to be damaged by power fluctuations or to be subject to improper viewing on a network.

Here's How

To shut down Windows 7 and your computer:

1. Click Start, and then click the Shut down button.

Step 1

2. If you have any unsaved files open, a dialog box will prompt you to save changes. Click Yes or Save (depending on the program in which you are saving), and repeat the process for every prompt that appears. Windows 7 will shut down and power down the computer completely.

 Exercise 5

Pausing and Restarting a Windows 7 Work Session

1. Click Start, click the arrow button to the right of the Shut down button, and then click *Lock*.
2. At the screen that appears, click the icon for your account, and then type your password and press Enter, if required.
3. Create a new user account with the account name **01 Ex5 User**. (Refer back to Steps 1–7 of Exercise 4 if you need to review the process, and then click the Control Panel window Close button. Use the same administrator password your instructor provided for that exercise. You need not create a password for this user.)
4. Click Start, click the arrow button to the right of the Shut down button, and then click *Switch user*. Click the icon for the **01 Ex5 User** account.
5. Click Start, click the arrow button to the right of the Shut down button, and then use the Print Screen function as described earlier to take a screen shot of the submenu. Use Paint, as described earlier, to save the file as **C01E05S05**. Submit the file to your instructor as a printout or e-mail attachment or on a thumb drive, and close Paint. Consult your instructor if you have any questions about saving, printing, or e-mailing the file.
6. Repeat Step 4, but this time switch back to your account.
7. Click Start, click the arrow button to the right of the Shut down button, and then click *Log off*.
8. Log back on to your account.
9. Click Start, click the right arrow button beside the Shut down button, and then click *Restart*. At the message that reminds you that others are logged on to the computer, click Yes to continue restarting.
10. Log back on to your account when the system restarts.

Getting Help and Support

It took Microsoft programmers some years to develop and finalize the features in Windows 7. An end user would have to have a photographic memory to know about every feature available, how it works, and where to find its settings. Because persons with a photographic memory form a limited universe indeed, Windows 7 includes a built-in Windows Help and Support system supplemented by online help downloaded from the Microsoft Web site on the Internet. Round out your basic skills now by learning how to find help when you have a problem using Windows 7.

Browsing in Windows Help and Support

Like earlier Windows versions, Windows 7 includes a built-in Windows Help and Support System (Figure 1.30). This system combines help information that installs on your computer system along with help provided online by Microsoft. The online portion of the help system ensures that the help you receive is the most timely and up-to-date help available. Online help typically downloads automatically as you browse or search.

Help and Support home button   Browse Help button

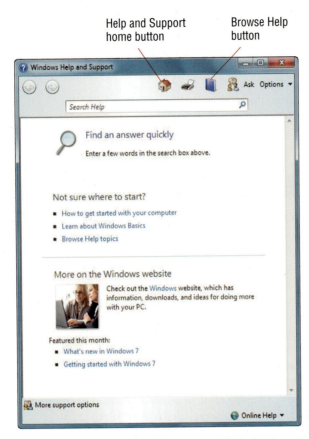

Figure 1.30 Access different forms of Help in the Windows Help and Support window.

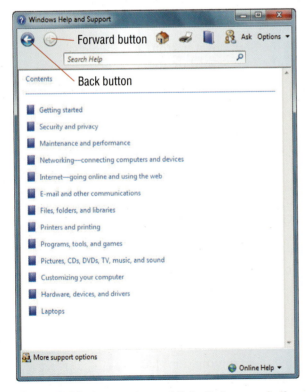

Figure 1.31 Click topics and links that appear in the Windows Help and Support window to browse.

To open the Windows Help and Support window, click Start, and then click *Help and Support.*

Note: *The first time you start Windows Help and Support, Windows 7 displays a message box asking whether it should check for new online content when searching Help. Click Yes to have it do so.*

Once you have opened the Windows Help and Support window, you can browse for help in three main ways:

- Click the link to one of the topics under Not sure where to start?.

- Click the Browse Help button in the toolbar at the top of the window. In the list that appears (Figure 1.31), click a link to an overall topic area, and then click subsequent topics and links until you arrive at the help information you need. Click the Back and Forward buttons as needed to move between information in the window.

- Type a topic to search for in the *Search Help* text box at the top of every Help window, and then press Enter. You can then click a topic in the list of results to see help information about it.

Searching for Help on the Windows Web Site

The Microsoft Knowledge Base searchable Web site represents years of cumulative information about the Microsoft products. Even more than the Windows 7 Help system's online component, it provides detailed, up-to-date information about how to perform more advanced operations in Windows 7 and troubleshoot problems you may encounter. When you cannot find the information you need in the Windows Help and Support system, you can search the Knowledge Base.

To go to the Windows Web site:

1. Click Start.
2. Click *Help and Support*.
3. Near the bottom of the initial Windows Help and Support window, click the Windows link under More on the Windows website. (Refer to Figure 1.30 if needed.)
4. Type a question or topic in the *Search this website* text box at the top of the page, and then press Enter.
5. Browse the resulting topics as desired.

Using Other Types of Help

Like other functions in Windows 7, the Windows 7 Windows Help and Support system has become more robust and functional, making it an excellent resource for users to both explore and to learn more about working with Windows 7 and the computer. The initial Windows Help and Support window offers a variety of other links that you can click to explore additional forms of help when you need it, including:

- **Troubleshooting.** If you click any Troubleshooting link you find in the Windows Help and Support window, the Help system displays a troubleshooter that walks you through steps to help correct such problems as repairing the system's Internet connection.

- **Ask button.** Click the Ask button to display a button with links to information about ways to get more specific assistance online, such as how to enable a friend to access your computer over the Internet to provide you with assistance.

 ## Exercise 6

Browsing and Searching Windows Help and Support

1. Click Start.
2. Click *Help and Support*.
3. Click the *Learn about Windows Basics* link. Scroll down in the window, if needed, and then click the *Working with files and folders* link.
4. To print this Help information, click the Print button (it has a printer on it) in the toolbar at the top of the Windows Help and Support window. Click a printer as indicated by your instructor, and then click Print to send the topic to the printer. Write *C01E06S04 Your Name* at the top of the printout to label it, and turn it in to your instructor as required.
5. Click the Help and Support home button at the top of the window to return to the initial Help content.
6. Click the *Search Help* text box near the top of the window, type log on, and press Enter.
7. Scroll down the list of results, and click one of the topics.
8. Click the Print button again. Select the printer indicated by your instructor, and click Print. Label this printout *C01E06S08 Your Name*, and submit it to your instructor.
9. Click the Back button in the upper left corner of the window twice.
10. Click the Windows link. The system's Web browser launches and displays the Windows 7 Help and Support page. (Of course, the system must have a live Internet connection for this to work.)

11. Review the information and Help options on the page.
12. Click the Web browser window Close (X) button to close the Web browser window.
13. Click the Windows Help and Support window Close (X) button.
14. Use the Start menu to shut down the computer.

CHAPTER Summary

- Microsoft Windows 7 is a new operating system for computers. The operating system enables you to tell the computer hardware and software what to do.

- You use a mouse or touchpad to interact with Windows 7, in most cases. Key mouse/touchpad skills include clicking, double-clicking, right-clicking, and dragging.

- When you start Windows 7, power on the system and then log on to your user account by clicking the account icon at the introductory screen. If the account is password-protected, type your password in the text box that appears and press Enter.

- The Start menu enables you to access the programs, features, and folders installed with Windows 7. Click the Start button to open the Start menu. You can click a program or folder in the initial menu, click *All Programs* to find more, or type the program name in the *Search* text box.

- The taskbar along the bottom of the Windows 7 desktop provides icons for launching some programs and for managing active system programs and features.

- Click an icon to select it or double-click an icon to open it. Drag over text to select it.

- Click a menu on a menu bar or command bar to open the menu, point to a command that displays a submenu, if needed, and then click the command to choose. An ellipsis (...) beside the command name means that clicking the command opens a dialog box.

- Dialog boxes contain controls such as text boxes and drop-down lists that are used to specify more detail about how a command should execute.

- A window is essentially a frame that holds content such as a program, file, or folder on the desktop. You can open multiple windows and click the taskbar button for a window to switch to that window.

- Click a taskbar button to switch to that window. Or, if a program has multiple windows open, point to the taskbar button, point to one of the preview thumbnails to temporarily display the window contents, and then click the preview thumbnail to open the window. The preview behavior is called Aero Peek.

- Press Ctrl+Windows logo key+Tab to display open windows in a preview stack with Aero Flip 3D. Press Tab to cycle the windows through the stack. When the window you want to work with is on top, press Enter.

- Click the Show desktop button to minimize or reduce all open windows to taskbar icons.

- Minimizing a window reduces it to a taskbar icon. Maximizing a window expands it to fill the desktop. Restoring a window returns it to its prior non-maximized size.

- Use the Minimize, Restore, Maximize, and Close buttons in the upper right corner of a window to manipulate its size.

- Drag a window by its title bar to move it.

- The Shake feature enables you to minimize all windows except the one you are working on. Drag the desired window's title bar rapidly left and right, as if you are shaking it, to accomplish this.

- The Snap feature enables you to resize a window on the fly. Drag the window up to the top of the screen to maximize it. Drag a window halfway off the left or right side of the screen to size it for side-by-side viewing.

- Windows 7 enables you to add standard and administrator user accounts to the system. Most user accounts are standard accounts.

- User accounts work with User Account Control, a security feature that prevents unwanted system changes. You must be logged on with an administrator account or have an administrator password to make changes that affect all users of the system.

- You can add a password to a user account, remove or change the password, or change the account picture.

- When you delete a standard user account, you can choose whether to keep the user's folders. Other user settings and information like e-mail will be deleted when you delete the account.

- You can put the computer into the power-conserving sleep mode to save your files and program status when you need to leave the computer. Click the arrow button beside the Shut down button on the Start menu and then click *Sleep* to put the system to sleep. Pressing the hardware Power button quickly wakes it up.

- Fast User Switching enables a new user to log on without forcing another user to close programs and log off. Click the arrow button to the right of the Shut down button, and then click *Switch user* to make the switch.

- You can use the Lock command found when you click the arrow button to the right of the Shut down button on the Start menu to hide your desktop from other users. Click your account icon and enter your password, if prompted, to unlock the system.

- Shutting down the system both logs all users off and powers down the computer. Click Start, and then click *Shut down*.

- You can use the Windows Help and Support window to browse for help, search for help, or go online to find more information. Click Start, and then click *Help and Support* to open Help.

CONCEPTS Check

Completion: Answer the following questions on a blank sheet of paper.

MULTIPLE CHOICE

1. To display the Start menu, click the _____ button.
    a. Open
    b. Prt sc
    c. Start
    d. Launch

2. Click _____ to browse for more programs on the Start menu.
    a. More
    b. All Programs
    c. Browse
    d. Next

3. The _____ appears along the bottom of the desktop by default.
    a. taskbar
    b. command bar
    c. button bar
    d. sidebar

4. The _____ in a window holds drop-down lists of commands.
    a. taskbar
    b. command bar
    c. menu bar
    d. Both b and c

5. The _____ organizes commands into tabs and groups.
    a. command bar
    b. menu bar
    c. Ribbon
    d. taskbar

6. A dialog box holds _____ that you use to give details about how a command should work.
    a. buttons
    b. choices
    c. lists
    d. controls

7. To close a program or window, press Alt+ _____ .
    a. F1
    b. F2
    c. F3
    d. F4

8. Click the _____ button to reduce a window to a taskbar button.
    a. shrink
    b. minimize
    c. small window
    d. reduce

9. Use the _____ command accessed via the Start menu to put the system to sleep.
   a. power
   b. sleep
   c. pause
   d. blink

10. Clicking _____ in the menu that appears when you click the arrow button located next to the Shut down button hides your desktop and requires you to log back on.
   a. Log off
   b. Lock
   c. Both a and b
   d. None of the above

Part 2 SHORT ANSWER

11. How do you find a program on the Start menu?

   _____

12. Why does Windows 7 require each system user to have a separate account?

   _____

13. What keyboard combination do you use to switch windows?

   _____

14. Name the buttons you can use to work with window sizing.

   _____

15. What is the difference between a standard user account and an administrator account?

   _____

16. How do you put the system to sleep, and what happens when you do?

   _____

17. How do you wake up the system?

   _____

18. What is the advantage of fast user switching?

   _____

19. What command do you use to restart the system?

   _____

20. Name two types of help you can get or ways to get help.

   _____

SKILLS Check

Save all solution files to the default Documents folder, or any alternate folder specified by your instructor.

Guided Check

STARTING UP AND OPENING FOLDERS AND PROGRAMS

1

1. Log on to the system.
   a. Power on the system.
   b. Click the icon for your user account.
   c. Type your password.
   d. Press Enter.
2. Start the Paint program.
   a. Click the Start button.
   b. Click *All Programs*.
   c. Click *Accessories*.
   d. Click *Paint*.
3. Open the Documents library window.
   a. Click Start.
   b. Click *Documents*.
4. Start Calculator.
   a. Click Start.
   b. Type **Calculator** in the *Start Search* text box.
   c. Click *Calculator* in the Start menu.
5. Take a picture of your screen, paste it into Paint, save it as **C01A01**, and submit it to your instructor either as a printout or via e-mail or USB flash drive for grading.

WORKING WITH OPEN WINDOWS

2

1. Minimize all windows to taskbar buttons.
   • Click the Minimize button on each window.
   OR
   • Click the Show desktop button on the taskbar.
2. Redisplay the Documents window.
   • Click the Documents library window taskbar button.
   OR
   • Press Alt+Tab, hold down Alt and press the Tab key repeatedly until the Documents library window is previewed, and then release the keys.
3. Drag the Documents window to the top of the screen to maximize it.
4. Maximize the Paint window from the taskbar.
   a. Click the Paint button on the taskbar.
   b. Right-click the preview thumbnail.
   c. Click *Maximize*.
5. Click the Paint window Restore Down button.
6. Take a picture of your screen, paste it into Paint, save it as **C01A02**, and submit it to your instructor either as a printout or via e-mail or USB flash drive for grading.
7. Close the Documents library, Calculator, and Paint windows.
   a. Right-click each program's icon on the taskbar.
   b. Click *Close window* in the Jump List.

SLEEPING AND WAKING THE SYSTEM

3

1. Put the system to sleep.
   a. Click Start.
   b. Click the right arrow button beside the Shut down button.
   c. Click *Sleep*.
2. Wake the system.
   a. Press the Power button on the computer case quickly.
   b. Click the icon for your user account.
   c. If needed, type your password in the *Password* text box and then press Enter or click the blue right arrow button to the right of the *Password* text box.

BROWSING WINDOWS HELP AND SUPPORT

4

1. Start Windows Help and Support.
   a. Click Start.
   b. Click *Help and Support*.
2. Go to a topic.
   a. Click the Browse Help button in the window toolbar.
   b. Click the Security and privacy category.
   c. Click the Understanding security and safe computing topic.
3. Print a topic.
   a. Click the Print button in the window toolbar.
   b. Select the printer indicated by your instructor and click Print.
   c. Label this printout **C01A04** *Your Name*, and submit it to your instructor.
4. Click the Close (X) button for the Help and Support window to close the window.

On Your Own

USE MENUS AND DIALOG BOXES

5

1. Restart the Paint program.
2. Use the Print Screen key to take a picture of your screen.
3. On the Home tab of the Ribbon in Paint, click the bottom part (with the arrow) of the Clipboard button, and then click *Paste*.
4. On the Home tab, click the Resize button in the Image group. Type 75 in the *Horizontal* text box and press Tab. Type 75 in the *Vertical* text box if necessary. Click OK.
5. Click the Rotate button in the Image group, and then click *Rotate left 90°*.
6. Maximize the Paint window.
7. Click the View tab on the Ribbon.
8. In the Zoom group, click the Zoom Out button.
9. Click the Home tab on the Ribbon to redisplay it.
10. Click the Save button on the Quick Access Toolbar and save the file as **C01A05**, and submit it to your instructor either as a printout or via e-mail or USB flash drive for grading.
11. Click the window Close (X) button to close Paint.

Assessment

6

WORKING WITH PROGRAM WINDOWS

1. Use the method of your choice to open the following programs and windows, in the order listed:
   Paint
   Internet Explorer
   WordPad
2. Right click the taskbar, and click *Show windows stacked*.
3. Press and hold Ctrl+Windows logo key+Tab.
4. Take a picture of your screen.
5. Press Enter.
6. Maximize the Paint window. Paste in the screen shot, save it as **C01A06**, and submit it to your instructor either as a printout or via e-mail or USB flash drive for grading.
7. Close all the open program windows.

Assessment

7

PAUSING A WORK SESSION

1. Click Start, then click the arrow button to the right of the Shut down button.
2. Take a picture of your screen, use Paint to save it as **C01A07**, and submit it to your instructor either as a printout or via e-mail.
3. Lock the system.
4. Log back on to the system.
5. Log off from your account.
6. Log back on to your account.
7. Restart the system.

Assessment

8

GROUP ACTIVITY: SEARCHING THE WINDOWS WEB SITE

Note that this assessment requires a working Internet connection.

1. As a group, agree on three help topics to search for.
2. Open the Windows Help and Support window.
3. Click the Windows link in the area titled More on the Windows website in the Windows Help and Support window. Maximize the browser window if needed when it opens.
4. Type the first topic to search for in the *Search this website* text box, and then press Enter.
5. Click a topic in the Search results list.
6. Right-click the page in the Web browser window, click Print, select a printer in the dialog box, and then click the Print button.
7. Repeat Steps 3 through 6 to find and print information about your other two selected help topics.
8. Label the printouts with the name of all the members of your group, and submit the printouts to your instructor for grading.

CHALLENGE Project

Your company has just bought a new computer with the Windows 7 operating system, and you have been asked to share the system with a coworker. Set up a password-protected account for the coworker and test it by logging on to it now.

1. Open the Control Panel, and create a new user account with the following settings:
   - Type: standard
   - User name: Buddy
   - Picture: marbles
   - Password: %Windows01*Challenge
   - Password hint: Chapter 1

Note: *Ask your instructor for an administrator password to complete this activity, if needed.*

2. Close Control Panel, and switch to the Buddy account.
3. Click the Start menu button so that you can see the user name at the top of the menu. Take a picture of your screen, save it as C01A09, and submit it to your instructor either as a printout or via e-mail or USB flash drive.
4. Log off from the Buddy account, and sign back to your account.
5. Delete the Buddy account and the 01 Ex5 User account you created in Exercise 5.

Working with Disks and Other Removable Media

PERFORMANCE OBJECTIVES

Upon successful completion of Chapter 2, you will be able to:

- Understand and select storage
- Obtain information about PC disks
- Assign a volume label
- Work with USB flash drives and other flash media
- Copy files and folders to a flash drive
- Work with CD and DVD media
- Change the AutoPlay setting of a drive
- Copy files to a writable CD or DVD
- View disk usage information
- Turn on disk compression
- Check a disk for errors
- Check disk partitioning
- Work with an external hard disk

The files and folders you access from Windows are stored on disk drives. These disk drives form the basis of the storage system on a PC, and can include hard disk drives, CD drives, and USB flash drives. Windows enables you to check and protect disks, view usage statistics on a disk, assign volume labels to disks, and much more. Windows also includes built-in utilities for partitioning and formatting new disks to prepare them for use.

Understanding and Selecting Storage

Files can be stored on a variety of media types, including flash random access memory (RAM) devices, CDs/DVDs, and hard disks. As you save and manage data files, you must evaluate the available storage options on the PC you are using and select the best one for the job. Storage can be categorized according to several different criteria.

The most popular type of storage device is a ***disk drive***. A disk drive is a mechanical device that reads and writes disks. It spins the disk platters past one or more read/write heads, which work with the operating system to retrieve and store files. See Figure 2.1. A wide variety of disk drives are available, including hard drives and CD drives.

Disk drive: A mechanical device that reads and writes disks

Disk platter

Read-write head

Figure 2.1 **A disk drive stores data on spinning platters.**

Some drives read and write data magnetically to disk; others read and write optically (with light). A ***magnetic disk*** stores data in patterns of positive and negative magnetic polarity in metallic particles on the surface of the disk platters, and a magnetic head in the drive changes the polarity on the disk surface to write data to it. Hard disks and floppy disks are magnetic. An ***optical disc***, such as a CD-R or DVD-R, stores data in patterns of greater and lesser reflectivity on the shiny surface of a disc. A laser changes the surface reflectivity in certain spots to write the data.

Note: *For magnetic storage, the correct spelling is "disk;" for optical it is "disc."*

A ***floppy disk*** is a type of magnetic disk. It consists of a 3.5-inch thin plastic disk, encased in a flat square casing. It fits into a floppy drive in a computer. Floppy disks and drives are mainly obsolete, but you still may encounter them in older PCs. Their limited storage capacity (only 1.44MB) and tendency toward developing errors make them less desirable to use than other media.

Flash RAM storage is becoming increasingly popular as an alternative to disk drives. ***Flash RAM*** is a type of static (***nonvolatile***) memory that retains its content even when the device is unpowered. The term "flash" comes from the way the data is updated—a "flash" of electricity erases and reprograms them.

Some types of disks, such as CDs, DVDs, and floppies, can be removed from the drive. For those disk types, the terms "disk" and "drive" are separately defined: the drive is the read/write mechanism and the disk is the platter on which it reads and writes.

Hard disks, on the other hand, are stacks of disk platters permanently sealed inside a drive unit. As far as the end-user is concerned, there is no hard disk separate from the hard drive, and vice-versa. Therefore the terms hard disk and hard drive are often combined as **hard disk drive**.

The most common type of flash RAM device is a **USB flash drive**, shown in Figure 2.2 (also called a thumb drive or jump drive). The flash RAM is permanently embedded in the plastic casing, and cannot be separated from the drive unit. USB flash drives are inexpensive and easy to carry, but if you want more capacity you must buy a whole new drive.

A **flash card reader** (Figure 2.3) is a drive that reads and writes data to flash RAM on removable plastic wafers, such as the flash memory cards from digital cameras and portable music players. Because a card reader is separate from the memory it reads, you can buy new flash memory cards at any time, or swap out one memory card for another as you would floppy disks. Card readers come built into many PCs, and USB-based card readers can also be purchased separately. Some PCs even have multiple card readers, each for a different type of card.

Hard disk drive: A sealed drive unit that contains a set of metal disks

USB flash drive: A USB drive with a flash RAM chip permanently embedded

Flash card reader: An internal or USB drive that reads and writes removable flash RAM cards

Photos courtesy of Macally Peripherals

Figure 2.2 Flash RAM devices store data on nonvolatile memory chips.

Figure 2.3 A card reader reads and writes data on removable flash RAM cards.

Note: *There are many types of memory cards, and not all card readers are compatible. The major types include SmartMedia, CompactFlash, and Secure Digital. Make sure you buy the right type for the card reader you have.*

Almost all storage media are portable. You can carry CD-Rs, DVD-Rs, USB flash drives, flash memory cards, and floppies from PC to PC freely, provided the other PC has an appropriate drive or port for it. Only internal hard disks are non-portable.

Tip: Hard disks can sometimes be portable too. An internal hard disk in the PC case can be removed and transported to another PC, although it requires opening up the case and disconnecting some cables. External hard disks are also available that work via a USB or FireWire port with any PC, and drive enclosures can be purchased that will convert an internal hard disk to an external USB model.

Each time you need to save a data file, or transfer a file from one PC to another, you must evaluate the available storage media on the system and choose which is the most appropriate to use. Table 2.1 provides some pros and cons of the major storage types discussed in this chapter. Not all PCs have all types of drives available, so your choice of storage medium depends on your system's capabilities.

Table 2.1   Storage Types

Storage Type	Attributes	Pros	Cons
Internal hard disk	Magnetic, internal, non-removable	High capacity, reliable, fast	Not easily portable
External hard disk	Magnetic, external, removable	High capacity, reliable, portable	Usually slower than internal, requires free USB or FireWire port, requires separate power source
Floppy drive and disks	Magnetic, portable	Compatible with older PCs	Slow, very low capacity, unreliable, newer PCs do not have floppy drives
Writable CD or DVD drive and discs	Optical, portable	Almost every PC has a CD drive, CD blanks are inexpensive	Slow to write to compared to other media CD-R blanks can be written only once; multi-write CD-RW and DVD-RW blanks are more expensive
USB flash drive	RAM-based, portable	Connects to a USB port, which almost every PC has, light-weight, compact to carry	Capacity is limited, more expensive per megabyte of storage than writable CDs or DVDs
Flash card reader and flash memory cards	RAM-based, portable	Connects to a USB port, lightweight, compact to carry, memory cards can be swapped out for additional storage	Capacity is limited, memory cards are expensive and are so tiny that they are easy to misplace.

Obtaining Information about PC Disks

Now that you know what types of storage are possible in a PC, the next step is to find out which storage types your PC supports. The easiest way to find this information is to look in the Computer window at a list of available drives.

The Computer window, which you open by clicking the Start button and clicking *Computer*, shows all the built-in drives in the PC (hard drives, CD drive, and so on) plus any external drives that have been temporarily plugged into USB ports or other ports. See Figure 2.4. If a drive is built in that is compatible with removable disks, the drive itself appears in the Computer window even if it does not currently contain a disk.

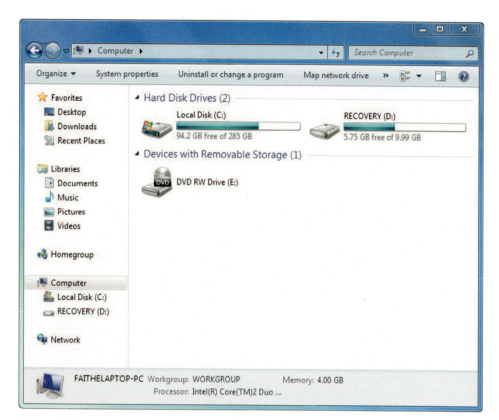

Figure 2.4 From the Start menu, click *Computer* to open a list of the drives on the PC.

Each drive has a unique letter identifier. Windows assigns these letters automatically based on the drive type, as follows:

- **A and B.** Floppy drives, if present
- **C.** Primary hard disk drive
- **D through Z.** Other drives

For each drive, the Computer window shows an icon that reflects the drive type. The name associated with the icon is either a generic label such as Local Disk, Floppy Disk, or a specific name (called a *volume label)* that has been assigned to it. You will learn to assign volume labels later in this chapter. The hard disk on which Windows is installed has a special Windows symbol on its icon to indicate that.

When deciding which drive to use to store files, it is important to know how much space is left on the disk so you will know whether the files will fit on it. Knowing how much space remains on your hard disk(s) can also help you determine whether it is time to add another hard disk to your system or upgrade to a larger hard disk.

Data is stored on a computer in ***binary*** format—that is, in collections of 1s and 0s. Each individual 1 or 0 is called a ***bit***, which is short for binary digit. Even the most complex data is broken down for storage into logical collections of bits.

A PC recognizes each group of eight bits as a ***byte***. A byte represents a single character of information; each number, letter, and symbol has its own unique binary code. The capacity of a disk, the size of a file, and the amount of memory installed in a PC are all described in terms of bytes. A single file can consist of thousands or even millions of bytes, and a disk drive can hold billions of bytes.

Binary: A numbering system consisting of only 1 and 0

Bit: A single binary digit

Byte: A group of eight bits forming a single character of information

Because it is so common to work with bytes in large quantities, names for various byte quantities are commonly used. These are described in Table 2.2.

Table 2.2 Terms for Groups of Bytes

Term	Number of Bytes	How Calculated
Kilobyte (KB)	1,024	2 to the 10th power bytes
Megabyte (MB)	1,048,576	A kilobyte of kilobytes
Gigabyte (GB)	1,073,741,824	A kilobyte of megabytes
Terabyte (TB)	1,099,511,627,776 (1,024 gigabytes)	A kilobyte of gigabytes

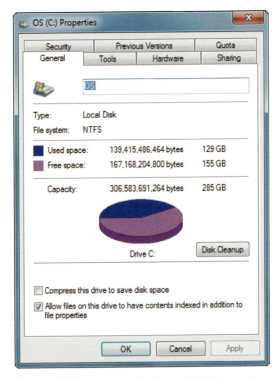

Figure 2.5 **More detailed capacity information is available from the drive's Properties box.**

When you select a drive in the Computer window, the drive's capacity information appears in the details pane at the bottom of the window, as shown in Figure 2.4. When the view is set to Tiles (as it is by default, and in Figure 2.4), the same information also appears below each drive.

The space used on the drive appears as a graphic, rather than as an exact number, in the details pane. The shaded portion of the bar shows the proportion of the total space that has been used. If you need to know the exact amount of space used, you can get this information from the Properties box for the drive, as shown in Figure 2.5. To view the Properties box, right-click the drive, then click *Properties*.

Assigning a Volume Label

A *volume label* is a text description that you can optionally assign to a disk. If present, it shows up in the disk properties in Windows. Both floppy disks and hard disks can have volume labels. You can change the volume label only on a writable disk; for example, you cannot change a volume label on a CD-ROM. (A CD or DVD might have a volume label preassigned to it, however.) Volume labels can be up to 11 characters in length, and can contain any letters or numbers, plus some symbols (but not any of these: * ? = + [ ] | \/).

If a hard disk or CD/DVD has a volume label, it appears in the Computer window along with the drive letter. In Figure 2.6, drive D has a volume label "RECOVERY." If no volume label is present, or if the drive does not contain a disk at the moment, a generic name appears that describes the general type of drive it is. In Figure 2.6, drive C has no volume label, so it appears as "Local Disk."

Volume label: A text description stored on the disk and displayed in the disk properties in Windows

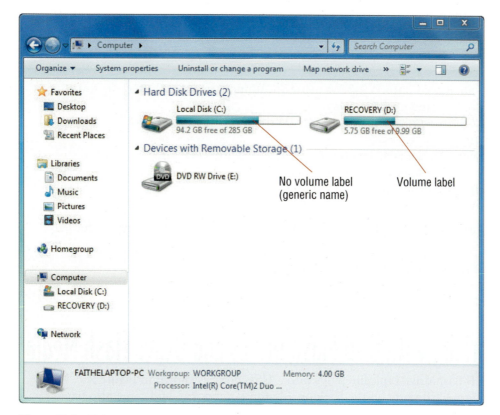

Figure 2.6 Volume labels appear in the Computer window.

Note: *Windows does not use the volume label internally to refer to the disk; the volume label is for human use only. Windows refers to disks only by their drive letters (and in some cases their internal serial numbers).*

Depending on the security settings on your computer, when you attempt to change the volume label for a drive, an Access Denied box may appear that reads "You will need to provide Administrator permission to rename this drive." If you logged onto Windows with an Administrator-level user account, you can click Continue to move past this dialog box and complete the name change. If you are logged on with a Standard or Guest user account, you will need to log on with an Administrator-level user name and password to complete this operation.

To set or change a disk's volume label:

Here's How

1. Make sure you are logged onto Windows using an Administrator-level user account.
2. In the Computer window, right-click the drive.
3. Click *Properties*.
4. Click in the top text box on the General tab.
5. Delete any existing text.
6. Type the new volume label.
7. Click OK.
8. If an Access Denied box appears, click Continue.

Exercise 1
Changing a Volume Label

1. Make sure you are logged onto Windows using an Administrator-level user account.
2. Click the Start button and click *Computer*.
3. Right-click the *C drive* icon and click *Properties*. Write down the current volume label, as you'll need it later.
4. Type your last name in the label box on the General tab and click OK.
5. If an Access Denied box appears, click Continue.
6. Capture a screen print of the Computer window. Name it **C02E01** *Your Name* and submit it to your instructor for grading.

   Tip: See "Capturing a Screen Picture to Complete an Assignment" in Chapter 1 for help, if needed.

7. Remove the volume label. Repeat Steps 2–5 to put the original volume label back in.
8. Close all open windows.

Working with USB Flash Drives and Other Flash Media

A USB flash drive typically plugs into a USB port, as shown in Figure 2.7. Most PCs have USB ports on the back or side (on notebooks), and some also have them on the front, as well. USB connectors fit only one direction, so if the connector does not fit easily, try turning it over.

When you connect a USB flash drive, Windows might open an AutoPlay window like the one shown in Figure 2.8. You can click on the choice that best suits the activity you want to do with the disk. In most cases, the correct choice is *Open folder to view files*.

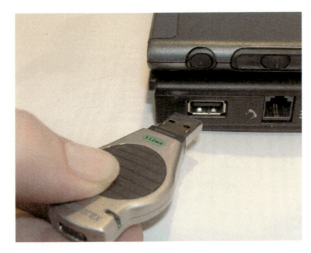

Figure 2.7 **Connect a USB device to a USB port. Windows will automatically detect it.**

Figure 2.8 **An AutoPlay window appears when Windows detects a new storage device and needs to know what you want to do with it.**

Note: *An option shown in Figure 2.8, Speed up my system using Windows ReadyBoost, is a feature that enables you to use flash RAM as a cache to speed up system performance.*

Tip: You can suppress an Autorun box by holding down the Shift key as you connect the drive or insert the disk.

Copying a File or Folder to a Flash Drive

Flash drives, being removable, are useful for moving files from one PC to another. The files must be less than the drive's capacity in size, of course. Most flash drives have a capacity of somewhere between 1GB and 16GB.

You can do any of the following to copy files to a flash drive:

* Open separate Computer windows for the source and the destination and drag and drop between them, as in Figure 2.9.

* Select the file or folder, copy it to the Clipboard (Ctrl+C), and then paste it into the destination (Ctrl+V).

* Right-click the file or folder, click *Send To*, and click the name of the flash drive.

Note: *The first time you connect a particular flash drive, Windows may need a few minutes to recognize the new device and install a driver for it. The appearance of an icon in the notification area indicates that is occurring. You won't be able to use the drive until that process completes.*

Drag and drop files from one window to the other

Figure 2.9 **Copy a file or folder to a flash drive by dragging and dropping it into the destination.**

To copy a file or folder to a flash drive (right-click method):

1. Connect a flash drive to the USB port on the PC.
2. Click Start and click *Computer*.
3. Navigate to the location containing the file or folder to be copied.
4. Right-click the file or folder and point to *Send To*, and then click the flash drive name on the list.

To copy a file or folder to a flash drive (drag-and-drop method):

1. Connect a flash drive to the USB port on the PC.
2. Click Start and click *Computer*.
3. Double-click the icon for the flash drive.
4. Repeat step 2 to open a second Computer window.
5. Navigate to the location containing the file or folder to be copied.
6. Drag the file or folder to the window for the flash drive.

To copy a file or folder to a flash drive (copy-and-paste method):

1. Connect a USB flash drive to the PC.
2. Click Start and click *Computer*.
3. Double-click the flash drive's icon.
4. Repeat Steps 2 – 3 to open a second Computer window.
5. Navigate to the location containing the file or folder to be copied.
6. Select the file or folder to be copied and press Ctrl+C.
7. Display the Computer window for the flash drive.
8. Press Ctrl+V.

Safely Removing Flash Media

When you are finished working with a removable storage device such as a USB flash drive or external hard disk, in most cases it is safe to simply disconnect it. Wait 30 seconds or so after the last usage to make sure all file operations have finished.

When data integrity is critical, however, you might want to take an extra safety precaution and use the Eject feature to stop the device before you unplug it. Windows waits for the device to finish any current operations and then stops it, so you are assured that it has no pending read or write operations before you disconnect it. To stop the device, right-click it in the Computer window and select *Eject*.

Alternatively, you can click the *Windows Explorer* icon in the notification area. A pop-up menu of the drives eligible for removal (any USB or other externally connected drives) appears, as shown in Figure 2.10. In Figure 2.10 it's "Eject DataTraveler 2.0."

Note: Depending on the settings of your notification area, the Windows Explorer icon may not appear there. You may need to click the up-pointing arrow on the notification area to open a palette of additional icons to find it. For information about the notification area's settings, see Chapter 6.

Figure 2.10 Click the *Windows Explorer* icon in the notification area and then click the drive to be removed.

When you see the message shown in Figure 2.11, disconnect the flash drive from the PC.

Windows Explorer icon

Figure 2.11 When you see this message, it is safe to disconnect a removable storage device.

To safely remove a USB or other removable storage device (Computer window method):

1. Right-click the removable drive icon in the Computer window.
2. Click *Eject*.
3. Wait for the Safe to Remove Hardware message to appear in the notification area.
4. Disconnect the device.

Here's How

To safely remove a USB or other removable storage device (notification area method):

1. Click the *Windows Explorer* icon in the notification area. You might need to click the arrow to display hidden icons to see it.
2. Click the device to remove.
3. Wait for the Safe to Remove Hardware message to appear in the notification area
4. Disconnect the device.

QUICK FIX

Getting Back In
To access the content of a flash drive after having used the Eject feature on it, disconnect it physically and reconnect it.

 ## Exercise 2
Working with a Flash Drive

1. Locate an unused USB port on your PC and connect the flash drive to it.
2. If an AutoPlay window appears, click Open folder to view files using Windows Explorer. If AutoPlay does not appear, click the Start button, then click *Computer*.
3. Locate Student Data Files at www.emcp.net/windows7. If you have not already done so, download files to your computer or to your USB flash drive. Ask your instructor for assistance, if needed.
4. Navigate to the Chapter 2 folder and locate the file named **Estate**. Navigation is explained in Chapter 3.
5. Right-click the file, point to *Send To*, and click the name and letter of the USB flash device. Then click the Close (X) button to close the window.
6. In the notification area, click the *Windows Explorer* icon.
7. Click the name of the flash drive. Verify that the file you copied is on the flash drive.
8. Right click and eject the device and submit it to your instructor for grading.
9. Close all open windows.

Working with CD and DVD Media

Most PCs have at least one optical drive, such as a CD or DVD drive. These discs store data in patterns of reflective and nonreflective areas on a shiny surface. A laser shines light on the surface of the disc, and a sensor measures the amount of light that bounces back.

Types of Optical Media

Optical media vary depending on the type (CD, DVD, or Blu-ray), the capacity per side (single layer or double layer), the number of readable sides (one or two), and, if writable, the number of times it can be written (once or multiple) and the type of writing standard it supports (for example, DVD+R or DVD-R). Later in the chapter you will learn the specifics of each of these variations. Both the discs and the drives that read them vary in these ways, although most modern drives support multiple types of discs.

Table 2.3 lists the capacities for basic non-writable discs. Later in this chapter you will learn about the specs for writable discs.

Table 2.3 Types of Optical Media

Type	Capacity
CD-ROM	700 MB
DVD-ROM	4.7 GB
DVD-ROM Dual Layer	8.5 GB
Blu-ray	25 GB
Blu-ray Dual Layer	50 GB

Changing the AutoPlay Setting of a Drive

Optical drives read on inserted discs and automatically perform a specified action. You can control what that action is by setting the AutoPlay setting of the drive. If you have not set a default action, the AutoPlay box opens every time you insert a CD or DVD, asking what you want to do with the disc. The options differ depending on the type of content the disc contains. Figure 2.12 shows the options for a writable data DVD; Figure 2.13 shows the options for an audio CD. There are other

Figure 2.12 When a data CD is inserted, the AutoPlay choices pertain to working with data.

Figure 2.13 When an audio CD is inserted, the AutoPlay choices pertain to audio files.

AutoPlay settings for other types of discs, such as blank CDs, video DVDs, and software installation CDs and DVDs. If you have other programs installed for working with those content types, options for those programs might appear in the AutoPlay box too.

You can set defaults for the various types of content via the Control Panel. When a default is set, Windows does not ask when a disc of that type is inserted; it simply performs the action. For example, by default Windows 7 plays audio CDs automatically rather than displaying the AutoPlay box (Figure 2.13). Figure 2.14 shows the Control Panel interface for setting AutoPlay options.

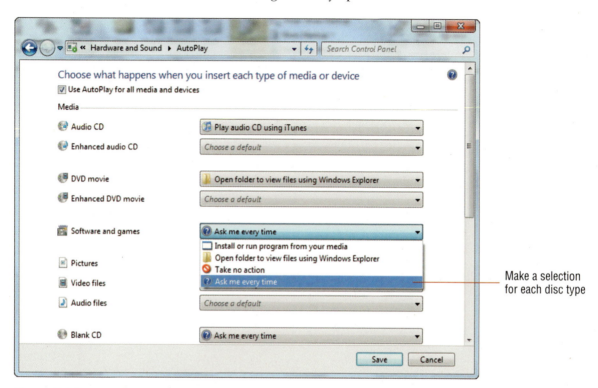

Make a selection for each disc type

Figure 2.14 Control the AutoPlay behavior here for each type of disc.

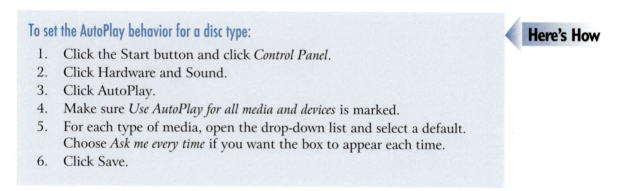

To set the AutoPlay behavior for a disc type:

1. Click the Start button and click *Control Panel*.
2. Click Hardware and Sound.
3. Click AutoPlay.
4. Make sure *Use AutoPlay for all media and devices* is marked.
5. For each type of media, open the drop-down list and select a default. Choose *Ask me every time* if you want the box to appear each time.
6. Click Save.

Here's How

Exercise 3

1. Click the Start button, and click *Control Panel*.
2. Click Hardware and Sound.
3. Click AutoPlay.
4. Open the drop-down list for Audio CD and click *Play audio CD using Windows Media Player*.
5. Capture a screen print of this window and submit it to your instructor for grading. Name the file **C02E03** *Your Name*.
6. Return to the AutoPlay window, then click Save.
7. (Optional) If you have an audio CD, insert it in the drive. It plays automatically.
8. Close all open windows.

Copying Files to Writable CD or DVD

CD: Compact Disc, a removable, optical disc that stores about 700 MB of data

DVD: Digital Versatile Disc (or Digital Video Disc), a removable, optical disc that stores about 4.7 GB of data per layer

Blu-ray: A high-capacity type of DVD disc that stores 25 GB of data per layer

Most computers include a writable **CD**, **DVD**, or **Blu-ray** drive that you can use to store files on writable discs. There are many types and variants of these discs, and it is important to match up the type of blanks you buy with the write capabilities of the drive. Table 2.4 lists popular writable discs currently available in stores and their specifications.

Table 2.4 Types of Optical Media

Type	Capacity	Writability
CD-R	700 MB	Once
CD-RW	4.7 GB	Multiple
DVD-R	4.7 GB	Once
DVD-RW	4.7 GB	Multiple
DVD+R	4.7 GB	Once
DVD+RW	4.7 GB	Multiple
DVD+R Dual Layer	8.5 GB	Once
DVD-R Dual Layer	8.5 GB	Once
BD-R Blu-ray	25 GB	Once
BD-R Blu-ray Dual Layer	50 GB	Once
BD-RE Blu-ray	25 GB	Multiple
BD-RE Blu-ray Dual Layer	50 GB	Multiple

The main differentiating factors between blanks are:

- **CD, DVD, or Blu-ray?** CDs are the lowest capacity; DVDs are mid-range, and Blu-ray are the highest capacity.

- **Recordable (R) or Rewritable (RW)?** Recordable discs can be written to only once, not erased and rewritten. Rewritable discs can be rewritten up to 1000 times and are more expensive. For Blu-ray discs, the abbreviations are BD-R for recordable and BD-RE for rewritable.

- **Plus or Minus?** There are two competing standards for DVD writing: +R (or +RW) and –R (or –RW). Many—but not all—drives support both. This is not a factor for CD or Blu-ray discs.

- **Single or dual layer?** DVD discs can be either single-layer (holding 4.7 GB of data) or *dual-layer* (holding 8.5 GB of data). For each disc type there are again two competing standards: plus and minus. Dual layer drives are sometimes called DVDR9 drives (either +R9 or –R9). Blu-ray discs can also be either single layer or dual layer with 25 GB or 50 GB capacity, respectively.

When you insert a new blank disc, the Windows AutoPlay window opens, providing a choice of burning a music CD or a data disc. See Figure 2.15.

Dual-layer disc: A type of DVD that stores data in two layers, enabling it to approximately double its capacity

Live File System: A type of CD and DVD file system that enables discs to be written to multiple times

If you choose *Burn files to disc using Windows Explorer*, Windows walks you through a Burn a Disc process in which you prepare the disc. You have a choice of two kinds of data disc:

- Like a USB Flash Drive: Using the *Live File System* in Windows, you can treat the disk like a flash drive, freely writing, editing, and deleting files from it. Formerly available only for rewritable discs, this file system now allows even plain CD-R discs to be changed and erased, so you can write to a disc just as if it were a USB flash drive. The drawback to this format is that the disc might not be able to be read on older computer systems. Earlier versions of Windows do not support this technology, although on many older systems a third-party CD writing program added that capability.

Figure 2.15 **Select which type of disc you want to create.**

- With a CD/DVD Player: This is the backward-compatible *mastered* file system, enabling only single writes to a blank disc. You must write all the content to the disc in one pass, and that content cannot be edited later. However, such a disc is compatible with virtually every CD player and CD drive.

Mastered: A type of CD and DVD file system that requires files to be written to the disc all at once

If you insert a blank DVD into a DVD-R drive, the AutoPlay dialog box includes *Burn a DVD data disc using Windows Media Player* and *Burn a DVD video disc using Windows DVD maker*. (See the Windows Help system to learn more about creating these various types of media discs.)

Note: *The Live File System format simulates multiple writing and erasing from a CD-R, but technically it is not really erasing and rewriting—it is simply writing to a new section of the disc and creating a new table of contents that ignores the older version. Therefore, the more times you make a change to the content of a CD-R, the smaller the disc capacity becomes. For true rewriting capability, in which the disc capacity does not erode, use a CD-RW disc.*

If you choose the Live File System, Windows formats the disc. When it is finished, an AutoPlay dialog box appears, as if you had just inserted a new USB flash drive. If you go with the mastered data disc, no formatting takes place (because the disc will be formatted when it is eventually written to).

To write files to the disc, drag and drop files and folders into the Explorer window of the disc. With a Live File System disc, the files are immediately written to the disc as you place them in the window.

With a mastered disc, the files and folders are not written to the disc right away, but instead they are placed in a holding area. When you are ready to write the files to disc, click the *Burn to Disc* icon on the command bar. All files are then written to the disc. A Burn to Disc window appears, in which you specify a disc title and a recording speed (see Figure 2.16). Enter that information and click Next to complete the process.

Note: *If the recording speed chosen is too fast for the drive or for the disc, errors might occur that will abort the entire process and render the disc unusable. Most discs list the maximum recording speed on the face of the disc.*

After writing files to a disc, you will probably want to label the disc so you will remember what is stored on it. Use only a soft-tipped marker, such as a Sharpie®, to label discs. Ball-point pens can damage the disc.

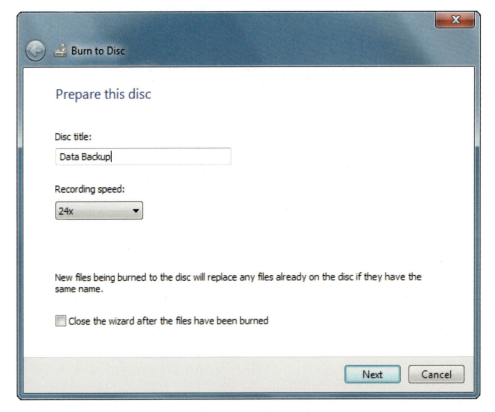

Figure 2.16 If writing a mastered disc, you will need to specify a recording speed.

To write files to a CD or DVD (Live File System):

1. Insert the blank disc.
2. Click Burn files to disc.
3. (Optional) Type a disc title.
4. Click Like a USB Flash Drive.
5. Click Next.
6. Wait for the disc to be formatted and then click OK.
7. Drag and drop files to the disc window. The files are copied to the disc immediately.

To write files to a CD or DVD (Mastered):

1. Insert the blank disc.
2. Click Burn files to disc.
3. (Optional) Type a disc title.
4. Click With a CD/DVD Player.
5. Click Next.
6. Drag and drop files to the disc window. The files are copied into a holding area.
7. Click Burn to Disc on the command bar.
8. In the Burn to Disc window, type a disc title (optional) if you did not specify one in Step 3.
9. Select a Recording Speed.
10. Click Next.
11. Wait for the files to be transferred to the disc. A completion message appears when the burn process finishes.
12. Click Finish. You can then close the disc Explorer window and eject the disc.

 ## Exercise 4

Backing Up Documents to a CD

1. Insert a blank CD-R or CD-RW disc into your writable CD or DVD drive.
2. Click Burn files to disc.
3. In the *Disc title* text box, type Backup.
4. Click Like a USB flash drive, if it is not already selected.
5. Click Next.
6. Wait for the disc to be formatted. When it is finished, click Open folder to view files. An Explorer window opens for the disc.
7. Click Start, and click *Pictures* to open the Pictures window.
8. Double-click the *Sample Pictures folder shortcut* icon.
9. Make sure you can see both windows at the same time. Drag and drop all the data files (not folders) from the Sample Pictures window to the CD's window.
10. Eject the disc, and label it **Sample Pictures Backup** with a soft-tipped marker. Submit the disc to your instructor for grading.
11. If the Pictures window is still open, close it now.

Working with Hard Disks

Although you will occasionally work with removable media such as flash drives and optical discs, the majority of your work in Windows will probably involve a hard disk. Hard disks are the most reliable form of storage, have the fastest access time, and provide the most capacity for the money.

Figure 2.17 Get information about disk usage from the Computer window.

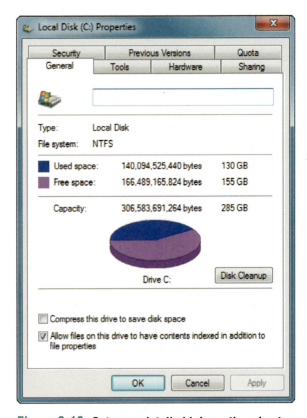

Figure 2.18 Get more detailed information about disk usage from the Properties window.

Viewing Disk Usage Information

In the Computer window, blue bars appear to show the percentage of the space occupied on each hard disk, and beneath the bar the amount free and total space appears. In addition, when a drive is selected, its information also appears in the details pane at the bottom of the Computer window, showing the same space information plus reporting the file system in use. In Figure 2.17, for example, the file system is NTFS.

Note: *NTFS (New Technology File System) is the default file system in Windows versions XP and higher for hard disks. Older file systems such as FAT32 and FAT are also recognized, for backward compatibility. USB flash drives use FAT32. CDs and DVDs use CDFS, which stands for CD File System.*

For more detailed information about the drive, such as the exact number of bytes of capacity and free space, display the Properties dialog box for the drive, as in Figure 2.18. You can display this dialog box by clicking Start, clicking *Computer*, and then right-clicking a hard drive and clicking *Properties*.

Turning on Disk Compression

If available disk space is in short supply, you might want to turn on disk compression for one or more hard disk drives. **Disk compression** enables the drive to store files so that they take up less space by running a simple compression algorithm on them. A **compression algorithm** is a mathematical formula used to remove wasted space in a file so it takes up less space on the disk. For example, it might identify strings of a certain number, like 00000000, and abbreviate them using fewer characters, like 0x8. It is available only on drives that use NTFS (the default file system).

Disk compression can be enabled for entire drives or for individual folders, and can be enabled for just the chosen location or all subordinate folders under it. When you enable compression, a Confirm Attribute Change box appears asking whether the change should affect subfolders and files too.

> **Tip:** Using disk compression causes a very minor slowdown in disk access because of the extra step involved in compressing and decompressing data on the fly. Therefore, you should not enable it if you still have plenty of room left on your hard disk drive.

To enable or disable disk compression for a hard disk:

1. Click Start, and click *Computer*.
2. Right-click a hard drive and click *Properties*.
3. Mark or clear the *Compress this drive to save disk space* check box.
   If the check box is unavailable, the NTFS file system is not in use and the drive cannot be compressed.
4. Click OK to display the Confirm Attribute Changes box.
5. Click the option to apply the changes either to the current location only or to all subfolders and files too.
6. Click OK.
7. If a warning box appears that you need administrator permission, click Continue.

Here's How

Disk compression: A means of decreasing the amount of space that files occupy on a disk by storing them more compactly

Compression algorithm: A mathematical formula used to remove wasted space in a file so it takes up less space on the disk

Checking a Disk for Errors

Over time, disks (especially hard disks) can develop errors in the storage system. These errors can be either physical, caused by bad spots on the surface, or logical, caused by improper shutdown or crashes in which files fail to be properly closed. Disk errors manifest themselves in problems reading or writing files or folders, or program crashes.

To check a disk for errors, use the **Check Disk** utility. To run it, open the drive's Properties box, click the Tools tab, and click the Check Now button.

By default, Check Disk fixes errors automatically. If you want to see what errors are found, you might choose to turn that option off so that Check Disk prompts you for confirmation each time it finds an error.

The Check Disk utility does two things: it always repairs logical errors in the file system, and it optionally scans for and recovers data from physically bad spots on the disk. The latter takes a long time (often an hour or more), so it is not a

Check Disk: A Windows-based utility for finding and fixing physical and logical errors on a disk

check you would want to run every time. Run a physical check only if you are seeing error messages that refer to data errors reading or writing to the disk. Logical errors are much more common.

Note: *Check Disk refers to areas on the disk surface as sectors. Sectors are numerically named areas of the surface that can be individually referenced by the drive controller. When there is an error within a sector, the entire sector is marked as "bad" and rendered unusable. Having a few bad sectors on a disk is normal.*

Here's How ▶ **To check a disk for errors:**

1. Click Start and click Computer.
2. Right-click a hard drive and click Properties.
3. Click the Tools tab and click Check Now.
4. (Optional) Mark or clear Automatically fix file system errors.
5. (Optional) Mark or clear Scan for and attempt recovery of bad sectors.
6. Click Start.
7. If the message appears "Windows can't check the disk while it's in use," click Schedule disk check. Then restart your computer and allow the check to run. Otherwise, wait for the check to complete and then click OK.

Sometimes a disk cannot be checked because parts of it are in use. In that situation, you will see a warning like the one in Figure 2.19. Click Schedule disk check to continue, and restart your PC to perform the check.

Figure 2.19 You might need to schedule the disk check to begin the next time you start your computer.

Partition: To logically divide the space on a physical hard disk into one or more logical drives

Primary partition: A bootable partition. A disk drive must have at least one primary partition

Extended partition: A secondary partition, in addition to the primary partition(s)

Checking Disk Partitioning

A physical hard disk drive is divided into logical disk drives, each with its own drive letter assigned. This is known as *partitioning*. Hard disks must be partitioned before they can be formatted, even if that partitioning simply consists of creating a single partition that occupies the entire physical disk.

Each physical disk must have at least one *primary partition*, which is a bootable partition. If there is only one partition on the drive, it is a primary one. Each primary partition can have only one logical drive on it, represented by one letter. In addition, a disk can have an *extended partition*. Extended partitions can have multiple logical drives, each with its own letter.

Note: *Your current hard disk is already correctly partitioned and formatted; otherwise, it would not be running Windows.*

To get information about the partitions of your drives, use the Disk Management utility, accessed from the Control Panel. Figure 2.20 shows an example in which there is one physical hard disk: Disk 0. Disk 0 has four partitions. However, only two of the partitions have a logical drive letter assigned to it (C: and D:). Disk 1 is a removable flash drive. The system's DVD drive is also listed (CD-ROM 0); it currently contains a disc that uses the CD file system

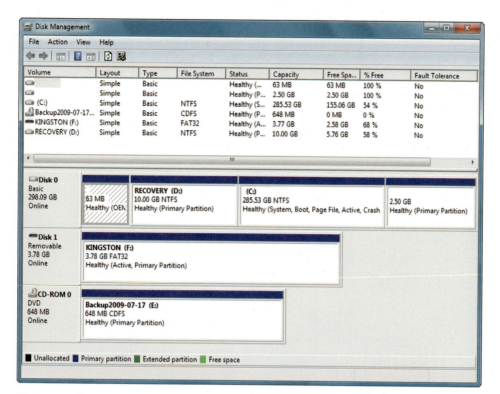

Figure 2.20 Examine partition information from the Disk Management utility.

(CDFS). If this drive were empty, the drive would appear at the left but the space to the right would be blank.

> **To examine the partition information for your system's disks:**
> 1. Click Start, and click *Control Panel*.
> 2. Click System and Security.
> 3. Under Administrative Tools, click Create and format hard disk partitions.
> 4. Examine the partition and drive information.

◄ **Here's How**

Working with an External Hard Disk

External hard disks have some things in common with internal ones, and some things in common with removable devices like USB flash drives.

External hard disks are like regular hard disks in that they appear as hard disks in the Computer window, and they can be partitioned and formatted like any other hard disk. They are like USB flash drives in that they can be connected at any time, and an AutoPlay window opens when you connect one unless you have set a default behavior for it. You can also use Eject to stop one before disconnecting it.

In addition to external hard disks that connect directly to a PC, there are also external hard disks that connect directly to a network, called *network addressable storage (NAS)*.

Network addressable storage (NAS): An external hard disk that is accessed through a network interface rather than locally through the Computer window

Exercise 5

Working with Hard Disks

1. Click the Start button, and click *Computer*.
2. Right-click the *C drive* icon and choose *Properties*.
3. Click the General tab if not clicked. Click *Compress this drive to save disk space* and click Apply.
4. Click *Apply changes to C:\drive only* and click OK. If a warning box appears that you need administrator permission, click Continue.
5. Click the Start button, and click *Control Panel*, and click System and Security
6. Under Administrative Tools, click Create and format hard disk partitions.
7. Determine the number of partitions on each of your hard disks, and the total space occupied by each one.
8. Capture a screen print of this window. Name it **C02E05** *Your Name* and submit it to your instructor for grading.
9. Close the Disk Management window and close any other open windows.

CHAPTER Summary

- File storage devices include floppies, CDs/DVDs, flash RAM devices, and hard drives.
- Magnetic disks, including hard drives and floppies, store data in patterns of magnetic polarity on the surface of one or more metal-coated platters. Optical discs store data in patterns of lesser and greater reflectivity on a smooth reflective platter.
- Flash RAM devices store data in nonvolatile RAM. These devices can have the RAM built-in (flash drive) or removable (flash card reader).
- To examine the drives on your system, open the Computer window from the Start button.
- Storage capacity is measured in bytes. A kilobyte is 1,024 bytes; a megabyte is 1,048,576 bytes. Hard disk capacity is measured in gigabytes (kilobytes of megabytes).
- A volume label is a text description stored on a disk and displayed in its properties. It can be assigned in the Properties window of the disk.
- To copy a file or folder to a removable storage location such as a USB drive, you can drag and drop it, copy and paste it, or right-click it and choose *Send To*.
- Before removing a flash drive (or external hard drive) from the PC, use the Eject utility (in the notification area) to stop the device so no data is lost.
- Optical disc types can be broken down by type (CD/DVD), capacity, ability to be written to once or multiple times, and support for dual layers.
- Usage and capacity information for hard disks is available from the Computer window. You can also right-click the icon and choose *Properties*.
- NTFS drives can use disk compression, which makes it possible to fit more files on the drive. To turn this on, mark the *Compress this drive to save space* check box in the properties for the drive.

- The Check Disk utility finds and fixes errors in the storage information for your drive. Use the Check Now button on the Tools tab of the drive's Properties box.
- To examine the partition information for each physical hard disk drive in your system, use the Disk Management tool. Choose *Control Panel*, System and Security, Administrative Tools, Create and format hard disk partitions.
- External hard disks work like internal ones, but can be connected and disconnected like flash RAM drives.
- Data CDs and DVDs can be burned in either of two formats: Live File Format or Mastered. Live File Format is more flexible, but Mastered is more backward-compatible.

CONCEPTS Check

Completion: Answer the following questions on a blank sheet of paper.

Part

1

MULTIPLE CHOICE

1. Which is an example of a magnetic disk?
   a. Flash RAM drive
   b. CD-ROM
   c. Hard disk
   d. All of the above

2. A group of eight bits is a _____ .
   a. kilobit
   b. byte
   c. megabit
   d. terabyte

3. How many bytes in a megabyte?
   a. 1,024
   b. 1,048,576
   c. 1,073,741,824
   d. 1,099,511,627,776

4. A floppy disk holds _____ of data.
   a. 700 MB
   b. 1 GB
   c. 1.44 MB
   d. 1 terabyte

5. Which of these symbols is not allowed in a volume label?
   a. @
   b. #
   c. %
   d. *

6. Which type of disc has a capacity of 8.5 GB?
   a. CD-R
   b. DVD-RW
   c. DVD-R Dual Layer
   d. CD-RW

7. What utility can you use to check your drives' partitioning and formatting?
   a. Disk Management
   b. Device Manager
   c. Partition Manager
   d. Services

8. What setting determines what happens when you insert a CD?
   a. Device Status
   b. AutoPlay
   c. Audio Manager
   d. None of the above

9. Which file system is most appropriate for a data CD you will be sharing with someone who uses some operating system other than Windows XP or higher?
   a. Live File System
   b. CDRW
   c. Mastered
   d. +R

10. One way to copy a file to a USB flash drive or floppy is to right-click the file and point to _____ on the menu that appears, then click the desired destination.
    a. Move
    b. Send To
    c. Transfer
    d. X-Copy

Part 2

SHORT ANSWER

11. What drive letter is assigned to the floppy disk drive, if present?

   _____

12. Why would you want to use the Mastered file system on a CD rather than Live File System?

   _____

13. With which type of CD writing do you need to specify a recording speed?

   _____

14. What does the Check Disk utility check for?

   _____

15. What type of port does a flash drive usually connect to on a PC?

   _____

16. What does the Eject command guard against?

   _____

17. What file system needs to be in use in order to use disk compression in Windows?

_____

18. What are symptoms of disk errors that can be fixed by running Check Disk?

_____

19. How many partitions must a hard disk have, at a minimum?

_____

20. How is an external hard disk similar to a flash drive, and how is it different?

_____

21. What is network addressable storage?

_____

SKILLS Check

Save all solution files to the default Documents folder, or any alternate folder specified by your instructor.

Guided Check

Assessment COPYING A FILE TO A FLASH DRIVE

1

1. Connect a USB flash drive to the PC.
2. Copy the file named **Sewing** from the Chapter 2 folder to the USB drive.
   a. Click Start.
   b. Click *Computer*.
   c. Double-click the *C drive* icon.
   d. Double-click the EMCP folder.
   e. Double-click the Chapter 2 folder.
   f. Right-click Sewing.
   g. Point to *Send To*.
   h. Click the USB flash drive.
   i. Wait for the file to be copied.
3. Use Eject to stop the flash drive.
   a. In the notification area, click the *Windows Explorer* icon.
   b. Click the flash drive's name (varies depending on model).
   c. Click OK.
4. Submit the flash drive for grading.

Assessment 2 SETTING DEFAULTS FOR MEDIA TYPES

1. Open the AutoPlay settings in the Control Panel.
   a. Click Start.
   b. Click *Control Panel*.
   c. Click Hardware and Sound.
   d. Click AutoPlay.
2. Set all the media types so that Windows will prompt you each time one is connected by opening each drop-down list and clicking *Ask me every time*.
3. Capture a screen print of this window and submit it to your instructor for grading. Name the file **C02A02 *Your Name.***

   Tip: See "Capturing a Screen Picture to Complete an Assignment" in Chapter 1 for help if needed.

4. Click Save.
5. Close all remaining open windows.

Assessment 3 GETTING INFORMATION ABOUT HARD DISKS

1. Display the Properties box for the C drive.
   a. Click Start.
   b. Click *Computer*.
   c. Right-click the *C drive* icon.
   d. Click *Properties*.
2. Capture a screen print of this window and name the file **C02A03S02 *Your Name.*** See "Capturing a Screen Picture to Complete an Assignment" in Chapter 1 for help if needed.
3. Check the C drive for errors.
   a. Click the Tools tab.
   b. Click Check Now.
   c. Click Start.
   d. If prompted that the check needs to be scheduled, capture a screen print of this message and name the file **C02A04S03 *Your Name.*** Then click Schedule Disk Check and then restart your PC. Otherwise, wait for the disk check to complete. Then capture a screen print of the completed disk check window and name the file **C02A04S03 *Your Name.***

On Your Own

Assessment 4 USING A FLASH DRIVE TO COPY FILES BETWEEN PCS

1. Connect a flash drive to the PC.
2. Copy the Chapter 2 folder containing student files for Chapter 2 to the flash drive.
3. Take the flash drive to another PC.
4. Copy the Chapter 2 folder from the flash drive to the other PC's hard drive.
5. Submit your flash drive to your instructor for grading.

Assessment 5 GROUP ACTIVITY: SHOPPING FOR OPTICAL DISCS

Note that this assessment requires a working Internet connection, or a trip to a store that sells discs, and a CD or DVD drive that can write to blank discs.

1. As a group, determine the type(s) of writable blank discs your PC will write to.
2. Have each team member spend 15 minutes shopping for the best prices on each type of disc.
3. Prepare an informal written report summarizing your findings and reporting the best available prices for discs you could find and the Web site(s) where you found them. Submit your report on paper or in a Word document named **C02A05**.

Assessment 6 ASSESSING HARD DISK USAGE

1. Use Disk Management to view the system's current hard disk partitions. Note if there is any unallocated space on any of the physical drives.
2. In the Computer window, examine the amount of free space available on each hard disk drive letter. Note how much space is available.
3. Assuming a disk should never get more than 85 percent full (except for a Recovery disk, if there is one), and assuming you were generating 200 MB of new data per week, at what point would you need to add another hard disk to this PC? Explain your answer and show how you calculated it.
4. Submit an informal written report with your findings to your instructor on paper or in a Word document named **C02A06**.

CHALLENGE Project

A small insurance agency is going to buy three new PCs for its clerical workers and set them up on a small local network. Recommend the types of drives or other storage devices that the PCs should have, and look up prices on the Internet for PCs with various configurations to determine how much each of the drives you recommend contributes to the overall cost. Write an informal report with your recommendations. Submit your report on paper or in a Word document named **C02A07**.

CHAPTER 3

Learning about Files, Folders, and Libraries

PERFORMANCE OBJECTIVES

Upon successful completion of Chapter 3, you will be able to:

- Use the Windows Explorer interface to browse files and folders
- Work with libraries and user folders
- Select multiple files and folders
- Create and rename folders
- Move and copy files and folders
- Sort, filter, group, and arrange file listings
- Create a library and manage library settings
- Find files and folders
- Create shortcuts for easier file and folder access
- Delete items and retrieve them from the Recycle Bin

Files are the basis of almost everything in computing. Whatever you do—whether it's running a program, typing a memo, or optimizing system performance—you are working with files. Most of the files on your system are there to run Windows 7 and your applications, but you can also create data files to store the work you do. You can then manipulate those data files in any way you like—rename them, copy them, organize them into folders, or even delete them altogether.

Using the Explorer Interface

Folder: An organizing unit for storing related files together in groups, also known as a location

Windows Explorer: The main file management interface in Windows 7

Disks can hold hundreds and even thousands of files, so some organizational structure is usually needed. *Folders* help organize a disk by creating logical groupings of files. In this section, you will learn how to use the Windows Explorer interface to browse the folders (also called locations) on your system and to display listings for different locations.

Understanding Windows Explorer

The Computer window that you used in Chapter 2 to examine the disks on your system is part of a larger file management interface called *Windows Explorer*. Each Explorer window (also called a *folder window*) displays the contents of a location you select. You can browse through a disk's content in a single window, or you can open multiple Explorer windows at once to compare the content of two locations or to move or copy between them.

Figure 3.1 shows an Explorer window, including the navigation and file management features built into Windows 7. Later sections in the chapter will cover using these features in greater detail:

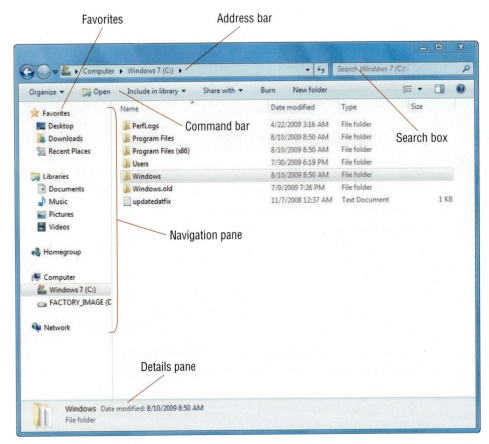

Figure 3.1 The Windows Explorer window provides several ways of accessing the files, folders, and disks on your PC.

- **Address bar.** Shows the name of the folder (location) whose contents appear in the folder window, as well as the folder(s) holding that folder. You can use this bar, as well as the Back and Forward arrow buttons to the left of it, to navigate to other folders.

- **Search box.** Enables you to enter a file or folder name to tell Explorer to find that file or folder.

- **Command bar.** Contains buttons for performing common tasks on the displayed content. Its buttons change depending on the content type; Figure 3.1 shows one set of buttons, but the bar would show a different set of buttons for a folder holding pictures. Some command bar buttons open menus with additional choices.

- **Navigation pane.** Enables you to move between locations, like different disks and folders.

- **Favorites.** Provides shortcuts for jumping to frequently used folders and re-running saved searches.

- **Details pane.** Displays basic information about the currently selected disk, folder, or file at the bottom of the window.

Displaying the Menu Bar

In addition to the command bar and other aids shown in Figure 3.1, Windows 7 also provides a menu bar for the folder window. It provides access to a menu system similar to the one that was available in previous Windows versions. The menu bar remains hidden until you need it. To display the menu bar, press the Alt key while the folder window is active. Then click a menu name to open a menu. Figure 3.2 shows the Edit menu open.

The menu bar remains visible until you select a command from it or until you click away from it.

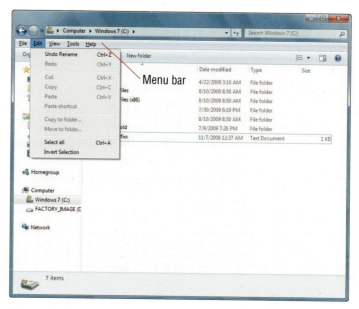

Figure 3.2 A traditional style menu bar can be activated by pressing the Alt key.

Displaying the Folder List

The folder list displays the drives and folders for the Computer in a hierarchical tree in the navigation pane. It provides an alternative method of browsing and navigating between locations that is more visual than the Address bar. See Figure 3.3. Note that the Favorites and Libraries sections in the navigation pane (Figure 3.1)—as well as the Homegroup and Network, if present—each also feature a similar list that works like the folder list.

To display the contents of a particular folder, click the folder's name in the navigation pane. The contents of the folder appear in the *file list* area of the window. Using the folder list, you can quickly jump to any drive or folder on your system.

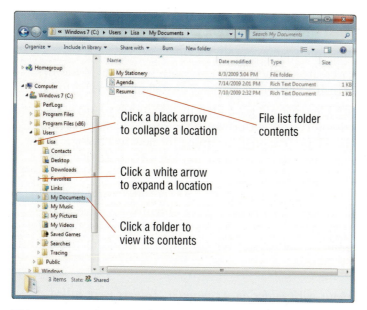

Figure 3.3 The folder list enables you to move between locations via a hierarchical tree.

You can collapse or expand a branch of the tree by double-clicking the drive or folder in the folder list. When the mouse pointer is in the navigation pane, a triangle appears to the left of each folder in the folder list to indicate the location's status. A black triangle means the item is expanded; a white triangle means it is collapsed. You also can click the black and white triangles to collapse and expand locations, respectively.

QUICK FIX

Menu Bar Does Not Appear
If the menu bar does not appear when you press Alt, the folder window may not be active. Click anywhere within the window to make it active, and then press Alt again.

File list: The area in a folder or library window that shows the files and folders in the folder or library

QUICK FIX

Navigation Pane Does Not Appear
If the navigation pane does not appear, click Organize on the command bar, point to Layout, and click navigation pane.

1. If needed, double-click *Computer* in the navigation pane to display the available disks.
2. Expand the desired drive by double-clicking it or clicking the *white triangle* beside it.
3. Expand/collapse folder levels as needed.
   a. Click a *white triangle* to expand a branch.
   b. Click a *black triangle* to collapse a branch.
4. Click the folder whose contents you want to view.

Tip: When you move the mouse pointer over a triangle, a highlight appears on the triangle to show you what drive or folder will be expanded or collapsed when you click.

Moving between Locations

Root directory: The top level of a disk, outside of any of its folders

In addition to using the folder list in the navigation pane to view the contents of a disk, you can open the Computer window by clicking Start and then clicking *Computer*, and then double-click the desired drive icon in the Computer window. A list appears of files and folders at its top level of organization—its ***root directory***. Figure 3.1 shows the root directory on the C drive of a PC. It contains these items:

- **Program Files and in some cases Program Files (x86)**. The folder(s) that stores the installed applications; on a system with the 64-bit version of Windows 7 installed, the Program Files folder holds 64-bit applications, while the Program Files (x86) folder holds 32-bit programs. A system with the 32-bit version of Windows 7 installed will have only the Program Files folder, which in that case holds 32-bit applications.

- **Users**. The folder that stores information and settings for each local user.

- **Windows**. The folder that stores the files Windows 7 itself needs to operate.

  Other items the root directory might contain include:

- **Windows.old**. A folder created if there was a previous version of Windows installed on the system or if a custom Windows 7 installation was performed.

- **PerfLog**. Holds the data files that are generated by a Windows 7 program called the Windows Reliability and Performance monitor. This advanced program is often used by IT professionals planning for new technology, as the program can monitor various system activities and identify those that have a negative impact on how the system operates.

- **Other Driver and System Software Folders**. The root may contain folders holding files for special software that helps a piece of hardware, such as the display, run. Software like this is typically provided by the manufacturer of a particular system component, and you or the computer system's manufacturer installs it in Windows 7.

Note: *Directory is synonymous with folder on a computer. Folders were called directories in MS-DOS, the original operating system for the IBM Personal Computer, back in the 1980s. The term was changed to folder in Windows because a folder is a more fitting metaphor.*

Browsing a Folder

To browse the contents of one of the folders, double-click the folder. For example, if you double-click the Users folder in the root directory of C, the folders that have been set up for each individual user on the PC appear. In Figure 3.4, there are three user folders: Lisa, Public, and Steve. Notice that the Address bar shows the *path* taken to the current location: first Computer, then the local disk [called Windows 7: (C) in this case], and then Users. The location immediately above or preceding a location is called is *parent*. For example, the C drive is the parent of the Users folder.

Note: The name that appears for the hard disk (Windows 7 in this chapter's examples) is called its volume label. You can change the volume label if desired. Chapter 2 provides more information about volume labels.

Windows 7 shows paths in the Address bar as links with arrows between them (refer to Figure 3.4). The traditional description of a path is the disk letter, a colon, and backslash (\), and then the folder names separated by backslashes, like this:

   C:\Users\Public

In the Address bar, each level of the path is a clickable link; you can jump to that location by clicking its name in the Address bar. You can reach other locations at any level of the path by clicking the arrow to the right of a link in the Address bar, and then clicking the desired folder in the menu that appears.

If you want to see the path of the current location displayed in its original format, click any blank area of the Address bar to temporarily change the path to the old-style notation. Click in the file list to return the Address bar to its normal notation.

Here are some tips for moving to other locations:

- **To jump to a location** listed in the Favorites section of the navigation pane, click it.

- **To return to the previously viewed location**, click the Back button. To go back several locations, click the Back button repeatedly, or click the Recent Pages button (the down arrow to the right of the Back and Forward buttons) and select a previously viewed location from the menu that appears. See Figure 3.5.

Path: The complete location of a file, including its disk letter and the folders in which it is located

Parent: The location immediately above the current one in the drive hierarchy

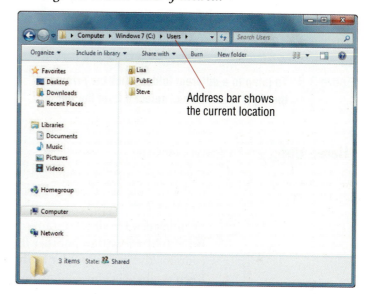

Address bar shows the current location

Figure 3.4 To browse folders within folders, double-click the desired folder.

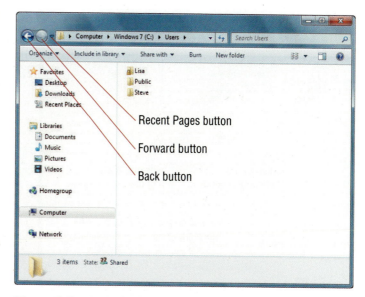

Recent Pages button

Forward button

Back button

Figure 3.5 The Back button goes back one location at a time, and the Recent Pages button opens a menu of previous locations.

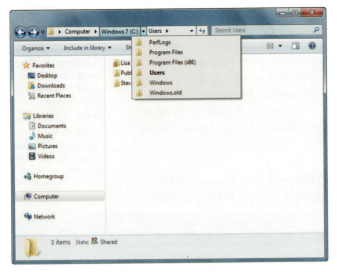

Figure 3.6 To jump to a different folder, click the arrow to the right of its link and select it from the list.

- **To go forward again** after going back, click the Forward button.
- **To jump to one of the higher-level folders in the current location's path**, click that folder's name in the Address bar. For example, in Figure 3.5, you could click Windows 7 (C:) to return to the root directory.
- **To jump to a different folder at a certain level**, click the arrow to the right of its link in the Address bar and select from the list. For example, in Figure 3.6, to jump to a different top-level folder on the C disk, click the arrow to the right of Windows 7 (C:) and then click another folder.

Here's How ➤ To browse a location:

1. Click Start, and click *Computer*. Or double-click *Computer* or click a folder under one of the other sections in the navigation pane. If you do the latter, skip to Step 3.
2. Double-click the disk containing the folder.
3. If the folder is within another folder, double-click the folder that contains the desired folder in the file list.
4. Keep double-clicking folders until you arrive at the folder containing the desired file.

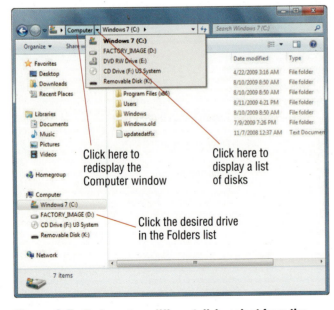

Click here to redisplay the Computer window

Click here to display a list of disks

Click the desired drive in the Folders list

Figure 3.7 To jump to a different disk, select from the folder list or use the Start menu or link on the Address bar.

Browsing a Different Disk

You can display the content of a different disk in Windows Explorer in several ways:

- Click Computer in the Address bar to return to the Computer window, which displays icons for all the available disk drives, and then double-click the desired disk.
- In the Address bar, click the arrow button to the right of Computer to display a drop-down list of disks and then click the desired disk. See Figure 3.7.
- Click the desired disk in the folder list under Computer in the navigation pane. Double-click Computer first if the disks do not appear.
- Open a new Computer window from the Start menu (Start, *Computer*).

Exercise 1
Browsing Locations

1. Click the Start button and click *Computer*. The Computer window appears.
2. Double-click the C: drive in the file list. (Remember, there will likely be a volume label along with the drive letter.) Its folders and files appear.
3. Double-click the Users folder. Its folders and files appear.
4. Double-click your user name folder, and then double-click the Favorites folder, and then the Microsoft Websites folder.
5. Take a screen shot of your desktop and name it **C03E01S05**. Print, e-mail it, or submit it to your instructor on a USB flash drive (thumb drive) for grading as required.
6. Click your user name in the Address bar to jump back your user name folder.
7. Click *Users* in the Address bar to jump back to the Users folder.
8. Click the Back button to return to your user name folder.
9. Click the Back button again to return to the Microsoft Websites folder.
10. Click the arrow to the right of your user name in the Address bar to display a menu of folders within that folder.

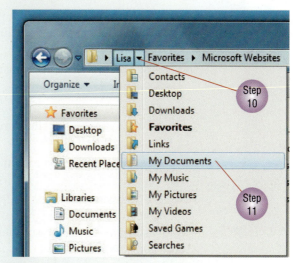

11. Click My Documents. The My Documents folder's content appears.
12. If the folder list does not appear under Computer in the navigation pane, double-click *Computer* to display the folder list.
13. In the navigation pane, click the white triangle beside the C: drive in the folder list. (The triangles appear when the mouse pointer is over the navigation pane.)
14. Click the white triangle beside *Users* in the folder list.
15. Click Public in the folder list.
16. Take a screen shot of your desktop and name it **C03E01S16**. Print, e-mail it, or submit it to your instructor on a USB flash drive (thumb drive) for grading as required.
17. Collapse all the expanded levels beneath Computer in the folder list in the navigation pane by clicking the black triangle next to *Computer*. You may need to scroll up in the pane to find the Computer listing.
18. Close the Explorer window.

Using Your Windows 7 Personal Folder

You learned in Chapter 1 that if more than one person uses a PC, you can create different user accounts to keep each user's data and gaming files separate. For each user added on the system, Windows 7 creates special folders. Each user's account folders are contained in a ***personal folder,*** which has the same name as the account name.

Personal folder: The parent folder holding folders for a user's account

Each folder within the personal folder is designed for a specific type of content:

- **Contacts**. For stored contact information used by e-mail and some other programs
- **Desktop**. Holds files and folders you have created or saved on your desktop
- **Downloads**. Holds files you have downloaded from the Internet
- **Favorites**. Holds items that you have identified as favorite places in the Internet Explorer Web browser
- **Links**. Holds the shortcuts that you have added to the Favorites section in the navigation pane
- **My Documents**. For data files from information-based business and productivity applications such as word processing, spreadsheet, and presentation programs
- **My Music**. For digital music clips and audio books
- **My Videos**. For video clips transferred to your system and video projects you create
- **Saved Games**. For the games that come with Windows 7, as well as games you install yourself
- **Searches**. For searches you have created and saved

To access any of these folders, click the Start button and then click the user name at the top of the right pane. This opens a folder window for your personal folder, displaying all the subfolders it contains. See Figure 3.8. Note that installing additional Windows programs and features may add folders within your personal folder or any of the folders it contains.

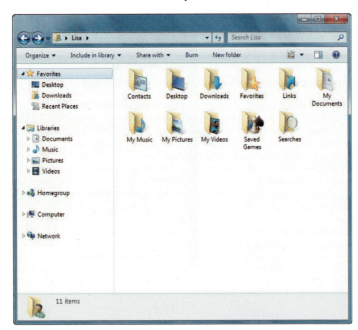

You also can navigate to any of the personal folders using the navigation pane or Address bar. To see this for yourself, navigate to the following path in any folder window: Computer > C: > Users > (your name). All the folders listed in this location are for your own data, for example Computer > C: > Users > (your name) > My Documents.

Note: *This book uses Windows 7 Address-bar-style notation to indicate paths, with arrows between the locations like this: C: > Users. On the Web and in other books, you might see DOS-style notation, with slashes separating the locations like this: C:\Users.*

Note: *When you are using the Explorer window to navigate to different folders, you cannot open the personal folder for another user.*

Figure 3.8 **For quick access to any of the four default folders Windows 7 creates for data, shown here, select your user name from the Start menu.**

Here's How

To open your personal folder:

- Click Start, and click *your user name* at the top of the right pane of the Start menu.

  OR

- Navigate to Computer > C: > Users > (your user name) using the Address bar or folder list in the navigation pane in a folder window.

Understanding Libraries

Libraries are a new feature in Windows 7. As a reminder, a library is a place for working with a particular type of file. Windows 7 offers Documents, Music, Pictures, and Video libraries by default, each for managing the type of file that its name suggests. A library does not store any files itself. Instead, it shows you all the contents of specified folders, so that you can view and work with the files in those folders at the same time. For example, say you are a commercial photographer who has taken digital photos of a number of products for a client. On your computer's hard disk, you have organized the photos of each product in a separate folder named for the product. This aids you in finding the digital photos of a particular product when the client needs the images or wants you to edit an image in some way. However, there may be other instances where you want to see all the digital photo files at once, such as if you need to burn a selection of photos of multiple products to a CD or DVD. In such a case, it would be easier to have the contents of all the individual product photo folders shown in a single library window, so that you can easily select images from a variety of locations and burn them to a disc.

The default libraries are each set up to monitor two locations holding a same file type: the one in your personal folder and the one in the Public folder. For example, the Documents library shows the contents of both C:>Users>Lisa>My Documents and C:>Users>Public>Public Documents. Likewise, the Music library is set up to show you the music files from both the personal and public location on your system, and so on for the Pictures and Videos folders.

You can display the contents of the Documents, Pictures, or Music library by clicking its library name listed below your user name on the right pane of the Start menu. You also can select a library in the Libraries section of the navigation pane in any window to open a library. A third way to open a library is via the Libraries window, shown in Figure 3.9. To open your Libraries window, showing the available libraries, click the Windows Explorer button on the taskbar. Then double-click the icon for the library that you want to open.

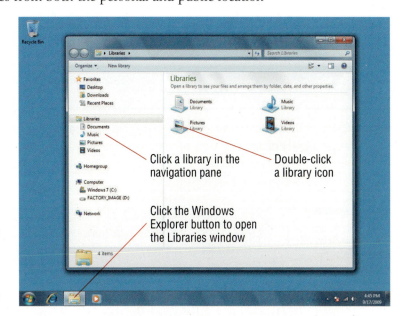

Figure 3.9 You can access your libraries in a variety of ways.

Here's How

To open a library:

- Click Start, and click the desired library near the top of the right pane of the Start menu.

OR

- Click the desired library in the Libraries section of the navigation pane in any folder window. (Double-click Libraries first if you do not see the individual libraries listed below it.)

OR

- Click the Windows Explorer button on the taskbar to open the Libraries window, and then double-click the icon for the desired library. If another folder window is already open on-screen, then right-click the Windows Explorer button and click *Windows Explorer* in the Jump List.

Tip: To open a second library window, right-click on the *Windows Explorer* icon on the taskbar, and click *Windows Explorer*.

Library pane

Figure 3.10 **A library looks like a regular folder but includes a library pane.**

Once a library window is open, it looks and works much like any other folder window. One key way to tell the difference between a folder window and a library is that you will see the **library pane** above the file list, like the example shown in Figure 3.10. You can work with the files and folders in a library just as you would work with them in the folder where they are actually stored. You can cut, copy, paste, and so on as described in this and other chapters. The "interface" between the library and a particular file's location will require no special actions on your part. Windows 7 does not limit you to working with the default libraries and their settings. You can customize one of the existing libraries to monitor additional locations, and you can create and customize your own libraries. You will learn how to do so later in this chapter.

Library pane: The area above the file list in a library window that shows the library's name and how many locations it monitors, as well as presenting a menu for arranging the library contents

Tip: If you need to go quickly to the location where a particular file in a library is actually stored, right-click the file, and then click *Open file location* in the shortcut menu that appears.

Opening Additional Folder Windows

To view two or more locations simultaneously, you might want to open more windows. You can do this by choosing *Computer* from the Start menu again, or by opening one of the default data or library folders described in the preceding two sections. Then size and arrange the windows so that both are visible at once. As you learned in Chapter 1, you can use Snap (also called Aero Snap) to arrange windows side by side, or the taskbar shortcut menu to choose various window arrangements, in addition to resizing and positioning windows manually.

Changing How Folders and Files Appear

Changing the view in a folder window enables you to control how the window presents files and folders. The various views present more or less information, and use smaller or larger thumbnails or icons. Smaller generic icons might be appropriate, for example, if a folder holds many files, and you want to see as many of them as possible in the folder window. In another case, seeing more information about a file or folder might help if you are looking for a file you last worked with on a particular date. Here are the views available to apply to any folder or library window:

- **Extra Large Icons**. This view shows items as very large thumbnails with just the disk, folder, or file name below. This view can be useful for looking at previews of pictures, for example. (Windows 7 is sometimes able to display a preview thumbnail of a data file rather than a generic icon, depending on the file type.)

- **Large Icons**. This view shows thumbnails that are slightly smaller than the Extra Large ones, with the disk, folder, or file name below.

- **Medium Icons**. This view reduces the thumbnail size even further and lists the disk, folder, or file name below each icon.

- **Small Icons**. In this view, generic icons appear the same height as the text, with the disk, folder, or file name to the *right* of each icon (not below it).

- **List**. This view shows the same information as the Small Icons view, but arranges the items in multiple columns.

- **Details**. This view also retains the small icons approach, but lists several columns of additional information to the right of each item's icon and name. The columns that appear by default will vary depending on the type of files being viewed, but may include such columns as Date or Date modified, Tags, Size, or Contributing artists. To change the width of a column, drag the divider between that column and the one to its right.

    Note: *Some of these properties, such as Type, are assigned when you create the file in a program such as a word processor.*

- **Tiles**. This view shows disk icons of the same size as Medium Icons, but shows the file name and some additional information about the file below. The information that appears depends on the type of icon. For drives, disk usage information appears. For document files, the file type and file size appears.

- **Content**. This view shows larger icons with larger names for easier reading.

To cycle through five of the available views—List, Details, Tiles, Content, and Large Icons—click the Views button itself. Each time you click the button, the folder window will display the next of those three views.

Figure 3.11 Use the Views button's menu to change the view for the current folder.

Click the down arrow button to the right of the Views button to open a menu listing the available views, as shown in Figure 3.11. Click the desired view. Or, if you want to experiment with an icon size that falls between the sizes designated by two particular views, drag the slider. When you release the mouse button, the icons will take on that custom size. The selected view applies to the current folder only. If you browse or jump to another folder, it will display its default view or the view most recently applied to it.

Note in Figure 3.11, also, that when folders display at larger thumbnail sizes, you can tell via the thumbnail whether the folder is empty or contains files. The thumbnail will include a folder and file within the folder if the folder has contents, or the thumbnail will show an empty folder when the folder is empty.

Here's How

To toggle between List, Details, Tiles, Content, and Large Icons views:

- Click the Views button.

To select from a menu of views:

1. Click the down arrow to the right of the Views button.
2. Click the desired view or drag the slider up or down on the list.

Note: *If you want to apply the same icon size to all folders of the same type (for example, folders that hold document files versus folders that hold pictures), click Organize on the command bar of an Explorer window, and then click Folder and search options. Click the View tab, click Apply to Folders, and then click OK.*

Tip: Additional viewing options are available from the View menu. Press Alt to display the menu bar, and then open the View menu and select the options desired. For example, you can turn the Status bar on or off and you can choose whether to automatically arrange the icons into orderly rows and columns.

In a library window, you can reset the window to its default view. To do so, click the Arrange by button in the library pane to open a list of arrangement choices, and click *Clear changes.*

Exercise 2
Viewing Personal Folders and Libraries

1. Click the Start button and click your user name in the right pane. A window for your personal folder appears.
2. Click the Views button three times to toggle between views.
3. Open the Views button's menu and click *Large Icons*. The view changes to display the larger icons.
4. Take a screen shot of your desktop and name it **C03E02S04**. Print, e-mail it, or submit it to your instructor on a USB flash drive (thumb drive) for grading as required.
5. Open the Views button's menu and drag the slider halfway between Medium Icons and Large Icons. Icons display at a custom size midway between the two sizes.
6. Open the Views button's menu and click *Medium Icons*.
7. Right-click the Windows Explorer button on the taskbar, and click *Windows Explorer* in the Jump List.
8. Take a screen shot of your desktop and name it **C03E02S08**. Print, e-mail it, or submit it to your instructor on a USB flash drive (thumb drive) for grading as required.
9. In the window you opened in Step 7, double-click the *Documents library* icon.
10. In the navigation pane, click *Music* in the Libraries section to display the Music library.
11. Open the Views button's menu and click *Tiles*.
12. In the library pane, open the Arrange by menu, and click *Clear changes*.
13. Close the open windows.

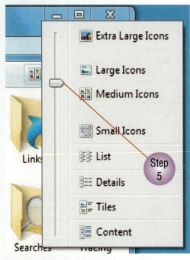

Managing Files and Folders

Now that you know how to control the Windows Explorer interface and how to navigate to various locations, this section describes what you can do when you get to a location. In this section you will learn how to select, rename, move, and copy files and folders.

Selecting Files and Folders

Before you can perform an action on a folder or file, such as deleting or renaming it, you must select it. Any commands you issue affect the selected item(s). Some commands can be performed on multiple items at once, such as moving or copying; other commands work only on individual items, such as renaming.

A selected file or folder appears with a blue or gray selection highlight over it, and information about it appears in the details pane. When multiple items are selected, they all appear with the same selection highlight, and the details pane reports the total number of items selected and summary information for them, such as the total aggregate file size.

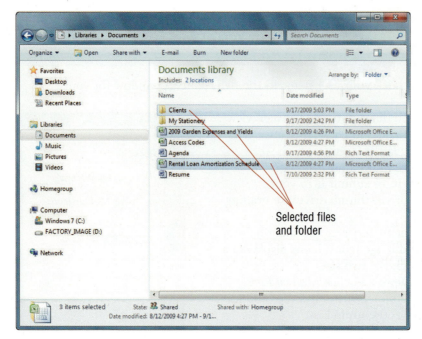

A group of selected files and/or folders can be either contiguous (all together) or noncontiguous. It makes no difference except in the technique used to select them. To select a contiguous block of items, hold down Shift as you click the first and last file in the group to select; to select a noncontiguous block, hold down Ctrl as you click each file you want. Figure 3.12 shows a noncontiguous selection. To remove a selection, click a blank area in the folder list.

Figure 3.12 Select noncontiguous items by holding down Ctrl as you click each one.

> **Tip:** You can force files to be contiguous with one another by sorting, filtering, or grouping them according to the property they have in common. For example, to select all Microsoft Word documents, sort the list by Type so they are all together on the list.

Here's How

To select a single item:
- Click the item.

To select multiple contiguous items:
1. Click the first item.
2. Hold down the Shift key and click the last item.

To select multiple noncontiguous items:
1. Click the first item.
2. Hold down the Ctrl key and click the next item.
3. Repeat Step 2 for additional items.

To select all the items in the current location:
- Press Ctrl+A.

To cancel (deselect) a selection:
- Click away from the selection.

Creating a New Folder

As you begin creating data files in various applications and for various purposes, you will probably want to create new folders to organize your work. You can create folders on a hard disk, on removable media, such as USB flash drives, on an external hard disk, or in a library. You can also create folders on any shared network location to which you have access. Once you have created a folder, you can save a document you have created from another program or copy or move files into the folder.

Some people choose to create their data folders as subfolders within the Documents library, so that they can easily access their folders from the Documents command on the Start menu. The Documents library is also the default storage location for most applications; however, you are free to create folders nearly anywhere you like. Because a library is not an actual location but instead almost a mirror that reflects the contents of other physical folder locations on the hard disk, any folder or file you create or save in a library will be stored in a specified folder location. You will learn more about designating the save folder for a library later in the chapter.

Note: *If you are logged on as a standard user, you may be prevented from creating folders in certain locations or need to supply an administrator password. All users will be prompted to confirm the operation when creating a folder in certain locations, such as the Windows folder. These restrictions are part of the Windows 7 User Account Control security scheme.*

For example, you work as a salesperson and want to use folders to organize your files for faster access. You might create a folder on your office computer called *Clients*. Within that *Clients* folder, you could then create a specific folder to hold the files you create for each client account, such as *Smith Electronics*, *Argyle Aggregates*, or *Kelly Appliances*. Then, when you needed to work on a file you created for a particular client, you would know exactly which folder it's in.

To create a folder:

1. Open the Computer window, your personal folder, or the main Windows Explorer window.
2. Display the location (folder or library) in which you want to create the folder.
3. Right-click a blank area of the folder window, point to *New*, and click *Folder*.
   OR
   On the command bar, click New folder.
4. Type a name for the new folder.
5. Press Enter.

Here's How

Renaming a File or Folder

If you made a typo when creating a folder or file name or need to update its name, you can do so at any time in a folder window, either by using the Organize button's menu or by right-clicking the file or folder. File and folder names can be up to 255 characters and can include spaces and most punctuation marks (but not any of these: / \ * ? " | < >). Every file name includes a ***file name extension***, added

File name extension: A period and additional letters appended to the file name to identify the file format automatically when the file is saved. (Chapter 5 covers saving files.) The file name extension consists of a period and additional letters added at the end of the file name and identifies the type of file and program used to create it. If the file name extension is visible when you rename the file, be sure not to delete or change it. Doing so means you will no longer be able to open the file by double-clicking it, and the program in which you created the file may no longer recognize the file.

Note: *Do not rename any of the folders that Windows 7 or your applications created, such as Windows, Program Files, or Users, or Windows will not work correctly. It is safe to rename only user-created folders and files.*

Here's How ▶

To rename a file or folder:

1. Open the Computer window, your personal folder window, or the main Windows Explorer window, and navigate to the folder or file to be renamed.
2. Right-click the folder or file and click *Rename*.
   OR
   On the command bar, click Organize and click *Rename*.
   OR
   Press F2.
3. Type a new name or edit the existing name.
4. Press Enter.

Tip: To undo a Rename operation, press Ctrl+Z immediately afterwards, choose Organize > *Undo* on the command bar, or press Alt to display the menu bar and then choose Edit > *Undo Rename*.

Copying or Moving a File or Folder

Copying a file or folder makes a duplicate of it and places that duplicate in a new destination. For example, you might have a flash memory card from your digital camera that has some recent pictures. When you place that card in the appropriate removable media disk drive connected to your computer, you can copy the image files to a folder on the hard disk. The original images remain on the flash card, until you decide to remove them.

You can copy files or folders in two ways: with the Windows Clipboard (via the Cut, Copy, and Paste commands) or via drag-and-drop.

Copying or Moving with the Clipboard

The Windows Clipboard is a temporary internal storage area in Windows 7. You can place things into that storage by selecting them and issuing either the Cut or Copy command. Cut removes the original; Copy leaves the original in place. You can then navigate to the new location and issue the Paste command to insert the Clipboard's content. Figure 3.13 illustrates how the Clipboard works.

One advantage of the Clipboard method of moving and copying is that multiple pastes are possible. After you have cut or copied something, you can then paste it into multiple different locations without having to re-cut or re-copy it. Another advantage is that you do not have to be able to see both the original and the destination locations at the same time. You can perform the cut or copy operation, and then open up the destination location at your leisure.

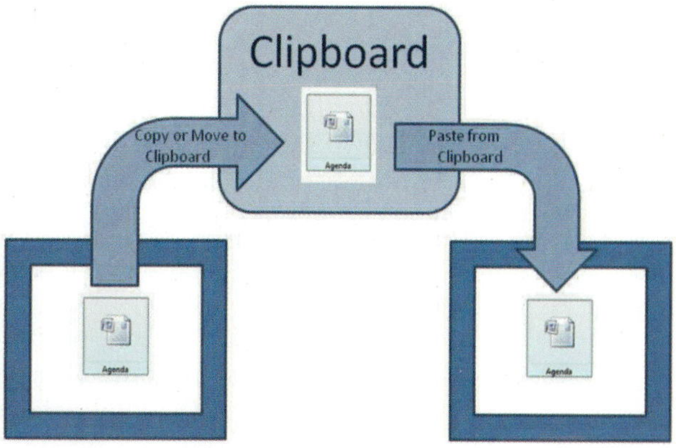

Clipboard

Copy or Move to Clipboard

Paste from Clipboard

Figure 3.13 **The Clipboard enables you to move and copy from one location to another.**

Tip: The Clipboard does much more than just move and copy files. You can use the Clipboard within most Windows applications to move and copy content between data files. For example, you could use the Clipboard to copy a drawing from a graphics program and paste it into a word processing document.

There are many ways to issue the Cut, Copy, and Paste commands, including mouse methods, keyboard methods, and menu methods.

To move a file or folder (or a group) with the Clipboard:

1. Select either the files(s) or folder(s).
2. Issue the Cut command in any of these ways:
   - Press Ctrl+X.
   - Right-click the selection and choose *Cut*.
   - Click Organize and click *Cut*.
   - Press Alt and choose Edit, *Cut*.
3. Display the destination location.
4. Issue the Paste command in any of these ways:
   - Press Ctrl+V.
   - Right-click an empty area of the destination location and choose *Paste*.
   - Click Organize, and click *Paste*.
   - Press Alt, and then choose Edit, *Paste*.

To copy a file or folder (or a group) with the Clipboard:

1. Select the files(s) and/or folder(s).
2. Issue the Copy command in any of these ways:
   - Press Ctrl+C.
   - Right-click the selection and choose *Copy*.
   - Click Organize and click *Copy*.
   - Press Alt and then choose Edit, *Copy*.
3. Display the destination location.
4. Issue the Paste command in any of these ways:
   - Press Ctrl+V.
   - Right-click an empty area of the destination location and choose *Paste*.
   - Click Organize, and click *Paste*.
   - Press Alt, and then choose Edit, *Paste*.

Here's How

Copying or Moving with Drag-and-Drop

This method requires having both the source and the destination locations visible at the same time. The locations can be in two separate Windows Explorer windows, or the destination location can be a folder or location icon in the navigation pane.

What happens when you drag-and-drop: does it move, or does it copy? That depends on the relationship between the source and destination locations. If the source and destination are on the same disk, drag-and-drop actions move the material. If the source and destination material are on different disks, drag-and-drop actions copy the material. To override this default behavior, hold down the Ctrl key if you want to copy, or hold down the Shift key if you want to move.

Here's How

Accurate Dropping
If you are dragging a selection into a folder in the Favorites section or the folder list in the navigation pane, make sure you position the mouse accurately over the folder before releasing the mouse button. When the mouse pointer is in the correct spot for dropping on that location, a large icon appears over the location with a Move To indicator under it, as shown in this figure.

To copy a file or folder (or a group) with drag-and-drop:

1. Select the file(s) and/or folder(s).
2. If the destination is on the same disk as the source, hold down the Ctrl key.
3. Drag the selection to the new location and drop it.

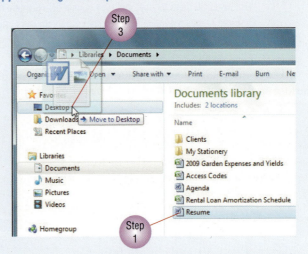

To move a file or folder (or a group) with drag-and-drop:

1. Select the file(s) and/or folder(s).
2. If the destination is on the same disk as the source, hold down the Shift key.
3. Drag the selection to the new location and drop it.

 ## Exercise 3

Creating and Managing Folders and Files

1. Click Start, and then click *Documents*. The Documents library opens.
2. Create a new folder named **Practice** there. One possible method:
   a. Click New folder on the command bar.
   b. Type **Practice**.
   c. Press Enter.
3. Rename the folder **Transport**. One possible method:
   a. Right-click the new folder.
   b. Click *Rename*.
   c. Type **Transport**.
   d. Press Enter.
4. Click Start, and then click *Computer*. The Computer window opens.

5. Arrange the two windows side-by-side so both are visible.
6. Locate Student Data Files at www.emcp.net/windows7. If you have not already done so, download files to your computer or to your USB flash drive. Ask your instructor for assistance, if needed.
7. Navigate to the folder for Chapter 3, and select the **Airline** file.
8. Copy the Airline file to the Documents library. One possible method:
   a. Hold down the Ctrl key.
   b. Drag the file to the Documents library.
9. In the Documents library window, rename the copied file:
   a. Right-click the Airline file.
   b. Click *Rename* in the shortcut menu.
   c. Type Railroad.
   d. Press Enter.
10. Move Railroad into the Transport folder. One possible method:
    a. Select Railroad and press Ctrl+X to cut it.
    b. Double-click the Transport folder to open it.
    c. Press Ctrl+V to paste Railroad into the Transport folder.
11. In the Railroad file's properties, use metadata to specify your name as the Author:
    a. Right-click Railroad and choose *Properties*.
    b. On the Details tab, point to the space to the right of Authors (and to the right of any existing name there) and click.
    c. Type your name in the text box, replacing any existing text.
12. Enter a Completed status and today's date:
    a. Continue working on the Details tab.
    b. Scroll down to the *Content* section.
    c. Point to the space to the right of Content status and click.
    d. Type Completed and then today's date.
    e. Click OK.
13. Close all open Windows Explorer windows.

Organizing Files and Folders

When a location contains many files, it can be difficult to make a meaningful evaluation of what is there. How many different file types are present? Are there any files that were recently modified? Which files are occupying the most disk space?

These important questions and more can be answered by applying *sorting*, *grouping*, *filtering*, or *arranging* to the display of files. Each of these techniques is useful for answering different questions about the data or browsing it in a different way.

Sorting the File and Folder Listing

Sorting arranges the items in a folder or library window according to a file property, such as alphabetically by name or in ascending order by size. When you have changed to the Details view in a folder or library window, some common sort criteria appear in a column headings bar immediately above the file listing: *Name*, *Date modified*, *Type*, and *Size*. (See Figure 3.14.) These represent the columns that appear when viewing the file list in Details view, but the column headings remain visible even in other views. Click any of those column headings to sort by that criterion. Click the same column heading again to toggle between ascending and descending sort order.

Sorting: Arranging items in a particular order based on a property

Grouping: Arranging items into grouped sections of a list based on a property

Filtering: Displaying only certain items based on a property

Arranging: Summarizing the items in a library into stacks based on a property

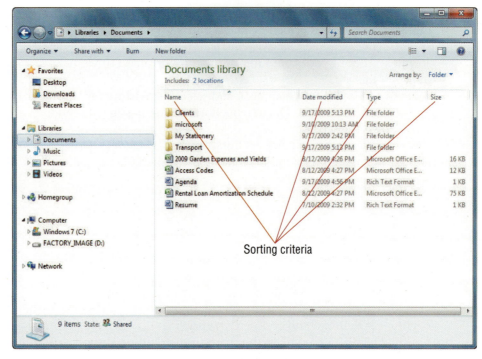

Figure 3.14: To sort a file and folder listing, click the column heading that describes the criterion for sorting.

To sort by a property other than the column headings listed, you can add the desired property as a column heading in the Windows Explorer window. To add a column, right-click any column heading and then click *More*. In the Choose Details dialog box, mark or clear check boxes to indicate which properties should be column headings, and then click OK.

> Tip: You also can press Alt and then choose View > *Choose details* to open the Choose Details dialog box where you select which columns appear on-screen.

Here's How

To sort by a column heading's criterion:
1. Display the Details view, if needed.
2. Click the column heading. Click it a second time to reverse the order.

To sort by a property not shown as a column heading:
1. Display the Details view, if needed.
2. Right-click any visible column heading.
3. Click *More*.
4. Mark the check box for the property by which you want to sort.
5. Click OK.
6. Click the column heading. Click it a second time to reverse the order.

Grouping Files and Folders

Grouping is like sorting except the items are divided into separate sections of the window based on their membership in one group or another. The groups depend on the criterion by which you are grouping; for example, in Figure 3.15, the files are shown grouped by Date modified. The groups in the figure are Today, Last week, and Earlier this year.

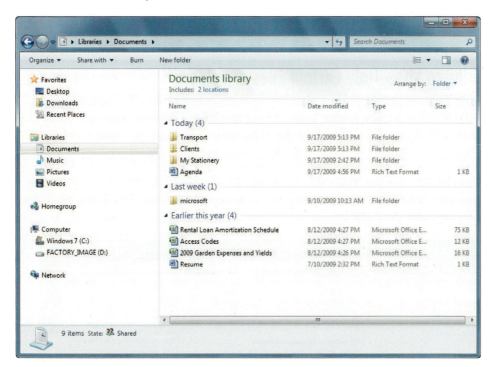

Figure 3.15 **This grouped listing shows files and folders placed in different sections based on their Date modified.**

Tip: You can expand and collapse groups in the file list using the triangles to the left of the group name or by right-clicking and using the *Expand all groups* and *Collapse all groups* in the shortcut menu.

To group by a column heading's criterion:

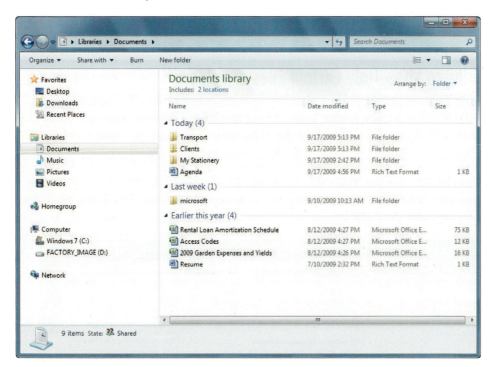

1. Right-click the file list.
2. Point to *Group by*.
3. Click the criterion to group by from the choices at the top of the submenu.

To group by a property not shown as a column heading:

1. Right-click the file list.
2. Point to *Group by*.
3. Click *More*.
4. Mark the check box for the property by which you want to group.
5. Click OK.
6. Right-click the file list.

Here's How

Here's How

7. Point to *Group by*.
8. Click the property (criterion) you selected in Step 4.

To remove grouping:

1. Right-click the file list.
2. Point to *Group by*.
3. Click *(None)*.

Filtering to Show Only Certain Files or Folders

Filtering displays only files that match particular criteria, such as a particular file type. To filter, move the mouse pointer over one of the column headings above the folder and file icons. Click the drop-down list arrow that appears, and then click the check boxes for one or more criteria in the drop-down menu, and press Enter or click outside the menu to close the drop-down box. Figure 3.16 shows *Earlier this year* chosen from the Date modified list, showing only the files created during the current week. To remove the filtering, open the drop-down list again, clear the check boxes, and close the list.

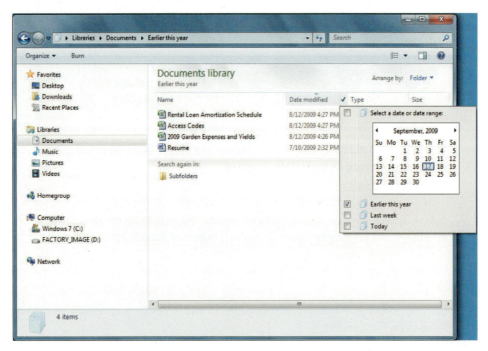

Figure 3.16 To filter the file list, open the menu for one of the column headings and mark a check box that represents the filter to apply.

Virtual folder: A temporary logical grouping of files, such as the files resulting from filtering or searching

A filter creates a ***virtual folder***, which is a temporary means of grouping files. Notice in Figure 3.16 that the Address bar indicates that you are in the folder called Earlier this year. That folder does not actually exist; it was created by the filter. When you remove the filter, the virtual folder will go away. If you want to save a filter specification, create a reusable virtual folder (see "Saving a Search" and "Using Saved Searches" later in this chapter).

To filter the file list in Details view:

1. Point to a column heading, and then click its down arrow to open its menu.
2. Click the desired filter criteria to place a check mark in its check box. Check multiple criteria if desired.
3. If needed, click the file list to close the menu.
4. Repeat Steps 1–3 to specify additional filtering for additional columns.

To remove a filter in Details view:

1. Point to the column heading for the filtered column (it will have a check mark to the right of its name), and then click the check mark to open its menu.
2. For each filter to remove, click its check box to clear the check mark.
3. Click the file list to close the menu.
4. Repeat Steps 1–3 to remove filtering from additional columns.

Arranging Items in a Library

A library window provides the ability to arrange items, hiding the individual items and instead showing icons or folders that represent various categories of the items. Arrange the items by opening the Arrange by menu in the library pane, and then clicking the desired category. The categories depend on which library you are working in. For example, in Figure 3.17, items in the Documents library are stacked by *Type*. In the Music library, you can arrange items by other categories such as *Artist*. The arranged items might appear as stacks, as in Figure 3.17, or they may appear as icons. To view the contents of an arranged stack or icon, double-click it. Each stack is a virtual folder (a temporary folder). To go back to all of the stacks or icons, click the Back button. To remove an arrangement, open the Arrange by menu and click *Folder*.

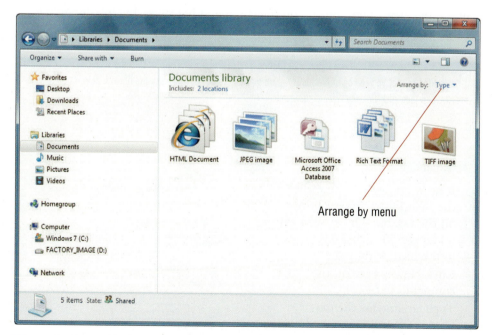

Figure 3.17 Arranging creates a series of virtual folders and displays them instead of the individual items.

To arrange a library:

1. Click the Arrange by menu in the library pane.
2. Click the desired category.

To remove the arrange setting:

1. Click the Arrange by menu in the library pane.
2. Click *Folder*.

Working with Libraries

You have already had an introduction to how each of the default libraries in Windows 7 keeps track of a particular type of file and folders stored in designated locations. The Documents library collects your data-oriented work, the Music library collects digital songs, the Pictures library presents digital images, and the Videos library is for movie clips and projects. As with folders, Windows 7 provides you the option of creating additional libraries to meet your file management needs and to customize a number of aspects of how any library—including any of the default libraries—operates.

Making or Deleting a Library

You can add a new library to create a central location for files pertaining to, say, a particular topic or client. Windows 7 enables you to add and remove libraries on an as-needed basis. Once you have created a new library, you need to set it up to monitor particular folders and choose other settings controlling how it behaves. After that point, you can copy and move files and folders into your custom library just as you would one of the default libraries. You need to be working in the main Windows Explorer window, which shows the default libraries, to create a new library. There, you can use the New library button on the command bar to get the job done.

> **Tip:** After you create and configure your own library, you can add a shortcut for it to the Windows 7 desktop so that you can open the library more quickly. To do so, right-click the library, point to *Send to*, and then click *Desktop (create shortcut)*.

To create a library:

1. If no windows are open, click the Windows Explorer button on the taskbar. Or, in an open folder window, click Libraries in the navigation pane.
2. Click New library on the command bar.
3. Type a name for the new library.
4. Press the Enter key.

Libraries

Open a library to see your files and arrange them

Documents
Library

Pictures
Library

Step 3

Client Photos
Library

Controlling Which Folders a Library Monitors

Each of the default libraries initially monitors and displays a pair of folders. For example, the Documents library shows the contents of the My Documents folder in your personal folder and the Public Documents folder in the Public folder. Each of the other default libraries monitors the pair of personal and public folders corresponding to the library's name. One of the folders set up for each library is designated as the ***save location***. A library functions as a virtual folder and does not really store the files or folders you create or copy in it. Instead, those files or folders are physically created in another folder on a disk, the save location.

Save location: The folder where a library will physically store any file or folder created or copied to the library.

Initially, a new folder you create monitors no folders. You must include one or more folders in the list of locations that the library shows. If you try to open a library for which no folders have been included, Windows 7 will prompt you to include a folder, as shown in Figure 3.18. Simply click the Include a folder button, browse to and select the desired folder in the dialog box that appears, and then click Include folder. The first folder you include for a library becomes the save location by default. If you remove the save location folder from the library, Windows 7 designates the next folder as the save location. You can add as many folders as desired and change the save location for any library, including the default libraries, at any time in the Properties dialog box for the library. To open the properties dialog box, right-click the library's icon in a file list or its name in the navigation pane, and click *Properties*.

Windows 7 places a few restrictions on which folders you can include in a library. Of course you can include the folders on your computer and its internal hard disk(s). You cannot include a folder from optical media (readable and writable CDs and DVDs) or any other type of removable media, such as a USB flash drive. You can include folders from an external hard drive, as long as the drive is connected to the system, powered on, and fully recognized. If your computer can connect to folders elsewhere on a network, such a network folder must be made available offline so it will be added to your computer's index in order to be included in the library. (You will learn about working with offline folders in Chapter 16.)

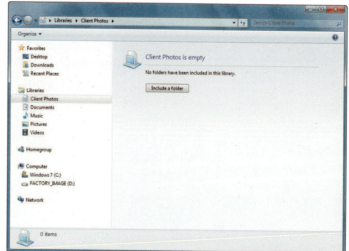

Figure 3.18 **You must include one or more folders in a new library.**

Here's How

To include a folder in a library:

- If the library is brand new and has no folders included, open the library and then click Include a folder. Navigate to and select a folder in the Include Folder dialog box that appears, and then click Include folder.

OR

1. In the main Windows Explorer window, right-click the library, and then click *Properties*. Or, in an open folder window, right-click the library in the navigation pane, and then click *Properties*.
2. Under Library locations, click the Include a folder button.
3. In the Include Folder dialog box that appears, navigate to and select the desired folder.
4. Click the Include folder button.

To change the save location in a library:

1. In the main Windows Explorer window, right-click the library, and then click *Properties*. Or, in an open folder window, right-click the library in the navigation pane, and then click *Properties*.
2. Under Library locations, click the folder that you want to set as the save location. (It will not have a check mark beside it.)
3. Click the Set save location button.
4. Click OK.

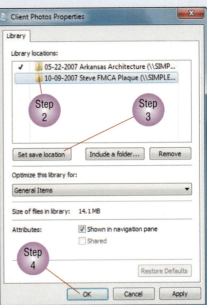

To remove a location from a library:

1. In the main Windows Explorer window, right-click the library, and then click *Properties*. Or, in an open folder window, right-click the library in the navigation pane, and then click *Properties*.
2. Under Library locations, click the folder that you want to remove.
3. Click the Remove button.
4. Click OK.

Changing Other Library Settings

Two other important library settings need to be specified for new libraries and can be changed for existing libraries. First, a library needs to be optimized for the types of files being managed by the library. The default optimization setting, General Items, groups files by folder location in the file list by default and shows items in the Details view. A better arrangement for photos is the Large Icons view; if you optimize a library for Pictures, it will use the Large Icons view by default. Other library optimization choices are Documents, Music, and Videos. The second setting you may wish to control is whether a custom library appears in the navigation pane or not. If you have added a shortcut for a library to the desktop or often work in the main Windows Explorer window that shows all your libraries, you may decide that having a library appear in the navigation pane (the default setting) is overkill. You can work with both of these settings in the Properties dialog box for the library.

Here's How

To optimize a library and control its navigation pane display:

1. In the main Windows Explorer window, right-click the library, and then click *Properties*. Or, in an open folder window, right-click the library in the navigation pane, and then click *Properties*.
2. Click the *Optimize this library for* drop-down list to open it, and then click the desired optimization.
3. Beside Attributes, click the *Shown in navigation pane* check box. Marking the check box specifies that the library will appear, while clearing it removes the library from the navigation pane.
4. Click OK.

Finding Files and Folders

As you use Windows 7 features and applications, you will likely create many data files such as reports, spreadsheets, photos, video clips, and so on. As the number of folders and files grows, the difficulty increases in remembering where you saved a particular file or in which location you created a particular folder. In this section you will learn some ways of locating a file or folder on your system.

Note: *The search features of Windows 7 find more than just files and folders; they also find information within an Outlook data file, including e-mails, contacts, calendar items, and tasks on to-do lists. This chapter focuses mainly on files and folders, but as you perform searches, some of the results you get will likely be Outlook data items.*

Not Getting Expected Search Results
If you do not get the search results you expect, make sure you started in a high enough level location. To search across all drives at once, start at the Computer window.

Performing a Quick Search by Name, Content, or Keyword

The *search* box in the top right corner of a folder or library window enables you to perform quick searches on a word or phrase you enter. Simply navigate to the drive or folder from which you want to start the search and type the criteria for your search, such as part of the file name or a keyword, into the *search* box. The search will be performed on that location and all its subordinate locations.

Type the search word(s) here

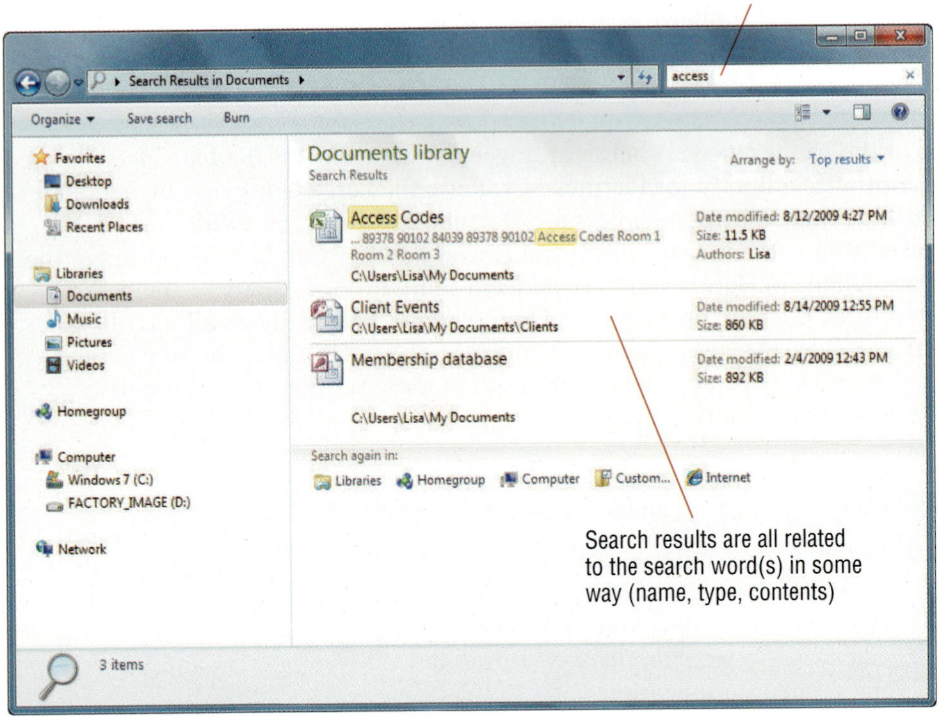

Search results are all related to the search word(s) in some way (name, type, contents)

Figure 3.19 A search filters to find all files and folders related to the word(s) you search for.

In Figure 3.19, for example, the word *access* was used as the search term, and Windows 7 has found files and folders that contain *access* in their file or folder name, or that were created in Microsoft Access, or that have the word *access* in their content.

Search results begin appearing immediately; the view in the current window is filtered to show the files and folders that match the text you have typed so far. It may take a few seconds or even a few minutes to see the full results if the search scope encompasses many locations, such as the entire contents of a large hard disk.

> **Tip:** You can speed up searches of locations that you frequently search by indexing them. Indexing a location creates an internal lookup table that the Search tools in Windows 7 can use to search the location more efficiently. Indexing is covered later in this chapter.

Here's How ▶ **To perform a search:**

1. Click in the *search* box in the folder or library window.
2. Type the file name, type, date, key words, or other criterion.
3. When you have typed as much of the search term as needed, press Enter.

Tip: The *search* box on the Start menu also enables you to perform a file and folder search. Click the Start menu button to open the menu, type all or part of the name of the desired file or folder, and then press Enter.

Tip: You can use wildcards (? and *) and comparison operators (< and >) with a search in a search box. For example, you can enter ??bb to find files that have any character as the first two characters and bb as the third and fourth characters. Or enter *.htm to find all files of the .htm file type (file extension). Entering <7/20/09 would find all files created before 7/20/09.

Repeating a Search

The *search* box tracks terms that you have performed over time. After you have performed a search, the next time you click in the *search* box, a drop-down list with the previous searches appears. Click one of those searches to run it again.

To repeat a search:

1. Click in the *search* box in the folder window.
2. Click one of the previous searches that appears.

Here's How

Tip: If the list of prior searches becomes too cluttered for practical use, you can delete items from the list. Click the *search* box, point to an item to delete, and then press the Delete key on your keyboard.

When you perform a search, you have the option of repeating the same search in another location. As shown in Figure 3.19, Windows 7 displays a Search again in section below the filtered search results in the window. To expand the search to one of those larger locations, click an icon. For example, click Libraries to rerun the search in all the libraries, or click Computer to search all locations on the computer.

Using Search Filters

Filters

Figure 3.20 **You can include a filter with a search.**

As you type an entry in the *search* box at the top of a folder or library window, the drop-down list that appears also includes filter categories along the bottom that you can use to build the search (Figure 3.20). You can either use a filter alone, or use it in conjunction with a search term that you enter. To apply one of the filters, select it, and then click one of the criteria that appears. For example, say you want to search for Access database files in a particular location. You could click the *search* box, type access, click the Type: filter, and then click the appropriate file name extension. When using the Date modified: filter, you can use the calendar that's among the choices to choose a date or date range. To change a filter criterion, click it in the *search* box, and then make a new choice in the list.

Note: *Windows 7 determines a file's type by its extension. An extension is a code that follows the file name, separated from it by a period—for example, myfile.docx or yourfile.txt. Windows 7 maintains a list of common file extensions and the types of files they represent, and uses this information to perform searches by general category of file such as music or pictures.*

Setting Search Options

The *search* box makes certain assumptions about what you want. In particular, it assumes that you want to search the entire contents of every file in an indexed location, that you want to search all the subfolders of every location, and that you want to include partial matches. The latter two of these choices slow down the search results considerably but provide the most thorough results. You can change those settings and more in the Search tab of the Folder Options dialog box (Figure 3.21). You can change to searching both file names and contents in non-indexed locations and turn on/off other options for indexing and search methods here.

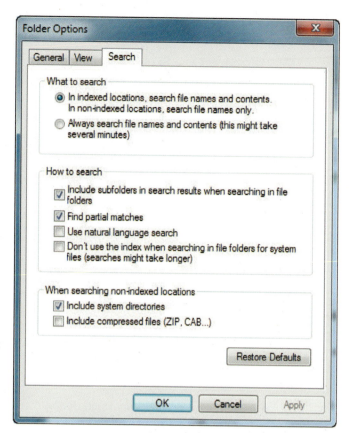

Figure 3.21 Set options for how Search will behave on the Search tab of the Folder Options dialog box.

To set search options:

1. Click Organize on the command bar of the folder or library window.
2. Click *Folder and search options*.
3. Click the Search tab in the dialog box.
4. Mark or clear check boxes for the options as desired.
5. Click OK.

◀ **Here's How**

Indexing a Location for Faster Searching

As you are performing some searches, you might notice that the search progress bar across the Address bar moves slowly, because the location being searched is not indexed. To avoid this, you can index the locations that you search most frequently.

Indexing creates a table of contents of the location that includes all the properties of all the files and folders within it. So when you search that location later, Windows 7 can refer to that table of contents rather than the actual file properties, and the search can take place much more quickly. Indexing occurs automatically behind the scenes when it is enabled for a location. All user folders and libraries and some special folders like those that store Start menu and Internet browsing history information are indexed by default, but you will need to enable indexing for other locations where you may store a lot of files, such as a storage folder on second hard disk installed in your system.

Indexing: A process that creates an index, an internal information set about a location, used to enable faster searching

Here's How ▶ **To enable or disable indexing for a location:**

1. Click Start, and then click *Control Panel*.
2. In the *search* box in the Control Panel window, type **index**.
3. Click *Indexing Options* in the Control Panel window.
4. In the Indexing Options dialog box, click Modify.
5. In the Indexed Locations dialog box, click the Show all locations button, and then click Continue in the User Account Control dialog box if you are not using an administrator account.
6. Click to mark or clear the check mark next to a location.

OR

Click the triangle next to a location to expand it and then mark or clear check boxes for individual folders within that location.

7. Click OK.
8. Close the other open dialog boxes and windows, clearing the search in the Control Panel window before closing it.

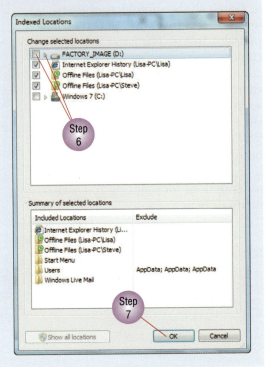

QUICK FIX

Slow Searches After Indexing
Indexing too many locations on your computer actually works against search performance. If you index the Windows folder or Program Files folder, the index will include loads of entries about files you will seldom, if ever, need to view or edit. If you have included these folders in the index, remove them to have a more efficient index.

When an indexed location is searched, the actual content of the location is ignored by default, and the search uses only the index as a reference. Therefore, if the index is out-of-date, the search results will not be accurate. Windows 7 attempts to keep the index current by indexing in the background as you work, but it sometimes requires an hour or more to index a complex location initially. If you must have accurate results at all times and do not mind that the search speed is slower because of it, you have two options:

• Turn off indexing for the location. This prevents Windows 7 from continuing to index this location, so if you re-enable indexing for it later, it might take awhile to update.

• In the Folder Options dialog box's Search tab (Figure 3.21), check the Always search file names and contents (might be slow) option button. This leaves indexing enabled but forces the search to look at the actual files, not just the index.

Here's How ▶ **To force Search to look at the actual location, not just the index:**

1. Click Organize on the command bar of the folder or library window.
2. Click *Folder and search options*.
3. Click the Search tab in the dialog box.
4. Mark the *Always search file names and contents (might be slow)* check box.
5. Click OK.

Saving a Search

After creating a search, you might wish to save it so you can rerun the same search again without having to set it up again manually.

To save a search, run the search and then click the Save search button on the command bar. Specify a name for the saved search in the Save As dialog box and click Save. See Figure 3.22. Do not change the save location. Saving the search to the default folder will make it easier to use, as described next. After you do that, the search is available in the saved searches list (accessible in the Searches folder in your personal folder).

Using Saved Searches

Your personal folder includes a Searches folder, where you can select from the saved searches you've created to find files. Each of these searches is a virtual folder. A virtual folder is like a query; every time you open it, you get the most recent results based on its search specifications.

Searches that you save will be added to the Searches folder, unless you specify another save location, which is best to avoid. Click the Start button, click your user name, and then double-click the Searches folder to display a list of saved searches, as shown in Figure 3.23. Double-click any of the saved searches to run it and display the results. Windows 7 also adds saved searches to the Favorites section of the navigation pane in a folder or library window. Click a search there to display the search results in the file list.

Figure 3.22 Save a search specification for later reuse by clicking the Save search button on the command bar and then assigning a name to the search.

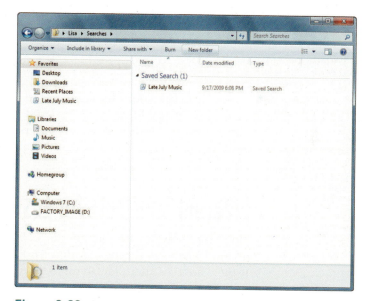

Figure 3.23 Saved searches appear in the Searches folder, ready for use.

Note: The path to the Searches folder is in your personal folder within Users. Each user has his or her own separate set of Searches. That's good because you can create your own custom saved searches that nobody else can access but you.

Creating Libraries and Searches

1. Click the Windows Explorer button on the taskbar.
2. Click the New library button on the command bar.
3. Type **Assignments** and press Enter.
4. Right click the *Assignments library* icon, and click Properties.
5. Click the Include a folder button. Navigate to and click the Public Documents folder. Click Include folder.
6. Choose *Documents* from the *Optimize this library for* drop-down list, and then click OK to close the library's Properties dialog box.
7. Take a screen shot of your desktop and name it **C03E04S07**. Print, e-mail it, or submit it to your instructor on a USB flash drive (thumb drive) for grading as required.
8. Click in the search box at the upper-right corner of the window.
9. Click the Date modified: filter.
10. Click *Earlier this month* in the menu that appears.
11. Group the search results by file type (extension):
    a. Right-click the file list.
    b. Point to *Group by* in the shortcut menu.
    c. Click *Type*.
12. Take a screen shot of your desktop and name it **C03E04S12**. Print, e-mail it, or submit it to your instructor on a USB flash drive (thumb drive) for grading as required.
13. Click the Save search button on the command bar.
14. Enter **Current Month Files** in the *File name* text box, and click Save.
15. Close the current window.
16. Click Start, and then click your user name in the Start menu.
17. Double-click the Searches folder.
18. Double-click the *Current Month Files* search to rerun it.
19. Click the Close (X) button to close the Windows Explorer window.

QUICK FIX

No Matching Files Appear
If no matching files appear, clear the current search and then reapply the search filter using the *Earlier this year* choice.

Creating Shortcuts for Easier File and Folder Access

Now you know how to find any file or folder on your system, but you probably do not want to go through all that trouble every time you want a particular item. If there are files and folders you use frequently, you might find that you can save time by creating a shortcut for that file or folder.

A *shortcut* provides you with an alternative way to navigate to a folder or library or open a file. For example, you could put a shortcut to your My Documents folder on the desktop so you do not have to open the Start menu every time you want to access it. Double-clicking a shortcut opens the disk, folder, library, or file that it represents.

Shortcut: A pointer icon to the original file that it represents

A shortcut is not the original file; it is just a pathway to it. Shortcuts can be distinguished from the original files in several ways:

- They usually have curved arrows in their bottom left corner, as shown in Figure 3.24.
- Sometimes they have "Shortcut" as part of their name—for example, MyDoc – Shortcut or Shortcut to MyDoc.
- If you right-click a shortcut and choose *Properties*, the Properties dialog box that appears has a Shortcut tab.

Creating a Desktop Shortcut to a File, Folder, or Library

You can create shortcuts in any folder, but the most common and convenient location for shortcut icons is the desktop. You can have as many shortcuts as you like on the desktop (although it might start to seem cluttered at some point). The easiest way to create a shortcut on the desktop is with drag-and-drop; hold down the Alt key as you drag any file or folder to the desktop to create a shortcut for it there.

Desktop shortcuts can be arranged in any way you like. Just drag them where you want them. By default, icons automatically snap to an invisible grid on the desktop, so that they do not overlap each other sloppily. You can turn that feature on/off by right-clicking the desktop and choosing *View, Align icons to grid*.

You can also have Windows 7 automatically arrange the desktop icons in orderly columns along the left side of the desktop. To enable this feature, right-click the desktop and choose *View, Auto arrange icons*.

Document shortcuts

Program shortcut

Figure 3.24 A shortcut icon usually has an arrow on it, and may also have the word "shortcut" in its name.

To create a desktop shortcut (drag-and-drop method):

1. Open the Computer window or another folder or library window.
2. Navigate to the folder holding the item for which you want to create a shortcut, if needed.
3. Select the item for which you want to create a shortcut.
4. Hold down the Alt key.
5. Drag the item to the desktop.

To create a desktop shortcut (Clipboard method):

1. Open the Computer window or another folder or library window.
2. Navigate to the folder holding the item for which you want to create a shortcut, if needed.
3. Select the item for which you want to create a shortcut.
4. Copy the item to the Clipboard in any of these ways:
   - Press Ctrl+C.
   - Right-click the selection and choose *Copy*.
   - Click Organize, and click *Copy*.
   - Press Alt, and then choose Edit and then *Copy*.
5. Right-click the desktop.
6. Choose *Paste Shortcut*.

▶ **Here's How**

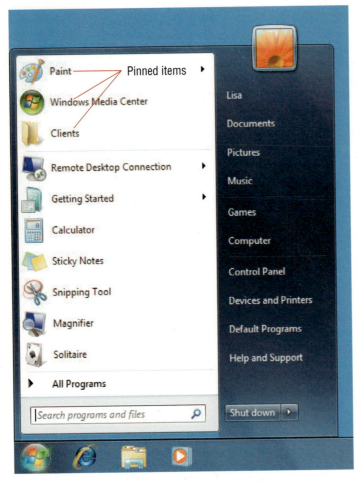

Pinning a Shortcut to the Start Menu

The Start menu contains many shortcuts; all the names of programs on its All Programs menu are actually shortcuts to those programs, for example, and all the names of locations along the right side of the Start menu are actually shortcuts to those locations.

You also can add your own shortcuts to the Start menu. This is called *pinning* them to the Start menu. A pinned shortcut appears in the upper left pane of the Start menu, above a divider line that appears after you pin the first item, where it is always available to you. In Figure 3.25, for example, there are three pinned shortcuts: for a folder named Clients, for Paint, and for Windows Media Center.

As you work in Windows 7, shortcuts appear to applications you have been using recently or frequently in the bottom part of the left pane of the Start menu. This area's shortcuts are constantly changing as you work. If you would like one of these programs to always have its shortcut available from the top level of the Start menu, pin it to the Start menu in either of these ways:

Figure 3.25 Pinned items appear at the top of the left pane of the Start menu, above the divider line.

- Drag it up into the upper left pane of the Start menu with the other pinned items.
- Right-click it and choose *Pin to Start Menu*.

Here's How ▶ To pin a shortcut to the Start menu (right-click method, for application shortcuts):

1. Create the shortcut if it does not already exist.
2. Right-click the shortcut.
3. Click *Pin to Start Menu*.

To pin a shortcut to the Start menu (drag-and-drop method, for any shortcut):

1. Create the shortcut on the desktop, if it does not already exist.
2. Drag the shortcut onto the Start button and continue holding down the mouse button.
3. When the Start menu opens, drag the icon onto the upper left portion of the Start menu.
4. Release the mouse button.

You also can pin shortcuts that are currently on the desktop to the Start menu. For a shortcut to an application, right-click the shortcut on the desktop and choose *Pin to Start Menu*. This method works only for application shortcuts, however. For data files, folders, and disks, the *Pin to Start Menu* command does not appear on the right-click menu, so you must instead use a drag-and-drop method. Drag the shortcut onto the Start button, and pause, still holding down the mouse button, until the Start menu opens. Then drag the shortcut upward, onto the upper left pane of the Start menu, and drop it there.

Adding a Shortcut to the Favorites List

As you saw at the beginning of this chapter, the navigation pane in any Windows Explorer window contains a Favorites section at the top, containing shortcuts to frequently used locations. You can define what locations appear here by adding and removing shortcuts from the list.

To add a location to the Favorites list, drag it from any file list, or from any other location (such as the desktop or the Start menu) and drop it onto the Favorites section name. The only restriction is that it must be a folder, library, or a drive, not an individual file.

Here's How

 ## Exercise 5

Creating Shortcuts

1. Open the Libraries window. (Click the Windows Explorer button on the taskbar.)
2. Drag the icon for the Assignments library you created in Exercise 4 to the Favorites list in the navigation pane.
3. Take a screen shot of your desktop and name it **C03E05S03** Print, e-mail it, or submit it to your instructor on a USB flash drive for grading, as required.
4. Remove the shortcut from the Favorites section:
   a. Right-click Assignments under Favorites.
   b. Click *Remove*.
5. Place a shortcut to the Assignments library on the desktop:
   a. Hold down the Alt key.
   b. Drag the *Assignments library* icon to the desktop.
   c. Drag the new shortcut icon up near the top right corner of the desktop.
6. Pin the Assignments library to the Start menu:
   a. Drag the icon for the library from the Libraries window onto the Start button and pause.
   b. When the Start menu opens, drag the icon to the top of the left pane of the menu.
7. Close the Libraries window.
8. Click Start to open the Start menu, take a screen shot of your desktop and name it **C03E05S08**. Print, e-mail it, or submit it to your instructor on a USB flash drive for grading as required.
9. Remove the shortcut from the Start menu:
   a. Click Start to open the Start menu.
   b. Right-click the shortcut for the Assignments library.
   c. Click *Remove from this list*.
   d. Press Esc to close the Start menu.

Deleting and Retrieving Files and Folders

How many times have you thrown something into a trash can, only to realize that you needed it again? Although digging through a trash can is no fun, it sure beats the alternative of losing your valuable item. Windows 7 has its own trash can you can dig through—the Recycle Bin. When you delete files and folders in Windows 7, they are not destroyed right away; instead they are moved to a hidden folder. The *Recycle Bin* icon on the desktop is a shortcut to that folder. From it, you can retrieve files and folders that were accidentally or ill advisedly deleted, or you can purge the Recycle Bin contents so that others cannot see what you have been deleting.

Note: *Only files and folders deleted from a hard disk are placed in the Recycle Bin. The Recycle Bin cannot hold or restore the files from removable media.*

Deleting a File or Folder

Deleting a file or folder moves it to the Recycle Bin. You can delete individual files, individual folders, or groups. (Select multiple items before issuing the command to delete.) Deleting a folder deletes everything within the folder too.

To delete a file or folder:

1. Select the file(s) and/or folder(s) to be deleted.
2. Do any of the following:
   - Right-click the selection and choose *Delete*.
   - Press the Delete key on the keyboard.
   - Click Organize, and click *Delete*.
   - Press Alt, and then choose Edit, *Delete*.
3. At the confirmation box, click OK.

To delete a file or folder permanently (bypassing the Recycle Bin):

1. Select the file(s) and/or folder(s) to be deleted.
2. Hold down the Shift key.
3. Press the Delete key on the keyboard.
4. At the confirmation box, click OK.

Here's How

QUICK FIX

Cannot Delete a File
If a file or folder cannot be deleted for some reason (for example, perhaps its Read-Only attribute is turned on, or perhaps it is in use by an application), an error message appears. Make sure all applications are closed that might be using the file, and check the file's properties to make sure *Read-only* is not set for it.

Restoring a File or Folder

The *Recycle Bin* icon on the desktop changes to include wadded up paper once you have deleted one or more items. This cues you to the fact that the Recycle Bin holds some items that are available for retrieval. As with a real-life trash can, you can "reach in" the Recycle Bin to take out (*restore*) any item that is in there. When you restore a file or folder from the Recycle Bin, Windows 7 places the item in its original folder location.

To view the contents of the Recycle Bin, double-click its icon on the desktop. Figure 3.26 shows a Recycle Bin with a few items in it. It resembles a regular Windows Explorer window, but it has different buttons on the command bar.

To see information about a deleted item, select it and look in the details pane at the bottom of the window. For example, Figure 3.26 shows information about a deleted spreadsheet document, including the date it was modified, the size, and the original author.

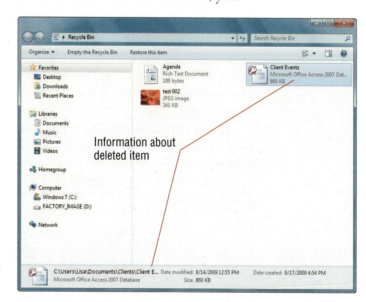

Figure 3.26 **Get information about a deleted item in the Recycle Bin by selecting it and looking in the details pane.**

Here's How

To open the Recycle Bin:

- Double-click the *Recycle Bin* icon on the desktop.

To view information about a deleted item:

1. Select the item in the Recycle Bin.
2. View the information in the details pane.
   OR
1. Double-click the item.
2. View the information in its Properties dialog box.
3. Click OK.

To restore an item to its original location:

1. Select the item in the Recycle Bin.
2. Click Restore this item on the command bar.
   OR
1. Right-click the item in the Recycle Bin.
2. Choose *Restore*.
   OR
1. Double-click the item in the Recycle Bin.
2. In its Properties box, click *Restore*.

To restore an item to another location:

1. Select the item in the Recycle Bin.
2. Drag-and-drop the item to another location (desktop or a folder window).

Permanently Deleting the Recycle Bin Contents

You can really "take out the trash" by emptying the Recycle Bin. Just as emptying a trash can and putting the trash on the curb for the garbage collector means you will not ever be able to get that trash back, emptying the Windows Recycle Bin permanently deletes its files and folders, making them unrecoverable. You can permanently delete a single item, selected items, or everything at once.

If you just want to delete everything at once from the Recycle Bin, you do not need to open its window; you can do it by right-clicking the icon and choosing *Empty Recycle Bin*. If you want to be selective about what gets purged, you must open the Recycle Bin window and delete files from it as you would delete files from any other location. The difference is that rather than going to the Recycle Bin as normal files would, these files are destroyed.

Here's How

To permanently delete a single item, or selected items:

1. Select the item(s) to delete permanently.
2. Do any of the following:
   - Press the Delete key.
   - Right-click the selection and choose *Delete*.
   - Click Organize and click *Delete*.
3. At the confirmation box, click Yes.

To empty the Recycle Bin (Recycle Bin window open):

- Click Empty the Recycle Bin on the command bar.
  OR
1. Press Alt.
2. Click File and click *Empty Recycle Bin*.
3. Click Yes in the Delete Multiple Items dialog box.

OR

1. Right-click any blank area of the Recycle Bin window.
2. Click *Empty Recycle Bin*.
3. Click Yes in the Delete Multiple Items dialog box.

To empty the Recycle Bin (Recycle Bin window closed):

1. Right-click the *Recycle Bin* icon on the desktop.
2. Click *Empty Recycle Bin*.
3. Click Yes in the Delete Multiple Items dialog box.

Configuring the Recycle Bin

The Recycle Bin will store deleted files until the space is needed or until the maximum Recycle Bin size has been reached; then it will start deleting files, starting with the ones that have been there the longest. You can control the maximum size of the Recycle Bin through its Properties dialog box, and you can also choose to turn the Recycle Bin off completely, so files are deleted immediately.

To access the Recycle Bin's properties, right-click its icon and choose *Properties*. A list of locations appears for which the Recycle Bin is active. Unless any disk quotas have been set for the system, all locations have the same amount of space available. See Figure 3.27.

To change the maximum size allocated to the Recycle Bin, enter a different number in the *Maximum size (MB)* text box. Or, to turn off the Recycle Bin completely, select *Don't move files to the Recycle Bin*.

To suppress the delete confirmation dialog box that appears each time you delete a file, clear the *Display delete confirmation dialog* check box.

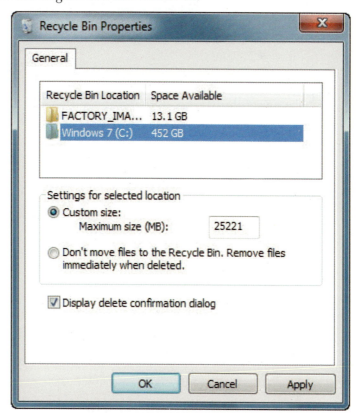

Figure 3.27 Configure how the Recycle Bin works from its Properties box. You can suppress the delete confirmation, set its maximum size, and even turn it off completely.

To turn off the Recycle Bin completely:

1. Right-click the Recycle Bin and click *Properties*.
2. Click the disk for which you want to turn off the Recycle Bin in the list at the top.
3. Click *Don't move files to the Recycle Bin*.
4. Click OK.

To change the maximum size of the Recycle Bin:

1. Right-click the Recycle Bin and click *Properties*.
2. Click the disk for which you want to change the Recycle Bin's size in the list at the top.
3. Change the *Maximum size (MB)* value.
4. Click OK.

To enable or suppress the delete confirmation message when deleting:

1. Right-click the Recycle Bin and click *Properties*.
2. Mark or clear the *Display delete confirmation dialog* check box.
3. Click OK.

Exercise 6

Deleting and Restoring Items (Files, Shortcuts, Folders, or Libraries)

1. Drag the desktop shortcut for the Assignments library that you created in Exercise 5 to the *Recycle Bin* icon.
2. Click the *Windows Explorer* icon on the taskbar to open the main Libraries window.
3. Move the Assignments library to the Recycle Bin:
   a. Select the icon.
   b. Press the Delete key to delete it.
   c. Click *Yes* in the dialog box that asks you to confirm moving the folder to the Recycle Bin.
   d. Close the Libraries window.
4. Display your personal folder using the Start menu.
5. Double-click the Searches folder to open it.
6. Move the Current Month Files search to the Recycle Bin:
   a. Select the icon.
   b. Press the Delete key to delete it.
   c. Click *Yes* in the dialog box that asks you to confirm moving the folder to the Recycle Bin.
   d. Close the window.
7. Restore the Current Month Files search to the Searches folder:
   a. On the desktop, double-click the *Recycle Bin* icon.
   b. Take a screen shot of your desktop and name it **C03E06S07**. Print, e-mail it, or submit it to your instructor on a USB flash drive for grading, as required.
   c. Click the *Current Month Files* icon.
   d. Click Restore this item in the command bar.
8. Select the Assignments library and shortcut icons using Ctrl+click or another selection method.
9. Click Restore the selected items in the command bar.
10. Close the Recycle Bin window.

11. Repeat Steps 1-6 to delete the items again, and then close all windows.
12. Empty the Recycle Bin:
   a. Right-click the *Recycle Bin* icon on the desktop.
   b. Click *Empty Recycle Bin*.
   c. Click Yes in the Delete Multiple Items dialog box.
13. Close any other open windows.

CHAPTER Summary

- Key navigational tools in an Explorer window include the Address bar, the *search* box, the command bar, and the navigation pane.

- To display the menu bar in a folder or library window, press Alt.

- Windows 7 includes four main libraries for each user's own files: Documents, Pictures, Music, and Videos. These are all accessed by clicking the Windows Explorer button on the taskbar, among other methods.

- Clicking the user name in the Start menu opens the personal folder, which holds a number of subfolders for organizing various types of files and information.

- To select multiple contiguous files or folders, hold down Shift as you click; for noncontiguous selection, hold down Ctrl.

- To create a new folder, right-click, point to *New*, and click *Folder*.

- To rename a file or folder, right-click it, click *Rename*, and type the new name.

- To move or copy, use the drag-and-drop method. Hold down Shift to move or Ctrl to copy.

- You also can move or copy with the Clipboard: Ctrl+X to cut, Ctrl+C to copy, and Ctrl+V to paste.

- Grouping and filtering are methods in Windows 7 for organizing file listings. Use the drop-down menu for a column heading to enable any of them.

- You can arrange items in a library using the Arrange by menu in the library pane.

- Add a library by clicking New library on the command bar of the Libraries window.

- Control which folders the library monitors and other library settings in the Properties dialog box for the library.

- You can save a search to rerun it later.

- The *search* box in the top right corner of any Explorer or library window performs quick searches based on the word(s) you enter.

- You can also use one of the filters that appear when you click the *search* box to build the search criteria.

- Indexing a location makes searching it go faster.

- To create a shortcut, Alt+drag the original to the desired location.

- Deleting a file or folder (by selecting it and pressing Delete) sends it to the Recycle Bin. You can restore items from the Recycle Bin to their original locations.

- To empty the Recycle Bin, right-click its icon on the desktop and choose *Empty Recycle Bin*.

CONCEPTS Check

Completion: Answer the following questions on a blank sheet of paper.

MULTIPLE CHOICE

1. To display the menu bar in an Explorer window, press the _____ key.
   a. Ctrl
   b. Alt
   c. Shift
   d. Insert

2. To copy a file from one location to another on the same disk with drag-and-drop, hold down the _____ key as you drag.
   a. Ctrl
   b. Alt
   c. Shift
   d. Insert

3. When an item is pinned to the Start menu, where on the Start menu does it appear?
   a. Bottom left
   b. Bottom right
   c. Top left
   d. Top right

4. To select multiple noncontiguous files, hold down the _____ key as you click each one.
   a. Ctrl
   b. Alt
   c. Shift
   d. Insert

5. To copy the selected files to the Clipboard, press Ctrl+_____ .
   a. V
   b. D
   c. C
   d. X

6. A(n) _____ monitors the contents of multiple locations, making it easier to find and work with files of a particular type.
   a. Explorer window
   b. Recycle Bin
   c. Personal Folder
   d. Library

7. _____ arranges a list of files into sections, with each individual file shown.
   a. Sorting
   b. Grouping
   c. Filtering
   d. Stacking

8. _____ shows only the files matching one or more specified criteria.
   a. Sorting
   b. Grouping
   c. Filtering
   d. Stacking

9. To permanently delete a file, bypassing the Recycle Bin, hold down _____ as you press Delete to delete it.
   a. Ctrl
   b. Alt
   c. Shift
   d. Insert

10. Which of these files would the search term cats find?
    a. cats.txt
    b. My Cat.docx
    c. category.xlsx
    d. all of the above

Part 2

SHORT ANSWER

11. What is your personal folder?

    _____

12. What is the benefit of indexing a location?

    _____

13. List three of the four default libraries in Windows 7.

    _____

14. List the six of the eight available views in Windows Explorer.

    _____

15. Name three locations where you can place shortcuts to a folder.

    _____

16. What does the Arrange by menu in a library window do?

    _____

17. What is a parent folder?

    _____

18. How can you sort items in a folder or library?

    _____

19. How do you find and rerun your saved searches?

    _____

20. Is it possible to restore files deleted from removable media, and why/why not?

    _____

SKILLS Check

Save all solution files to the default Documents folder, or any alternate folder specified by your instructor.

Guided Check

Assessment 1 — DELETING AND RESTORING A FILE

1. Open the Chapter 3 Student Data Files folder.
2. Move the **Recycle** file into the Recycle Bin.
   a. Click the Recycle file.
   b. Press Delete.
   c. Click Yes.
3. Minimize the folder window by clicking its Minimize button.
4. Double-click the *Recycle Bin* icon.
5. Take a screen shot of your desktop and name it **C03A01**. Print, e-mail it, or submit it to your instructor on a USB flash drive for grading, as required.
6. Restore the Recycle file from the Recycle Bin window.
   a. Click the Recycle file.
   b. Click *Restore this item*.
7. Close the Recycle Bin window by clicking its Close (X) button.
8. Open the Chapter 3 folder by clicking the Windows Explorer taskbar button.
9. Verify that the Recycle file again appears in the window.
10. Leave the window with the Chapter 3 files open for the next Assessment.

Assessment 2 — PINNING AND UNPINNING A START MENU ITEM

1. Pin the Recycle file to the Start menu.
   a. Drag the *Recycle file* icon from the Chapter 3 window over the Start button.
   b. When the Start menu opens, drag the file up to the top of the left pane of the menu and release the mouse button.
2. Click outside the Start menu to close it.
3. Close the Chapter 3 folder window by clicking its Close (X) button.
4. Click the Start button to open the Start menu, take a screen shot of your desktop, and name it **C03A02**. Print, e-mail it, or submit it to your instructor on a USB flash drive for grading, as required.
5. Unpin the Recycle file.
   a. Click the Start button.
   b. Right-click the *Recycle file* shortcut.
   c. Click *Remove from this list*.
   d. Click outside the Start menu to close it.

Assessment CREATING FOLDERS AND COPYING FILES

3

1. Open the Documents window.
   - Click Start, and click *Documents*.
2. In the Documents library, create a new folder called Construction and open it.
   a. Click New folder on the command bar.
   b. Type **Construction**.
   c. Press Enter.
   d. Double-click the icon for the new Construction folder to open it.
3. Open the Chapter 3 Student Data Files folder.
4. Copy the file **Townsend** into the Construction folder.
   a. In the data files folder window, click Townsend.
   b. Hold down the Ctrl key and drag Townsend into the Construction folder.
   c. Close the chapter's data files folder window, leaving the Construction folder open.
5. Copy the Construction folder onto a USB flash drive.
   a. In the Address bar for the Construction folder window, click Documents.
   b. Select the Construction folder's icon.
   c. Press Ctrl+C to copy it to the Clipboard.
   d. In the Address bar, click Computer to display a list of drives.
   e. Insert a USB flash drive.
   f. Double-click the icon for the drive.
   g. Press Ctrl+V to paste the copied folder from the Clipboard.
6. Submit the USB flash drive to your instructor for grading, if required.
7. Close all open windows.

Assessment FINDING FILES

4

1. Use a saved search to determine what documents have been modified recently on your computer.
   a. Click Start and click your user name.
   b. Double-click Searches.
   c. Double-click *Current Month Files* (You saved this search in Exercise 4.)
   d. Look in the details pane for the number of items found.
      The number of items is: _____ .
   e. Close the window.
2. Run a search that shows only WordPad documents.
   a. Click Start and then click your user name.
   b. Click the *search* box, and then click the Type: filter.
   c. Click *.rtf* in the menu.
   d. Look in the details pane for the number of items found.
      The number of items is: _____ .
4. Create and save a custom search that finds files containing "Town".
   a. Click the x in the *search* box to clear the previous search.
   b. Type **Town** in the *search* box.
   e. Click Save search on the command bar.
   f. Type **Town Search**.
   g. Click Save.

5. Copy the saved search you just created to a USB flash drive.
   a. Insert a USB flash drive.
   b. Click Start, and then click your user name.
   c. Double-click Searches.
   d. Click *Town Search*, and press Ctrl+C to copy it.
   e. Open the Computer window, and double-click the USB drive.
   f. Press Ctrl+V to paste the search file.
   g. Close the open windows.
6. Submit your answers from Steps 1 and 2 on a blank sheet of paper for grading, and submit your USB flash drive containing the file from Step 5.

On Your Own

Assessment 5 — MOVING, COPYING, AND RENAMING FILES AND FOLDERS

1. Insert a USB flash drive.
2. Copy all the graphics files (JPG extension) from the Chapter 3 data folder (in the data files for this book) to the USB drive.
3. Make a copy of **Estate**, and name the copy **MyEstate**.
4. Move the file MyEstate onto the USB drive.
5. In the properties for MyEstate, set the Manager to your name.
6. On the USB drive, make a copy of MyEstate, and name the copy **Backup**.
7. Copy Backup to the Chapter 3 folder.
8. Submit your USB flash drive to your instructor for grading.

Assessment 6 — CREATING VIRTUAL SEARCH FOLDERS

1. Create a new custom search that finds only files in which the Date created is later than 01/01/09, and save the search as **2009 and Newer**. (**Hint:** You will need to type the > wildcard in the search box.)
2. Create a new custom search that finds all files with the Medium Size: filter.
3. Run the Search, and then save it as **Large Files.**
4. Filter the results of the Large Files search to show only JPEG pictures.
5. Copy the saved searches to a USB flash drive or e-mail them to submit them to your instructor for grading.

Assessment 7 — CREATING DESKTOP SHORTCUTS

1. Open the folder containing the Chapter 3 files for this book.
2. Create shortcuts on the desktop to the following files:
   Blue Square
   Purple Squiggle
   Red Circle
3. Close any open folders.
4. Arrange the shortcut icons neatly on your desktop.
5. Take a screen shot of your desktop, and name it **C03A07**. Print, e-mail it, or submit it to your instructor on a USB flash drive for grading, as required.
6. Double-click the *Red Circle* shortcut.
7. Click the Paint window Close (X) button to close the program and file.
8. Delete the desktop shortcuts you created in Step 2.
9. Empty the Recycle Bin.

8

1. Open the Chapter 3 Student Data Files folder.
2. Make a copy of the file **Bowl.jpg**, but keep the name of the file secret. You can use any combination of letters and numbers, but do not change the file extension (.jpg).
3. Place that copy in any folder on your hard disk.
4. Make a note of the file's size and date modified, and write that information on a blank piece of paper.
5. Trade PCs with someone else in your class, and trade your pieces of paper.
6. Find your partner's missing file based on the information you know about it (its size, type, and date modified).
7. (If possible) Burn a CD containing the missing file and submit the CD to your instructor for grading.
8. Delete any saved searches listed in the Favorites section of the navigation pane.
9. Close all open windows.

CHALLENGE Project

As part of your company's marketing campaign, you have been asked to catalog all the high-resolution graphics files you have available on your PC. Use the Search feature in Windows 7 to find every JPEG and TIFF graphic file at least 1 MB in size.

1. Gather the following information, using any combination of the searching, filtering, sorting, and other techniques you learned in this chapter:
   - How many files are there of each file type (based on the extension)?
   - What is the largest file size, and what are the dimensions (in pixels) of that picture?
   - How much space would it require on a disc to copy all those files to it?

2. Burn a CD containing the pictures you found. If you found more than 700 MB of pictures, choose as many pictures as will fit on a single CD.

Organizing and Protecting Information

PERFORMANCE OBJECTIVES

Upon successful completion of Chapter 4, you will be able to:

- Change the Explorer window layout
- Customize how Explorer displays information
- Add and edit file properties
- Remove file properties and personal information
- Work with file and folder versions
- Set file and folder permissions

The Windows 7 file management interface, Windows Explorer, is very customizable. You can set it up to function in whatever way works best to match your working style. It also enables you to define properties and set or clear personal information for files and folders, and to recall earlier versions of files and control who can access them.

Changing the Explorer Window Layout

The Windows Explorer window can be set up to display or hide several types of listings and information. For example, you can show or hide panes that display folders, that show information about selected files, and that provide continuous access to the menu system.

Reviewing the Available Panes

The following panes are optional in Windows Explorer and can be turned on or off as needed. See Figure 4.1.

- **Menu bar.** Normally available only when you press the Alt key, the menu bar provides Windows XP-style menus for working with files and folders. It can be set to remain on all the time.
- **Details pane.** This pane appears at the bottom of the window, providing information about the selected file(s), folder(s), or drive(s).
- **Preview pane.** This pane shows a preview of certain types of data files when they are selected. This pane is hidden by default.
- **Navigation pane.** The navigation pane appears by default on the left, providing links to frequently accessed locations.

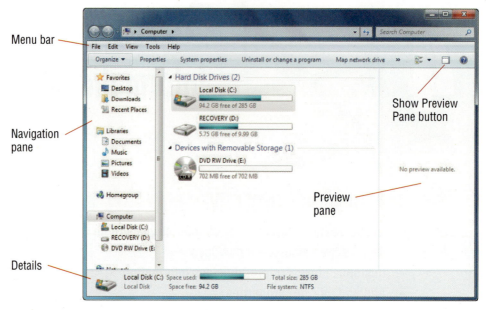

Figure 4.1 View the customizable parts of the Explorer window.

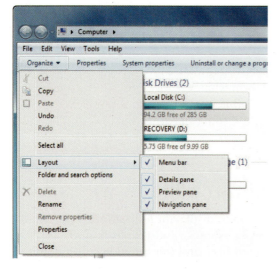

Figure 4.2 Turn window elements on or off from the Organize menu.

Tip: A quick way to toggle the preview pane on and off: click the Show the Preview Pane button, pointed out in Figure 4.1.

Hiding and Redisplaying Panes or the Menu Bar

You can display or hide some of the optional window panes and bars via the Organize menu's Layout command. Click Organize, and then point to *Layout*. Options appear for Menu bar, Details pane, Preview pane, and Navigation pane, as shown in Figure 4.2.

Here's How ▶ To display or hide the menu bar or an optional pane:

1. Click Organize.
2. Point to *Layout*.
3. Click the pane or bar to toggle on or off.

Resizing Panes

Several of the panes in the Explorer window can be resized. Resizing a pane does not change the overall size of the window, so space added to one pane means space subtracted from the adjacent one. Resizing panes can be useful when you need to see more of one pane's content than is currently displayed and you do not mind

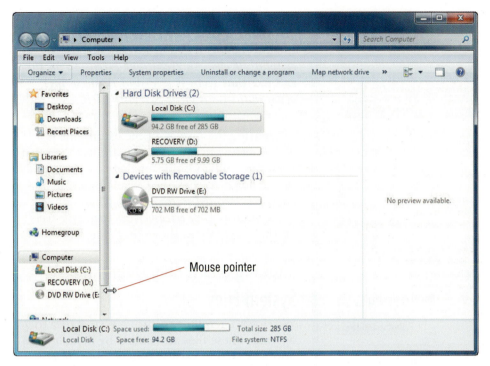

Mouse pointer

Figure 4.3 **Adjust the size of a pane by dragging the divider between it and an adjacent pane.**

if the adjacent pane's content has less room. If you need to see a larger portion of both panes, you must resize the entire window instead.

To resize a pane, drag the divider between two panes. The mouse pointer turns into a double-headed arrow, as shown in Figure 4.3. Once the double-headed arrow appears, hold down the mouse button and drag. Release the mouse button when the pane reaches the size you want.

Customizing How Explorer Displays Files and Folders

In addition to modifying the look of the Explorer window itself, you can also modify how the file and folder listings appear within that window. The following sections explain some of the modifications you can make.

Showing and Hiding File Extensions

By default, Windows 7 hides file extensions for known file types. As you learned in Chapter 3, an extension is a code that follows the file name, separated from it by a period. Windows 7 determines a file's type by its extension. For example, the file Memo.docx is a Word 2007 file because it uses the .docx extension. However, in a default Explorer window, that file would appear as Memo, not as Memo.docx. The file's type could be deduced by looking at its icon and noticing the "W" on it for "Word," but if you do not recognize the icons for all the applications you have on your system, that might not be useful. Instead, you might prefer to turn on the display of file extensions for all files.

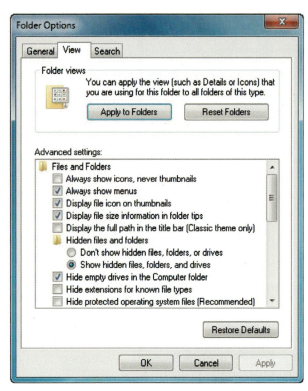

Figure 4.4 Use the View tab in the Folder Options dialog box to control whether file extensions are displayed or hidden for known file types.

Note: *Another benefit of turning on file extensions is that they make it more noticeable when a file has a double extension, such as graphic.gif.vbs. An executable extension on the end like that (.vbs is a Visual Basic script) often indicates a virus-carrying file.*

Setting the display of file extensions is a global setting for all locations and is controlled from the Folder Options dialog box. To display this dialog box, click the Organize button and choose *Folder and search options.* Then either mark or clear *Hide extensions for known file types* on the View tab, as shown in Figure 4.4.

Showing and Hiding Operating System Files

Windows 7 requires **operating system files** to operate. These files are hidden by default from normal Explorer listings so that they are not accidentally moved or deleted. At some point, you might need to see these files. For example, you might need to check a date on one of them as you are troubleshooting a problem. You can do this from the same View tab of the Folder Options dialog box shown in Figure 4.4.

Here's How

To display or hide extensions for known file types:

1. Click Organize.
2. Click *Folder and search options.*
3. Click the View tab.
4. Mark or clear *Hide extensions for known file types.*
5. Click OK.

To display or hide protected operating system files:

1. Click Organize.
2. Click *Folder and search options.*
3. Click the View tab.
4. Mark or clear *Hide protected operating system files (Recommended).*
5. Click OK.

Operating system files: Files that the operating system (Windows 7) needs to start the system and keep it running

Revealing Hidden Files and Folders

As you will learn in "Changing File Attributes" later in this chapter, one of the attributes you can apply to a file or folder is Hidden. When the Hidden attribute is turned on for a file or folder, that file or folder does not appear in the Explorer window—that is, unless you have specified that hidden files and folders be visible there.

In the Folder Options dialog box (Figure 4.4), you can set either of two values under Hidden files and folders:

- **Don't show hidden files, folders, or drives.** This is the default. Anything hidden does not appear.

- **Show hidden files, folders, and drives.** Hidden files and folders do appear, but with their icons slightly faded to distinguish them from unhidden ones. Figure 4.5 shows the difference.

You will probably want to leave this setting at *Don't show hidden files, folders, or drives* most of the time because otherwise there is not much point in having hidden files and folders. Files and folders are hidden to prevent others from knowing they exist. However, whenever you need to work with a hidden file or folder, you must temporarily turn on *Show hidden files, folders, and drives* so you can access it.

Figure 4.5 **A hidden file (left) appears dimmed compared to an unhidden one (right).**

To reveal hidden files and folders:

1. Click Organize.
2. Click *Folder and search options.*
3. Click the View tab.
4. Click *Show hidden files, folders, and drives.*
5. Click OK.

Here's How

Customizing a Folder Icon's Appearance

By default, for most folders, the folder's icon includes a preview of the folder's content. Not all types of content are necessarily previewed there, though; the type of content previewed depends on the type you have set for the folder.

The default type for most folders is General Items, which causes Windows 7 to use previews appropriate for each data type—text files for documents, pictures for graphics, and so on. The exact appearance of the icon depends on the number of files in the folder, their types, and whether or not there are subfolders. Figure 4.6 shows several examples of folders that use the General Items type.

Figure 4.6 **Several examples of folder icons when the type is set to General Items.**

Alternate types include Documents, Music, Videos, and Pictures. When you change to one of those folder types, files of the specified types are used for the previews on the folder's icon. For example, Figure 4.7 shows some icons for folders of the Pictures type.

Figure 4.7 **Several examples of folder icons when the type is set to Picture Icons.**

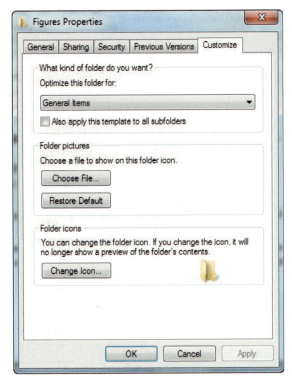

Figures Properties

General | Sharing | Security | Previous Versions | Customize

What kind of folder do you want?
Optimize this folder for:

General Items ▼

☐ Also apply this template to all subfolders

Folder pictures
Choose a file to show on this folder icon.

[Choose File...]

[Restore Default]

Folder icons
You can change the folder icon. If you change the icon, it will no longer show a preview of the folder's contents.

[Change Icon...]

[OK] [Cancel] [Apply]

Figure 4.8 Use the Customize tab in the folder's Properties box to set up how its icon will appear.

You can start by setting a basic folder type for a folder, using one of the predefined templates Windows 7 provides. Then you can fine-tune that template by choosing a specific file to be previewed on the folder icon or choosing a fixed icon to appear instead of a preview. See Figure 4.8.

The *Folder pictures* section of the Customize tab enables you to specify one of the files to function as the preview for the folder. If you choose a file from here, only that file's preview will appear, even if the folder contains other files as well.

The Restore Default button resets the folder's icon back to its default. This is useful to reverse the effect of having chosen a specific file.

If you want the folder's icon to be a fixed icon rather than a preview, you can click the Change Icon button and select an icon file. Icons come, by default, from a file called SHELL32.DLL, but other files can also contain icons you can use. When you specify a fixed icon, the folder's preview capabilities are disabled until you use Restore Default to put the folder back to using previews.

Here's How ▶ **To customize the folder icon's appearance:**

1. Right-click the folder and choose *Properties*.
2. Click the Customize tab. If there is no Customize tab, this folder cannot have its icon appearance changed.
3. Open the *Optimize this folder for* list and click a template type.
4. (Optional) Do any of the following:
   • Click Choose File, select an image file to be previewed on the icon, and click OK.
   • Click Restore Default to return the folder to its default setting.
   • Click Change Icon, select an icon to use instead of a folder preview, and click OK.
5. Click OK.

 ## Exercise 1

Customizing the Explorer Interface

1. Open the Computer window.
2. Make notes about the current on/off status of all the customizable panes and bars. Then make the following settings changes to the Explorer window:
   • Turn on the menu bar.
   • Turn on the navigation, preview, and details panes.

3. Make the following changes to the way Windows 7 displays files and folders:
   - Display file extensions for known file types.
   - Show hidden files and folders. You may be required to click Yes in response to the Warning pop-up dialog.
4. Display the properties for the folder containing the data files for this chapter (Chapter 4) on your USB drive. Ask your instructor for help, if needed, in locating the folder.
5. Display the EMCP folder, so you see the Chapter 4 folder as an icon.
6. Capture a screen print of this window and submit it to your instructor for grading. Name the file **C04E01** *Your Name*. See "Capturing a Screen Picture to Complete an Assignment" in Chapter 1 for help, if needed.
7. Check with your instructor, and, if needed, return all settings for Windows Explorer and for the affected folders to their original settings.

Working with File Properties

File properties are information about a file or attached to a file. Properties include two types of information:

- **Metadata.** Information attached to a file that states something about that file, such as its author name and keywords. Metadata is most often associated with data files, such as Word documents.

- **Attributes.** On/off flags set for a file that determine such things as whether the file is read-only, indexed, hidden, modified since being backed up, compressed, and/or encrypted. All files have these, not just data files.

File properties: Information about a file or information attached to a file

Metadata: Information attached to a file that provides descriptive data such as the author's name

Attributes: On/off flags set for a file, such as read-only

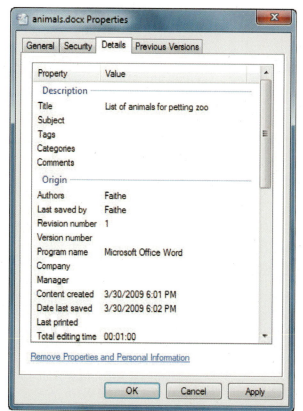

Adding and Editing Metadata

Depending on the file type, a Details tab might be available in the file's Properties box. On the Details tab you can define values for various metadata properties.

Some of the metadata for a file is not editable, such as Content created, Total editing time, Program name, and so on. If you click in the Value column for one of these, the entire row is highlighted and there is no insertion point. For other items, however, you can click to move the insertion point into the text box and type a new value, as in Figure 4.9.

Figure 4.9   **Examine a file's metadata in its Properties box and change any details, as needed.**

Here's How ▶ **To view and change metadata for a file:**

1. Right-click the file and choose *Properties*.
2. Click the Details tab.
3. Click in the Value column for any of the properties you want to set, and type a new value.
4. Repeat Step 3 as needed and then click OK.

QUICK FIX

No Details Tab
If there is no Details tab, you might not be working with a data file that contains metadata. Try using a file from a Microsoft Office application, for example.

Changing File Attributes

A file's attributes define basic yes/no facts about it. Depending on the file system the drive is using, you might have access to some or all of these attributes:

- **Read-only**. The file cannot be deleted or modified.

- **Hidden**. The file does not appear in Explorer file listings (unless hidden files are set to be shown, as you learned how to do earlier in this chapter).

- **Archive (File is ready for archiving)**. The file has changed since it was backed up with a backup program that sets the archive flag to off.

- **Indexed (Allow this file to have contents indexed in addition to file properties)**. The content of the file is included in Windows 7 index of the disk's contents, so any searches for words it contains will find the file.

- **Compressed (Compress contents to save disk space)**. The file has been compressed with NTFS compression. This is available only on drives that use the NTFS file system. When you apply this to a folder, rather than a file, you are prompted to choose whether to apply the change to the selected folder only or all its subfolders and files as well.

- **Encrypted (Encrypt contents to secure data)**. This file has been encrypted with NTFS encryption. This is available only on drives that use the NTFS file system. Read-only and Hidden attributes can be turned on or off from the General tab of the file's Properties box. For other properties, you must click the Advanced button on the General tab to open the Advanced Attributes dialog box. See Figure 4.10.

Figure 4.10 Set the attributes for the file from the General tab of its Properties box and from the Advanced Attributes dialog box.

To set or clear the Read-only and/or Hidden attributes:

1. Right-click the file and choose *Properties*.
2. On the General tab, mark or clear the *Read-only* check box.
3. Mark or clear the *Hidden* check box.
4. Click OK.

To set or clear the Archive, Indexed, Compressed, or Encrypted attributes:

1. Right-click the file and choose *Properties*.
2. On the General tab, click Advanced.
3. Mark or clear the *File is ready for archiving* check box.
4. Mark or clear the *Allow this file to have contents indexed in addition to file properties* check box.
5. Mark or clear the *Compress contents to save disk space* check box.
6. Click OK.
7. Click OK.
   If you changed the *Compress contents to save disk space* check box's status for a folder:
8. Click Apply changes to this folder only OR click Apply changes to this folder, subfolders and files.
9. Click OK.

Removing File Properties and Personal Information

Before you share files with others, you might want to remove any personally identifiable information in its metadata, such as the author's name or keywords you have added. Windows 7 provides an easy way to remove this metadata.

You can remove all the metadata that might in any way identify you (by clicking Select All), or you can be selective and choose individual properties to remove, as shown in Figure 4.11. Alternatively, you can choose to create a copy that lacks the properties, leaving the original intact.

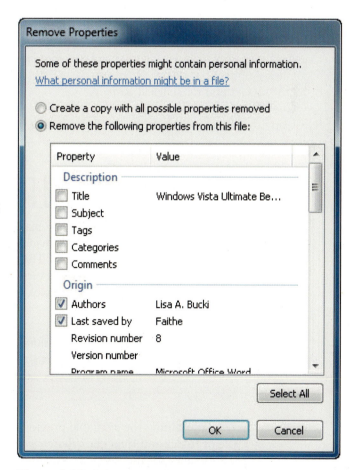

Figure 4.11 Select properties to remove from the file before distributing it.

Here's How ▶ **To remove file properties and personal information from a file:**

1. Right-click the file and choose *Properties*.
2. Click the Details tab.
3. Click Remove Properties and Personal Information.
4. Click *Create a copy with all possible properties removed.*
   OR
   Click *Remove the following properties from this file* and then mark the check boxes for the properties to remove.
   OR
   Click Select All.
5. Click OK.

Exercise 2

Working with File Metadata and Attributes

1. Locate Student Data Files at www.emcp.net/windows7. If you have not already done so, download files to your computer or to your USB flash drive. Ask your instructor for assistance, if needed.
2. Open the Chapter 4 folder. Copy the file **Townsend.doc** and name the copy **C04E02S02.doc**.
3. Display the Properties box for C04E02S02.doc.
4. Display its Details tab, and set the following metatags:
   Title: Townsend
   Authors: *delete the existing author and type your own full name*
5. Click Apply.
6. On the General tab, click *Read-only*.
7. Click OK.
8. Copy the file to a flash drive, and submit it to your instructor for grading.

Working with File and Folder Versions

Windows 7 includes a feature that enables you to restore a file or folder to a previous version. For example, if you have made and saved changes to a file, you may decide you no longer want those changes. The application you used to change the file may not enable you to retrieve the previous versions. However, Windows 7 tracks the changes you have made to the file and enables you to select an earlier version to reinstate.

> **Tip:** Versioning is available for almost all files, but it is useful to the end-user primarily for data files. You would not usually want to restore an earlier version of a system file, for example, because it was probably updated for a reason, such as Windows Update activity.

To examine the available previous versions for a file or folder, right-click the file or folder and then click *Restore previous versions*. The file or folder's Properties box opens with the Previous Versions tab displayed, as in Figure 4.12. From here, you can open the previous version, copy it to a separate file with its own name, or restore the file to the earlier version (deleting the current version).

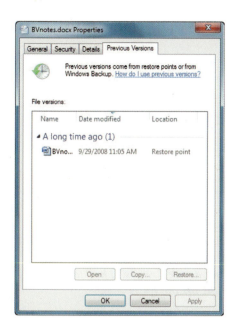

Figure 4.12 **View version information for a data file from its Previous Versions tab in its Properties box.**

Here's How

To view a file or folder's version information:

1. Select the file or folder.
2. Right-click the file and choose *Restore Previous Versions*.

To open a previous version for viewing in its original application:

1. Select the desired version from the Previous Versions tab.
2. Click Open.

To copy a previous version out into its own separate file:

1. Select the desired version from the Previous Versions tab.
2. Click Copy. The Copy Items dialog box opens.
3. Select the location to which to copy.
4. Click Copy.

To overwrite the newer version with the older version's data:

1. Select the desired version from the Previous Versions tab.
2. Click Restore.
3. At the warning, click Restore.
4. At the confirmation box, click OK.

QUICK FIX

No Version Controls Available
If you do not have any version controls available for a file or folder, the file or folder is probably stored on a disk that uses the FAT32 file system, not Windows 7 default NTFS file system. Versioning is available only on NTFS disks.

Setting File or Folder Permissions

There are two types of permissions you can assign to files and folders:

- **Local file permission**. Permission for users on the same local PC to access each other's files. The user is determined by the logon used when starting up Windows 7. Local file permissions are covered in the following sections.

- **Network sharing**. Permission to access a file that is stored on a computer other than the one you are working with.

Understanding Groups and Users

In addition to any network account, each PC has one or more local user accounts. When a particular user is logged on, that user automatically has permission to access all files and folders that he or she has created. The user can, if desired, restrict access by other individuals or groups by changing the permissions on the file or folder.

Groups provide a convenient way of assigning the same permissions to multiple users at once. If you define a group and set up a list of users to be part of it, then you can assign permissions to the group rather than to the individuals. Individual users can be part of multiple groups, and can also have individual permissions assigned in addition to any inherited from the group(s).

Local file permission: The permission to access a file belonging to another user on the same PC

Network sharing permission: Permission to access a file stored on a different PC

Group: A named set of individual users to which the same permissions should be assigned

Note: *Local permissions can be set only on drives that use the NTFS file system, not FAT32.*

There may already be multiple users set up on your system, and several predefined groups exist by default:

- **Everyone**. A group that includes all users. Assign permissions to this group to affect every user, including guests.

- **Administrators**. A group that includes all users who have Administrator rights.

- **Users**. A group that includes all users who have User rights, which are less powerful than Administrator rights.

Note: *Microsoft recommends that you operate Windows 7 from a User-level account on a day-to-day basis, and switch to an Administrator-level account only to make changes such as installing new software or updating device drivers. Therefore, a single person might have more than one user account on the PC.*

QUICK FIX

No Security Tab
If there is no Security tab, the drive does not use the NTFS file system, and you will not be able to set local permissions for files and folders on that drive.

Viewing Local Permissions for a File or Folder

To view the permissions for a file or folder, open its Properties box and look on the Security tab. Click a group or user name in the top of the dialog box, and the permissions appear in the bottom section. See Figure 4.13. Check marks that appear in gray represent permissions inherited from higher levels in the folder structure; black check marks represent permissions set for the specific folder or file.

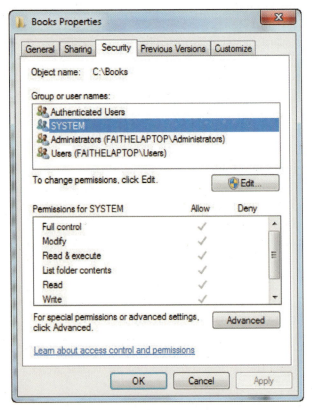

Figure 4.13 View the local user and group permissions for a folder or file.

Adding or Removing a Permission

You can set permissions at the file level, but it is better to set them at a folder level. Then whatever you put into that folder inherits its permissions. That way you have fewer permissions to keep track of and you do not have to reset the permissions for files individually.

Note: *In most cases, to allow or not allow a permission, you should mark or clear the Allow check box for an item. The absence of "allow" is in effect a denial. Use the Deny check box only rarely, to specifically override an inherited permission for a particular individual or group. Troubleshooting problems caused by forgotten Deny settings can be difficult.*

To add or remove a permission for a file or folder:

1. Right-click the file or folder and choose *Properties*.
2. Click the Security tab.
3. Click Edit. The Permissions dialog box opens.
4. Click the desired group or user name.
5. In the *Permissions for* section, mark or clear the *Allow* check boxes for each permission, as needed.
6. Click OK.
7. Click OK.

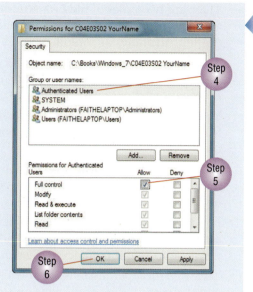

Exercise 3

Working with Permissions

1. Open the Computer window and navigate to the folder containing the data files for this chapter.
2. Copy the Chapter 4 folder to your hard drive, and rename the copy **C04E03S02**.
3. Grant full control of the folder to the Authenticated Users group.
4. Capture a screen print of the C04E03S02 Properties window and submit it to your instructor for grading. Name the file **C04E03 *Your Name***.
5. Delete the C04E03S02 folder from your hard drive.

Tip: See "Capturing a Screen Picture to Complete an Assignment" in Chapter 1 for help, if needed.

CHAPTER Summary

- The customizable parts of an Explorer window include the menu bar, details pane, preview pane, and navigation pane. To turn these on or off, use the Organize button's menu.

- To resize the panes within an Explorer window, drag the dividers between panes. The overall window size does not change.

- To customize how files and folders appear, such as hiding extensions for known file types, hiding operating system files, and showing hidden files and folders, choose *Folder and search options* from the Organize button's menu and set the options on the View tab.

- To customize the appearance of a folder's icon, right-click the folder and choose *Properties* and on the Customize tab, choose a template, and, if desired, customize the settings for the template by selecting a specific icon or picture.

- There are two types of file properties: metadata and attributes. Metadata is assigned mostly to data files; it includes text descriptions of properties such as Author. Attributes are on/off switches for qualities such as Read-only.

- To remove personally identifiable information from a file, right-click it and choose *Properties*. On the Details tab, click Remove Properties and Personal Information, choose what to remove, and click OK.

- You can retrieve earlier versions of a file or folder with the Previous Versions feature in Windows 7. Use the Previous Versions tab in the Properties box for the file or folder.

- There are two kinds of access you can grant to content on your hard disk: network and local. Local permissions can be assigned only to files and folders on NTFS volumes, not FAT32.

- For ease of administration, it is often preferable to assign permissions to a group of users rather than to individual ones. It is also easier to assign permissions to entire folders rather than individual files.

- To assign local permissions, right-click the file or folder and choose *Properties*, and then set up the permissions on the Security tab.

CONCEPTS Check

Completion: Answer the following questions on a blank sheet of paper.

Part

1

MULTIPLE CHOICE

1. If the menu bar does not appear in the Explorer window, what key on the keyboard can you press to make it appear?
   a. Ctrl
   b. Shift
   c. Alt
   d. Any of the above

2. Where does the preview pane appear, if present?
   a. Left
   b. Right
   c. Top
   d. Bottom

3. When you drag the divider between two panes in the Explorer window, how is the overall size of the window affected?
   a. It does not change.
   b. It changes vertically but not horizontally.
   c. It changes horizontally but not vertically.
   d. It changes both horizontally and vertically.

4. To reveal hidden files and folders, click Organize, *Folder and search options*, click the _____ tab, and click *Show hidden files, folders, and drives*.
   a. Hide
   b. View
   c. Custom
   d. Advanced

5. To set a folder's type, and thereby affect the folder's icon appearance, right-click the folder and choose _____ , and then click the _____ tab.
   a. *Customize,* Folder
   b. *Properties,* Customize
   c. *Change,* Icon
   d. *Setup,* Image

6. Which of these is an example of file metadata?
   a. Compressed
   b. Read-only
   c. Author
   d. Hidden

7. Compression and encryption are available only if _____ .
   a. you are using Windows 7, not an earlier version of Windows
   b. the drive uses the NTFS file system
   c. you are logged on as a user named Guest
   d. the drive uses the FAT32 file system

8. On which tab of a file's Properties dialog box can you restore a previous version?
   a. Backup
   b. Repair
   c. Previous Versions
   d. System

9. What does it mean when a file has the *File is ready for archiving* check box marked?
   a. File has been changed since backed up with a backup utility.
   b. File has *not* been changed since backed up with a backup utility.
   c. File's creation date was more than six months ago.
   d. File has not been accessed in more than six months.

10. Which two attributes are available directly on the General tab in a file's Properties box?
    a. Hidden and System
    b. Archive and Encrypt
    c. Read-only and Hidden
    d. Indexed and Read-only

Part 2

SHORT ANSWER

11. In an Explorer window, which button's menu contains the Layout command, which opens a submenu from which you can choose which panes to view?

    _____

12. How can you display file extensions for known file types in Explorer windows?

    _____

13. Why might you want to display hidden files and folders?

    _____

14. List five ways to customize the Explorer window interface (*not* the display of the files within the window).

    _____

15. What is the difference between metadata and attributes for a file?

    _____

16. From which tab of a file's Properties dialog box can you remove properties and personal information?

    _____

17. What is the difference between local file permission and network sharing?

    _____

18. What are the advantages of assigning local file permissions to folders rather than to files?

    _____

19. If no Security tab appears in a folder's Properties box, what can you assume about the drive's file system?

    _____

20. Why should you avoid using the Deny check box to remove permission for a file or folder?

    _____

SKILLS Check

Save all solution files to the default Documents folder, or any alternate folder specified by your instructor.

Guided Check

Assessment **CHANGE THE EXPLORER WINDOW LAYOUT**

1

1. Open the Computer window and turn off all optional Explorer window components except the navigation pane.
   a. Click the Start button.
   b. Click *Computer*.
   c. Click Organize.
   d. Point to *Layout*.
   e. Note which options are selected: menu bar, details pane, preview pane, and/or navigation pane.
   f. Click one of the options that is currently selected to turn it off.
   g. Repeat Steps c through f as needed until everything optional is off except navigation pane.
2. Display the drive icons as Large Icons.
   a. Click Views.
   b. Click *Large Icons*.
3. Widen the navigation pane so that no entries are horizontally cut off.
4. Capture a screen print of this window and submit it to your instructor for grading. Name the file **C04A01** *Your Name*.

5. Return the Explorer window to the following settings:
   - View setting: Medium Icons
   - Layout: Details and navigation panes only

Assessment 2   CUSTOMIZING HOW EXPLORER DISPLAYS FILES AND FOLDERS

1. Check to see whether file extensions are hidden or not; if they are not, hide them.
   a. Click Start.
   b. Click *Computer*.
   c. Click Organize.
   d. Click *Folder and search options*.
   e. Click the View tab.
   f. Make sure the *Hide extensions for known file types* check box is marked; click it to mark it, if needed.
   g. Click OK.
2. Check to see whether hidden files are visible or not; if not, make them visible.
   a. Click Organize.
   b. Click *Folder and search options*.
   c. Click the View tab.
   d. Make sure *Show hidden files, folders, and drives* is selected; if not, click it to select it.
   e. Click OK.
3. Display the contents of the Users folder on your primary hard drive.
   a. Click Start.
   b. Click *Computer*.
   c. Double-click the C drive (or the drive that contains Windows).
   d. Double-click the Users folder.
4. Set the view to Large Icons.
   a. Click Views.
   b. Click *Large Icons*.
5. Make sure the Default folder (a hidden folder) is showing. If it is not, recheck your work on Step 2.
6. Capture a screen print of this window and submit it to your instructor for grading. Name the file **C04A02** *Your Name*.
7. Close all remaining open windows.

Assessment 3   ASSIGNING METADATA TO A FILE

1. Open the Chapter 4 Student Data Files folder. Ask your instructor for help in locating the folder, if needed.
2. Copy the file **Estate.xlsx** and name the copy **C04A03.xlsx**.
   a. Select Estate.xlsx.
   b. Press Ctrl+C to copy.
   c. Press Ctrl+V to paste.
   d. Right-click the copy and click *Rename*.
   e. Type C04A03 and press Enter.

   Note: *If file extensions are hidden, do not type .xlsx on the end; if file extensions are visible, then do type that extension.*

3. Open the Properties for C04A03.xlsx.
   a. Right-click C04A03.xlsx.
   b. Click *Properties*.

4. On the Details tab, enter a title of Estate, a subject of Estate, a tag of Financial, and a comment of Preliminary Draft.
   a. Click the Details tab.
   b. Point to the area to the right of Title, so that the placeholder Add a Title appears, and then click and type Estate.
   c. Point to the area to the right of Subject, and then click and type Estate.
   d. Point to the area to the right of Tags, and then type Financial.
   e. Point to the area to the right of Comments, and then type Preliminary Draft.
5. Change the Authors entry to your own name.
   a. Next to Authors, select Ashley Colvin and press Delete.
   b. Type your full name.
6. Capture a screen print of this window and submit it to your instructor for grading. Name the file **C04A03** *Your Name*.
7. Click OK.
8. Submit C04A03 *Your Name* to your instructor for grading.
9. Close all remaining open windows.

Assessment 4 — REMOVING PERSONAL INFORMATION FROM A FILE

1. Open the Chapter 4 Student Data Files folder.
2. Open the properties for Estate.xlsx.
   a. Right-click Estate.xlsx.
   b. Click *Properties*.
3. Create a copy of the file that contains no personal metatdata.
   a. Click the Details tab.
   b. Click Remove Properties and Personal Information.
   c. Click *Create a copy with all possible properties removed*.
   d. Click OK.
   e. Click OK.
4. Rename the copy **C04A04.xlsx**.
5. Submit the file to your instructor for grading.

Assessment 5 — ASSIGNING PERMISSIONS TO A FOLDER

1. Create a new folder with your last name as its name in the root directory of your C drive.
   a. Click Start.
   b. Click *Computer*.
   c. Double-click the C drive.
   d. Click *New Folder*.
   e. Type your last name.
   f. Press Enter.
2. Set the permissions on that folder so that the Users group has full control of it.
   a. Right-click the folder you created in Step 1.
   b. Click *Properties*.
   c. Click the Security tab.
   d. Click Edit.
   e. Click Users.
   f. Mark the *Allow* check box for Full Control.
   g. Click OK.

3. Click the Users group so that its permissions show up as check marks.
4. Capture a screen print of the Security tab in the Properties dialog box and submit it to your instructor for grading. Name the file **C04A05** *Your Name*.
5. Click OK to close the Properties box.

On Your Own

Assessment 6 TURNING ON ALL OPTIONAL EXPLORER WINDOW ELEMENTS

1. Display the Computer window.
2. Make a note of which optional elements are displayed.
3. Turn on every available optional pane and menu bar.
4. Capture a screen print of the Explorer window and submit it to your instructor for grading. Name the file **C04A06** *Your Name*.
5. Return the window to its original condition using the notes you made from Step 2.

Assessment 7 DISPLAYING OPERATING SYSTEM FILES

1. In the Folder Options dialog box, make sure that the *Hide protected operating system files (Recommended)* check box is marked.
2. Display the root directory of the C drive and count the number of files.
3. Return to the Folder Options dialog box and clear the *Hide protected operating system files (Recommended)* check box.
4. Display the root directory of the C drive again and count the number of files.
5. On a blank piece of paper, write down the counts from Steps 2 and 4, and the names of at least four files that appeared only when operating system files were not hidden, and submit it to your instructor for grading.

Assessment 8 CUSTOMIZING APPEARANCE OF A FOLDER

1. In the Chapter 4 folder, create five new folders, named All Items, Documents, Pictures and Videos, Music Details, and Music Icons.
2. Copy the following files from the Chapter 4 folder into each of the new folders: **Distance.wma, bowl.jpg, Estate.xlsx, Townsend.doc.**
3. Set up each of the folders with the folder template that matches its name.
4. Submit an informal written report describing the differences in the way the folder icons appear.

Assessment 9 EXPERIMENTING WITH ATTRIBUTES

1. In the Chapter 4 folder, select and copy the file **Register.txt** to the Clipboard, and then paste it onto a USB flash drive.
2. On the flash drive, open the properties for Register.txt and set its File is ready for archiving attribute to Off.
3. Open Register.txt in Notepad and make a minor change to the file. Save and close the file.
4. Examine the attributes for Register.txt and note that the Archive attribute has been turned back on.
5. Write a paragraph explaining how this attribute might be useful to a computer user.

CHALLENGE Project

Suppose you want to give a copy of all of the data files for this chapter to an acquaintance, but you first want to remove as much personal information as possible from them. Not all of the files used for this chapter's exercises and assignments store personal information, however. Some of them only have details that are fixed, such as file size, or on/off attributes such as Archive.

Create a copy of the data files for this chapter. Then remove the personal information for as many of them as it is possible to do so for, and copy the files to a USB flash drive to submit for grading.

Using Windows 7 Programs

PERFORMANCE OBJECTIVES

Upon successful completion of Chapter 5, you will be able to:

- **Start and exit a program**
- **Create and save a new file**
- **Open and resave an existing file**
- **Print a regular or XPS file**
- **Send a file via fax**
- **Create unformatted and formatted documents with Notepad and WordPad**
- **Use the Math Input Panel**
- **Create a graphic picture in Paint**
- **Use the Snipping Tool**
- **Copy content from one application to another**
- **Launch an application from the command prompt**
- **Find and launch a program with the Start menu**

As your computing workspace, the Windows desktop offers a number of application tools or programs geared to help you accomplish specific computing tasks. For example, you can use the Calculator to crunch numbers and use WordPad to create documents like letters and reports. Applications enable you to create, save, and print files and, in some cases, to perform special activities like faxing a file. Still other applications track information, such as the Windows Live Mail program that you can use to manage your e-mail and schedule, as described in Chapter 9. You can start and close applications as needed and have multiple programs open on-screen to work with them as needed.

Performing Basic Application Activities

Application (program):
A set of instructions for performing a particular task or set of tasks, such as word processing or drawing a picture

The Windows 7 operating system enables you to install and use numerous types of *applications* or *programs*, each developed to handle a special type of activity. An application consists of a fixed set of instructions that the computer can execute, so, for the most part, each application or program stands alone and is used individually. In addition to enabling you to install applications that you need, Windows 7 includes a number of its own applications, some of which you will learn about later in the chapter.

Learning to use a variety of programs is easier than ever, because the majority of programs have some operations in common and even use similar menus and commands.

Starting and Exiting a Program

RAM (random access memory): The working menu that holds programs and unsaved work

Exiting or shutting down: Closing a program to remove its instructions and open files from RAM

Starting a program loads its instructions into the computer's **RAM (random access memory)**, the "working memory" that contains instructions for running programs and unsaved file information. Use the Windows 7 Start menu to start a program.

Exiting or **shutting down** a program removes it from the screen and from RAM. Shutting down a program not only frees up RAM for use by other programs and processes, but it also secures your work so that no unwanted viewer can see your work in a particular program. You typically can use one of a few different methods to shut down a program.

Here's How

To start a program:

1. Click the Start button.
2a. If you have used the program frequently and its name appears at the left side of the Start menu, click the program's name. The program will start and you can skip the rest of the steps.
    OR
2b. Click *All Programs*. A list of available programs and subfolders with additional programs appears in the left column of the start menu.
3. Click the folder holding the program to start, if needed. Otherwise, skip to Step 4.
4. Click the name of the program to start. The program will start, and its program window will appear on-screen.

To shut down a program and any open files in the program:

1. Click File or the button that you click to display file commands.
2. Click the *Exit* or *Quit* command.

OR

- Click the program window Close (X) button.

OR

- Press Alt+F4.

3. If a dialog box asks whether to save your changes to the current file, click Yes or Save to save, or click No or Don't Save to close without saving.

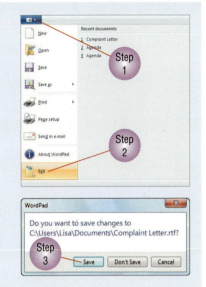

Note: Rather than the File menu name, the recent versions of many Microsoft Office applications and some Windows 7 applications have a button at the far left of the Ribbon tabs that you click to open the menu or screen with commands for working with files. In the recent versions of Office applications, this button is called the Office button. In other Windows 7 applications, the button name varies to match the application name. For example, in WordPad, it is called the WordPad menu button.

Making a Blank File

In many cases, starting a program automatically creates a new, blank file in the program. For example, when you start the Notepad application, it opens with a new, blank document file. However, if you have already added information to the current file or are working in a file that you previously saved and reopened, then you will need to take action to open a new file if you need one.

To open a new, blank file, click the File menu or the button that displays the file commands, and then click *New* (Figure 5.1), or press Ctrl+N. In many of the applications that are part of Windows 7, a blank file appears immediately.

Some applications, like recent versions of Microsoft Office Word, may prompt you to choose a *template* with starter content and formatting for the new file when you use the *New* command. As shown in Figure 5.2,

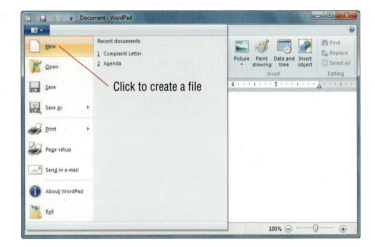

Figure 5.1 **The New command creates a new, blank file.**

you have the option of looking for templates on your computer or on the Web. Just click the applicable link, and select or search for the desired template. Other applications may prompt you to select a document type (like WordPad) or to name and save the file immediately (like Microsoft Access). Many applications, like the Microsoft Office applications, assign a temporary numbered file name to a new file until you save the file and give it a more descriptive name.

Template: A file with formatting and possible starter content that becomes the basis for a new file

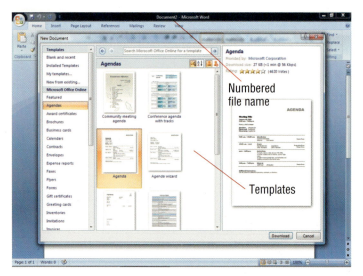

Figure 5.2 **Some applications give you the option to use a template or choose a document type when you create a new file.**

Note: *Pressing Ctrl+N almost always creates a blank file without asking you to choose a template. Older versions of some applications also have a New button on a toolbar that you can click to create a blank file without needing to choose a template.*

Saving a New File and Closing

Once you have created the blank file, you can begin adding content into it, as needed. Of course, the type of content you create will vary depending on the nature of the application. In word processing programs such as Windows 7 NotePad or WordPad, you type the text for your document. In a spreadsheet program, you enter values and formulas. In a graphics program such as Windows 7 Paint, you create an image using program tools.

Save: Preserve a file's information on disk

As you are working, the information you are creating exists only in RAM. To retain the ability to later open and work with the content you have already created, you have to *save* the file to disk.

During the process of saving a new file, you also assign a name to the file. Note that the application will also append a period plus a three- to five-letter file name extension that identifies the file format. Typically, each program creates files in a unique format, such as .txt for Notepad and .rtf for WordPad, but many programs can create and read files in a variety of formats. For example, Word can save documents in its own format, plus .html (Web page) format and others.

> **Tip:** Try to make your file names unique and descriptive to make it easier to find the file you need at a later time. For example, *Letter* is too generic, while *Benson Engine Sales Letter* gives you more information about the file's contents. Including a date in the file name helps you keep track of files that you may update from time to time so that you can tell updated versions of the files apart, as in *Resume 5-1-10* and *Resume 9-1-10*.

Here's How ▶ To save a new file:

1. Click File or the button that displays the file commands, and then click *Save*; or press Ctrl+S. If the program has a toolbar with a Save button, you can click that button, instead.
2. If you want to save in a location other than your default Documents library and you do not see a navigation or other pane at the left side of the Save As dialog box, click the Browse Folders button. This expands the Save As dialog box to include a pane at the left.

3. As in an Explorer window folder list (see Chapter 3), navigate to and select the folder where you want to store the saved file in the navigation pane. If there is no navigation or left pane, the dialog box will offer other methods for navigating to and selecting a folder.

4. Click the *File name* text box, and type the desired file name.

5. Click Save.

When you finish working in a file, you typically will no longer want it open in the program window, nor taking up usable RAM capacity. In such a case, you can *close* the file. In most programs, each file exists in its own program window, so you can close the file by closing the program window. To do so, click the Close (X) button for the file window, which typically appears below the program's Close button and is sometimes called the Window Close button. Many programs also include a *Close* command on the File menu (or the menu with file commands) that you can click to close a file. In other programs, you have to click the Close (X) button for the program window itself to perform the close. As when you exit a program, if you have any unsaved work in the file being closed, the program prompts you to save your changes.

Close: To remove a file from the program window and working memory

Opening an Existing File

If you have already saved a file in a folder on your system's hard disk, you can *open* the file in the program where you created it to resume working with the file, to print it, to copy information from it, and more. Opening the file loads the saved information into the system's working memory. To open the existing file, you must know the disk and folder location where it was saved.

Open: To load a file into the program window and working memory

To open an existing file:

1. Click File or the button that displays the file commands, and then click *Open*; or press Ctrl+O. If the program has a toolbar with an Open button, you can click that button, instead.

2. If you saved the file in a location other than your default Documents library or one of its subfolders, navigate to the save location in the pane at the left or by other means available in the Open dialog box for the program that you are using, and select the location (folder).

Here's How

3. Double-click the file icon. Or, click it once, and then click the Open button.

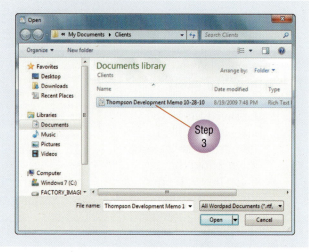

Tip: Double-click a file's icon in any folder or library window to both start the application used to create the file and open the file itself.

Saving Changes Made to an Existing File

Even though you will see a prompt to save file changes when you close the file or exit the program, you should still save your work periodically. Then, if some type of power surge or other problem causes your system to stop working, you will have preserved at least some of your most recent work. Get in the habit of saving every 10 minutes or so.

To save your work in an existing file, click File or the button for the file commands, and then click *Save*. If the menu includes both Save and Save As commands, click the *Save* command. Most applications also enable you to press Ctrl+S to save your work.

Note: *Some programs include an automatic saving feature that you can set to save your file automatically at an interval you specify, such as every five or ten minutes. However, this type of feature can sometimes cause the program to "pause" while the save takes place, slightly interrupting your work.*

Printing a File

Printing a file creates a paper or hard copy version of the file's contents, so that you can mail, overnight, or otherwise give the document to someone who needs it. Most organizations also still preserve most documents in hard-copy format for record-keeping purposes. The emergence of inexpensive, high-quality color printers in the last several years enables not only more attractive, eye-catching business document printouts, but also the ability for users to print their own digital photos and create other personal projects that were previously unattainable.

Another type of printout does not involve paper at all. When you ***print to a file***, Windows 7 essentially converts the file contents to another format, typically one that can be read or printed by more programs or even a specialized ***viewer application***. You will learn about this type of printout shortly.

Print to a file: A method of converting a file to a more easily shared format

Viewer application: An application that can read files printed or converted to a particular type of file format

Regular File Formats Because different printer models require different printing instructions, installing a printer under Windows 7 installs a **printer driver** file. The printer driver translates the information about a file format from a particular application in such a way that the printer can print the file correctly. So, when you send a printout or print job to the printer, the printer driver handles the file information and passes it along to the printer. If you have multiple printers installed on a system, then the print process includes selecting the desired printer (and therefore its printer driver) for the current print job.

Printer driver: The printer control file that interprets print information from an application

Note: *Printing requires that a printer be installed to work with Windows 7 and that it be connected to your system or network, be powered on, and have a supply of paper. Click Start, and then click Devices and Printers, where you can use the Add a printer button to install a printer. You also can change printer settings in the Devices and Printers window, and if the printer is recognized under the new Device Stage feature, you can in some cases perform even more activities. Chapter 13 provides more information about adding and removing a printer.*

Printing also includes choosing other settings for the specific print job, such as the number of copies you would like to print and which pages in the file you would like to print. Some applications and printers enable you to choose other settings, such as whether to collate the printed pages.

Some applications also include a *Print Preview* command that enables you to see how your file will look when printed. Check the File menu or the application toolbar to see if it offers a *Print Preview* command or button. Choose the command or button to open the preview. If the preview needs no changes, you can typically click a Print button at the top of the view to open the Print dialog box (see Step 2, below). If the document needs further changes, click the Close or Close preview button to return to the regular view and make those changes before printing.

To print a file:

Here's How

1. Open the file to print in the application used to create it.
2. Click File or the button that displays the file commands, and then click *Print*; or press Ctrl+P. The Print dialog box appears. The settings in this dialog box vary depending on the application and printer being used.
3. Select the printer to use in the *Select Printer* list, printer *Name* drop-down list, or the applicable list of printer choices in the dialog box that appears.
4. If you want to change settings for the selected printer, click the Preferences or Properties button. The dialog box that appears offers more detailed settings pertaining to the selected printer. For example, for a color inkjet printer, the dialog box may offer the choice of whether to print in black and white or color, and what type of paper (such as photo paper) to use for the printout. The dialog box may offer multiple tabs of options and may also include an Advanced button that you can click to see even more settings. Click OK after making your changes to close the open printer settings or properties dialog boxes.
5. Select the settings for the pages or area to print in the dialog box section named *Page Range* or something similar. Typically, if you choose to print a selection of pages, you type in the page numbers separated by a hyphen (for continuous pages) or a comma (for noncontiguous pages).

6. Change the *Number of copies* value to print more copies, if desired. You can select the initial entry and type a new value or click the up spinner button.

7. Change any other dialog box settings, as desired. Again, the available settings may vary depending on your program and printer.

8. Click Print or OK. The Print dialog box closes, and the program sends the printer job to the printer.

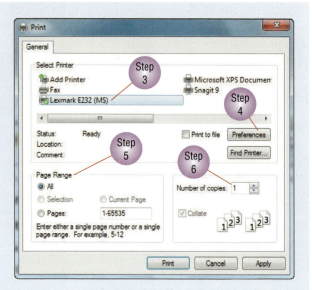

Understanding XPS Documents *XPS* stands for *XML Paper Specification*, a type of document format intended to be portable—that is, easily viewed by a variety of users and providing a consistent appearance when viewed on-screen or printed. Windows 7 includes the built-in Microsoft XPS Document Writer printer driver. So, when you select Microsoft XPS Document Writer as the printer for a print job from any program, the printed result is a file with the .xps file name extension (an XPS file or document) rather than a hard copy printout. Once you create the .xps file, you can share it with others, make it available for download from a Web page, and so on.

XPS (XML Paper Specification): A portable document format from Microsoft that enables you to create an XPS (.xps) document from any program by printing to the Microsoft XPS Document Writer

Figure 5.3 **Selecting Microsoft XPS Document Writer "prints" an XPS file.**

To convert the current file you are working on in any application to an XPS file, click File (or the button that displays the file commands), and then click *Print*, or press Ctrl+P, as usual. In the Print dialog box, select *Microsoft XPS Document Writer* as the printer to use from the *Select Printer* list, printer *Name* drop-down list, or the applicable list of printer choices, as shown in Figure 5.3. Choose other print settings as desired, and then click Print or OK. In the Save the file as dialog box that appears, specify the file name and location to save to, as you would for any other file, and then click Save. The XPS printer driver generates the file and automatically assigns the .xps file name extension.

To view an XPS document, double-click the document icon in any folder or library window. The document opens in the Windows 7 XPS Viewer application. (In

Windows Vista, XPS documents open in Internet Explorer, which has a built-in XPS viewer.) You also can open the XPS Viewer by choosing *Start*, *All Programs*, *XPS Viewer*.

Note: *Once you have opened an XPS file in the XPS Viewer application, you can use its command bar to work with the file and perform advanced operations like applying a digital signature or setting file permissions.*

Faxing a File

One method for faxing works much like generating an XPS file. To fax, you "print" a file to the fax printer driver (Microsoft Windows Fax and Scan) built in to Windows 7 by choosing *FAX* from the *Select Printer* list, printer *Name* drop-down list, or the applicable list of printer choices in the Print dialog box. When you then click Print or OK, the fax driver generates the electronic fax document and opens the New Fax window, where the document being faxed appears as an attachment in the *Attach* text box.

To start a fax from scratch rather than initiating it from the Print dialog box, choose Start, *All Programs*, *Windows Fax and Scan*. In the Windows Fax and Scan window that opens, click New Fax on the toolbar below the menu bar.

Note: *If the Windows Firewall has been enabled on your system, a Windows Security Alert dialog box may appear to inform you that incoming network connections have been blocked for Microsoft Windows Fax and Scan. To send faxes, you can click Keep Blocking to leave the blocking enabled.*

Type the recipient's fax number in the *To* text box, as shown in Figure 5.4, enter the fax topic in the *Subject* text box. Type and format additional text in the message body area, and then click Send. Enter information such as your area code and line access number if the Location Information dialog box appears, and then click OK twice. The Microsoft Windows Fax and Scan application dials the system's fax modem and sends the fax.

Note: *The first time you fax a document, a Fax Setup dialog box appears. Click the Connect to a fax modem or Connect to a fax server on my network choice, as applicable, and then respond to the additional dialog boxes that appear to specify fax settings. These steps assume that the fax modem hardware has been properly installed in the system and is connected to a phone line, if needed.*

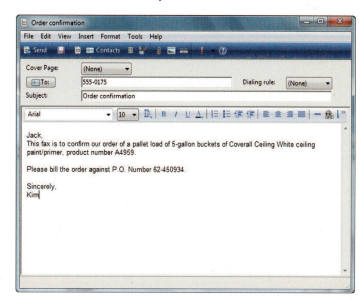

Figure 5.4 Print to the FAX driver to fax a document or use the Windows Fax and Scan application to create a fax from scratch.

 Exercise 1

Using WordPad to Create, Save, and Print a Letter

1. Click the Start button, and then click *WordPad* if it appears in the left pane of the Start menu. Otherwise, click Start, click *All Programs*, click *Accessories*, and then click *WordPad* to launch the WordPad application.
2. Click the Line spacing button in the Paragraph group of the Home tab, and click *1.0* in the drop-down list.
3. Click the Line spacing button in the Paragraph group of the Home tab again, and click *Add 10pt space after paragraphs* in the drop-down list to clear the check box beside it.
4. Type today's date, and then press Enter four times.
5. Type the following addressee information, and then press Enter four times:

   Accounts Payable Department
   Allen Products
   222 82nd St.
   Indianapolis, IN 46222

6. Type the following salutation, body, and closing text, pressing Enter twice after the salutation and body text, and four times after the closing:

   To Whom It May Concern:

   Enclosed find my check number 1162 in the amount of $296.42, payment in full for your invoice 3232.

   Sincerely,

7. Type your name.
8. Click the WordPad menu button, and then click *Save*. Enter C05E01 as the file name, and click Save to save the file in the default Documents library.

   Note: *If your instructor asks you to save your file in another location, save it there instead of the Documents folder.*

9. Click the WordPad menu button and then click *Exit* to exit WordPad.
10. Restart WordPad.
11. Click the WordPad menu button and then the *C05E01* file in the Recent documents list at the right to reopen the file. (If the file does not appear in the Recent documents list, click Open, navigate to the location where you saved the file, and double-click the file in the file list of the Open dialog box.)
12. Click the WordPad menu button, click the right arrow beside *Print* in the menu, and then click *Print preview*. The Print Preview view of the file appears. Click the Close print preview button in the Close group of the Print Preview tab of the Ribbon to return to the regular view of the file.
13. Click the WordPad menu button, and then click *Print*. Select the printer specified by your instructor, and click Print to print the file. Submit the finished printout to your instructor, if required.
14. Close WordPad and the file.

Using Calculator

Calculator is a small, special-purpose application that has been a part of all released versions of Windows. Like a separate hand-held calculator, the Calculator in Windows 7 can perform basic calculations such as addition, subtraction, multiplication, and division, as well as more advanced scientific calculations.

Start Calculator with the Start menu, just as you would any other application. You can choose Start, *All Programs*, *Accessories*, *Calculator*.

> Tip: An accessory or helper application like Calculator is sometimes called an applet.

Calculator's default view enables you to perform basic math computations in what is called its Standard mode. However, if you click the Calculator View menu, you can click one of three additional views or modes for performing more complex calculations. For example, if you click *Scientific*, the Calculator expands to display buttons for more complex calculations, as shown in Figure 5.5. Click View and then *Standard* to change back to the regular view for Calculator.

Figure 5.5 The Standard (left) and Scientific (right) modes of Calculator.

> Tip: To open a second window of a program like Calculator or Internet Explorer, right-click its taskbar button and click the program name.

To use the on-screen keys for the Calculator, you can click with the mouse. Most users can work faster with Calculator using the keyboard. As long as the NUM LOCK key is active, pressing the numbered keys above the letters on the keyboard enters the number in Calculator, and the period key enters a decimal place. Use the following keys for mathematical operators, pressing Shift as needed:

Parentheses to group values	( )
Addition	+
Subtraction	−
Multiplication	*
Division	/
Equals	Enter

> Tip: If you are using a desktop system and the keyboard has a 10-key keypad at the right end, you can use that keypad to make entries in Calculator with one hand.

So, for example, if you want to enter the equation $(6 \times 5)+(2 \times 8)=$ into Calculator, you would type (6*5)+(2*8) and then press Enter for the equals sign. Calculator will display the subtotal *30* after you type the first close parenthesis, but simply continue entering the rest of the equation to arrive at the total.

Here are some other useful techniques to know when you use Calculator:

- Click the C button to clear the most recent calculated total.

- To store a number in Calculator's memory, click the MS button.

- To recall a stored number, click the MR button. For example, you can add 10 numbers together, and then press MS to store the total. Then, you could multiply two numbers, press +, and then click MR and press Enter to add the stored total to the multiplied numbers.

- MC clears the stored value from memory.

- To add a newly calculated value to the stored total in memory, click the M+ button, and then MR to see the new stored total.

- To copy the number currently displayed in Calculator and paste it into another application, press Ctrl+C (Edit, *Copy*) to copy the value, and then Ctrl+V (Edit, *Paste*) to paste in the destination application.

The Windows 7 version of Calculator has been upgraded to include Programmer and Statistics modes, shown in Figure 5.6, that are also accessible from the View menu. Programmer mode offers the ability to perform calculations as well as choose the number format and data type, common needs in the programming field. Use the top group of option buttons at the left to change the number format: hexadecimal (*Hex*), decimal (*Dec*), octal (*Oct*), and binary (*Bin*). Use the second set of option buttons to change the data type: QWORD (*Qword*), DWORD (*Dword*), WORD (*Word*), and BYTE (*Byte*). This mode also displays integers only, discarding decimals. Similarly, Statistics mode includes added function buttons that are useful to any professional who needs to perform statistical calculations, such as summing, averaging, and finding the standard deviation in a group of values. For example, if you want to average some values, you would enter each value and click the Add button to add it to the dataset. You then would click the button for the statistical operation to perform.

Calculator offers even more improvements. You can choose either *Unit conversion* or *Date calculation* from the View menu to expand the calculator window. You can perform a variety of unit conversions, such as converting between various weight units or between various other types of measure like power, length, date, and more. For example, as Figure 5.7 shows, a jeweler

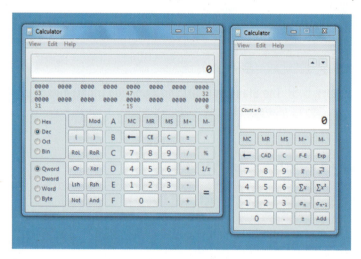

Figure 5.6 **The Programmer (left) and Statistics (right) modes of Calculator.**

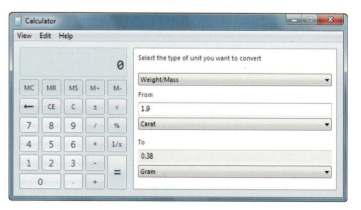

Figure 5.7 **Using Calculator to convert a weight.**

could convert a weight in carats to the equivalent weight in grams. Available date calculations include finding the difference between two dates or adding and subtracting days to a date you specify.

Lastly, Calculator now includes four worksheets—Mortgage, Vehicle lease, Fuel economy (mpg), and Fuel economy (L/100 km)—available from the *Worksheets* submenu of the View menu. You can use each worksheet to calculate the type of data suggested by its name, such as calculating a mortgage payment. After displaying a worksheet, enter data in the worksheet fields, and then click the Calculate button to display the result in the box at lower right.

To hide a converter or worksheet and return to the default for the current Calculator mode, click View, and then click *Basic*. Click the Calculator window's Close (X) button to close Calculator.

Creating a Plain Text File with Notepad

Like Calculator, Notepad has been part of every Windows version. Use Notepad to create document files in ***plain text (.txt)*** format. What that means is that while you can change the type of lettering used for text on-screen in Notepad, saving the file wipes out that special formatting, saving only the text content. Thus, Notepad creates about the most basic and compact type of document.

Plain text (.txt): A file format for document files that does not allow for or save any text formatting information

You need to know about using Notepad to create and work with plain text files because the plain text file type is still used in a variety of ways with computers. For example, some programs use tracking-log files or startup-settings files that have various file name extensions but are really plain text files that you can open and edit in Notepad. Similarly, because the language used to create Web pages depends on special text codes or tags like <head> and </table>, you actually can create and edit basic Web pages using Notepad. Finally, because Notepad files are so small, you may prefer to use Notepad to create simple documents in any situation where file size or storage space is an issue.

Start Notepad from the Start menu by choosing Start, *All Programs*, *Accessories*, *Notepad*. From there, the same File menu commands discussed so far in this chapter—New, Open, Save, Print, and Exit—work essentially the same in Notepad as in other applications. Type the text that you want, pressing Enter or Tab and using capital letters to set off or highlight information, as needed. Figure 5.8 shows the Notepad window with a file open in it. Note that you need to click Format, and then click *Word Wrap* to have lines of text wrap (move to the next line) within the window size.

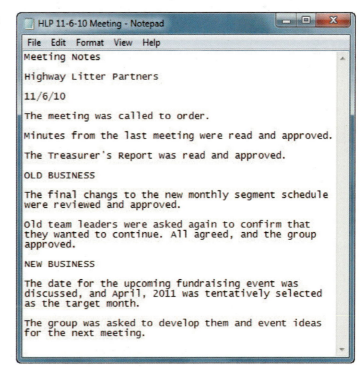

Figure 5.8 **Create plain, basic, compact text files in Notepad.**

Creating a Text File with Formatting in WordPad

Font: A typeface, a style of lettering, appearing either on the screen or in print

Rich Text Format (.rtf): A basic document file format that preserves some text formatting

WordPad represents a step up from Notepad in that it enables you to apply, save, and print basic text formatting. WordPad enables you to not only change the text *font* (type of lettering), but a variety of other settings that apply to text and paragraphs.

Select Start, *All Programs, Accessories, WordPad* to start WordPad. Use commands as for other applications to create and manage files. By default, saving a WordPad file saves it in ***Rich Text Format (.rtf)***, a format name that indicates that file formatting will be preserved.

After you drag over text to select it for formatting, WordPad enables you to work with these formatting settings, some of which are illustrated in Figure 5.9:

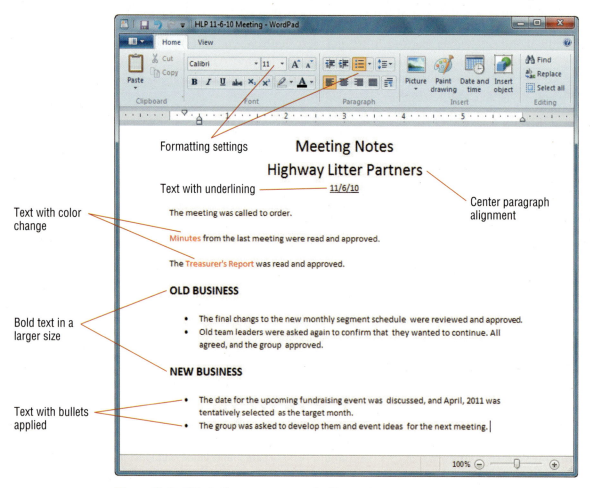

Figure 5.9 This is the same text as the Notepad document in Figure 5.8, but this example in WordPad has formatting applied, starting with a different font.

- **Font**. Use the buttons and lists in the Font group of the Home tab of the Ribbon to change the text font family, font size, style (Bold, Italic, and so on), size, effects (Strikethrought, Underline, and so on), and other settings such as text color.

- **Bullets**. The Start a List drop-down in the Paragraph group, by default, turns bullets on or off for the paragraph holding the insertion point, or the selected paragraphs. Use the drop-down arrow for this button to change to another list style, such as a numbered list.

- **Alignment**. The Paragraph group of the Home tab of the Ribbon enables you to add or remove indents for paragraphs, set line spacing, and choose a paragraph alignment (Align text left, Align text right, Center, or Justify).

- **Other**. Click a ruler location to create a custom tab stop, or use the tools in the Insert group of the Home tab of the Ribbon to incorporate elements such as the date and time and graphics in the document.

Note: *The ruler appears above the document text and shows measurements in 1/8-inch increments.*

 ## Exercise 2

Creating a Meeting Flyer in WordPad and Converting with Calculator

1. Click the Start button, click *All Programs*, click *Accessories*, and then click *WordPad* to launch the WordPad application.
2. Click the Line spacing button in the Paragraph group of the Home tab, and click *1.0* in the drop-down list.
3. Click the Line spacing button in the Paragraph group of the home tab again, and click *Add 10pt space after paragraphs* in the drop-down list to clear the check box beside it.
4. Type the following basic information, press Enter twice after each line and press Tab after each colon, and type your name where indicated by *Student Name* in the last line:

   Highway Litter Partners
   New Team Member Meeting
   When: 7 p.m. November 4
   Where: Regent Community Center
   Contact: Student Name, 555-0606

5. Press Enter one more time, and then type the following text:

   Highway Litter Partners is a volunteer organization dedicated to keeping roadsides clean in our community. If you can spare two hours a month to join a cleanup team, we need you! Last year, volunteers removed 7.5 tons of roadside waste.

6. Press Enter twice, and then type the following two lines, pressing *Enter* after each line:

   Cleaner communities
   A better world

7. Click Start, click *All Programs*, click *Accessories*, and click *Calculator*.
8. Click View, and then click *Unit conversion*.
9. Select *Weight/Mass* from the *Select the type of unit you want to convert* drop-down list.
10. Enter *7.5* in the *From* text box, select *Short ton* from the accompanying drop-down list, and select *Pound* from the *To* drop-down list.
11. Drag over the result in the *To* text box and press Ctrl+C to copy it.
12. Click View, and then click *Basic* to hide the converter, and then close Calculator by clicking its Close (X) button.

13. Use the taskbar to redisplay the WordPad document, if needed.
14. Paste the copied value:
    a. Select *7.5 tons* in the body text.
    b. Press Ctrl+V to paste the value and replace the selection.
    c. Type a space and pounds.
    d. Add a thousands comma in the pasted value.
15. Click the WordPad menu button and click *Save* or click the Save button. Enter C05E02 as the file name, and click Save to save the file in the default Documents library.

    Note: *If your instructor asks you to save your file in another location, save it there instead of the Documents folder.*

16. Drag over all text in the document or press Ctrl+A. This selects all of the text. Open the *Font family* drop-down list in the Font group of the Home tab of the Ribbon, and click *Georgia*. Open the *Font size* drop-down list and click *14*.
17. Drag over the first two lines in the document. Use the tools in the Font group of the Home tab on the Ribbon to change the Font family to *Arial* and the Font size to *20*. Also, click the Center alignment button in the Paragraph group to center the text.
18. Format the words *When:*, *Where:*, and *Contact:* in boldface by dragging over each selection, and then clicking the Bold (B) button in the Font group.
19. Drag over the When:, Where:, and Contact: paragraphs to select them. Click the 1.5-inch mark on the ruler above the document text. The text to the right of the new tab stop shifts to the right based on the new tab.
20. Click anywhere in the paragraph of text starting with *Highway Litter Partners*, and then click the Increase indent button in the Paragraph group of the Home tab. All lines of the paragraph are indented at the left.
21. Drag over the last two lines of text to select them, and then click the Start a list button in the Paragraph group on the Home tab of the Ribbon. The paragraphs change to a bulleted list.
22. Press Ctrl+S to save your changes to the file.
23. Click the WordPad menu button, click the arrow to the right of *Print*, and then click *Print preview*. The Print Preview view of the file appears. Click the Close print preview button in the Close group of the Print Preview tab to return to the regular view of the file.
24. Click the WordPad menu button and then click *Print*. Select the printer specified by your instructor, and click Print to print the file. Submit the finished printout to your instructor if required, or instead e-mail the file or submit it on your USB flash drive as required.
25. Close WordPad and the file.

Using the Math Input Panel

Tablet PC: A type of laptop computer on which you can select commands and give other user input using a stylus (tablet pen) or sometimes a finger

Graphics tablet: An external input device, which generally connects to the computer via a USB port, and with which you can select commands, give user input, and draw images using a stylus (pen)

The Math Input Panel is a new Windows 7 feature. If you have a **tablet PC** or have a **graphics tablet** connected to your computer (either with or instead of a mouse), Windows 7 can recognize handwritten content that you create in a special new application called the Math Input Panel. The Math Input Panel recognizes and converts the symbols and equations you draw into a nicely formatted digital equation that you can insert into documents you create, as in the example in Figure 5.10. The Math Input Panel recognizes symbols and equation types commonly used in high school- and college-level math topics, such as calculus, functions, algebra, geometry, sets, and more. Students and professionals in a variety of fields, or anyone else who needs to create technical documents that include complex math, can benefit by attaching a graphics tablet to their computer and using the Math Input Panel.

After you enter an expression in the Math Input Panel and Windows 7 digitizes the expression, you can then insert the converted expression into a document in another program. The target program has to support a standard called *MathML* (Mathematical Markup Lanuguage), an XML-based language for creating and sharing mathematical expressions between programs. MathML was originally developed to facilitate presenting complex math on Web pages, and it is now supported by a host of programs designed for editing and using math in documents, as well as OpenOffice, an open source software suite. (A list of supported programs is available via the W3C Web site: www.w3.org/Math. Support for MathHTML was incorporated into Microsoft Office Word 2007, and although Word uses its own similar XML-based standard for mathematical expressions, the transition between the two standards is seamless when you use the Math Input Panel and Word 2007. Figure 5.11 shows an expression that has been inserted into a Word 2007 document from the Math Input Panel. You can edit and format the expression in Word and even use the Equation Tools Design tab of the Ribbon to change the expression, shown in Figure 5.11. The expression disappears from the Math Input Panel after being inserted, but you can reopen it there using the History menu.

After you finish using the Math Input Panel and click its window Close (X) button, it remains an active application accessible via the notification area. This allows you to reuse any equation that is in the History for the current work session. To exit the Math Input Panel completely, click the Show hidden icons button at the left end of the notifications area, right-click on the *Math Input Panel* icon in the list that appears, and then click *Exit* in the shortcut menu.

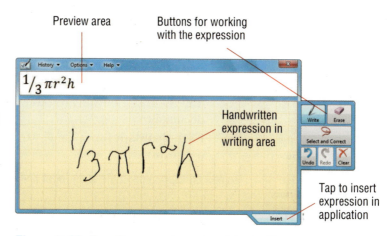

Preview area   Buttons for working with the expression

Handwritten expression in writing area

Tap to insert expression in application

Figure 5.10   A math expression entered in the Math Input Panel.

MathML: An XML-based standard for describing mathematical expressions in programs, published by the W3C Math Working Group (www.w3.org/Math)

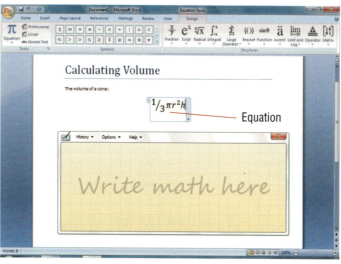

Equation

Figure 5.11   A math expression inserted into a Word 2007 document.

Here's How

To create a math expression and insert it into a document:

1. Open or create the document (in a program that supports MathML) into which you want to insert a math expression, and position the insertion point at the location where you would like the expression to appear.

2. Click Start, click *All Programs*, click *Accessories*, and then click *Math Input Panel*.

3. Using the pen or stylus, start writing in the writing area, which initially displays the message *Write math here*.

4. Tap the Undo button at the right to undo any stroke or character or the Redo button to redo actions.

5. Tap the Insert button, at lower right, to insert the equation into the document.

6. Click the Math Input Panel window Close (X) button to hide the application.

To edit an expression in the Math Input Panel

1. Reopen the Math Input Panel by clicking the Show hidden icons button at the left side of the notifications area, and then click the *Math Input Panel* icon in the list that appears.

2. If needed, select the equation to edit from the History menu.

3. Tap the Select and Correct button at the right.

4. Drag with the pen to draw a circle around the symbol or character that you would like to correct. When the symbol or character turns red, it will be selected for correction.

5. When you release the mouse button, a list of possible corrections appears. You can either tap one of the suggestions in the list, or draw a replacement character within the selection marquee.

6. To remove extraneous content, tab the Erase button at the right, and then drag over the content to erase in the writing area.

7. Click Write to resume adding more to the expression.

*Note: **Some Web browser programs can't display MathML correctly. For example, Internet Explorer typically needs an added plug in (mini program) such as MathPlayer to add the needed support.***

Creating a Basic Picture with Paint

The Paint applet enables you to create basic graphics and save them in a variety of file formats, such as PNG (Portable Network Graphics, the default format) or JPEG (.jpeg or .jpg) file format. Because *compression* in these file formats makes the files fairly compact, many files on Web pages are created or converted as PNG or JPEG files. The compression used in PNG files is lossless, meaning all the original data is contained in the compressed file, while the JPEG compression is lossy, meaning it can make smaller files by discarding some of the original data. Other file formats Paint can save, such as TIFF (Tagged Image File Format), use no compression at all.

The Paint program includes several groups of tools on the Home tab of the Ribbon, with simple tools that you can use to create lines, shapes, and text to build an image like the example shown in Figure 5.12. The Home tab also includes selection tools, an eraser, a tool you can use to fill a color, a color picker, and a magnifier.

Note: *Depending on the size of the Paint window, the Shapes choices either appear as a button as shown in Figure 5.12, or as a scrolling list that previews the shapes.*

Like most of the other applications discussed in this chapter, Paint is also in the Accessories group of applications. Choose Start, *All Programs, Accessories, Paint* to start Paint. Paint opens with a new, blank file, and you also can use the New command on the Paint menu to create a file.

Figure 5.12 Layer shapes, lines, and text to create a Paint image.

One of the first things to do for each Paint file you create is to specify its size. Click the Paint menu button and then click *Properties* (Ctrl+E) to open the Image Properties dialog box, where you can specify the Width and Height for the file in Units of *Inches, Centimeters,* or *Pixels*. You also can specify whether the image should be *Black and white,* or *Color*. Click OK to finish establishing the image size.

Once you have created the image, you can use these basic techniques to add and work with its contents:

- **Add a line or shape.** Click the arrow below the Shapes button in the Shapes group, and then click the line or desired shape in the palette that appears. Use the Shape outline and Shape fill drop-downs to select the shape outline and fill type, and the Size drop-down list to choose a line or outline width. Click the Color 1 button in the Colors group, and then click the desired color for the line or shape outline. To select the color for the specified shape fill, click the Color 2 button in the Colors group, and then click the desired color for the line or shape outline. To create the shape or line, drag diagonally on the image. (Note that the Polygon and Curve tools require some extra techniques you can learn about in Help.) To make freeform lines, use the Pencil tool in the Tools group.

- **Add text.** Click the Text button in the Tools group. Click the Color 1 button in the Colors group, and then click the desired text color. Drag diagonally on the image to specify the area where you want the text to appear. Choose a font, font size, and attributes in the Text Tools Text tab of the Ribbon, and then type the desired text.

- **Make and change a selection.** Click the arrow at the bottom of the Select button in the Image group, and then click the type of selection you want to make. Drag on the image to make the selection. Drag the selection to move it, press Delete to delete it, or use another Image group choice such as Rotate or flip to make a change.

- **Erase and fill.** Click the Eraser tool, select an eraser Size, and then drag on the area to erase. Or, select a Color 2 color, click the Fill with color tool in the

Undoing a Change
Because any change you make either removes or paints over existing pixels, press Ctrl+Z immediately to undo any unwanted change.

Deselecting
To deselect an object you have just created, click another tool. Otherwise, you may inadvertently apply changes such as color changes to your new object.

Tools group, and then click the area to fill. Note that the area to fill must be a continuous area of the same color.

Do not forget to save your changes to any Paint file you create.

Note: *Graphics programs that paint work differently from those that draw. Paint programs change individual dots or pixels of color in the image file, while draw programs create shapes based on easily changed shape outlines. Paint programs are also called raster programs, and draw programs are also called vector programs.*

Using the Snipping Tool

Windows 7 includes a new application called the Snipping Tool that enables you to capture an image of all or part of what is on screen. You can paste what you have snipped into another program or save it as a PNG, JPEG, GIF (another graphic format), or MHT (single file Web page) file. The Snipping Tool is a great way to share content between applications when doing so might otherwise not be possible, such as when copying and pasting directly between applications does not work. Images you create and save with the Snipping Tool can be inserted into a document or e-mail message, for example in an instance where you want to show a colleague how to complete an action in an application. The Snipping Tool is fairly easy and straightforward to use.

Here's How ▶ **To take a screen shot with the Snipping Tool**

1. Make sure that the information you want to capture appears on-screen.
2. Click Start, click *All Programs*, click *Accessories*, and then click *Snipping Tool* to open the Snipping Tool window.
3. To change the snip type from the default *Rectangular* type, click the down-arrow at the right of the New button, and click *Free-form snip*, *Window snip*, or *Full-screen snip*.
4. A full-screen snip will be taken immediately. For a window snip, click the window to snip. For the other snips, drag on-screen to select the area to snip.
5. When you release the mouse button, the snip appears in the Snipping Tools window. You can use the tools there to save, copy, e-mail, or annotate the snip. Click the New button to create a new snip.
6. Click the window Close (X) button to close the Snipping Tool. If prompted to save the snip, choose the appropriate option.

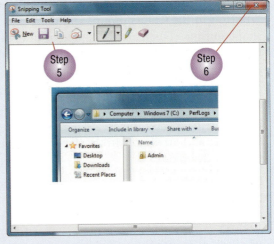

Exercise 3

1. Click the Start button, click *All Programs*, click *Accessories*, and then click *Math Input Panel* to open the Math Input Panel.
2. In the writing area, write the calculation for the area of a circle: πr^2. Correct the expression as needed.
3. Click the Start button, click *All Programs*, click *Accessories*, and then click *Snipping Tool* to open the Snipping Tool.
4. With the default (*Rectangular snip*) snip type selected, drag to select the expression in the preview area of the Math Input Panel.
5. Close the Math Input Panel by clicking its window Close (X) button, and then clicking Show hidden icons in the notification area, right-clicking the *Math Input Panel* icon, and clicking Exit.
6. Click the Start button, click *All Programs*, click *Accessories*, and then click *Paint* to launch the Paint application.
7. Click the Paint menu button, and then click *Properties*. Leave the Units set to Pixels, and enter 240 in both the *Width* and *Height* text boxes. Also, leave the *Colors* option selected. Click OK.
8. Use the taskbar to switch back to the Snipping Tool window, click its Copy button on the toolbar, and then click the window Close (X) button. Click No if prompted whether to save the snip.
9. Back in Paint, click the Paste button to paste the math expression snip. Drag the lower-right handle of the pasted item's selection box to increase its size slightly. Then move the mouse inside the selection, and when you see the four-arrow mouse pointer, drag the selection to center it about one-third of the way from the top of the file.
10. Add more text:
    a. Click the Text tool in the Tools group of the Home tab of the Ribbon.
    b. Make sure that black is selected for the Color 1 box in the Colors group.
    c. Click below the pasted expression. Select *Times New Roman* from the font family list in the Font group of the Text Tools Text tab of the Ribbon, and also change the font size to *28*.
    d. Type Media.
    e. Size and drag the selection box for the text so that the text is centered below the pasted expression.
    f. Click outside the text to deselect it.
11. Add a circle shape:
    a. Click the Color 1 box and then click the indigo color (second from right on the top row) in the Colors group.
    b. In the Shapes group, click the down arrow at the bottom of the Shapes button, and click the *Oval* shape. Or simply click the oval shape if the selection of shapes is visible in the Shapes group.
    c. Click Shape fill, and make sure that *No fill* is selected.
    d. Drag to draw a circle around the logo text, pressing and holding the Shift key as you drag to create a perfect circle.
    e. Resize and reposition the finished circle as needed, and then click away from it.
12. Fill the circle:
    a. Click the Color 1 box and then click the light turquoise color (third from right on the middle row) in the Colors group.
    b. Click the Fill with color tool in the Tools group.
    c. Click inside the indigo circle to fill it. Also click in the open parts of the *e, D,* and *a* to fill them.

13. Click the Paint menu button, and then click *Save*. Enter C05E03 as the file name, leave PNG (*.png) selected as the *Save as type*, and click Save to save the file in the default Documents library.

    Note: *If your instructor asks you to save your file in another location, save it there instead of the Documents folder.*

14. Click the Paint menu button, and then click *Print*. Select the printer specified by your instructor, and click Print to print the file. Submit the finished printout to your instructor if required, or instead e-mail the file, or submit it on your USB flash drive, as required.

15. Close Paint and the file.

Copying Data between Files and Applications

As you learned in Chapter 3, Windows 7 manages a special storage location in your system's memory called the *Clipboard*. In that chapter, you saw how you could cut or copy a file from a folder to the Clipboard, and then paste the file into a new location from the Clipboard.

Just as you can use the Clipboard to copy or move files between folders, you can use the Clipboard to copy or move information from *within* a file to a location within another file—even a file within another program in many instances. For example, Figure 5.13 shows a range of cells from an Excel 2007 worksheet pasted to a memo document in Word 2007. You can use one of two methods to get the job done, as you will learn here.

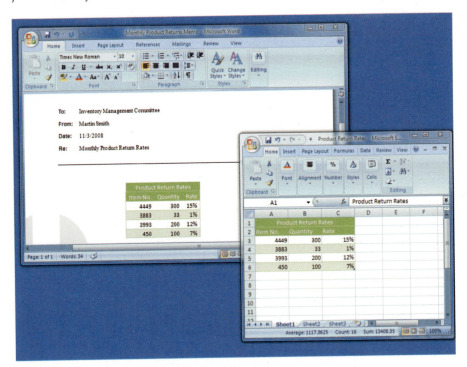

Figure 5.13 The selected cells in Excel have been pasted into Word (left).

Using the Clipboard

Cutting and pasting information moves it from one location to another, removing the original selection and placing it in a new destination. Copying and pasting copies information, leaving the original selection in place and inserting a copy of that information in the destination that you specify.

Start the move or copy by selecting some text or cells (typically by dragging over them) or by clicking an object to select it. Then, use the *Cut*, *Copy*, and *Paste* commands on the Edit menu to perform the move or copy. Cut or copy the selection, choose the destination for the cut or copied information, and then paste. While some applications offer toolbar buttons that provide shortcuts for copying and pasting, the following keyboard shortcuts work in almost all Windows-based applications, including those in Windows 7 itself:

- Cut   Ctrl+X
- Copy   Ctrl+C
- Paste   Ctrl+V

QUICK FIX

Pasting is Unsuccessful
If you try to move or copy information between incompatible files or applications, the pasted information will not appear, and you may see an error message. You can try pasting the information in another format. To do so, open the Edit menu and click the *Paste Special* command, if it appears. Then choose an available format for the paste.

To copy or move a selection with commands:

Here's How

1. Open the file that holds the information to copy or move.
2. Select the information to copy or move by dragging over it (text and cells) or clicking it (graphics and other objects).
3. Click Edit, and then click *Copy* to copy the selection or *Cut* to cut the selection. Or, in a program that uses the Ribbon, click the Copy or Cut button on the Home tab. You also can press Ctrl+C to copy or Ctrl+X to cut, or use any Copy or Cut button available on a toolbar.
4. Open or switch to the file where you want to place the copied or moved information. Or, if you are copying or moving within the same file, scroll to or display the location where you would like to place the copied or cut information.
5. Click to position the insertion point in the location, often called the destination location, where you want to insert the pasted information.
6. Click Edit, and then click *Paste* or press Ctrl+V. In a program that uses the Ribbon, click the Paste button on the Home tab. The selection appears in the destination location.
7. If desired, you can repeat Steps 4–6 to paste the Clipboard contents into additional destinations. The copied or cut selection remains on the Clipboard until you copy or cut another selection or shut down the system.

Note: *Be careful to examine the area in the document where you have cut or pasted a selection. In some cases, you may need to add extra spaces or lines to make sure the document still looks good and reads correctly.*

Tip: The top Microsoft Office applications have their own special Clipboard called the Office Clipboard. The Office Clipboard can hold up to 24 different copied items, and you can select which item to paste into a destination document.

Using Drag-and-Drop

Just as you can drag and drop a selected file between folder or library windows, you can drag and drop a selected text or object between documents. Use this technique if you prefer using the mouse to copy or move selections.

Here's How ▶

Dragging and Dropping within a Document
Drag-and-drop does not work as well if you need to move or copy information to different pages within a particular document. Often, the document will appear not to scroll as you are dragging, and then jump beyond the location where you wanted to stop. If this is the case, use the Edit menu commands or shortcuts, instead, to perform the copy or move.

To copy or move a selection with drag-and-drop:

1. Open the file that holds the information to copy or move.
2. If you are copying or moving information to another file, open that file.
3. Size and position the open file (or application) windows on the Windows desktop so that both windows are at least partially visible.
4. Return to the window for the file that contains the information to copy or move, and select the information by dragging over it (text and cells) or clicking it (graphics and other objects).
5. Drag the selection from the source file over to the window of the destination file; when the destination file window becomes active, drag up and down as needed to position the insertion point at the specific location where you want to place the copied or cut information. Note that you have to press and hold Ctrl when you drag to copy. If you do so, the mouse pointer will include a plus sign for the copy; if not, the mouse pointer will include only a selection box.
6. Release the mouse button. The moved or copied information appears in the destination location.

Step 5

Exercise 4
Using a Picture and Calculated Values in a Memo

1. Click the Start button, click *All Programs*, click *Accessories*, and then click *WordPad* to launch the WordPad application.
2. Type **Memorandum**, and press Enter.
3. Insert the date:
   a. Type **Date:**
   b. Press the Tab key.
   c. Click Date and time in the Insert group of the Home tab of the Ribbon.
   d. In the *Available formats* list of the Date and Time dialog box, click the format that resembles *August 21, 2012*. (The formats reflect the current date.) Click OK.
   e. Press Enter.
4. Type the following text, pressing Enter twice after each line except the last one, adding your name in the place of *Student Name*, and pressing Tab after each colon:

To: Al Smith, Pi R-Squared Media

From: Student Name

Re: New Logo

The new logo is complete and appears below. At our hourly design rate of $35, the total fee comes to

5. Click the WordPad menu button, and then click *Save*. Enter C05E04 as the file name, and click Save to save the file in the default Documents folder.

   Note: *If your instructor asks you to save your file in another location, save it there instead of the Documents folder.*

6. Click the Start button, click *All Programs*, click *Accessories*, and then click *Paint* to launch the Paint application.

7. Open the **C05E03** file you created in Exercise 3.

8. Click the bottom portion of the Select button (with the arrow) in the Image group of the Home tab of the Ribbon, and then click *Select all* or press Ctrl+A. Paint selects the whole logo image.

9. Click the Copy button in the Clipboard group or press Ctrl+C. This copies the selection to the Clipboard.

10. Click the Paint menu button, and then click *Exit* or press Alt+F4 to close Paint. The copied information remains on the Clipboard.

11. Click at the end of the **C05E04** memo file and press Enter twice.

12. Click the Paste button in the Clipboard group of the Home tab of the Ribbon or press Ctrl+V. The logo appears.

13. Click the Start button, click *All Programs*, click *Accessories*, and then click *Calculator* to launch the Calculator application.

14. Use the keyboard or click Calculator keys to multiply 3 x 35.

15. Press Ctrl+C or choose Edit, *Copy* to copy the calculated amount to the Clipboard.

16. Click the window Close (X) button to close Calculator. The copied information remains on the Clipboard.

17. Click to position the insertion point at the end of the last line of the memo. Press the spacebar to add a space if needed, and then click the Paste button on the Ribbon.

18. Add a dollar sign to the left of the pasted value and a period after.

19. Press Ctrl+S to save your changes to the memo file.

20. Click the WordPad menu button, and then click *Print*. Select the printer specified by your instructor, and click Print to print the file. Submit the finished printout to your instructor if required, or instead e-mail the file or submit it on your USB flash drive as required.

21. Close WordPad and the file.

Using the Command Prompt

The most prevalent operating system prior to Windows, called DOS, required the user to enter all commands at a ***command prompt***, which initially looked like **C:\>** on most systems. The user had to enter all commands as typed codes or words, some of which could be rather obscure, like *chkdsk*. As you might imagine, this command prompt or command line interface made computers daunting to use for many people who did not have the time to learn to navigate to folders from a prompt or to remember lists of commands.

The Windows operating system has done away with the command prompt—almost. There still may be instances where you need to work from the command prompt, especially to perform certain system maintenance and troubleshooting tasks. For example, if your system is having trouble connecting to your school or company network, the Help Desk staff member might ask you to run the *ipconfig* command to gather some diagnostic information.

To use the command prompt, you open a command prompt window in Windows 7. Once that window is open, you type the desired command, along with any ***switches*** to specify another detail about how the command should run. A switch

Command prompt: A line of text displayed by an operating system to indicate that it is prepared for you to type in commands

Switch: A forward slash and a letter or phrase code that specify a further aspect of how a command line command should run

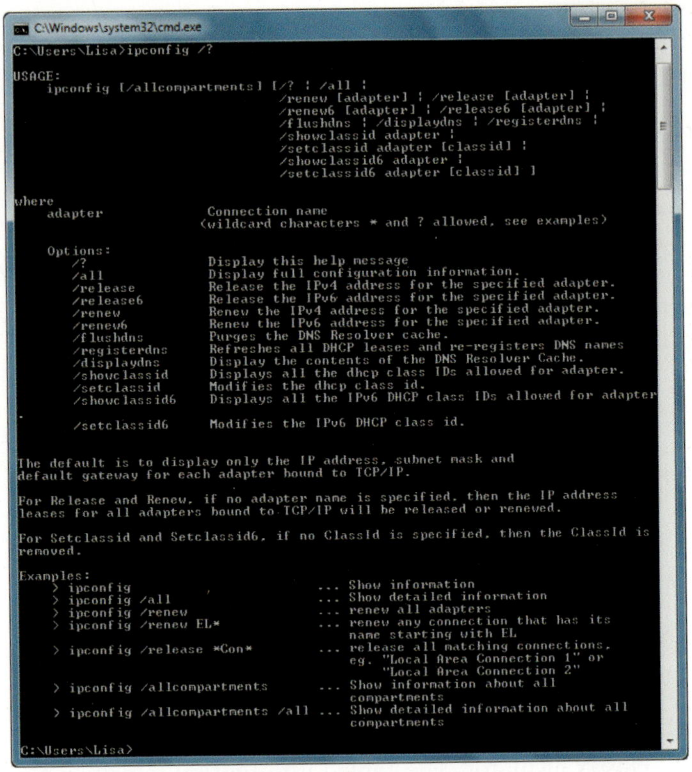

Figure 5.14 Viewing the available switches for ipconfig by typing ipconfig /? and pressing Enter.

usually consists of a forward slash plus a letter, word, or phrase, all typed after the command on the command line. To see the available switches for a particular name, type the command name at the prompt, press spacebar, type /?, and then press Enter. For example, Figure 5.14 shows the information about switches that appears when you type *ipconfig /?* at the command prompt and press Enter.

By default, the command line shows the path to your user folder. To navigate to other folders and view files, you can use these commands at the command line:

- **cd** *directory name* Changes to a subfolder within the current folder.

- **mkdir** *directory name* Makes a new subfolder within the current folder.

- **cd.** Moves up a directory level.

- **dir** Lists the files and folders in the current folder. If you include the /p switch, the listing pauses at each full window, so you can review the list and then press spacebar to continue.

If you include the /w switch, the command lists the files in a wide, multi-column format. You also can include both /p and /w.

You can run a variety of other commands from the command prompt, including but not limited to:

- **copy** *old file name new file path and name* Copies a file. To copy within the same folder, omit the path from the new file name, but do use a different file name.

- **del** *file name* Deletes the specified file. You can use wildcards with this command to delete multiple files.

- **help | more** (the center symbol is the pipe symbol, or the Shifted Backslash) Lists the available commands and pauses at a full window listing. Press spacebar to continue.

Note: *When you enter a file name at the command prompt, you must include the period and file name extension.*

In addition to running commands with a limited scope from the command prompt, you also must start certain full programs from the command prompt. For example, you type *mmc* at the command line to start the Microsoft Management Console, including the path and name of a snap-in module, if required. Typing *msinfo32* starts a System Information application, while *secpol.msc* starts the Local Security Policy application.

To open a command prompt window and use a command or start a program:

1. Click the Start button, click *All Programs*, click *Accessories*, and then click *Command Prompt* to open a command prompt window

OR

   Click Start, type **cmd** in the *search* box, and then press Enter.
2. Type the command or program name, including any switches and parameters (such as a file name), as required.
3. Press Enter. The command executes or the program starts.
4. Enter additional commands, if required.
5. Click the command prompt window Close (X) button, or type **exit** and press Enter to close it when you finish.

Note: *It is possible to elevate the command prompt session to the administrator level when needed. To do so, type cmd in the search box on the Start menu, press Ctrl+Shift+Enter, and click Yes in the User Account Control dialog box that appears.*

Exercise 5

Getting Help in the Command Prompt Window

1. Click Start and type **cmd** in the search box.
2. Press Enter. The command prompt window opens.
3. Type **help | more** and press Enter. (You can include spaces before and after the pipe symbol or leave them out. The command will run either way.)
4. Capture a screen shot, paste it into Paint, and save the file as **C05E05S04**.
5. Press the spacebar, and then review the next screen of commands.
6. Press the spacebar as many times as needed to scroll to the end of the list.
7. Type **exit** and press Enter to close the command prompt window.
8. E-mail your screen shot to your instructor or submit it on your USB flash drive, as required.

Searching for a Program with the Start Menu

While the Start menu is an easier way to start programs than hunting through folders on a system to find a program startup command, it still can take you several steps to launch a program that you do not use often with the Start menu.

To save time in such a case, you can use the *search* text box at the bottom of the Start menu to jump to the program's startup command and use it. Typing an entry in that text box not only lists matching files, but also matching program names.

Here's How ▶ To find and start a program with the *search* box on the Start menu:

1. Click the Start button.
2. Type the beginning or all of the command name in the *search* box. The left column pane of the Start menu displays matching programs at the top of the list, in the *Programs* section.
3. Click the name of the program to start.

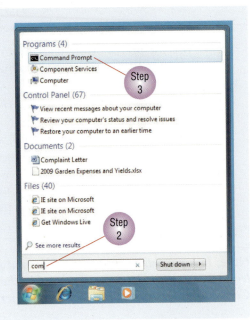

 ## Exercise 6

Finding and Starting Programs with the Start Menu

1. Click Start and type **media**.
2. Click *Windows Media Player* in the list of programs that appears.
3. Close *Media Player*.
4. Click Start and type **ex**.
5. Capture a screen shot, paste it into Paint, and save the file as **C05E06S05**.
6. Click *Internet Explorer* in the Programs list at the top of the left pane of the Start menu.
7. Close Internet Explorer.
8. E-mail your screen shot to your instructor or submit it on your USB flash drive, as required.

CHAPTER Summary

- Use the Windows 7 Start menu to start a program.
- Use the *New* command (Ctrl+N) on the File menu or the menu with file commands that appears when you click the program button to the left of the Ribbon tabs to start a new file. If prompted, select a file type or template.
- Use the *Save* command (Ctrl+S) on the File menu or the menu with file commands that appears when you click the program button to the left of the Ribbon tabs to save and name a file. Use the *Save As* command when you want to save an existing file under a new name, and press Ctrl+S to save ongoing work to an existing file.
- Click the window Close (X) button to close the file, program, or folder window.
- Use the *Print Preview* command on the File menu or menu with the file commands to review a document before printing.

- Choose the *Print* command (Ctrl+P) on the File menu or the menu with the file commands to start a print job, choose a printer and other settings such as the number of copies in the Print dialog box, and then click Print or OK.
- Print to the Microsoft XPS Document Writer printer (driver) to create an XPS file.
- Print to the FAX printer (driver) or start Windows Fax and Scan application to send a fax.
- Use Calculator to calculate mathematical and scientific values. Input values and operators with the keyboard or its 10-key keypad, if available.
- Calculator offers new Programmer and Statistics modes with even more conversion and calculation functions.
- Calculator also includes new converters and worksheets for performing common activities like calculating a mortgage payment.
- Use Notepad to create plain text (.txt) documents.
- Use WordPad to create Rich Text Format (.rtf) documents, which save some text and paragraph formatting.
- The Math Input Panel works with a tablet PC or graphics tablet and converts math expressions you write into digital versions that you can paste into other applications.
- Use the Paint program to create simple graphics files saved by default in the JPEG (.jpg) format.
- Tools on the Ribbon in WordPad and Paint enable you to format text and objects.
- The Snipping Tool enables you to take a screen shot of all or part of what is on-screen and to save that content for use in other documents.
- To make a selection in a document, drag over text or cells, or click the item to select.
- To move or copy with the Clipboard: Ctrl+X to cut, Ctrl+C to copy, and Ctrl+V to paste, switching to the destination window and clicking to position the insertion point before pasting.
- To move or copy using drag-and-drop: hold down Ctrl to copy.
- Open the command prompt window to enter operating system commands and start programs at the command prompt.
- When using the command prompt, type the desired command along with any switches or parameters, and then press Enter.
- Including the /? switch with a command at the command prompt displays information about using the command, including switches you can use with it.
- To find a program, type its name into the *search* text box at the bottom of the Start menu. Then click the name of the program to start in the list of programs that appears.

CONCEPTS Check

Completion: Answer the following questions on a blank sheet of paper.

MULTIPLE CHOICE

1. To start a program, use the _____ menu.
   a. Program
   b. Open
   c. Start
   d. Launch

2. To create a file, choose the _____ command.
   a. Open
   b. New
   c. Save
   d. Print

3. To save a file, choose the _____ command.
   a. Open
   b. New
   c. Save
   d. Print

4. To work with a file you have previously saved and closed, choose the _____ command.
   a. Open
   b. New
   c. Save
   d. Print

5. Use the _____ to see how a file will look when printed.
   a. Print Review
   b. Print Overview
   c. Print Preview
   d. Print Purview

6. To select a printer and create a print job, choose the _____ command.
   a. Open
   b. New
   c. Save
   d. Print

7. To copy the selected text or object to the Clipboard, press Ctrl+ _____ .
   a. X
   b. C
   c. D
   d. V

8. To copy a selection from one location to another with drag-and-drop, hold down the _____ key as you drag.
   a. Ctrl
   b. Alt
   c. Shift
   d. Insert

9. Which program do you use to create a plain text (.txt) file?
   a. WordPad
   b. TextPad
   c. Notepad
   d. PlainPad

10. Which program do you use to add numbers?
    a. PlusPad
    b. Add
    c. Command Prompt
    d. Calculator

Part 2 — SHORT ANSWER

11. Why start a program?

_____

12. What happens in some programs when you create a new file?

_____

13. When do you assign a name and location for a stored file?

_____

14. How do you display a worksheet in Calculator?

_____

15. Explain the basic difference between a plain text (.txt) and RTF (.rtf) file, and name the programs used to create each.

_____

16. Name the primary tab that appears in most applications with the Ribbon.

_____

17. Describe the difference between copying and moving a selection.

_____

18. How do you create an expression in the Math Input Panel?

_____

19. Explain how to open the command prompt window.

_____

20. Name one command you can use in the command prompt window.

_____

SKILLS Check

Save all solution files to the default Document folder, or any alternative folder specified by your instructor.

Guided Check

Assessment 1 — STARTING AND EXITING PROGRAMS

1. Start Windows Update.
   a. Click Start.
   b. Click *All Programs*.
   c. Click *Windows Update*.
2. Start WordPad.
   a. Click Start.
   b. Click *All Programs*.
   c. Click *Accessories*.
   d. Click *WordPad*.
3. Start Notepad.
   a. Click Start.
   b. Type **no**.
   c. Click *Notepad* in the list of programs.
4. Start Calculator.
   a. Click Start.
   b. Type **calc**.
   c. Press Enter.
5. Close the Windows Update window.
   a. Click the taskbar button for the window.
   b. Click the window Close (X) button.
6. Close the Calculator window.
   a. Click the taskbar button for the window.
   b. Click the window Close (X) button.
7. Close the Notepad window.
   a. Click the taskbar button for the window.
   b. Click the File menu.
   c. Click Exit.
8. Close the WordPad window.
   a. Click the WordPad menu button.
   b. Click Exit.

Assessment 2 — CREATING AND SAVING A FILE

1. Start WordPad.
   a. Click Start.
   b. Type **wordpad**.
   c. Press Enter.
2. Type the following text into the document, pressing Enter once after the first two paragraphs and twice at the end of the last line:
   Saving a File
   Saving a file enables you to specify both a file name and disk and folder in which to save the file. Use the Save command or press Ctrl+S to start the save.

Use the Open command or press Ctrl+O to open the dialog box you can use to choose a file to reopen.

3. Select the first line in the file, and then apply formatting.
   a. Open the Font family drop-down list in the Font group of the Home tab of the Ribbon, and click *Arial Black*.
   b. Open the Font size drop-down list in the Font group, and click *20*.
4. Apply bold to the selected words in the body paragraphs, as shown below:
   Saving a file enables you to specify both a file name and disk and folder in which to save the file. Use the **Save** command or press **Ctrl+S** to start the save.
   Use the **Open** command or press **Ctrl+O** to open the dialog box you can use to choose a file to reopen.
5. Save the file as **Saving**.
   a. Click the WordPad menu button to the left of the Home tab.
   b. Click *Save*.
   c. Type Saving.
   d. Navigate to the library or folder to save to, if required.
   e. Click Save.
6. Click the WordPad menu button, and then click Exit to close WordPad.
7. E-mail the file to your instructor or copy it to your USB flash drive and submit it as required.

Assessment **OPENING, EDITING, AND PRINTING A FILE**

3

1. Start WordPad.
   a. Click Start.
   b. Type wordpad.
   c. Press Enter.
2. Open the Chapter 5 Student Data Files folder. Ask your instructor for assistance, if needed. Open the **WordPad Document Formats** file.
   a. Click the WordPad menu button.
   b. Click *Open*.
   c. Navigate to the folder with the student data files for this book.
   d. Double-click the WordPad Document Formats file.
3. Copy the text in the file.
   a. Press Ctrl+A to select all the text in the document.
   b. Press Ctrl+C.
4. Open the **Saving** file.
   a. Click the WordPad menu button.
   b. Click *Open*.
   c. Navigate to the folder where you saved the file in Assessment 2.
   d. Double-click the Saving file. (Do not save the WordPad Document Formats file.)
5. Add text to the end of the document.
   a. Press Ctrl+End to move the insertion point to the end of the document.
   b. Type WordPad can open and resave documents in other formats.
   c. Press Enter.
6. Paste the copied text into the **Saving** file by pressing Ctrl+V.
7. Reformat the pasted text.
   a. Drag over the pasted text to select it.
   b. Open the Line spacing drop-down list in the Paragraph group of the Home tab of the Ribbon, and click *1.0*.
   c. Click at the right end of each line and press Delete to remove the extra hard returns (extra lines of space).

8. Save the edited file with a new name.
   a. Click the WordPad menu button.
   b. Click *Save As*.
   c. Type Saving 2.
   d. Navigate to the folder to save to, if required.
   e. Click Save.
9. Preview the printout.
   a. Click the WordPad menu button.
   b. Click *Print Preview*.
   c. After reviewing the preview, click Close.
10. Print the file.
    a. Click the WordPad menu button.
    b. Click *Print*.
    c. Choose the printer specified by your instructor.
    d. Click Print to send the printout to the printer. Write your name on the printout and submit it to your instructor as required.
11. Click the WordPad menu button, and then click *Exit* to close WordPad.

Assessment 4 — CREATING AN XPS DOCUMENT

1. Start WordPad.
   a. Click Start.
   b. Type wordpad.
   c. Press Enter.
2. Open the **Saving 2** file.
   a. Click the WordPad menu button.
   b. Click *Open*.
   c. Navigate to the folder where you saved the file in Assessment 3.
   d. Double-click the **Saving2** file.
3. Print the file as an XPS document.
   a. Click the WordPad menu button.
   b. Click *Print*.
   c. Click *Microsoft XPS Document Writer* in the *Select Printer* list.
   d. Click Print to send the printout to the printer.
   e. Type Saving 3.
   f. Navigate to the folder to save to, if required.
   g. Click Save.
4. Click the WordPad menu button, and then click *Exit* to close WordPad.
5. View the XPS document.
   a. Click the Windows Explorer button on the taskbar.
   b. Navigate to the folder or library where you have saved the XPS file.
   c. Double-click the file.
6. Click the XPS Viewer window Close (X) button to close the file.
7. E-mail the file to your instructor or copy it to your USB flash drive and submit it as required.

On Your Own

Assessment 5 — CALCULATING AND PASTING VALUES

1. Start Notepad.
2. Start Calculator.
3. Perform the following calculation, using the appropriate keyboard keys for the math operators:
   $(197+202) \div (1+2.45)=$

4. Copy the result, paste it into the first line of the Notepad file, and press Enter.
5. Switch back to Calculator and clear the previous total.
6. Find the square root of 236.
7. Copy the result, paste it into the next line of the Notepad file, and press Enter.
8. Switch back to Calculator and clear the previous total.
9. Select *Scientific* from the View menu.
10. Find 11^3 (11 to the 3rd power or 11 cubed).
11. Copy the result, and close Calculator.
12. Paste the result into the next line of the Notepad file.
13. Save the file as **Calculations**.
14. E-mail the file to your instructor or copy it to your USB flash drive and submit it as required.

Assessment 6 SNIPPING AND EDITING A GRAPHIC

1. Open the Pictures library.
2. Open the Sample Pictures folder.
3. Double-click the sample picture of your choice to open it in Windows Photo Viewer. (Ask your instructor to supply an example picture if the Windows sample photos are not available.)
4. Start the Snipping Tool application.
5. Snip a rectangular area at least 2 inches in height and width from the picture.
6. Switch back to the Windows Photo Viewer window, and close it.
7. Click the Copy button on the Snipping Tool toolbar.
8. Start Paint.
9. Click the Paste button in the Clipboard group of the Home tab.
10. Click the Text button in the Tools group of the Home tab.
11. Click on the image, type Snip!, and format and position the text as desired.
12. Save the file as **Snipped Image** in the PNG format, in the folder or library specified by your instructor.
13. E-mail the file to your instructor or copy it to your USB flash drive and submit it as required.
14. Close the open applications and windows. Do not save the Snipping Tool content if prompted.

Assessment 7 USING THE COMMAND PROMPT TO START PROGRAMS AND COMMANDS

1. Click Start, type cmd, and press Enter.
2. Close the command prompt window.
3. Click Start, type secpol.msc, and press Enter. Click *Continue in the User Account Control* dialog box, if it appears.
4. Close the Local Security Policy window.
5. Click Start, type cmd, and press Enter.
6. Type secpol.msc at the command prompt, and press Enter. Click *Continue in the User Account Control* dialog box, if it appears.
7. Close the Local Security Policy window.
8. Type ipconfig and press Enter.
9. Take a screen shot of the desktop (increase the size of the command prompt window and scroll up as needed to display the full results of the ipconfig command). Paste the shot into Paint, save it as **C05A07**, and submit it to you instructor via e-mail or on your USB flash drive as required.
10. Type exit and press Enter to close the command prompt window.

PARTNER ACTIVITY: WRITING AND PRINTING A REPORT

1. Find a partner, and pick a topic about which you would like to write a brief report. Pick a topic for which a simple Paint graphic would be appropriate.
2. Decide which of you will enter the text, and which will create the graphic.
3. Open WordPad and create the text first. Decide on the contents together while the designated typist enters the information. Save the file as **Assessment 8 Report**.
4. Now switch users, and share ideas on how to create the illustration for the report in Paint. Only the designated "artist" should create the actual Paint graphic, however. Save the file as **Assessment 8 Graphic**.
5. Press Ctrl+A, and then Ctrl+C to copy the graphic in Paint.
6. Switch back to the WordPad document, click to position the insertion point at the destination location, and then press Ctrl+V.
7. Add both of your names into the bottom of the document and apply any text and paragraph formatting desired.
8. Save the file.
9. Print a copy of the file and submit it to your instructor for grading.

CHALLENGE Project

As a member of the sales team in your company, you have been asked to develop a proposed schedule and agenda for an upcoming meeting with a client, and to send a memo to the sales team members to gather feedback and move the plan along.

1. Open Paint, and create a picture of the product (or service) that you will be presenting to the client. For example, you can combine shapes to create a car, cell phone, or coffee cup. (Don't worry too much about creating a perfect drawing. Developing advanced drawing skills can take months or years.)
2. Open WordPad, and create a memo document with the proposed agenda, including your name on the *From* line. Copy the product image from Paint and paste it into the memo document.
3. Save the document as **Challenge Client Meeting Agenda**, and print it, if required by your instructor.
4. Imagine that you need to post the document to the Web for the clients involved, so "print" it as an XPS file. Because some of the sales people in your company's group will not have access to a hard copy or the Web, start the process for faxing the file to see how it works. (Note that you probably will be unable to send a fax, so simply close the window after reviewing how the fax would look.)
5. If required, supply the final memo document to your instructor in hard copy format, or submit both the WordPad document and the XPS file via e-mail or on your USB flash drive to your instructor.

CHAPTER 6

Customizing the Desktop

PERFORMANCE OBJECTIVES

Upon successful completion of Chapter 6, you will be able to:

- Use the Control Panel to change settings
- Change how the keyboard and mouse work
- Change the desktop background, color scheme, theme, and icon size
- Work with display settings
- Specify a screen saver
- Adjust system sounds
- Control icons on the desktop
- Adjust the Start menu
- Change the taskbar and its toolbars
- Use gadgets
- Make the system accessible for users with disabilities
- Specify or synchronize the system date and time

Changing the appearance and function of a desk can take real work. You can refinish it, maybe take out or reconfigure some drawers, and add new handles. But those tasks all take a lot of work and leave the desk unusable for a while. Because Windows 7 offers a virtual desktop, in contrast, you can change its looks and some aspects of its operation in mere moments. You can customize the overall appearance of the desktop or fine-tune individual items such as the taskbar or the system time. You can access most of the choices you need for customizing the desktop in Control Panel or on the desktop itself.

Understanding the Control Panel

The Windows 7 Control Panel provides a central location where you can access and change system settings. You will use the Control Panel to perform essential system operations, from adding users to adjusting the desktop's appearance to adding and removing hardware. Many of the more specific tasks you will learn about later in this chapter and the book require that you can move around and find desired settings in Control Panel.

Opening the Control Panel

Use the Start menu to open the Control Panel. The command for starting Control Panel is in the right column on the Start menu, as shown in Figure 6.1, so all you need to do is click Start and then *Control Panel*. The Control Panel window opens.

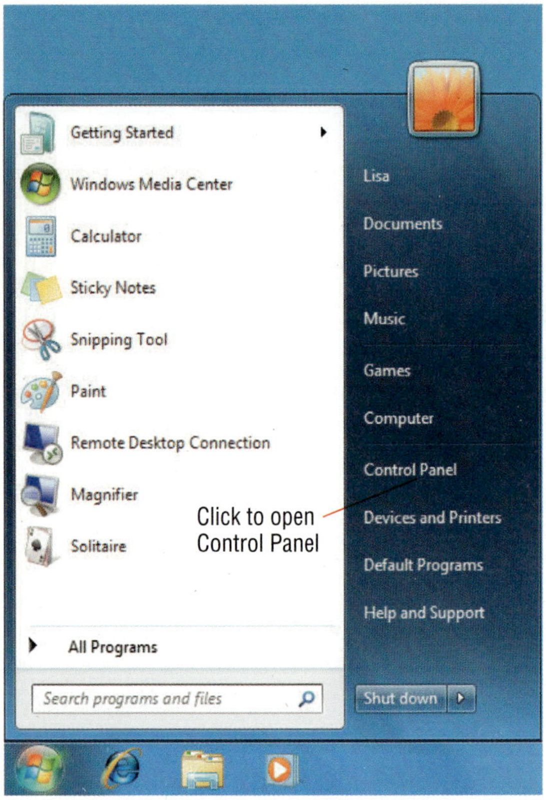

Control Panel organizes its settings into categories to make them easier to find. Figure 6.2 shows the main Control Panel screen, which shows categories by default. You will find an icon and accompanying link for each of these categories:

- **System and Security**. This category offers the choices for viewing system performance, viewing hardware information and working with hardware, making backups, and viewing and adjusting system performance-related settings, among other settings. It also includes the Action Center for protecting, updating, troubleshooting, and recovering the system, as well as other tools for maintaining the system, such as Windows Update and administrative tools.

- **Network and Internet**. Go here to access the Network and Sharing Center, where you can view and set up your network, as well as handle tasks like working with a network homegroup and changing Internet browser settings.

- **Hardware and Sound**. Change system sounds and work with hardware such as the mouse, keyboard, and scanners, cameras, sound, and the display using settings from this category, as well as working with some specialized settings such as power settings, pen or touchpad settings, and tablet PC settings.

Figure 6.1 Choosing Start and then *Control Panel* opens the Control Panel.

- **Programs**. In this category, find the choices for installing and uninstalling programs and Windows 7 features, specifying default programs, and working with gadgets.

- **User Accounts and Family Safety**. As you learned in Chapter 1, this category in Control Panel provides the settings for working with user accounts. It also offers parental control settings, among other choices.

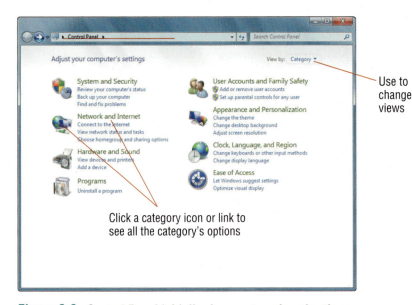

Figure 6.2 Control Panel initially shows categories of options.

- **Appearance and Personalization**. The choices here enable you to make the desktop your own—choose from fun stuff like specifying your own background and adding fonts. Make the system friendlier by customizing the taskbar, Start menu, and folder settings.

- **Clock, Language, and Region**. Look in this category when you need to make sure the system is set to the proper date, time, and time zone, or even to work with language settings for Windows 7 and the keyboard.

- **Ease of Access**. Use the settings found in this category to customize the system for a user with special needs. For example, you can replace sounds with visual cues or turn on speech recognition.

Some settings appear in multiple categories. For example, Power Options choices appear in the System and Security and Hardware and Sound categories. This enables you to find the desired settings via any of the categories to which they are relevant.

Many Control Panel settings, such as the Appearance and Personalization settings, apply to the currently logged-on user only. This enables each user to set up the desktop to work exactly as he or she prefers.

There are some Control Panel options that you cannot access via the Category view in Control Panel. To find those options, open the *View by* list and click either *Large icons* or *Small icons*. (Choosing *Category* redisplays the categories.) Other Control Panel icons are accessed most easily by right-clicking the desktop. This book will use the easiest method for selecting the particular Control Panel settings under discussion.

Working with the Control Panel Window

The Control Panel home window (Figure 6.2) enables you to move quickly to the system task that you want to perform. Clicking a category icon displays all of the available subcategories and tasks in the category. However, if the task you want to perform appears on the Control Panel home window below a category name, you can click the task link to begin the task immediately.

After you click a category icon, Control Panel displays lower-level categories and the tasks within each of them. For example, Figure 6.3 shows how Control Panel appears when you click the *Appearance and Personalization* category icon. You can click a task link under any category to start performing that task. To back up to the

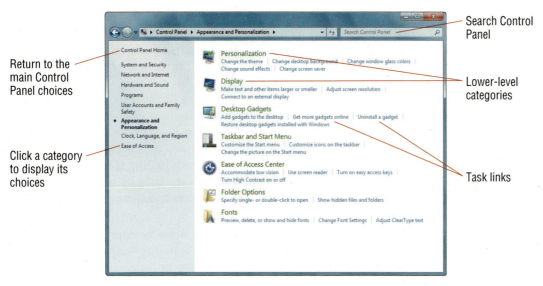

Figure 6.3 Navigate Control Panel by clicking categories and tasks.

Control Panel home window, either click the Back (left arrow) button as you would for any Explorer window, or click the Control Panel Home link at the top of the list at the left side of the window. Or, if the task you want does not appear in the selected category, you can click another category in the list at the left side of the window.

When you finish your work with the Control Panel, click the window's Close (X) button to close it.

Changing Keyboard and Mouse Settings

As ***user input devices***, the mouse and keyboard enable you to give commands to and enter information into your computer. Using these devices effectively requires manual dexterity in the hands and wrists. Because dexterity levels vary from user to user and are affected by other factors such as whether one is left-handed or right-handed, Windows 7 provides settings for adjusting how the mouse and keyboard respond to user actions.

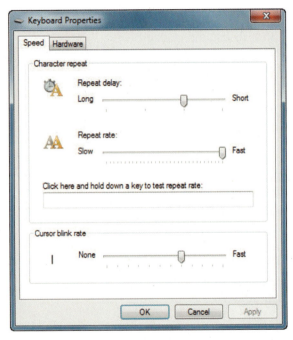

Figure 6.4 **You can change the repeat delay and repeat rate for the keyboard, as well as the cursor blink rate.**

In the Keyboard Properties dialog box (Figure 6.4), you can adjust the *Repeat delay* slider (the length of time that you can press and hold a key before the computer starts repeating the character on-screen) and the *Repeat rate* slider (how quickly a character repeats when you press and hold a key) for the keyboard. Increasing the keyboard repeat delay and reducing the repeat rate can reduce repeated characters for any user with stiffness in the hands and fingers. You also can drag the *Cursor blink rate* slider to the left to slow down the flashing speed of the vertical insertion point, making it easier to see.

The Mouse Properties dialog box (Figure 6.5) offers four tabs of settings that may be active (the fifth tab is for the driver), depending on the type of mouse (or touchpad or trackball) installed with the system. The tabs and the settings they offer include:

- **Buttons**. You can check the *Switch primary and secondary buttons* check box to flip the functions of the left and right mouse buttons, making the right mouse button the primary button for clicking and double-clicking. This makes the mouse easier for a left-handed person to use. You also can drag the *Speed* slider to change how fast a user must perform a double-click for the system to recognize it; slower speeds work better for users with stiff fingers. Marking the *Turn on ClickLock* check box enables you make selections or drag by briefly pressing and holding the mouse. You can then reposition the mouse and click to finish the drag or select. Use the Settings button to control how long you must press and hold the mouse to activate ClickLock.

- **Pointers**. On this tab, you can choose different mouse pointers, either for functional or fun reasons. In Windows, the mouse pointer's appearance changes to cue you about the current activity going on, such as when the mouse is in the right position to resize a window. Use the *Scheme* drop-down list to choose new pointers overall. For example, you can choose one of the schemes with (Large) in its name to make the pointers easier to see on-screen. To change any individual pointer, click the pointer in the *Customize* list, and then click the Browse button. Use the Browse dialog box that appears to find and select a new pointer, and then click Open. Clicking Use Default returns a pointer to its original appearance. If you have changed several pointers, you can use the Save As button in the Scheme area to save your own scheme. Leaving *Enable pointer shadow* active (marked) makes the pointer easier to see on the screen by placing a shadow under it for contrast.

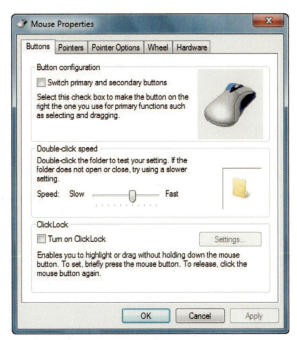

- **Pointer Options**. The options on this tab control the mouse pointer's Motion, Snap To behavior, and on-screen Visibility. Drag the *Select a pointer speed* slider under Motion to make the pointer move faster or slower relative to how quickly you drag the mouse. Choose a slower speed for users who have trouble using the mouse. If you have the pointer speed set to a fast speed, leave *Enhance pointer precision* checked so the mouse will move less

Figure 6.5 You can set up the mouse for a left-handed user, choose new pointers, and more.

quickly when you move the mouse more slowly or stop it. To save work, click *Automatically move pointer to the default button in a dialog box*; this enables a feature that snaps the mouse to the button. To make the pointer easier for those with vision difficulties to see, click *Display pointer trails* to enable this feature, and *Hide pointer while typing* to disable it. To enable a way to highlight a lost pointer on-screen, click the *Show location of pointer when I press the CTRL key* check box.

- **Wheel**. This final tab of settings applies only when a wheel mouse or touchpad that mimics wheel behaviors is installed on the system. To change the Vertical Scrolling speed for the scroll wheel button when you move it, either change the specified number of lines under *The following number of lines at a time* or click the *One screen at a time* option to select it, instead. If the wheel also has Horizontal Scrolling capability, you can change the setting under *Tilt the wheel to scroll the following number of characters at a time*, as desired.

To work with keyboard and mouse settings in Control Panel:

Here's How

1. Click the Start button and then click *Control Panel*.
2. In the search box, type **keyboard**.
3. Click the *Keyboard* link or icon.
4. Change settings on the Speed tab of the Keyboard Properties dialog box (Figure 6.4) as desired, and then click OK.
5. Back in the Control Panel window, click the Back button.
6. Click the *Hardware and Sound* category icon or link.
7. Under *Devices and Printers*, click the *Mouse* task link.
8. Change the settings on various tabs of the Mouse Properties dialog box (Figure 6.5) as desired, and then click OK.
9. Click the Close (X) button for the Control Panel window.

Note: *When you have a graphics tablet attached to the system or the system is a tablet PC, the Hardware and Sound category in Control Panel offers the lower-level Pen and Touch and Tablet PC Settings categories that you can use to adjust how user input works for those devices. For example, under Pen and Touch, you can work with handwriting personalization and the meaning of "flicks." Under Tablet PC Settings, you can calibrate the screen or set up button behavior.*

Exercise 1

Using Control Panel to Slow Down the Keyboard and Mouse

1. Click the Start button and then click *Control Panel* to open the Control Panel home window.
2. In the search box, type keyboard.
3. Click the *Keyboard* icon to open the Keyboard Properties dialog box.
4. Drag the *Repeat delay, Repeat rate*, and *Cursor blink rate* sliders all the way to the left.
5. Capture a screen shot, paste it into Paint, and save the file as **C06E01S05**.
6. Click Cancel to close the dialog box without applying those changes.
7. Click the Back button to return to the Control Panel home window.
8. Click the *Hardware and Sound* icon or link.
9. Click the *Mouse* task link under *Devices and Printers* to open the Mouse Properties dialog box.
10. Drag the *Speed* slider on the Buttons tab all the way to the left, and click the *Turn on ClickLock* check box to check it.
11. Capture a screen shot, paste it into Paint, and save the file as **C06E01S11**.
12. Click the Pointer Options tab, drag the *Select a pointer speed* slider all the way to the left, and then click the *Display pointer trails* check box.
13. Capture a screen shot, paste it into Paint, and save the file as **C06E01S13**.
14. Click Cancel to close the dialog box without applying those changes.
15. Click the window Close (X) button to close Control Panel.
16. E-mail your screen shots to your instructor or submit them on your USB flash drive, as required.

Changing Display Settings

Any time you look at the computer screen for a long period of time, its contents can have an impact on both your mood and your eyesight. You can change a variety of appearance-oriented settings, such as the background color or picture used and the default color for windows, the Start menu, and the taskbar. You also can change settings that affect the viewing quality and function of the display, such as the resolution, screen saver, and text size. The Control Panel enables you to work with these Appearance and Personalization settings, and more.

Aero desktop experience: The default appearance for Windows 7 on fully compatible systems, featuring a transparency feature called glass

The default screen appearance for Windows 7 running on a system meeting hardware requirements is called the ***Aero desktop experience***. Aero not only gives a 3-D appearance for many screen elements, but it also features glass or transparent window borders and other features for more easily switching between and managing windows. If your system does not include the hardware to support the Aero features, the most telltale sign is that window borders will not be transparent. In this case, the appearance for the screen is called Windows 7 Basic. For other systems that have the right hardware, the Aero interface features may be turned off, but they can be redisplayed using Control Panel.

To display the Appearance and Personalization settings in Control Panel, you can use one of two methods:

- Click Start, and then *Control Panel*. In the Control Panel home window, click the *Appearance and Personalization* icon, and then click *Personalization*.

- Right-click the Windows 7 desktop, and then click *Personalize* in the shortcut menu.

The Personalization settings for the desktop appear in Control Panel, as shown in Figure 6.6.

Changing the Background

Windows 7 displays the desktop background specified by the theme set up when Windows 7 was installed. You can change the selected background at any time to use one of the other available pictures or to use your own picture. You also can choose a solid color to use as the background, which can make icons on the desktop easier to see.

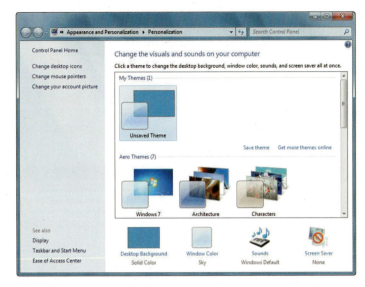

Figure 6.6 Use these Personalization choices to specify your desktop appearance.

To change the desktop background in Control Panel:

1. Right-click the desktop, and click *Personalize*.
2. Click *Desktop Background* at the bottom of the window.
3. Click the *Picture location* drop-down list and click the desired type of background to apply.
4. Choose the background to use. The method you choose will vary slightly depending on the choice you made in Step 3.
   - **Windows Desktop Backgrounds**. This choice lists all the desktop background wallpaper images included with Windows 7. Scroll through the available wallpapers and click the one to use.
   - **Pictures Library**. This choice lists the images in the Pictures library. Scroll through the available pictures and click the picture to use.
   - **Top Rated Photos**. This choice displays the Pictures library photos with the highest ratings assigned.
   - **Solid Colors**. This choice displays thumbnails of solid colors that you can apply to the desktop as a background. Scroll down and click the desired thumbnail, or click More to open the Color dialog box, where you can select a custom color.
   - **Browse**. If you clicked one of the first four choices above but did not find the desired picture, you can click the Browse button beside the *Picture location* drop-down list to navigate to another folder and find a picture to use.

Here's How

5. If you chose a picture as the desktop background, click one of the options on the *Picture position* drop-down list. *Fill* increases the image's width until the image can fill the screen vertically. *Fit* increases the image's width to match the horizontal dimension of the screen. *Stretch* changes the image proportions as needed and sizes the image to fill the screen. *Tile* repeats a small image as many times as needed to fill the desktop. And the *Center* option places the image in its original size in the center of the desktop.

QUICK FIX

Gaps in the Background
Some of the Windows Wallpaper choices are sized for wide-format displays. Choose one of those background choices if you see black gaps at the left and right of the screen after applying another image as the background.

6. Click Save changes to apply the new desktop background.
7. Click the Close (X) button for the Control Panel window.

Note: *To assign a rating to a picture in the Pictures library, click the picture. In the details pane, click the desired number of stars beside Rating, and then click Save.*

Checked pictures appear in the slideshow

Specify how frequently the slideshow picture should change

Playing a Desktop Slideshow

If a static desktop background fails to offer the interest that you are seeking, you can play a series of selected desktop backgrounds or pictures as a desktop slideshow. Select the overall type of background image you want to apply from the *Picture location* drop-down list in Desktop Background settings in Control Panel. Use the Select all or Clear all button to select or deselect all the picture thumbnails, and then click individual thumbnails as needed to refine your selection. (See Figure 6.7.) Only checked pictures will appear in the slideshow. Make a choice from the *Change picture every* drop-down list to specify how long each picture should appear on-screen, and then click Save changes to start the show. Close the Control Panel window if you are finished working with settings.

Figure 6.7 **Set up a desktop screen show here.**

Changing the Window Color and Appearance

Windows 7 applies a specific color to window borders, the Start menu, and the taskbar. You can choose another color for these items, and enable or disable transparency. Windows 7 also applies specific colors and settings to every other element on-screen.

The default colors for fully Windows 7-compatible systems (that is, systems with advanced display adapters or graphics cards) is the Sky window color with transparency enabled. Systems using older display equipment will by default use the colors specified by the Windows 7 Basic theme. No matter what color your system uses by default, or if Aero has been turned off on your system, you can change the color applied to window borders, the Start menu, and the taskbar.

Here's How

To change window color and appearance in Control Panel:

1. Right-click the desktop, and click *Personalize*.
2. Click *Window Color* near the bottom of the window.
3. Click another color at the top of the Window Color and Appearance window.
4. Drag the *Color intensity* slider to make the color more or less intense, as desired.
5. To customize the color, click *Show color mixer*; drag the *Hue, Saturation*, and *Brightness* sliders that appear to adjust the color; and then click *Hide color mixer*.
6. To work with transparency, click the *Enable transparency* check box to turn on (check) or turn off (uncheck) transparency.

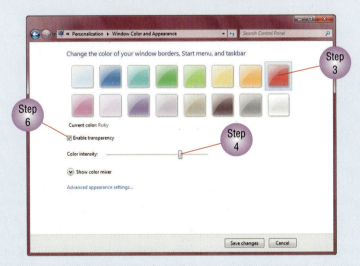

7. Click Save changes to apply the new color settings.
8. Click the Close (X) button for the Control Panel window.

A Dialog Box Instead
On systems that do not have the hardware required by Aero, a Window Color and Appearance dialog box appears. You can use it to work with color settings for various window elements.

Changing the Display Resolution, Refresh Rate, and Other Settings

Display or monitor settings can have a big impact on comfort when you are viewing the screen. If on-screen items are too large or small, you can have difficulty reading and finding information. If the monitor uses a *refresh rate* that is too low, you may see an unpleasant screen flicker. You also may have to change resolution and refresh rate settings if you need to connect the computer to an

Refresh rate: The rate at which the display redraws the image on the screen

external projector. For example, the projector may only work with lower resolution or refresh rate settings or may not display a readable on-screen image unless you choose a low resolution.

Resolution is expressed as a measurement of width by height, in pixels. Pixel is a short version of "picture element," referring to each dot of color that the monitor displays. So, a monitor set to display at 800 x 600 is showing an image 800 pixels wide by 600 pixels tall. A 1024 x 768 display is 1,024 pixels wide by 768 pixels tall. The available settings vary depending on the capabilities of the system's installed display adapter card.

You also can specify the colors the monitor displays, choosing from options such as Medium or Highest. A higher color setting makes pictures appear more realistic on-screen, but also consumes more system resources. If you notice that your system slows down after you choose a higher-quality color setting, you may want to rethink that setting.

Here's How

To change display settings in Control Panel:

1. Right-click the desktop, and click *Screen resolution*.
2. Open the *Resolution* drop-down list and click the desired resolution.
3. Click *Advanced settings*.
4. Click the *Monitor* tab.
5. Click the *Colors* drop-down list, and click the desired color setting.
6. Open the *Screen refresh rate* drop-down list and click the desired rate, and then click OK to close the dialog box.
7. Click OK to apply the new display settings.
8. Click the Close (X) button for the Control Panel window.

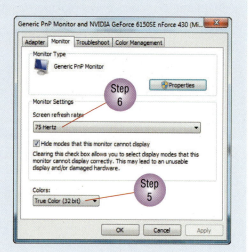

Choosing a Screen Saver and Delay

A screen saver appears on-screen when your computer has been idle for a designated period of time. Screen savers serve important privacy and security functions, as well as helping prevent images from "burning in" on some newer flat-panel monitors. Having a screen saver come on when you step away from your computer hides the contents of sensitive documents or private e-mails. You can set up the screen saver to prompt the user to log on when anyone attempts to stop the screen saver, providing the security that only you can log back on to the system.

In choosing a screen saver, you specify how long the system must be idle before the screen saver starts, and whether the logon screen appears when a user attempts to resume the system. You also can choose settings for some screen savers, and preview the selected screen saver at full-screen size.

Note: *Windows 7 comes with several preinstalled screen savers available via the Screen Saver drop-down list in the Screen Saver Settings dialog box. The Photos choice actually displays the picture files in the Pictures library.*

To choose a screen saver in Control Panel:

1. Right-click the desktop, and click *Personalize*.
2. Click *Screen Saver* to open the Screen Saver Settings dialog box.
3. Click the *Screen saver* drop-down list, and click the desired screen saver.
4. Click the Settings button, choose the desired settings in the Settings dialog box that appears, and then click OK. For example, for the 3D Text screen saver, you can enter custom text, work with size and rotation settings, adjust the surface style, and more. If the screen saver has no options, you can click OK in the No Options message box that appears.
5. To preview the screen saver at full-screen size, click the Preview button. Wiggle the mouse or tap the touchpad to return to the Screen Saver Settings dialog box.
6. Change the *Wait (x) minutes* text box entry, as needed, to specify how many minutes the system must be idle before the screen saver displays. You can drag over the existing entry and type a new entry or click the spinner arrow buttons to change the entry.
7. To require log on after resuming the screen saver, click the *On resume, display logon screen* check box to check it.
8. Click OK to apply the new screen saver settings.
9. Click the Close (X) button for the Control Panel window.

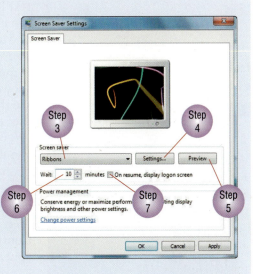

When you need to resume using your system after the screen saver has kicked in, wiggle the mouse, tap the touchpad, or press a key. If you specified that the screen saver should require you to log back on, click the icon for your user account. If your account is password-protected, type your password in the *Password* text box, and then press Enter or click the blue right-arrow button to the right of the *Password* text box.

Choosing a Theme

A *theme* specifies a variety of appearance settings for the desktop, including the desktop picture or background, icons, window appearance, and so on. Choosing a theme applies all the settings stored in that theme to the Windows 7 desktop. In this way, a theme makes it easy for you to change the desktop appearance in a snap.

To apply another theme using the Control Panel, right-click the desktop and click *Personalize*. Scroll down through the list of available themes (Figure 6.8) and click the theme you want to apply. It appears on the desktop immediately, so all you have to do next is close the Control Panel Personalization window.

If you have changed a variety of desktop appearance settings such as the background and window color, you can save those changes as your own theme that you can reapply at any time. To do so, click *Save theme* in the Personalization

Theme: A named collection of appearance settings you can apply to the Windows 7 desktop

Figure 6.8 The Personalization window enables you to select a theme.

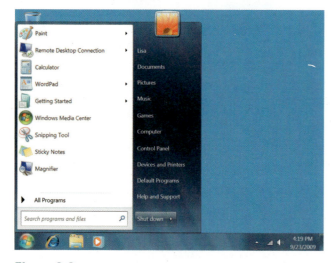

Figure 6.9 A larger text size also increases icon and menu size.

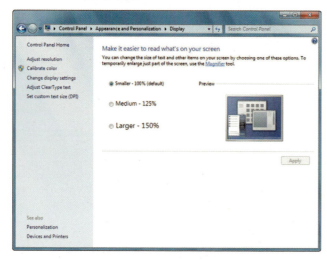

Figure 6.10 Choose an existing text size or use the *Set custom text size (DPI)* link at left to specify your own.

window, type a name for the theme in the *Theme Name* text box of the Save Theme As dialog box that appears, and then click Save. You can then select the theme from the Personalization settings in Control Panel, just as you would any other theme.

Changing Text and Icon Size

By default, text in Windows 7 displays at a 96 pixels per inch (ppi) size. If you change the display resolution for the system and text looks too small at its default size, you can change the text size to an enlarged size of Medium - 125% (120 ppi) or Larger – 150% (144 ppi). The larger sizes make icons, menus, and dialog boxes look larger, too, as shown in Figure 6.9. In the figure, you can see that the Start menu is almost as tall as the screen. With the normal Smaller – 100% (96 ppi) font size, the Start menu is only about two-thirds as tall as the screen.

To change the font size (in DPI), click Start and click *Control Panel*. Click *Appearance and Personalization*, and under *Display* click *Make text and other items larger or smaller*. The Control Panel settings shown in Figure 6.10 appear.

Click one of the size settings to choose it. Or, click the *Set custom text size (DPI)* link at the left, enter a new scale percentage in the *Scale to this percentage of normal size* text box or use its drop-down list to click a preset percentage, and then click OK. Back in the Control Panel window, click Apply to apply your change. A message box appears to inform you that you must log off your computer to apply these changes. Click Log off now to do so immediately, or Log off later to have the new font size take effect the next time you shut down and start up or restart the system.

Note: *You also can increase icon size and various text sizes separately. To do so, right-click the desktop and click Personalize. Click Window Color. Click the Advanced appearance settings link to open the Window Color and Appearance dialog box. Select Icon from the Item drop-down list, and then change the item Size and font Size settings, as desired. You also can select other items from the Item drop-down list to change their font Size settings. For example, you can increase or decrease the size of the text in any Active*

Title Bar, Inactive Title Bar, or Menu. Click OK twice to close the dialog boxes and apply your settings, then close the Control Panel window.

Customizing Sound Settings

In addition to the mouse pointer changing to give you visual cues about your actions in Windows 7, the operating system plays sounds to alert you when certain events occur, such as to warn you when battery power is getting low on a mobile computer or to alert you when you have received an e-mail message. You can change the sound for any individual program event and turn the Windows 7 startup sound on and off via Control Panel.

Right-click the desktop, and then click *Personalize*. Click *Sounds* near the bottom of the window. On the Sounds tab of the Sound dialog box, click an event in the *Program Events* list. As shown in Figure 6.11, the *Sounds* list at the bottom of the dialog box becomes active. Click the *Sounds* list to open it, and click another sound to use; you also can click the Browse button and use the Browse for New *Event Name* Sound dialog box that appears to navigate to and double-click a .wav sound file to assign to the event. Click the Test button to test the new sound. If you want to

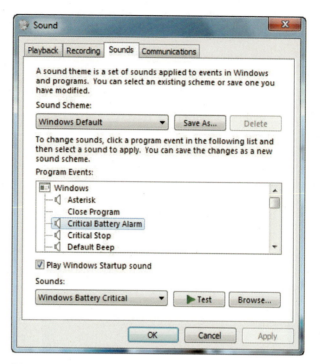

Figure 6.11 You can change the sound played for a program event.

turn off or reenable the sound that plays when you start up the system, click the *Play Windows Startup sound* check box to clear or check it, as desired. Then click OK to apply the sound changes, and close the Control Panel window.

Note: *As with a theme, you can save the set of sounds you have assigned to the various program events as your own custom sound scheme using the Save As button on the Sounds tab of the Sound dialog box.*

Exercise 2

Changing the Window Color, Desktop Background, and Sounds

1. Right-click the desktop, and click *Personalize*.
2. Click *Window Color* at the bottom of the window. Write down the current color settings so that you can refer to them later.
3. Click the *Pumpkin* color, drag the *Color intensity* slider all the way to the right, and click Save changes.
4. Back in the Personalization settings in Control Panel, click *Desktop Background*.
5. Select *Windows Desktop Backgrounds* from the *Picture location* drop-down list, if needed, and then scroll down to the *Scenes* section and click one of the images there. Click Save changes, which returns you to the Personalization settings.
6. Capture a screen shot, paste it into Paint, and save the file as **C06E02S06**.
7. Click *Sounds* in the Personalization settings in Control Panel.
8. Click *Close Program* in the Program list, open the *Sounds* drop-down list, and click *tada*. Click the Test button to test the sound playback.

9. Capture a screen shot, paste it into Paint, and save the file as **C06E02S09**.
10. Click Cancel to close the Sound dialog box without applying the sound change.
11. Use the *Window Color* and *Desktop Background* choices to return to the default window color and the previous desktop background.
12. Click the Close (X) button to close the Control Panel window.
13. E-mail your screen shots to your instructor or submit them on your USB flash drive, as required.

Working with Desktop Icons

Desktop shortcut icons are meant to provide you with an easy and convenient way to launch files and open programs. However, if the icons overlap or you cannot find the one you want, then you do not experience the convenience you were seeking by creating the icons in the first place. You can take steps to control the display and arrangement of icons on the desktop to set them up for maximum convenience.

Icon size choices

Toggles icons on and off

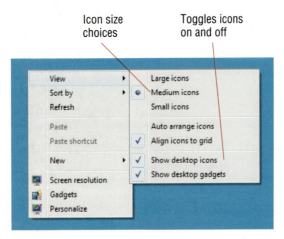

Figure 6.12 **Right-click the desktop and point to** ***View*** **for sizing and display choices.**

Setting Icon Display

Icons are visible on the desktop by default, but you can hide the desktop icons temporarily, when needed. For example, if you want to hide the icons so that others do not see that you are using a particular program or file, you can do so. You also can change the icon size for desktop icons.

To make either of these changes to the desktop icons, start by right-clicking the desktop. Then, to work with icon size and visibility, point to the *View* command to display the submenu shown in Figure 6.12. Click one of the three icon sizes above the top divider line on the View submenu to set a new icon size. (Classic icons is a small size; this choice does not change the icon pictures.) To hide or redisplay desktop icons, click *Show desktop icons* to uncheck it (hide icons) or check it (display icons).

> Tip: If you right-click the desktop and click *Personalize*, you can click *Change desktop icons* in the list of tasks at the left to open a dialog box that enables you to specify which system icons appear on the desktop by default and even to change the picture used by a system desktop icon.

Arranging Icons

Align icons to grid: A feature that snaps an icon into alignment with a desktop grid when you move the icon

Auto arrange icons: A feature that arranges desktop icons to fill the desktop grid slots in order

You can move a desktop icon to any position by dragging it with the mouse. By default, the icon will align or snap to an invisible grid, which helps keep the desktop neat and prevents one icon from overlapping and hiding another. If you prefer, you can turn off the **Align icons to grid** feature to give you total control of where icons appear. You also can turn an **Auto arrange icons** feature on and off. This feature automatically arranges icons to fill the desktop grid positions in order, and places each new icon in the next available grid position.

To turn the Align icons to grid and Auto arrange icons features on and off, right-click the desktop, point to the *View* command, and then click either *Auto arrange icons* or *Align icons to grid*, as needed. If a check appears beside either of these choices on the submenu, the feature is already enabled.

You also can sort the icons on the desktop just as you can sort the icons in an Explorer window. In the case of desktop icons, you can sort by *Name, Size, Item type*, and *Date modified*. To sort the desktop icons, right-click the desktop, point to *Sort by*, and click one of the sort order choices shown in Figure 6.13.

View	▶	
Sort by	▶	Name
Refresh		Size
		Item type
Paste		Date modified
Paste shortcut		
New	▶	
🖥 Screen resolution		
🖼 Gadgets		
🖼 Personalize		

Figure 6.13 **When you click one of the sort order choices on this submenu, Windows 7 immediately places the desktop icons in the new order specified.**

QUICK FIX

Losing an Icon
If you turn off both *Align icons to grid* and *Auto arrange icons*, it becomes possible to drag an icon all the way off the desktop. If you mistakenly do so, right-click the desktop, point to View, and then click either *Auto arrange icons* or *Align icons to grid* to pop the icon back onto the desktop.

Customizing the Start Menu

Even though the Start menu makes your libraries and favorite applications easier to find and open, you can customize the Start menu to specify exactly what links and choices it lists. You also can specify whether some items, such as the Computer choice, appear as links or as menus. If you change an item to a menu, clicking the item name displays a menu of the item's contents. You also can add items to the right pane of the Start menu that do not appear there by default. For example, you can add a Favorites menu and a Recent Items list for direct access to Web sites and files you use often. You also can add choices for accessing the Network, the Homegroup, your Downloads folder, and more.

You also can control whether the left pane of the Start menu tracks recently opened files and programs, the number of programs it displays, and how many items Jump Lists display.

To customize the Start menu:

Here's How

1. Right-click the Start menu button, and click *Properties*. The taskbar and Start Menu Properties dialog box appears with the Start Menu tab selected.
2. Click check boxes in the *Privacy* section, as desired, to control whether Windows 7 tracks recently opened files and/or programs and displays them on the Start menu and taskbar. (Clearing these check boxes enhances privacy by preventing others from knowing what you have worked on recently.)
3. Click the Customize button. The Customize Start Menu dialog box appears.

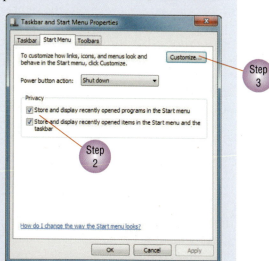

Here's How

4. In the list of Start menu items, click a check box beside an item to hide or redisplay it. Or, if an item lists three option buttons, as for Computer, click *Display as a link*, *Display as a menu*, or *Don't display this item*, as needed.

5. Change the *Number of recent programs to display* text box entry to indicate how many recent programs you want to appear in the left pane of the Start menu. You can drag over the existing entry and type a new entry or click the spinner arrow buttons to change the settings.

6. Change the *Number of recent items to display in Jump Lists* text box entry to indicate how many recent files you want to appear in the Jump List for a program. You can drag over the existing entry and type a new entry or click the spinner arrow buttons to change the settings.

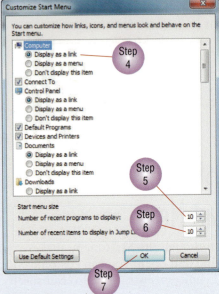

7. Click OK to apply the new Start menu settings.
8. Click OK to close the Taskbar and Start Menu Properties dialog box.

Note: ***Click the Use Default Settings button in the Customize Start Menu dialog box to return the Start menu to the default choices.***

Exercise 3
Customizing the Desktop by Working with Icons and the Start Menu

1. Right-click the desktop, point to *View*, and click *Show desktop icons*. Windows 7 hides the icons on the desktop.
2. Right-click the desktop, point to *View*, and click *Show desktop icons* to redisplay the icons.
3. Drag the *Recycle Bin* icon somewhere to the right side of the desktop.
4. Right-click the desktop, point to *View*, and click *Large icons*.
5. Capture a screen shot, paste it into Paint, and save the file as **C06E03S05**.
6. Right-click the desktop, point to *View*, and click *Medium icons*.
7. Right-click the desktop, point to *View*, and click *Auto arrange icons*. The Recycle Bin should snap back to its default position.
8. Right-click the desktop, point to *View*, and click *Auto arrange icons* to turn that feature off.
9. Right-click the Start menu button and click *Properties*.
10. Click Customize, click *Display as a menu* under Computer in the list of Start menu items, and then click OK twice to close both dialog boxes.
11. Click Start, and then *Computer* to open the menu that now appears for that Start menu item.
12. With the Computer menu still open, take a screen shot, paste it into Paint, and save the file as **C06E03S12**.
13. Close the Start menu, if needed.
14. Right-click the Start menu button and click *Properties*.

15. Click Customize, click Use Default Settings, and then click OK.
16. Click OK again to close the Taskbar and Start Menu Properties dialog box.
17. E-mail your screen shots to your instructor or submit them on your USB flash drive, as required.

Customizing the Taskbar and Notifications Area

Like the desktop, the taskbar provides you with a variety of ways to launch and work with programs and Windows 7 features. By default, the taskbar displays icons (for Internet Explorer, Windows Explorer, and Windows Media Player) at the left and the notification area (also called the system tray) at the right. You can customize the icons that appear in either location, as well as hide and display other desktop toolbars.

Pinning a Program to the Taskbar

Adding an icon for a program to the taskbar is called pinning the program to the taskbar. This enables you to open that program via the taskbar and to open its documents via a Jump List even if the program is not running. For example, Figure 6.14 shows WordPad pinned to the taskbar; you can see the command for unpinning it in the displayed Jump List. You also can unpin any program you have added to the taskbar.

To pin a program to the taskbar, you can use one of three methods, depending on whether or not the program is running. Unpinning a program is easy, as well.

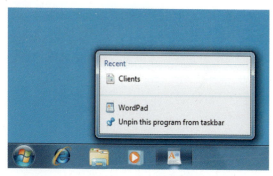

Figure 6.14 **Pin an application to the taskbar so its icon always appears.**

To pin a program to the taskbar:

- If the program is running, right-click its taskbar icon and click *Pin this program to taskbar*.
  OR
- If the program is not running, find it the on the Start menu, right-click it, and click *Pin to Taskbar*.
  OR
- Open a folder window and navigate to the folder holding the executable (startup) file for the program, and drag it onto the taskbar to the right of the other icons. When a yellow pop-up tip that reads Pin to taskbar appears, release the mouse button.

To unpin a program from the taskbar:

- Right-click the program's taskbar icon and click *Unpin this program from taskbar*.

Here's How

To pin a file to a pinned program's Jump List, drag the file's icon over the pinned program's icon on the taskbar, and when you see the Pin to (*program name*) pop-up tip, release the mouse button. To unpin the file, right-click the program's icon on the taskbar to open its Jump List, right-click the file in the Pinned section at the top of the Jump List, and click Unpin from this list.

Adding a Toolbar to the Taskbar

You can display one of several other default toolbars on the taskbar: Address (Address bar), Links, Tablet PC Input Panel, and Desktop. In most cases, these "toolbars" appear as an additional text box or a menu button that you can click. For example, Figure 6.15 shows how the Address toolbar looks when added to the taskbar. You can enter a Web page address in the Address toolbar text box and press Enter to open that page in your system's browser.

Figure 6.15 Display another toolbar on the taskbar to add functionality, such as the ability to type in a Web page address.

Figure 6.16 Moving the taskbar to another position on-screen may make it easier for you to use.

To display or hide any taskbar toolbar, right-click the taskbar, point to Toolbars in the menu that appears, and then click the name of the desired toolbar. A checkmark appears beside the name of any displayed toolbar in the submenu.

Moving the Taskbar

The taskbar appears along the bottom of the desktop by default, because when it is in that position, you need to move the mouse the least distance to select any item on the taskbar. Still, your preference for the taskbar location might be different. For example, if you are a left-handed user and you have already flipped the functions of the mouse buttons, you might find it more natural to make selections when the taskbar is positioned along the left side of the screen, as shown in Figure 6.16. Notice that when you move the taskbar, Windows 7 shifts the desktop icons out of the way automatically and reorients the pinned icons and notification area contents to reflect the new taskbar position.

You can use one of two methods to move the taskbar. You can drag it to the desired location on-screen. Or, you can right-click the taskbar, and click *Properties*. Choose the desired taskbar location from the *Taskbar location on screen* drop-down list on the Taskbar tab of the Taskbar and Start Menu Properties dialog box, and then click OK.

QUICK FIX

A Locked Taskbar
If you can't drag the taskbar, that means it is locked. Right-click the taskbar, and then click *Lock the taskbar* to unlock it. Repeat the process to relock the taskbar after you have dragged it to the desired location.

Tip: You can drag the dotted dividers that appear when the taskbar is unlocked to resize the toolbars displayed on the taskbar.

Auto-hiding the Taskbar

When enabled, the *auto-hide* feature tells Windows 7 not to display the taskbar unless you move the mouse pointer over the location where the taskbar should normally appear. Enabling auto-hide provides a bit more room on-screen for you to work with the files and applications you are using.

To auto-hide the taskbar, right-click the taskbar and click *Properties*. Click the *Auto-hide the taskbar* check box to check it as shown in Figure 6.17, and then click OK. To redisplay the taskbar at any time, move the mouse pointer over the location where you have set up the taskbar to appear. To turn off the auto-hide feature, click that check box again on the Taskbar tab of the Taskbar and Start Menu Properties dialog box.

Setting Up Icon Display in the Notification Area

You can control how the icons work in the notification area. You can set up all or some of the icons to display all of the time, not at all, or only when in use. You also can specify whether notification icons for the Action Center, Network, Volume, Windows Explorer, and other applications appear. You also can turn off the display of the *Clock, Volume, Network, Power,* and *Action Center* icons, or turn their display back on altogether.

Auto-hide: A feature that hides the taskbar unless the mouse pointer is over the taskbar location

Figure 6.17 Click the *Auto-hide the taskbar* check box to turn auto-hiding on and off.

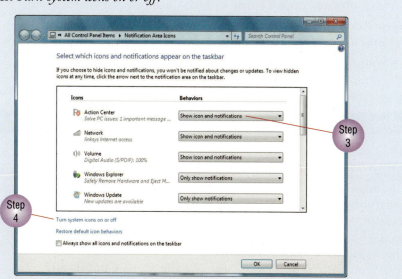

To customize the notification area icons:

1. Right-click the taskbar, and click *Properties*.
2. On the Taskbar tab in the Taskbar and Start Menu Properties dialog box, click the Customize button under *Notification area*.
3. For each icon listed, choose one of the available Behaviors using the accompanying list: *Show icon and notifications, Hide icon and notifications,* or *Only show notifications*.
4. Click *Turn system icons on or off*.

Here's How

5. For each icon listed, turn the icon *On* or *Off* using the accompanying Behaviors list.
6. Click OK twice to close the Control Panel windows.

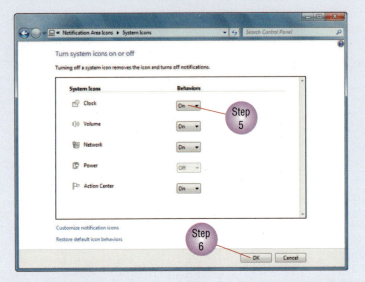

7. Click OK to close the Taskbar and Start Menu Properties dialog box.

Choosing Other Taskbar Properties

There are a few remaining settings on the Taskbar tab of the Taskbar and Start Menu Properties dialog box (refer to Figure 6.17) that you should be aware of in case you want to turn them off to suit your working style. You can right-click the taskbar and click *Properties*, click these settings to uncheck (disable) or check (enable), as needed, and then click OK to apply your changes:

- **Use small icons**. Displays taskbar icons in a smaller size, so the taskbar itself displays at a smaller size.

- **Taskbar buttons**. If you often have a lot of files open, you can choose an option here to specify whether Windows 7 should consolidate all the open files from a program onto a single taskbar button.

- **Use Aero Peek to preview the desktop**. When this option is enabled, moving the mouse over the Show desktop button hides open windows so that you can see the desktop.

 Exercise 4

Updating the Taskbar

1. Click the Start menu button, and type **calc**.
2. Right-click *Calculator* in the list of Programs at the top of the left pane of the Start menu, and click *Pin to Taskbar*.
3. Click the Calculator button on the taskbar to start Calculator.
4. Click the Calculator window Close (X) button to close Calculator.
5. Right-click the taskbar and click *Lock the taskbar*.
6. Drag the taskbar to the right side of the desktop.
7. Capture a screen shot, paste it into Paint, and save the file as **C06E04S07**.

8. Drag the taskbar back to its default position at the bottom of the screen.
9. Right-click the taskbar and click *Lock the taskbar*.
10. Right-click the *Calculator* icon on the taskbar, and click *Unpin this program from taskbar*.
11. Right-click the taskbar and click *Properties*. Click *Auto-hide the taskbar* to check it, and then click OK.
12. Move the mouse pointer over and away from the taskbar area at the bottom of the screen a few times to see how auto-hide works. Finish by moving the mouse pointer off the taskbar area, so that the taskbar autohides.
13. Capture a screen shot, paste it into Paint, and save the file as **C06E04S13**.
14. Right-click the taskbar and click *Properties*. Click *Auto-hide the taskbar* to uncheck it, and then click OK. This turns auto-hide off. The desktop should now look as it did when you started the exercise.
15. E-mail your screen shots to your instructor or submit them on your USB flash drive, as required.

Using Gadgets

Windows 7 continues to offer *gadgets*, or mini-programs, that sit on the desktop and perform ongoing functions, provide updating information from an online source, or enable you to have fun. Each gadget provides a unique tool or function. For example, the Clock gadget shows the current system time, the Slide Show gadget displays an on-screen slide show of the digital picture files stored in a particular folder on the hard disk. Other gadgets that come with Windows 7 show the date; show system performance; show news or stock or weather information from online sources; enable you to convert currency or play a puzzle game; and play Windows Media Center content. In addition, you can find and download dozens of additional gadgets from a variety of authors online. The available gadgets vary from games to a gadget for displaying Facebook messages to tools for securely shredding files or generating passwords. Most gadgets are free, and they provide a great way to customize Windows 7 with functions you want and need.

> **Gadgets:** The mini-programs that deliver information and tools on the desktop

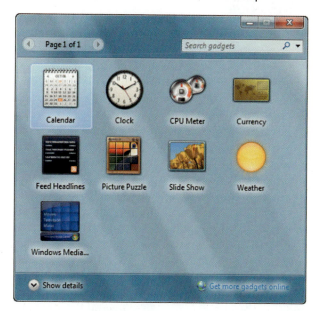

Figure 6.18 Use the Gadget Gallery to add a gadget to the desktop.

Adding and Removing a Desktop Gadget

The Windows Gadget Gallery enables you to add gadgets to the desktop and find more gadgets. On the desktop, each gadget takes on a different appearance depending on its function. Many gadgets appear in mini-windows, but other gadgets might take on a shape unique to its function, such as the Clock appearing as a round clock face. Initially, there are no gadgets on the desktop, so you have to open the Gadget Gallery (see Figure 6.18) and choose one or more gadgets to add. Figure 6.19 shows the Currency and Clock gadgets added to the desktop. The available gadgets include the

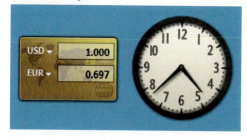

Figure 6.19 Convert currencies, get the time, and more with gadgets.

Calendar, Clock, CPU Meter, Currency (exchange monitor), Feed Headlines (news feeds), Picture Puzzle, Slide Show, Weather, and Windows Media Player. You can add and remove gadgets as desired to make the desktop display information you need or prefer to have available.

Note: *Many of the gadgets require an active Internet connection to receive updated data.*

Here's How ▶ **To add a gadget to the desktop:**

1. Right-click the desktop and click *Gadgets* in the shortcut menu.
2. Double-click each gadget that you want to add to the desktop.
3. Click the Close (X) button in the upper-right corner of the Gadget Gallery window to close the window when you have finished adding gadgets.

If you no longer need or want to work with a gadget on the desktop, you can close it. After you close a gadget, you can reinstate it from the Gadget Gallery at any time.

Here's How ▶ **To close a gadget to remove it from the desktop:**

1. Right-click the gadget.
2. Click *Close gadget*.

Tip: If you right-click the desktop and point to *View*, you can then click *Show desktop gadgets* to hide all gadgets without removing them from the desktop. You can then repeat the command to redisplay all the gadgets.

Changing Gadget Settings

Because each gadget does something different, the options for working with each gadget are specific to that gadget. For example, you can choose how the Clock gadget looks, specify the folder that holds the pictures for the Slide Show gadget, or choose a different news source for the Feed Headlines gadget. You can right-click any gadget and then click *Options* to find the choices for using the gadget.

Figure 6.20 shows the window with the options for the Clock. For this gadget, you can click an arrow button in the top section to choose a different clock appearance, enter a *Clock name*, select another *Time zone*, or *Show the second hand*. In some cases, you can click directly on the gadget to change a setting. For example, you can click one of the boxes on the Currency gadget and select another currency from the list that appears.

Figure 6.20 You can determine how to use a gadget by setting options for the gadget.

Note: *If you point to the blank area beside the upper-right corner of any gadget, a toolbar with small buttons pops up. Clicking what is usually the middle button, which has a small wrench on it, also opens the window with options for the gadgets.*

Here's How

To change options for a gadget:

1. Right-click the gadget on the desktop, and then click *Options* in the shortcut menu.
2. Change settings as desired in the window that appears. (The choices vary depending on the selected gadget.)
3. Click OK.

Finding Gadgets Online to Customize the Desktop

In addition to the gadgets that install with Windows 7, Microsoft and other software developers offer additional new gadgets online. To see what other gadgets are available at any given time, right-click the desktop and click *Gadgets*. In the Gadget Gallery window that opens, click the *Get more gadgets online* link in the lower-right corner.

Your system's Web browser will launch and display the Windows Web page that offers a sampling of additional gadgets for download. Scroll down the page, and click the *Get more desktop gadgets* link. This displays a page where you can find the full range of available gadgets. Click a category at the left to view available gadgets, as shown in Figure 6.21, and then click the Download button for any gadget that you want to download. In the security alert pop-up that appears, click Install. In the File Download dialog box, click Open, and then click Run in the Internet Explorer – Security Warning dialog box. In the Desktop Gadgets – Security Warning dialog box, click Install to (at last) download and add the gadget. You can then close the Web browser window, and add the gadget to the desktop by double-clicking it in the Gadget Gallery window before closing that window, as well.

Note: *Because the available gadgets will change over time, you may see different offerings if you click the Fun and games category than the ones shown in Figure 6.21.*

Figure 6.21 Browse and download additional gadgets offered on this Web page.

Click to resize

Figure 6.22 Some gadgets can appear in two sizes.

Moving and Sizing Gadgets

Like desktop icons, you can control where gadgets appear on the desktop using the mouse. Drag the gadget to the desired position. When you release the mouse button, the gadget drops onto the specified position. You also can adjust some gadgets to use a larger size. Move the mouse pointer over the upper-right corner of the gadget so its toolbar appears, and click the Larger size button (see Figure 6.22). To return the gadget to its prior size, display its toolbar and click the Smaller size button.

Keeping Gadgets on Top

If you want to make sure that a gadget always appear in front of other open application windows—such as when you want a stock-price feed or news feed to always be visible—right-click the gadget and click *Always on top*.

Note: *The figures in the rest of this book will not show gadgets unless they are being discussed in the text.*

 ## Exercise 5

Working with Gadgets

1. Right-click the desktop and click *Gadgets* to display the Gadget Gallery window.
2. Double-click the Feed Headlines gadget. If your classroom does not have a live Internet connection, choose an alternate gadget if indicated by your instructor.
3. Click the Gadget Gallery window's Close (X) button to close the window.
4. Click *View headlines* in the gadget to start the feed, if necessary.
5. Right-click the Feeds gadget and click *Options*.
6. Open the *Display this feed* drop-down list, and review the available feeds.
7. Press Esc to close the list of feeds and the gadget options.
8. Move the mouse pointer over the upper-right corner of the gadget, so its toolbar appears.
9. Capture a screen shot, paste it into Paint, and save the file as **C06E05S09**.
10. Display the Feeds gadget toolbar, and click the Larger size button.
11. Capture a screen shot, paste it into Paint, and save the file as **C06E05S11**.
12. Right-click the Feeds gadget, and click *Close gadget*.
13. E-mail your screen shots to your instructor or submit them on your USB flash drive, as required.

Using the Ease of Access Center

The Ease of Access Center in Windows 7 enables you to set up a system for use by someone with visual impairments and other special challenges. For example, the system can be optimized for use without a display at all, where the Narrator reads on-screen information aloud. The system can be optimized to make the screen easier to see, or to be set up for a form of input other than the mouse or keyboard—Speech Recognition or an On-Screen Keyboard. You also can change settings to make the mouse and keyboard easier to use, as you already learned earlier in the chapter.

Starting the Ease of Access Center turns on a Narrator and offers initial settings that you can use to begin to set up the system for a user with special needs. From there, you can choose different pages of information to perform different optimizations. As Figure 6.23 shows, the *Quick access to common tools* section at the top of the Ease of Access Center gives the option of starting four common accessibility features. The four common accessibility features include:

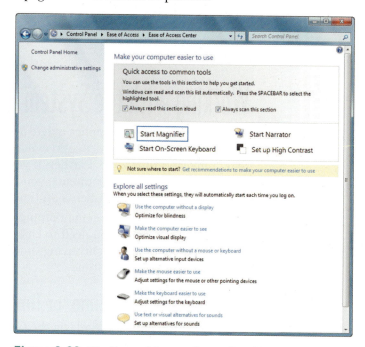

- **Magnifier**. A pane which shows an enlarged version of the screen area around the mouse. This feature can help those who have trouble seeing.

- **On-Screen Keyboard**. A keyboard that appears on-screen so that you can "type" by clicking or tapping letters rather than using a keyboard for input. This feature can help users who find it difficult or painful to use the keyboard.

- **Narrator**. Turns on the Narrator feature, which reads on-screen content to the user. This feature helps users unable to see a display.

- **High Contrast**. Sets up the screen to make it easier to read by making colors more distinct. This is another feature that can help anyone who has difficulty reading the screen.

Figure 6.23 The Ease of Access Center Narrator makes some initial suggestions about accessibility settings, but also offers a variety of additional settings.

Below the *Quick access to common tools* section, the *Explore all settings* area (Figure 6.23) in the Ease of Access Center offers additional categories of accessibility settings that you can use to set up the computer as desired, including settings for working with the Narrator, Speech Recognition, and more.

Note: *To use audio features like Narrator and Speech Recognition, the computer must be equipped with speakers and a microphone.*

To open and start using the Ease of Access Center:

1. Click Start, and then click *Control Panel*.
2. Click the *Ease of Access* category icon.
3. Click the *Ease of Access Center* icon. (Note that you can work with Speech Recognition settings from this point, instead.)
4. Listen as Narrator reads the Quick access to common tools choices. To select one of the choices, press spacebar after Narrator reads its name. Or, click the desired choice with the mouse.
5. Scroll down, if needed, and click any of the icons in the Explore all settings area.

Here's How

6. Use the settings that appear to adjust system accessibility. For example, if you clicked Make the mouse easier to use in Step 5, the Ease of Access Center displays options such as *Change the color and size of mouse pointers*.
7. Click the Back button to return to the Ease of Access Center.
8. Repeat Steps 5–7 to choose additional settings, as desired.
9. Click the Close (X) button to close the Ease of Access Center (Control Panel) window.

Working with the System Date and Time

Because your computer applies a date and time "stamp" to every file and e-mail you create, it is a good practice to make sure that the computer is set to the right date, time, and time zone. Further, if you rely on calendar software to track and remind you of your appointments, you want the time to be accurate so that you will arrive at your appointments on time.

Windows 7 installation may prompt the user to set up the date, time, and time zone for the system. If you need to change that information, such as if the system fails to update for a daylight saving time change, you can change the date, time, or time zone yourself at any time

Changing the Date, Time, or Time Zone

You can set the date and time via the Control Panel by clicking *Clock, Language, and Region* in the Control Panel home window, and then by clicking one of the tasks under *Date and Time* in the Control Panel window that appears. You also can change the date, time, and time zone directly from the clock display in the notification area.

To change the system date, time, and time zone:

1. Right-click the clock (time) in the notification area at the right end of the taskbar, and click *Adjust date/time*.
2. Click Change date and time on the Date and Time tab of the Date and Time dialog box. If a User Account Control dialog box appears, enter an administrator password, and click Yes.
3. Click another date on the calendar, if needed. To change months, click the arrows beside the month and year or click the month and year itself and then click another month in the zoomed view of the calendar that appears.
4. To set each segment of the time (hour, minute, second, AM/PM), click in that segment and then click spinner arrow buttons, as needed to change the time.

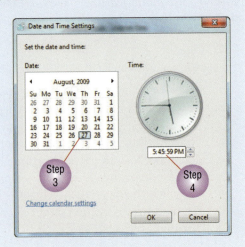

5. Click OK to apply the time change and return to the Date and Time dialog box.
6. Click Change time zone on the Date and Time tab of the Date and Time dialog box.
7. Choose the desired time zone from the *Time zone* drop-down list in the Time Zone Settings dialog box, and click OK.
8. Click OK to close the Date and Time dialog box and apply the changes.

Tip: If you need to track the time in multiple time zones for business purposes, such as if you work on the East Coast but serve clients on the West Coast, you can use the Additional Clocks tab in the Date and Time dialog box to display up to two additional clocks set to different time zones.

Synchronizing to an Internet Time Server

Like other timepieces, the system clock within your computer may not always keep perfect time. So, if you have an always-on Internet connection, you can ensure that the system is always set to an accurate time by synchronizing it with an **Internet time server**.

Internet time server: A Web site that provides highly precise times

Windows 7 by default uses this feature, synchronizing the system time to the Windows Internet time server: time.windows.com. If you prefer to use another server, Windows 7 lists some additional government time servers such as time.nist.gov. Or, you can turn off Internet time synchronization if you do not have an always-on Internet connection or want to set the time yourself.

To work with Internet time settings, right-click the clock (time) in the notification area at the right end of the taskbar, and click *Adjust date/time*. Click the Internet Time tab in the Date and Time dialog box, and then click the Change settings button. If a User Account Control dialog box appears, enter an administrator password, and click Yes. If you want to leave time synchronization on but use another server, choose the alternate server from the *Server* drop-down list, and then click Update now. To turn off Internet time synchronization, click the *Synchronize with an Internet time server* check box to clear it. Click OK twice to close the dialog boxes and apply your changes.

 ## Exercise 6

Changing Date and Time Settings

1. Look at the clock in the notification area. Write down the current time and the current date.
2. Right-click the clock (time) in the notification area at the right end of the taskbar, and click *Adjust date/time*.
3. Click *Change date and time* on the Date and Time tab of the Date and Time dialog box. If a User Account Control dialog box appears, enter an administrator password, and click Yes. (Your instructor can provide an administrator password to use.)
4. Click the current month and year at the top of the calendar. Click *June* in the zoomed calendar to display the calendar for June of the current year. Click *21* to set the date to June 21.
5. Click the hour within the time in the text box to the right, and click the spinner arrow buttons as needed to change it to *12*.

6. Click OK twice to close the dialog boxes and apply the new time.
7. View the new date and time settings in the notification area as in Step 1. Compare the current date and time with the values you recorded earlier.
8. Now, reset the date and time by synchronizing to an Internet time server. Right-click the clock (time) in the notification area at the right end of the taskbar and click *Adjust date/time*.
9. Click the *Internet Time* tab, and then click *Change settings* on the tab. If a User Account Control dialog box appears, enter an administrator password, and click Yes.
10. Make sure that the *Synchronize with an Internet time server* check box is checked, and then click *Update now*.
11. After the Internet Time Settings dialog box informs you that the synchronization has finished, click OK twice to close the dialog boxes and apply the time change.
12. View the new date and time settings in the notification area as in Step 1. Compare the current date and time with the values you recorded earlier.

CHAPTER Summary

- The Control Panel provides a central location for accessing system settings.
- Click Start and then click *Control Panel* to open Control Panel. Click a category icon or link to find lower-level categories of actions, and then click the task to perform. You also can click a category or task in the list at the left side of Control Panel.
- You can adjust such settings as the keyboard repeat rate, the mouse double-click speed, or the functions of the mouse buttons.
- Right-click the desktop and click *Personalize* to find settings for customizing the desktop.
- You can change window colors and transparency, the picture or background on the desktop, screen saver, theme, and system sounds. You also can choose the right resolution and refresh rate for the display (monitor).
- You also can change the sounds Windows 7 plays for system events, such as when you shut down the system.
- Right-click the desktop and use the *View* and *Sort By* submenu choices to choose icon size, alignment settings, and sort order.
- Right-click the Start button and click *Properties* to display the settings for customizing the Start menu.
- You can control whether Start menu items display as menus, and add more items such as Favorites and Recent Files.
- Right-click the taskbar and click *Properties* to display the settings for customizing the taskbar.
- You can pin a program to the taskbar to add a button for the program there.
- Display and hide various toolbars on the taskbar, or unlock the taskbar and move it to a new position. You also can set up the taskbar to remain hidden (auto-hide) unless you point to it with the mouse.
- The icons in the notification area can be set up to be hidden when inactive.
- Gadgets are mini-programs that make data or special functions available on the desktop.

- Right-click the desktop and click *Gadgets* to open the Gadget Gallery. Double-click a gadget to add it to the desktop. You also can click the link in the lower-right corner of the window to search for more gadgets online.

- Drag gadgets into any position you want on the desktop. To close a gadget, right-click it and click *Close gadget*.

- The Ease of Access Center in Control Panel offers settings for customizing the system for users with special needs.

- When you open the Ease of Access Center, the Narrator starts and prompts you to enable one of the four most common accessibility features. You also can scroll down and choose individual features as desired.

- Right-click the time in the notification area and click *Adjust date/time* to open the Date and Time dialog box where you can choose a new date, time, or time zone.

- The Date and Time dialog box also offers a tab that you can use to synchronize the system with an Internet time server.

CONCEPTS Check

Completion: Answer the following questions on a blank sheet of paper.

Part

1

MULTIPLE CHOICE

1. To change system settings, use the _____ .
   a. Start menu
   b. taskbar
   c. Control Panel
   d. desktop

2. Click the _____ command on the Start menu to access system settings.
   a. Start menu
   b. taskbar
   c. Control Panel
   d. desktop

3. To make the mouse easier to use, you can _____ .
   a. slow the double-click speed
   b. flip mouse buttons
   c. slow the pointer speed
   d. Any of the above

4. The _____ feature snaps an icon you are moving to the nearest available slot in the invisible desktop grid.
   a. Align icons to grid
   b. Auto arrange icons
   c. Show desktop icons
   d. Line up icons

5. The _____ feature moves icons to fill available slots in the invisible desktop grid.
   a. Align icons to grid
   b. Auto arrange icons
   c. Show desktop icons
   d. Show desktop

6. When customizing the Start menu, choose the _____ option to be able to access an item's contents directly from the Start menu.
   a. Don't display this item
   b. Display as a link
   c. Display as a menu
   d. Display contents

7. The _____ feature removes the taskbar from view until you point to its location.
   a. Auto-hide
   b. Glass
   c. Aero
   d. Cloaking

8. A gadget set up to be _____ remains visible no matter which program windows are open and what their sizes are.
   a. floated
   b. always open
   c. maximized
   d. always on top

9. How many extra clocks can you display on the taskbar?
   a. Zero
   b. One
   c. Two
   d. Three

10. Synchronizing to an _____ keeps the system date and time accurate.
    a. online dating site
    b. alternate time zone
    c. Internet time location
    d. Internet time server

Part 2

SHORT ANSWER

11. Name one of the two primary keyboard settings you can change.

    _____

12. Name at least two types of backgrounds that you can apply to the desktop.

    _____

13. Describe what a screen saver is and why you might use one.

    _____

14. Describe what a theme is.

    _____

15. Explain how to hide the icons on the desktop.

_____

16. Name at least two of the toolbars you can display on the taskbar.

_____

17. Describe a situation when you need to unlock the taskbar.

_____

18. Describe how to pin a program to the taskbar.

_____

19. Name at least three of the available gadgets.

_____

20. Explain what the Ease of Access Center is and how to use it.

_____

SKILLS Check

Save all solution files to the default Documents folder, or any alternate folder specified by your instructor.

Guided Check

Assessment

1

SLOW DOWN THE MOUSE AND DISPLAY MOUSE TRAILS

1. Start Control Panel.
   a. Click Start.
   b. Click *Control Panel*.
2. Find Mouse Settings.
   a. Click *Hardware and Sound*.
   b. Click *Mouse* under Devices and Printers.
3. Slow down the mouse.
   a. Drag the *Speed* slider under Double-click speed to the left, until it is an increment or two to the left of the center point.
   b. Take a screen shot of the desktop, paste the shot into Paint, and save it as **C06A01S03**.
4. Turn on pointer trails.
   a. Click the Pointer Options tab in the Mouse Properties dialog box.
   b. Click the *Display pointer trails* check box to check it.
   c. Drag the slider to the desired setting for the pointer trails length.
   d. Take a screen shot of the desktop, paste the shot into Paint, and save it as **C06A01S04**.
5. Click OK to apply the changes.
6. Drag the mouse on-screen to see how it behaves.
7. Repeat Steps 2–5 to undo the settings changes you made.

8. Click the window Close (X) button to close Control Panel.
9. Submit the screen shots via e-mail or on your USB flash drive to your instructor, as required.

CHANGE THE SCREEN RESOLUTION AND COLORS

2

1. Find screen resolution settings.
   a. Right-click the desktop.
   b. Click *Screen resolution*.
2. Change display resolution.
   a. Click the *Resolution* drop-down list. Make a note of the current setting.
   b. Drag the resolution slider to the highest or lowest available setting, as you prefer.
   c. Click OK in the Screen Resolution window.
   d. Click Keep changes when asked to keep the new display settings.
3. Find personalization settings.
   a. Right-click the desktop.
   b. Click *Personalize*.
4. Change window colors.
   a. Click *Window Color*. Make a note of the current color.
   b. Click *Ruby*.
   c. Click the *Enable transparency* check box to clear (uncheck) it.
   d. Click Save changes.
5. Take a screen shot of the desktop, paste the shot into Paint, and save it as **C06A02**.
6. Close the Control Panel window, and then repeat Steps 1–4 and change back to the settings you made a note of while completing the Assessment.
7. Click the window Close (X) button to close Control Panel.
8. Submit the screen shot via e-mail or on your USB flash drive to your instructor, as required.

HIDE AND REDISPLAY DESKTOP ICONS AND THE TASKBAR

3

1. Hide desktop icons.
   a. Right-click the desktop.
   b. Point to *View*.
   c. Click *Show desktop icons*.
2. Turn on auto-hide for the taskbar.
   a. Right-click the taskbar.
   b. Click *Properties*.
   c. Click the *Auto-hide the taskbar* check box to check it.
   d. Click OK.
3. Take a screen shot of the empty desktop, paste the shot into Paint, and save it as **C06A03**.
4. Repeat Steps 1–2 to undo the settings changes you made.
5. Submit the screen shot via e-mail or on your USB flash drive to your instructor, as required.

UNLOCK AND MOVE THE TASKBAR

4

1. Unlock the taskbar.
   a. Right-click the taskbar.
   b. Click *Lock the taskbar*.
2. Drag the taskbar to the top of the screen.
3. Click the Start menu button on the moved taskbar.

4. With the Start menu open, take a screen shot of the desktop, paste the shot into Paint, and save it as **C06A04**.
5. Close the Start menu by clicking a blank area of the desktop.
6. Drag the taskbar back to the default location at the bottom of the screen.
7. Lock the taskbar.
   a. Right-click the taskbar.
   b. Click *Lock the taskbar*.
8. Submit the screen shot via e-mail or on your USB flash drive to your instructor, as required.

On Your Own

Assessment 5 — DISPLAY COMPUTER AND GAMES AS MENUS ON THE START MENU

1. Right-click the Start button, and then click *Properties*.
2. Click Customize.
3. Click the *Display as a menu* choice for both Computer and Games.
4. Click OK twice to close the dialog boxes and apply the changes.
5. Open the Start menu and point to *Games*.
6. Take a screen shot of the Games menu, paste the shot into Paint, and save it as **C06A05S06**.
7. If needed, reopen the start menu and point to *Computer*.
8. Take a screen shot of the Computer menu, paste the shot into Paint, and save it as **C06A05S08**.
9. Redisplay the Taskbar and Start Menu Properties dialog box, click the Start Menu tab, click Customize, and click Use Default Settings. Click OK twice.
10. Submit the screen shots via e-mail or on your USB flash drive to your instructor, as required.

Assessment 6 — DRAW PICTURE AND DISPLAY ON DESKTOP

1. Start Paint.
2. Use the Paint button, *Properties* command to set the image size to 100 x 100 pixels.
3. Draw some simple shapes or lines in the graphic. You are free to be as creative as you want.
4. Save the file as **Background**, as a JPG image, in your default Pictures library, and close Paint.
5. Right-click the desktop and click *Personalize*, then click *Desktop Background*.
6. Apply the new picture you just created and saved in the Pictures folder as the new desktop background, using the *Tile* option to repeat it on the desktop.
7. Close Control Panel.
8. Take a screen shot of the new desktop, paste the shot into Paint, and save it as **C06A05**.
9. Return to the prior desktop background, as desired.
10. Submit the screen shot via e-mail or on your USB flash drive to your instructor, as required.

Assessment 7 — PUT THE WEATHER GADGET ON THE DESKTOP

1. Right-click the desktop, and click *Gadgets*.
2. Double-click the Weather gadget in the Gadget Gallery window.
3. Close the Gadget Gallery window.
4. Right-click the Weather gadget and click *Options*.

5. Enter your school's city and state in the *Select current location* text box, press Enter, and click OK.
6. Take a screen shot of the gadget on the desktop, paste the shot into Paint, and save it as **C06A07**.
7. Right-click the Weather gadget, and click *Close gadget*.
8. Submit the screen shot via e-mail or flash USB drive to your instructor, as required.

Assessment 8 — GROUP ACTIVITY: CUSTOMIZATION ASSESSMENT

1. Divide into teams of four. Imagine that you are computer consultants hired to set up a number of new Windows 7 systems for a company.
2. Create a WordPad document and save it as **Recommendations**.
3. Type the following categories into the document:
   Mouse and Keyboard:
   Desktop Background:
   Screen Saver:
   Taskbar:
4. As a group, share ideas on how to set up the systems with regard to each of the listed categories.
5. Type in your setup ideas beside or below each category.
6. Save the file.
7. Print the file and submit it to your instructor for grading.

CHALLENGE Project

As a special education teacher, you will be teaching a computer class to high-school students who have a variety of disabilities. You need to prepare specific computers in the computer lab for each student based on his or her unique capabilities.

1. Open WordPad and create a new file named **Student Setup Needs**.

   Imagine that you have three students. Jane cannot see at all. Tim has a disability that makes it difficult for him to use his hands. And Sam has both limited hearing and some trouble using his hands. Type each student's name into the WordPad file.

2. Open the Ease of Access Center and research settings you might change and other recommendations you might make to set up a system for each student.

3. Type your system setup suggestions as a bulleted list under each student's name in the WordPad file. Include the general steps or process for implementing each setup suggestion.

4. Save your changes to the document.

5. If required, supply the final document to your instructor in hard-copy format or via e-mail or on your USB flash drive.

Part 2

Windows® 7

Using the Internet and Multimedia with Windows 7

➤ Browsing with Internet Explorer

➤ Ensuring Your Safety and Privacy on the Internet

➤ Using Windows Live Mail

➤ Working with Digital Photographs and Music

CHAPTER 7

Browsing with Internet Explorer

PERFORMANCE OBJECTIVES

Upon successful completion of Chapter 7, you will be able to:

- Start and exit Internet Explorer
- Understand what a URL is
- Display a Web page
- Browse through Web pages
- Use tabs to open multiple Web pages
- Search for a topic
- Use accelerators and Web Slices
- See content when not connected
- Deal with the Information bar
- Set up and read an RSS feed

With Windows 7 and an Internet connection, a nearly unlimited store of information and content becomes available. From reading online news to learning how to manage your money or plant a garden, to finding reviews about the new TV that you want to buy, to shopping for nearly anything you want, to selling stuff that you want to get rid of, the World Wide Web offers it all. This chapter shows you how to use Internet Explorer, the built-in Web browser for Windows 7.

Starting and Exiting Explorer

Web browser: A program that enables you to view and retrieve information from the World Wide Web

World Wide Web: A structure of linked documents stored on Web server computers connected to the Internet

Windows 7 includes the Internet Explorer 8 *Web browser* program that you can use to view and retrieve information from the *World Wide Web*. Web server computers connected to the Internet store and deliver the linked documents that make up the Web.

The documents on the Web are primarily based on a language called HTML: HyperText Markup Language. HTML is called a markup language because it uses tags to "describe" the contents of a document, identifying titles, lists, tables, and so on. Internet Explorer can read the tag information and display each document correctly on-screen.

Figure 7.1 **Use one of two ways to start Internet Explorer.**

You can start Internet Explorer, also called IE, in one of two ways, which are shown in Figure 7.1:

- Click Start, click *All Programs*, and then click *Internet Explorer* in the left pane of the Start menu. If your system has a 64-bit version of Windows installed, you may have the 64-bit version of Internet Explorer installed as well, so you can click *Internet Explorer (64-bit)*, instead, to use the browser that is optimized for your version of Windows.

- Click the Internet Explorer button, which appears on the taskbar by default.

When you start Internet Explorer, it will connect to the Internet and display the designated home page, the page set up to display first. By default, this page is the MSN Web page or site, but on your system it may be another page set up by the computer's maker or your school.

Note: *The first time IE is started on a system, the Set Up Windows Internet Explorer 8 window opens. You can click Ask me later to skip the process, or Next to step through a series of screens where you can specify whether certain features are active or not.*

Note: *If your computer uses a dial-up Internet connection, you may see a dialog box prompting you to start the connection process. Click the Connect button to do so.*

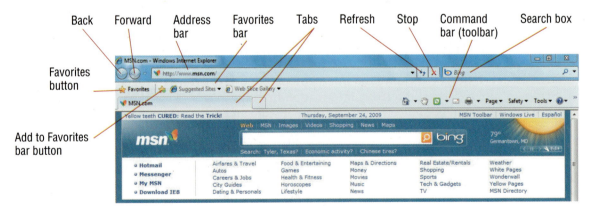

Figure 7.2 **Key parts of the Internet Explorer window.**

The Internet Explorer window has a number of features (Figure 7.2) that you use to find and display Web documents and information. These features include:

- **Address bar**. Make an entry here to go directly to a Web location.
- **Back and Forward buttons**. Become active after you begin browsing. These buttons give you another way to move around.
- **Refresh button**. Reloads the current Web location.
- **Stop button**. Stops the loading of the current location.
- **Search box**. Enables you to search for information online.
- **Favorites bar**. Displays buttons for favorite sites you have added, so you can click a button to go to the favorite site.
- **Favorites button**. Opens the Favorites Center, which lists your favorite Web locations and more.
- **Add to Favorites bar button**. Adds the displayed Web location as a button on the Favorites bar.
- **Tabs**. Each tab holds a single Web location, but you can use multiple tabs to have more than one location open at a time.
- **Command bar (Toolbar)**. Offers additional buttons for working in IE.

When it is open, Internet Explorer behaves like any other program, meaning you can minimize, restore, resize, and maximize its window. You also can close the program when you finish working by clicking the window Close (X) button. Alternately, you can press Alt+F4 to close the program and its window.

> Tip: If you want to access IE commands using a menu bar, you can right-click the command bar (toolbar) and click *Menu Bar*.

Understanding URLs

You learned in Chapter 3 how each computer document exists as a separate named file stored in a specific folder, and the "directions" to that location are known as the the file's path. Similarly, each Web document or *Web page* you view is a separate file stored in a particular location on the Web. To open the document, you have to specify its address and file name, known as its *URL (Uniform Resource Locator)*.

Web page: An HTML file (Web document) stored in a particular location

URL (Uniform Resource Locator): The address of a Web page

Each URL has distinctive parts that communicate information about the location and nature of the Web page it represents. Figure 7.3 illustrates these parts of a URL:

- **Protocol**. Represents the communication standards used by the location identified. Web page URLs use the http (HyperText Transfer) protocol. Sometimes, the protocol for a URL will be *https://*, meaning that the site uses extra security features and is verified as trusted via a certificate and certificate authority; a secure Web site typically requires you to log on for security.

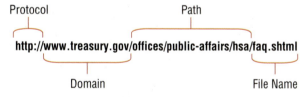

Figure 7.3 **Key parts of a URL.**

- **Domain**. This part of the URL identifies the overall Web site that holds the specific Web page being referenced. In the example in Figure 7.3, *www.treasury.gov* is the Web site for the United States Department of the Treasury. The *.gov* suffix at the end of the domain name is its top-level domain (TLD) name that identifies the type of organization operating the domain. Table 7.1 lists some common top-level domains. If you leave off the path and file name in the URL, the home page of the domain will load by default. Other top-level domains represent countries, such as the .au domain for Australia or .ca for Canada.

- **Path**. The folder path to the Web page file.
- **File name**. The file name for the Web page. The file name may have a file name extension of .htm, .html, or some variation like .shtml, or it may have an extension such as .asp if it is a different type of Web page.

Table 7.1   Most Common Top-Level Domains (TLDs)

Name	Type
.biz	business
.com	business or information
.edu	school or other educational institution
.gov	government
.info	informational
.mil	military (U.S. Department of Defense)
.name	individual person or family
.net	business or ISP
.org	non-profit organization
.us	federal agency (U.S.)

Note: *Some URLs have additional information, such as including a port and query to request more specific information from the Web server.*

URLs cannot include spaces, so in some cases, you will see the underscore (_) character used to separate words. Make sure that you type the URL just as specified, including any underscore characters. If the page does not load and you see an error message in the browser window, you may have mistyped the URL. Select the Address bar contents, retype the URL entry, and press Enter to try again.

Going to a Web Page

To go directly to a Web page—that is, to open or load the Web page directly in the Internet Explorer Web browser—you use the Address bar at the top of the IE window. Note that when you type in a URL, IE lets you leave off the *http://* protocol portion, for example you can type *www.msn.com* instead of *http://www.msn.com*. In some cases, you also can leave off the *www.* portion of the domain, simply entering *msn.com* rather than *www.msn.com*.

Windows 7 includes what Microsoft calls a smarter Address bar. When you start typing an Address bar entry, the Address bar reviews sites you have previously visited, called the **history** or browsing history, your favorites, and RSS feeds (which you will learn about later in this chapter) and suggests possible matches. As shown in

History: An IE feature that tracks Web sites and pages you have visited within a recent time period—by default the previous 20 days

Figure 7.4, you can either click one of the suggested matches or press the keyboard shortcut, when present, to jump to that page. The list shows you both the site or page name in addition to its URL, making it easier to select the desired destination.

Keyboard shortcut

Figure 7.4 The smarter Address bar suggests matching sites.

Note: *When you load a Web page, the status bar displays the URL and a progress bar as the page loads. In place of the domain, you may see an IP (Internet Protocol) address such as http://192.168.1.1.*

Note: *In some instances, when you open a Web page for the first time, the Microsoft SmartScreen filter displays a blocking Web page and shows the Address bar in red. This means that the Web site has been found on a list of sites known to have content that can infect and damage your computer. You have the option of going to your home page or proceeding to the blocked page. You will learn more about the SmartScreen filter, what it does, and how to change its settings in the next chapter.*

To go to a Web page: **Here's How**

1. Select the URL currently in the Address bar. In some cases, clicking the URL once selects it. If that does not work, you can either drag over the URL, or right-click the Address bar and click *Select All*.
2. Type a different URL into the Address bar. If one of the matches that appear is the page you want to visit, click it in the list. Otherwise, continue to Step 3.

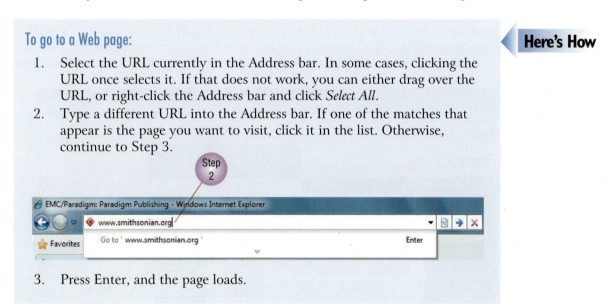

3. Press Enter, and the page loads.

 ## Exercise 1
Going to a Web Page

1. Click the Internet Explorer button on the taskbar.
2. If needed, click or drag over the URL in the Address bar to select it.
3. Type finance.yahoo.com and press Enter. The Yahoo! Finance page appears.
4. Click or drag over the contents of the Address bar again.
5. Type www.smithsonian.org and press Enter. The Smithsonian Institution's Web site appears.

6. Click or drag over the contents of the Address bar again.
7. Type http://en.wikipedia.org/wiki/Jackson_Pollock and press Enter. The Jackson Pollock article on the Wikipedia Web site opens.
8. Click the Print button drop-down arrow on the command bar and click Print. In the Page Range area, click Pages, leave 1 entered, and click Print to print a copy of the first page of Web page information. Write your name on it and submit it to your instructor for grading, if required.
9. Click the window Close (X) button to close the Web site and browser.

Browsing Pages

Browsing: Displaying and reading Web pages in whatever order suits you

Imagine if all the billions of pages on the Web were crammed onto a single page that you had to review from top to bottom, like a long scroll of paper. It would take forever to find any information you needed! That is why the contents of the Web were engineered as discreet pages that you can "flip" to as needed, in a nonlinear fashion, more like the pages in a magazine. When a topic catches your eye, you can *browse* to the page that covers that topic by following a link.

Following a Link

Hypertext: A document format or system in which the document contains links to other content

Hyperlink: An item on a Web page that you can click to display another Web page or to download information

The term *hypertext*, referred to in the HTML file-type acronym and http:// protocol, means that a Web page document contains links, called *hyperlinks*, to other pages and files. Clicking a hyperlink displays the destination Web page or, in some cases, begins a file download.

While hyperlinks originally only appeared as specially formatted text on a Web page, today's Web pages also include links in the form of graphics (pictures), buttons, navigation bars or tabs, drop-down lists, even buttons for expanding lists of links, and

Navigation bar hyperlinks

Mouse pointer over hyperlink

Button hyperlink

Text hyperlink

URL for linked page

Graphic hyperlink

Figure 7.5 **Different types of hyperlinks.**

even online advertisements. Traditionally, hyperlinked text was blue and underlined, but Web page designers no longer adhere to that style. Hyperlinks may be any color, may be bold, and may lack an underline. How can you identify hyperlinked text if you are not certain how the Web page designer has formatted it? You can typically point to the text with your mouse. If the text is a hyperlink, it may change color or appearance, and the mouse pointer will change from an arrow to a hand, as shown in Figure 7.5. The status bar displays the URL to the linked destination page, in case you want to check it to verify where the link will take you before you follow it.

To follow any hyperlink, click it with the mouse. The contents of the destination page will download and appear in IE. After you follow a text hyperlink, it typically changes to another color or style; the default is generally for hyperlinks to start out blue and turn purple when followed.

Note: *A link that starts a download opens the File Download dialog box. Click the Save button, specify the save location in the Save As dialog box, then click Save to download the file.*

Backing Up or Going Forward

When you initially start Internet Explorer, the Back and Forward buttons in the upper-left corner are disabled or grayed out. That is because you have not done any browsing yet. Once you move to the first page beyond your IE home page, the Back button becomes active, and you can click it to back up to the previously viewed page.

After you click Back at least once, the Forward button becomes active, and you can click it to move forward to the page from which you have backed up. When you have backed up or moved forward multiple times, the Recent Pages drop-down list arrow, beside the Back and Forward buttons, becomes active. You can click the button to open the Recent Pages menu of previously visited pages (Figure 7.6), and then click one of the listed pages to redisplay it. The drop-down list saves you from having to click the Back or Forward button numerous times.

Figure 7.6 Use the Recent Pages menu to redisplay a previously visited page.

Note: *The History command that appears at the bottom of the Recent Pages menu opens the Favorites Center pane with the History tab selected at the left side of Internet Explorer. You can use that pane to go back to pages visited on previous days (Figure 7.7). Click a day to list the pages you viewed, and then click the page to redisplay. Click the pane's Close (X) button to close the pane.*

Going to Your Home Page

You can redisplay the Internet Explorer home page at any time. To do so, click the Home button on the command bar or press Alt+M+Enter.

To change the home page or add a new home page to the Home button's drop-down menu, first browse to the page that you want to use as a home page. Click the Home button drop-down list arrow on the IE command bar, and then click *Add or Change Home Page*. Click one of the options for adding the home page in the Add or Change

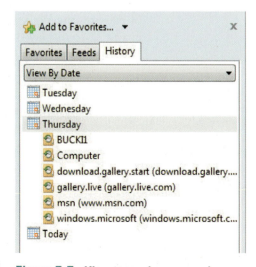

Figure 7.7 View pages from a previous day in the Favorites Center History tab.

Home Page dialog box that appears (Figure 7.8), and then click Yes. If you added the Web page as an additional home page tab, you can then click the Home button drop-down list arrow and click the new page's name on the menu at any time to display that alternate home page. When you start up IE, each home page will appear on a separate tab. Note that some Web pages include a link for setting the displayed page as the IE home page.

Figure 7.8 **You can change the home page or add the current page as an additional home page.**

Note: *Use the Remove submenu of the Home button drop-down list to remove any previously marked home page.*

Using the Refresh Button
Click the Refresh button if you load a page and it displays information from a prior day. Or, if you are viewing a Web page that updates frequently, such as a page with stock quotes, clicking Refresh ensures that the page will display the latest available data.

Refreshing or Stopping a Page

If you have problems with a page loading correctly, the Refresh and Stop buttons at the far-right end of the Address bar (Figure 7.9) come in handy. If a page does not load completely, some or all of its text may not appear, or you may see a box with a red *x* inside a frame where a graphic did not load. In such a situation, clicking the Refresh button to reload the page can help the missing information appear. If a page loads too slowly or you realize you have clicked the wrong link, click the Stop button to stop the page load. Then you can browse to another location.

Figure 7.9 **The Compatibility View (left), Refresh (center) and Stop (right) buttons found at the far-right end of the Address bar.**

Compatibility View: A view in Internet Explorer that enables it to better display sites and pages designed for older browser versions

Using Compatibility View

A third button, shown at the left in Figure 7.9, appears when you visit some Web pages. This is the *Compatibility View* button. It appears whenever IE identifies a site that was designed for an older browser version. Because Web site programming methods and standards change over time, a site created for a set of standards supported by earlier browsers may not display correctly in the latest IE browser. If the Compatibility View button appears and menus, images, or text appear out of place on the Web page, click the Compatibility View button. Doing so should enable IE to display the page more accurately. You need not click the Compatibility View button if a page appears to be loading and displaying everything correctly.

 ## Exercise 2

Browsing the Yahoo! Web Site

1. Click the Internet Explorer button on the taskbar.
2. If needed, click or drag over the URL in the Address bar to select it.
3. Type **www.yahoo.com** and press Enter. The main Web page for the Yahoo! site appears.
4. Click the HotJobs link in the list along the left.
5. Capture a screen shot, paste it into Paint, and save the file as **C07E02S05**.
6. Click one of the category tabs (such as Job Search) at the top of the page.
7. Click the Back button.
8. Click the Forward button.
9. Click the Recent Pages drop-down list button beside the Back and Forward buttons, and then click *Yahoo!* to return to the main Yahoo! Web site page.

10. Scroll down, and browse to any news topic of interest using the World tab in the middle section of the page.
11. Click the Compatibility View button.
12. Capture a screen shot, paste it into Paint, and save the file as **C07E02S12**.
13. Click the Home button on the command bar to return to the home page.
14. Close Internet Explorer.
15. E-mail your screen shots to your instructor or submit them on your USB flash drive, as required.

QUICK FIX

Finding the Compatibility View Button
If you don't see the Compatibility View button, right-click near the command bar and click *Compatibility View Button.*

Working with Tabs

Tabs is a feature that has made the latest versions of Internet Explorer, and many other browsers, much more flexible to use and more magazine-like. The tabs feature enables you to display multiple Web pages at once within the IE window, rather than having to open a separate IE window for each Web page you would like to view. The tabs feature can be quite helpful when you are performing research, for example, or when you need to compare prices for an item from two different Web sites.

Adding a Tab for a URL

Tabs appear at the top of the IE window, on the same row as the command bar and directly below the Address bar. The rightmost tab is always blank and ready for you to use it to display another Web page.

To open a Web page in a new tab:

1. Click the blank tab to the right of the active Web page tab(s) at the top of Internet Explorer (called the New Tab button) or press Ctrl+T. The tab activates, and a description of using tabs appears. The about:Tabs entry in the Address bar appears highlighted by default.
2. Type a different URL into the Address bar.

Here's How

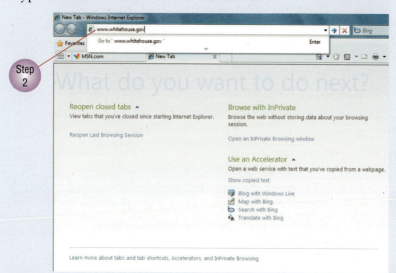

3. Press Enter. The page loads, and the page content appears on the new tab.

Switching between Tabs

Quick Tabs: A feature that displays a thumbnail of each open Web page (tab) from which you can select the tab to open

As with a tab in a dialog box, you click an Internet Explorer Web page tab to bring that tab to the forefront and display its content. You also can click the Tab List drop-down arrow button (Figure 7.10) that appears to the left of the first tab, and then click the name of the page to display in the list that appears. Either of these approaches works fine when you have a few tabs open.

Quick Tabs button   Tab List button   Tab Close button

Figure 7.10 **Buttons for working with tabs.**

However, if you have many tabs open and cannot remember what type of content each of the open Web pages holds, you might want to use the **Quick Tabs** feature to preview and switch to a tab.

To display the Quick Tabs, click the Quick Tabs button shown in Figure 7.10. The page thumbnails appear, as shown in Figure 7.11. Click the thumbnail of the page to display to make it the active tab.

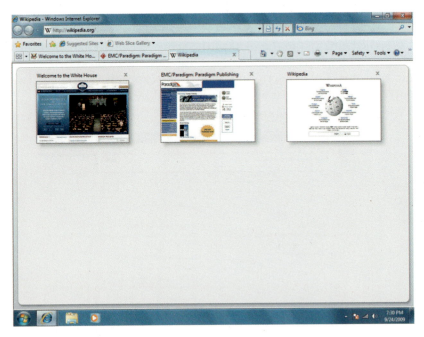

Figure 7.11 **Click a thumbnail to go to that Web page (tab).**

Note: To close any individual tab, click the Close (X) button that appears on the tab itself. If you have multiple tabs running when you exit Internet Explorer, the program prompts you to confirm that you want to close all tabs. Click Close all tabs to do so.

Exercise 3

1. Click the Internet Explorer button on the taskbar.
2. Click the New Tab button to the right of the tab for the home page.
3. Type www.whitehouse.gov in the Address bar and press Enter. The main Web page for the White House site appears.
4. Click the New Tab button to the right of the tab for the White House page.
5. Type www.wikipedia.org in the Address bar and press Enter. The main Web page for the Wikipedia free encyclopedia appears.
6. Click the home page tab. The home page becomes the active Web page.
7. Click the White House page tab. That tab becomes active.
8. Click the Quick Tabs button.
9. Capture a screen shot, paste it into Paint, and save the file as **C07E03S09**.
10. Click the Quick Tabs button again, and then click the tab for the Wikipedia Web site.
11. Click the tab Close (X) button to close the Wikipedia tab.
12. Click the tab Close (X) button to close the White House tab.
13. Leave IE open for the next exercise.
14. E-mail your screen shot to your instructor or submit it on your USB flash drive, as required.

Searching the Web

Internet Explorer has a built-in search feature located in the upper-right corner of the program window. As with the built-in search boxes in the Start menu and Explorer windows, the search box in IE provides a direct, convenient way to search for information on the Web. In this case, the search box by default uses the ***Bing*** Internet ***search engine*** operated by Microsoft to search the Web for the word or phrase you specify.

Bing: The latest Internet search engine from Microsoft

Search engine: A Web site/service that uses an index method to track and retrieve Web documents that match specified terms

To search the Web:

Here's How

1. Click in the search box near the upper-right corner of the IE window, to the right of the Address bar. Alternately, you can press Ctrl+E.
2. Type the word, words, or phrase you want to search for.
3. Use one of the following methods to run the search:
    *   Press the Enter key or click the Search (magnifying glass) button to display the search results in the current tab.
    *   Press Alt+Enter to display the search results in a new tab.

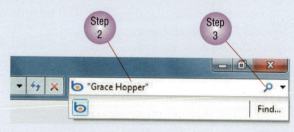

Step 2   Step 3

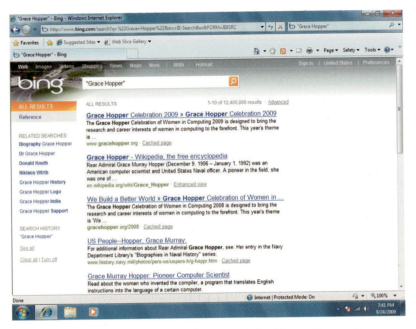

Search lists the search results links and includes a brief description of each. For example, Figure 7.12 shows the results that appear after a search for *"Grace Hopper."* (More on the quotation marks next.) When there are numerous results, you can scroll down to the bottom of the page and click a number link to display another page listing additional results. The navigation bar above the search results list actually enables you to find different types of information about the search term. For example, you could click the Images choice to see pictures of the person or item you searched for. Bing also includes links for Related

Figure 7.12 **The results listed after a search for "Grace Hopper."**

Searches along the left. Click any link in the list of search results or in the lists at the left to display information about the search subject.

Note: Internet Explorer can be customized to use another search engine such as Google, Yahoo, Ask.com, dogpile.com, or any other. Your school may have customized its computers to use another search tool, in which case you can simply use the search engine that appears. Most search engines work in the same way.

Note: Other search engines may present search results differently. For example, some search engines rank results or give you estimates about how well a result matches the search text you entered.

Because of the vast volume of information now available on the Web, searching for a single-word, generic term yields such a long list of results that you may never find the particular bit of information that you need. For example, searching for *flower* on the day this chapter was written yielded 36,804,755 matching results! So, Bing and other search engines enable you to use a number of techniques to make your search more specific so that you see a more targeted (better matching) list of search results.

For starters, use more specific words and phrases, and include the search phrase in quotation marks. The search box can accept entries up to 150 characters long. Adding the quote marks means that the search engine will look for the exact phrase you specify. So, for example, a search for *yellow ladyslipper* returns more than 6.4 million matches, while adding the quotes to search for *"yellow ladyslipper"* reduces the matches to about 4,500. In either case, those results are a lot more narrow than the 118+ million matches returned for *flower*.

Most search engines, including Bing, enable you to use operators to specify whether the results should match any or all of the words entered in cases where you leave out the quotation marks. Table 7.2 lists the basic operators. You must enter the operators in all capital letters.

Table 7.2 Web Search Operators

Operator	Use	Example	Alternatives in Other Search Engines
AND	Results must match all words; typically assumed if omitted.	knicks and pistons	and, and sometimes + (plus)
OR	Results may match any of the words.	knicks or pistons	or, and sometimes | (pipe)
NOT	Results will include the first word, but not the second one (the word preceded by the operator).	knicks not pistons	- (minus)

> **Tip:** Most search engines ignore other common words like *the* or *in*. So, use the most descriptive words that you can when performing a search. Most search engines also ignore capitalization.
>
> Many Web sites include a search box for searching the site's contents. In many instances, you also can use quotation marks and operators for more specific searches using a site-based search box.

You also can include keywords or meta words with a search term when using some search engines. The keywords make the search more specific, enabling you to search by location or file type. Table 7.3 lists often-used search keywords; most search engines use the same or very similar keywords. (Most search engine pages have a Help link that you can click to learn about techniques, like using keywords.)

Table 7.3 Most Common Search Keywords

Keyword	Use	Example
contains:	Specifies that matching sites must have links to the specified file type.	"yellow ladyslipper" contains:jpg
site:	Finds all documents on a domain (Web site) and its subdomains.	"yellow ladyslipper" site: www.fs.fed.us
intitle: or inbody:	Finds all documents that have the search text in the document title (intitle:) or body text (inbody:).	inbody:"yellow ladyslipper"
url:	Searches to check whether a specific domain or file is indexed by the search engine.	url:www.purdue.edu

Tip: Bing also recognizes Instant Answers, special search terms that you can use to get answers to common questions. For example, you can type area code followed by a city and state, and Bing will tell you the area code(s) for the specified location.

Figure 7.13 Search suggestions appear by default.

Using Search Suggestions

The search box now offers a form of built-in assistance called *search suggestions*. When you type a search word or phrase in the search box, the search suggestions pane appears below the box. The pane lists suggestions that further refine the the search term(s) you typed and help you narrow your search, as in the example in Figure 7.13. Click one of the suggestions in the list to perform that search.

Tip: You can turn search suggestions off and back on. In Internet Explorer, click the down arrow at the right end of the search box, and then click Manage Search Providers. Click a provider in the list, such as Bing, click Disable suggestions in the section at the bottom, and then click Close.

Adding a Visual Search Provider

For even more robust searches, you can set up a visual search provider. Doing so enables the search suggestions list to include *visual suggestions*, images and information about a potential search match, so you can go directly to a result that best answers your question or provides the information you need. Once you have installed one or more visual search providers, you can display and select from visual suggestions in the search suggestions pane.

Here's How ▶ **To add a visual search provider in IE:**

1. Click *Tools* on the command bar, and then click *Internet Options*.
2. On the General tab of the Internet Options dialog box, click the Settings button in the Search section.
3. In the Manage Add-ons window, click *Search Providers* in the Add-on Types list at the left.
4. Click *Find more search providers* at the bottom of the window.
5. Scroll through the search providers that appear, and find the one you want that includes the *Visual Search* icon below it.
6. Click the Add to Internet Explorer button for the desired visual search partner. The Add Search Provider dialog box appears.
7. In the Add Search Provider dialog box, click Add.
8. Close the Internet Explorer window with the gallery of search providers.

9. Click Close to close the Manage Add-ons window. (The search provider may not appear there, even though you have added it.)
10. Click OK to close the Internet Options dialog box.

To perform a visual search:

1. Type the search term(s) in the search box.
2. At the bottom of the search suggestions pane, click the icon for the visual search provider, if that provider isn't already selected. The visual search suggestions appear. (Click the *Bing* icon to switch back to normal search suggestions when desired.)
3. Click the desired visual suggestion.

 ## Exercise 4

Searching for a Topic Online

1. Click in the search box above the command bar.
2. Type **thomas edison phonograph**, and press Enter.
3. Capture a screen shot, paste it into Paint, and save the file as **C07E04S03**.
4. Click Images on the navigation bar above the search results.
5. Capture a screen shot, paste it into Paint, and save the file as **C07E04S05**.
6. Click in the search box again.
7. Type **thomas edison**, and click one of the search suggestions.
8. Capture a screen shot, paste it into Paint, and save the file as **C07E04S08**.
9. Click one of the results links.
10. Click the Back button.
11. E-mail your screen shots to your instructor or submit them on your USB flash drive, as required.

Working with Favorites

You have already seen that Internet Explorer enables you to set up multiple home pages. Because most users quickly develop a list of sites they visit frequently to perform research, get news and entertainment, handle finances or shop online, and so on, IE offers an even better way to record and even organize sites you visit often. You can mark a frequently visited site as a *favorite page*. You can use a listed favorite to quickly jump back to the corresponding page or site without having to remember its name.

Favorite page: A frequently visited Web site or page that is saved in the list in the Favorites Center for easy access

Using the Favorites Bar

The Favorites bar that appears above the page tabs provides the fastest way for marking and using a Favorite, although you should reserve this technique for the sites you use very frequently. Browse to the page that you want to add to the Favorites bar, and then click the Add to Favorites bar button on the Favorites bar (Figure 7.14). To remove a favorite from the Favorites bar, right-click it, click *Delete*, and then click Yes in the Delete Shortcut dialog box.

Add to Favorites
bar button

Button for
a favorite

**Figure 7.14 You can populate the Favorites bar with buttons
for jumping to favorite pages.**

> **Tip:** The Suggested Sites button on the Favorites bar enables you to turn on the suggested sites feature, which gives you ideas about sites you can check out that might have similar offerings to sites you have visited.

Marking a Favorite Page

The upper-left corner of Internet Explorer includes a Favorites button to the left, on the Favorites bar above the page tabs. You use this button to open the Favorites Center, which you can use to mark a Web page as a favorite on the Favorites Center list.

Here's How ▶ **To add a Web page to the Favorites list:**

1. Jump or browse to the page that you want to mark as a favorite.
2. Click the Favorites button on the Favorites bar.
3. Click the Add to Favorites button. The Add a Favorite dialog box opens.
4. Edit the favorite name listed in the *Name* text box, if needed.
5. If you want to store the favorite in an existing folder, choose the desired folder from the *Create in* drop-down list. To place the favorite in a new folder, click New Folder, make an entry in the *Folder Name* text box of the Create a Folder dialog box, make a choice from the *Create in* drop-down list to designate the new folder as a subfolder, and then click Create.
6. Click Add to close the Add a Favorite dialog box and finish creating the favorite.

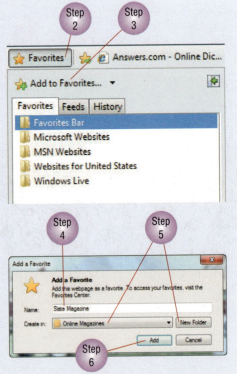

Organizing Favorites

You can think of a favorite (and even a folder for favorites) as a temporary setting, because you can make changes to your favorites at any time. You can delete, rename, and move favorites and folders to suit your changing needs.

To handle these tasks, click the Favorites button on the Favorites bar, click the Add to Favorites button drop-down arrow, and click *Organize Favorites* in the menu that appears. The Organize Favorites dialog box appears. If the favorite you want to work with is in a folder, click the folder, and then click the item to change. (To change a folder, just click the folder.) As shown in Figure 7.15, you can use the buttons at the bottom to make a change, as follows:

Figure 7.15 **Change favorites here.**

- **Move the favorite or folder**. Click the Move button, select or create the folder where you would like to place the selected item in the Browse for Folder dialog box that appears, and then click OK.

- **Rename the favorite or folder**. Click the Rename button, type the new name, and press Enter.

- **Delete the favorite or folder**. Click the Delete button, and then click Yes in the Delete File confirmation dialog box that appears.

When you finish making your changes to favorites, click the Close button in the Organize Favorites dialog box.

Going to a Favorite Page

The favorites remain hidden in the Favorites Center until you need to use them. Once you display the Favorites Center, you can open a folder and click the favorite page that you want to display.

To display a favorite Web page:

1. Click the Favorites button to the far-left of the Web page tabs, or press Alt+C.
2. If the list of favorites does not appear in the pane that opens, click the Favorites tab.
3. Click the folder that holds the favorite to display. If needed, click additional subfolders, too.

Here's How

4. Click the desired favorite. The Favorites Center pane closes, and the favorite page opens in Internet Explorer.

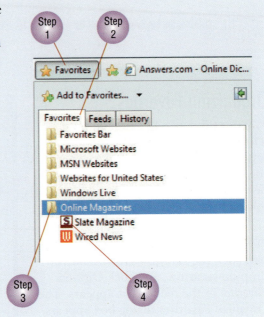

Exercise 5

Marking and Using a Favorite

1. Click the Home button on the command bar to return to the home page.
2. If needed, click or drag over the URL in the Address bar to select it.
3. Type www.refdesk.com, and press Enter. The Refdesk.com Web site offers links to dozens of research, writing, news, and information sites, making it a great resource for students, writers, researchers, and anyone else with a healthy dose of curiosity.
4. Click the Favorites button, and then click *Add to Favorites*.
5. Edit the *Name* text box entry to read Refdesk.com … Reference, Facts, News.
6. Click the New Folder button.
7. Type Research Resources in the *Folder Name* text box of the Create a Folder dialog box that appears. Make sure that *Favorites* is selected as the *Create In* drop-down list choice, and then click Create.
8. Back in the Add a Favorite dialog box, click Add to finish adding the new favorite.
9. Click Home on the command bar to redisplay the home page.
10. Click the Favorites button, and click the Favorites tab, if needed.
11. Click the Research Resources folder to display the Refdesk.com favorite.
12. Capture a screen shot, paste it into Paint, and save the file as **C07E05S12**.
13. Click the Favorites button to redisplay the Favorites Center, and then click the Favorites tab, if needed. Click the Research Resources folder if needed to display the Refdesk.com favorite, and then click the favorite. The Refdesk.com Web site appears.
14. E-mail your screen shot to your instructor or submit it on your USB flash drive, as required.

Using Accelerators

As fast as researching any topic on the Web has become, in IE 8, Microsoft introduces a way to make it even faster: *accelerators*. You can select text on a Web page, click the *Accelerator* icon that appears, and point to or click the desired task. For example, in Figure 7.16, a geographical location is selected on the Web page. To view a map of the location, you can click the *Accelerator* icon and point to *Map with Bing* to display a pop-up map. Clicking *Map with Bing* opens a separate tab with more map information. Pointing to *All Accelerators* displays a submenu with choices including a choice to find more accelerators.

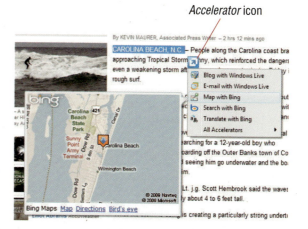

Accelerator icon

Figure 7.16 **Using an accelerator.**

Using a Web Slice

A **Web Slice** works somewhat like a favorite except that with a Web Slice, you are marking a particular type of Web content that updates as a favorite. Using a Web Slice is much like using a weather or news feed gadget, because you are subscribing to a particular segment of information. When a Web page contains a Web slice, the green Add Web Slices button becomes active on the IE command bar. To subscribe to the slice, you can click that button, or click the green icon that appears when the mouse pointer is over the slice content, or press Alt+J. Then click Add to Favorites bar in the dialog box that appears, as shown in Figure 7.17. From that point on, you can click the Web Slices button on the Favorites bar to view the slice. When the slice is open, click the right-arrow button in the lower-left corner to open the Web page for this Web Slice.

Accelerators: A new feature in IE 8 that enables you to perform tasks with selected content, such as mapping or blogging about a selected location

Web Slice: A form of favorite that enables you to subscribe to updating content from a particular Web site

Add Web
Slices button

Figure 7.17 **Subscribing to a Web Slice.**

Viewing Web Content Offline

If for some reason you want to limit your time online—to offset the cost of your Internet connection, for example, you can go offline once you have opened the page or pages that you want to read. This technique also can enhance security if you are using a public network or you need to view information but are unsure about the safety of the Web site you are viewing.

Figure 7.18 Internet Explorer prompts you to reconnect to the Internet when you click a link to browse from offline status.

To "take it offline" after you have displayed one or more Web pages in separate tabs, click the Tools button at the right end of the Internet Explorer command bar, and then click *Work Offline*. This step disconnects or disables the Internet connection.

When you are ready to go back online, you can click Tools, and then *Work Offline* again. Or, you can click a link or go to a URL; when you do so, Internet Explorer prompts you to reconnect, as shown in Figure 7.18. Click Connect to resume your online work. (IE will redial your Internet connection, if needed.)

Responding to the Information Bar

Active content: Online content that is interactive or animated, also loosely including pop-ups and certain downloads that may be required to run such content

Internet Explorer by default is set up to protect your system by taking a cautious approach toward any type of active content or controls. ***Active content*** typically refers to interactive or animated elements on a Web page, including such items as pop-ups and self-playing movies. Receiving and using or displaying this type of content often requires the transfer of software add-ins, such as the Flash Player, or other executable code. While you may welcome some of this content and the accompanying code or programs, such as an ActiveX control or Adobe Flash Player, because they make Web pages livelier, you need to keep in mind that these seemingly harmless transfers may be hiding malicious code intended to damage your system. (More about this in Chapter 8.)

Figure 7.19 The Information bar appears below the page tabs.

When a Web page wants to download or display some type of active content on a page, the Information bar pops up below the Web page tabs, and you hear an alert beep. You also may see a message like the one in Figure 7.19. Click the Close button to close the message.

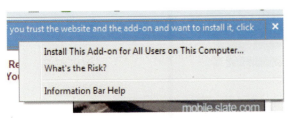

Figure 7.20 Click the Information bar, and then click one of the options to determine how to handle the flagged content.

To see choices for dealing with the Information bar message, click the Information bar. Then click a choice in the menu that appears (Figure 7.20). From there, you also might need to choose settings from a dialog box. All the choices depend on the nature of the content being flagged as potentially harmful.

If you prefer to dismiss the Information bar without performing any action, click the Close (X) button at the far-right end of the bar.

Note: *While it is not a good security practice, if you find the Information bar annoying, you can turn it off. Click the Tools button on the IE command bar, and then click Internet Options. Click the Security tab, and then click Custom Level. Scroll down to the Downloads section, and then click Enable under Automatic Prompting for File Downloads. Also scroll to the ActiveX controls and plug-ins section, and click Enable under Automatic prompting for ActiveX controls.*

Note: *In some cases, in addition to the Information bar, a dialog box will appear immediately, asking you whether to install software needed by the Web site. Make sure the software is from a trusted source before doing so.*

Working with RSS Feeds

When you find favorite Web sites that are useful and informative, you might get into a routine of visiting those sites on a regular basis. But even then, you have to browse through the site to find the relevant content that you want to read. Internet Explorer solves this problem by enabling you to subscribe to *RSS feeds*. An RSS feed delivers specially designated content on a Web site.

While you can certainly browse to and read RSS content, you save even more time by subscribing to have the content delivered to Internet Explorer. Having the latest content delivered directly to your system saves time, as you might imagine. You do not have to visit a site and review its contents to see if you have read the latest.

> **RSS (Really Simple Syndication) feeds:** Regularly updated Web site information such as news or pictures, which a user can visit or subscribe to; also called XML feeds, syndicated content, and Web feeds

Adding a Feed

Internet Explorer automatically alerts you when you browse to a Web site that offers an RSS feed. The View Feeds on This Page button becomes active, and you can use it to subscribe to the feed.

To subscribe to an RSS Feed:

1. Click the View feeds on this page button's drop-down list arrow on the IE command bar when it becomes active (turns orange).
2. Click the feed to view.
3. Click the Subscribe to this feed link on the page. Or click the Favorites button on the Favorites bar, and then click the Subscribe to this Feed button.
4. Edit the *Name* text box entry, if desired, and optionally make a new subfolder of the Feeds folder to hold the feed.

Here's How

Step 1

No Web Slices Found

2003 Training/Demos Help and How-to [RSS] (new)
2007 Training/Demos Help and How-to [RSS] (new)
Clip Crabby Office Lady [RSS] (new)

Step 2

5. Click Subscribe. The feed subscription is added.

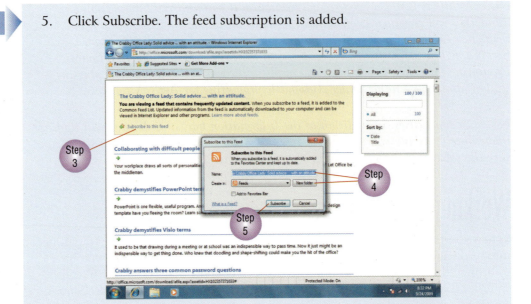

Note: *The Feed Headlines gadget gives you the ability to view news and sports headline feeds outside of Internet Explorer, right on the desktop. Choose the RSS feed to view from the gadget's options. You also can download additional gadgets for viewing feeds that you choose rather than the headline feeds made available by the default gadget. Refer to Chapter 6 for a review of working with gadgets.*

Reading a Feed

The Favorites Center where you list your favorite Web pages for easier access also is the location where you select and view RSS feeds.

> **Tip:** You can use a keyword search to find Web sites with feeds about a topic of interest. For example, search for *rss feeds: stocks* to find feeds about stocks and the stock market.
>
> Many Web sites display an *RSS* icon like the one in the IE command bar next to any link that leads to an RSS feed. Click the link, and then click Subscribe to This Feed, if desired, on the page that appears.

To display a subscribed feed:

1. Click the Favorites button on the Favorites bar, or press Alt+C.
2. Click the Feeds tab.
3. If needed, click the folder that holds the feed to display any subfolders.
4. Click the desired feed. The Favorites Center pane closes, and the feed page opens in Internet Explorer.

Exercise 6

Setting Up an RSS Feed

1. Click the Home button on the command bar to return to the home page.
2. If needed, click or drag over the URL in the Address bar to select it.
3. Type money.cnn.com, and press Enter. The CNNMoney.com Web site offers information about financial markets and personal finance. The View feeds on this page button on the IE command bar becomes active.
4. Click the View feeds on this page drop-down list arrow button, and then click *CNNMoney.com - Most Popular [RSS]*. This RSS feed delivers the most popular stories of the day for the site.
5. Click the Subscribe to this feed link on the page. Or click the Favorites button on the Favorites bar, and then click the Subscribe to this Feed button.
6. Edit the *Name* text box entry to read **CNNMoney Daily Favorites**, and click Subscribe. The feed subscription is added.
7. Click the Favorites button or press Alt+C.
8. Click the Feeds tab.
9. Capture a screen shot, paste it into Paint, and save the file as **C07E06S09**.
10. Click the Favorites button to redisplay the Favorites Center, click the Feeds tab, and then click the *CNNMoney Daily Favorites* feed.
11. Click Home on the command bar to redisplay the home page.
12. E-mail your screen shot to your instructor or submit it on your USB flash drive, as required.
13. Close Internet Explorer.

CHAPTER Summary

- The World Wide Web consists of HTML-formatted documents that can be viewed using a Web browser program connected to the Internet.

- The Internet Explorer Web browser is included as part of Windows 7. Start IE using the Start menu or a button on the taskbar. Close the IE window to close the program.

- The Internet Explorer window includes a command bar (toolbar) for selecting commands, as well as other features for navigating and browsing.

- A Web site's URL identifies its location on the Internet, including domain (Web site), folder, file name, and the communications protocol used to retrieve it.

- To go directly to a Web page, type its URL in the Address bar and press Enter.

- Click links or hyperlinks to browse between Web pages. Use the Back and Forward buttons to visit pages previously viewed during the current IE work session, and click the Home button on the command bar to redisplay the home page.

- Change to Compatibility View to display Web pages designed for earlier browsers if text, menus, or other objects appear out of place.

- The tabs feature enables you to have multiple Web pages open at once. Click the blank tab, type a URL in the Address bar, and press Enter to activate a new tab.

- Click a tab to view its contents.

- To search for information on the Web, type the search term(s) in the search box to the right of the Address bar, and then press Enter.

- Include quotation marks to search for an exact phrase, or use operators or keywords to make a search more specific.

- As you type a search term, search suggestions appear. Click a Search Suggestion to select a more detailed search.

- You can set up a visual search provider to enable the search suggestions list to display images and information as search suggestions.

- If you view a Web page often, you can add it to the Favorites bar or mark it as a favorite, which lists it in the Favorites Center. To view a favorite, click it on the Favorites bar or open the Favorites Center, click the Favorites tab, and click the favorite.

- Select content on a Web page and click the blue *Accelerator* icon to perform a task using that data.

- Subscribe to a Web Slice when you see the green Add Web Slices button on the command bar.

- If you want to reduce Internet connection time, view content offline by clicking the Tools button and then clicking *Work Offline*.

- The yellow Information bar pops up below the Web page tabs to alert you when a Web page wants to download active content to your system. Click the Information bar to see a list of choices for continuing.

- An RSS feed delivers specially formatted content to which frequent readers can subscribe.

- Use the *View feeds on this page* drop-down list on the Favorites bar, when it becomes active, to choose a feed. Then use the Subscribe to This Feed link to begin the subscription process.

- To view a feed to which you have previously subscribed, open the Favorites Center, click the Feeds button, and click the feed.

CONCEPTS Check

Completion: Answer the following questions on a blank sheet of paper.

Part 1

MULTIPLE CHOICE

1. The Web organizes information into _____ of information.
   a. blocks
   b. pages
   c. categories
   d. libraries

2. To start Internet Explorer, use the _____ .
   a. Start menu
   b. taskbar
   c. navigation pane
   d. Both a and c

3. URL stands for _____ .
   a. Uniform Resource Label
   b. Unisource Reform Location
   c. Uniform Resource Locator
   d. Under Radar Level

4. To go directly to a Web page, type its URL in the _____ and then press Enter.
   a. Address bar
   b. URL box
   c. navigation bar
   d. browse bar

5. A hyperlink on a Web page can be _____ .
   a. linked text
   b. a linked graphic
   c. a linked button
   d. Any item from a through c

6. Click the _____ and _____ buttons to view a Web page already viewed during the current Internet Explorer work session.
   a. Browse, Return
   b. Back, Forward
   c. Reverse, Continue
   d. Up, Down

7. The _____ feature enables you to open multiple Web pages in Internet Explorer.
   a. Pages
   b. Aero
   c. Tabs
   d. Reveal

8. A _____ enables you to find information on the Web.
   a. find bar
   b. navigation bar
   c. search monitor
   d. search engine

9. Use the _____ to return to a favorite Web page.
   a. Favorites Center
   b. Favorites Menu
   c. Favorites List
   d. Favorites Dialog Box

10. RSS stands for _____ .
    a. Random Statistic Service
    b. Really Simple Syndication
    c. Relative Service System
    d. Retrieving Statistics Service

SHORT ANSWER

11. What does HTML stand for?

    _____

12. What are hyperlinks in a hypertext document?

    _____

13. Describe how to open a Web page in a new tab.

    _____

14. Explain how to switch between open tabs.

    _____

15. What is a Search Suggestion?

    _____

16. Explain why you would mark a page as a favorite.

    _____

17. What is an Accelerator on a Web page?

    _____

18. What is the purpose of the Information bar?

    _____

19. Explain what an RSS feed is.

    _____

20. How do you know if a Web page that you have displayed has an RSS feed?

    _____

SKILLS Check

Save all solution files to the default Documents folder, or any alternate folder specified by your instructor.

Note: *If the Information bar appears at any point during these exercises, click the Close (X) button at the far-right end of the bar to close it.*

Guided Check

DISPLAY A WEB PAGE

1

1. Click the Internet Explorer button on the taskbar.
2. Display another Web page.
   a. Click in the Address bar. (Drag over the text there to select it if IE does not select the whole entry for you.)
   b. Type www.cnn.com.
   c. Press Enter.
   d. Take a screen shot of the desktop, paste the shot into Paint, and save it as **C07A01S02**.
3. Display another Web page.
   a. Click in the Address bar. (Drag over the text there to select it if IE does not select the whole entry for you.)
   b. Type www.senate.gov.
   c. Press Enter.
   d. Click the Compatibility View button.
   e. Take a screen shot of the desktop, paste the shot into Paint, and save it as **C07A01S03**.
4. Redisplay the home page by clicking the Home button on the IE command bar.
5. Click the window Close (X) button to close Internet Explorer.
6. Submit the screen shots via e-mail or on your USB flash drive to your instructor, as required.

BROWSING ON THE WEB

2

1. Click the Internet Explorer button on the taskbar.
2. Display another Web page.
   a. Click in the Address bar. (Drag over the text there to select it if IE does not select the whole entry for you.)
   b. Type www.wsj.com.
   c. Press Enter.
3. Browse on the page.
   a. Click the MarketWatch tab link near the top.
   b. Click the Personal Finance tab link, which is on the tab bar about one-third of the way down from the top of the page that appears.
   c. Take a screen shot of the desktop, paste the shot into Paint, and save it as **C07A02**.
   d. Click the Back button.
   e. Click the Forward button.
   f. Click the link for the lead story on the page.
4. Redisplay the home page. (Click the Home button on the IE command bar.)
5. Submit the screen shot via e-mail or on your USB flash drive to your instructor, as required.

Assessment 3 — USING WEB PAGE TABS AND WORKING OFFLINE

1. With IE still open, display another Web page.
   a. Click in the Address bar. (Drag over the text there to select it if IE does not select the whole entry for you.)
   b. Type www.moma.org.
   c. Press Enter.
2. Activate another tab and display a page in it.
   a. Click the New Tab button to the right of the active tab.
   b. If the Address bar contents are not selected automatically, click or drag to select them.
   c. Type www.guggenheim.org.
   d. Take a screen shot of IE with the multiple tabs open, paste the shot into Paint, and save it as **C07A03S02**.
3. Switch tabs.
   a. Click the tab for the MoMA page. The page becomes active.
   b. Take a screen shot of IE with the MoMA tab active, paste the shot into Paint, and save it as **C07A03S03**.
4. Close a tab.
   a. Click the Guggenheim Museum tab.
   b. Click the tab's Close (X) button to close the tab.
5. Redisplay the home page by clicking the Home button on the IE command bar.
6. Submit the screen shots via e-mail or on your USB flash drive to your instructor, as required.

Assessment 4 — SEARCHING THE WEB

1. Perform a broad search.
   a. Click in the search box.
   b. Type T Rex.
   c. Press Enter.
   d. Take a screen shot of the search results, paste the shot into Paint, and save it as **C07A04S01**.
2. Perform a more narrow search with an operator.
   a. Drag over the contents of the search box.
   b. Type "T Rex" NOT dinosaur AND band. This tells the search to eliminate results that exclude the word *dinosaur* but to ensure that matches do have the word *band*.
   c. Press Enter.
   d. Take a screen shot of the search results, paste the shot into Paint, and save it as **C07A04S02**.
3. Search for a particular type of content with a keyword.
   a. Drag over the contents of the search box.
   b. Type "T Rex" AND band contains:MP3. This tells the search to find results that include the word *band* and music files in the MP3 file format.
   c. Press Enter.
   d. Take a screen shot of the search results, paste the shot into Paint, and save it as **C07A04S03**.
4. Redisplay the home page by clicking the Home button on the IE command bar.
5. Submit the screen shots via e-mail or on your USB flash drive to your instructor, as required.

On Your Own

Assessment ## BROWSE AND USE TABS

5

1. Go to the www.nasa.gov Web site.
2. Click the NASA IN YOUR LIFE button.
3. Take a screen shot of the Web page, paste the shot into Paint, and save it as **C07A05S03**.
4. Click the Back button.
5. Right-click the MOON AND MARS button, and then click *Open in New Tab*. Click the new page tab if it does not activate on its own.
6. Take a screen shot of the Web page, paste the shot into Paint, and save it as **C07A05S06**.
7. Close the second tab.
8. Go to moneycentral.msn.com/detail/stock_quote.
9. Type MSFT in the *Name or symbol(s)* text box, and then click Go.
10. Wait at least five minutes, and then click the Refresh button to update the stock quote.
11. Redisplay the home page.
12. Submit the screen shots via e-mail or on your USB flash drive to your instructor, as required.

Assessment ## MARK AND USE FAVORITE SITES

6

1. Go to the cnet.com Web site. (Remember, in some cases you can skip typing the *www.* part of a URL.)
2. Save the site as a favorite in the Favorites Center, naming it CNET and placing it with a new folder named Computers that you create.
3. Go to the zdnet.com Web site.
4. Save the site as a favorite in the Favorites Center, naming it ZDNET and placing it in the Computers folder.
5. Open the Favorites Center, click the Favorites tab, and click the Computers folder.
6. Take a screen shot with the Favorites Center open, paste the shot into Paint, and save it as **C07A06**.
7. Use the Favorites Center to go to the CNET favorite page.
8. Use the Favorites Center to go to the ZDNET favorite page.
9. Redisplay the home page.
10. Submit the screen shot via e-mail or on your USB flash drive to your instructor, as required.

Assessment ## SUBSCRIBE TO AND VIEW A FEED

7

1. Use the Favorites Center to go to the ZDNET favorite you created in Assessment 6.
2. Click the News & Blogs choice in the navigation bar.
3. Browse to the page for a featured blogger under ZDNet Perspective at the right.
4. Click the View feeds on this page button on the command bar.
5. Click the Subscribe to this feed link, name the feed **ZD BLOGGER**, leave the Feeds folder selected, and click Subscribe.
6. Redisplay the home page.
7. Open the Favorites Center and click the Feeds tab.
8. Take a screen shot with the Favorites Center open, paste the shot into Paint, and save it as **C07A07**.

9. Use the Favorites Center to go to the ZD BLOGGER feed.
10. Redisplay the home page.
11. Submit the screen shot via e-mail or on your USB flash drive to your instructor, as required, and delete the subscribed feeds if requested to do so by your instructor.

Assessment **GROUP ACTIVITY: RESEARCH A TOPIC**

8

1. Pair off with another student to complete this project.
2. Select a topic that you want to research from another class or your job. For example, you might research a particular leader discussed in a history or political science class, or a particular plant species covered in a botany class.
3. Use Internet Explorer to find and print at least five Web pages covering the selected topic.
4. Write a paragraph or two summarizing the key points in the pages you found and print your summary.
5. Label all the printouts with your names and submit them to your instructor, as required.

CHALLENGE Project

You are the IT manager for a small company, and you need to purchase some new notebook computers with the Windows 7 operating system. Use Internet Explorer to find an online computer retailer, and select a notebook model to purchase. Take a screen shot of the Web page with the model and price for the system, saving it as **C07A09S01**. Now, find three other sites offering the same model or one with comparable features, and take screen shots of the Web pages with those systems and prices, saving the files as **C07A09S02**, **C07A09S03**, and **C07A09S04**. Submit the screen shots via e-mail or on your USB flash drive to your instructor, as required.

CHAPTER 8

Ensuring Your Safety and Privacy on the Internet

PERFORMANCE OBJECTIVES

Upon successful completion of Chapter 8, you will be able to:

- Adjust Internet Explorer security settings
- Manage Web site logons
- Configure privacy preferences
- Protect the system with Windows Firewall
- Protect against spyware with Windows Defender
- Select virus protection

The Internet is a wonderful resource, but it also poses some hazards. Hackers can take control of your system, your data can be destroyed or stolen, and your PC can be damaged by malicious programs such as viruses and malware. Windows 7 protects you from many of these hazards via several built-in utility programs.

Evaluating Your System's Overall Security Status

Throughout this chapter you will learn about the various security measures Windows 7 provides for your protection. The Action Center offers an overview of the statuses of each of these utilities and provides easy-to-use buttons for enabling any of them that are not currently operational.

To view the Action Center, click Start, and then *Control Panel*. Then click *Review your computer's status*. There are two categories: Security and Maintenance. Any unresolved issues appear beneath a category heading. For example, in Figure 8.1, there are two Maintenance issues that need resolution: Set up backup and System Maintenance. For a quick fix, you can click the button for one of the items. For example, under System Maintenance in Figure 8.1, you could click Perform system maintenance. Postpone making any fixes yet, though, because the rest of the chapter details how you cannot only enable but also fine-tune the settings of the various utilities.

Clicking the Expand button (down pointing arrow) for a category expands it to reveal what exactly is included and what the statuses of the various utilities are. For example, in Figure 8.1, the Maintenance category has been expanded to reveal, among other things, that Check for solutions to problem reports is turned on.

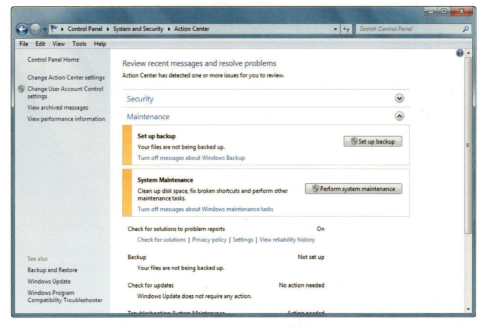

Figure 8.1   Examine the system's overall security status in the Action Center.

Adjusting Internet Explorer Security Settings

Internet Explorer (IE) requires security because some Web pages run applications that can potentially harm your PC, make unwanted changes to its settings, or compromise your data. The security settings in Internet Explorer help minimize those risks by specifying what types of programs Web pages can run and under what circumstances.

Configuring Internet Security Zones

Internet Explorer classifies all Web sites (and HTML-based local content, such as a Web page stored on a local area network) in one of four zones. Each zone can be separately configured for security:

- **Internet.** The standard setting, used unless otherwise specified.

- **Local intranet.** Pages on your local *intranet*.

- **Trusted sites.** Sites you have designated as safe, to be granted extra permissions.

- **Restricted sites.** Sites you have designated as unsafe, to receive extra restrictions.

  For each zone, there is a slider you can adjust to set a basic level, as shown in Figure 8.2. The settings available on the slider depend on the zone. For example, the lowest level of the Internet zone is Medium,

Intranet: A private network, usually within a company or organization, using the same types of content and the same protocols as the Internet

Selected zone

Figure 8.2   Set a security level for each of the four security zones.

because untested and untrusted sites are at that level. In contrast, the Trusted Sites zone can be set for any of several levels from High to Low. For each zone you can also click Custom Level to fine-tune the settings for the chosen level.

For each zone except Internet, you can click the Sites button to specify which sites—or which types of sites—will be included. You can optionally restrict the list (or not) to only *secure sites*—that is, sites that begin with https://, rather than http://. The rationale here is that only secure sites can be trusted to be what they appear to be, and therefore only secure sites should be subject to loosened security. However, if you need a specific non-secure site to have looser security in order to work properly, you might want to override that limitation.

Secure site: A Web site that uses a secure protocol, https://, rather than the usual http:// to ensure that the communication is not intercepted or hacked

All procedures in this section are from within Internet Explorer.

Here's How

To adjust the basic security level for a zone:

1. From Internet Explorer, click Tools, *Internet Options*.
2. Click the Security tab.
3. Click the icon for the zone to configure.
4. Drag the slider up or down.
5. (Optional) Repeat Steps 3–4 for other zones.
6. Click OK.

QUICK FIX

The Slider Doesn't Appear
If the slider does not appear, it means that custom settings have been defined for that level; click Default Level to reset the custom settings and get the slider back.

To customize the security level for a zone:

1. From Internet Explorer, click Tools, *Internet Options*.
2. Click the Security tab.
3. Click the icon for the zone to configure.
4. Click Custom level.
5. Change any settings desired in the Security Settings dialog box.
6. Click OK.
7. (Optional) Repeat Steps 3–6 for other zones.
8. Click OK.

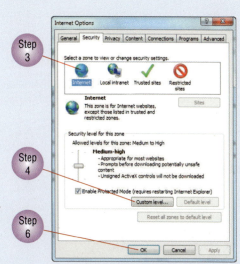

To specify sites to be included in a zone:

1. From Internet Explorer, click Tools, *Internet Options*.
2. Click the Security tab.
3. Click the icon for the zone to configure (Trusted Sites, Restricted Sites, or Local intranet).
4. Click Sites.
5. If you chose Local intranet in Step 3, click Advanced. This step is not necessary if you chose Restricted Sites or Trusted Sites.
6. Type a site in the *Add this website to the zone* text box.

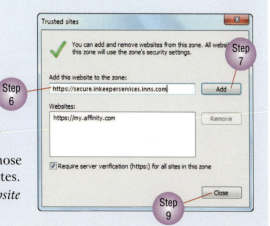

QUICK FIX

Server Verification
If the *Require server verification (https:) for all sites in this zone* check box is marked (available for Trusted Sites or Local intranet only), the Web site you enter in Step 6 must begin with https://, not http://. The "s" indicates that it is a secure site.

7. Click Add.
8. Repeat Steps 6–7 for additional sites, if needed.
9. Click Close.

Configuring the Pop-Up Blocker

Pop-up: An extra window that appears auto-matically as a result of a certain Web page being displayed

Pop-ups are extra windows that automatically open as a result of a certain Web page being displayed. Their use in Web design is controversial. Some sites use them to display useful information, but they are mostly used to display unwanted advertisements. Internet Explorer includes a built-in pop-up blocker that prevents most pop-ups from appearing.

When the pop-up blocker is on, you can temporarily allow pop-ups on a specific page by holding down the Shift key as you click the link that triggers the pop-up to appear. To permanently allow a certain site to use pop-ups, you can add it to the Exceptions list for the pop-up blocker.

After turning on the pop-up blocker, you can set a filter level:

- **High.** Blocks all pop-ups; hold down Ctrl+Alt to override.
- **Medium.** Blocks most pop-ups (the default).
- **Low.** Allows pop-ups from secure sites.

All procedures in this section are from within Internet Explorer.

To enable or disable the pop-up blocker (menu method):

- Click Tools, *Pop-up Blocker, Turn On Pop-up Blocker*.
  OR
- Click Tools, *Pop-up Blocker, Turn Off Pop-up Blocker*.

To enable or disable the pop-up blocker (dialog box method):

1. Click Tools, *Internet Options*.
2. Click Privacy.
3. Mark or clear the *Turn on Pop-up Blocker* check box.
4. Click OK.

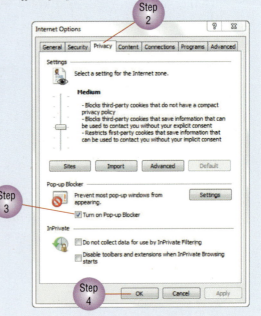

To configure the filtering level for the pop-up blocker:

1. Click Tools, *Pop-up Blocker*, *Pop-up Blocker Settings*.
2. Open the *Blocking level* list and choose a level of blocking (Low, Medium, or High).
3. Click Close.

To allow pop-ups from a certain site:

1. Click Tools, *Pop-up Blocker*, *Pop-up Blocker Settings*.
2. Type the address of the site in the *Address of website to allow* text box.
3. Click Add.
4. Repeat Steps 2–3 for other sites, if needed.
5. Click Close.

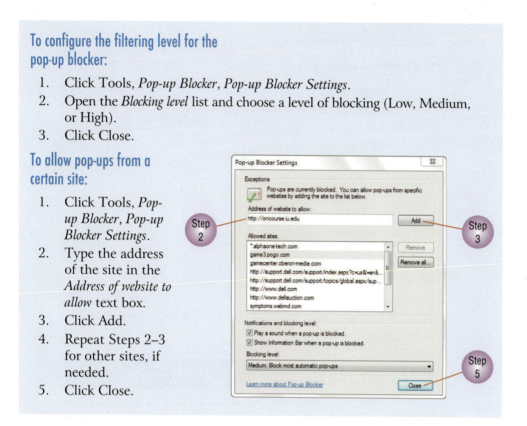

Enabling or Disabling the SmartScreen Filter

The **SmartScreen filter** is a built-in safety check for known-unsafe Web sites—in other words, sites that are set up to harm your computer or violate your privacy. One of the most common types of unsafe sites is a phishing site. *Phishing* is a trick whereby someone sends an e-mail or directs you to a Web site that simulates a legitimate one, usually one that requires the user to log on and provides financial transactions, such as PayPal or the Web site of a bank. Unsuspecting users type their user names and passwords into this fake Web site, which then harvests that information and uses it to steal money.

A phishing site usually has telltale signs that indicate it is not legitimate, such as URLs that do not match the underlying link, failure to show your correct user name, and so on. Experienced users can look for these signs themselves, but Internet Explorer includes a phishing filter that looks for these indicators automatically and warns you if a site appears to be a phishing site.

SmartScreen compares the address of the site you are browsing to a list of known-dangerous sites that Microsoft maintains online, and if it is found to be dangerous, it alerts you and blocks the site from displaying. You can leave SmartScreen automatic site checking turned on, or you can have Internet Explorer check individual sites that you suspect on an as-needed basis.

Phishing: Using a fake Web site or e-mail to steal username and password information

To turn off automatic SmartScreen filtering:

1. Choose Safety, *SmartScreen Filter, Turn Off SmartScreen Filter*.

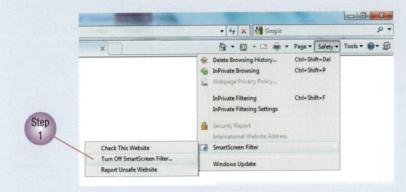

2. Click OK.

Tip: The SmartScreen Filter command is also available from the menu bar's Tools menu (but not from the Tools button's menu). To display the menu bar, press the Alt key.

To turn on automatic screening:

1. Choose Safety, *SmartScreen Filter, Turn On SmartScreen Filter*.
2. Click OK.

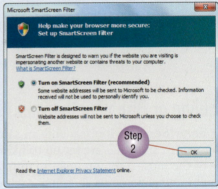

To check a Web site (if automatic screening is off):

1. Choose Safety, *SmartScreen Filter, Check this Website*.
2. If a confirmation appears, click OK.
3. When the results appear, click OK.

To completely disable the SmartScreen filter:

1. Choose Tools, *Internet Options*.
2. Click the Advanced tab.
3. Scroll down to the *Security* section.
4. Clear the *Enable SmartScreen Filter* check box.
5. Click OK.

Managing Your Stored Logon Information

When you enter logon information at a Web site, Internet Explorer asks if you want it to remember that information. That way when you revisit the same Web site, it fills in your username and password automatically, saving you time.

The Credential Manager feature in Windows 7 enables you to modify or delete those stored logons to prevent others who might be using your computer from gaining access to those secure Web sites. It is available from the Control Panel, under User Accounts and Family Safety. From the Credential Manager you can manage individual saved logons, or back up or restore all your logons at once.

> **Tip:** To easily move all your logons from one PC to another, back them up to a USB flash drive, take them to the other PC, and then restore them in Credential Manager there.

To delete stored logon information

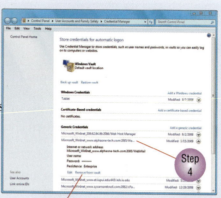

Here's How

1. Click Start, and then click *Control Panel*.
2. Click User Accounts and Family Safety.
3. Click Manage Windows Credentials
4. Click the stored logon to delete. Its listing expands.
5. Click Remove from Vault.
6. Click Yes.

Step 4

Step 5

To edit stored logon information

1. Click Start, and then click *Control Panel*.
2. Click User Accounts and Family Safety.
3. Click Manage Windows Credentials.
4. Click the stored logon to edit. Its listing expands.
5. Click Edit.
6. Retype the user name and password.
7. Click Save.

Step 6

Step 7

To back up all stored logon information

1. Click Start, and then click *Control Panel*.
2. Click User Accounts and Family Safety.
3. Click Manage Windows Credentials.
4. Click Back Up Vault.
5. Click Browse, and select a storage location.
6. Type a file name in the File name box, and click Save.
7. Click Next.
8. Press Ctrl+Alt+Delete.
9. Type and retype a password for the backup.
10. Click Next.
11. Click Finish.

To restore backed-up logon information

1. Click Start, and then click *Control Panel*.
2. Click User Accounts and Family Safety.
3. Click Manage Windows Credentials.
4. Click Restore Vault.
5. Click Browse, select the file containing the backup, and click Open.
6. Click Next.

7. Press Ctrl+Alt+Delete.
8. Type the password for the backup.
9. Click Next.
10. Click Finish.

Exercise 1

Configuring Internet Explorer Security

1. On a blank piece of paper or in a Word document, write your name and write or save the file as **C08E01**.
2. Display the Action Center, and evaluate your PC's current security status. Record any issues you find. Close the Action Center window when you are finished.
3. Set the security settings for the Internet zone to Medium-High:
   a. Start or switch to Internet Explorer, then choose Tools, *Internet Options*.
   b. Click the Security tab.
   c. Click *Internet*.
   d. Drag the slider to Medium-High if not already at that setting.
   e. Click OK.
4. Turn off the pop-up blocker in Internet Explorer:
   - Choose Tools, *Pop-up Blocker*, *Turn off Pop-up Blocker*. If the Pop-up Blocker warning dialog box appears, click Yes.
5. Navigate to a Web site that uses pop-ups. For example, try www.popuptest.com and click one of the pop-up test hyperlinks there.
6. Record the URL of the Web site you tested on your paper or in your Word document, and record whether the pop-up(s) were blocked.
7. Close the pop-up window(s) if any opened, but keep the original popuptest window open.
8. Turn on the pop-up blocker in Internet Explorer.
9. Reload the page by pressing F5, and then click on a pop-up link to retest. Observe whether the pop-up window reappears.
10. Record whether the pop-up(s) were blocked.
11. Visit a known phishing site. You can find a list of recently identified phishing sites at www.phishtank.com.
12. Choose Safety, *SmartScreen Filter*, *Check this Website*, and click OK.
13. Record the URL, and whether Internet Explorer identified it as a phishing site.
14. If a message appears that the site is not a reported phishing site, do the following:
    a. Click OK.
    b. Choose Tools (menu, not button), *SmartScreen Filter*, *Report Unsafe Website*. Press Alt to display the menu bar if needed.
    c. Mark the *I think this is a phishing website* check box.
    d. Type the characters shown in the picture.
    e. Click Submit.
    f. Close the browser window.
15. Submit your paper or Word document to your instructor for grading.

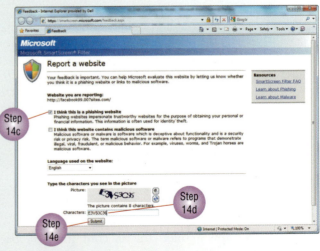

Configuring Privacy Preferences

Whereas security settings help protect your PC and data from harm, privacy settings keep your data safe from anyone who might want to snoop. This is especially useful on PCs that multiple people share.

Note: *When you log on to the local PC with a different user name, Internet Explorer's history, cookies, and AutoComplete settings are all stored separately, so it is not necessary to take privacy precautions to prevent one user from accessing another user's Internet usage information. You may find it easier to simply log on as a different user than to clear all the settings described here.*

Blocking and Allowing Cookies

Cookies are small plain text files stored on your hard disk to keep track of your settings for certain Web sites. For example, when you shop for items at an online store, the information about the items in your shopping cart are stored in a cookie until you are ready to check out. Web sites that use cookies create them automatically for you as needed. A cookie can be either a session cookie or a persistent one. A *session cookie*, also called a *temporary cookie,* is deleted when you close the browser window; a *persistent cookie*, also called a *saved cookie,* remains on your hard disk indefinitely, and usually stores logon information to help a Web site identify a return visitor.

Cookies: Small plain text files that store your settings for certain Web sites

Session cookie: A cookie that is automatically deleted when the browser window is closed

Persistent cookie: A cookie that remains on your hard disk indefinitely

A cookie can be read only by the Web site that created it, so there is little risk of anyone gathering any information about you remotely by browsing your cookies online. However, other local users on the PC can potentially browse cookies simply by opening the cookie files in Notepad. (Cookie files have .txt extensions.)

Note: *Internet Explorer can operate without cookies, but many Web sites will not display correctly, especially those involving buying and selling.*

Cookies can be either first-party or third-party. A *first-party cookie* is one that has been created by the Web site you are viewing. A *third-party cookie* is one created by an advertisement on the Web site you are viewing, owned by some other company and used to track your Web usage for marketing purposes. Third-party cookies are less likely to be useful to you.

First-party cookie: A cookie placed on your hard disk by the Web site you are visiting

Third-party cookie: A cookie placed on your hard disk by an advertisement on a Web site you are visiting

Anyone with access to your PC can look inside cookie files to gather information you have entered at various Web sites, such as your user name and password to access those sites. You can prevent this by deleting the cookie files and then preventing cookies from being saved in the future. However, you will not automatically be logged onto those Web sites anymore when visiting them if the cookies no longer exist, and some Web sites will not work if you do not allow cookies.

You can optionally choose to retain the cookies for Web sites that are on your Favorites list, while deleting all other cookies. This enables you to retain data for sites you use often while still preserving your privacy for other sites.

►

To delete existing cookies:

1. From Internet Explorer, choose Tools, *Internet Options*.
2. Click the General tab.
3. Under *Browsing history*, click Delete.
4. (Optional) Mark the *Preserve Favorites website data* check box.
5. Make sure the *Cookies* check box is marked.
6. Click Delete.
7. Click OK.

QUICK FIX

Returning to Default
To return to the default settings, you can click the Default button on the Privacy tab.

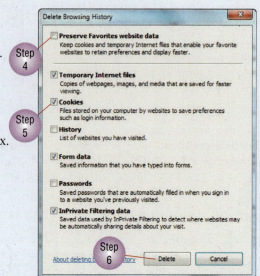

To specify a cookie-handling policy:

1. From Internet Explorer, choose Tools, *Internet Options*.
2. Click the Privacy tab.
3. Drag the Settings slider up or down.
4. (Optional) To override default cookie handling:
   a. Click Advanced.
   b. Click *Override automatic cookie handling*.
   c. In the First-party Cookies section, click a setting.
   d. In the Third-party Cookies section, click a setting.
   e. Mark or clear the *Always allow session cookies* check box.
   f. Click OK.
5. (Optional) To block or allow cookies from a certain Web site:
   a. Click Sites.
   b. Type the address of the site.
   c. Click Block, or click Allow.
   d. Repeat Steps a–c for another site, if needed.
   e. Click OK.
6. Click OK.

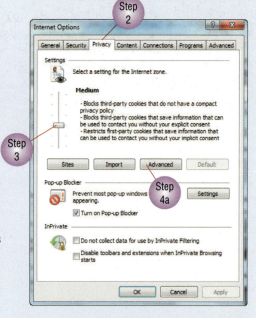

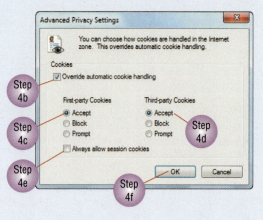

Using InPrivate Browsing

InPrivate browsing is a mode in Internet Explorer 8 that enables you to browse Web sites in privacy. When using this mode, Internet Explorer does not retain any information about the browsing in cookies, history, or temporary Internet files, so someone snooping at your computer for information about your browsing habits would not find anything.

When you activate InPrivate browsing, a new IE window opens up for the private session. The Address bar shows an InPrivate indicator (Figure 8.3) to remind you of the mode you are using. A message about InPrivate browsing also appears.

Figure 8.3 **A new InPrivate Browsing window.**

To open an InPrivate Browsing Window:

1. From Internet Explorer, choose Safety, *InPrivate Browsing*.
2. Enter the address of the page you want to display into the Address bar and press Enter.

Here's How

Using InPrivate Filtering

As you browse Web pages that contain ads, sometimes those ads have codes in them that track your online usage and send information back to their sponsors. Large ad companies may have ads on hundreds of different sites, and they gather data whenever the same computer accesses more than one of their sites. This enables the ad companies to figure out, among other things, what site content people tend to have in common. For example, if they notice that a high percentage of people who shop for office supplies also shop for sporting goods, they might run extra ads for office supplies on a sporting goods client's site. The information that these advertisers gather from you does not contain personally identifiable data; it works in aggregate with data from thousands of other people. However, some people prefer to block their Web usage from being sent to the advertisers.

The feature in IE 8 that allows you to block advertisers from gathering data on you is called **InPrivate Filtering**. When you turn on InPrivate Filtering, IE refers to an internal list of advertisers that it maintains; if a page you display contains an ad from that company, IE prevents the display of that ad from triggering any information being sent to the advertiser. You can turn InPrivate Filtering on and off, and you can also control the list of advertisers, blocking or allowing individual ones.

You can also specify how many different sites that you visit an advertiser has to be linked in with for the InPrivate Filtering feature to take effect. The default is 10, but you can set this at anywhere between 3 and 30. The lower the number, the more advertising companies will be blocked.

Here's How

To turn InPrivate filtering on or off

From Internet Explorer, choose Safety, *InPrivate Filtering*.

To control which advertisers are affected by InPrivate filtering

1. From Internet Explorer, choose Safety, *InPrivate Filtering Settings*.
2. Click *Choose content to block or allow*.
3. Click an individual advertiser.
4. Click Block or Allow.
5. Repeat steps 3–4 for other advertisers.
6. (Optional) Increment the number up or down for the *Show content from providers used by this number of websites you've visited* setting.
7. Click OK.

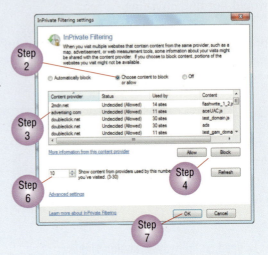

Clearing the History and Other Personal Information

To make it easier to use the Web, Internet Explorer stores a variety of personal information on your hard disk:

- **Temporary Internet files.** Copies of Web pages, images, and media that are cached from previous viewing for quicker reloading of pages.

- **Cookies.** Text files containing settings specific to a Web site, covered earlier in this chapter.

- **History.** A list of the pages you have visited, so you can return to a page even if you have forgotten its address as long as you remember what day you accessed it.

- **Form data.** Information you have typed into Web-based forms, accessible via drop-down lists in form fields.

- **Passwords.** Passwords you have stored for accessing secure sites.

- **InPrivate Filtering Data.** Information about which advertisers have ads at sites you have visited, used to determine InPrivate Filtering settings (covered earlier in this chapter).

If you like, you can exclude data from Web sites that are on your Favorites list from deletion. This enables you to clear the data for most sites but still retain the passwords and quick-loading capabilities for sites you use most often.

You can clear any of this information at any time so that others who use your computer will not be able to access it. You can also tell Internet Explorer how many days of history it should store. The default is 20 days.

Note: *To view the browsing history, choose View, Explorer Bars, History, or press Ctrl+Shift+H.*

To clear personal information:

1. Choose Safety, *Delete Browsing History* or press Ctrl+Shift+Delete.
2. (Optional) If you want to preserve stored data for sites on your Favorites list, mark the *Preserve Favorites website data* check box.
3. Mark the check box for the types of content you want to delete.
4. Click Delete.

To specify the number of days of history to store:

1. From Internet Explorer, choose Tools, *Internet Options*.
2. Click the General tab.
3. In the *Browsing History* section, click Settings.
4. In the *Days to keep pages in history* section, enter a number of days.
5. Click OK.
6. Click OK.

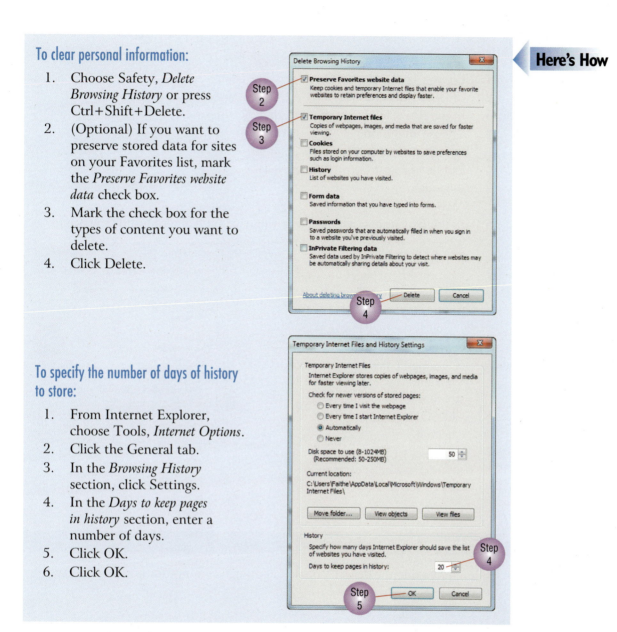

Temporary Internet files can take up a substantial amount of space on the hard disk, but they can make pages that you have previously accessed load faster. You can control the amount of caching that is done and how often Internet Explorer checks for a new version of the pages by clicking the Settings button on the General tab of the Internet Options dialog box. See Figure 8.4. You can also change the location where such pages are stored (by default it is in C:\Users*username*\AppData\Local\Microsoft\Windows\Temporary Internet Files), and you can view the files and other objects that are stored.

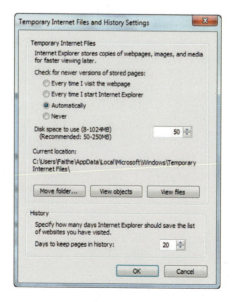

Figure 8.4 You can specify the amount of caching of temporary Internet files.

Here's How ▶ **To specify caching settings for temporary Internet files:**

1. Choose Tools, *Internet Options*.
2. Click the General tab.
3. In the *Browsing History* section, click Settings.
4. Choose an option:
   Every time I visit the webpage
   Every time I start Internet Explorer
   Automatically
   Never
5. In the *Disk space to use* box, type the maximum amount of disk space to use for cached pages.
6. (Optional) To change the location where pages are cached:
   a. Click Move folder.
   b. In the *Browse for Folder* box, click the new location.
   c. Click OK.
7. (Optional) Click View objects or View files to view the currently stored temporary files.
8. Click OK.
9. Click OK.

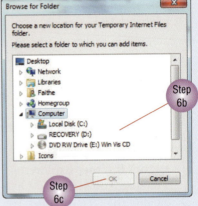

Step 6b

Step 6c

Exercise 2

Configuring Internet Explorer Privacy

1. In Internet Explorer, override the default cookie handling to prompt for both first-party and third-party cookies:
   a. Choose Tools, *Internet Options*.
   b. Click the Privacy tab.
   c. Click Advanced.
   d. Mark the *Override automatic cookie handling* check box, if not already marked.
   e. Under First-party Cookies, click *Prompt*.
   f. Under Third-party Cookies, click *Prompt*.
   g. Click OK.
   h. Click OK.
2. Navigate to a site that uses cookies. Use a site designated by your instructor, or use www.msn.com.
3. When the Privacy Alert window opens, capture a screen shot of the window, and save it as **C08E02S03**. Click Allow Cookie as many times as prompted to do so.
4. Change the cookie handling settings so that automatic cookie handling is no longer overridden:
   a. Choose Tools, *Internet Options*.
   b. Click the Privacy tab.
   c. Click Advanced.
   d. Clear the *Override automatic cookie handling* check box.
   e. Click OK.
   f. Click OK.

5. Delete all the temporary Internet files and cookies from your browser:
   a. Choose Tools, *Internet Options*.
   b. Click the General tab.
   c. Click Delete.
   d. Make sure the *Temporary Internet files* check box is marked.
   e. Click Delete.
   f. Click OK.

QUICK FIX

Allowing Cookies
If the Privacy Alert window reappears, mark the *Apply my decision to all cookies from this website* check box. And click Allow Cookie.

Protecting the System with Windows Firewall

Have you ever wondered how it is that your PC's Internet connection can deliver various types of content without getting confused? It always sends your e-mail to your e-mail program, Web pages to your browser, and so on. This works because each application—and in some cases each function within an application—uses a different port. A *port* is a numbered software channel that directs network input and output. For example, e-mail typically goes out on port 25 and comes in on port 110.

When a port is unused, any application can use it, and therein lies the security problem. Malicious programs can use unsecured ports to send commands to your system that compromise it. A *firewall* can prevent this from happening. Firewall software blocks port access requested by unknown programs, allowing only the programs you specify to get through. There are also hardware-based firewalls, especially in larger corporate networks.

The Windows Firewall is enabled by default, but on some systems it is turned off because it is not needed. This might be the case, for example, on a system with a third-party firewall program installed, or on a system connected to a network that has a hardware firewall solution installed. To check the firewall's status, view the Windows Firewall page of the Control Panel. (It's in the System and Security section.) In Figure 8.5, for example, the firewall is turned off. You can turn it back on again by clicking *Turn Windows Firewall on or off*, or by clicking *Use recommended settings*.

New in Windows 7, you can have separate firewall on/off settings for public versus private networks. In most cases you will probably want the firewall to remain on for both. A **public network** is one in which you don't know or trust all the other computer users, such as a public café. A **private network** is one in which you do trust the others, such as in a home office network.

Port: A numbered software channel that directs network input and output

Firewall: Software or hardware that prevents unauthorized access to ports

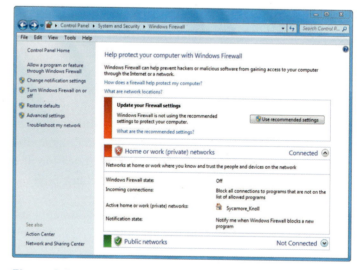

Figure 8.5 **Check the status of the Windows Firewall via the Control Panel.**

Here's How

To check the status of the Windows Firewall:
1. Click Start, and then click *Control Panel*.
2. Click System and Security.
3. Click *Check Firewall Status*.

Here's How ▶ **To turn the Windows Firewall on or off:**

> Note: *If you are using a third-party firewall program on your computer, you might not be able to complete these steps.*

1. Click Start, and then click *Control Panel*.
2. Click System and Security.
3. Click Windows Firewall.
4. Click *Turn Windows Firewall on or off*.
5. Under Home or Work Network Location Settings, click *Turn on Windows Firewall* or *Turn off Windows Firewall*.
6. Under Public Network Location Settings, click *Turn On Windows Firewall* or *Turn Off Windows Firewall*.
7. Click OK.

The Windows Firewall blocks incoming requests from connecting to your system except for programs that are specifically set up as exceptions. Windows sets up some programs as exceptions for you; you can fine-tune these settings on your own for more control. For each program or service, you can choose whether it should be allowed through the firewall for public and/or private networking. You can also add other programs to the list, and specify settings for them too.

Here's How ▶ **To allow a program through the firewall:**

1. Click Start, and then click *Control Panel*.
2. Click System and Security.
3. Under Windows Firewall, click *Allow a program through Windows Firewall*.
4. Click the Change Settings button.
5. Find the desired program on the list.
6. Mark or clear its *Home/Work (Private)* check box.
7. Mark or clear its *Public* check box.
8. If the program does not appear on the list, do the following:
   a. Click Allow another program.
   b. Click the desired program name.
   c. Click Network Location Types
   d. Mark or clear the check boxes as desired.
   e. Click OK. The program appears on the list now.
9. Click OK.

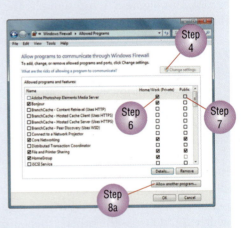

To prevent all incoming connections:

1. Click Start, and then click *Control Panel*.
2. Click Safety and Security.
3. Click Windows Firewall.
4. Click *Turn Windows Firewall on or off*.
5. For both Home/Private and Public networks, click *Block all incoming connections, including those in the list of allowed programs*.
6. Click OK.

QUICK FIX

Blocking All Incoming Connections
If the firewall is set to Off, the *Block all incoming connections* check box is not available. Click *On* to enable it.

Protecting against Spyware with Windows Defender

Windows Defender is a utility that protects your system against malware. *Malware* is a shortening of the term "malicious software," software that is designed to harm your computer in some way. Malware includes both spyware and adware. *Spyware* is software that secretly spies on your usage habits and collects information about you, sometimes including your passwords and credit card information, and sends it back to its owner. *Adware* is software that pops up ads or redirects your Web browser.

Windows Defender operates by comparing the installed programs, drivers, and other helper files against a list of known threats (definitions). It then removes or prompts you to confirm removal of any items it finds that could potentially cause your system harm.

Malware: A generic term meaning software designed to harm your computer in some way

Spyware: A type of malware that spies on your computer usage

Adware: A type of malware that pops up ads or redirects your Web browser

> Tip: Because Windows Defender is only as good as its most recent list of definitions, it is important to allow Windows Update to download and install the latest Windows Defender updates.

Windows Defender offers three types of protection:

- **Scans.** Windows Defender can be set for automatic system scans on a scheduled basis, and you can also manually initiate extra scans at any time.
- **Real-time protection.** Windows Defender monitors the system and alerts you when potentially unwanted software attempts to install itself or run, or when a program attempts to change an important Windows 7 setting.
- **SpyNet community.** If you choose to join this community, you can see how other people have responded to software that has not yet been classified for risk.

Windows Defender is available from the Control Panel, but is not assigned to any of the categories you see in Categories view. To find it, you must switch to the Large Icons or Small Icons view of the Control Panel.

To open Windows Defender (Control Panel method):

1. Click Start, and then click *Control Panel*.
2. In the upper right corner, click *Category*, opening a menu of views, then click *Large Icons*.
3. Click *Windows Defender*.

To open Windows Defender (Start menu method):

1. Click Start.
2. Type Defender. Windows Defender appears on the menu above the Start button.
3. Click *Windows Defender*.

Here's How

Performing a Windows Defender Scan

Windows Defender automatically scans your system according to a schedule you set up (covered later in this chapter), but you can also initiate an additional scan at any time that you suspect a problem. You can choose to run any of these three types of scans:

- **Quick Scan.** Scans only the locations on your hard disk that spyware is most likely to affect. Use this scan type on a routine basis.
- **Full Scan.** Scans all files on your hard disk and all currently running programs, but might make your computer run more slowly as it scans. Use this scan type when you suspect a problem.
- **Custom Scan.** Scans only certain drives and folders.

Here's How

To perform a quick scan:

1. Open Windows Defender if it is not already open.
2. In the toolbar of the Windows Defender window, click Scan.

To perform a full scan:

1. Open Windows Defender if it is not already open.
2. In the toolbar of the Windows Defender window, click the down arrow to the right of Scan.
3. Click *Full scan*.

To perform a custom scan:

1. Open Windows Defender if it is not already open.
2. In the toolbar of the Windows Defender window, click the down arrow to the right of Scan.
3. Click *Custom Scan*.
4. Click Select.
5. Click the check boxes for the locations to check.
6. Click OK.
7. Click Scan Now.

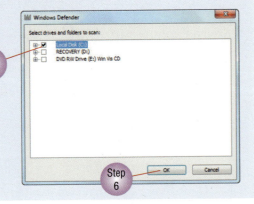

Joining the SpyNet Community

SpyNet is an online community of users. When you encounter an unknown threat, if you are a SpyNet member, your system sends information to the SpyNet database about how you responded to it. In return, you can see how other users responded to the same threat. This helps users learn from one another and helps Microsoft decide which threats are most common so they can develop solutions for them to incorporate into Windows Defender.

You can join Microsoft SpyNet at either a basic or an advanced level. At a basic level, the system takes care of threats automatically based on the best information available. At an advanced level, the system notifies you about unknown threats found and lets you decide how to handle them.

To join Microsoft SpyNet:

1. Open Windows Defender if it is not already open.
2. Click Tools.
3. Click Microsoft Spynet.
4. Click Join with a Basic Membership or Join with an Advanced Membership.
5. Click Save.

Here's How

Dealing with Threats Found by Windows Defender

When Windows Defender finds a potential threat, it classifies the threat in one of the ways listed in Table 8.1. Different levels of threat are subject to different default actions.

Table 8.1 **Windows Defender Alert Levels**

Alert Level	Explanation	What to do
Severe	A very harmful program that will damage your PC or compromise your security.	Remove this software immediately.
High	A program that might cause a system problem by changing a setting in Windows 7 or collecting your personal information.	Remove this software immediately.
Medium	A program that might make changes or compromise your privacy, but not necessarily.	Review the alert details to see where the software came from and why it is running. Then block or remove it if needed.
Low	A program that may collect information about you or change system settings, but only in agreement with the licensing terms it displayed when you installed it.	If you intended to install this software, it is probably benign. Check the alert details to make sure you recognize the program's name and publisher.
Not yet classified	Programs that are typically harmless unless they were installed without your knowledge.	If you recognize the software and trust its publisher, allow it to run. If you are a SpyNet community member, check the community ratings for this program to see what others have done.

Windows Defender warns you when a malware attack is occurring. You can choose to Remove All, Review, or Ignore.

If you click Review, information about the item appears. From there you can Remove All or Apply Actions. The latter refers to the action selected in the Action column in the upper part of the window.

When Windows Defender finds an unclassified threat, a message about it appears in the main Windows Defender window. Click Review and take action to get information about it.

Here's How ▶ **To review and respond to a threat from Windows Defender:**

1. Click Review and take action.
2. Read the information about the threat.
3. In the Action column, open the drop-down list and choose *Deny* or *Permit*.
4. Click Apply Actions.
5. Close the Windows Defender window.

Scheduling Automatic Scans

You can adjust the way Windows Defender automatically scans your system for threats. By default, it scans once a day at 2:00 a.m., checks for updated definitions before scanning, and applies default actions to items it detects during the scan.

Here's How ▶ **To schedule an automatic scan:**

1. Start Windows Defender.
2. Click Tools.
3. Click *Options*.
4. Make sure the *Automatically scan my computer* check box is marked.
5. (Optional) Adjust the Frequency, Approximate time, and Type settings.
6. Make sure the *Check for updated definitions before scanning* check box is marked.
7. At the left, click Default actions.
8. Make sure *Apply recommended actions* is marked.

   Note: *You can define the default actions for High, Medium, and Low alert items, but in most cases it is best to leave them set at the Default action, so that Windows Defender can take action based on what the definition files recommend.*

9. Click Save.

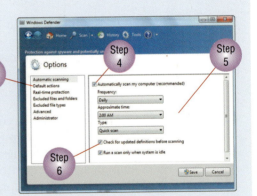

Exercise 3

1. Open the Windows Firewall Settings dialog box:
   a. Choose Start, *Control Panel*.
   b. If not already in Category view, set View By to Category.
   c. Click System and Security.
   c. Click *Check firewall status*.
2. Make sure the Windows Firewall is turned on. If it is not:
   a. Click *Turn Windows Firewall on or off*.
   b. Click *Turn On Windows Firewall* in the Home or work network location settings and the Public network location settings sections.
   c. Click OK.
3. Click *Allow a program or feature through Windows Firewall*.
4. Mark the check box in the Public column for *Windows Media Player*.
5. Look on the Start/All Programs menu for a program that does not appear on the list of allowed programs and features.
6. Add this program to the Exceptions list:
   a. Click Add program.
   b. Click the desired program.
   c. Click Add.
7. Capture a screen shot of newly added program on the list, and save it as **C08E03S07**.
8. Close the Windows Firewall Settings dialog box and the Control Panel.
9. Open Windows Defender and do a quick scan:
   a. Open the Start menu and type Defender, and then click the shortcut for Windows Defender to run it.
   b. Click the Scan button.
10. When the scan is completed, review and respond to any threats found. If you found any threats, take a screen shot of the information for one of them and save it as **C08E03S10**. If it found nothing, take a screen shot of the screen telling you that no threats were found.
11. Submit your screen captures to your instructor for grading.

Considering Virus Protection

A *virus* is a self-replicating, self-spreading malicious program that moves from one executable file to another. A related threat, called a *worm*, is similar but moves from PC to PC, infecting the PC itself rather than any individual file. Both can cause your system to behave strangely, to slow down, to delete files, and even to stop working altogether.

Windows 7 comes with almost every utility you need to keep your system safe, but there is one exception: it lacks antivirus software. Therefore, you will need to purchase (or acquire for free) a third-party virus protection package to install.

Microsoft offers a free program called Microsoft Security Essentials that you can download and install from http://www.microsoft.com/Security_essentials. It provides virus protection as well as spyware and malware protection, and because it is a Microsoft product, it works seamlessly with the Windows 7 utilities and features.

If you prefer a more full-featured antivirus solution, consider a third-party antivirus or full-system security product. However, not all antivirus programs are compatible with Windows 7, so carefully read the system requirements on the box of the program you are considering, or look up the system requirements online. Following are some products that are designed for Windows 7:

Virus: A self-replicating malicious program that spreads from one executable file to another

Worm: A self-replicating malicious program that spreads from one PC to another, infecting the PC itself rather than any individual file

- Norton Antivirus (www.symantec.com)
- McAfee VirusScan (www.mcafee.com)
- CA Anti-Virus (www.ca.com)
- F-Secure Anti-Virus for Windows 7 (www.f-secure.com)
- AVG Anti-Virus (www.grisoft.com)
- Trend Micro AntiVirus (www.trendmicro.com)

CHAPTER Summary

- To display the Windows Action Center, open the Control Panel and click System and Security, and then click Action Center.
- There are four security zones for Internet Explorer: Internet, Local intranet, Trusted sites, and Restricted sites. From inside Internet Explorer, click Tools, *Internet Options* and click the Security tab to configure them.
- To enable or disable the pop-up blocker in Internet Explorer, choose Tools, *Pop-up Blocker, Turn on (off) Pop-up Blocker*. You can also block pop-ups from a certain site (Tools, *Pop-up Blocker, Pop-up Blocker Settings*).
- A phishing site pretends to be a legitimate Web site in order to steal personal information. To check a Web site for phishing, choose Safety, *SmartScreen Filter, Check this Website*.
- Manage your stored logon information for various Web sites with the Credential Manager. Access it from the Control Panel's User Accounts and Family Safety section.
- Cookies are small plain text files stored on your hard disk to keep track of your settings for certain Web sites. They are necessary for some pages to operate properly.
- Session (temporary) cookies last only as long as the browser window is open; persistent (saved) cookies carry over between sessions. First-party cookies are created by the Web site being viewed. Third-party cookies are created by ads on the page.
- To delete existing cookies from IE, choose Tools, *Internet Options*, and on the General tab, under Browsing History, click Delete, mark the *Cookies* check box, and click Delete.
- Cookie handling policy is set on the Privacy tab by dragging the Settings slider up or down.
- An InPrivate browsing session retains no information about your browsing habits. To open one, choose Safety, InPrivate Browsing or press Ctrl+Shift+P.
- InPrivate filtering prevents bulk advertisers from receiving information about your browsing habits. To turn it on or off, choose Safety, InPrivate Filtering or press Ctrl+Shift+F.
- To clear personal information from IE, choose Tools, *Internet Options*, and on the General tab, in the Browsing History section, click Delete. Mark the *History* check box, and any other check boxes desired, and click Delete.
- A firewall blocks port access requested by unknown programs to keep hackers out of your system. The Windows Firewall is enabled by default. To check its status, choose Start, *Control Panel*, System and Security, *Windows Firewall*.

- Windows Defender protects your system against spyware and adware. It scans for existing threats and provides real-time protection.
- To run a Windows Defender scan, open Windows Defender, either from the Control Panel (Large Icons or Small Icons view) or from the Start menu (type Defender to find it). Then click Scan.
- Windows 7 does not come with virus protection, but many third-party programs are available that will provide it.

CONCEPTS Check

Completion: Answer the following questions on a blank sheet of paper or in a Word document.

Part 1

MULTIPLE CHOICE

1. What does the Action Center do in Windows 7?
   a. Suggests system maintenance actions you can take to improve your system.
   b. Reports spyware and adware alerts.
   c. Reports viruses detected.
   d. All of the above.

2. What does it mean if there is no slider shown on the Security tab in the Internet Options dialog box?
   a. Custom settings have been specified for the chosen zone.
   b. Cookies have been disabled.
   c. There are no current security threats.
   d. You are logged on as a Standard user and therefore cannot make security changes.

3. A secure Web site is one that begins with _____ rather than http://.
   a. ftp://
   b. smtp://
   c. https://
   d. shttp://

4. If a Web site creates its own cookie on your hard disk, such as a merchant site creating a shopping cart cookie for you, it is considered a _____ cookie.
   a. first-party
   b. provisional
   c. third-party
   d. residual

5. From which tab of the Internet Options dialog box do you delete cookies?
   a. General
   b. Security
   c. Privacy
   d. Advanced

6. From which tab of the Internet Options dialog box do you specify a cookie-handling policy?
   a. General
   b. Security
   c. Privacy
   d. Advanced

7. What does Windows Defender protect your system from?
   a. Port hacking
   b. Malware
   c. Viruses
   d. UAC

8. Windows Defender is able to protect your system against the latest threats because Windows Update regularly downloads the latest _____ .
   a. definitions
   b. kernels
   c. INIT files
   d. backups

9. What does a Full Scan do in Windows Defender that a Quick Scan does not?
   a. Scans each location more rigorously.
   b. Scans more locations.
   c. Connects to the Internet to get the latest scan information.
   d. All of the above.

10. What is the one type of threat that Windows 7 does *not* include protection for?
    a. Firewall attacks
    b. Spyware
    c. Viruses
    d. Malware

Part 2 — SHORT ANSWER

11. What are the two categories in the Windows Action Center?

    _____

12. What are the four security zones for Internet Explorer?

    _____

13. What is phishing and how can it be harmful to a user?

    _____

14. What is the difference between a session cookie and a saved cookie?

    _____

15. What are the pros and cons of regularly deleting temporary Internet files from your hard disk?

    _____

16. What kind of danger does a firewall protect your computer from?

    _____

17. Why is it important to use Windows Update regularly to get updates for Windows Defender?

_____

18. What is the difference between spyware and adware?

_____

19. What is the SpyNet community and what is the advantage of joining it?

_____

20. Name three antivirus programs that you could use with Windows 7.

_____

SKILLS Check

Save all solution files to the default Document folder, or any alternative folder specified by our instructor.

Guided Check

Assessment **EXPERIMENTING WITH COOKIES**

1

1. On a blank piece of paper, write your name and C08A01, or in a Word document, type your name and save the file as **C08A01**.
2. Delete all cookies and temporary Internet files.
   a. Choose Tools, *Internet Options*.
   b. Click the General tab.
   c. Click Delete.
   d. Mark the Temporary Internet Files and Cookies check boxes.
   e. Click Delete.
   f. Click OK.
3. Block any future cookies from being stored on your PC.
   a. Choose Tools, Internet Options.
   b. Click the Privacy tab.
   c. Click Advanced.
   d. Click *Override automatic cookie handling*.
   e. Set both first-party and third-party cookies to *Block*.
   f. Click OK.
   g. Click OK.
4. Visit the following Web page to test Internet Explorer's cookie acceptance, and click Continue:
   www.tempestech.com/cookies/cookietest1.asp.
   On your paper or in a Word document, record the message that appeared.

5. Set first-party and third-party cookies to Prompt:
   a. Choose Tools, *Internet Options*.
   b. Click the Privacy tab.
   c. Click Advanced.
   d. Set first-party and third-party cookies to *Prompt*.
   e. Click OK.
   f. Click OK.
6. Visit the following Web page to test Internet Explorer's cookie acceptance, and click Continue: www.tempestech.com/cookies/cookietest1.asp.
7. When a prompt appears, record the message in the prompt on your paper or in your Word document, and then click Allow Cookie. If the prompt repeats, click Allow Cookie again.
8. Locate a cookie on your hard disk that was saved by the cookie test you just performed. To do so, follow these steps:
   a. From an Explorer window, choose Organize, Folder and search options.
   b. Click the View tab.
   c. Click show hidden files, folders, and drives.
   d. Clear the hide protected operating system files check box.
   e. Click OK to close the dialog box.
   f. navigate to C:\users*username*\AppData\Roaming\Microsoft\Windows\Cookies\Low. where *username* is your Windows user name.
   g. Locate username@www.tempesttech.com.
9. Open the found cookie in Notepad, and record the contents of that file. Then close the file.
10. Return Internet Explorer to its default cookie-handling setting.
    a. Choose Tools, *Internet Options*.
    b. Click the Privacy tab.
    c. Click Advanced.
    d. Clear the *Override default cookie handling* check box.
    e. Click OK.
    f. Click OK.
11. Submit your paper or Word document to your instructor for grading.

Assessment 2 CLEARING AND VIEWING INTERNET EXPLORER HISTORY

1. In Internet Explorer, delete your browsing history.
   a. Choose Safety, *Delete Browsing History*.
   b. Mark the *History* check box and click Delete.
2. Visit at least five different Web sites of your choice.
3. View the browser history (Ctrl+Shift+H), and click *Today*.
4. Capture a screen shot of the history list showing only the sites you visited in Step 2, and save the file as **C08A02**. Submit it to your instructor for grading.
5. Delete the browsing history again, as in Step 1.

Assessment 3 EXPERIMENTING WITH POP-UP BLOCKER SETTINGS

1. In Internet Explorer, set the pop-up blocker filtering level to Low.
   a. Click Tools, *Pop-up Blocker, Pop-up Blocker Settings*.
   b. Open the Blocking level list and choose Low.
   c. Click Close.
2. Go to www.popuptest.com, click Multi-PopUp Test, and count the number of pop-ups that get through the pop-up blocker. Record the answer on a piece of paper or in a Word document named **C08A03**.

3. Set pop-up blocker filtering to Medium (see Step 1).
4. Repeat Step 2, and count the number of pop-ups. Record your answer.
5. Set the pop-up blocker filtering to High.
6. Repeat Step 2, and count the number of pop-ups. Record your answer.
7. Hold down Ctrl+Alt and repeat Step 2, and count the number of pop-ups. Record your answer.
8. Turn off the pop-up blocker entirely.
   a. Click Tools, *Internet Options*.
   b. Click Privacy.
   c. Clear the *Turn on Pop-up Blocker* check box.
   d. Click OK, and then click Yes in the Pop-up Blocker dialog box.
9. Repeat Step 2, and count the number of pop-ups. Record your answer.
10. Based on your experiments, write a short paragraph summarizing what you learned about pop-up blocking in Internet Explorer.
11. Submit your paper or Word document to your instructor for grading.

Assessment 4 PERFORMING A SCAN WITH WINDOWS DEFENDER

1. Start Windows Defender.
   • Choose Start, *All Programs, Windows Defender*.
2. Perform a custom scan that scans only your main hard disk (C).
   a. Click the down arrow next to Scan.
   b. Click *Custom Scan* and then click the Select button.
   c. Mark the check box for the *C* drive.
   d. Click OK.
   e. Click Scan Now.
3. While the scan is running, do a Web search on a product called Winfixer. What is this product? Is it spyware? What do experts recommend you do if it is on your system? Write your answers on a blank piece of paper or in a Word document named **C08A04**.
4. Describe the results of the Windows Defender scan. Did it find any threats? If so, how did you respond to them?
5. Submit your paper or Word document to your instructor for grading.

On Your Own

Assessment 5 LETTING A PROGRAM THROUGH THE FIREWALL

1. Identify a program installed on your system that accesses the Internet.

   Note: *Your instructor may tell you what program to use for this exercise. If not, choose any e-mail, Web, or FTP program, or any program that automatically updates itself over the Internet, such as an antivirus program.*

2. Determine whether this program is set up as an exception, able to bypass the Windows Firewall.
3. If the program is not yet set up as an exception, make it so.
4. Capture a screen shot of the Allow Programs to Communicate Through Windows Firewall screen with that program's check box marked. Save it as **C08A05** and submit it to your instructor for grading.

CONFIGURING THE TRUSTED SITES ZONE

1. For the Trusted Sites zone in Internet Explorer, customize the settings in the following ways:
   - Allow Scriptlets: Prompt
   - Download unsigned ActiveX controls: Prompt
   - Logon: Prompt for user name and password.
2. Identify a secure Web site that you trust.

   Note: *You can use any secure site—that is, one whose URL begins with https://. It can be an online store, a school site, or some other site. Your instructor may tell you which site to use. If you cannot find a secure site to use, use an unsecure site and clear the Require server verification check box so that Internet Explorer will allow it.*

3. Add that site to the Trusted Sites zone.
4. Capture a screen shot of the Trusted Sites dialog box with the added URL visible. Save it as **C08A06** and submit it to your instructor for grading.

TRACKING A PERSON'S INTERNET USAGE (PARTNER ACTIVITY)

1. Delete all browsing history information from Internet Explorer (all categories).
2. Visit at least five popular Web sites. At least one of the sites you visit should use cookies.
3. Switch PCs with a classmate.
4. Using the History, Cookies, and Temporary Internet Files on the PC, determine as much information as possible about the other person's browsing history.
5. Write a brief report on a piece of paper or in a Word document named **C08A07** summarizing the information you gathered in Step 4, and submit it to your instructor for grading.

EXPLORING OTHER MALWARE PROTECTION PROGRAMS

Windows Defender is only one of several anti-malware programs you can use. Others include Spybot Search & Destroy and Ad-Aware.

Using the Web, research the above-mentioned two programs, and find out:

- The program's cost (if not free).
- Whether there are multiple versions available (for example, a free version and a pay version).
- Whether it will work with Windows 7.
- The program's benefits over Windows Defender, if any.

CHALLENGE Project

Your supervisor has asked you to determine the most cost-effective virus protection solution for your company, which consists of 20 employees, each with their own Windows 7 PC.

Gather information about two or more brands of Windows 7-compatible virus protection programs. Write a one- or two-page report summarizing your findings.

Using Windows Live Mail

PERFORMANCE OBJECTIVES

Upon successful completion of Chapter 9, you will be able to:

- Understand how to get and install Windows Live Mail
- Start and exit Windows Live Mail
- Add an e-mail account
- Create and send a message
- Create a photo e-mail message
- Receive, read, and respond to a message
- Manage messages
- Handle junk mail
- Set up a signature to add to your messages
- Add, manage, and e-mail a contact
- Learn and get help about Microsoft software from newsgroups
- Track events with Calendar

Windows 7 enables you to take advantage of one of the most significant capabilities that the Internet has made widely available: e-mail. You can pound out an electronic message on your keyboard, send it, and within minutes (usually), it can travel across the room, country, or globe to its recipient. This chapter shows you how to use the Windows Live Mail e-mail program to send, receive, read, respond to, and organize messages. You will also learn how to work with junk mail, signatures, contacts, online newsgroups , and calendar features.

Starting and Exiting Windows Live Mail

E-mail: Short for "electronic mail," e-mail provides the ability to send and receive messages via a wired or wireless network, or more broadly, the Internet

Snail mail: Slang term for postal mail, derived from the fact that postal mail is very slow relative to e-mail

The ability to send *e-mail* messages over a network of computers emerged sometime during the mid-1960s. At that point, networks typically enabled communications within the organization's limited environment. When the Internet emerged as a widely available communications system during the 1990s, users could suddenly e-mail people other than colleagues on the company network. Customers could e-mail questions to businesses, friends could e-mail friends, partners from different companies could discuss a project with e-mail messages, and so on. Because e-mail messages typically arrive in a matter of minutes rather than the days or weeks required for postal mail (or *snail mail*, as it is now often called), e-mail, for the first time, made it possible for colleagues in different physical locations to work together in near-real time and for friends and family members to share information across the miles.

Sending e-mail today requires an Internet connection via an organization network or ISP. You also need to have an e-mail account with an ISP if one is not provided by another organization such as your school or employer. Many e-mail account providers enable access to e-mail via the Web and a Web browser, called **Web mail.** Web mail is convenient because it provides the ability to access e-mail from any computer with an Internet connection and browser, such as when using a computer at a library. The downsides to Web mail are that you have to be connected to the Internet to read the mail, which also slows the process; features offered by the Web mail site may be limited; and the provider may limit the amount of online storage provided with the account, meaning that you have to pay more to be able to store more e-mail online. For these reasons, most e-mail providers—even ones thought of as Web mail providers like Hotmail and Gmail— give you the option of retrieving and storing your e-mail on your system via an e-mail program. An e-mail program also provides the added benefit of enabling you to retrieve and store messages from multiple e-mail accounts in a single location.

Older versions of the Windows operating system included the Outlook Express e-mail program, but Windows Vista migrated to a new program called Windows Mail. Windows 7 no longer includes Windows Mail, but you download an updated free version called Windows Live Mail from download.live.com. When you start the download, you can click the Run button in the File Download – Security Warning dialog box to perform the download, and then Yes in the User Account Control dialog box after the download completes to start the install process. Choose the programs to install in the Windows Live window if it appears, click Install, and respond to any other prompts as needed during the install process.

Windows Live Mail enables you to compose, send, and receive messages; reply to and forward messages; file and manage messages; it also works with another program that enables you to store and retrieve recipient information.

Note: *Some operations require that Windows Live Mail be set up as the default e-mail program for your system. To set Windows Live Mail as the default e-mail program, click Start, and then Default Programs. In the Default Programs window, click Set your default programs. Click Windows Live Mail in the Programs list, click Set this program as default in the right pane, and then click OK. If the procedure for setting Windows Live Mail as the default e-mail program doesn't work correctly, it may mean that you have another e-mail program installed that is causing a conflict; try uninstalling that program to fix the problem.*

You can start Windows Live Mail using the Start menu. Click Start, and then click *Windows Live Mail* in the left pane of the Start menu. If the Windows Live Mail choice does not appear on the left pane of the Start menu, click *All Programs*, click *Windows Live*, and then click *Windows Live Mail* as shown in Figure 9.1.

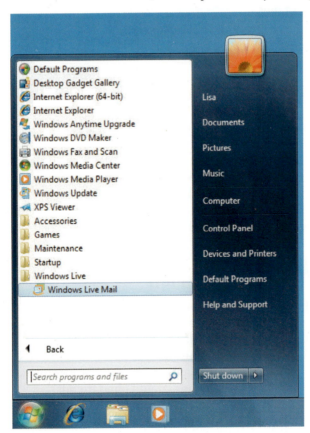

Figure 9.1 **Starting Windows Live Mail.**

The first time you start up Windows Live Mail, it prompts you to set up an e-mail account and displays a dialog box from the setup wizard that walks you through that process. Start from Step 4 in the next section, "Setting Up Your E-mail Account," to learn how to complete the wizard or restart it manually.

After you have set up your e-mail account, each time you start Windows Live Mail, it connects to the Internet and downloads any new messages to the Unread e-mail folder. Figure 9.2 shows the key features of the Windows Live Mail window, which include:

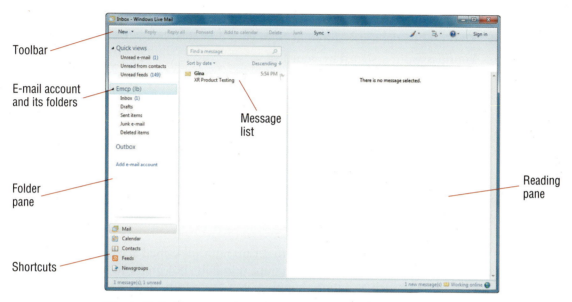

Figure 9.2   Key parts of the Windows Live Mail window.

Note: *If your computer uses a dial-up Internet connection, you may see a dialog box prompting you to start the connection process when you start Windows Live Mail. Click the Connect button to do so.*

- **Toolbar**. Contains buttons for working with messages.
- **Folder pane**. Shows the default e-mail folders for Windows Live Mail and custom folders that you create.
- **Message list**. Lists the messages contained in the folder that is selected in the Folder pane.
- **Reading pane**. Shows a preview of the contents of the message selected in the Message list.
- **Shortcuts**. Shows different functions available in Windows Live Mail. Click a choice in this list at the bottom of the Folder pane to specify which type of information you want to work with.

You can minimize, restore, resize, and maximize the Windows Live Mail program window as for any program. In particular, you might want to leave the program minimized on the taskbar, so that you can check your mail quickly every so often. You also can close the program when you finish working by clicking the window Close (X) button. Alternately, you can press Alt to open the menu bar, click File and then click *Exit*, or press Alt+F4 to close the program and its window.

Setting Up Your E-mail Account

Mail server: A computer with software that enables it to manage e-mail sending, receiving, and storage

E-mail account: In Windows Live Mail, a collection of settings that enables the program to send and receive e-mail via your ISP's mail servers (or to work with newsgroup messages)

E-mail address: The identifier that specifies where an e-mail address should be delivered, including a name, an @ symbol, and the ISP domain. For example, janet22@emcp.com (pronounced "janet 22 at emcp dot com") could be the e-mail address for a user signed up with an ISP that has the emcp.com domain

To enable Windows Live Mail to interact with your ISP's *mail servers*, you have to provide both your logon information and server information. You set up an *e-mail account* in Windows Live Mail to hold the proper logon information that enables Mail to interact with your ISP's mail servers to send and receive your e-mail messages. Before you start the process of setting up your e-mail account, you need to ensure you have the following information from your ISP:

- Your *e-mail address* assigned by the ISP.

- Your user name, if it is different from your e-mail address.

- Your password assigned by your ISP.

- The incoming mail server used by your ISP, which is usually a POP3 (Post Office Protocol version 3) or IMAP (Internet Message Access Protocol) server. The incoming mail server name will be similar to pop.isp.com or mail.isp.com.

- The outgoing mail or SMTP (Simple Mail Transfer Protocol) server used by your ISP, which will have a name similar to smtp.isp.com or smtpauth.isp.com.

Note: *If you will be using Windows 7 on your employer's or school's network, chances are the organization's IT (Information Technology) department will configure your Windows Live Mail e-mail account for you.*

Windows Live Mail enables you to set up multiple e-mail accounts, as needed. For example, if you use one e-mail account normally, but prefer to use another for a special purpose such as online shopping, you can set up each e-mail account in Windows Live Mail to manage messages for both accounts. The setup process will create a separate set of message folders for each account.

Here's How

To set up an e-mail account in Windows Live Mail:

1. Press the Alt key, click Tools, and then click *Accounts*. The Internet Accounts dialog box appears. Or, click the Add e-mail account link in the Folder pane at the left, and skip to Step 4

2. Click the Add button.

3. Leave *E-mail Account* selected in the Select Account Type list of the next dialog box, and then click Next.

4. In the Add an E-mail Account dialog box, type the e-mail address assigned by your ISP in the *E-mail address* text box.

5. Type the password assigned by your ISP in the *Password* text box. (Leave *Remember password* checked.)

6. Type the display name (your name or nickname) you want to use in the *Display Name* text box.

7. Click Next.

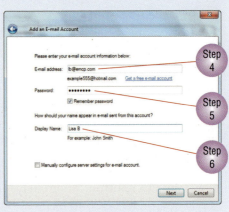

8. If your ISP's incoming mail server is not a POP3 server, open the incoming e-mail server type drop-down list, and click *IMAP*.

9. Type the name of your ISP's incoming mail server in the *Incoming server* text box.

10. If your ISP requires authentication (logon) information that differs from your e-mail address, click the *Login ID (if different from e-mail address)* text box entry and edit it as needed.

11. Type the name for your ISP's outgoing mail server in the *Outgoing server* text box. Note that due to acquisitions and mergers between ISP companies, the POP3 and SMTP server names might not be consistent.

12. If your ISP requires authentication (logon) information for outgoing e-mail, click the *My outgoing server requires authentication* check box to check it. When the SMTP server's name includes "auth," as in smtpauth.emcp, com, it usually requires authentication. Checking the check box tells Windows Live Mail to supply the user name and password automatically when needed to send mail.

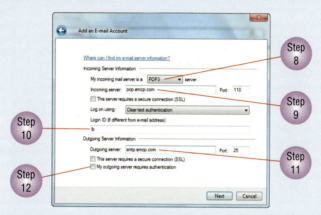

13. Click Next.

14. The final dialog box confirms that you have successfully set up the account. Click Finish.

QUICK FIX

Using Your Web-Based E-mail Account with Windows Live Mail

To set up Windows Live Mail to work with a Windows Live Hotmail account, you just need to supply the e-mail address and password during the account setup process. After that, you will be prompted to click Download to download message folders, and you will be able to log on and off your account using the profile that appears in the upper-right corner. For some Web-based (http://) mail services, such as Gmail, you have to enable your Web mail account for POP3 mail. Gmail's Help system includes information about the POP and SMTP server entries and other set-tings needed to config-ure an e-mail program like Windows Live Mail. In other cases, as with Yahoo! Mail, you can upgrade to a paid version of the service that supports POP mail transfer.

Note: *The exercises in this chapter assume there is an e-mail account set up on the computer system you are using for the purposes of this course, whether your own system or one in a computer lab. If you need information about which e-mail account you should be using or how to set up an e-mail account for use for the exercises in this chapter, consult your instructor.*

Creating an E-mail Message

You can compose an electronic e-mail message in Windows Live Mail and send that message to one or more **recipients**. The message you create can include text and other electronic content. You can send as many messages as needed. No matter what the content or purpose of the message, you follow the same overall process for creating the message, as described in this section.

Recipient: A person to whom you are sending an e-mail message

Opening the Message Window

Message window (or composition window): The window where you compose and address an e-mail message in Windows Live Mail; also refers to the window where you read and respond to a received message

Message header: Also called the e-mail header, this is the information that appears at the head (top) of the message, including date sent, sender, recipient(s), and subject

You compose a message in Windows Live Mail using the New Message window, which is generically called a ***message window*** or ***composition window***. Shown in Figure 9.3, the New Message window contains its own menu bar and toolbar with commands and tools for creating and sending the e-mail message. It includes text boxes where you can address the message and specify a topic, collectively called the ***message header***, as well as a large text box where you can enter the message content. You can use one of a few different methods to open the New Message window after clicking Mail in the list of functions at the bottom of the Folder pane.

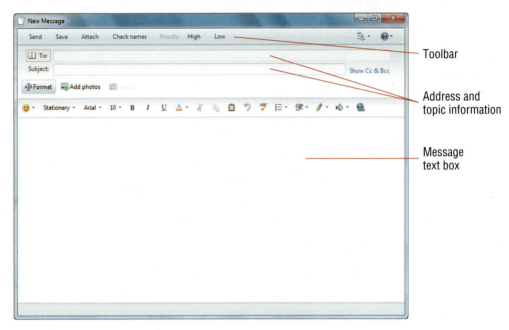

Figure 9.3   Key parts of the New Message window.

Here's How

> To open the New Message window in Windows Live Mail, use one of these methods after clicking Mail at the bottom of the Folder pane:
>
> - Press Alt to open the menu bar, click File, point to *New*, and then click *E-mail message*.
> - Click the New button at the left end of the Mail window toolbar.
> - Press Ctrl+N.

Specifying Recipients and Subject

You need to supply the e-mail address for each recipient who is to receive an electronic copy of the message. The top of the new message window lists two text boxes for entering recipient information:

- **To**. Enter the e-mail address(es) for the primary recipient(s).
- **Cc and Bcc**. Click *Show Cc & Bcc* beside the *Subject* text box. Enter the e-mail address(es) for any secondary recipients to whom you want to send a reference copy (Cc is considered a carbon copy and Bcc is considered a blind carbon copy in traditional business terminology) of the message.

To address the message, click in the *To* text box, and type each recipient's e-mail address, separating the addresses with a semicolon as shown in Figure 9.4. If you need to send a copy of the message to another interested person, click *Show Cc & Bcc*, and then click in the *Cc* text box and enter his or her e-mail address. To send a copy of the message to a recipient whose e-mail information will not be visible to other recipients, enter that recipient's e-mail address in the *Bcc* text box. (To hide the *Cc* and *Bcc* text boxes when you no longer need to specify additional recipients, click *Hide Cc & Bcc*.) Finally, click in the *Subject* text box and type a subject for the message. Notice that once you type a subject for the message, that subject text replaces *New Message* in the message window title bar.

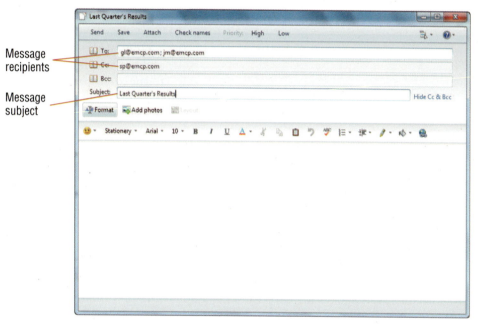

Figure 9.4 Use the message header text boxes near the top of the message window to address the message and specify its subject.

If you are entering the e-mail address for a recipient from whom you have previously received and replied to an e-mail message, the Windows Live Mail feature for automatically completing e-mail addresses displays a drop-down list with suggested matching recipient names, as shown in Figure 9.5. To finish your entry, you can click one of the listed e-mail addresses and save yourself some typing.

Figure 9.5 If Windows Live Mail displays one or more recipient names, you can click the name to use.

If you have saved e-mail recipient addresses, as described in the later section in this chapter called "Working with Contacts," or if your system was upgraded from

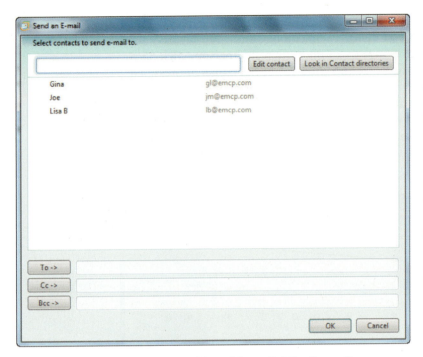

a previous Windows version where your e-mail addresses were previously stored, you can specify e-mail recipients using the Send an E-mail dialog box. To open the dialog box, click *To* at the top of the message window. In the Send an E-mail dialog box that appears (Figure 9.6), click the recipient to add in the list at the left, and then click the To, Cc, or Bcc button at the bottom of the dialog box to add the selected e-mail address to the appropriate recipient box at the right. Repeat the process to add as many recipients as desired, and then click OK.

Figure 9.6 **Click a recipient to add, and then click To, Cc, or Bcc.**

Adding and Formatting Text

Message body: The text for an e-mail message, entered or viewed in the message window

The text you add to the message is called the ***message body***. When e-mail emerged, all messages contained only plain, unformatted text because that was the only type of text that e-mail servers and software supported. This limitation actually provided an advantage during earlier days when network and Internet transfer capacities were smaller. Plain text messages are smaller and therefore would not exceed network capacity.

Now, many servers and e-mail programs support what Windows Live Mail calls Rich Text (HTML) formatted messages, which can include background images, different fonts, attributes like bold and colored text, and even automatic bulleted and numbered lists. By default, the Rich Text (HTML) format is specified for all new messages unless you change the message format. For simplicity, you can refer to the Rich Text (HTML) format as simply HTML.

To change from HTML to a plain text message, press Alt in the message window, click the Format menu, and then click *Plain text*. Click OK in the message that appears warning you that you will lose message formatting. If you choose a plain text message, you can then simply type the desired text in the message text box. The tools for formatting text disappear when you change to the Plain text message format, so you will not be able to use them.

Stationery: A set of background, font, and color selections applied to an e-mail message

When you want to send an e-mail message in the Rich Text (HTML) format, you do not have to change the default message format. You can also apply a variety of formatting features to your message text. You can even apply ***stationery*** if you did not do so (by using the Stationery button in the message window) when creating the message.

To enter and format text in a Rich Text (HTML) message:

Here's How

1. To apply message stationery if you did not do so earlier, click Stationery in the toolbar of formatting choices above message text, and click More stationery. In the Select Stationery dialog box that appears, click a stationery choice, review its Preview, and then click OK to apply it to the message.

2. Click in the message text box and type the message text.

3. To apply formatting to any text, drag over the text to select it, and then use the desired formatting tool on the toolbar above the message body. For example, you can select a list of items, click the Formatting as list button, and then click one of the list choices to convert the items to a numbered list or bulleted list.

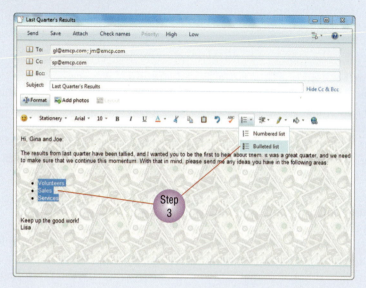

QUICK FIX

Using Proper E-mail Etiquette
Most people use the e-mail medium to communicate for both personal and business purposes, so it is important to be mindful of the recipients and the purpose of your message and set the appropriate tone. A message that is intended to address a serious business matter should not include emoticons and abbreviations, for example. Also, typing in ALL CAPS is considered impolite—it is the equivalent of screaming in all forms of electronic communication. Enclose a word or phrase in *asterisks* for emphasis, instead, when sending a message in plain text format.

> **Tip:** You can copy and paste information into the body of an e-mail message. You even can select and copy information from a Web page, such as a URL, and paste it into the message. Use the Insert a link button above the message body to properly insert a URL. When the message in the Rich Text (HTML) message format, you even can paste some non-text information, such as a selection of cells from a spreadsheet or a picture file.

Attaching One or More Files

When a file such as a word processing document or spreadsheet includes extensive information and you do not want to or cannot recreate the information in the body of an e-mail message, then you can send the file as a *file attachment* to the e-mail message. The attachment travels along with the message to the recipients, who can then view the message and save its attachment to their system's hard disk, if needed.

File attachment: A file created in a program other than your e-mail software that you designate to be sent along with an e-mail message

While adding an attachment to an e-mail message takes only a moment or two, you need to keep these considerations in mind with regard to file attachments:

- While there is no real limitation on the size of file that you can attach to an e-mail message, keep Internet connection speeds (yours and the recipient's)

and the size of the recipient's e-mail storage in mind. Large files will take too long to transmit over slow dial-up connections. Some ISPs limit individual messages to 5MB to 10MB, so any message exceeding or overflowing the limitation will be rejected.

- In most cases (with notable exceptions being common graphic file formats, which can be opened by a variety of programs), the recipient must have the software used to create the attached file installed on his or her computer to open the file. Make sure any file attachment you send is in a format that the recipient's computer can open.

- Some e-mail programs and/or corporate mail servers screen for executable files (with .exe, .bat, and .inf file name extensions) and prevent the user from opening or receiving attached files in those formats. Computer viruses and other malicious software can be transmitted in executable files, so you may need to use another means, such as an online file sharing site, to transmit this type of file to a recipient.

> **Tip:** If you have a very large file or group of files that you must send as an e-mail attachment, you can often compress the file(s). Compressing can not only combine several files into a single file or folder for easier sending, but it also can significantly reduce the size of the included file(s). In an Explorer window in Windows 7, select the files to compress, right-click, click Send To in the shortcut menu, and click Compressed (zipped) folder in the submenu. Type a name for the new folder when it appears, and press Enter. You also can use a third-party program such as WinZip to compress files.

To attach a file to an e-mail message, click the Attach button on the message window toolbar. Use the Open dialog box that appears to navigate to the location that holds the file to attach. Click the file (or Ctrl+click to select multiple files), and then click Open. The header area at the top of the message expands to show a paper clip icon beside the name(s) of the attached file(s) as shown in Figure 9.7.

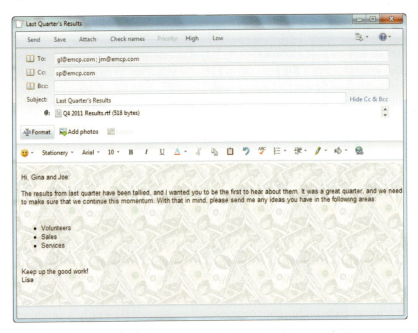

Figure 9.7 A paper clip icon appears beside the name of the file attachment.

Creating a Photo E-mail

When you attach a digital photo to a message, it generally arrives as a file attachment in the message recipient's Inbox. This means the recipient will not see the image on selecting the message. You can paste a photo into the message body, but when you do so, Windows Live Mail gives you few options for formatting the image. Windows Live Mail now enables you to create a *photo e-mail message* by adding a photo using the Add photos button above the message body. Using this method not only inserts the photo in the message body (rather than as an attachment), but also offers additional ways to format the image, such as adding a border or caption, as shown in Figure 9.8. After you click the Add photos button, use the Add Photos dialog box that appears to navigate to and select one or more photos to insert. Click each photo and then click the Add button. When you have selected all the photos to attach, click Done. You then can use the tools that appear above the message body (refer to Figure 9.8) to format the photo. To add a caption, click the photo and then type the caption in the area below it.

Photo e-mail message: A message where the Add photos button has been used to include a photo, making special formatting options, such as adding a photo caption, available.

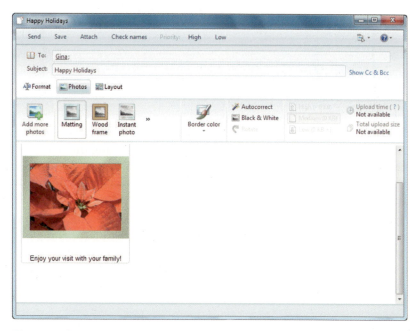

Figure 9.8 **Photo e-mail messages support enhanced photo formatting.**

Sending and Receiving Messages

Sending an e-mail message initially closes the message window and places the message in the *Outbox* folder in the Folder pane of Windows Live Mail. At that point, you can either wait until Windows Live Mail automatically checks for messages (an interval of 30 minutes by default) so that the message will send, or you can send and receive messages manually to ensure that your outgoing mail leaves the Outbox promptly.

Outbox: The Windows Live Mail folder that holds e-mail messages you have composed, but not sent

> **Tip:** You can press F7 in the message window to start spell check to check the contents of your message before sending it. Typos and sloppy grammar in e-mail messages can reflect negatively on your professionalism, so always make sure you proof and spell check important messages.

To send an e-mail message and check for incoming messages:

1. Click the Send button on the message window toolbar.
2. Click the Sync button on the Windows Live Mail window toolbar. Received messages will be placed in the Inbox folder for your e-mail account in the Folder pane.

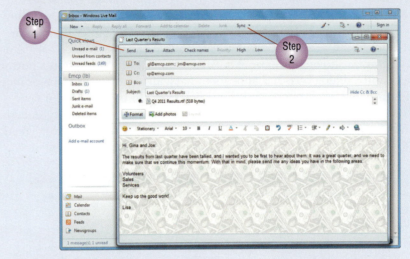

The e-mail server at your ISP stores e-mail messages addressed to you until you receive the messages. By default, receiving messages by clicking the Sync button on the Windows Live Mail window toolbar downloads them from the e-mail server to your computer. Click the Inbox folder under your e-mail account name in the Folder pane. The Message list shows a row of header information for each received message.

You can have multiple e-mail accounts set up on a single system. For example, if you run a small business and have one e-mail account set up for company use and another set up for personal use, you can choose the account for which you want to send and receive messages. To do so, click the drop-down list arrow for the Sync button and click the name of the mail account to check in the menu that appears.

Exercise 1

Sending a Message

1. Click Start, click *All Programs*, click *Windows Live*, and then click *Windows Live Mail.*
2. Click Mail in the list of choices at the bottom of the Folder pane.
3. Click the New button on the Windows Live Mail window toolbar.
4. Type your instructor's e-mail address in the *To* text box.
5. Click in the *Subject* text box, and type **Chapter 09 Exercise 01**.
6. Click the Stationery button, click *More stationery*, and double-click the *Bamboo* stationery.
7. Click in the message text box, if needed.
8. Type the following message:

So far in this chapter, I have learned how to:

Start and exit Windows Live Mail
Set up an e-mail account
Compose a message
Send and receive messages

9. Drag over the list of items in the message body, click the Format as list button in the formatting tools, and then click *Numbered list* to apply numbering to the list.
10. Click the Send button in the message window.
11. Click the Sync button on the Windows Live Mail window toolbar.
12. Click File, and then click Exit to close Windows Live Mail.

Reading and Responding to Messages

When you click the Sync button on the Windows Live Mail window toolbar, Mail signs on to your e-mail account, checks for messages, and downloads any new messages. This is also called *checking* your e-mail. To view your received messages in your **Inbox**, click Mail in the list of choices at the bottom of the Folder pane, and then click the Inbox folder under your e-mail account. Your messages appear in the **Message list** in the center, as shown in Figure 9.9.

Inbox: The Windows Live Mail folder that holds e-mail messages you have received

Message list: The pane that lists the e-mail messages in the currently selected folder of the Folder pane

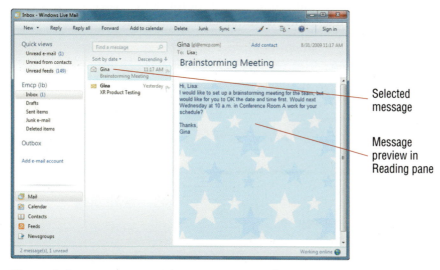

Selected message

Message preview in Reading pane

Figure 9.9   Use the Message list to preview and open messages from the Inbox.

To preview a message, click it in the Message list. The message preview appears in the Reading pane that appears, by default, at the right side of Windows Live Mail. After a default interval of five seconds, the selected message listing will change from bold to regular text in the Message list to indicate that you have read the message. If the Reading pane does not show enough of the message contents for your needs, you can open the message in its own window by double-clicking the message in the Message list. Both the Reading pane and the message window include scroll bars for scrolling down to read more of the message.

Tip: To print a message, right-click it in the Message list and click the Print button. This opens the Print dialog box, where you can select settings for the printout. These settings work as in any other application.

If an HTML message has embedded pictures, they, by default, do not download for security reasons. If you trust the source of the message, you can click the *Show images* link in the yellow Information bar at the top of the Reading pane or the message window to download and view the pictures in the message. If the message with pictures is not from a trusted source, you can click *Delete and block* instead.

Whether you work with a selected message in the main Windows Live Mail window or its own message window, you can use the following toolbar buttons to specify how to respond to the received message:

*   **Reply**. Opens a reply message addressed to the message sender only. Includes Re: before the message subject.

*   **Reply all**. Opens a reply message addressed to the message sender and anyone else who received a copy of the message to which you are responding. Includes Re: before the message subject.

*   **Forward**. Opens a reply message not addressed to anyone. Includes Fw: before the message subject.

Whether you are replying to or forwarding information, add or change the *To* and *Cc* recipient information as needed, type response text in the message body area above the quoted text (Figure 9.10) from any prior message(s), and send the message as described earlier in this chapter. If you try to send or forward an e-mail message that includes pictures that cannot be sent or forwarded, click Yes at the message box that appears to continue with the send.

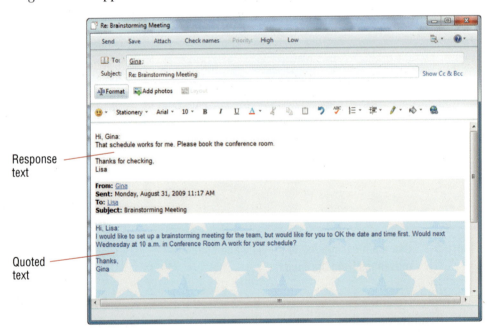

Figure 9.10 **Re: in the subject line indicates this is a reply message.**

Tip: Because e-mail is a nonverbal medium, a message can come across as more terse than you intended it to be. You can use the button at the far-left end of the tools above the message text area to insert *emoticons* to convey the real tone or spirit of your remarks. You also can insert typed emoticons such as: :-) for happy, :-(for sad, ;-) for winking, and :-D for laughing.

 **Exercise 2**

Receiving and Responding to a Message

1. Click Start, click *All Programs*, click *Windows Live*, and then click *Windows Live Mail*.
2. Click Mail in the list at the bottom of the Folder pane.
3. Click the New button on the toolbar.
4. Type your own e-mail address in the *To* text box.
5. Click in the *Subject* text box, and type **Chapter 09 Exercise 02**.
6. In the message window, click the Stationery button above the message text box, and click *More stationery*. Double-click *Mosaic 1* in the Select Stationery dialog box.
7. Click in the message text box. if needed.
8. Type the following message:

   I can respond to an e-mail message in one of three ways:
   > **Reply**
   > **Reply all**

9. Click the Send button in the message window.
10. Click the Sync button in the Windows Live Mail window.
11. Wait a few moments, and then click Sync again. The message should arrive in your Inbox.
12. Click the Inbox folder under your e-mail account in the Folder pane if needed, and then click the received *Chapter 09 Exercise 02* message in the Message list. When you read the text in the Reading pane, notice that you have left out one of the three response message types.
13. Click the Reply button on the Windows Live Mail window toolbar.
14. Click *Show Cc & Bcc* in the message window, click in the *Cc* text box, and type your instructor's e-mail address.
15. Click above the quoted text in the message text box, and type the following:

   I also can Forward the message.

16. Click the Send button in the message window.
17. Click the Sync button in the Windows Live Mail window. This sends the additional information to both you and your instructor.

Managing Messages

A busy person's e-mail Inbox might receive dozens of incoming messages per day. Just as incoming "stuff" can quickly clog the workspace on the desk in your office, incoming messages can clutter up your Inbox and make it tougher to find the messages you really need. Windows Live Mail offers features that enable you to organize the messages that hit your Inbox.

Filing and Viewing Messages

Most e-mail programs offer a feature that users should take advantage of more often: the ability to create folders to organize e-mail messages, in particular, received messages. Say you work for an advertising firm and you are managing three client accounts. To help you keep better track of the messages, you could create a folder for each client and move the messages pertaining to each client to the respective client folder. Create folders for received messages as subfolders of your Inbox folder.

Here's How ▶ **To create a folder, file a received message in it, and view the messages in a folder:**

1. Make sure that Mail is selected at the bottom of the Folder pane, and right-click the Inbox folder, and then click *New folder*. Or, click to select the Inbox, click the drop-down arrow beside New on the toolbar, and click *Folder*.

2. Type a name for the new folder in the *Folder name* text box of the Create Folder dialog box. (Note that if you wanted to create a subfolder for a subfolder previously created in the Inbox, you could select the desired subfolder in the list in the Create Folder dialog box.)

3. Click OK.

4. To move (file) a message in a subfolder of the Inbox, double-click the Inbox folder to expand its subfolders, if needed.

5. Drag the message to move it from the Message list over the folder into which you want to place the message. When you release the mouse button, the message will be moved into the folder. Repeat this process to move other messages into the folder, as needed.

6. To view the messages in the folder, click the folder. The messages you have moved into the folder appear in the Message list. You can select any message there to view its contents in the Reading pane.

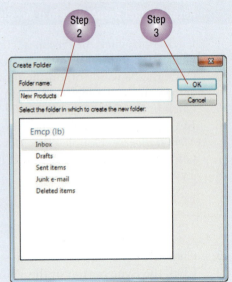

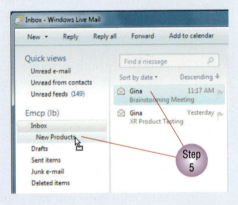

Tip: The boldface number in parentheses that appears to the right of a folder name in the Folder pane identifies the number of unread messages in the folder. If you check your e-mail and such a number appears to the right of a subfolder that you have created in the Inbox, click the folder to view the new messages.

Note: *You can set up a message rule that will automatically move a message from a particular recipient or with a particular type of content into the folder that you specify—even the Deleted items folder. To get started using this feature, press Alt, and then choose the Tools, Message Rules, Mail command.*

Exercise 2
Receiving and Responding to a Message

1. Click Start, click *All Programs*, click *Windows Live*, and then click *Windows Live Mail*.
2. Click Mail in the list at the bottom of the Folder pane.
3. Click the New button on the toolbar.
4. Type your own e-mail address in the *To* text box.
5. Click in the *Subject* text box, and type Chapter 09 Exercise 02.
6. In the message window, click the Stationery button above the message text box, and click *More stationery*. Double-click *Mosaic 1* in the Select Stationery dialog box.
7. Click in the message text box. if needed.
8. Type the following message:

   I can respond to an e-mail message in one of three ways:
   > Reply
   > Reply all

9. Click the Send button in the message window.
10. Click the Sync button in the Windows Live Mail window.
11. Wait a few moments, and then click Sync again. The message should arrive in your Inbox.
12. Click the Inbox folder under your e-mail account in the Folder pane if needed, and then click the received *Chapter 09 Exercise 02* message in the Message list. When you read the text in the Reading pane, notice that you have left out one of the three response message types.
13. Click the Reply button on the Windows Live Mail window toolbar.
14. Click *Show Cc & Bcc* in the message window, click in the *Cc* text box, and type your instructor's e-mail address.
15. Click above the quoted text in the message text box, and type the following:

   I also can Forward the message.

16. Click the Send button in the message window.
17. Click the Sync button in the Windows Live Mail window. This sends the additional information to both you and your instructor.

Managing Messages

A busy person's e-mail Inbox might receive dozens of incoming messages per day. Just as incoming "stuff" can quickly clog the workspace on the desk in your office, incoming messages can clutter up your Inbox and make it tougher to find the messages you really need. Windows Live Mail offers features that enable you to organize the messages that hit your Inbox.

Filing and Viewing Messages

Most e-mail programs offer a feature that users should take advantage of more often: the ability to create folders to organize e-mail messages, in particular, received messages. Say you work for an advertising firm and you are managing three client accounts. To help you keep better track of the messages, you could create a folder for each client and move the messages pertaining to each client to the respective client folder. Create folders for received messages as subfolders of your Inbox folder.

To create a folder, file a received message in it, and view the messages in a folder:

1. Make sure that Mail is selected at the bottom of the Folder pane, and right-click the Inbox folder, and then click *New folder*. Or, click to select the Inbox, click the drop-down arrow beside New on the toolbar, and click *Folder*.

2. Type a name for the new folder in the *Folder name* text box of the Create Folder dialog box. (Note that if you wanted to create a subfolder for a subfolder previously created in the Inbox, you could select the desired subfolder in the list in the Create Folder dialog box.)

3. Click OK.

4. To move (file) a message in a subfolder of the Inbox, double-click the Inbox folder to expand its subfolders, if needed.

5. Drag the message to move it from the Message list over the folder into which you want to place the message. When you release the mouse button, the message will be moved into the folder. Repeat this process to move other messages into the folder, as needed.

6. To view the messages in the folder, click the folder. The messages you have moved into the folder appear in the Message list. You can select any message there to view its contents in the Reading pane.

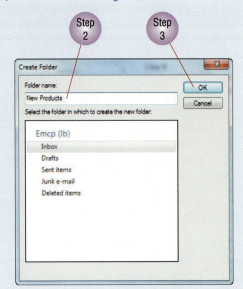

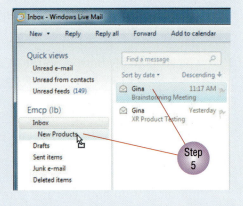

Tip: The boldface number in parentheses that appears to the right of a folder name in the Folder pane identifies the number of unread messages in the folder. If you check your e-mail and such a number appears to the right of a subfolder that you have created in the Inbox, click the folder to view the new messages.

Note: *You can set up a message rule that will automatically move a message from a particular recipient or with a particular type of content into the folder that you specify—even the Deleted items folder. To get started using this feature, press Alt, and then choose the Tools, Message Rules, Mail command.*

Saving a Message Attachment

When you receive a message that has a file attached, a paper clip icon appears to the right of the message name in the Message list. To save the attached file to your computer's hard disk, click the message in the Message list. In the Reading pane, right-click the file's icon above the message title, and then click *Save as*. If you have opened the message in its own window, you also can right-click the file icon in the upper-left corner of the window, and then click *Save as*. If needed, use the Save Attachments As dialog box to select the folder in which you want to save the file attachment, edit the *File name* if desired, and then click Save.

Dealing with Junk Mail

One particular type of e-mail calls for special handling. *Junk e-mail* or *spam* messages can clog up your Inbox and distract your attention from more important incoming e-mail messages. In some cases, commercial or sales-oriented messages might be legitimate messages from online sites for which you have signed up to receive e-mail messages about sales and new items or even e-mail newsletters. In other cases, the messages come from entities that send unsolicited messages to large groups of users without prior request or agreement by the user.

Even benign spam messages will clog up your Inbox. Even more troubling is the fact that some spam messages represent activities many users find questionable or objectionable, and a certain percentage of junk e-mails are outright scam attempts to solicit money, or dupe you into providing personal information that can lead to identity theft, or to deliver messages intended to infect your computer with a virus or other malware (malicious software). So, by default, Windows Live Mail has its *junk e-mail filter* enabled to provide a low level of protection, which tells Windows Live Mail to place obvious incoming spam messages directly into the Junk e-mail folder in the Folder pane rather than the Inbox.

To mark a message as junk mail, click it in the Message list and click Junk on the Windows Live Mail window toolbar. This immediately moves the message to the Junk e-mail folder in the Folder pane. You can right-click any other message from a sender for whom you want to set junk e-mail handling, and move the mouse pointer over the *Junk e-mail* menu choice to see the submenu shown in Figure 9.11. Clicking *Add sender to safe senders list* tells the junk e-mail filter never to treat e-mail from that sender as junk mail. In contrast, clicking *Add sender to blocked senders list* tells the junk e-mail filter to treat all messages from that sender as junk mail and to move received messages from that sender into the Junk e-mail folder. Clicking *Mark as junk* immediately moves the message to the Junk e-mail folder, but does not change settings for the sender.

Junk e-mail or spam: Like paper junk mail, these are commercial e-mail messages sent to you without request

Junk e-mail filter: A Windows Live Mail feature that automatically moves likely junk e-mail messages to the Junk E-mail folder

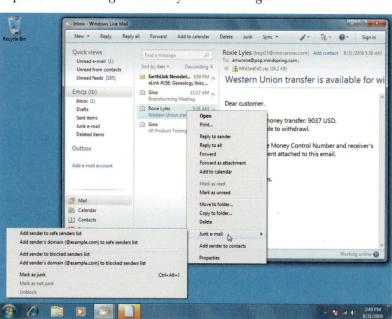

Figure 9.11 You can specify how the junk e-mail filter should treat messages from a particular sender by using this submenu.

Figure 9.12 By default, Windows Live Mail informs you when it moves a message to the Junk e-mail folder.

If you consider a message as junk e-mail, you can delete it manually just as for any message.

The first time you receive a suspected junk e-mail, the junk e-mail filter displays a message box (Figure 9.12) telling you that it has moved the junk e-mail message to the Junk e-mail folder. You can click Open Junk E-mail Folder to view the message; Junk E-mail Options to work with settings; or Close to simply close the dialog box without taking action on the junk e-mail. You can click the *Please do not show me this dialog again* check box before closing the dialog box to turn off this type of alert message.

You can press Alt, open the Actions menu, point to *Junk e-mail*, and click *Safety options* to set the level of junk e-mail protection and work with your Safe Senders and Blocked Senders lists. You also can click the Menus button on the Windows Live Mail window toolbar and click *Safety options* to find those options.

It's a good practice to click your Junk e-mail folder in the Folder pane from time to time to check it for messages that are not junk. If you find a message there that is not junk, right-click it, point to *Junk e-mail* in the menu, and click *Mark as not junk*. This immediately moves the message back to your Inbox.

> **Tip:** Some ISPs have e-mail servers set up to trap junk mail and spam in special online folders and prevent it from ever downloading to your computer. When an ISP offers such protection, you generally have to log on to your Web mail account and set the preferences for handling spam and suspect e-mail there.

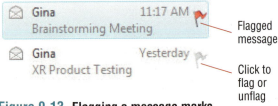

Figure 9.13 Flagging a message marks it for later attention.

Flagging and Deleting Messages

You may apply a *flag* to other received messages that you want to revisit at a later time, such as if a message includes an important meeting date or statistic. To flag a message, click the grayed-out flag icon beside its header in the Message list, as shown in Figure 9.13. The flag icon turns red. Repeat the process to remove the flag.

Flag: Identifies received messages that might require further attention by applying a flag icon

> **Tip:** You can sort the Message list by a variety of criteria, including the receipt Date, who messages are From, and the Flag setting. Use the Sort by (Criterion) list above the Message list to apply the sort.

Even if you do a good job of managing your incoming e-mail messages with filing, spam filtering, and flagging, messages may stack up to an unruly number rather quickly. Coupled with the fact that many organizations limit the volume of e-mail messages you can store means that you will need to remove old and irrelevant messages from time to time.

You can delete a message from the Inbox or any other folder when you no longer need the message. Select the message in the Message list and then press the

Delete key or click the Delete button on the Windows Live Mail window toolbar to delete it. Deleting a message at first merely moves it to the Deleted items folder in the Folder pane. If you mistakenly move a message there, click the Deleted items folder, then drag the message back to the Inbox or another folder. (You also can right-click a message and click *Move to folder* to use the Move dialog box to move the message to another folder.)

When you want to delete messages permanently, you have to empty the Deleted items folder after moving the messages there. Emptying the Junk e-mail folder to delete its messages also deletes the messages permanently.

To empty the Junk e-mail folder to delete its messages permanently:

Here's How

1. After clicking Mail in the list at the bottom of the Folder pane in the Windows Live Mail window, click the Junk e-mail folder in the Folder pane. Review the messages in the folder to ensure that you indeed want to delete them permanently.
2. Once you have verified that you do want to delete all the folder's contents, right-click the Junk e-mail folder, and then click *Empty 'Junk e-mail' folder*.

To empty the Deleted items folder to delete its messages permanently:

1. After clicking Mail in the list at the bottom of the Folder pane in the Windows Live Mail window, click the Deleted items folder in the Folder pane. Review the messages in the folder to ensure that you indeed want to delete them permanently.
2. Once you have verified that you do want to delete all the folder's contents, right-click the Deleted items folder, and then click *Empty 'Deleted items' folder*. You also can find *Empty 'Deleted items' folder* on the Edit menu that appears when you press Alt.
3. In the message box that asks whether you want to delete the folder's contents permanently, click Yes.

To delete an individual message from either the Deleted items or Junk E-mail folder, first click the folder in the Folder pane. Right-click the message in the Message list, click *Delete*, and then click Yes in the message box that asks you to confirm that you want to delete the message.

Exercise 3

Managing Messages

1. After clicking Mail in the list at the bottom of the Folder pane, right-click the Inbox folder in the Folder list, and then click *New folder*.
2. Type **Chapter 09 Exercises** in the *Folder name* text box, and then click OK.
3. Click the Inbox folder again, if needed.
4. In the Message list, click the message that you sent in Exercise 2 of this chapter (subject: *Chapter 09 Exercise 02*), and then Ctrl+click the received response message (subject: *Re: Chapter 09 Exercise 02*).
5. Drag the selected messages over the Chapter 09 Exercises folder in the Folder list.
6. Click the Chapter 09 Exercises folder.
7. Capture a screen shot, paste it into Paint, and save the file as **C09E03S07**.

8. Right-click each message in the Chapter 09 Exercises folder and click *Delete*.
9. Right-click the Chapter 09 Exercises folder in the Folder list, and click *Delete*. Click Yes to confirm the deletion.
10. Click the Deleted items folder in the Folder list.
11. Capture a screen shot, paste it into Paint, and save the file as **C09E03S11**.
12. Right-click the Deleted items folder, and click *Empty 'Deleted items' folder*.
13. Click Yes in the dialog box that asks you to confirm the permanent deletion.
14. Submit the screen shots via e-mail or USB flash drive to your instructor.

Adding a Signature Block and Message Priority

While e-mail in some respects emerged as a substitute for typed or handwritten letters, the way in which it has so accelerated communication has led to a number of "shortcuts" like the emoticons mentioned previously. This section shows you how to add your personal identifier at the end of each e-mail and how to inform a message recipient about a message's importance.

Creating a Signature

Sig: Short for signature block, this is identifying text that Windows Live Mail adds to the bottom of every e-mail message

Another example of a shortcut is the ability for Windows Live Mail to tack on a *sig* or *signature block* to the end of every message you send. The sig can be as simple as your name, or it can include not only your full contact information (name, title, address, e-mail address, phone number, fax number, and so on), but also any other type of text-based information you want to include; or, if you have already set up your sig information in a plain text (.txt) file created with Notepad that includes text or a graphic image created from alphanumeric characters (formerly called ASCII art), you can use it as the sig instead. Creating the sig and telling Windows Live Mail to assign it to all outgoing messages saves you the trouble of having to type a closing at the end of every message.

After completing the following steps, the sig will be added to the bottom of every outgoing e-mail message you create.

Here's How

To create a sig and tell Windows Live Mail to append it to every message:

1. After clicking Mail in the list at the bottom of the Folder pane, click the Menus button on the toolbar, and then click *Options*. You also can press Alt to display the menu bar, click Tools, and then click *Options*.
2. Click the Signatures tab in the Options dialog box.
3. Click New. (You can then optionally click Rename, type a more descriptive name for the signature, and then press Enter.)
4. In the *Edit Signature* section of the text box, click in the *Text* text box, and type the text portion of the signature. Or see Step 5 to apply a sig file, instead.
5. Click the File option button. Click the Browse button, using the Open dialog box that appears to select a text file to use as the signature, and click Open. Note that the Open dialog box assumes you are looking for a plain text (.txt) file and displays only files of that type. If you want to include additional formatting with a sig file, you can use an application such as Word to create the file and save it in HTML format, and then select that file format in the Open dialog box when finding the sig file.

6. Click the *Add signatures to all outgoing messages* check box to check it, signifying that you want to include the signature at the bottom of all outgoing messages.
7. Click OK.

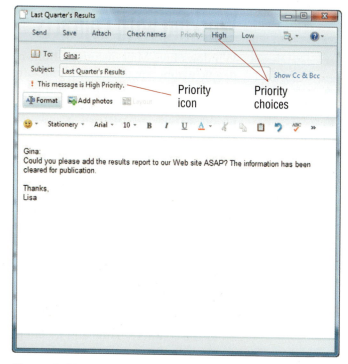

Setting Message Priority

In addition to setting up a sig so that a message will always automatically include your sender information, you can assign a priority setting to tell the message recipient whether imminent or delayed action is required. By default, all messages are set to a Normal Priority. You can change the message to High Priority or Low Priority in the message window. To do so, click the High or Low button on the message window toolbar. (See Figure 9.14.) You also can press Alt, click Tools, point to *Set priority*, and then click a priority in the submenu that appears.

As shown in Figure 9.14, when you apply either High or Low Priority to an outgoing message, an icon and message appear to identify the priority. The icon corresponds to the priority setting: a red exclamation point for a High Priority message, and a blue down arrow for a

Figure 9.14 Change a message to High or Low Priority to alert the recipient to its importance.

Low Priority message. This icon shows up in the flag column of the Message list in the recipient's Inbox folder (refer to Figure 9.13) so the recipient can see the priority at a glance.

 Exercise 4

1. Make sure Mail is selected in the list at the bottom of the Folder pane in Windows Live Mail. Click the Menus button on the toolbar, and then click *Options*.
2. Click the Signatures tab of the Options dialog box.
3. Click the New button.
4. Leave the Text option button selected in the *Edit Signature* section of the dialog box, and type your name and e-mail address in the text box, pressing Enter after your name to place the e-mail address on a separate line.
5. Click the *Add signatures to all outgoing messages* check box to check it.
6. Capture a screen shot, paste it into Paint, and save the file as **C09E04S06**.
7. Click OK to finish creating the sig and close the Options dialog box.
8. Click the New button on the Windows Live Mail window toolbar. Your sig should appear in the message text box of the New Message window.
9. Enter your instructor's e-mail address in the *To* text box.
10. Click in the *Subject* text box and type Chapter 09 Exercise 04.
11. Click the Attach button on the message window toolbar, and then, in the Open dialog box that appears, select the **C09E04S06** file as the message attachment.
12. Click the High button on the toolbar. If desired, type a brief message to your instructor in the message body area.
13. Click Send on the message window toolbar to send the message.
14. Click Sync in the Windows Live Mail window to send the message from your Outbox.

Working with Contacts

Contact: A listing with e-mail address and other contact information for a person entered into the Contacts feature in Windows Live Mail

Windows Live Mail includes a built-in Contacts feature for managing contacts—people whom you e-mail or phone often. You can use Contacts to track mailing, phone, fax, e-mail, job title information, personal details, notes, and tracking ID information for anyone with whom you interact. Once you have added a *contact* into Contacts, that contact shows up in the Send an E-mail dialog box (refer to Figure 9.6) whenever you use it to address an e-mail message. Building a list of contacts not only serves as a handy reference list when you need to make a call or send a letter, but it also enables you to address e-mails more quickly.

To start working with Contacts in Windows Live Mail, click Contacts in the list at the bottom of the Folder pane. Windows Live Mail opens a separate Windows Live Contacts window, which you can use to add and work with your contacts.

Adding a Contact

When you add a contact, you can specify as few or as many details as you want. To set up a contact to whom you want to send e-mail, at a minimum, you should enter the contact's name and e-mail address.

To add a new contact:

1. In the Windows Live Mail window, click Contacts in the list at the bottom of the Folder pane.
2. Click the New button on the Windows Live Contacts window toolbar. The Add a Contact window opens, with its Quick add fields displayed.
3. Click *Contact* in the list at the left to display a more thorough list of contact fields.
4. Enter information in the *First name*, *Middle name*, and *Last name* text boxes, as desired, pressing Tab to move between the boxes.
5. Click in the appropriate e-mail text box, and type the contact's e-mail address.
6. If you enter multiple e-mail addresses, select the one to use by default from the *Primary e-mail address* drop-down list.
7. Click other choices at the left and enter additional information about the contact as desired, such as a Windows Live Messenger Address in the IM category.
8. Click the Add contact button. The new contact appears in the list in the Windows Live Contacts window.

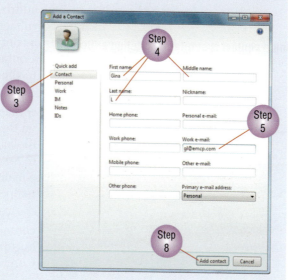

Note that the contacts in Windows Live Mail initially exist separately from the contacts you can create in the Contacts folder found in your personal folder in Windows 7. (Use the New Contact button on the command bar in that Contacts folder window to add a contact.) In particular, you may have a number of contacts in that Contacts folder if your system was upgraded to Windows 7 from an earlier version. It is easy to import one of your personal folder Contacts folder contacts into Windows Live Contacts for use with Windows Live Mail. In the Windows Live Contacts window, click the Menus button on the toolbar, click *Import*, and then click *Address book for current Windows user*. Click OK at the message window that informs you of the number of contacts imported. The imported contacts then appear in the Windows Live Contacts window.

Changing or Deleting a Contact

You can edit the properties (information) for a contact at any time to ensure you are using the most up-to-date information possible and prevent returned e-mails or letters. To edit a contact, double-click the contact in the list in the Windows Live Contacts window, make the changes you want in the Edit Contact window, and then click Save.

Deleting a contact deletes the contact permanently, so make sure that you have verified that you want to delete the contact. To delete the contact, you can

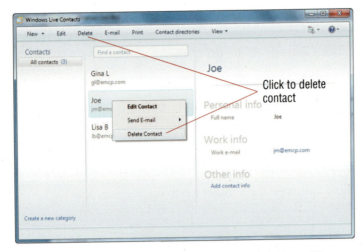

Figure 9.15 Deleting a contact is similar to deleting a file.

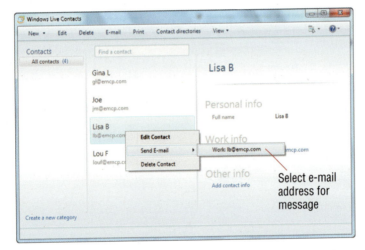

Figure 9.16 You can create an e-mail message to a contact from the Windows Live Contacts window.

either click the contact and then click the Delete button on the Windows Live Contacts window toolbar, or you can right-click the contact and click *Delete Contact* as shown in Figure 9.15. In the message box asking you to confirm the deletion, click OK. The contact is permanently deleted.

E-mailing a Contact

Windows Live Mail and Windows Live Contacts work together to enable you to address e-mail messages more quickly. In fact, you can create a new message to a contact from within the Windows Live Contacts window rather than going back to the Windows Live Mail window.

Click the contact in the list of contacts, and then click the E-mail button on the Windows Live Contacts window toolbar. Or right-click the contact, point to *Send E-mail*, and then click the desired e-mail address, as shown in Figure 9.16, to open a New Message window.

When you finish working with contacts, click the Window Close (X) button to close the Windows Live Contacts window.

Note: *You also can right-click a contact in the Contacts folder of the personal folder, point to* Action, *and click* Send E-mail *to send an e-mail in Windows Live Mail. However, for this to work, Windows Live Mail has to be set as the default e-mail program in Windows 7 as described earlier.*

Using Microsoft Help Groups

Newsgroup: An online message forum where users can read and post discussion topics, questions, and responses

Post: A message submitted to a newsgroup

The bottom of the Folder pane at the left side of Windows Live Mail has an entry called Newsgroups. If you click it, you will see an entry called *Microsoft Communities* higher up in the Folder pane. This entry represents a different type of electronic messaging called a *newsgroup*. *Posts* (messages) that users send to the newsgroup are visible to other users, who can read and reply to the post as desired. In this way, users can provide support and help to one another, for free. Microsoft Communities is a collection of newsgroups about Microsoft programs like Windows 7.

To begin using Microsoft Communities, click *Microsoft Communities* in the Folder list in Windows Live Mail after clicking Newsgroups. (If a message appears asking whether you want to make Windows Live Mail the default news reader for your system, respond as desired.) Click *View Newsgroups* to download the community newsgroups. The available newsgroups will download and appear in the Newsgroup Subscriptions dialog box. To be able to read the messages in a newsgroup, you must **subscribe** to the group. You can scroll down the list of groups (type a search term in the *Display newsgroups that contain* text box to narrow the list of newsgroups), click the desired newsgroup as shown in Figure 9.17, and then click Subscribe to subscribe to it. You can repeat the process to subscribe to other newsgroups, and then click OK to finish setting up subscriptions.

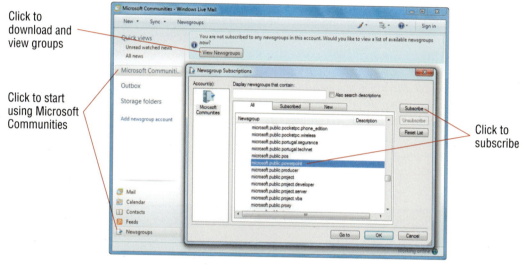

Click to download and view groups

Click to start using Microsoft Communities

Click to subscribe

Figure 9.17 Subscribing to a Microsoft Communities newsgroup.

Note: *To go to a Web-based discussion group about Windows Live Mail, click the Help button on the toolbar, and then click* Search the Mail discussion group.

Tip: Right-click Microsoft Communities, and then click Newsgroups to reopen the Newsgroup Subscriptions dialog box so you can change which newsgroups you subscribe to, or click Reset List to check for new newsgroups.

To read newsgroup messages in Windows Live Mail, double-click *Microsoft Communities* in the Folder list to display the subscribed newsgroups, if needed, and then click the name of the group to read. Windows Live Mail downloads the messages in the group and displays them in a Message list, just as for e-mail messages. To view a message, click it in the list. The message contents appear in the Reading pane at the bottom of the window. Clicking a plus to the left of a message expands the responses to the message. You can click a response to view its contents, as well.

As with an e-mail message, you can click the Reply button on the Windows Live Mail window toolbar to respond to the newsgroup message's sender, or click Forward to forward the message via e-mail. If you want to respond to the message publicly—that is, to post your response back to the newsgroup—click the Reply group button. The first time you do so, a User Information dialog box will appear to ask you to verify the *Display Name* and *E-mail Address* to use for your post; change those if needed, and then click OK. Then type your response in the message window, and click Send.

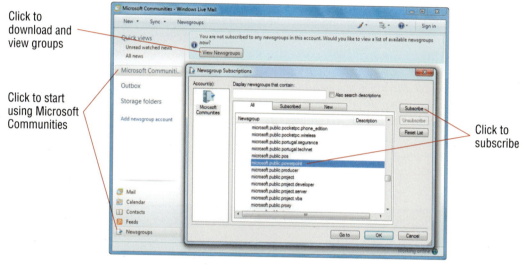

Subscribe: To indicate that you want to download and receive messages from a particular newsgroup in Windows Live Mail

To create a brand-new post to the group, click the New button at the far left end of the toolbar. Confirm your User Information, enter a message Subject, and add the Message text, just as you would for an e-mail message, and then click Send to send the message to the newsgroup. Be aware it may take a few hours for your message to show up, depending on the speed with which the news server handles messages.

After you finish working with newsgroups, click Mail in the list at the bottom of the Folder pane to return to using Mail.

Note: *Some ISPs host a news server that offers access to thousands of other public newsgroups. You can access those newsgroups by setting up an account for the news server in Mail. Choose Tools, Accounts. Click Add, click Newsgroup Account, and then click Next. Follow the wizard screens to set your display name and e-mail address, enter the news server name (usually in the format mail.isp.com), and specify logon information, if required. After you set up the news server account, it will appear in the Folder list so you can select it to subscribe to its newsgroups and view messages. Many users supply anonymous display names and e-mail addresses when participating in public newsgroups to avoid spam and identity theft.*

 Exercise 5

Adding, E-mailing, and Deleting a Contact

1. In the Windows Live Mail window, click Contacts in the bottom of the list in the Folder pane.
2. Click New on the Windows Live Contacts window toolbar.
3. Click Contact in the list at the left side of the Add a Contact window.
4. Enter your instructor's name in the *First name* and *Last name* text boxes.
5. Click in the *Work e-mail* text box, and type your instructor's e-mail address.
6. Click Add contact to finish adding your instructor as a contact.
7. Click the instructor contact in the list of contacts.
8. Capture a screen shot, paste it into Paint, and save the file as **C09E05S08**.
9. Minimize the Windows Live Contacts window.
10. Click Newsgroups at the bottom of the Folder pane. (If a message about setting the default news client appears, click No to continue.)
11. Right-click Microsoft Communities in the Folder pane, and then click *Newsgroups*.
12. In the Newsgroup Subscriptions dialog box, scroll through the list of newsgroups, click one, click Subscribe, and then click Go to.
13. If needed, double-click the new newsgroup in the Folder pane to download its messages.
14. Read and select a particular post or response, and then click Forward in the toolbar.
15. A New Message window appears. Use the To button to select your instructor as the contact to whom you want to forward the message.
16. Click in the *Subject* text box to the right of the existing subject text, and type Chapter 09 Exercise 05 to add that information to the existing text.
17. Click Send on the message window toolbar to send the message.
18. Reopen the Windows Live Contacts window from the taskbar.
19. Click the instructor contact, if needed, click Delete on the Windows Live Contacts window toolbar, and click OK to confirm the deletion.
20. Click the Close (X) button for the Windows Live Contacts window.
21. Click the Menus button on the Windows Live Mail window toolbar, and then click Options.
22. Click the Signatures tab, select the signature you created in Exercise 4 in the *Signatures* list, and click Remove. Click OK.
21. E-mail your screen shot to your instructor or submit it on a USB flash drive, as required.

Managing Your Time with the Calendar

Windows Live Mail includes a useful calendar function, which you can use to manage your appointments and events to attend. The Windows Live Mail calendar can help a typical person organize his or her home, student, or professional life.

To display the Calendar, click Calendar in the list at the bottom of the Folder pane in Windows Live Mail. The Calendar opens in Windows Live Mail, showing the current date, as shown in Figure 9.18.

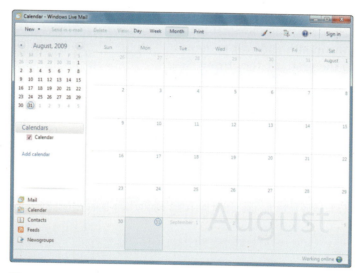

Figure 9.18 Track appointments using the Windows Live Mail Calendar.

The Folder pane shows the current overall calendar and a Calendars section where you can create calendars for different purposes, such as Home, Work, and Kids. You can use the calendar at the top to select the date to display or to add tasks. You can use the *Add calendar* choice under Calendars to add a calendar for each person or purpose as you desire. The appointments for each calendar will be color-coded with the color you assign to the calendar when you create it, so that you can see, at a glance, which activities pertain to a particular calendar.

To create a new calendar, click the *Add calendar* link under Calendars in the Folder pane. In the Add a Calendar dialog box that appears, type a *Calendar name* entry for the new calendar, click a color chip, enter an optional *Description*, and click OK.

Displaying a Date

With any luck, you will be using Calendar in Windows Live Mail to plan your activities well in advance of when you need to attend an appointment. This means that you need to be able to display the future date on which an appointment will occur to schedule that date in Calendar. Use the calendar at the top of the Folder pane to display a particular date for scheduling.

If the date on which you need to schedule an appointment occurs during the month currently displayed, click the desired date on the calendar. If the calendar shows the wrong month, use the arrows at the top, to the left and right of the month and year, to scroll to another month. You also can click the month and year at the top to "zoom" the calendar so you can jump more quickly to another month.

To select another date:

1. Click the left or right arrow beside the month and year at the top of the calendar in the Folder pane to display the desired month.
   OR
   Click the month and year at the top to "zoom out" to a listing of months for the current year, and then click the *desired month*. Or, click the month and year to zoom out to the year, use the arrows to the left and right of the year to move to the desired year, and then click the desired month.

2. Click the *desired date*. The schedule for that date appears.

Tip: Click Go to today below the calendar in the Folder pane to jump to the current date.

Changing the View

When you are trying to keep on track for a particular day, viewing the calendar in the default Month view does not provide the needed level of detail. You may want to change the view of your calendar to see a single day, or a week, like the example shown in Figure 9.19. Click the desired view button on the Calendar – Windows Live Mail window toolbar to select the view.

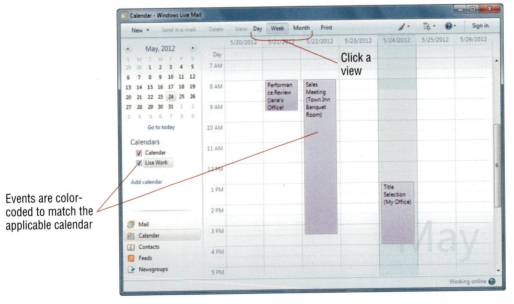

Figure 9.19 Change to Day view or Week view, shown here.

Adding an Event

An *event* is a period of time identified in the Calendar during which you are scheduled for a specified activity in a certain location. You schedule events in the Calendar so that you can see your commitments and avoid making overlapping commitments.

The Day and Week views show each event's name and location, and graphically identify the time schedule for the event. Each event is also color-coded to match the calendar to which it belongs and is marked as an all-day event, if applicable.

Event: A time period for which you have scheduled a particular activity in Windows Live Mail Calendar

To create an event:

Here's How

1. Change to Day or Week view, and display the date on which you want to add the event.
2. Double-click the time for the appointment in the day's schedule. (Click the time for the desired day when working in Week view.) The New Event window opens.
3. Type the event's topic in the *Subject* text box, and press Tab.
4. Enter additional event information as applicable:
   - **Location**. Type the location for the appointment.
   - **Start and End**. Use the calendar and time controls to specify a specific starting and ending date and time for the event, if it is not an all-day event.
   - **All day**. Check this check box if you want to block out the whole day for the event.
   - **Calendar**. Use the drop-down list to choose another person's calendar, if applicable.
   - **Select availability**. Indicate whether to mark the event time period as *Busy*, *Free*, *Tentative*, or *Away*.
   - **Notes**. Click in the large text box below the other settings and type notes about the event, such as materials you need to remember to bring.

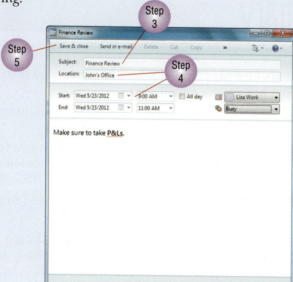

5. Click Save & close on the window toolbar to finish adding the event.

To view the details of an event, navigate to the date on which the event occurs, and then double-click the event. To remove an event, click the event on the schedule, and then click the Delete button on the toolbar.

> Tip: After you open an event in its window by double-clicking the event, you can click the Send in e-mail button on the toolbar to e-mail information about the event to anyone who needs it, such as event participants.

Exercise 6
Setting Up Events in Calendar

1. With Windows Live Mail open, click Calendar in the list at the bottom of the Folder pane.
2. Using the calendar at the top of the Folder pane, click the month and year at the top, click the right arrow button once to display the months for the following year, and then click *September*.
3. Click Week on the toolbar.
4. On the calendar at the top of the Folder pane, click the Monday of the second full week of September.
5. On the main calendar page in the window, double-click *2 PM* on the Tuesday's schedule listing.
6. In the New Event window, type **Staff Meeting** as the *Subject*.
7. Click in the *Location* text box, and type **Conference Room C**.
8. Use the *End* drop-down list to select an end time of *3:30 PM*.
9. Click Save & close on the toolbar.
10. Capture a screen shot, paste it into Paint, and save the file as **C09E06S10**.
11. Close Windows Live Mail by clicking its window Close (X) button.
12. E-mail your screen shot to your instructor or submit it on a USB flash drive, as required.

CHAPTER Summary

- Download Windows Live Mail from download.live.com and install it with Windows 7 to send and receive e-mail messages.
- Choose Start, *All Programs*, *Windows Live*, *Windows Live Mail* to start Windows Live Mail.
- The first time you start Windows Live Mail, it will prompt you to set up your e-mail account. You will need server and logon information to set up the account.
- Press Alt, and then choose Tools, *Accounts* and then click Add to begin the process for adding an e-mail account at a later time.
- Click Mail in the list at the bottom of the Folder pane at the left side of the Windows Live Mail window any time you want to work with e-mail messages.
- With the Mail feature displayed, click New on the toolbar to open a message window for a new message.

- Address the e-mail message by entering recipient e-mail addresses in the *To* text box. Include a semicolon after each address when typing multiple e-mail addresses into one of the text box. Display the *Cc* and *Bcc* text boxes to include additional recipients.

- If you have entered the e-mail address of a recipient into Contacts, you can click the To button to address the message by selecting the contact.

- Enter the message subject in the *Subject* text box, and the message text in the large message text box of the message window.

- If you want to apply stationery and formatting to message text, the message must be the using Rich Text (HTML) format rather than Plain Text format. Choose the message format by pressing Alt and using the Format menu in the message window.

- Use the buttons above the message body in the message window to apply formatting to selected text in the message body.

- Attach one or more files to send along with the message using the Attach button on the toolbar.

- Click Send on the message window toolbar to send the message to your Outbox.

- Click the Sync button on the Windows Live Mail window toolbar to send outgoing messages and receive incoming messages.

- Click the Inbox folder in the Folder pane, if needed, and then click a message in the Message list to preview its contents in the Reading pane. Double-clicking a message opens it in its own window.

- Use the Reply, Reply all, or Forward buttons to respond to a message.

- To create a new subfolder of the Inbox folder, right-click the Inbox folder in the Folder pane, click *New Folder,* type a new folder name, and then click OK.

- Select the Inbox folder, and then drag a message from the Message list onto a new folder to move the message to that folder in the Folder pane.

- To save the attachments for a selected message, right-click the attachment icon in the Reading pane or message window, and click *Save as*.

- Junk mail or spam e-mail messages are commercial messages sent to you without request.

- Because junk mail messages clog your Inbox and may include malicious software, Windows Live Mail, by default, uses its junk e-mail filter to move suspect messages to the Junk e-mail folder.

- Select a message in the Message list and press Delete to move the message to the Deleted items folder. To delete messages permanently, right-click the Deleted items folder in the Folder list and then click *Empty 'Deleted items' folder*.

- Click the Menus button, click *Options* and then click the Signatures tab to set up a signature block that you can use to sign your outgoing messages automatically.

- Click the High or Low button on the message window toolbar to specify the desired priority to inform a message recipient of the message's relative importance.

- Click Contacts in the list at the bottom of the Folder pane to open the Windows Live Contacts window, which you can use to manage information about people whom you contact often.

- Click the New button on the Windows Live Contacts window toolbar, and then enter information in the Properties dialog box that appears to set up a new contact.

- Double-click a contact to edit contact information, or to delete the contact, click the contact and then click the Delete button on the Windows Live Contacts window toolbar.
- To e-mail a contact, click the contact in the list of contacts, and then click the E-mail button on the toolbar.
- Microsoft Communities in Windows Live Mail represents newsgroups where you can post messages to get help and share information about Microsoft products.
- To begin using Microsoft Communities, click Newsgroups in the shortcut list at the bottom of the Folder pane, and then *Microsoft Communities* in the Folder pane. Right-click Microsoft Communities and click *Newsgroups* to open the Newsgroup Subscriptions window, where you can download (Reset List) newsgroups and subscribe to the groups you want to read.
- To read newsgroup messages in Windows Live Mail, double-click *Microsoft Communities* in the Folder list to display the subscribed newsgroups, and then click the name of the group to read. To view a message, click it in the Message list.
- To track upcoming events, click Calendar in the list at the bottom of the Folder pane. Click Day, Week, or Month to select a view, and use the calendar at the top of the Folder pane to navigate between dates. Double-click the desired date and time to open the New Event window and schedule an event.

CONCEPTS Check

Completion: Answer the following questions on a blank sheet of paper.

Part 1   MULTIPLE CHOICE

1. E-mail is short for _____ .
   a. effective mail
   b. event mail
   c. electronic mail
   d. effortless mail

2. Download and install the _____ program with Windows 7 to send, receive, and read e-mail.
   a. Outlook Express
   b. Eudora
   c. Outlook
   d. Windows Live Mail

3. A person to whom an e-mail message is addressed is called a _____ .
   a. receiver
   b. recipient
   c. postal resident
   d. box owner

4. Bcc: stands for _____.
   a. blind carbon copy
   b. backup carbon copy
   c. backward carbon collection
   d. beneficial cyber communication

5. Before a message sends from Windows Live Mail, it goes to the _____ folder.
   a. Send
   b. Hold
   c. Outbox
   d. Forward

6. A received e-mail message is placed in the _____ folder in Windows Live Mail.
   a. Receive
   b. Inbox
   c. To Read
   d. Incoming

7. _____ a file to send it along with an e-mail message.
   a. Insert
   b. File
   c. Pin
   d. Attach

8. Create a _____ to organize messages in Windows Live Mail.
   a. folder
   b. folio
   c. dropbox
   d. message center

9. The _____ function in Windows Live Mail helps you manage the names and e-mail address of people you e-mail frequently.
   a. Address Book
   b. Mailing List
   c. Contacts
   d. People

10. A _____ holds public messages that users can read and respond to using Windows Live Mail.
    a. newsgroup
    b. message list
    c. e-forum
    d. server

SHORT ANSWER

11. How do you start Windows Live Mail?

_____

12. How do you create a new e-mail message?

_____

13. How can you use an e-mail address that is one of your contacts from within Windows Live Mail?

_____

14. How do you send and receive messages?

_____

15. How do you read a received message?

_____

16. What button do you click if you want to send a response to all original recipients of the message?

_____

17. What button do you click to send a message to someone who was not one of the original message recipients?

_____

18. Name at least one reason why junk e-mail might be a problem.

_____

19. How do you create a new contact?

_____

20. How do you create an event in the Calendar function?

_____

SKILLS Check

Save all solution files to the default Documents folder, or any alternative folder specified by our instructor.

Guided Check

START MAIL AND SEND A MESSAGE

1

1. Trade e-mail addresses with another student, and use your partner's e-mail address to complete this exercise. He or she should use your e-mail address to complete the exercise.
2. Start Windows Live Mail.
   a. Click Start.
   b. Click *All Programs*.
   c. Click *Windows Live*.
   d. Click *Windows Live Mail*.
3. Create and address a new message.
   a. Click Mail in the list of shortcuts at the bottom of the Folder pane.
   b. Click New on the toolbar
   c. Click in the *To* text box.
   d. Type your partner's e-mail address.
   e. Click *Show Cc & Bcc* if the Cc and Bcc text boxes do not appear.
   f. Click in the *Cc* text box.
   g. Type your instructor's e-mail address.
4. Enter a subject.
   a. Click in the *Subject* text box.
   b. Type Chapter 09 Assessment 01.
5. Enter the message body.
   a. Click in the message text box.
   b. Type Thank you for receiving my practice message.
   c. Press Enter twice.
   d. Type your name.
6. Format the message text.
   a. Drag over all the text in the message body.
   b. Open the size drop-down list, which displays 10 by default, and click the *18 pt.* choice.
   c. Open the Font color drop-down list, and click Indigo (the next to last color on the top row).
   d. Click at the end of your name to deselect the text.
   e. Take a screen shot, paste the shot into Paint, and save it as C09A01.
7. Send the message.
   a. Click the Send button on the message window toolbar.
   b. Click the Sync button in the Windows Live Mail window toolbar.
8. Submit the screen shot via e-mail or on a USB flash drive to your instructor, as required.

SEND A PHOTO E-MAIL MESSAGE WITH A FILE ATTACHMENT

1. Create another message to your student partner. Click New on the Windows Live Mail window toolbar.
2. Address the message.
   a. Click in the *To* text box.
   b. Type your partner's e-mail address.
   c. Click in the *Cc* text box.
   d. Type your instructor's e-mail address.
3. Enter a subject.
   a. Click in the *Subject* text box.
   b. Type **Chapter 09 Assessment 02**.
4. Create the photo e-mail.
   a. Click the Add photos button above the message text box.
   b. Open the Chapter 9 Student Data Files folder.
   c. Double-click the **WLM** JPEG file in the Add Photos dialog box.
   d. Click Done in the dialog box.
5. Format the image.
   a. Click the image in the message body.
   b. Click the double-right arrow button to the right of the matting and frame choices, and click *Brushed edges*.
   c. Scroll down to see the bottom of the photo, click where it says *Click here to add text*, and type **See attached file for description**.
   d. Click above the photo to deselect it.
6. Attach the file.
   a. Click the Attach button on the message window toolbar.
   b. In the Open dialog box, navigate to the Chapter 9 Student Data Files folder.
   c. Click the **WLM** text document file and click Open. The file name and paper clip icon appear in the message header area, below the *Subject*.
   d. Size the message window so that the picture caption is visible.
   e. Take a screen shot, paste the shot into Paint, and save it as **C09A02**.
7. Send the message.
   a. Click the Send button on the message window toolbar.
   b. Click the Sync button on the Windows Live Mail window toolbar.
8. Submit the screen shot via e-mail or on a USB flash drive to your instructor, as required.

RECEIVE A MESSAGE AND SAVE A FILE ATTACHMENT

1. Receive messages in Windows Live Mail. Click the Sync button on the toolbar. The message(s) from your class partner should arrive.
2. Read a message.
   a. Click the Inbox folder in the Folder pane, if needed.
   b. Click the Chapter 09 Assessment 01 message in the Message list.
   c. View the message contents in the Reading pane.
   d. Take a screen shot, paste the shot into Paint, and save it as **C09A03**.
3. Save a message attachment.
   a. Click the Chapter 09 Assessment 02 message in the Message list.
   b. Right-click the attachment file icon in the Reading pane, and then click *Save as*.
   c. Use the Browse button to change to the folder specified by your instructor, if needed.
   d. Click Save.

4. Submit the screen shot via e-mail or on a USB flash drive to your instructor, as required.

Assessment 4 — VIEWING AND CHANGING JUNK E-MAIL FILTER SETTINGS

1. Open junk e-mail filter settings. With Mail still selected in the list at the bottom of the Folder pane, click the Menus button on the toolbar, and click *Safety options*.
2. Increase the protection level.
   a. On the Options tab, click *High*. This choice will move a greater number of suspicious e-mails into the Junk e-mail folder.
   b. Take a screen shot, paste the shot into Paint, and save it as **C09A04**.
   c. Click OK.
3. Reopen junk e-mail filter settings. Click the Menus button on the toolbar, and click *Safety options*.
4. Reset the protection level to the previous level.
   a. On the Options tab, click *Low*.
   b. Click OK.
5. Submit the screen shot via e-mail or on a USB flash drive to your instructor, as required.

On Your Own

Assessment 5 — CREATE AND DELETE A SIG AND SEND ANOTHER MESSAGE

1. Open the Chapter 9 Student Data Files folder, then open the **Diamond Sig.txt** file. The file should open in the Notepad application.
2. Edit the file to replace the Student Name placeholder text with your name.
3. Save the file as **C09A05** (use the File, *Save As* command) in the folder where you are saving your exercise solution files, and then close Notepad.
4. In Windows Live Mail, click the Menus button, click *Options*, and then click the Signatures tab.
5. Click New in the *Signatures* section.
6. Click the File option button under *Edit Signature*, and then use the Browse button to select the **C09A05** file you saved in Step 3 as your new sig.
7. Under *Signature settings*, click the *Add signatures to all outgoing messages* check box to check it.
8. Click OK to apply the change and close the dialog box.
9. Create a new e-mail message addressed to your instructor. Type Chapter 09 Assessment 05 as the message subject. The edited sig should appear in the message body. You can optionally type additional message text if desired.
10. Click *Hide Cc & Bcc*, if needed, so that only the *To text* box appears.
11. Send the message.
12. Click the Menus button, click *Options*, and then click the Signatures tab.
13. In the *Signatures* section, click the signature you created in Step 3, and then click Remove.
14. Click OK to finish removing the sig and close the dialog box.

FILE AND DELETE YOUR CLASS MESSAGES

1. Right-click the Inbox folder in the Folder pane, and click *New Folder*.
2. Type Chapter 09 Assessment 06 as the folder name, and then click OK.
3. Select the two messages you have received during these Assessments, and drag them into the Chapter 09 Assessment 06 folder you created in Step 2.
4. Click the Chapter 09 Assessment 06 folder to display its contents. Take a screen shot, paste the shot into Paint, and save it as **C09A06S04**.
5. Click the Chapter 09 Assessment 06 folder again, and then press Delete. Click Yes in the message box that asks you to confirm the deletion.
6. Double-click the Deleted items folder in the Folder pane to display the deleted folder. Click the Chapter 09 Assessment 06 folder to display its contents. Take a screen shot, paste the shot into Paint, and save it as **C09A06S06**.
7. Right-click the Deleted items folder, and click *Empty 'Deleted items' folder*. Click Yes to confirm the deletion.
8. Submit the screen shots via e-mail or on a USB flash drive to your instructor, as required.

ADD A CONTACT AND AN EVENT

1. Click Contacts in the list at the bottom of the Folder pane.
2. Click the New button on the toolbar.
3. Enter contact information about the student you partnered with for earlier assessments. Click Add contact to finish entering the contact.
4. Click the new contact in the list of contacts. Click the Menus button in the Windows Live Contacts window, point to Export, and click *Business card (.VCF)*. This command enables you to save the contact information for each contact as a "virtual business" card that you can later send to any e-mail recipient. Save the card in the folder where you are saving exercise files for this book.
5. Click the Windows Live Contacts window Close (X) button.
6. Click Calendar in the list at the bottom of the Folder pane in the Windows Live Mail window.
7. Select the date May 24, 2013. Add an all-day event for that date with Last Day of School as the *Subject* and Campus as the *Location*. Click Save & close to finish the event.
8. Right-click the event on the main calendar and click *Send in e-mail*.
9. In the New Message window, enter your instructor's e-mail address in the *To* text box.
10. Apply the High priority flag to the message and attach the contact file for your student partner that you created earlier. (You can delete other contacts from the folder, if desired.)
11. Click Send, click Mail in the Folder pane, and then click Sync to send the message.
12. Close the Windows Live Mail application.

CLASS ACTIVITY: CREATE AN E-MAIL EMOTICON AND SHORTCUT COLLECTION

Your instructor will start this project. Your instructor will create a Notepad file that lists the e-mail address for each student in the class. The instructor will save the file as **Emoticons and Abbreviations**, and will send an e-mail message to the first student on the list with **Emoticons and Abbreviations** attached as a file.

The student who receives the file first will save the **Emoticons and Abbreviations** file to the system hard disk. He or she will then open the file, type in an emoticon or common messaging abbreviation (such as LOL for Laugh Out

Loud), and delete his or her own e-mail address from the file. He or she should then note the e-mail address for the next student on the list, save and close the file, and then e-mail the file to the next student on the list.

In this way, the **Emoticons and Abbreviations** file will be forwarded to each student in the class, so he or she can add an emoticon or shortcut (that has not already been added by another student), delete his or her own e-mail address, and then e-mail the updated file to the next student on the list.

The final student should e-mail the file back to the instructor after adding the last emoticon or shortcut and deleting his or her own name.

Note that you are allowed to research emoticons and abbreviations on the Web, so feel free to do so.

CHALLENGE Project

You are self-employed, and you just started using the Windows 7 operating system, but you have questions about using Windows Live Mail. Subscribe to the microsoft.public.windows.live.mail.desktop newsgroup that is part of Microsoft Communities. Post a question to the group. Cc: your instructor when you post the message. After a day or so, check the newsgroup to see if there have been any responses to your question. If there are, forward at least one of those messages to your instructor.

CHAPTER 10

Working with Digital Photographs and Music

PERFORMANCE OBJECTIVES

Upon successful completion of Chapter 10, you will be able to:

- Import pictures from a digital camera
- Use the Pictures library and preview a picture
- Play pictures on-screen as a slide show
- Copy images into Windows Live Photo Gallery
- Organize, tag, and arrange images in Windows Live Photo Gallery
- Find, print, and e-mail images
- Build a music library in Media Player
- Rip your songs from an audio CD
- Build and play a playlist
- Sync with a portable music player
- Copy the songs from a playlist to CD-R
- Stream music

The Web and more powerful computers have paved the way for more rich and interactive electronic communications. Even everyday business communications, like a letter, might contain a picture, and other communications, like e-mail, might include sounds. Media capabilities also make your computer more personal and pleasing to use, such as displaying on your desktop a digital picture you took or playing some favorite music while you work. Business communications increasingly include more media, as well, from newsletter e-mails that include product information and photos to presentations with audio and video. This chapter shows you how to use the digital media management capabilities featured in Windows 7.

Importing Pictures from a Digital Camera into Windows 7

Digital picture: An image or picture saved in digital format for use in computer documents and Web pages

Digital camera: A device that captures pictures and stores them on digital storage media

Documents that integrate pictures, as well as text, have become more of the norm rather than an exception in business and personal communications. Most commercial Web pages include at least one **digital picture**. Windows 7, like its predecessor Windows versions, enables you to transfer digital images from a **digital camera** and store and organize those images on your computer's hard disk for use in your business and personal documents.

A digital camera works in a way that is similar to a traditional film camera. Light comes through the lens and an opening called the aperture when you press a button to take the picture (open the shutter). Rather than striking film to create the image, in a digital camera the light strikes an optical sensor that then enables the camera to digitize the image and store it on digital storage media within the camera.

Besides the fact that you can use a digital camera with your computer, three factors really have contributed to the fast rise in popularity of digital cameras. First, there is immediacy. You don't have to wait for film to be developed to see your pictures. With a digital camera, you can view a picture immediately on the LCD on the back of the camera. Second, storing images on removable media, a hard disk, or a CD-R is extremely cheap compared with the costs of film and film development. And third, digital images are more easily shared and used than prints from a photo camera. You can e-mail your images, post them online, include them in documents, combine them in a collage, and manipulate them in any number of ways depending on the software you have available.

Transferring Pictures from a Digital Camera or Removable Media

Most digital cameras connect to the computer via a USB port. Generally speaking, if your camera model is supported by Windows 7, all you do is make the connection and Windows 7 will enable you to transfer the images to your system's hard disk. If you prefer to remove the Secure Digital (SD), Compact Flash (CF) or other removable flash memory card from the camera and insert it into a card reader, Windows 7 also will recognize images stored on CD-R. Windows 7 can transfer images from there, as well. Many notebook and desktop computer models have built-in flash media card readers.

Here's How ▶ To transfer digital photos from a digital camera or storage card:

1. Connect the camera to the computer via the camera's USB cable, or connect the digital card reader to the system via its cable. If your digital card reader is integrated into the system, as on some newer "media center" or mobile PCs, you need not connect it.

2. Power the camera on, and put it in its Playback or Transfer mode. If you are working with a digital card reader, insert the card into the reader or slot. The AutoPlay dialog box appears.

3. Click *Import pictures and videos using Windows*.

4. In the Import Pictures and Videos dialog box, enter a **tag** to identify the pictures in the *Tag these pictures (optional)* text box. The tag you enter becomes the name of the folder where Windows 7 places the imported digital photos.

5. Click Import. The import begins.

Tag: A file property that you assign to identify a folder or file in more detail so you can find information more easily

6. While the import proceeds, an *Erase after importing* check box appears in the Import Pictures and Videos dialog box. You can check that check box to have Windows 7 delete the original shots from the camera's storage after the pictures are imported, if you need to do so to free up storage space in the camera. During the import, Windows also compares the pictures on the camera or card with pictures that you have already imported, and skips any duplicate images.

7. After the import finishes, which may take several minutes depending on the number of images stored in your camera, Windows 7 automatically displays the imported pictures in a virtual folder named Imported Pictures and Videos. You can work with them there as described later in the chapter. Power off and disconnect the camera. Or, use the Safely Remove feature in Windows 7 to secure the storage card, and then remove it from the reader slot and disconnect the reader, if needed.

Note: *Rather than importing the pictures from the camera, you can copy them. To do so, click Open device to view files using Windows Explorer in the AutoPlay dialog box. This opens an Explorer window for the camera or storage card. In that window, you can select and copy image files and paste them to any other folder on your system, just as you would for any other file.*

Note: *Some digital cameras may be compatible with a feature called Device Stage, which enables you to not only import pictures, but also perform other hardware functions. If your camera is compatible with Device Stage, Device Stage will open instead of AutoPlay when you connect your camera. If that happens, click the task link for importing or copying pictures and videos from the camera.*

Viewing Pictures in the Pictures Library

By default, images that have been transferred to your system are placed in a subfolder of the My Pictures folder in your personal folder, meaning they will also appear in the Pictures library by default. To open the Pictures library, click Start on the taskbar and then click *Pictures* in the right pane of the Start menu.

Each time you use Windows 7 to import images automatically, as just described, it creates a folder and assigns the date of the import along with any specified tag as the folder name, as shown in the example in Figure 10.1. To view the pictures in any folder, double-click the folder icon.

Figure 10.1 The folder holding imported pictures is named with the import date and any tag you specified.

As shown in Figure 10.2, the icon for each imported picture shows a preview of the picture. Using the Views menu to choose a larger icon size will enable you to preview the pictures more easily in the Pictures library. The import process assigned a name to each photo that includes the tag, if you specified one, and a sequential number. Most digital cameras save images in the JPEG (.jpg) or TIFF (.tif) format automatically.

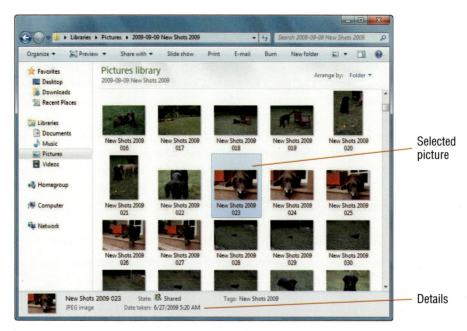

Figure 10.2 The name of each imported picture includes the tag you entered during the import and a sequential number.

To select a photo, click it. To preview a digital photo at a larger size, double-click it in the Pictures library. By default, the picture opens in Windows Photo Viewer. If you instead want to view it in another application, select the picture, click the drop-down list arrow beside the Preview button on the toolbar, and click the name of the application in which you want to open the picture.

> Tip: You can right-click any image in a Pictures library or a subfolder and then click *Set as desktop background* to place the image on the desktop.

Exercise 1

Transferring Digital Camera Images

1. Take some pictures with your digital camera or a digital camera being made available for this class by your instructor. (Ideally, you won't have any other images stored on the camera when you start.)
2. Connect the camera or a card reader to the system via its cable.
3. Power the camera on and put it in its playback or transfer position. Or, remove the storage card from the camera and place it in the card reader.
4. Click *Import pictures and videos using Windows* in the AutoPlay dialog box.
5. Type **Chapter 10 Exercise 01 Import** in the *Tag these pictures (optional)* text box in the Import Pictures and Videos dialog box.
6. Click Import.
7. When the window with the imported pictures opens, Click the Close (X) button to close it.
8. Power down and disconnect the camera, or safely remove the storage card from the card reader.
9. Click Start, and then click *Pictures* in the list under your user name.
10. Double-click the folder icon for the folder that holds the pictures you just imported, which will have the date plus the Chapter 10 Exercise 01 tag in its name.
11. Capture a screen shot, paste it into Paint, and save the file as **C10E01S11**.
12. Click the Close (X) button to close the Pictures library window.
13. Submit the screen shot via e-mail or a USB flash drive to your instructor, as required.

Showing a Slide Show of the Pictures in a Folder

While you have the option of using a digital picture you have taken as the Windows 7 desktop background image to personalize your computer, why settle for one image? You can instead play back the images stored in any subfolder of your Pictures folder as an on-screen **slide show**.

Not only does a slide show make a nice decorative statement on the desktop, but you can use a slide show to present pictures of a subject or topic during a presentation if you lack a true presentation graphics program.

Slide show: A feature that automatically displays each picture from a folder on-screen in sequence

Note: Even if a folder holds picture files of the same file formats typically used by digital cameras (JPEG or TIFF), you will not be able to play the folder's contents as a slide show unless the folder is properly customized. Windows 7 only recognizes subfolders of the My Pictures folder (in your user folder) and the Pictures library as pictures windows, by default. To optimize a folder to offer all the picture features, right-click in the folder's Explorer window and click Properties in the shortcut menu. On the Customize tab of the Properties dialog box, open the Optimize this folder for drop-down list, click Pictures, and click OK.

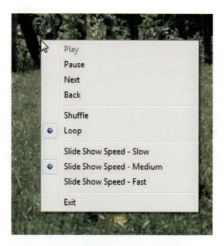

Figure 10.3 Right-click a slide show to see a menu of options for controlling its playback.

To start a slideshow, open the Pictures library (Start, *Pictures*), and then navigate to the folder that holds the picture files to play. Click the Slide show button on the command bar. The slide show begins playing immediately.

To control the slide show, right-click any slide. As shown in Figure 10.3, a shortcut menu with options for controlling the show appears.

- **Pause**. Click to stop the slide show, freezing it at the current image. To resume the slide show, right-click the screen and then click *Play*.

- **Next and Back**. Jump ahead to the next image or go back to an already-displayed image.

- **Shuffle or Loop**. Click one of these options to determine whether the slide show displays images in random order (Shuffle) or each in order, repeating the sequence after all images have been displayed (Loop).

- **Slide Show Speed—Slow, Slide Show Speed—Medium, or Slide Show Speed—Fast**. Click one of these choices to specify how quickly Windows 7 should move from one image to the next in the slide show.

- **Exit**. Click to exit the slide show.

In addition to using the Exit command on the shortcut menu to end the slide show, you can press Esc on the keyboard.

Note: *The Desktop Gadget Gallery includes a Slide Show gadget, by default, that plays back the contents of the Pictures library and its subfolders. You can use the Options for this gadget to play pictures from another folder.*

 Exercise 2

Play a Slide Show and View Your My Pictures Folder

1. Click Start, and then click *Pictures*.
2. Double-click the Chapter 10 Exercise 01 Import folder you created in the last exercise.
3. Click the Slide show button on the command bar.
4. Right-click the slide show. With the shortcut menu open, capture a screen shot. Click Exit to leave the slide show. (You cannot work in applications with the slide show running.)
5. Paste the screen shot you made in Step 4 into Paint, and save the file as **C10E02S05**.
6. Go back to the Chapter 10 Exercise 01 Import folder window.
7. Click the Slide show button on the command bar to run the show again.
8. Press Esc to finish the slide show.
9. Click the Close (X) button to close the Pictures library window.
10. Click Start, and then click your user name.
11. Double-click the My Pictures folder.
12. Double-click the folder icon for the folder that holds the pictures you just imported, which will have the date plus the Chapter 10 Exercise 01 tag in its name.
13. Capture a screen shot, paste it into Paint, and save the file as **C10E02S13**.
14. Click the Close (X) button to close the My Pictures window.
15. Submit the screen shots via e-mail or a USB flash drive to your instructor, as required.

Using Windows Live Photo Gallery

Windows Live Photo Gallery provides a centralized location where you can view and organize digital images that you have shot with a digital camera or obtained from another source. It offers all of the features that the Pictures library does, plus some additional features like the ability to fix a photo or add additional information such as a caption or more tags. Like Windows Live Mail, you can download Windows Live Photo Gallery for free at Microsoft's download.live.com Web site and install it at any time.

Note: *If your media needs include working with video, the download.live.com site also offers a free download of Movie Maker, a program you can use to create your own movies from your video clips, digital photos, and music.*

Starting and Exiting Windows Live Photo Gallery

You can start Windows Live Photo Gallery, shown in Figure 10.4, by clicking Start, clicking *All Programs*, clicking *Windows Live*, and then clicking *Windows Live*

Photo Gallery. Of course, if the Windows Live Photo Gallery startup command already appears in the left pane of the Start menu because you have used it often, then you can click it directly after clicking Start. If the Sign in to Windows Live dialog box opens, you can enter your Windows Live ID and password and click Sign In, or simply click Cancel to bypass the dialog box. Signing in with a Windows Live ID enables you to take advantage of additional features such as automatically publishing your photos online.

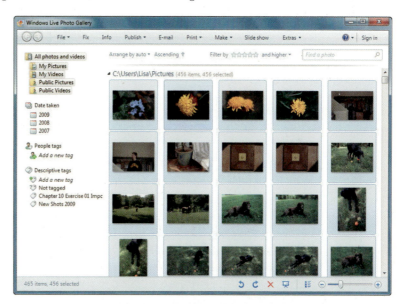

To exit Windows Live Photo Gallery, you can click File on the toolbar and then click *Exit*, click its window Close (X) button, or press Alt+F4.

Figure 10.4 Windows Live Photo Gallery enables you to work with and organize the images you have imported.

Importing Images in Windows Live Photo Gallery

By default, Windows Live Photo Gallery shows all the pictures in your My Pictures folder, as well as those in the Public Pictures folder, just as the Pictures library does. (It also shows all the videos stored in the corresponding folders for videos.) Windows Live Photo Gallery enables you to import images from either a scanner or a digital camera into the *gallery*. A *scanner* uses an optical device to read the analog (continuous) information in a picture hard copy and converts that information into a digital copy that can be stored on a computer. While several types of scanners have been available over time, the most prevalent type is the flatbed scanner, where you place the image facedown on the glass scanner bed for scanning.

Scanner: A device that optically reads a hard copy of a picture to create a digital copy

Gallery: The images that Windows Live Photo Gallery tracks (displays) because you have either imported the images or added the folder holding the images

Start out by connecting the digital camera (or card reader) or scanner, and power the device on. In the case of the camera, also put it in Playback or Transfer mode. In the case of the scanner, place the image to import facedown on the scan surface. Then, in Windows Live Photo Gallery, click File on the toolbar and then click *Import from a camera or scanner*.

Note: *After you install Windows Live Photo Gallery and connect a digital camera or insert a flash media card with pictures, the AutoPlay window that appears includes a View pictures using Windows Live Photo Gallery command that you can click. Then, you can click the Import to gallery button on the command bar of the window that appears to import the images into Photo Gallery.*

In the Import Photos and Videos dialog box that appears (Figure 10.5), click the scanner or camera from which you want to import, and then click the Import button. When importing from a camera or card reader, Windows Live Photo

Figure 10.5 **Select the device for the import.**

Gallery indicates the number of items found for import. You can leave the *Review, organize, and group items to import* option selected and then click Next; then you can use the expanded dialog box that appears (Figure 10.6) to check and uncheck groups to import, click an *Enter a name* prompt and type a name for a group, or click an *Add tags* prompt and type additional descriptive tags to help with organizing and finding images. Click Import when you finish making your choices. Or, if you click *Import all new items now* in the Import Photos and Videos dialog box, you can type in a name and add tags directly, and click Import to import all images under the specified name and tags. When importing from a scanner, you will get the opportunity to choose settings for the scan, such as whether to scan in color or grayscale. Respond to the prompts as needed for either type of import. When the import finishes, you can power down and disconnect the device, if desired.

Choose groups
to import

Work with names
and tags

View individual
photos

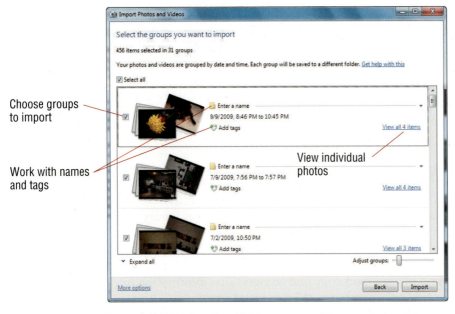

Figure 10.6 **Choosing which groups and images to import.**

Note: *Graphic images from existing sources like magazines or online sites like Flickr are typically protected by copyright law. Make sure you understand fair use laws and different forms of licenses such as Creative Commons before you download or scan and use an image for any commercial purpose.*

Adding a Folder of Images

If images have already been stored elsewhere on your system or network, you can add that folder to the gallery. No matter where an image is actually stored, adding it to the gallery means that you can work with it just like an image that you have imported directly.

Here's How

To add a folder to the gallery:

1. Click File on the Windows Live Photo Gallery command bar, and then click *Include a folder in the Gallery*. The Include a Folder in the Gallery dialog box appears.
2. In the folder tree, select the folder that holds the images to add.
3. Click OK. A message box informs you when the photos have been added to the gallery.
4. Click OK to close the message box.

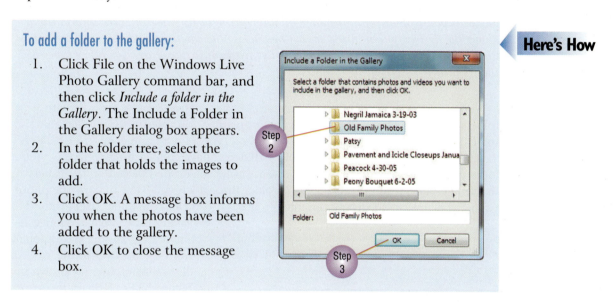

To remove a folder, right-click it in the pane at the left and click *Remove from the gallery*.

Viewing Images and Organizing within Photo Gallery

Windows Live Photo Gallery organizes the images in the gallery according to the year the photos were taken. The pane at the left lists the years that imported photos were taken, as shown in Figure 10.7.

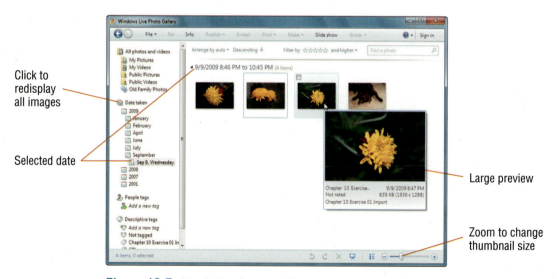

Click to redisplay all images

Selected date

Large preview

Zoom to change thumbnail size

Figure 10.7 **Displaying images taken on a particular date.**

You can display only photos with a particular tag or rating or photos that were taken on a particular date. To do so, double-click the year and month and then click the desired date under Date taken, or click the desired tag under Descriptive tags in the pane at the left. For example, in Figure 10.7 a particular date was selected in the pane, so only images taken on that date appear. To redisplay all images, click *Date taken* or *All pictures and videos*.

To select an image, click its thumbnail. If you want to see a larger preview of any image, move the mouse pointer over its thumbnail. Figure 10.7 also shows an example of this type of preview. You also can drag the slider at the bottom-right corner of the window to resize all the thumbnails.

Note: *If you cannot find an image by navigating to it, you can enter information about the desired photo in the search box below the command bar, as in the Pictures library window. Searching for picture files works just like search for other types of files, which is described in Chapter 3.*

You can use the folder tree that appears under *All photos and videos* to create folders in which you might want to further organize your photos. Right-click any folder or subfolder there, click *Create new folder*, type a folder name, and press Enter. To copy or move a photo into any folder that you have created, first go to the location or choose the display method that shows the desired picture in the gallery list. In the pane at the left, display the folder into which you want to copy the photo using the arrows to the left of the folder icons. (If you click the folder itself, the gallery list of images changes.) Then, drag an image thumbnail from the list over to the destination folder, as shown in Figure 10.8. If the folder is on the same disk, it will be moved rather than copied.

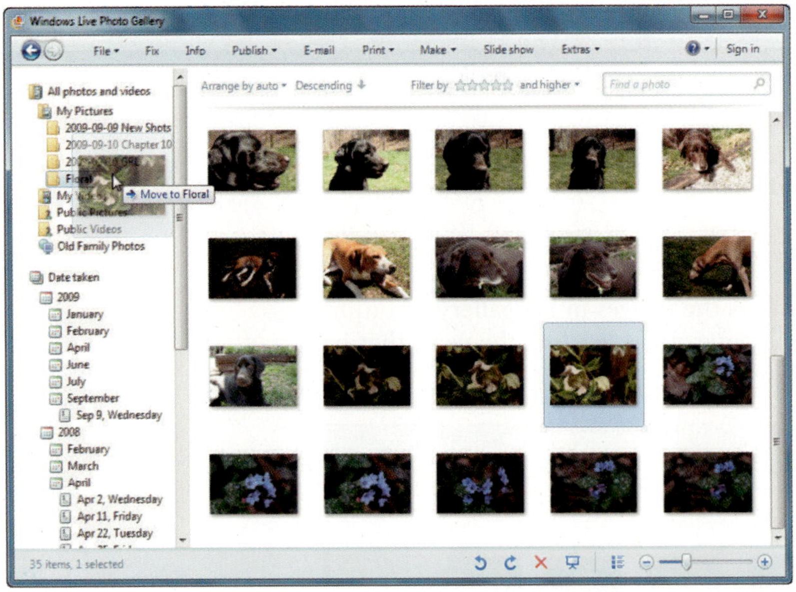

Figure 10.8 Drag an image over a folder to move or copy the image there.

To delete an image from any location in Photo Gallery, click its thumbnail and press the Delete key. Click Yes to confirm the deletion in the Delete File dialog box. Remember, if you imported an image from a location other than your computer, such as a network location, deleting an image deletes it permanently. Deleting an image stored on your system's hard disk moves the image to the Recycle Bin.

Making Basic Photo Fixes

Both the Pictures library and Windows Live Photo Gallery enable you to correct a photo's orientation. You might need to do this, for example, if you rotate the camera so that you can shoot a picture with a portrait (tall) orientation to fit in a subject that is vertically oriented. When you do that, the photo appears to be lying on its side in the Pictures library or Photo Gallery. To correct this situation in either location, right-click the photo and click either *Rotate clockwise* or *Rotate counterclockwise*. The photo immediately snaps to the corrected orientation and keeps that orientation until you rotate it again.

Photo Gallery offers the advantage of enabling you to make additional corrections to a selected photo. You can adjust exposure (apparent brightness and contrast), color, cropping, or fix red-eye—when the subject appears to have glowing red or green eyes in a photo.

Here's How

To correct a photo:

1. Select the category or location that holds the photo to edit in the pane at the left.
2. Click the photo to fix in the gallery list.
3. Click Fix on the command bar. The photo opens by itself for editing, then the Fix pane appears at the right.
4. Use the choices in the Fix pane to fix the photo as desired. You can use one or any combination of the fixes, but Microsoft recommends that if you plan to make multiple changes, make them in the order in which the Fix pane lists them. To collapse an option, click the option name again. The fixes listed in the Fix pane are:
   - **Auto adjust**. Click to have Photo Gallery fix exposure and color by making choices for you.
   - **Adjust exposure**. Click this choice, and then drag the *Brightness, Contrast, Shadows,* and/or *Highlights* sliders until the image looks as desired.
   - **Adjust color**. Click this choice, and then drag the *Color Temperature, Tint,* and/or *Saturation* sliders until the image looks as desired.
   - **Straighten photo**. Click this choice, and then drag the slider until the image looks as desired.
   - **Crop photo**. Click this choice, drag the handles on the crop frame until it identifies the portion of the image that you want to keep, and then click Apply.
   - **Adjust detail**. Click this choice, and then drag the *Sharpen* and *Reduce Noise* sliders. Clicking the Analyze button provides a suggested *Reduce Noise* setting.
   - **Fix red eye**. Click this choice, and then drag over the eye to fix in the image.
   - **Black and white effects**. Click this choice, and then click one of the thumbnails that appear to colorize the image accordingly.

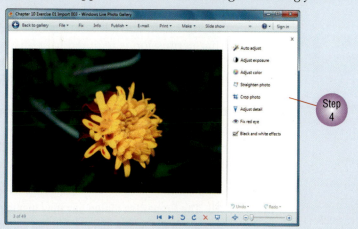

5. To undo and redo changes as you make them, click *Undo* or *Redo* at the bottom of the Fix pane.

6. When the image looks the way you want, click Back to gallery on the command bar to return to the regular Gallery display. Photo Gallery automatically saves the changes you made to your image. Click OK if a dialog box notifies you that you can revert the changes.

Applying Tags, Ratings, and Other Info

Rating: Assigning a certain number of stars to a file to identify how much you like it or how important it is

As with rotating a photo, you can work with some photo information (properties) in either the Pictures library or Windows Live Photo Gallery.

If you click a picture in its folder in the Pictures library, you can add a tag or a *rating* using the Tags or Rating choices in the details pane at the bottom of the window. Click to the right of Tags so that you see *Add a tag*, type the new tag, press Enter or click Save. If you start typing a tag name that exists, a drop-down appears; click to place a check mark beside the desired tag, and click Save.

Added rating   Added tag

Figure 10.9 You can apply a rating to a photo in the details pane of the Pictures library window.

To add a rating, point to the number of stars you want to add beside Rating in the details pane. When the correct number of stars are highlighted, as in Figure 10.9, click the start under the mouse pointer and then click the Save button.

You can work with tags, ratings, and even more file information in the Properties dialog box for an image file, just as for any other file, which you learned about in Chapter 4. Right-click the image file in the folder, and click *Properties*. Click the Details tab, change settings as desired, and click OK to apply the changes. Special settings you may want to pay attention to here include adding a photo Title, Subject, and Authors to help better identify the photo if it will be distributed for use by other parties. In such a scenario, adding a *Copyright* field entry is also a good idea to put others on notice that permission is required for re-using the image. Note that if you scroll down the Details tab, you can see information about the image size, the camera and settings used to create the image (Figure 10.10), and more, assuming your camera stores those kinds of details with each image file.

And, as with any other file, you can rename a picture file in a folder window by right-clicking the file, clicking *Rename*, typing the new name, and pressing Enter.

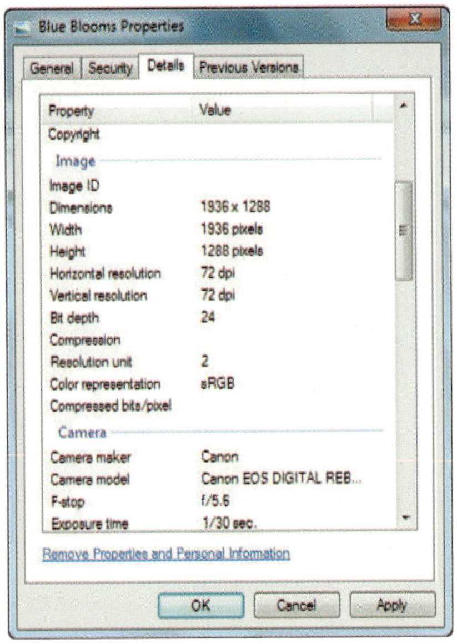

Figure 10.10 The Properties dialog box may display more details about the image and the camera settings used to take it.

In Windows Live Photo Gallery, you also can change a variety of settings, but there, you use the Info pane. Click the photo for which you want to change settings in the gallery list, and then click Info in the command bar. The Info pane appears at the right side of the window, as shown in the example in Figure 10.11.

Changing settings in the Info pane primarily consists of clicking and typing. You can click the file's name, date, time, *Add descriptive tags*, or *Add caption*; type the desired new entry or changes; and then press Enter. The only exception is assigning a rating. In that case, just click the desired number of stars under the image size information. When you finish updating the image information in Photo Gallery, click the Info button again to close the Info pane.

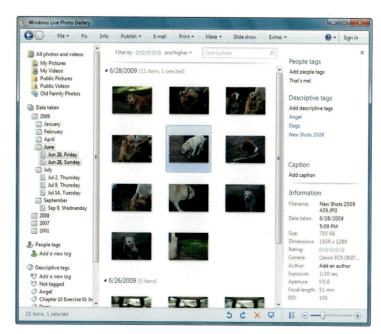

Figure 10.11 Use the Info pane in Photo Gallery to change image settings.

 Exercise 3

Fixing and Tagging an Image

1. Click Start, click *All Programs*, click *Windows Live*, and then click *Windows Live Photo Gallery*.
2. Click File on the toolbar, and then click *Include a folder in the gallery*.
3. Locate Student Data Files at www.emcp.net/windows7. If you have not already done so, download files to your computer or to your USB flash drive. Ask your instructor for assistance, if needed.
4. Use the folder tree in the Include a Folder in the Gallery dialog box to select the folder that holds the student data files for Chapter 10, and then click OK. Click OK again at the message that tells you the import has been completed.
5. Click the **Yellow Rose** file thumbnail in the gallery list.
6. Click Fix on the toolbar.
7. Click *Adjust exposure* in the Fix pane.
8. Drag the *Brightness* slider slightly to the right.
9. Click *Adjust color* in the Fix pane.
10. Drag the *Color temperature* slider slightly to the right.
11. Click the Back to gallery button on the toolbar to close the pane and apply your changes. Click OK if a dialog box notifies you that you can revert the changes.
12. With the image still selected, click Info on the command bar.
13. Click to apply a rating of four stars in the Info pane.
14. Click *Add descriptive tags* in the Info pane, type Floral, and press Enter.
15. Capture a screen shot, paste it into Paint, and save the file as **C10E03S14**.
16. Submit the screen shot via e-mail or a USB flash drive to your instructor, as required. Leave Windows Live Photo Gallery open for the next exercise.

Wrong Date Taken
If Photo Gallery cannot identify when an imported picture was taken, it assigns a default date and time of 12:00 a.m. January 1, 1980. To correct that date, select the image(s) to update in the Gallery, click Info to display the Info pane at the right. Click the date below the image thumbnail, edit the date that appears, and then click a blank part of the page. Click Info again to hide the Info pane.

Printing an Image

You can print the selected image from either Windows Live Photo Gallery or the Pictures library window by using the Print button on the command bar. In either case, Windows 7 displays the Print Pictures dialog box, which offers special settings for making photo prints. For example, you can print an image at standard photo sizes such as 4 x 6 inches, 5 x 7 inches, and wallet size.

Here's How ▶ To print a photo:

1. Select the photo to print in the Pictures library or Windows Live Photo Gallery. You can select multiple photos, too.
2. Click Print on the command bar. In Photo Gallery, you have to click *Print* again in the drop-down menu that appears. The Print Pictures dialog box opens.
3. Click the *Printer* drop-down list and then click the printer to use.
4. Click the *Paper size* drop-down list and then click the paper to use.
5. Click the *Quality* drop-down list and then click the quality setting to use.
6. Click the *Paper type* drop-down list and then click the paper to use. This setting is only available if the selected printer is an inkjet printer or another type of printer that changes ink or toner usage based on paper type.
7. Scroll down the list of available print layouts at the right, and click the layout to choose.
8. If you selected a single photo in Step 1 and the selected layout has a position for more than one image, increase the *Copies of each picture* text box entry to a number that matches the number of photo positions on the layout. This will repeat the image to fill all the spots on the layout.
9. Click Print. The Print Pictures dialog box sends the picture(s) to the printer.

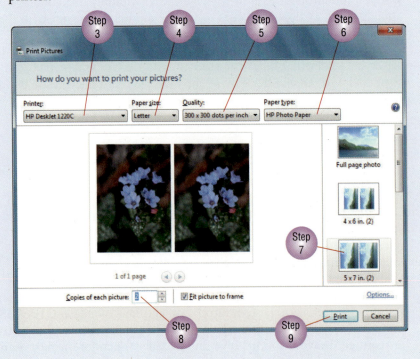

Photo Gallery offers an additional print feature. If you click Print and then *Order prints*, the Order Prints dialog box appears with a list of online printing companies. You can select a company and send digital pictures to it to have prints made, which typically requires that you set up an account and provide credit card payment information. This can be a good option when you need to make high-quality prints or even specialty items like a mug from a digital photo.

E-mailing an Image

Both the Pictures library window and Windows Live Photo Gallery enable you to e-mail one or more selected images without having to start your e-mail program first, although you do need to install and configure an e-mail program such as Windows Live Mail in order for this process to work. When you send one or more images, you can select a smaller image size to reduce transmission time. Windows 7 will then resize the images accordingly for the message.

◀ **Here's How**

To e-mail a photo:

1. Select the photo to e-mail in the Pictures library or Windows Live Photo Gallery. You can select multiple photos, too.
2. In the Pictures library, right-click the image, point to *Send to*, and click *Mail recipient*. In Windows Live Photo Gallery, click E-mail on the command bar. If you are sending the e-mail from the Pictures library, the Attach Files dialog box opens; continue to Step 3. If you sent it from Windows Live Photo Gallery, jump to Step 5.
3. Click the *Photo size* drop-down list, and then click the size to use. The dialog box shows a Total estimated size of the picture(s) when set to the selected dimensions.

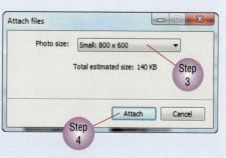

4. Click Attach. Windows 7 prepares the files to send them, and opens an e-mail message window.
5. Enter the recipient's e-mail address in the *To* text box. Change other addressing, subject, and body text information as needed, and then click Send. The message sends.

Exercise 4

Printing and E-mailing an Image

1. In Windows Live Photo Gallery, click Chapter 10 Exercise 01 Import under Descriptive tags in the navigation pane. This displays the photos you imported in Exercise 1 of this chapter.
2. Click the thumbnail for any of the images there.
3. Click Print and then *Print* on the command bar.
4. Select a printer from the *Printer* list, if needed. Leave Letter selected as the *Paper size*.
5. Scroll down the layouts, and click *3.5 × 5 in. (4)*.
6. Increase the Copies of each picture value to 4.
7. Click Print.

8. Write your name and **C10E04S08** on the printout and submit it to your instructor for grading.
9. Select another photo in the folder.
10. Click the E-mail button on the command bar.
11. Enter your instructor's e-mail address in the *To* text box, enter Chapter 10 Exercise 04 as the *Subject*, and click Send.
12. If needed, start your e-mail program (such as Windows Live Mail) and complete the send from your Outbox.
13. Close your e-mail program.
14. Click the Windows Live Photo Gallery window Close (X) button to exit the program.

Using Windows Media Player

After working with digital photos moved into the spotlight as a top use for computers, the next wave—digital music—hit. The Windows Media Player application, built into Windows 7, enables you to listen to digital music and view digital video. On the music side, you can do much more than simply listen. You can convert songs from your audio CDs to digital music, build a list of songs from different artists for playback, and even burn your own music CDs.

Starting and Exiting Media Player

Windows Media Player is pinned to the taskbar by default. To start it, you can click its taskbar icon. Or, you can click Start, click *All Programs*, and then click *Windows Media Player* in the list at the top of the left pane of the Start menu.

Player Library: The collection of songs and other media items added into Windows Media Player

Note: *The first time you start Windows Media Player, it asks you to choose initial settings, such as making Media Player the default music and video player. You can click Recommended settings and then click Finish to continue working.*

To exit Windows Media Player, you can press Alt to open the menu bar, click File, and then click *Exit*; click its window Close (X) button; or press Alt+F4.

Figure 10.12 **Windows Media Player enables you to organize your digital songs.**

Adding Files to the Player Library

Media Player tracks all your digital music and other media in its ***Player Library***. (The Player Library is within Media Player and is different from the Windows Explorer libraries, such as the Music library.) Once a song is in the library, you can play it, add a rating, add it to a list of songs for playback, and so on. To display the Music library (see Figure 10.12), click Music under Library in the navigation pane at the left side of the Media Player window. Note that the Player Library also manages other types of content, including Videos, Pictures, and Recorded TV.

Adding files to the Player Library is more of an automatic process than you might think. By default, Media Player monitors the contents of your libraries, including your Music library. Any time you add a song file to that library or any of the folders it monitors, Windows Media Player automatically adds the file to the Player Library. Media Player also adds any file you play from another location on your computer or network to the library. And, when you add songs from a CD or buy them from an online music service, they become part of the library.

Windows Media Player can store and play music files in the **Windows Media Audio**, MP3, and WAV formats.

In most instances, then, you do not have to take any action to add songs to the library. You can change the folders that Media Player monitors. Click Organize on the command bar, point to *Manage libraries*, and click *Music* in the submenu. In the Music Library Locations dialog box, use the Add button that appears to open the Include Folder in Music dialog box, select the folder to add, and click Include folder. When you finish adding folders, click the OK button in the Music Library Locations dialog box to close the dialog box. Note that you also can remove a folder in the Music Library Locations dialog box by clicking the folder and using the Remove button.

Windows Media Audio (wma): The default file format to which Windows Media Player converts and saves song files

Tip: When you play music, a list pane automatically appears at the right to give you information about what is playing.

Browsing and Rating Songs

As you perform different activities in Media Player, you will use the navigation pane choices and the tabs along the top to move between functions. Remember to click Music in the navigation pane to return to your music in the Player Library.

You can use the Library choices in the navigation pane at the left to choose how the library lists music and to help find songs. For example, to list music by artist, click *Artist*. You can then double-click any artist that appears to see the songs by that artist. To list music by type, you can click *Genre*, and then double-click any category that appears to see the songs in that category.

After you have browsed to a particular list of songs, you can click a song to select it, or double-click a song to play it. You can click the Back button in the upper-left corner, which looks and works just like the Back button in an Explorer window, to back up from the location to which you browsed. Or, to return to viewing a list of songs, click *Music* in the navigation pane.

As with pictures, you can apply or change the star rating for a song. To do so, browse to the song in the library. Move the mouse pointer over the desired number of stars in the Rating column (Figure 10.13), and then click with the mouse.

QUICK FIX

Don't Need the List
If Media Player is displaying the list pane at the right and you want to close it, click Organize, point to *Layout*, and click *Show list* to uncheck it. Or, click the tab that's displayed to hide the list.

Figure 10.13 Click the rating to apply to the song.

Ripping a CD

Some of us are old enough to still have a sizeable collection of music (audio) CDs lying around. Swapping CDs in and out of the computer to play them gets a bit tiresome, and if you are traveling with your mobile PC, you do not want to add the weight of a pile of CDs.

Use Windows Media Player to *rip* music from a CD and store the music in digital format in the library. By default, Media Player saves each ripped song file in the Windows Media Audio file format. The songs ripped from each CD are placed in a separate subfolder of your My Music folder, which is monitored by the Music library, by default. Windows Media Player creates a folder for each artist, and then within that folder, a folder for each CD (album).

Note that you use this process only for audio CDs published by a music company. If you have a CD with songs that you own that have already been converted to MP3 format, for example, you should copy them to your system's hard disk in a subfolder of your Music folder. Be sure to observe all copyright laws; do not share your songs with others illegally.

Here's How ▶

To rip songs from an audio CD:

1. Make sure that your system has a live Internet connection so that Windows Media Player can assign accurate song information to each song file.
2. Insert the audio CD into the system's CD or DVD drive. Windows Media Player downloads information about the artist, album, and songs, and starts playing the CD.
3. Click the Rip CD button on the command bar. Windows Media Player displays progress information about the song being ripped.
4. When the ripping operation finishes, all the songs show Ripped to library in the *Rip status* column, and the Stop rip button changes back to Start Rip. At this point, you can click the Stop playback control button, eject the CD (right-click the CD name in the upper-left corner, point to *Play*, and click *Eject*), and rip additional CDs, if desired.

No Rip CD Button
If you can't see the Rip CD button, be sure that the list pane at the right is closed. Click the List options button in the upper-right corner of the list pane and then click *Hide list* to hide the pane.

Format Changes
To rip a CD to a format other than WMA, click the Rip settings button, point to *Format* in the menu that appears, and click the desired format before starting the rip. You also can use the *Audio Quality* submenu to choose a different quality setting.

Note: *If the AutoPlay dialog box appears when you rip a CD, you can click its Close (X) button to close it.*

Note: Windows Media Player in Windows 7 does not rip inserted CDs automatically. If you want to set it up to do so, click Organize on the command bar, and then click Options. Click the Rip Music tab, click the Rip CD automatically check box to mark it, and click OK.

Creating a Playlist

Using Windows Media Player as your digital jukebox breaks through some of the limitations of traditional audio CD players. Even though some models can play multiple CDs and use a special mode to play songs in a random order, they sometimes take a while to switch between discs and the song order may not suit you.

In Windows Media Player, you create a *playlist* to set the order in which a group of songs play. A playlist offers a number of advantages, including the fact that you can combine songs from different artists and albums, and make the playlist as long or short as you would like. For example, if your company is sponsoring a party and you want music at the event, you can create a playlist that runs for a few hours, so the music will run all through the event without the need for someone to change CDs.

Playlist: A list that specifies a group of songs for Media Player to play and the order in which it should play them

To build a playlist in Media Player:

1. Click the Play tab, and then click *Clear list* if the list pane shows previously played songs.
2. Navigate to a song to add in the library.
3. Drag the song from the library into the desired position on the list pane.
4. Repeat Steps 2 and 3 to add additional songs to the list.
5. After you add all the songs, drag them to position them in the desired order.
6. Click Save list.
7. Type a name for the list, and press Enter.
8. Click the Stop playback button to stop the playlist, if desired.

Here's How

9. Click the List options button in the upper-right corner of the list pane and then click *Hide list* to hide the pane. Or, click the Play tab again.

Playing a Playlist

You can play any individual song in the library by double-clicking it. To play a playlist, double-click *Playlists* in the navigation pane, and then double-click the name of the playlist to play. The music begins playing immediately. Note that if you try to play a song that was licensed from another source and your system does not have the correct permissions or logon installed, playback stops and a Media Usage Rights Acquisition error message appears.

> **Tip:** The lower-right corner of the Windows Media Player window includes a Switch to Now Playing button, which you can click to change to Now Playing mode, which has a smaller window. Move the mouse pointer over that window and click the Switch to Library button that appears to redisplay the Player Library.

 ## Exercise 5

Ripping a CD and Making a Playlist

1. Click the *Windows Media Player* icon on the taskbar. Or, click Start, click *All Programs,* and click *Windows Media Player.* Make sure the system is connected to the Internet.
2. Insert an audio CD (one of your own or one provided by your instructor) into the system's drive.
3. If the rip process does not start automatically, click Rip CD.
4. When the rip process finishes, capture a screen shot, paste it into Paint, and save the file as **C10E05S04**.
5. Click the Stop button to stop playback.
6. Right-click the CD name in the upper-left corner, point to *Play*, and click *Eject*.
7. Click the Play tab.
8. Navigate to the songs for the CD you just ripped, starting by clicking Music in the navigation pane.
9. Drag at least three of them to the playlist in the list pane.
10. Click Save list above the new list.
11. Type **Chapter 10 Exercise 05 List,** and press Enter to name the playlist.
12. Capture a screen shot, paste it into Paint, and save the file as **C10E05S12**.
13. Submit the screen shots via e-mail or a USB flash drive to your instructor, as required.
14. Click the Stop playback control to stop the playlist, and leave Windows Media Player open for the next exercise.

Syncing with a Portable Device

The ability to play back songs or audio information on a portable device like a digital music player is more than just a luxury. If you can play back some vital information like an audio book file during a long commute, you can make good use of time that would otherwise have been wasted. Given that many schools are starting to distribute lectures and other class materials via audio files, you might even have need to sync study materials to a device for listening on the go.

Sync: To make sure a connected device or mobile computer has the same up-to-date files as your main computer

Windows Media Player supports a wide variety of portable devices to which you can transfer your music and other audio files. Connect the device, power it on, start Media Player, and click the Sync tab to get ready to *sync*. The first time you connect, Media Player checks your device and selects the best sync method based on its capabilities and storage capacity. Devices with more than 4 GB of capacity will be set up to sync automatically, meaning that all content in the library will sync, so you can just click the Start sync button on the Sync tab at the right.

Figure 10.14 Place items to sync to the device in the list pane at the right.

For a device that you or Media Player set up to sync manually (click the Sync options button on the Sync tab, point to the device name, and click *Select settings* to open the device's properties, and click the *Start sync when this device connects* check box if available), you choose which items (songs and other forms of audio content) and playlists to add. After you click the Sync tab, drag items and playlists from the library to the list pane (Figure 10.14). If you have more than one device connected, click the applicable device in the navigation pane first, before you choose songs, other audio, and playlists. If your device is low on capacity, make sure to check at the top of the tab to verify that you have enough space remaining before you add additional items. Then, click Start Sync to sync the music and/or other audio.

Note: *Windows Media Player in Windows 7 doesn't support iPod devices automatically. However, through the use of a Windows Media plug-in (added application) available from another software publisher for a reasonable fee, Windows Media Player can see and sync with many iPod models, as in the example in Figure 10.14. If you plan to get a plug-in to sync your music with your iPod, make sure you rip the music in an audio file format supported by iPods. Usually, the MP3 format is a safe bet.*

When the sync finishes, the list pane displays a message that says the sync is complete and you can now disconnect the device. At that point, you can eject the device using the safely remove hardware feature in Windows 7 and power off and remove the device.

> **Tip:** Some downloadable content on the Web are called *podcasts*, referring to the fact that they were originally developed for playback on Apple iPod player models. However, many podcasts are distributed in MP3 format, which means you can download and play them from Media Center, and sync them from there with your non-iPod device.

Burning a Playlist to CD-R or DVD-R

Once you have created a playlist, you can burn it to a CD-R for your own personal use on other machines and audio devices. Again, copyright law applies, so burning song copies to give away to friends is not appropriate use of this functionality.

Here's How

To burn a playlist to a CD-R in Media Player:

1. Click the Burn tab.
2. Insert a blank CD-R in the drive. If the AutoPlay dialog box opens, you can click its Close (X) button to close it.
3. Drag a playlist from the navigation pane to the list pane at the right.
4. Add additional songs or playlists, checking to ensure that you have time (space on the disc) remaining before adding each.
5. Click Start burn in the list pane. After the burn finishes, Media Player automatically ejects the CD-R. You can insert another one and use the Start Burn button to create another copy, if desired.

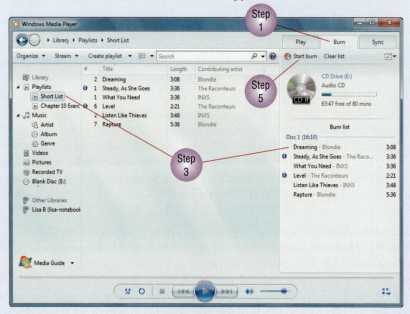

6. Click Burn to close the list pane.

Working with Media Streaming

Stream: To play back music from another computer or digital media receiver on your network

Windows Media Player can **stream** music over a network. This means that one computer can play back the music stored in another computer's Media Player Library. Network devices called digital media receivers also can play back the music from a computer's Player Library. To stream media from your system, media streaming must be turned on in Windows Media Player. This enables other computers and devices on the network to "see" or access your system's digital content. In order to stream music between computers, they must be using the Windows Vista operating system or later.

To turn on streaming, click the Stream button on the command bar, and then click *Turn on home media streaming*. If you previously set up a homegroup and made music sharing available, streaming may already be turned on, and that command won't appear. The next step is to determine which other computers and devices on your network can access your content for streaming. To allow all devices and users access, click the Stream button on the command bar, and then click *Automatically allow devices to play my media*. Confirm this choice by clicking *Automatically allow all computers and media devices* in the Allow All Media Devices dialog box. To limit access to only select computers and devices, click Stream, and then click *More streaming options*. In the *Show devices on* list, choose Allowed or Blocked as applicable for each choice or computer, and then click OK.

Once the media on another computer is shared for streaming, that computer will appear in the navigation pane in Windows Media Player, as shown in Figure 10.15. Double-click the name of the other library to open it, and then select and play music just as you would on the library stored on your own computer.

Select the other computer's libraray here →

Figure 10.15 **Music can be streamed (played) from the library on another computer.**

Note: *You can change options for streaming by clicking the Stream button and then clicking More streaming options in the menu that appears. For example, you can specify a name for your media library and change what devices and programs can access shared media.*

 Exercise 6

Burning a Music CD-R

1. Click the Burn tab.
2. Insert a blank CD-R disc (one of your own or one provided by your instructor) into the system's CD-R or DVD-R drive.
3. Drag the Chapter 10 Exercise 05 List playlist that you created in Exercise 5 of this chapter from the navigation pane to the list pane.
4. Click Start burn.
5. When the burn process finishes and the disc ejects, write your name and **C10E06S05** on the CD-R with a soft-tip marker and submit it to your instructor for grading.
6. Click the window Close (X) button to close Windows Media Player.

CHAPTER Summary

- You can import pictures from a digital camera or a storage card inserted in a media card reader. Just attach the device, power it on, and use the *Import pictures and videos using Windows* choice in the AutoPlay dialog box that appears.

- The tag you assign when importing pictures becomes part of the name of the folder where the pictures are copied and the file name for the imported pictures.

- Imported pictures are placed in a new subfolder of the My Pictures user folder, which is monitored by the Pictures library. This folder window has special features for working with picture files.

- Click the Slide Show button on the command bar in a Pictures library window to play the pictures as a slide show. Right-click the slide show to see commands for controlling it.

- Imported pictures are also available for viewing, editing, and printing in Windows Live Photo Gallery. Download the program from download.live.com. Start this application by choosing Start, *All Programs, Windows Live, Windows Live Photo Gallery*.

- To change how Photo Gallery lists images, click a choice in the pane at the left.

- Use the File, *Include a folder in the gallery* command in Photo Gallery to include pictures from other folders.

- Click a photo in Photo Gallery and then click the Fix button to see choices for editing the photo in the Fix pane.

- In the Pictures library, click an image and add a tag or rating in the details pane. Or, right-click it, click *Properties*, and click the Details tab. In Photo Gallery, click an image, and then click the Info button on the toolbar to work with the file name, rating, tags, and other information.

- Click the Print button in either the Pictures library or Windows Live Photo Gallery to prepare and send a print job.

- You can size and e-mail pictures using the E-mail button in Windows Live Photo Gallery.

- Manage your digital music in Windows Media Player. Start this application by clicking the Windows Media Player button on the taskbar or by choosing Start, *All Programs, Windows Media Player*.

- Use the pane at the left to navigate in Media Player.

- Music in the Music folder of your user folder becomes a part of the Player Library in Windows Media Player automatically. Or, you can insert an audio CD and use the Rip CD command to rip it.

- To save a group of songs as a playlist that you can replay at any time, click the Play tab. Drag songs from the library into the list pane at the right, and click Save list.

- To play a song or playlist, double-click it.

- You can take songs or other audio information with you by syncing from Media Player to a device.

- Click the Burn tab, insert a blank CD-R, drag songs or playlists to the list pane, and then click Start burn to burn a CD-R.
- Click Stream, and then click *Automatically allow devices to play my media* to enable other systems and devices on your network to stream music from your Player Library. Select a shared library in the navigation pane to stream its music.

CONCEPTS Check

Completion: Answer the following questions on a blank sheet of paper or in a Word document.

Part 1   MULTIPLE CHOICE

1. The My Pictures folder in your personal folder is also called the _____ .
   a. Pictures locker
   b. Digital drawer
   c. Pictures library
   d. Pictures finder

2. The _____ application also enables you to work with your digital photos.
   a. Windows Digital Photo Editor
   b. Windows Live Photo Gallery
   c. Windows Pictures Explorer
   d. Windows Pictures Finder

3. Adding a _____ assigns a category to a digital picture.
   a. rating
   b. label
   c. tag
   d. caption

4. Adding a _____ assigns stars to a digital picture.
   a. rating
   b. label
   c. tag
   d. caption

5. Playing a _____ show displays the images from a folder on-screen.
   a. photo
   b. desktop
   c. folder
   d. slide

6. Clicking the _____ button enables you to make changes to a digital photo.
   a. Correct
   b. Fix
   c. Edit
   d. Retouch

7. The _____ application enables you to play digital songs.
   a. Windows Song Player
   b. Windows CD Player
   c. Windows Media Player
   d. Windows Audio Player

8. Importing a song from an audio CD is called _____ the song.
   a. importing
   b. digitizing
   c. converting
   d. ripping

9. Create a _____ to select songs that you want to hear together.
   a. playlist
   b. song list
   c. favorites list
   d. replay list

10. You can _____ songs or a playlist from Media Player to a portable device.
    a. transfer
    b. trade
    c. sync
    d. push

Part **SHORT ANSWER**

2

11. Explain how to start transferring images from a digital camera to your computer.

    _____

12. In what folder does Windows 7 place the imported pictures?

    _____

13. How do you start the picture import process from the Windows 7 desktop?

    _____

14. When you print digital photos, what do you select to control the size for the printed image(s)?

    _____

15. Explain one method for adding a tag to a digital photo.

    _____

16. Which pane in Windows Media Player do you use to display certain pictures or songs?

    _____

17. Explain how to starting adding music from an audio CD to the library in Windows Media Player.

    _____

18. In what folder does Windows 7 place the imported songs?

    _____

19. Name one reason to create a playlist.

_____

20. True or False: It is legal to share digital photos you have scanned or found online or digital songs copied from an audio CD with other users.

_____

SKILLS Check

Save all solution files to the default Documents folder, or any alternate folder specified by your instructor.

Note: *If the Information bar appears at any point during these exercises, click the Close (X) button at the far-right end of the bar to close it.*

Guided Check

Assessment **PLAY A SLIDE SHOW OF SAMPLE PICTURES**

1

1. View the sample pictures that install with Windows 7.
   a. Click Start.
   b. Click *Pictures*.
   c. Double-click the Sample Pictures folder.
2. View picture information.
   a. Click a picture thumbnail.
   b. Review the information in the details pane.
3. Start and pause a slide show.
   a. Click Slide show on the command bar.
   b. Right-click the fourth image that appears, and click *Pause*.
   c. Right-click again and click *Play*.
4. Stop the slide show.
   a. Take a screen shot of the desktop.
   b. After viewing several more images, press Esc.
   c. Paste the shot into Paint, and save it as **C10A01**.
5. Click the window Close (X) button to close the folder for the Sample Pictures in the Pictures library.
6. Submit the screen shot via e-mail or a USB flash drive to your instructor, as required.

Assessment **IMPORT PICTURES INTO PHOTO GALLERY**

2

1. Start Windows Live Photo Gallery.
   a. Click Start.
   b. Click *All Programs*.
   c. Click *Windows Live*.
   d. Click *Windows Live Photo Gallery*.

2. Import the pictures.
   a. Click File on the toolbar.
   b. Click *Include a folder in the gallery*.
   c. Use the folder tree in the Include a Folder in the Gallery dialog box to select the folder holding the data files for this assessment.
   d. Click OK.
   e. Click OK again at the message that tells you the import has been completed.
   f. Take a screen shot of the desktop, paste the shot into Paint, and save it as **C10A02**.
3. Leave Windows Live Photo Gallery open for the next Assessment.
4. Submit the screen shot via e-mail or a USB flash drive to your instructor, as required.

Assessment EDIT PHOTO INFO AND MAKE A FIX

3

1. Add your name as a photo caption.
   a. Drag to select the thumbnails of all three of the photos imported in Assessment 2.
   b. Click the Info button on the command bar.
   c. Click *Add caption* in the Info pane.
   d. Type your name and press Enter.
2. Add a tag.
   a. Click *Add descriptive tags* in the Info pane.
   b. Type Floral, and press Enter.
3. Fix the color in a photo.
   a. Click the **Rhododendron.jpg** image thumbnail.
   b. Click Fix on the command bar.
   c. Click *Auto adjust* in the Fix pane.
   d. Take a screen shot, paste the shot into Paint, and save it as **C10A03**.
4. Exit Windows Live Photo Gallery.
   a. Click Back to gallery on the command bar.
   b. Click the window Close (X) button to close the program.
5. Submit the screen shot via e-mail or a USB flash drive to your instructor, as required.

Assessment RIP AND RATE MUSIC

4

1. Start Windows Media Player.
   a. Click Start.
   b. Click *All Programs*.
   c. Click *Windows Media Player*.
2. Rip an audio CD.
   a. Insert the audio CD.
   b. Click Rip CD if the rip does not start automatically.
   c. After the ripping concludes, click the Stop playback button.
   d. Right-click the CD title at upper left, point to *Play*, and click *Eject*.
3. Rate songs.
   a. Double-click Music in the navigation pane to expand it, if needed.
   b. Click *Album* under Music.
   c. Double-click the album (CD) you ripped in Step 2.
   d. In the Rating column, click to assign a star rating to at least three of the songs.
   e. Take a screen shot, paste the shot into Paint, and save it as **C10A04S03**.

4. View the rated songs.
   a. Click Music in the navigation pane.
   b. Click Organize, point to *Sort by*, and click *Rating*.
   c. Take a screen shot of the results, paste the shot into Paint, and save it as **C10A04S04**.
   d. Click Organize, point to *Sort by*, and click *Album*.
5. Exit Windows Media Player. Click the window Close (X) button to close the program.
6. Submit the screen shots via e-mail or a USB flash drive to your instructor, as required.

On Your Own

Assessment IMPORT, TAG, AND E-MAIL PICTURES

5

1. Use a digital camera (your own or one provided by your instructor) to shoot at least three pictures for this exercise. (Ideally, you won't have any other images stored on the camera when you start.)
2. Connect the camera to your computer, power it on, and change to its Playback or Transfer mode, if required.
3. Click *Import pictures and videos using Windows* in the AutoPlay dialog box and complete the import.
4. Type Chapter 10 Assessment 05 in the *Tag these pictures (optional)* text box of the Import Pictures and Videos dialog box that appears and click Import.
5. In Windows Live Photo Gallery, navigate to the location that holds the newly imported pictures.
6. Select two pictures by using Ctrl+click or dragging over the thumbnails.
7. Click the E-mail button on the command bar.
8. Address the e-mail to your instructor, enter Chapter 10 Assessment 05 as the message subject, and send it.
9. Leave Windows Live Photo Gallery open for the next Assessment, but close your e-mail program.

Assessment PRINT PICTURES

6

1. Working in the Windows Live Photo Gallery, reselect the pictures you imported and e-mailed in Assessment 5.
2. Click Print on the command bar, and click *Print* again.
3. Select the Printer specified by your instructor, leaving the Paper size and Quality settings as is.
4. Scroll down the list of layouts, and click the *3.5 x 5 in. (4)* choice.
5. Increase the *Copies of each picture* setting to 2.
6. Click Print.
7. Write your name and **C10A06** on the printout, and submit it to your instructor for grading, as required.
8. Close the Windows Live Photo Gallery.

Assessment MAKE A PLAYLIST AND BURN A CD-R

7

1. Start Windows Media Center.
2. Rip another CD.
3. Create a playlist named Chapter 10 Assessment 07.
4. Burn the playlist to CD-R.
5. Write your name and **C10A07** on the CD-R with a soft-tipped marker and submit it to your instructor for grading.

8

1. Close Windows Media Player if it is running.
2. Start Internet Explorer, and go to www.cnet.com or www.zdnet.com.
3. Find the section on the Web site that offers downloadable podcasts. On the CNET site, scroll down and look for the Podcasts tab on the right. On the ZDNet site, scroll down to the bottom, and click the Podcasts choice under ZDNet News & Blogs.
4. Navigate to a podcast of interest. (If needed, try clicking on a few links first to identify different podcasts.)
5. Right-click the download link and then click *Save Target As*.
6. In the Save As dialog box that appears, choose to save the file in the Music library, and then click Save. The podcast downloads to your computer.
7. Click Close to close the dialog box that tells you that the download is complete.
8. Close Internet Explorer.
9. Start Windows Media Player.
10. Navigate to the podcast file (click Music in the navigation pane) in the library. Double-click it, or click it and click the Play button in the playback controls at the bottom of Media Player.
11. Take a screen shot, paste the shot into Paint, and save it as **C10A08**.
12. Stop the playback and close Media Player.
13. Submit the screen shot via e-mail or a USB flash drive to your instructor, as required.

CHALLENGE Project

You are organizing a client seminar to be held in meeting rooms at a local hotel. On the morning of the seminar, continental breakfast will be offered to participants. Your boss has asked you to provide some music to play during the breakfast to set a nice tone for the event. Use Windows Media Player to create a mix CD for the event. Rip several songs, arrange them in a playlist, and burn the playlist to a CD-R. Write your name and **C10A09** on the CD-R, and submit it to your instructor.

Part 3

Windows® 7

Basic Networking and System Maintenance

➤ Using Your System on a Network

➤ Maintaining Your System

➤ Ensuring Your Safety and Privacy on the Internet

Using Your System on a Network

PERFORMANCE OBJECTIVES

Upon successful completion of Chapter 11, you will be able to:

- **Connect to a network**
- **Create and use a VPN connection**
- **View network locations**
- **Map a network drive**
- **Share files and folders on the network**
- **Work with network printers**
- **Troubleshoot a network**
- **Set up an Internet connection**

Most PCs do not stand alone—they are connected to one or more other PCs either via cables or via wireless connections. When two or more computers connect, they form a network. In this chapter, you will learn how to use networks to share information between PCs, and how to set up shortcuts to your favorite network locations.

Networking Basics

Network: A group of connected computers

Local area network (LAN): A network in which the computers are nearby one another, such as in the same building

Wide area network (WAN): A network in which the computers are physically separated, such as in different buildings or cities

A *network* is a group of connected computers. Networked computers can share files and printers with one another, and can share an Internet connection. When connected computers are in the same room or even the same building, they are part of a *local area network (LAN)*. When the computers are spread out over a greater distance, such as in different buildings or even different cities, they are part of a *wide area network (WAN)*.

Most business networks are *client/server* networks. They consist of one or more end-user computers, which are the *clients,* and one or more computers that handle the administration of the network, which are the *servers.* On a very small network, a single server handles all the administrative tasks; on larger networks, there are separate servers for tasks such as file storage (file servers) and printer sharing (print servers). A client/server network that uses Windows Server software is known as a *domain*.

Very small networks (consisting of fewer than 20 computers) can be set up to be *peer-to-peer (P2P)*. In a P2P network, there is no server; all the clients share the administrative burden of maintaining the network. A P2P network is also known as a *workgroup*.

Windows 7 computers on a workgroup can also be part of a homegroup. A *homegroup* consists of two or more computers running Windows 7 on a P2P network. Homegroups make file and printer sharing especially easy between computers. Only Windows 7 computers can be a part of a homegroup. (However, you can still share files and printers on a workgroup between computers running different Windows versions.) Being part of a homegroup is optional, and is a choice only for computers in workgroups, not domains. A computer can be a part of only one homegroup at a time.

Wired versus Wireless Networks

A computer can connect to a network either via a cable (wired) or via a wireless connection. Different computers on the same network can connect to it in different ways. For example, your desktop PC might connect via a cable and your notebook via wireless.

The most popular type of wireless network is a radio frequency (RF) type, conforming to a standard known as IEEE 802.11, or *Wi-Fi*. There have been several versions of the 802.11 standard, including 802.11b, 802.11g, and 802.11n. The latter is the most recently developed and fastest, operating at up to 600 Mbps at a range of about 200 feet (more or less, depending on walls, floors, or other obstructions).

Wireless connections are more convenient than wired connections because there are no cables, but they are also slower and less robust. A typical wired connection runs at about 1 Gbps. A typical wireless one runs at about three-fifths of that (and that's best-case speed with 802.11n, which not all computers support). In addition, a wireless connection can sometimes temporarily lose the signal, especially when you are at the edge of the range.

Wireless networks also are more subject to security breaches than wired ones. With a wired network, an intruder must have access to your router or switch to plug a cable into it. With a wireless network, however, anyone within the vicinity can tap in. Therefore, wireless networks require security measures to ensure that only authorized PCs can connect. There are several types of wireless security, including the following, listed here in order of oldest (and least secure) to newest (and most secure): Wired Equivalent Privacy (WEP), Wi-Fi Protected Access (WPA), and WPA2. Each of these is a different method of requiring a PC to provide an access code before it can connect.

Figure 11.1 An RJ-45 jack connects a PC to a wired network.

What You Need to Connect to a Network

Most PCs today have an *RJ-45 connector* for plugging the PC into a wired network. This connector looks like a telephone plug except it is slightly wider (see Figure 11.1). To connect to an existing wired network, you run a cable from that plug to the router or switch. In many offices, wired ports are built into the wall, just as telephone and electrical outlets are; if your office has one of these, you can simply connect a cable from your PC to that jack.

The RJ-45 connector on the PC is a part of the PC's **network interface card** (NIC), which can be a separate add-on card inside the PC or can be built into the motherboard itself. It works the same either way. (A PC with a wireless NIC does not have an RJ-45 jack; instead it has a small antenna.) If your computer does not have a NIC, you can add a NIC to the PC, or have a technician add one for you.

Note: *Your NIC appears in the Device Manager under the Network Adapters category. You will learn how to use the Device Manager in Chapter 13. If it does not appear there, you might not have a NIC installed.*

If you are setting up a new network, you will also need a box that each of the PCs' network cables plugs into, a central gathering point such as a **switch**. This box directs the traffic between the PCs in the network, delivering packets of data to the correct location. (A more sophisticated form of a switch, called a **router**, is able to direct traffic between network segments on a larger network and to share an Internet connection on a home network.) For a wireless network, the connector box is called a **wireless access point** (WAP).

Note: *If you are installing a new NIC, you must set it up to work in Windows by installing a device driver. In Chapter 13, you will learn how to install new hardware and make sure it has a working device driver.*

Network interface card (NIC): A circuit board, or a built-in component on a motherboard, that provides network connectivity for a PC

Switch: A box into which PCs connect that directs network traffic among the PCs

Router: A type of switch that is able to direct traffic between different segments of a network

Wireless access point: A switch for wireless networking

Connecting to a Network

Windows 7 is very adept at detecting network connections, so provided you have a NIC installed and a wired connection established, Windows will simply start using the network, making its resources available to your PC.

With a wireless connection, the first time you use Windows 7 you must set up the connection. After that, the connection reestablishes itself automatically each time you turn on the PC and the network becomes available.

Using the Network and Sharing Center

The Network and Sharing Center provides a central location for checking network connectivity and network sharing settings. Figure 11.2 shows the Network and Sharing Center for a PC with a wireless network connection. For wireless connections, a Connect or disconnect hyperlink is available; this is not available for a wired connection.

Click here to see connection status

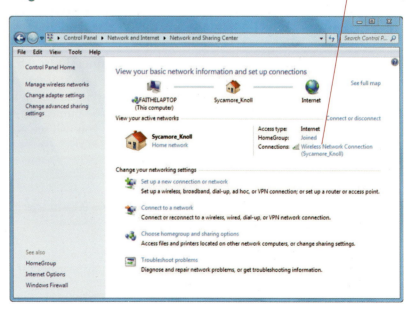

Figure 11.2 **The Network and Sharing Center shows network information.**

To display the Network and Sharing Center (Control Panel Method)

1. Choose Start, *Control Panel*.
2. Under Network and Internet, click *View Network Status and Tasks*.

To display the Network and Sharing Center (Windows Explorer Method)

1. Open any file management window. (For example, choose Start, *Computer*.)
2. In the navigation pane at the left, click Network.
3. On the toolbar at the top, click Network and Sharing Center.

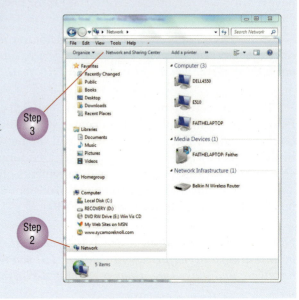

Figure 11.3 Details about the network connection appear in a Status window

Viewing the Status of a Network Connection

From the Network and Sharing Center window, you can get information about a connection by clicking the hyperlink to the right of *Connections*. In Figure 11.2, it is Wireless Network Connection (Sycamore_Knoll), for example.

Figure 11.3 shows the details for a wireless connection; wired connections do not have SSID or Signal Quality, nor do they have a Wireless Properties button.

The details displayed include:

- **IPv4 Connectivity.** This is the IP addressing type used for the Internet and for most LANs. If you are connected to the Internet, IPv4 shows Internet.

- **IPv6 Connectivity.** This is the IP addressing type used for newer LANs. If you are on a private local area network, this will show as Local; if you are on a public network, it will show as Limited. If the network you are on does not use IPv6, you will see No Internet Access.

Tip: If you want to see the exact IP address in use for either IPv4 or IPv6, click Details.

- **Media State.** Enabled should appear here if the connection is enabled.

- *SSID.* This identifier, used only in wireless networks, is the name specified by the wireless access point or wireless router. It is often, by default, the name of the manufacturer of the hardware, such as Linksys.

- **Duration.** This shows how long the connection has been up and running. When you restart the PC, it resets the counter.

- **Speed.** This states the speed of the network in megabytes per second (Mbps). For a wireless network, this is typically 11 Mbps or 100 Mbps; for a wired network it is usually either 100 Mbps or 1000 Mbps.

- **Signal Quality.** These bars, shown only for wireless networks, indicate the signal strength between the PC and the wireless access point.

- **Details.** Click this button for more detailed information about the connection.

- **Wireless Properties.** Available only for wireless connections; click this button for a Properties box in which you can determine whether the connection should be established automatically and whether security should be enabled.

SSID: The identifier for the wireless access point or router

Viewing and Changing the Workgroup or Domain Name

If connected to a network, your computer is either assigned to a domain or a workgroup. (If you see Homegroup: Joined in the Network and Sharing Center window, as in Figure 11.2, you can assume you are part of a workgroup.) Within that domain or workgroup, each computer is assigned a unique network name.

In most cases, it is not important what these names are. However, for certain troubleshooting activities, you may need that information. You may occasionally need to change it, too, if directed by a system administrator or technical support representative.

To determine the workgroup or domain name

Here's How

1. Choose Start, *Control Panel*.
2. Click System and Security.
3. Under the System heading, click *See the name of this computer*.

   System
   View amount of RAM and processor speed | Check the Windows Experience Index
   Allow remote access | See the name of this computer | Device Manager

   Step 3

4. Scroll down to the Computer name, domain, and workgroup settings section and examine the names there.

   Computer name, domain, and workgroup settings

Computer name:	FaitheLaptop	Change settings
Full computer name:	FaitheLaptop	
Computer description:		
Workgroup:	WORKGROUP	

   Step 4

To change to a different workgroup or domain:

1. Perform steps 1–4 of the preceding procedure.
2. Click Change Settings. The System Properties dialog box opens.
3. Click *Change*.
4. Click the Domain or the Workgroup option.
5. Type the name of the domain or workgroup.
6. Click OK.
7. At the confirmation box, click OK.
8. Click Close.
9. At the prompt to restart, click Restart Now or Restart Later.

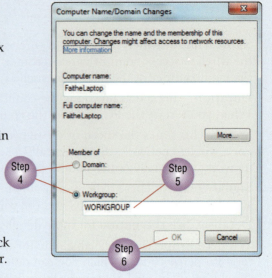

Setting a Network Location

A network location can be classified as Home, Work, or Public. The Public setting is appropriate when you are connecting to a network in a public place, such as when using a wireless Internet connection at a coffee shop or at a school. This setting prevents other PCs from discovering your computer and browsing its shared content. The Work or Home settings are appropriate when you are connecting to your home or business LAN; they allow you to see other computers and devices and allow others to see yours.

To specify a network location type:

1. From the Network and Sharing Center, click the hyperlink under your active network name. Depending on the current type, it may appear as Home network, Work network, or Public network.
2. Click Home network, Work network, or Public network.
3. Click Close.

Connecting and Disconnecting a Wireless Network

The first time your PC connects to a particular wireless access point, you must confirm that connection, and if it is a secure network, you must enter the security information needed for it. Then when your PC comes into range of that access point in the future, it automatically connects to that access point using those same settings (provided you have it set up for automatic connection).

To connect to a wireless network:

Here's How

1. From the Network and Sharing Center, click Connect to a network.
2. Click the network to which to connect.
3. Click the Connect button.
4. Click Close.

To allow or disallow automatic connection in the future:

1. From the Network and Sharing Center, click View Status.
2. Click Wireless Properties.
3. Mark or clear the *Connect automatically when this network is in range* check box.
4. Click OK.
5. Click Close.

To disconnect from a wireless network:

From the Network and Sharing Center, click Disconnect.

Configuring Wireless Network Security

When you connect to a wireless network in which the access point requires security, you are prompted to enter an access code. This code is generated by the configuration software for the access point. Depending on the brand and model of the access point, you can access that configuration software either via a utility you install on one of the attached PCs or via a Web browser interface (by entering the IP address of the access point).

As mentioned earlier in this chapter, there are several types of wireless security encryption, and the PC must use whatever type the wireless access point requires. The setup involves selecting the encryption type and entering a network security key, which is a string of characters that translates to a code.

To enable wireless network security:

Here's How

1. From the Network and Sharing Center, click the hyperlink for the desired connection. A Wireless Network Connection status box appears..
2. Click Properties.
3. Click the Security tab.
4. Open the Security type list and click the type of security to use.

   Tip: For WEP security, choose *Shared*.

5. Type the security key code to use in the *Network security key* text box.
6. Click OK.

Exercise 1

Getting Information about Your Network Connection

1. On a blank piece of paper, write your name and C11E01, or in a Word document, type your name and save the file as **C11E01**.
2. Determine the domain or workgroup to which your PC belongs, and write it on your paper or in your Word document:
   a. Click Start, and then click *Control Panel*.
   b. Click System and Security.
   c. Under the system category, click See the name of this computer.
   d. Look next to Workgroup or next to Domain for the information.
3. Determine your PC's IPv4 address and the duration of the connection:
   a. Open the Network and Sharing Center.
   b. Click the hyperlink for your connection, to the right of Connections.
   c. Record the duration listed next to Duration.
   d. Click Details.
   e. Record the address listed next to IPv4.
   f. Click Close.
   g. Click Close.
4. Submit your paper or Word document to your instructor for grading.

Creating and Using a VPN Connection

The Internet, by default, is not a secure transfer medium for sensitive data. You can connect to another PC, but you cannot guarantee that someone will not snoop on that connection. Because of this, many companies do not allow Internet access to their most sensitive data resources, such as customer databases and financial data.

Virtual private network (VPN): A secure software tunnel that runs from one computer to another using the Internet as its conduit

If you need to connect to your company's network but you are nowhere near it physically, you might choose to create a *virtual private network (VPN)* connection. A VPN connection is a secure software tunnel that runs from one computer to another using the Internet as its conduit. When you are connected to your workplace's LAN via a VPN connection, it is as if your PC were in the building where the LAN resides, and your connection to it is as secure as if you were using the network there. VPN connectivity might be necessary to use certain resources that are restricted to only local LAN users and not available via the Web, such as customer databases.

After you initially set up the VPN connection, you can easily reestablish it at any time without having to reenter the settings.

Here's How → **To set up a VPN connection:**

1. Open the Network and Sharing Center.
2. Click *Set up a new connection or network*.
3. Click *Connect to a workplace*.
4. Click Next.
5. Click *Use my Internet connection (VPN)*.

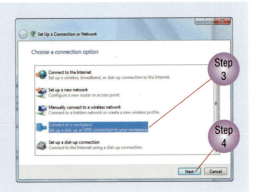

6. Type the Internet address into the box provided.

7. Mark any of the check boxes for special options for the connection.

8. Click Next.

9. Type the user name and password needed to connect.

10. (Optional) Mark the *Remember this password* check box.

11. (Optional) If the connection requires a domain, enter it in the Domain box.

12. Click Connect.

13. Wait for the connection to be established.

14. At the Successfully connected to VPN Connection box, click Close.
This does not disconnect the connection; it continues to run in the background. The connection remains established until you reboot, log off, or disconnect it manually.

To connect an existing VPN connection:

1. Open the Network and Sharing Center.

2. Click Connect to a network.

3. Click the VPN to which you want to connect.

4. Click Connect.

5. Type your user name and password if they are not already filled in.

6. If needed, type the domain if not already filled in.

7. Click Connect.

8. At the Successfully connected to VPN Connection box, click Close.

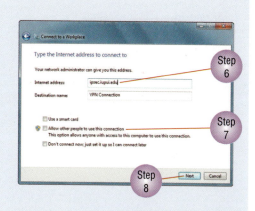

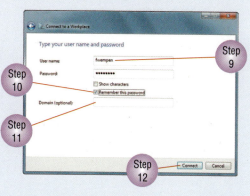

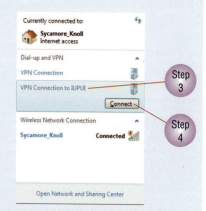

QUICK FIX

Requiring Advanced Settings
Many places of business require advanced settings to be configured on a VPN connection. If the connection does not work after going through these steps, check with your IT department to find out what additional settings may be required.

To disconnect a VPN connection:

1. Click the *Network* icon in the notification area, so that a pop-up menu appears.
2. Click the VPN connection.
3. Click Disconnect.
4. Wait for the connection to terminate.

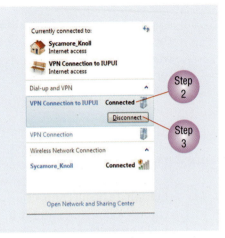

Figure 11.4 Browse the PCs on your network from the Network window.

Figure 11.5 The shared resources from the chosen PC appear as icons; double-click an icon to access that resource.

Viewing Network Locations

When a network connection is established—whether it be via a wired or wireless network or a VPN connection—you can access network locations that have been made available to you. These can include folders on a dedicated file server and/or folders on individual client PCs that the owners have chosen to share.

Browsing the Network

One way to access a network location is to browse for it. You can do this by choosing *Computer* from the Start menu and then clicking the Network link in the bottom left corner of the window; a list of computers appears that are part of your workgroup or domain. In Figure 11.4, the computers and other devices in the local workgroup appear.

The network locations available depend on the network connectivity of the PC. Depending on your network type, you may see PCs, network storage devices, network-aware printers, and other resources.

Double-click one of the icons to browse the available drives and folders. For example, in Figure 11.5, you can see that the PC called FAITHELAPTOP is sharing five folders and one printer driver. You can then access any of these by double-clicking it, just as if it were an icon on your own local system. Double-clicking a folder icon opens that folder and displays its files; double-clicking a printer icon opens the print queue for that printer.

Mapping a Network Drive

If you frequently access the same network location, you might want an easier way than browsing to access it. You could map that location to a drive letter. The new drive letter appears in the Computer window, along with your other local drives, and then you can double-click that drive letter to quickly access the referenced location. See Figure 11.6.

The mapped drive can be used in any program, even programs that do not ordinarily support reading/writing from network locations. Network drive mapping is also a good tool to use when setting up systems for less experienced computer users because it is much easier for them to remember a simple letter than a complete path to a network location.

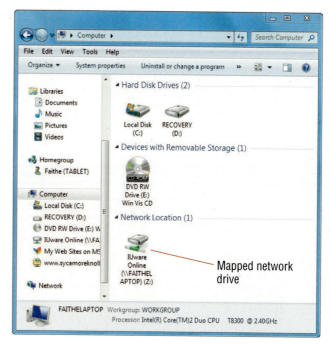

Figure 11.6 A mapped network drive letter appears in the Computer window, along with your other drives.

You can set up the mapping to reestablish itself automatically each time you log on, if desired. That way you never have to think about the location being located on the network; as far as your system is concerned, the location is simply another hard drive on your own system.

> **Tip:** An alternative to mapping a network drive is to create a shortcut on the desktop or in the navigation pane to the network location. The shortcut is as quick and easy to access as a drive letter.

To map a network location to a drive letter:

1. Click Start, *Computer*, and then click Network at the bottom of the navigation pane at the left.
2. Navigate to the location containing the folder to be mapped.
3. Right-click the folder and choose *Map Network Drive*.
4. Select the drive letter to use.
5. Mark or clear the *Reconnect at logon* check box.
6. Click Finish.

Here's How

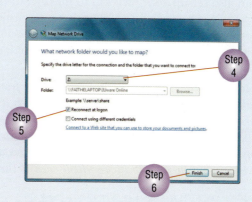

1. Click Start, and then click *Computer*.
2. Right-click the mapped drive.
3. Click *Disconnect*.

 ## Exercise 2

Accessing Files and Folders on the Network

1. On a blank piece of paper write your name and C11E02, or in a Word document, type your name and save the file as **C11E02**.
2. Click Start, and click *Computer*. Click Network in the lower left corner of the window.
3. Record the names of the network resources that appear at this top level of network browsing (up to six items), and their types (computers, network drives, network printers, and so on).
4. Double-click one of the items you see, and record what icons appear within it (up to six items).
5. Select one of the folders in Step 4, and map drive letter Y to it:
   a. Right-click the folder and choose *Map network drive*.
   b. Select *Y* as the drive letter.
   c. Clear the *Reconnect at logon* check box.
   d. Click Finish.
6. Capture a screen shot of the Computer window, showing the mapped network drive, and name the file **C11E02S06**.
7. Disconnect the drive mapping:
   a. From the Computer window, press Alt to display the menu bar if needed, and then choose Tools, *Disconnect Network Drive*.
   b. Click the *Y* drive.
   c. Click OK.
8. Submit your paper or Word document and your screen capture to your instructor for grading.
9. Close all open windows.

Sharing a File or Folder on the Network

In addition to using resources provided by other PCs on your network, you can also set up your own PC to make your drives or folders available. For example, suppose you are working on a project that several other people in your organization also need to contribute to. You could place the project files in a folder on your hard disk and then share that folder on the network.

Note: *Should you share a folder directly from your own PC or should you copy that folder to a network-accessible location such as your company's file server? There are pros and cons to each. If you copy the files to a location that is always available, such as a file server, others will be able to access them even if your own PC is turned off. On the other hand, if you keep the files on your own local hard disk, then you will always be able to access them even if the network goes down.*

Choosing Which Libraries to Share with Your Home Group

If your computer is part of a homegroup, you can specify which of your libraries you want to make available to others. To do this, open up the Network and

Sharing Center, and click *Choose Homegroup and Sharing Options*. From the controls that appear (see Figure 11.7), you can choose which libraries to share with others in your homegroup by marking or clearing check boxes. You can also choose to share additional libraries besides the ones represented by check boxes in Figure 11.7.

Note: As you learned in Chapter 3, you can add other files and folders to a library. The Documents library, for example, can consist not only of the Documents folder on your hard disk, but also any other folders that you have specified should be part of that library.

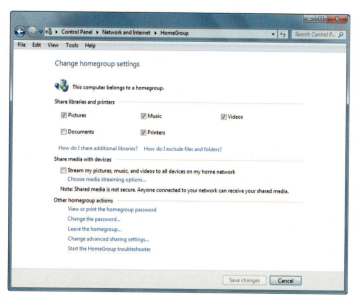

Figure 11.7 You can adjust what you will share with other members of your homegroup.

To choose default libraries to share:

1. Open the Network and Sharing Center.
2. Click *Choose homegroup and sharing options*.
3. If you have not previously shared any libraries, a message appears saying so. Click the hyperlink and choose what you want to share, to continue.
4. Mark or clear check boxes for each of the libraries under Share libraries and printers.

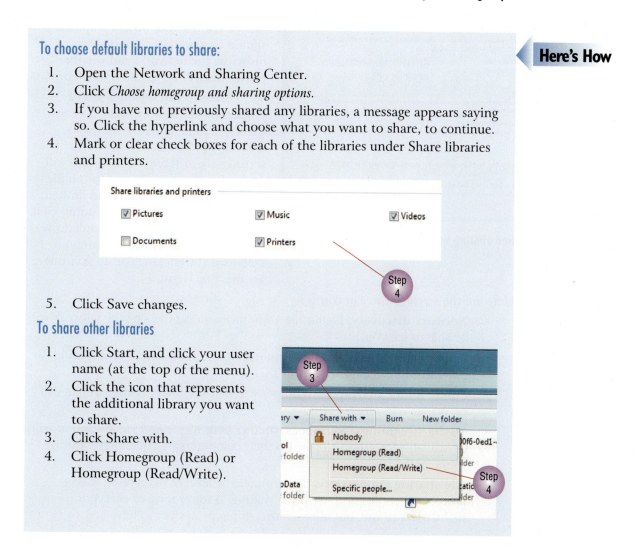

5. Click Save changes.

To share other libraries

1. Click Start, and click your user name (at the top of the menu).
2. Click the icon that represents the additional library you want to share.
3. Click Share with.
4. Click Homegroup (Read) or Homegroup (Read/Write).

Here's How

Include other folders in a library

1. Browse to the icon for the folder to be included.
2. Click Include in library.
3. Click the library it should be a part of.

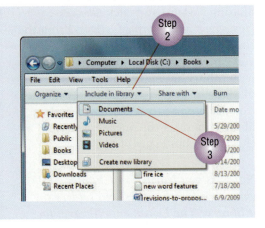

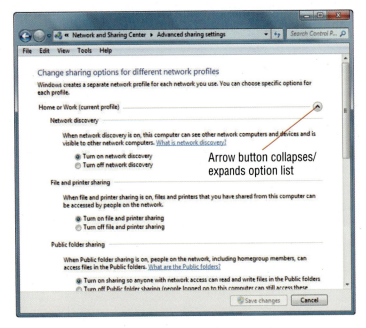

Figure 11.8 Fine-tune sharing settings.

Configuring Network Sharing

On all networked computers, regardless of whether you use a homegroup, you can fine-tune the network sharing permissions. This includes things like whether file and printer sharing is turned on, whether other computers should be able to see yours when browsing the network, and whether passwords will be required for sharing.

There are two separate sets of properties for network settings: one used for Home or Work networks, and one used for Public networks. The settings are different because you will probably want permissions for public networks to be very strict and limited, to prevent strangers from invading your privacy. Each set can be expanded (by clicking the down pointing arrow) or collapsed (by clicking the up pointing arrow). See Figure 11.8.

Here are the settings you can control:

- **Network discovery**. Determines whether others browsing the network will be able to see you.

- **File and printer sharing**. Determines whether file and printer sharing (in general) will be enabled on your PC.

- **Public folder sharing**. Determines whether the folder named Public will be available to others.

- **Media streaming**. Determines whether your music and video content will be available for others to play on their computers by streaming it from yours.

- **File sharing connections**. Determines the level of encryption used to protect the connection when file sharing. A lower level of encryption is slightly less secure, but allows more, different devices to have access.

- **Password-protected sharing**. Determines whether passwords will be required when others try to access your files, folders, or printers.
- **Homegroup connections**. Determines how homegroup connections will be authenticated.

Here's How

To change a network sharing setting:

1. Open the Network and Sharing Center.
2. Click Change advanced sharing settings (if part of a homegroup) or Change advanced sharing options (if not part of a homegroup).
3. Choose the options desired.
4. Click Save Changes.

Sharing with Public Folders

Each local user on a PC has a set of public folders. These folders exist for the specific purpose of file sharing. One way to share certain files, then, is to place the files to be shared in one of these public folders. These are not dependent on being part of a homegroup; they work on all network types, P2P or client/server.

Note: *Make sure Public folder sharing has been enabled in order for others to see your public folders. See the preceding section.*

To access your public folders, open any file management window (such as Computer) and click the Public link in the navigation pane. This opens a set of public folders, with names that reflect the suggested content for each one. See Figure 11.9. Then just drag and drop content from any location into one of these folders.

Note: *When you browse the content of someone else's PC via the network, as you learned to do earlier in the chapter, that user's Public folder appears as one of the resources associated with his or her PC.*

Figure 11.9 Place content in your public folders to share it with others on your network.

Sharing Individual Folders and Drives

There are several ways to share individual folders and drives. One way, as you just saw, is to place them in the Public area and then make public sharing available.

If you are using a homegroup, you can easily share folders, with either read-only or read/write access. Right-click the folder, point to *Share With*, and then click one of the homegroup sharing options.

If you are not using a homegroup, you can share the folder or drive via Windows' File Sharing interface. This works the same as it did under Windows Vista (in which there was no homegroup feature).

To share a folder with your homegroup:

1. Select the folder.
2. Click Share With.
3. Click one of the homegroup options:
   a. Homegroup (Read)
   b. Homegroup (Read/Write).

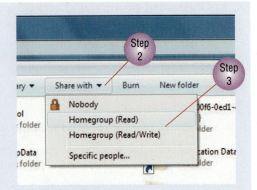

To share a folder (without a homegroup):

1. Select the folder.
2. Click Share With.
3. Click Specific People.
4. Click Share. A confirmation appears that your folder is shared.
5. Click Done.

To share a drive:

1. From the Computer window, right-click the drive and choose *Share with, Advanced Sharing*.
2. Click the Advanced Sharing button.
3. Mark the *Share this folder* check box.
4. (Optional) Change the Share name to something more descriptive. (By default it is the drive letter.)
5. Click OK.
6. Click Close.

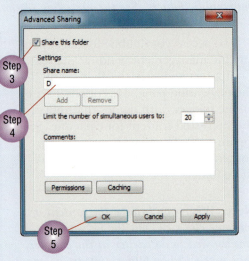

To unshare a folder:

1. Right-click the shared folder and choose *Share with, Nobody*.
2. Click *Stop sharing*.

To unshare a drive:

1. From the Computer window, right-click the drive and click *Share with, Advanced sharing*.
2. Click the Advanced Sharing button.
3. Clear *Share this folder*.
4. Click OK.
5. Click Close.

Setting Up User-Based Sharing Permission

By default, all network users can access shared folders with equal permissions. No user name or password is required. If you would prefer to fine-tune permissions based on the individual user, you can enable password-protected sharing and then set up permissions for each allowed user.

Note: *The users to whom you assign permissions must be set up as local users of your PC. Therefore, you should set up their user accounts in advance. (To do so, see "Working with User Accounts and Passwords" in Chapter 15.)*

A user can have any of these permission levels assigned for accessing a particular folder:

- **Reader**. The person may read the files, but not change them.
- **Contributor**. The person may read files, add files, and change or delete the files that they themselves add.
- **Co-owner**. The person may view, change, add, and delete files.

To enable password-protected sharing:

1. Open the Network and Sharing Center.
2. Click Change advanced sharing settings.
3. In the Home or Work section, click *Turn on password protected sharing*.
4. Click Save Changes.

To assign a user permission to a shared folder:

1. Right-click the shared folder and click *Share with, Specific people*.
2. Click Change sharing permissions.
3. Open the drop-down list to the left of the Add button and click the local user for which to add permission.
4. Click Add.
5. Open the drop-down list for the Permission Level for the user and set it to the desired level.
6. Click Share.

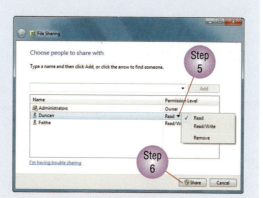

Exercise 3

Sharing Folders on the Network

1. On a blank piece of paper, write your name and C11E03, or in a Word document, type your name and save the file as **C11E03**.
2. Check the network sharing settings to make sure file sharing and public folder sharing are enabled and to make sure password protection is disabled:
   a. View the Network and Sharing Center.
   b. Click Change advanced sharing settings.
   c. If file and printer sharing is turned off, turn it on.
   d. Under Home or Work, if password protected sharing is on, turn it off.
   e. If public folder sharing is turned off, turn it on.
   f. Click Save Changes.
3. Share the Chapter 11 Student Data Files folder on your hard disk:
   a. Browse to the folder containing the data files for this course.
   b. Right-click the Chapter 11 data folder and click *Share with, Specific people*.
   c. Type Everyone and click Add.
   d. Click Share.
   e. Click Done.
4. Copy the Chapter 11 data folder to your Public Documents folder:
   a. Select the Chapter 11 data folder and press Ctrl+C to copy it.
   b. Navigate to c:\users\Public\Documents.
   c. Press Ctrl+V to paste.
5. Go to another PC on your network and attempt to access the Chapter 11 data folder on your hard disk (the original, not the copy in the Public Documents folder). On your paper or in your Word document, record the steps you took and whether it was successful.
6. From the other PC, attempt to open, make changes to, and save **Memo.docx**. On your paper or in your Word document, record the steps you took and whether it was successful.
7. From the other PC, repeat Steps 5 and 6 with the copy in the Public Documents folder. Record your results.
8. Return to your own PC and unshare the original Chapter 11 data folder:
   a. Right-click the Chapter 11 data folder and click *Share with*.
   b. Click Nobody.
9. Submit your paper or Word document to your instructor for grading.

Working with Network Printers

Network-aware printer:
A printer with a built-in network interface card, capable of connecting directly to the network without going through a PC

Two types of printers can be available on a network: those that are truly ***network-aware*** (that is, they have their own network interface card and their own address), and those that are shared with an individual PC. A network-aware printer can be connected directly to the network, so that it does not rely on any particular PC being active in order to be available. A shared printer is a locally installed printer on a PC that has been set up to be shared with others. When the PC sharing it is turned off or disconnected from the network, the printer becomes unavailable to network users.

Installing a Network Printer

Before you can print to a network printer, you must set up a driver for it on your PC. This is done using the Add Printer Wizard, and is covered in "Adding a New Printer" in Chapter 13 in greater detail.

The Add Printer Wizard enables you to select either local or network printers. If you choose to install a network printer, it scans the network and presents you with a list of the available printers, both network-aware ones and shared ones. You can tell the difference because a network-aware printer will have an IP address (a numeric address) listed for it; whereas, a shared printer will have a network path containing the name of the PC to which it is attached. For example, in Figure 11.10, the last printer on the list is network-aware and the rest are shared.

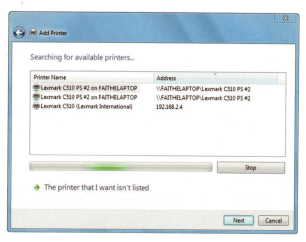

Figure 11.10 When browsing for network printers, both network-aware and shared printers are included in the list.

To set up your PC to use a network printer:

Here's How

1. Click Start, and then click *Control Panel*.
2. Under Hardware and Sound, click *View devices and printers*.
3. Click Add a printer.
4. Click Add a network, wireless or Bluetooth printer.
5. Wait for the wizard to search for available printers, and then click the printer you want to use.

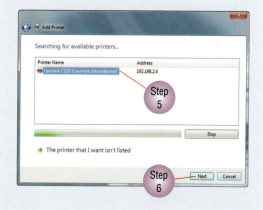

6. Click Next.

   Tip: If a driver for that printer is already installed on your PC, click *Use the driver that is currently installed (recommended)* and click Next.
7. If needed, change the printer's name in the Printer Name box. (This is possible only for network-aware printers, not shared ones.)
8. Mark or clear the *Set as the default printer* check box, as desired.

   Tip: For a network-aware printer only, you may be prompted whether to share the printer with others. Sharing a printer with others is not necessary because other PCs will also be able to access the printer directly, as you did, so click *Do not share this printer*, and click Next.
9. (Optional) Click Print a test page if you want to test the connection.
10. Click Finish.

Sharing a Local Printer

You can make your own local printer available to other network users so that they can set it up on their PCs as described in the preceding section. A shared printer shows a sharing symbol on its icon, the same as with a shared folder. See Figure 11.11.

Sharing symbol

Lexmark C510 PS (MS)

Figure 11.11 A shared printer's icon displays a sharing symbol.

If the other network users also run the same version of Windows, the needed driver is copied to their PCs automatically when they set up the printer. If there are people on the network who have other versions of Windows, however, you must make drivers available for those versions, or those users must supply their own drivers for the printer, to use the printer.

Here's How ▶ To share a local printer on the network:

1. Click Start, and then click *Control Panel*.
2. Under Hardware and Sound, click *View devices and printers*.
3. Right-click the printer and click Printer Properties.
4. Click the Sharing tab.
5. Mark the *Share this printer* check box.
6. (Optional) Change the Share name, if desired, to more accurately describe the printer.
7. (Optional) To make other drivers available:
   a. Click Additional Drivers.
   b. Mark the check boxes for additional Windows versions to support.
   c. Click OK.
   d. If prompted, insert a disc containing the driver for the other version and click OK.
   e. Follow the prompts to finish installing the additional driver(s).
8. Click OK.

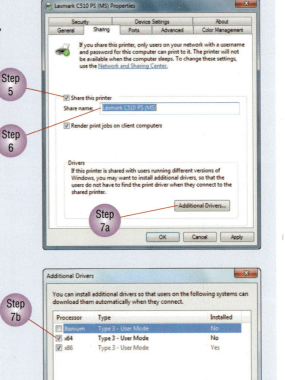

Exercise 4

Work with Network Printers

1. Share your local printer on the network, using your initials as the share name:
   a. Click Start, and then click *Control Panel*.
   b. Under Hardware and Sound, click *View devices and printers*.
   c. Right-click your local printer (if you have more than one, use any) and click Printer Properties.
   d. Click the Sharing tab.
   e. Mark the *Share this printer* check box.
   f. In the Share name box, type your initials.
   g. Click OK.

2. Go to another PC on your network (or trade with another student) and set up the shared printer from your original location as a network printer on that PC:
   a. Reopen the Printer window if it is not still open (Start, *Control Panel, Devices and printers*).
   b. Click Add a printer.
   c. Click Add a network, wireless or Bluetooth printer.
   d. Wait for the wizard to search for the printers and click the printer that has your initials as the name.
   e. Click Next.
   f. If prompted that a driver is already installed, click *Use the driver that is currently installed (recommended)* and click Next.
   g. Click Next.
   h. Click Print a test page.
   i. Click Finish.
3. Delete the printer driver from the Printers window. (To do so, click its icon and press the Delete key on the keyboard.)
4. Return to your original PC and unshare the shared printer.
5. Write your name on the test page that prints and submit it to your instructor for grading.

Troubleshooting the Network

As an end-user in a corporate network, you will seldom need to worry about troubleshooting because your network probably has a full-time network administrator or other IT expert who administers it. However, if you have a small peer-to-peer network in your home or business, you might not have professional help at your disposal, and you might need to troubleshoot any problems that occur yourself.

Diagnosing and Repairing a Network Connection Problem

When a network connection is not functioning correctly, Windows can help you determine why. The Windows Network Diagnostics utility can examine your network connection and suggest the probable causes for the current problem and possible solutions. It can also help you reset the network adapter, which can sometimes resolve an intermittent problem.

To diagnose a network problem:

1. Open the Network and Sharing Center.
2. Next to Connections, click the name of the current connection. The Status box for the connection appears.

Here's How

Here's How

3. Click Diagnose.
4. Evaluate the options that appear, and click the option most suited to your situation. For example, you might choose to reset the network adapter.
5. Click OK.

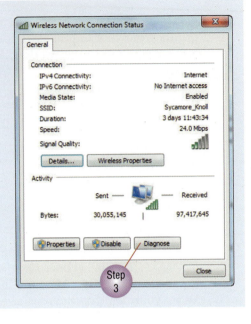

Determining the IP Address of a PC

An ***Internet Protocol (IP) address*** is a numeric identifier for the PC on the network. IP addresses can be local (that is, apply only to your LAN) or can apply to the PC's address on the Internet at large. Windows 7 can recognize two types of IP addresses: IPv4 addresses (the older style, currently used on the Internet) and IPv6 addresses (a newer type, not widely used now, but made available for future implementation). You will mostly work with the IPv4 addresses, which consist of a set of four numbers, each between 0 and 254, separated by periods, like this: 192.168.0.1. An IPv6 address is more complex; it consists of a series of hexadecimal numbers (that is, numbers that use not only digits 0 through 9 but also letters a through f).

You will not usually need to know your PC's IP address; Windows 7 handles it behind the scenes. However, if you are working with a technician to diagnose a connectivity problem, the technician may ask you to look up the IP address assigned to the PC.

You can find the IP address that your PC is using in two ways. You can either look at the network connection details, or you can use a command-line interface to run the IPCONFIG command.

If you are working with an IT professional on troubleshooting a problem, he or she might also ask you for the ***subnet mask***. This numeric code indicates what part of the IP address represents the subnet and what part represents the individual address of the PC. A ***subnet*** is a group of computers that share a common top-level identifier, similar to the telephone numbers in a certain area code. A subnet mask for an IPv4 addressing scheme consists of four numbers separated by periods, such as 255.255.255.0. Subnet masks are necessary because different networks divide up the available digits in the IP address differently.

A subnet mask is actually a long string of 1s and 0s with all the 1s at the beginning, like this: 11111111.11111111.11111111.00000000. The subnet mask carries only one useful piece of information: the point at which 1 turns to 0. For example, in the above string, it does so after the 24th 1. Each set of eight digits is considered a separate binary number, and is then converted to decimal. For example, 11111111 in binary is 255 in decimal. Because it is most common for

Internet Protocol (IP) address: A numeric address that uniquely describes the address of a PC or other network-aware component on a network or on the Internet

Subnet: A group of computers that share a common top-level identifier, similar to the telephone numbers in a certain area code

Subnet mask: A numeric code that indicates what part of the IP address represents the subnet and what part represents the individual address of the PC

a subnet mask to switch from 1 to 0 at one of the points where there is a decimal point, most subnet masks consist of only 255s and 0s. However, it is possible for a subnet mask to have a break point in other spots, like this: 11111111.11111 111.11110000.00000000, resulting in a subnet mask in decimal numbering of 255.255.240.0.

Besides the PC's IP address, you may also find it helpful to determine its *default gateway*. This is the address of the device that takes the network connection out of its local subnet and into the larger network (your company's network, or the Internet). Later in this chapter you will learn how to ping an address to determine if a connection exists to it, and you might want to ping the default gateway's address.

Default gateway: The IP address of the port that leads out of your local subnet and into the larger network or the Internet

To find the PC's IP address:

Here's How

1. Open the Network and Sharing Center.
2. Next to Connections, click the name of the current connection. The Status box for the connection appears.
3. Click Details. The Network Connection Details dialog box opens.
4. Note the IPv4 IP address.
5. Note the IPv4 subnet mask.
6. Note the IPv4 default gateway.
7. (Optional) If needed, note the Link-local IPv6 IP address.
8. Click Close.
9. Click Close.

To find the PC's IP address via command-line interface:

1. Click Start.
2. Type **cmd** and press Enter.
3. Type **ipconfig** and press Enter.
4. Note the IP addresses, the subnet mask, and the default gateway.
5. Click the X to close the command prompt window.

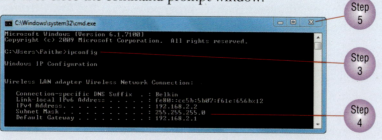

Using Ping to Check the Connection

Network problems are often not your PC's fault, but instead caused by a breakdown in the communication pipeline somewhere between your PC and the intended destination. That destination could be a Web site, a file server on your LAN, a shared printer on someone else's PC, or any other network-addressable location.

IT professionals use a command-line utility called PING to check the connectivity between a PC and another network location, and based on the results, they can narrow down where the breakdown in communication is occurring. For example, suppose your PC is connected to a router, which in turn is connected to a server, which in turn is connected to the Internet. If you cannot access the Internet, which component is at fault? You can figure this out by checking the connection between your PC and the router first. If that connection is working, then you can check between your PC and the server. You keep working through the connection, from closest to farthest away, until you find the part that is not working.

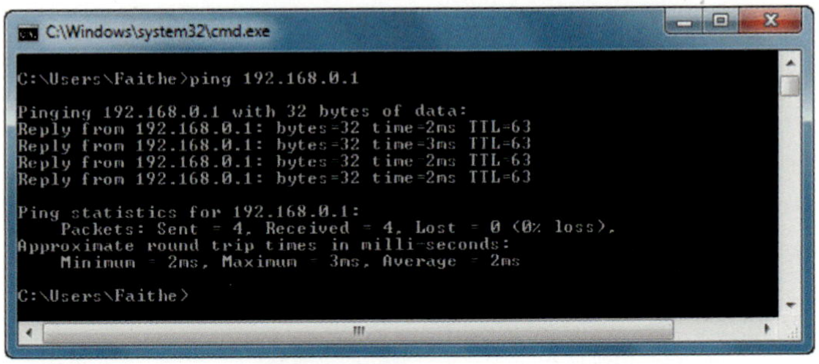

Figure 11.12 A successful ping results in replies.

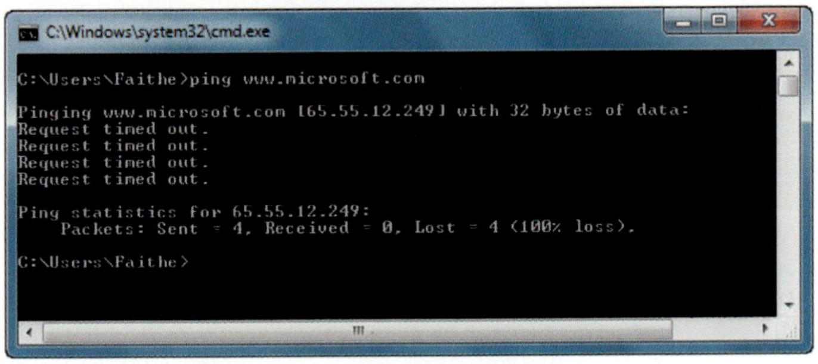

You can "ping" a device based on its IP address (the IPv4 one). Pinging sends an inquiry to that device, requesting a response. If the response comes back, you know the connection is working between your PC and that device.

If you see a reply, as shown in Figure 11.12, the connection is working. If a message appears indicating that the request timed out, as in Figure 11.13, either the connection is not working or the address you are pinging does not support ping requests (as is the case with www.microsoft.com, for example).

Figure 11.13 An unsuccessful ping times out.

Note: *You can ping either by IP address or by Web address (for example, www. emcp.com). If you ping a Web address, a Domain Name System (DNS) server on the Internet resolves (converts) the Web address to the equivalent IP address for you.*

What addresses should you ping? Start by pinging the loopback address: 127.0.0.1. If this works, then the PC's NIC is set up correctly. Then try pinging the PC's own IP address. If that works, ping the default gateway. From there, continue pinging addresses that are progressively farther away from your PC until you find the breakdown.

Here's How ▶ To ping an IP address or Web address:

1. Click Start.
2. Type **cmd** and press Enter.
3. Type **Ping**, a space, and then the IP address or Web address to check.
4. Press Enter.
5. Wait for a reply or for the connection to time out.

Understanding Internet Connections

The Internet is a big network of interconnected computers that communicate using the IPv4 addressing system that you learned about earlier in this chapter. Using the Internet you can exchange e-mail with others, visit Web pages, post your own Web content, and much more.

To connect to the Internet, you either need an always-on Internet connection via your company's LAN, or you need to sign up with an Internet Service Provider (ISP), which then provides you with a means of connecting. Different ISPs offer different means of connecting; some of the options that might be available to you in your home or business, depending on its location, include:

- **Digital Subscriber Line (DSL).** A high-speed connection that uses unused portions of regular telephone lines; requires a DSL terminal adapter.
- **Cable.** A high-speed connection that uses digital cable TV wires to carry Internet service; requires a cable modem.
- **Satellite.** A medium-speed connection that uses a two-way satellite dish to carry Internet service; requires a satellite dish with receiver/transmitter and a satellite terminal adapter.
- **Dial-up.** The oldest, slowest type of connection, but sometimes the only available method in isolated areas or due to a tight budget; requires a modem.

Each type of service requires its own unique type of modem or terminal adapter. A *modem* (short for modulator/demodulator) converts between digital data from the PC and analog (sound) data that can be sent over a telephone line or cable TV line. When a connection is all-digital, as with DSL and satellite, such that there is no conversion needed between analog and digital, the device is referred to as a *terminal adapter*.

To set up any type of Internet connectivity except dial-up, get a startup kit from the ISP, or schedule professional installation (necessary for satellite service, for example, because of FCC regulations governing transmitters). The PC sees one of these always-on connections as a network connection and treats it accordingly, making Internet services automatically available to your PC. You do not need to connect or disconnect.

Note: *You can share an always-on Internet connection with multiple PCs in your home or office by using a router. A router functions as a switch in the network, serving as a gathering point into which all the PCs in the network connect, but it also can manage an Internet connection. You connect the modem or terminal adapter to the router, and then the router shares that connection with all the PCs to which it is attached.*

Dial-up connectivity is different. With a dial-up connection, you must create a connection in Windows, and then activate that connection whenever you want to use the Internet. Then you disconnect that connection when you are finished.

Modem: Short for modulator/demodulator, a device that converts between digital computer data and analog sound wave data and can be transmitted via telephone lines

Terminal adapter: A communication device that sends and receives all-digital networking data, such as for a cable or DSL Internet connection

Here's How ▶ To create a new dial-up Internet connection:

1. Open the Network and Sharing Center.
2. Click *Set up a new connection or network*.
3. Click *Set up a dial-up connection* and click Next.
4. Enter the information for the dial-up connection from your ISP, including the phone number, user name, and password.
5. (Optional) Mark the *Remember this password* check box.
6. (Optional) Change the Connection name.
7. Click Connect.

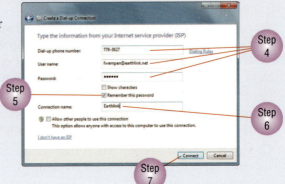

To use an existing dial-up Internet connection:

1. Open the Network and Sharing Center.
2. Click *Connect to a network*.
3. Click the desired existing connection.
4. Click Connect.

CHAPTER Summary

- A network is a group of connected computers. When in the same building, it is a local area network (LAN). When spread out over a greater distance, it is a wide area network (WAN).

- A client/server network consists of one or more end-user computers (clients) and one or more servers to handle the administration. A peer-to-peer network has no servers, and is typically very small.

- A wired network uses cables (typically with RJ-45 connectors, which are like wide telephone plugs) that plug into a PC's network interface card.

- A wireless network uses radio frequency (RF) or infrared signals. The most popular type of wireless is IEEE 802.11, also called Wi-Fi. It is a type of RF-based Ethernet.

- The computers of a network connect to a switch, router, or wireless access point.

- To display the Network and Sharing Center, click Start, *Control Panel*, *View Network Status and Tasks*.

- A network can be Public, Home, or Work. Security is higher on a public network. From the Network and Sharing Center, click the current network type (under the network name), and then click Home Network, Work Network, or Public Network to specify a network's status.

- To connect to a wireless network, from the Network and Sharing Center click *Connect to a network*. Click the network to which to connect, and then click the Connect button.

- Wireless networks typically employ security to keep unauthorized users out. From the Network and Sharing Center, click the network name next to Connections. Click Wireless Properties, click the Security tab, and from the *Security Type* list, click the type of security you want to use.

- To change the workgroup or domain name for a PC, from the Control Panel click System and Security and then click System. Click *Change Settings*, and on the Computer Name tab, click Change.

- A Virtual Private Network (VPN) connection is a secure software tunnel that runs between PCs using the Internet as its conduit.

- To set up a VPN connection, from the Network and Sharing Center click *Set up a new connection or network*, choose *Connect to a workplace*, and follow the prompts.

- To browse a network for available files, choose Start, *Computer* and then click Network in the navigation pane at the bottom left.

- Mapping a network drive assigns a drive letter to a network location. From any file management window (such as Computer), click *Map Network Drive*.

- To share your own files on the network, the network must first be set up as a Home or Work network (rather than public). To share public folders, enable public folder sharing in the Network and Sharing Center (click Advanced Sharing Settings).

- To share other folders than the public ones, right-click the folder and choose *Share with, Advanced Sharing* (for a drive) or *Share with, Specific People* (for a folder).

- To assign a user permission to a shared folder, right-click the folder and choose *Share with, Specific People*, and add users and permission levels for them.

- To use a network-shared printer, set up the printer with the Add Printer Wizard, the same as any other printer (Start, *Control Panel, View Devices and Printers, Add a printer*), except specify a network location for it.

- To share your own printer, right-click the printer's icon in the Printer window and choose Printer Properties, then click the *Sharing* tab. Mark the *Share this printer* check box and click OK.

- To diagnose a network problem, from the Network and Sharing Center, click network name next to Connections to view its status, and then click Diagnose.

- To determine a PC's IP address, look in the network connection details (see previous item) or use the IPCONFIG command at a command prompt.

- A subnet is a group of computers within a network segment. A subnet mask is a code that describes what part of an IP address refers to the subnet and what part refers to an individual PC.

- A default gateway is the IP address of the port that leads out of your local subnet.

- At a command prompt, you can use the PING command to check connectivity between your PC and another one.

CONCEPTS Check

Completion: Answer the following questions on a blank sheet of paper or in a Word document.

Part 1

MULTIPLE CHOICE

1. When network computers are in the same room or building, they are part of a(n) _____ .
   a. wide area network (WAN)
   b. local area network (LAN)
   c. client/server network
   d. enterprise network

2. A network that includes one or more servers is a _____ .
   a. wide-area network (WAN)
   b. local area network (LAN)
   c. client/server network
   d. P2P network

3. A network that consists only of peers is a _____ .
   a. wide-area network (WAN)
   b. local area network (LAN)
   c. client/server network
   d. P2P network

4. Another name for the IEE 802.11 standard is _____ .
   a. Wi-Fi
   b. infrared
   c. USB
   d. parallel

5. What kind of connector is common on a NIC?
   a. RJ-11
   b. RJ-14
   c. RJ-35
   d. RJ-45

6. Which IP address type is used for the Internet today?
   a. IPv2
   b. IPv4
   c. IPv6
   d. IPv8

7. An SSID is applicable only to what type of connection?
   a. client/server
   b. cable
   c. wireless
   d. wired

8. When connecting to a wireless network that provides Internet access at a local coffee shop, you should set the connection to be _____ network.
   a. Public
   b. Discoverable
   c. Private
   d. Work

9. Which of these is a valid IPv4 address?
   a. 192.168.0
   b. 192.168.0.1
   c. 192.266.851.22
   d. 192.168.0.1.1.6

10. What command checks the connectivity between your PC and another PC or network device based on the IP address?
    a. Ping
    b. Trace
    c. Ipconfig
    d. WindowsIp

SHORT ANSWER

11. What are three types of wireless network security?

    _____

12. What are the three permission levels you can set for sharing a folder with a particular user?

    _____

13. What error message will you see if Ping does not work?

    _____

14. What is the difference between a modem and a terminal adapter?

    _____

15. Which type of Internet connection is slowest and least preferable and why?

    _____

16. 255.0.255.0 is not a valid subnet mask. Explain why.

    _____

17. Suppose a printer has both a USB connector and a NIC, so you can choose to connect it directly to the network or share it from an individual PC. What are the benefits of connecting it directly to the network?

    _____

18. Would someone who runs a different version of Windows than you be able to use your shared printer? If not, why? If so, what would you need to provide, if anything?

    _____

19. When you share a folder on your hard disk, and you do not specify password-protected sharing, who will be able to access it?

    _____

20. If you can successfully ping the PC's loopback address but not its default gateway, what does that tell you about where the connection problem lies?

    _____

SKILLS Check

Save all solution files to the default Documents folder, or any alternate folder specified by your instructor.

Guided Check

Assessment 1 — DISCONNECTING AND CONNECTING A NETWORK

1. On a blank piece of paper, write your name and C11A01, or in a Word document, type your name and save the file as **C11A01**.
2. Disconnect all existing network connections.
   a. Click Start, *Control Panel, View network status and tasks*.
   b. If Disconnect appears next to any of the network connections, click it to disconnect them. (This does not appear for wired connections.)
   c. On the back of your PC, unplug any RJ-45 connectors, disconnecting any wired connections.
3. Record on your paper or in your Word document what you had to do to disconnect all the network connections.
4. Try to access the Internet. Record on your paper or in your Word document what error message(s) you see.
5. If you unplugged an RJ-45 connector in Step 2, reconnect it, and record what happens on-screen. Look both in the notification area and in the Network and Sharing Center window.
6. If you disconnected from a wireless network in Step 2, reconnect to that network.
   a. From the Network and Sharing Center, click *Connect to a network*.
   b. Click the wireless network to which to connect.
   c. Click the Connect button.
7. If applicable, record what messages appeared on-screen when you reconnected the wireless connection. Look both in the notification area and in the Network and Sharing Center window.
8. Try to access the Internet again. If it does not work, troubleshoot, and record what steps you took.
9. Submit your paper or Word document to your instructor for grading.

Assessment 2 — COLLECTING INFORMATION ABOUT YOUR NETWORK CONNECTION

1. On a blank piece of paper, write your name and C11A02, or in a Word document, type your name and save the file as **C11A02**.
2. Open the Network and Sharing Center.
   a. Click Start, and then click *Control Panel*.
   b. Click *View network status and tasks*.
3. Click the network name next to Connections.
4. Collect the following information, and record it on your paper or in your Word document.
   - Media state
   - Duration
   - Speed
5. Click Details.

6. Collect the following information, and record it on your paper or in your Word document.
   - Physical address
   - IPv4 IP Address
   - IPv4 Subnet Mask
   - IPv4 Default Gateway
7. Click Close to close the Details box.
8. Click Properties to see the connection properties, and look at the installed items on the *This connection uses the following items* list.
9. Record the items on your paper or in your Word document, then click OK.
10. Click Close to close the Properties box for the connection.
11. Submit your paper or e-mail your Word document to your instructor for grading.
12. Close the *Network and Sharing Center* window if it is still open.

Assessment 3   BROWSING THE NETWORK

1. On a blank piece of paper, write your name and C11A03, or in a Word document, type your name and save the file as **C11A03**.
2. Browse the network.
   a. Choose Start, *Computer*.
   b. In the navigation pane at the left, click *Network*.
3. Notice which items are available for browsing in the Network window, and record their names on your paper or in your Word document.
4. Pick one of the items, and double-click it. Record what happens.
5. Click the Back button to return to the Network window's list of items, and repeat Step 4 for another item. Again, record what happens.
6. Submit your paper or e-mail your Word document to your instructor for grading.
7. If you are able to view a shared folder on one of the PCs on the network, try the following:
   a. Select any data file within the shared folder. (For example, choose a Word document, an Excel file, or a plain text file.)
   b. Press Ctrl+C to copy it, and press Ctrl+V to paste the copy.
   c. Rename the copy to your last name. (Keep the same file extension.)
   d. Open the copy by double-clicking it. Make a change to the file, save the changes, and close the file.
   e. Delete the copy.
8. Note on your paper or Word file which parts of Step 7 you were able to accomplish and which parts did not work. Based on this experiment, how do you think the folder-sharing security settings are configured on that PC?
9. Submit your paper or Word document to your instructor for grading.

Assessment 4   PARTNER EXERCISE: WORKING WITH PUBLIC FOLDERS

1. On a blank piece of paper, write your name and C11A04, or in a Word document, type your name and save the file as **C11A04**.
2. Create a new text file in your Public Documents folder with your last name as the file name.
   a. Click Start, and then click *Computer*.
   b. In the navigation pane, click Public.
   c. Double-click Public Documents.
   d. Right-click a blank area and choose *New, Text Document*.
   e. Type your last name as the document's name, and press Enter.

3. Switch PCs with a partner, and attempt to find the text file you just created from that user's PC by browsing the network. When you find it, capture a screen shot of the window, and name the file **C11A04S03**.
If you are unable to find the text file, troubleshoot, and document your steps on your paper or in your Word document.
4. Open the text file in Notepad (by double-clicking it) and type your full name inside it. Save your changes to it and close it.
If you are unable to complete Step 4, troubleshoot, and document your steps on your paper or in your Word document.
5. View the Properties for the file (right-click the file and choose *Properties*).
6. Capture a screen shot of the Properties window, and name the file **C11A04S06**.
7. Submit your paper or Word document and your screen shots to your instructor for grading.

On Your Own

Assessment EXAMINING THE SECURITY SETTINGS ON A WIRELESS ACCESS POINT

5

1. On a blank piece of paper, write your name and C11A05, or in a Word document, type your name and save the file as **C11A05**.
2. Using your Web browser, access the setup utility for your wireless access point. On your paper or in your Word document, write the address you used. Enter the address in the Address bar on your Web browser preceded by http://, like this: http://192.168.0.254.

   Note: *You will need to know the IP address that the wireless access point uses for this purpose. It is usually an address in the 192.168.x.x range. Your instructor or the documentation that came with the device will tell you what to use.*

3. Look through the Web-based configuration utility at the settings available for the access point. What types of wireless security does this access point support? What options are available? Write the answer on your paper or Word document.
4. Submit your paper or Word document to your instructor for grading.

Assessment CHANGING THE WORKGROUP NAME

6

1. On a blank piece of paper, write your name and C11A06, or in a Word document, type your name and save the file as **C11A06**.
2. View the System Properties dialog box (Control Panel, System and Security, System, Advanced system settings), and on the Computer Name tab, make a note of the current workgroup or domain, and write it on your paper or in your Word document.
3. Click the Change button, and if the Workgroup option button is not selected, select it. Type **STUDENTS** as the workgroup name.
4. Save the changes and restart the PC.
5. Try to browse the network via the Network window, and record the results on your paper or in your Word document.
6. Change at least one other PC in your network over to this same STUDENTS workgroup.
7. Try again to browse the network, and record the results.
8. Change all the computers back to their original network membership (workgroup or domain).

9. Try again to browse the network in the Network window, and record the results.
10. Submit your paper or Word document to your instructor for grading.

Assessment **EXPERIMENTING WITH A VPN CONNECTION**

7

1. Establish a VPN connection to your work or school.
2. Look in the Network and Sharing Center, and in the Computer window, and in the Network window to see what differences you can observe when the VPN connection is established. You might need to disconnect and reconnect from the VPN connection several times to check for differences.
3. Write a brief report explaining the differences you observed, and label it **C11A07**.

Assessment **EXPLORING NETWORK PRINTER PROPERTIES**

8

1. Share a local printer on the network.
2. On another PC, set up the shared printer as a network printer.
3. On the PC to which the printer is directly connected, right-click the icon for the printer and choose *Properties*. Examine the printer settings available there.
4. Repeat Step 3 on the PC that uses the printer via the network, and examine the printer settings available there.
5. Write a brief report explaining the differences, and label it **C11A08**.

CHALLENGE Project

You work for a small business that has six PCs, and you have been asked to set up a network for file and printer sharing and for Internet connectivity. Your boss has purchased a commercial DSL package that comes with a single DSL terminal adapter.

He has also purchased a router that has six RJ-45 jacks, a connector for the incoming DSL line, and a wireless networking antenna, so that it can function both as a router and as a wireless access point. Two of the PCs in the office are laptops with both wired and wireless capability; the other four have RJ-45 jacks for wired connections but no wireless. You have plenty of cables available for connecting components to one another.

Draw a diagram showing how you would connect all the PCs, the router, and the DSL terminal adapter. Use dotted lines to represent wireless connections and solid lines to represent wired ones.

CHAPTER 12

Maintaining Your System

PERFORMANCE OBJECTIVES

Upon successful completion of Chapter 12, you will be able to:

- **Use Windows Update to keep Windows 7 current**
- **Add or remove a font**
- **Use Disk Cleanup to remove unneeded files**
- **Expand memory with Windows ReadyBoost**
- **Defragment a disk**
- **Configure power settings**
- **Back up files and folders**
- **Restore settings to an earlier time with System Restore**

To keep Windows 7 running optimally, you can run system utilities that improve system performance, safeguard your data, and fine-tune system settings. These tasks are optional, but can make Windows 7 run better and more efficiently.

Using Windows Update to Keep Windows 7 Current

Windows Update is a free service from Microsoft that downloads the latest patches, fixes, and updates from Microsoft's servers for Windows 7 and other Microsoft products. By default, Windows Update runs automatically behind the scenes, downloading updates as they become available. You can also trigger an update manually, and you can review updates that are already installed, and, in some cases, you can remove previously installed updates (for example, if a recent update has caused a problem with your system).

Windows Update: A free service from Microsoft that downloads the latest patches, fixes, and updates from Microsoft's servers for Windows 7 and other Microsoft products

Displaying Windows Update

You can access Windows Update via the *System and Security* section of the Control Panel. From the Windows Update screen, you can see when the system last checked for updates, when the last update was installed, and more. See Figure 12.1. Along the left side are links to common activities for working with Windows Update.

Figure 12.1 View and manage Windows Update settings via the Control Panel.

Here's How

To display the Windows Update screen:

1. Click Start.
2. Click *Control Panel*.
3. Click the *System and Security* category icon.
4. Click *Windows Update*.

Tip: If Internet Explorer is open, you can also access Windows Update by choosing Tools (from the menu bar), Windows Update. Press Alt to display the menu bar if it does not already appear.

Changing Windows Update Settings

When a PC is connected full-time to the Internet, as with a broadband, always-on connection, updates occur automatically. However, some people choose to turn off automatic updates for a variety of reasons. For example, some people prefer to control when updates are done because some updates require the PC to be restarted, and they do not want the PC automatically restarting itself (and possibly causing them to lose unsaved work in applications) when they are not expecting it.

For important updates, you can choose one of these actions:

- **Install updates automatically (recommended).** Updates are downloaded and installed at the specified time (unless the particular update requires user input or accepting a license agreement). If an update requires a restart, the restart occurs automatically. This is the default setting in Windows 7.

- **Download updates but let me choose whether to install them.** Updates are downloaded, but then they wait for the user to trigger their installation. This is useful for people who might not always want every update that is offered.

- **Check for updates but let me choose whether to download and install them.** An update notice appears, but the download does not occur until the user triggers it. This is useful for people on dial-up connections so that the download does not interfere with Internet performance at a critical time.

- **Never check for updates (not recommended).** Windows Update does not run automatically. This is useful in some managed corporate environments where updates are controlled by an administrator or provided by a company server rather than downloaded directly from Microsoft.

As shown in Figure 12.2, you can also choose at what date and time the preferred action should occur.

Some updates are more important than others to the system's functionality. For example, an update that patches a security hole is more important than one that slightly improves the functioning of a specialized utility that few people use. Windows Update categorizes the updates in one of three levels of priority:

Figure 12.2 Choose how Windows Updates should occur.

- **Important:** Affects the system's stability and security. These updates are always included.

- **Recommended:** Fixes a problem with or improves the performance of a nonessential Windows 7 component or add-on. These updates are included automatically only if the check box is marked under *Recommended Updates* (see Figure 12.2).

- **Optional:** Updates or enhances parts of Windows 7 that not everyone uses, such as support add-ons or foreign language packs. These updates are not downloaded automatically; you must manually run Windows Update (as described later in this chapter) to acquire them.

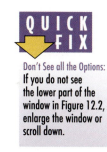

Don't See all the Options: If you do not see the lower part of the window in Figure 12.2, enlarge the window or scroll down.

Microsoft Update is a separate feature from Windows Update; it includes updates for Microsoft products other than Windows itself, such as Microsoft Office, Microsoft Visual Basic, and so on. If you would like to include updates for other products in the Windows Update process, make sure the check box under *Microsoft Update* is marked (see Figure 12.2).

To change Windows Update settings:

1. Choose Start, *Control Panel, System and Security, Windows Update.*
2. Click Change Settings in the list pane.
3. Click to open the drop-down list under Important Updates.
4. Click the desired update option.

Here's How

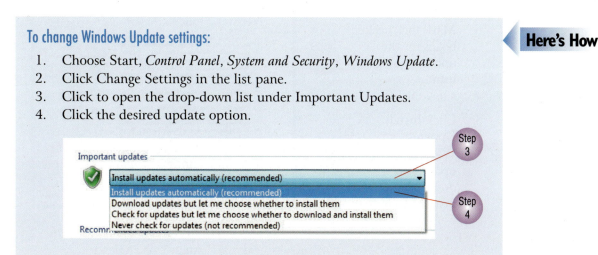

5. (Optional) Choose a different date and time for updates to occur.

6. Mark or clear the check box in the *Recommended Updates* section.
7. Mark or clear the check box in the *Microsoft Update* section. Leave other checkboxes set at their defaults.
8. Click OK.
9. If prompted, click Yes to restart the PC.

Checking for and Installing an Update

If your settings do not specify that Windows 7 will check automatically for updates, you must click the *Check for Updates* link in the Windows Update window to initiate a check. If any new updates are found, they appear in the Windows Update window. From there you can click Install Updates to download the important updates (if not already downloaded) and install them. Even if Windows Update reports that no important updates are available, there still may be useful updates you might want. For example, you might want a device driver update for a piece of hardware on your system. Therefore, you might want to use the following steps to select optional updates, in addition to installing the important ones.

To choose and install updates:

1. Choose Start, *Control Panel*, *System and Security*, *Windows Update*.
2. Click the link for optional updates. A list of available updates appears.
3. Mark the check boxes for the updates you want.
4. Click OK.
5. Click Install Updates.
6. Wait for the updates to download and install.

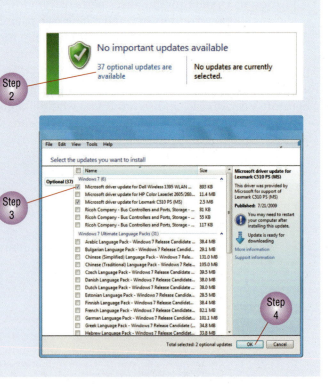

Reviewing the Update History

The *Update History* list shows the Windows 7 updates that have been installed on your system. To see it, click *View Update History* in the Windows Update window. You can then double-click any of the lines to open its details, as in Figure 12.3. If any of the updates do not have a Successful status, view its details and then click the link in the details under Help and Support.

Removing an Update

Not all updates can be removed; some of them, such as security patches, permanently affect Windows 7. Other updates, however, can be removed, and the files they affected rolled back to their previous versions. This might be useful, for example, if an update caused an unexpected problem with a device or application.

Figure 12.3 The update history shows the updates that have been installed.

To remove a Windows 7 update:

1. Choose Start, *Control Panel, System and Security*.
2. Under *Windows Update*, click Installed Updates.
3. Click an update to uninstall. If uninstall is available, an Uninstall button appears.
4. Click Uninstall or double-click the update to uninstall.
5. If prompted for confirmation, click Yes.

Here's How

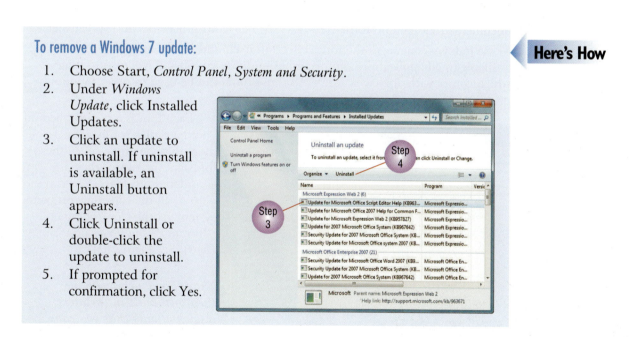

Exercise 1

Updating Windows

1. Open the Control Panel's *System and Security* section (Start, *Control Panel, System and Security*).
2. Under *Windows Update*, click the *Turn automatic updating on or off* link.
3. Under Important Update, open the drop-down list and choose *Check for updates but let me choose whether to download and install them*.
4. Click OK.
5. Under Windows update, click *View Installed Updates*.

6. Scroll down to the Microsoft Windows section. Click an installed update and observe whether an Uninstall button appears above the list.
7. For one of the updates that has an Uninstall button available, click Uninstall.
8. Click Yes to confirm, if prompted. If prompted to restart your computer, click Restart Now and wait for it to restart.
9. Open the Control Panel's *System and Security* section.
10. Under *Windows Update*, click *Check for Updates*.
    At least one update should appear available (the one you uninstalled). If no updates are available, try uninstalling a different update.
11. Click the Install Updates button and follow any prompts to install it.
12. When a message appears that the updates were successfully installed, capture a screen shot of this window, paste the shot into Paint, and save it as **C12E01**. See "Capturing a Screen Picture to Complete an Assignment" in Chapter 1 for help, if needed.
13. Check with your instructor, and if needed, return the *Windows Update* setting to its previous state (probably *Install updates automatically*).
14. Submit the screen shot via e-mail or on a USB flash drive to your instructor, as required.

Viewing, Installing, and Removing Fonts

Font: A typeface, a style of lettering, appearing either on the screen or in print

Soft font: A font that is stored as a file on a PC rather than stored internally in the printer

In its most generic definition, a *font* is a typeface, a style of lettering. Windows 7 uses fonts for on-screen display of text, and also in applications that produce documents that contain formatted text, such as word processors and spreadsheets.

Windows 7 manages the font collection itself and makes nearly all fonts available to all applications. For example, suppose you install Microsoft Office, which comes with dozens of fonts. All those fonts can be used in other Windows programs too, not just Office applications.

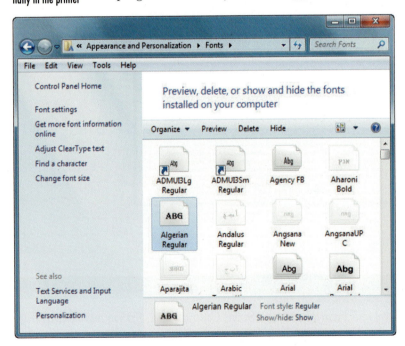

Each font is a file installed on your hard disk (or in some cases more than one file). Since these fonts are "software" they are considered *soft fonts*. You can see a list of all the soft fonts on your system via the Control Panel (*Appearance and Personalization, Fonts*). See Figure 12.4.

Note: *Some printers have their own built-in (printer-resident) fonts that you can use in some applications. The printer's driver defines these fonts to Windows 7; they are separate from the fonts you are learning about in this section. For information about your printer's built-in fonts, consult its documentation.*

Figure 12.4: To display a list of fonts on your system, from the Control Panel choose *Appearance and Personalization* and then click *Fonts*.

To see a sample of a font, double-click it to open a window containing sample text in that font at various sizes, as in Figure 12.5. Some font icons represent a group of fonts, so when you double-click them, more font icons appear; if that happens, double-click one of the ones that appears to see a sample of it.

To install a new font in Windows 7, open up an Explorer window for the folder containing the new font. Then right-click the font file and choose Install. Alternatively, you can drag-and-drop the font file into the Fonts window.

Figure 12.5 Double-click a font in the Fonts window to display a sample of it.

Many people like to have as many fonts as possible to choose from, but sometimes you might want to remove some font files. Each font file takes up some space on the hard disk, and if disk space is limited, the cumulative effect of having hundreds of fonts installed can be significant. Some people also prefer to keep the list of installed fonts small because it reduces the amount of scrolling through the font list they have to do in applications to find the font they want to apply.

The easiest way to remove a font is to delete its icon from the Fonts folder. Click it and press the Delete key to do so. If you think you might want to reinstall that font again at some point, copy the font to a backup folder (by dragging-and-dropping it from the Fonts folder into another folder).

If you aren't worried about disk space, but would like to make the font list more compact in applications, you can choose to hide one or more fonts from most programs that use fonts.

Note: A font file can take up as little of 8 KB of space or many megabytes of space depending on its complexity. TrueType collections can take up as much as 35 MB in some cases, for example. To find out which fonts are taking up the most space, view the Fonts window in Details view and then sort the display by Size. If Size is not one of the columns displayed, choose View, then Choose Details. Mark the Size check box and click OK. Then to sort by the Size column, click its column heading. Scroll the display to the right if you don't see the Size column after adding it.

To view the Fonts window:

1. Click Start and click *Control Panel*.
2. Click *Appearance and Personalization*.
3. Click *Fonts*.

To install a font:

1. From the Fonts window, right-click the font file.
2. Click Install.

To remove a font:

1. Click the font file in the Fonts window.
2. Press the Delete key.
3. Click Yes.

Here's How

To show or hide fonts not in your language:

1. In the Fonts window, click *Font settings*.
2. Mark or clear the *Hide fonts based on language settings* check box.
3. Click OK

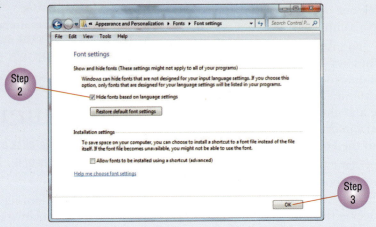

Step 2

Step 3

To hide an individual font from applications:

1. In the Fonts window, right-click the font to hide.
2. Click *Hide*.

To unhide a hidden font:

1. In the Fonts window, switch to Details view (View, *Details*).
2. Right-click a font that shows Hidden in the Show/hide column.
3. Click *Show*.

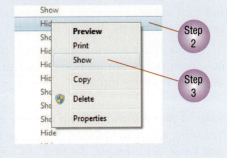

Step 2

Step 3

Exercise 2

Removing and Reinstalling a Font

1. Create a new folder on the C drive called FontBackup and leave it open.
2. Open the Control Panel's Fonts window (Start, *Control Panel, Appearance and Personalization, Fonts*).
3. Select a font and press Ctrl+C to copy it to the Clipboard.
   Different systems will have different fonts; you can use any font that is installed on your system. Make sure you do not pick one that has a curved arrow on its icon; those are font shortcuts, not actual font files.
4. Display the FontBackup folder, and press Ctrl+V to paste the font into it.
5. Capture a screen print of this window and submit it to your instructor for grading. Name the file **C12E02**. See "Capturing a Screen Picture to Complete an Assignment" in Chapter 1 for help, if needed.
6. Display the Fonts folder and delete the font you copied.
7. From the C:\FontBackup folder, right-click the font file(s) and choose Install.
8. Click Close.
9. Close the Fonts folder window.

Using Disk Cleanup to Remove Unneeded Files

Hard disks over time accumulate files that you do not need to keep, such as temporary Internet files, leftover files from software installations, and deleted files retained in the Recycle Bin. When a hard disk becomes almost full, system performance begins to suffer. Therefore, it is good housekeeping practice to run Disk Cleanup periodically to delete some of the files that Windows 7 no longer needs.

You can choose to clean up only your own files (that is, files associated with your user account) or system files for all users on the computer. The latter gets rid of more files, but you risk possibly cleaning up (that is, deleting) files that some other user on the PC might have intended to keep.

Disk Cleanup identifies files in various categories that you can delete to save space, as shown in Figure 12.6. You can mark or clear the check box for a category, or select it and click View Files to see exactly what the category contains.

Figure 12.6 Disk Cleanup identifies files that can be deleted to free up space on the hard disk.

To run Disk Cleanup:

> **Here's How**

1. Open the Computer window.
2. Right-click the desired drive to clean up and choose *Properties*.
3. On the General tab, click Disk Cleanup.
4. Wait for Disk Cleanup to calculate the space to be freed up.
5. In the Disk Cleanup window, mark or clear check boxes for each category of file to clean up.
6. (Optional) To clean up system files, click the Clean up system files button. Then wait for system files to be cleaned.
7. Click OK.
8. Click Delete Files to confirm. Then wait for the files to be cleaned up.

Defragmenting a Disk

When a file is stored on a disk, if there is room, the file is placed in contiguous clusters on the drive surface. This makes the file easily accessible to the disk's read/write head, since it is all in one place, and makes the disk access time as fast as it can be. Over time, however, as the file is modified, the additional pieces are written to nonadjacent areas, and the file becomes *fragmented*. The disk read/write heads must move around more to pick up the pieces, so the disk access time suffers. *Defragmenting* a disk can improve its performance by rewriting as many files as possible to contiguous clusters.

Windows 7 automatically defragments drives once a week, by default. You can initiate a manual defragment operation at any time, and/or change the interval and timing of the automatic activity.

You can start the Disk Defragmenter utility in two ways. You can run it from the Properties box for a particular drive (Tools tab) or from the Start, *All Programs*, *Accessories*, *System Tools* menu.

Fragmented file: A file that is stored in multiple noncontiguous clusters on a hard disk

Defragment: To reorganize the file storage on a disk drive so that as many files as possible are stored contiguously

To start the Disk Defragmenter utility (Properties method):

1. Open the Computer window.
2. Right-click the drive to defragment and click *Properties*.
3. On the Tools tab, click Defragment now.

To start the Disk Defragmenter utility (Start menu method):

1. Click the Start button.
2. Click *All Programs*.
3. Click *Accessories*, and then click *System Tools*, and then click *Disk Defragmenter*.

To run a manual disk defragmentation:

1. Start the Disk Defragmenter utility.
2. In the Disk Defragmenter dialog box, click Defragment disk.
3. Wait for the defragmentation to finish.

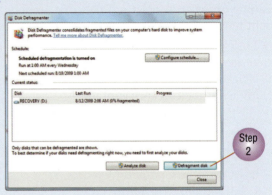

To schedule automatic defragmentation:

1. Start the Disk Defragmenter utility.
2. Click Configure Schedule.
3. Specify how often from the *Frequency* drop-down list.
4. Specify which day on the *Day* drop-down list.
5. Specify the time on the *Time* drop-down list.
6. Click OK.

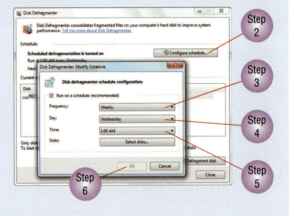

Exercise 3

Cleaning Up and Defragmenting a Hard Disk

1. Start Disk Cleanup for the C drive.
2. Mark the check boxes for all possible files to delete except Office Setup Files (if present), Setup Log Files, and Thumbnails, and complete the Disk Cleanup.
3. Start the Disk Defragmenter and start the defragmenting process now.
4. While you are waiting for the process to complete, capture a screen print of this window and submit it to your instructor for grading. Name the file **C12E03**. See "Capturing a Screen Picture to Complete an Assignment" in Chapter 1 for help, if needed.
5. Click Close. The defragmentation continues in the background.

Expanding Memory with Windows ReadyBoost

ReadyBoost enables you to use storage space from a removable media device, such as a USB flash drive, for additional RAM. When you connect a ReadyBoost-capable storage device, the AutoPlay dialog box includes an option to use the device to speed up your computer. You can then specify the amount of space that should be devoted to this purpose, so you can continue using the device for regular storage as well.

> **Tip:** A system can benefit from one to three times the amount of ReadyBoost storage as it has physical RAM. For example, if you have 1 GB of RAM in your system, a flash drive of 4 GB would be best allocated for 1 to 3 GB of storage for ReadyBoost and the remaining storage for regular file storage.

Note: *Not all USB flash drives work with ReadyBoost. Windows 7 will determine whether yours will or not.*

To expand memory with ReadyBoost:

Here's How

1. Connect the flash RAM drive and wait for the AutoPlay box to appear.
2. Click *Speed up my system using Windows ReadyBoost*.

3. Click *Dedicate this device to ReadyBoost* on the ReadyBoost tab.

   Or

   Click *Use this device*.
4. If you chose *Use this device* in Step 3, drag the slider to specify the amount of disk space to be used for ReadyBoost.
5. Click OK.

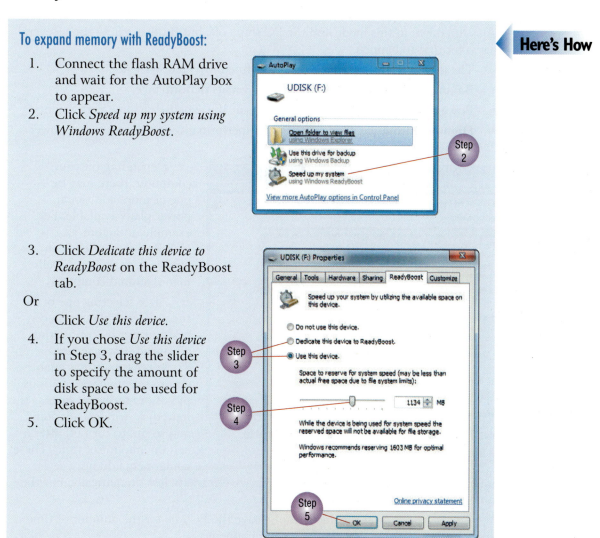

Configuring Power Settings

Many people leave their computers on most of the time, to avoid spending time rebooting every time they want to use it. However, leaving a computer on consumes a significant amount of power. On a PC that is plugged in all the time, this is merely a slight increase in the electric bill, but on a laptop PC running on batteries, full power usage can quickly drain the battery and decrease the amount of time the PC can be used before recharging.

Creating a Power Plan

A power plan defines whether and how the system will partially shut itself down to save power after a specified period of inactivity. You can configure a PC in two ways to save power: turn off the display after a time, and put the computer to sleep after a certain amount of time.

When a computer sleeps, everything except RAM and the CPU is shut down to save power. When the user wakes the PC up, the system comes back up quickly (compared to a full reboot) because Windows 7 is already in RAM and does not have to be reloaded. When the PC is running on batteries, eventually the battery does run down in this mode and the PC shuts off, but it takes a long time (several days) for that to happen.

The three preferred power plans predefined in Windows 7 are:

- **Balanced**. A balance of power savings versus performance
- **Power saver**. Aggressive power savings at the expense of some performance
- **High performance**. Consistently high performance at the expense of power savings

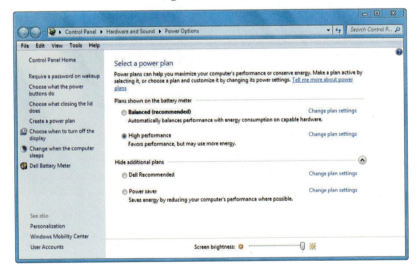

Depending on your computer, there may be one or more additional power plans available. For example, in Figure 12.7, Dell Recommended is an option because it is a Dell-manufactured computer.

After selecting one of the preferred plans, you can customize it by configuring advanced power settings. These power settings enable you to selectively set various pieces of hardware, such as the hard disk, wireless adapter, and so on, to turn off after a certain amount of time. These components do not use as much power as the monitor, so they will save electricity less dramatically, but they do contribute to power usage.

Figure 12.7 Windows 7 offers several preconfigured power plans to choose from.

To test your power settings, simply leave the PC idle for the amount of time specified in the power plan and see what happens.

To select a preferred power plan:

1. Open the Control Panel.
2. Click *System and Security*.
3. Click *Power Options*.
4. Click one of the power plans.

To customize a power plan (basic customization):

1. Open the Control Panel.
2. Click *System and Security*.
3. Click *Power Options*.
4. Click the *Change plan settings* link next to the power plan to customize.

   Note: *Perform steps 5–8 separately for On Battery and Plugged In if you are on a laptop computer. On a desktop computer there is only one set of controls.*

5. Open the *Dim the display* list and select an amount of time (or choose Never).
6. Open the *Turn off the display* list and select an amount of time (or choose Never).
7. Open the *Put the computer to sleep* list and select an amount of time (or choose Never).
8. Drag the *Adjust plan brightness* slider to adjust the screen brightness level.
9. Click Save Changes if finished, or go on to the next section to do advanced customization.

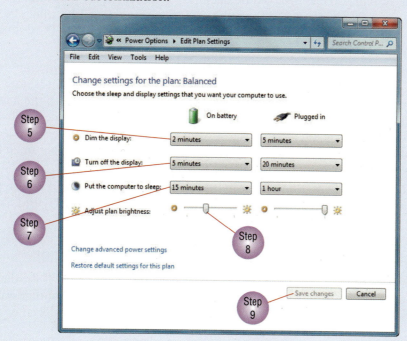

To customize a power plan (advanced customization):

1. Perform all steps in "To customize a power plan (basic customization)" above.

2. Click the *Change advanced power settings* link.

3. In the Power Options dialog box, click the plus sign next to a category to open it. Some categories may have sub-categories and require clicking additional plus signs.

4. Change the setting(s) for the selected category as desired.

5. Repeat Steps 3–4, as needed.

6. Click OK.

7. Click Save Changes.

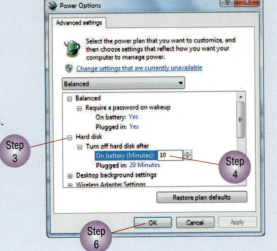

An even deeper Sleep mode called *Hibernate* uses no power at all and is useful when leaving a PC idle for longer periods of time. Hibernate is useful primarily for laptops running on batteries, and there are sometimes incompatibilities between it and some systems, so it is disabled by default. Hibernate copies the contents of RAM to a special region on the hard disk and then shuts down the whole PC. When you turn it back on, the data is copied back into RAM and the PC wakes up as if it were in Sleep mode.

New in Windows 7 is a mode called *Hybrid Sleep*, which is a combination of Sleep and Hibernate. It is used by default on desktop systems, and it is not available when you are working on a laptop. It saves the system state to the hard disk, just the way hibernation does, but then, instead of shutting down, it puts the computer in Sleep mode afterward. That way you can resume from Sleep mode quickly, but if something happens that causes the PC to shut down, your open files and settings are restored from hibernation.

You can enable hibernation and/or hybrid sleep from the Advanced Power Options, in the Sleep category. Set the Hibernate After and/or Allow Hybrid Sleep settings to something other than Never.

Defining Power Buttons and Turning On Password Protection

As you saw in the preceding section, one way for Sleep to be triggered is for the PC to sit idle for the amount of time specified in the power profile. Another way to trigger Sleep is to configure the power button(s) to place the PC in Sleep or Hibernate mode.

Some PCs have separate Sleep and Shut Down buttons; others have only a Power button. If the PC does not have a Sleep button, the Sleep setting is ignored. Sleep buttons are more common on notebook PCs, but can also be found on some multifunction keyboards.

The Power button can be defined in any of these states: Do Nothing, Shut Down, Sleep, or Hibernate. The Sleep button can be defined in any of those except Shut Down.

QUICK FIX

PC Goes into Hibernate instead of Sleep:
If your PC goes into Hibernate rather than Sleep, check the timing you have set for each one. If the Sleep time is less than the Hibernate time, the PC will switch from Sleep to Hibernate when the Hibernate time comes. However, if the Hibernate time is earlier, it will stay in Hibernate and the Sleep directive will be ignored.

When a PC wakes up from sleep or hibernation, anyone who wakes it up has full access to it unless you password-protect the wake-up. You can add some security to that by requiring the user's logon password to be reentered when the PC wakes up.

Note: *Password protection works only if the user account requires a password to log on to Windows 7, because the same password is used.*

To define power button settings and optionally require a password on wake-up:

◀ **Here's How**

1. Open the Control Panel.
2. Click *System and Security*.
3. Click *Power Options*.
4. Click *Require a password on wakeup* at the left side of the window
5. Open the *When I press the power button* list and select an action.
6. Open the *When I press the sleep button* list and select an action.
7. Open the *When I close the lid* list and select an action.
8. Click *Require a password (recommended)* or *Don't require a password*.
9. Click Save Changes.

To reset a preferred plan to its default:

1. Click the *Change Plan Settings* link next to the power plan's name.
2. Click the *Restore default settings for this plan* link.
3. Click Yes.
4. Click Cancel.

🌐 Exercise 4

Managing Power Settings

1. Open the Power Options in the Control Panel.
2. Redefine the Power saver plan to the following basic settings:

   Note: *If you are using a laptop, make these changes for the On Battery settings.*

   • Turn off the display in 3 minutes.
   • Put the computer to sleep in 5 minutes.
3. In the Advanced settings for the Power saver plan, under USB settings, set the USB selective suspend setting to Enabled and click OK.
4. Capture a screen print of this window and submit it to your instructor for grading. Name the file **C12E04**. See "Capturing a Screen Picture to Complete an Assignment" in Chapter 1 for help if needed.
5. Save the changes to the Power Saver plan.

6. Make sure the Power Saver plan is selected.
7. Wait 3 minutes to confirm the display turns off.
8. Wait two more minutes to confirm the PC goes into Sleep mode.
9. Press any key to wake up the PC again.
10. Redefine the Power Saver plan by resetting it to its default settings.
11. Close all open windows.

Backing Up Files and Folders

Windows 7 has a backup utility that makes it easy to automate the process of backing up your important data, as well as to perform manual backups and restores. The Backup utility allows you to do four main tasks:

- **Back Up Files**. You can set up an automatic file backup, do an extra backup at any time, and change backup settings. (Automatic backup is not included in Windows 7 Home Basic.)

- **Restore Files**. You can restore all the files from a backup set or only certain files from it.

- **Create a System Image**. You can back up your entire hard disk (in a process called *mirroring)*, creating an exact copy that you can later restore in the event of a catastrophic system crash.

- **Create a System Repair Disc**. You can create a bootable CD or DVD that will enable you to troubleshoot and repair your system in the event that Windows 7 cannot start normally.

Mirror: To copy the complete contents of a drive to another drive

To perform any of these activities, start by opening the Backup Status and Configuration window.

Here's How ▶ **To open the Backup Status and Configuration window:**
1. Click Start, and then click *Control Panel*.
2. Click *System and Security*.
3. Click *Backup and Restore*.

Setting Up an Automatic Backup

An automatic file backup, with its default settings, backs up most of the files on your system, including all data files, but excludes many of the files that you would not need in the event of a system crash because they would be loaded when you reloaded Windows 7 and your applications. That way it can save space on the backup disk while still providing you data protection.

As you are setting up automatic file backup, you are prompted to indicate where you will save the backup. You can save to a hard disk, CD, DVD, or to a network location. If you choose to back up to a network location, you can click Browse to browse your local area network for a location in which to store the backup.

To set up automatic file backup:

1. Open the Backup and Restore window.
2. Click *Set up backup*. If Set Up Backup has already been run on this PC, this option will not appear; instead choose *Change settings*.
3. Choose where to store the backup:

   3a. Save backup on: Click any of the drive letters in this list to store the backup there, on a local drive connected to the PC.

   3b. Save on a network: click this and then click Browse to open the Browse for Folder dialog box, and then navigate to the desired folder and click OK.

4. Click Next.
5. Select *Let Me Choose*.
6. Click Next.
7. Select the libraries, disks, and/or folders you want to include.
8. Clear the *Include a system image of drives* check box if it is marked.
9. Click Next.

10. (Optional) To change when the backup will occur, do the following:
    a. Click the *Change schedule* hyperlink next to the currently scheduled date and time.
    b. Change the How Often setting.
    c. Change the What Day setting.
    d. Change the What Time setting.
    e. Click OK.
11. Click *Save settings and run backup*.

    Note: *To change the backup settings at any time, follow the above steps, but in Step 2 choose Change Settings.*

If you are backing up to a CD or DVD and you are backing up more files than will fit on a single disc, you will be prompted one or more times after Step 10 to insert a new blank disc. Therefore, the backup cannot run completely unattended unless the entire backup will fit on one disc or you are backing up to a hard disk or network location with enough space for it.

After you set up the backup and enable it to begin running for the first time, as in the preceding steps, it runs in the background and you can continue working with Windows 7 normally as it runs.

> Tip: To delete a backup saved to an external hard disk or network location, navigate to the folder containing the backup you want to delete and delete that folder. Backup folders are named Backup Set plus the current date and time. For example, if the backup were performed at 9:00:00 a.m. on December 23, 2009, the folder would be named Backup Set 2009-12.23 090000.

Re-performing a Backup

After you have once defined the automatic backup settings, you can re-perform the same backup with the same settings without having to set it up again. Just click Back Up Now in the Backup Status and Configuration window. When you re-perform a backup, only the files that have changed since the previous backup are copied. Therefore, it will not take as long as the initial backup.

If you need to choose different files or a different location, see "Setting Up an Automatic Backup" earlier in this chapter.

Restoring Files

If you need to restore a single file, multiple files, or even *all* the files from your backup, you can easily do so with the Restore Files feature in the Backup Status and Configuration window.

You can restore files in two ways.

- **Restore files**. Restores your own files only (not files for all users) and only files backed up from the same PC. This is the method covered in this chapter. You can restore from the current backup or from an older backup.
- **Advanced Restore**. Restores files from a backup from another PC or for all users of the computer. This method is less frequently used and is not covered here.

After choosing the backup to restore, you can select the files and folders within that backup set to restore. When the Add Folder to Restore window appears, or the Add File to Restore window, it looks like a regular file navigation window for your system, but it is referring to the backup set, not to the actual files currently on your hard disk. The path that appears across the top of the dialog box points to the backup set.

> Tip: To quickly select all the files in the entire backup set, from the Add Files to Restore window, click Computer on the Favorites list and then select all the drive icons that appear and click Add.

Here's How ▶ To restore from the latest backup:

1. Open the Backup and Restore window.
2. Click *Restore my files.*
3. Add the desired folders to the list to be restored:
   a. Click Browse for Folders.
   b. Click a folder to restore. Hold down Ctrl to select multiple folders.

    c.   Click Add Folder.

    d.   Repeat as needed to add more folders.

4.   Add the desired individual files to the list to be restored:

    a.   Click Browse for Files.

    b.   Navigate to the file and select it. Hold down the Ctrl key to select multiple files.

    c.   Click Add Files.

    d.   Repeat as needed to add more files. You can also click Search to look for a particular file or folder by name.

5.   Click Next.

6.   Click *In the original location*, or click *In the following location* and then type a path or browse for one.

7.   Click Start Restore.

8.   Wait for the restore to finish. If any duplicates are found, respond to the prompt indicating what you want to do. Mark the *Do this for all conflicts* check box to repeat your answer without additional prompts appearing.

9.   At the Successfully restored files prompt, click Finish.

Creating a System Image

A system image is a backup that copies everything from all your hard drives to a specified backup location. You cannot select which files and folders to back up; it automatically backs up everything on all internal hard disks in the system.

One of the best uses for a system image is to preserve a copy of the original system state when you first acquire the PC. You can then return the system to its "factory fresh" state at any time when problems occur with it such as viruses or corrupted files.

To create a system image:

Here's How

1.   Open the Backup and Restore window.

2.   Click the *Create a system image* link.

3.   When prompted to choose where you want to save the backup, click *On a hard disk, On one or more DVDs*, or *On a network location*. Then select the drive or path of the chosen type.

4.   Click Next.

5.   If a list of drives appear, mark or clear the check boxes for the drives to include, and click Next.

6.   Click Start Backup.

7.   Follow the prompts to complete the backup. Depending on your choice in Step 4, you might be asked to insert, format, or label one or more discs.

This copy cannot be used selectively to restore files, as with the Restore feature; instead you must use the system recovery utility in Windows 7 (click Start, then type Recovery and press Enter), boot from a Windows 7 installation disc and use the Repair feature, or use a preinstalled recovery option (available on some PCs that do not come with a Windows 7 disc).

If you have a Windows 7 installation disc, insert it and restart the computer. Then choose to repair the computer and walk through the prompts to select the system image to recover.

If you do not have a Windows 7 installation disc, you still can restore the backup, but you must boot into the Advanced Boot Options menu. To do this, restart the PC and press F8 repeatedly until the Advanced Boot Options menu appears. (If you see the Windows 7 logo, you missed it; try again.) Then from there, select Repair Your Computer and follow the prompts.

Creating a System Repair Disc

A system repair disc is a bootable CD or DVD that you can use to start your PC if it will not start normally. It not only contains boot files, but also a variety of utilities that may be useful in troubleshooting and repairing. You can also use it to start the system as preparation for restoring using a system image (like the one you learned how to create in the previous section).

Here's How ▶

To create a system repair disc:

1. Open the Backup and Restore window.
2. Click the *Create a system repair disc* link.
3. Select the drive letter of your CD or DVD drive.
4. Insert a blank CD or DVD into the drive.
5. Click Create disc.
6. Wait for the disc to be created. When a message appears that it is done, click Close, and then click OK.

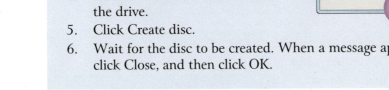

 ## Exercise 5

Backing Up Data

1. Place a blank writeable CD in the PC.
2. Open the Backup and Restore window.
3. Click Change Settings and then click Change Backup Settings. Or, if you have not already set up backup on this PC, click Set Up Backup.
4. Choose to back up to your CD drive.
5. When prompted to select the files to back up, click Let Me Choose, and then click Next.
6. Expand the list of locations and choose the Documents library only. (Deselect all other locations.)
7. Move through the rest of the backup configuration accepting the defaults, and start the backup.
8. When prompted to label and insert a blank disk, click OK.
9. When the backup is complete, write your name and CH12E05 on the disc with a soft-tipped marker and submit it to your instructor for grading.

Restoring Settings to an Earlier Time with System Restore

Backup works well for data files and other personal information, but it does not back up system files. When you experience problems such as Windows 7 not starting properly or running too slowly, it is often a problem with system files. Sometimes installing a new program replaces a system file, causing unintended problems with other programs that rely on it; other times a virus or other malicious program changes a Registry setting so that Windows 7 does not work as well or starts displaying unwanted ads or Web sites.

Note: *A system image does include system files, but it requires a more extreme restore process, so it is not a practical way to correct minor system problems.*

System Restore works by creating a backup of the Registry and other important system files. Windows 7 runs System Restore every day, creating regular restore points, and you can also manually create a restore point at any time. An ideal time to create a restore point would be before installing new software, for example. At any time you can revert the system to any available restore point, reversing all changes made to the Registry since that time, and usually reversing any problems that those later changes created.

In earlier Windows versions, the same utility, System Restore, was used both to create restore points and to restore them. In Windows 7, you create restore points via System Protection, and you restore them via System Restore.

To create a system restore point:

1. Click Start, and then right-click *Computer* and choose *Properties*. Alternatively, you can open the *Control Panel*, click *System and Security*, and click *System*.
2. Click the *System protection* link.
3. Click Create.
4. Type a description for the restore point.
5. Click Create.

6. When a message appears that the restore point has been created, click Close.

To restore a system restore point:

1. Save your work in any open programs, and close them.
2. Choose Start, *All Programs*, *Accessories*, *System Tools*, *System Restore*. Alternatively, you can perform Steps 1–2 from the preceding procedure and then click System Restore.
3. Click the desired restore point.
4. Click Next.

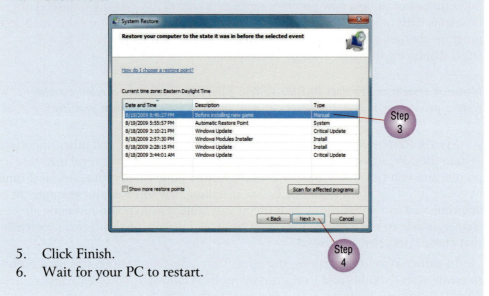

5. Click Finish.
6. Wait for your PC to restart.

CHAPTER Summary

- Windows Update works automatically to download and install the needed updates. You can configure it by way of the *System and Security* section of the Control Panel.

- Fonts are available Windows 7-wide, regardless of the program that originally supplied them. Many fonts are installed automatically with certain programs, such as Office.

- To install new fonts, drag-and-drop fonts into the Fonts folder or right-click a font file and choose Install.

- Disk Cleanup partially automates the process of selecting and deleting files that you no longer need, to save hard disk space. Run it from the disk drive's Properties box, on the General tab.

- Defragmenting a disk rearranges file storage so files can be accessed more quickly. It is done automatically at regular intervals. You can also manually initiate it from the drive's Properties box on the Tools tab.

- ReadyBoost enables you to connect a USB flash drive and use part of it to boost system performance by providing an extra memory cache. When you insert the flash drive, the AutoPlay box will present ReadyBoost as one of the play options.

- Power plans define the power management settings for Windows 7. There are three default plans: Balanced, Power saver, and High Performance. Each of these can be fully customized.
- To set power options, from the Control Panel go to *System and Security* and choose *Power Options*.
- The Backup utility in Windows 7 can back up or restore files or can make a complete backup (a system image) of the entire PC's contents on all internal hard disks.
- To access the Backup utility, choose Start, *All Programs, Accessories, System Tools, Backup and Restore.*
- System Restore backs up system files so you can return your PC settings to an earlier time to reverse bad Registry changes.
- To create a restore point, from the System properties, click System Protection.
- To restore a restore point, choose Start, *All Programs, Accessories, System Tools, System Restore.*

CONCEPTS Check

Completion: Answer the following questions on a blank sheet of paper.

Part 1   MULTIPLE CHOICE

1. What is the default setting for Windows Update?
   a. Do nothing
   b. Notify of updates but do not automatically download or install
   c. Download updates but do not automatically install
   d. Automatically install and download updates

2. What are the three levels of priority that a Windows 7 update can have?
   a. Important, Recommended, and Optional
   b. Critical, Important, and Recommended
   c. Important, Standard, and Extra
   d. High, Medium, and Low

3. From which screen do you remove Windows 7 updates?
   a. Uninstall Programs
   b. Installed Updates
   c. Device Manager
   d. Appearance and Personalization

4. To prevent a font from showing up in applications, but still leave it installed on your system, _____ it.
   a. mask
   b. hide
   c. restore
   d. clip

5. Where in the Control Panel is the Fonts folder located?
   a. System
   b. Appearance and Personalization
   c. Security
   d. Users

6. Which of these does Disk Cleanup do?
   a. Deletes unused icons from the desktop
   b. Deletes unneeded files from the hard disk
   c. Defragments the disk
   d. Repairs disk errors

7. Why is fragmentation a problem on a disk?
   a. Results in disk errors
   b. Makes the CPU run slower
   c. Degrades disk access time
   d. Clutters up desktop with unwanted icons

8. What do power plans control?
   a. Voltage generated by power supply
   b. Idle time before parts of the PC go into low power usage mode
   c. Speed of the CD-ROM drive
   d. All of the above

9. Which two things can you specify for a preferred power plan without going into the advanced settings?
   a. Turning off monitor and putting PC to sleep
   b. Turning off monitor and turning off hard disk
   c. Putting the PC to sleep and putting the PC in Hibernate mode
   d. Putting the PC to sleep and turning off the monitor

10. Where does the password that is needed come from when you provide a password on wake up?
   a. Administrator password
   b. User password for the logged-on user
   c. A separate screen saver password you specify
   d. None of the above

Part 2

SHORT ANSWER

11. Name three activities you can perform from the Backup and Restore window.

   _____

12. What power-saving mode is a combination of Sleep and Hibernate modes?

   _____

13. Why would you want to set up a power plan for a desktop PC, even though it never needs to run on batteries?

   _____

14. Give an example of a problem that System Restore might help you recover from, and give an example of a problem it would not help with.

   _____

15. Why would someone want to *not* have Windows Update always download and install updates automatically?

   _____

16. Explain the difference between a soft font and a printer-resident font.

   _____

17. What does the ReadyBoost feature do?

    _____

18. Why would you want to hide certain fonts from your applications?

    _____

19. List four types of files that Disk Cleanup can remove.

    _____

20. How does defragmenting improve system performance?

    _____

SKILLS Check

Save all solution files to the default Documents folder, or any alternative folder specified by your instructor.

Guided Check

Assessment REMOVE AND REINSTALL A WINDOWS UPDATE

1

1. On a blank sheet of paper, write your name and today's date.
2. Set Windows Update to not check for any updates automatically.
    a. Click Start, *Control Panel*, *System and Security*, *Windows Update*.
    b. Click Change Settings.
    c. Under Important Updates, choose Never check for updates.
    d. Click OK.
3. Remove one of the Windows 7 updates that have already installed, and write on your sheet of paper which one you removed.
    a. Click Installed Updates.
    b. Click an update to uninstall. Make sure you choose one for which an Uninstall button appears.
    c. Write down the name of the update on your paper.
    d. Click Uninstall, or double-click the update.
    e. If prompted to confirm, click Yes.
4. Check for and install updates.
    a. Click the Back button to return to the main Windows Update window.
    b. Click Check for Updates button.
    c. Click Install Updates.
5. Display your update history.
    • Click View Update History.
6. Take a screen shot of this window, paste the shot into Paint, and save it as **C12A01**.
7. Turn on automatic updates again.
    a. Click the Back button, and then click Change Settings.
    b. Click Install updates automatically (recommended).
    c. Click OK.
8. Submit the screen shot via e-mail or on a USB flash drive to your instructor, as required.
9. Close all open windows.

Assessment 2 — INSTALLING A NEW FONT

1. Check to see whether the font Tuffy is already installed on your PC. If it is, remove it. If it is not installed, go on to Step 2.
   a. Click Start, *Control Panel*, *Appearance and Personalization*, Fonts.
   b. Look for all font names that begin with "Tuffy" on the font list. If any appear, select them, press Delete, and click Yes to confirm.

   Note: *To more easily browse for the Tuffy font, view the list in Details view and then sort by the Name column.*

2. Install the Tuffy font from the Chapter 12 Student Data Files folder.
   a. Open the Chapter 12 folder.
   b. Open the Fonts window.
   c. Drag-and-drop all four variations of the Tuffy font into the Fonts window.
3. From the Fonts window, refresh the display, and then display a sample of Tuffy Medium Italic.
4. Capture a screen shot of this window, paste the shot into Paint, and save it as **C12A02**.
5. Close all remaining open windows. Do not save the changes to the document.
6. Submit the screen shot via e-mail or on a USB flash drive to your instructor, as required.

Assessment 3 — IMPROVE SYSTEM PERFORMANCE

1. Run a Disk Cleanup operation on the C drive, cleaning up as much as possible from the C drive.
   a. From the Computer window, right-click the C drive and choose *Properties*.
   b. On the General tab, click Disk Cleanup.
   c. Mark the check boxes for all categories except *Office Setup files* (if present).
   d. Click OK.
2. Defragment all internal hard disks.
   a. From the Computer window, right-click the C drive and choose *Properties*.
   b. On the Tools tab, click Defragment Now.
3. Set the defragmentation scheduling to once a week, at 3:00 a.m. on Wednesdays.
   a. Click Configure schedule.
   b. Open the *Frequency* list and click *Weekly*.
   c. Open the *Time* list and click *3:00 a.m.*
   d. Capture a screen shot of this window, paste the shot into Paint, and save it as **C12A03**.
   e. Click OK.
4. Click Defragment disk and then close all remaining open windows. The defragmentation will continue in the background.
5. Submit the screen shot via e-mail or on a USB flash drive to your instructor, as required.

Assessment 4 — CONTROLLING POWER SETTINGS

1. Open the Power Options. (Choose Start, *Control Panel*, *System and Security*, *Power Options*.)
2. Redefine the High Performance power plan to turn off the display after one hour.
   a. Click *Change plan settings* next to High Performance.
   b. Open the *Turn off the display* list and choose *1 hour*.

Note: *If working on a laptop, change the setting under Plugged In for this exercise.*

3. Customize the High Performance power plan to never turn off hard disks.
   a. Click *Change advanced power settings*.
   b. Click the plus sign next to Hard disk.
   c. Click the plus sign next to Turn off hard disk after.
   d. Change the Setting value to Never. (Type the word Never into the box.)

   Note: *If working on a laptop, change the setting for step 3d next to Plugged In.*

   e. Capture a screen shot of this window, paste the shot into Paint, and save it as **C12A04**.
   f. Click OK.
   g. Click Save Changes.
4. Submit the screen shot via e-mail or on a USB flash drive to your instructor, as required.
5. Close the Power Options window.

On Your Own

BACKING UP USER AND SYSTEM DATA

5

1. Open the Backup and Restore window.
2. Set up an automatic file backup with the following settings:
   - Back up to a writeable CD.
   - Back up only your own Pictures library.
   - Set this backup to be performed monthly on the fifth day at midnight.
3. Burn the backup to a writeable CD.
4. Label the CD **C12A05** with a soft-tipped marker and submit it to your instructor for grading.
5. Set a system restore point manually.
6. Install an application on your PC, such as a shareware utility, that makes changes to the Registry. Your instructor may provide you with a program to install; if not, find one from a download site such as www.cnet.com.
7. Restore the system restore point and allow it to restart your PC.
8. Try running the program you installed prior to restoring. Write notes about whether and how that worked, and submit them to your instructor for grading.

RESTORING FILES FROM A BACKUP

6

1. Create a document file in Microsoft Word called **test.doc** and save it to the Documents folder. In that file, type your name and today's date.
2. Use the Backup utility in Windows 7 to back up your Documents library.
3. Delete **test.doc** from the Documents folder.
4. Use the backup you created in Step 2 to restore **test.doc** to its original location.
5. Capture a screen shot of the window confirming that the restore operation has completed successfully, paste the shot into Paint and save it as **C12A06**.
6. Submit the screen shot via e-mail or on a USB flash drive to your instructor, as required.

EXPLORING OTHER SOURCES OF FONTS

1. Open a Web browser window and perform a Web search for public domain fonts.
2. Find a Web site that offers free public-domain fonts, and find a font that interests you.
3. Download that font and install it on your PC.
4. In your word processor, create a new document. Type your name and today's date in the new font. Save the file as **C12A07**.
5. E-mail the file to your instructor, or print it and submit the hard copy printout to your instructor. Your instructor may tell you which method is preferred.

EXPLORING DISK CLEANUP

1. On a blank sheet of paper, write **C12A08** and then record the information you gather in the following steps.
2. Open the Properties box for the C drive and note how much available space it reports that you have. Amount: _____
3. Start a Disk Cleanup operation, and choose to clean up only your own files. Mark all the check boxes and note how much space it reports that you will gain. Amount: _____
4. Run the Disk Cleanup operation.
5. Open the Properties box again for the C drive and note how much available space you have. Amount: _____
6. Based on this experiment, write a paragraph explaining how the estimate of the amount of space from Step 3 was or was not accurate compared to the amount of space actually freed up.

CHALLENGE Project

Suppose you are in charge of a small business's data backup. The business wants to back up all documents, pictures, and e-mails every night from each employee's PC, and store the backups on a network server. Write a report explaining how the company could use Windows 7 to perform these backups, and include step-by-step instructions that could be given to each employee explaining how he or she could set up the backup to occur every night at 11 p.m.

Adding Software and Hardware

PERFORMANCE OBJECTIVES

Upon successful completion of Chapter 13, you will be able to:

- Install a program
- Set default programs
- Control program startup
- Remove a program
- Install a program update
- Add a printer
- Work with hardware
- Configure a second monitor

To extend your computer's capabilities, you can install new software and hardware. New software enables you to perform different tasks with the computer, and new hardware makes the computer run better or faster or gives it additional storage or input/output functionality.

Installing and Removing Software

Windows 7 comes with a few handy programs that you can use for very basic operations, such as writing a letter with WordPad, adding numbers with Calculator, and drawing pictures with Paint. However, for most business tasks (and many personal ones as well), you will want to buy and install additional software.

New PCs sometimes come with extra software in addition to the default applications that come with Windows 7. Some of this software might be useful, but not all of it is helpful for every user's situation; you will likely want to remove some of the preinstalled software to free up the disk space. You might sometimes also want to remove software you have installed (for example, if you need to install a new version and the manufacturer recommends uninstalling old versions first, or if you decide you do not like the program and simply want to get rid of it).

Installing Software

Almost all programs come with a Setup utility that automates the installation. Setup utilities perform three functions:

- The utilities copy the needed files to your hard disk. In most cases, you will not need to have the program's CD inserted in the computer to use the program after it has been installed. However, some games do continue to require the CD, either because of the large size of its video clips or to prevent unauthorized duplication or sharing.

- The utilities also make needed changes to the Windows *Registry*. The Registry is a configuration database where system settings are stored—everything from display settings to information about installed hardware and software.
- They add a shortcut to the Start menu. Depending on the program, the shortcut might be directly on the All Programs menu or might be in a folder (submenu) within it.

When you buy software on a CD or DVD, the Setup utility and all the files to be copied to the hard disk are contained on the disc. The disc also typically contains an *Autorun* file that tells Windows 7 how to start the Setup utility automatically when the disc is inserted. When you insert the CD or DVD, an AutoPlay box might appear, as in Figure 13.1. Click Run Autorun.exe (or whatever the name of the file is) to start the Setup program. Then follow the prompts that appear onscreen. Notice in Figure 13.1 the check box for *Always do this for software and games*. If at some point someone has marked that check box, then you will not see the AutoPlay dialog box when inserting a disc; the Setup program will start automatically.

Figure 13.1 By default Windows 7 prompts for an action when you insert a disc; choose Run Autorun.exe to start the Setup utility.

When you download a program, it usually comes packaged in a single executable file that contains the Setup utility plus all the files to be installed. When you run that file, the Setup utility unpacks and installs the needed files.

A Setup program might ask if you want a Typical or Advanced installation. A typical installation uses a default location to store the files and installs a default set of options and settings. An advanced installation enables you to fine-tune the installation. In most cases, the default location is the best choice.

Adding a Program to the Start Menu Manually

Some programs, such as some free ones you download from the Web, are very simple, consisting of a single executable file. Such programs do not need to change the Registry or copy any files to your hard disk, so they do not require a Setup utility. For such programs, you must create a Start menu shortcut manually, if you want one.

There are several ways of adding a shortcut to the Start menu, but among the easiest is to create a shortcut on the desktop and then move that shortcut to the Start menu.

Here's How ▶ To create a Start menu shortcut:

1. Open an Explorer window and navigate to the folder containing the executable file for the program.
2. Hold down the Alt key and drag the executable file to the desktop. This creates a shortcut for it on the desktop.

3. Drag the shortcut from the desktop and hold it over the Start menu without releasing the mouse button. The Start menu opens.
4. Hover over *All Programs*. The All Programs menu opens.
5. If you want to place the shortcut in a folder on the Start menu, hover over that folder until it opens.
6. Release the mouse button, dropping the shortcut into the desired location on the Start menu.

Removing a Program

When you remove a program, Windows 7 does the following:

- It removes references to that program from the Registry.
- It deletes the program's files from the hard disk.
- It removes shortcuts to the program from the Start menu.

Windows 7 knows how to do these things because most applications come with an Uninstall file that provides advice about its removal. Windows 7 reads that information and performs the steps that the Uninstall file recommends.

Note: *In some cases an uninstall operation is performed imperfectly, either because the Uninstall file's instructions are not clear or because Windows 7 is unable to perform some of the functions due to security limitations or files being in use. After a program has been uninstalled, you might notice that a folder for it still exists on the hard disk, for example, or a shortcut to it (non-working) still appears on the Start menu. You can delete such remnants manually, as you would delete any folders, files, or shortcuts.*

You can access the Uninstall information for all installed programs via the Control Panel in Windows 7. From the Control Panel Home, under the Programs section click Uninstall a program to see the list of installed programs that are eligible for removal. Figure 13.2 shows an example, but your list will likely be different.

Different programs uninstall differently. Some have separate utilities for uninstalling and for changing the installation, for example. In Figure 13.2, the selected application, Bonjour, has separate buttons. Other applications have a single utility (and a single button) for changing and for uninstalling.

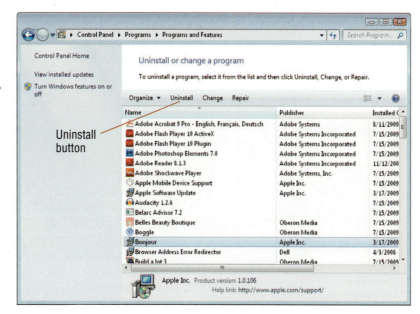

Figure 13.2 Windows 7 recognizes these programs as being installed. You can uninstall one by selecting it and then clicking Uninstall.

Figure 13.3 **After selecting a program to uninstall and clicking Uninstall, you are prompted to confirm that you really do want to uninstall it.**

Once you click the Uninstall button (or Uninstall/Change button), the uninstall instructions provided for that program launch an Uninstall process that varies greatly among applications. Some are very simple Yes/No prompts, as in Figure 13.3, with no user interaction required. In other cases you must specify options for the uninstall process, such as whether to keep your configuration files for the program.

Here's How ▸ To uninstall a program:

1. Click Start, and then click *Control Panel*.
2. Under Programs, click Uninstall a program.
3. Click the program to uninstall.
4. Click the Uninstall button or the Uninstall/Change button, whichever appears.
5. Follow the prompts to uninstall the program.

Incomplete Uninstall
If the uninstall , is not "clean," meaning there are some orphaned files and folders left on your hard disk after the uninstall, you can browse to the Program Files folder and delete them. However, they probably are taking up very little space and will not hurt anything if left on your hard disk.

Using Compatibility Mode

Some older programs designed for previous versions of Windows will not install correctly and/or will not run correctly under Windows 7 using default settings. Such programs can sometimes be tricked into running by employing the Windows 7 Compatibility Mode. You can use it on a Setup utility and also on the main executable that runs the program.

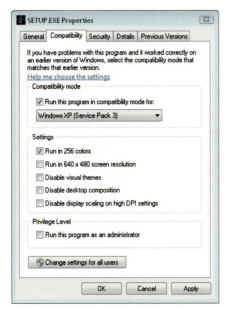

Figure 13.4 **Set compatibility options in the file's Properties box to help it run under Windows 7.**

Before resorting to Compatibility Mode, first try to install or run the program normally. If it does not work, then try to determine which version of Windows the program was designed for (Windows Vista, XP, Server 2003, 2000, NT 4, Windows 98ME, or 95). From there, set options on the Compatibility tab in the file's Properties box, as in Figure 13.4.

In addition to choosing an overall operating system to emulate for this program, you can also tweak some display options under the *Settings* area of the Properties box. For example, Windows 7 does not normally run in 256-color display mode, but some old programs require that display mode, so you can mark the *Run in 256 Colors* check box to force Windows 7 temporarily into that display mode when running that program.

Note: *Because running a setup program in Compatibility Mode does not automatically set up the application itself to run in Compatibility Mode, you must configure the application's executable file separately after the setup has completed.*

Exercise 1

1. In the folder containing the data files for this chapter, double-click **WinMem50.exe**.
2. If you see a security warning, click Allow.
3. Click Next.
4. Click I accept the agreement.
5. Click Next four times to move through the Install Wizard.
6. Click Install.
7. Click Finish.
8. Capture a screen of the WinCleaner Memory Optimizer page that appears, paste it into Microsoft Paint, and save the file as **C13E01**. Submit it to your instructor for grading. See "Capturing a Screen Picture to Complete an Assignment" in Chapter 1 for help, if needed.
9. Open the Control Panel, and click Uninstall a program.
10. Click WinCleaner Memory Optimizer Version 5.2, and click Uninstall.
11. Click Yes.
12. If prompted to restart your computer, click Yes to do so.

Setting Default Programs

Some tasks can be performed using your choice of programs. For example, a Web hyperlink can be opened in any Web browser you like, such as Internet Explorer, Firefox, or Opera, and music files can be played in Windows Media Player or in a third-party music application such as iTunes.

A file's extension indicates its type. For example, a .txt extension indicates a text file. Each extension is assigned to an application; that application takes ownership of all files of that type, so that when you double-click the file to open it, it opens in that application. By default, Notepad is the application associated with .txt files, so any .txt files you open appear in Notepad.

As you become proficient with your computer, you may develop strong preferences for one application over another. For example, you may prefer the Firefox browser, and want any clicked-on hyperlinks to open in that program rather than Internet Explorer.

There are two ways to examine and change the assignments of extensions to applications:

- You can browse a list of programs and tell a program that it should "own" (that is, be the default program for) all of the file types it supports, or you can tell it precisely which file types to own.

- You can browse a list of file extensions and change the programs that are assigned to one or more of them.

To choose a program as the default for all the file types it supports: ◀ **Here's How**

1. Click Start and then click *Control Panel*.
2. Click Programs.
3. Under Default Programs, click Set your default programs.
4. Click a program. Information about it appears.
5. Click Set this program as default.

6. Click OK.
7. Close the Control Panel window.

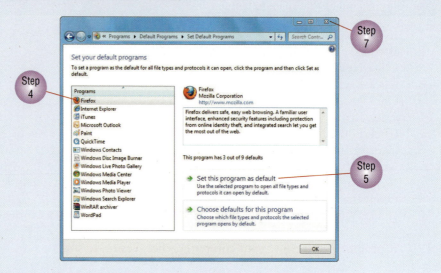

To choose a program as the default for individual file types it supports:

1. Click Start and then click *Control Panel*.
2. Click Programs.
3. Under Default Programs, click Set your default programs.
4. Click a program. Information about it appears.
5. Click Choose defaults for this program. A list of file types supported by this program appears.
6. Mark or clear the check boxes for the available file types.
7. Click Save.
8. Close the Control Panel window.

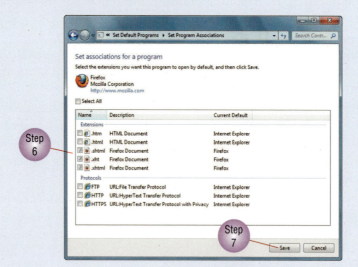

To set a file type to always open in a specific program:

1. Click Start and then click *Control Panel*.
2. Click Programs.
3. Under Default Programs, click Make a file type always open in a specific program.

4. Select a file extension.
5. Click Change program. A list of the installed programs that can handle this file type appears.

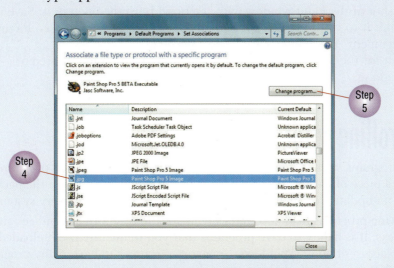

6. Click the program you want to use for this file type.
7. Click OK.

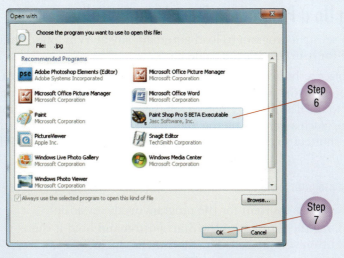

8. Click Close.
9. Close the Control Panel window.

Exercise 2
Changing the Default Program for a File Type

1. Click Start, and click *Control Panel*.
2. Click Programs.
3. Under Default Programs, click Make a file type always open in a specific program.
4. Select the .bmp file type.
5. Click *Change program*. Note the current default for that file type. It may be Windows Photo Viewer, Paint, or Windows Media Center, for example.
6. Click Paint.

7. Click OK, and then click Close.
8. Navigate to the folder containing the data files for this chapter and double-click **bowl.bmp**. The image opens in Paint.
9. Capture a screen shot of the Paint window with the **bowl.bmp** file open in it. Save it as **C13E02** and submit it to your instructor for grading. See "Capturing a Screen Picture to Complete an Assignment" in Chapter 1 for help, if needed.
10. Change the default for the .bmp file type back to the setting you noted in Step 5.
11. Close all open windows.

Controlling Automatic Program Startup

Some programs start automatically when Windows 7 starts. Such programs usually control a piece of hardware or keep some useful service running in the background such as an updater for an application or an instant message delivery system.

Having programs load automatically at startup has both advantages and drawbacks. It is handy to have programs that you frequently use preloaded, but it also places a drain on Windows 7 memory resources to have many programs loaded that are not actively being used. In addition, the more programs that load at startup, the longer it takes Windows 7 to start.

Setting Up a Program to Start Automatically

You can set up a program to load automatically at Windows 7 startup by placing a shortcut for it in the Startup folder.

To place a shortcut in the Startup folder, first create the shortcut. You can do this by pressing the Alt key and then dragging the executable file from any Explorer window to the desktop. Alternatively, if there is already a shortcut for that program elsewhere (such as already on the Start menu), you can press the Ctrl key and then drag the shortcut to create a copy of it. Then drag the shortcut into the Startup folder.

Here's How ▶ | To set a program to start automatically at Windows 7 startup:

1. Create a shortcut for the program on the desktop.
2. Drag the shortcut to the Start button and hold it there, with the mouse button still pressed. The Start menu opens.
3. Hover over *All Programs*. The All Programs menu opens.
4. Hover over *Startup*. The Startup submenu (folder) opens.
5. Drop the shortcut into the Startup submenu.

Tip: You might notice that other programs load at startup automatically in addition to those that have shortcuts in the Startup folder. Most programs that set themselves up for automatic startup do so by creating Registry entries for themselves that trigger the loading. End users should not attempt to set up such entries themselves; the Startup folder method works fine and is much safer.

Preventing a Program from Starting Automatically

Some programs set themselves up to load automatically at Windows 7 startup when you install them. Sometimes this is necessary, or at least highly recommended, for the optimal performance of the software or its related device. For example, antivirus software should always be loaded automatically at startup to prevent against virus infection, and if you need certain activities to happen when the PC is unattended, such as fax receiving, the controller for those activities should be loaded. Other times, it is just a waste of the PC's memory to keep the software, such as an instant messaging program that you very seldom use, loaded at all times.

You can prevent a program from loading automatically at startup in several ways. Depending on the situation, one of the easy methods might work, or you might have to resort to something more drastic.

First, check the All Programs\ Startup folder for a shortcut to that program. If you find such a shortcut there, delete it (right-click it and choose Delete). See Figure 13.5.

If you do not find the shortcut in the Startup folder, next try looking in the program itself to see if there is a setting that controls the program's startup. If there is, turn that setting off; the program will then make the needed change to the Registry automatically. For example, in Figure 13.6, Yahoo! Messenger can be configured to load automatically at startup or not via the check box at the top of the window.

If neither of those methods works, you can use the System Configuration utility to disable the automatic startup. This utility lists most of the applications that load at startup, and you can selectively enable or disable each one.

Right-click a shortcut and choose Delete

Figure 13.5 Delete a shortcut from the Start menu.

Look for an option that loads the program at startup

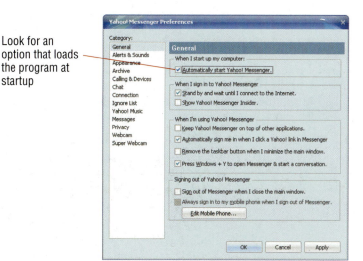

Figure 13.6 Some programs have a setting you can adjust that controls whether it loads at startup.

Note: *The main drawback to using the System Configuration utility is that sometimes it is not obvious what program a certain line represents. If you are not sure about an item, do a Web search on its name.*

To prevent a program from loading at startup using the System Configuration utility:

1. Click Start.
2. In the *Start Search* box, type msconfig and press Enter.
3. Click the Startup tab.
4. Clear the check box of the entry you want to disable.
5. Click OK.

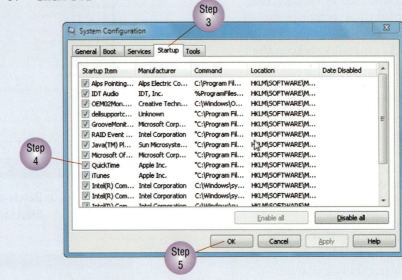

Step 3

Step 4

Step 5

Exercise 3

Enabling and Disabling Automatic Startup

1. Create a shortcut on the desktop for the Calculator program:
   a. Click Start, *All Programs, Accessories*.
   b. Hold down Alt and drag the Calculator shortcut to the desktop.
2. Drag the Calculator shortcut you just created into the Startup folder:
   a. Click and hold down the mouse button on the Calculator shortcut.
   b. Drag the shortcut to the Start menu and pause for the menu toopen.
   c. Drag the shortcut to *All Programs* and pause for the menu to open.
   d. Drag the shortcut to Startup and pause for the folder to open.
   e. Drop the shortcut beneath the word Startup.
3. Restart the PC and confirm that Calculator starts automatically.
4. Capture a screen print of the open Startup folder showing the Calculator shortcut in it. Name the file **C13E03**. See "Capturing a Screen Picture to Complete an Assignment" in Chapter 1 for help, if needed.
5. Delete the Calculator shortcut from the Startup folder.
6. Restart the PC and confirm that Calculator does not load.
7. Delete the Calculator shortcut from the desktop.

Installing a Program Update

Patch: A program update intended to fix a problem with the original version of the program

Manufacturers release updates for programs periodically to fix problems and to enhance capabilities. When an update is intended primarily to fix a problem, it is known as a *patch*.

The process for acquiring updates for a program depends on the program and its manufacturer. Some Microsoft programs can be updated automatically via the Microsoft Update feature in Windows 7, which works along with Windows Update (see "Using Windows Update to Keep Windows 7 Current" in Chapter 12).

Some programs have shortcuts to the company's Web site and to updates, available on a Help menu or via the program's properties or options. For example, in Figure 13.7, you can see that the Microsoft PowerPoint 2007 PowerPoint Options dialog box provides a Get Updates button.

Some programs, when they are installed, create a shortcut on the Start menu for the company's Web site. You can use that shortcut to go to a Web page where downloads are available.

PowerPoint 2007 enables you to check for updates within its options

Figure 13.7 **Some programs provide a way of getting updates from within the program itself.**

If none of the preceding options are available, you might want to check the manufacturer's Web site manually, by pointing your Web browser to the company's site and then browsing for downloads and updates. The company's Web site information is probably available on the box that the program came in, or in its documentation, or can be found by doing a quick Web search on the company's name.

Adding and Removing a Printer

One of the most common pieces of hardware to add to a system is a printer. Printers enable you to generate hard-copy printouts of your work. Printers come in many varieties, including laser and inkjet. Some printers are *multifunction devices (MFD)*, combining the functionality of a printer with that of a scanner, copier, and in some cases fax machine.

Most printers today use a USB interface, so they can easily be connected and disconnected at any time. USB devices are *hot-pluggable*, meaning you do not have to wait until the computer is turned off to connect or disconnect them. USB printers also fully support the *Plug and Play* (PnP) device-support standard. Windows 7 therefore recognizes them automatically, and either automatically installs a driver or prompts you for a driver location. Given a compatible device and system BIOS and a compatible Windows version (Windows 95 and higher), Plug and Play allows a PC to see and configure a device without having to manually tell Windows what resources to assign to the device.

Some older printers use a parallel interface, also known as an *LPT port.* LPT stands for Line Printer. This type of interface consists of a 25-pin plug at the PC end and a 36-pin Centronics plug at the printer end. This interface is not hot-pluggable; you should connect this type of printer only when the PC's power is turned off. Printers connected via this interface might automatically be detected in Windows 7, or you might need to run the Setup software that comes with the printer.

Multifunction device (MFD): A printer that also has other functions, such as scanner, copier, and fax machine

Hot-pluggable: Able to be connected or disconnected while the PC is up and running

Plug and Play: A standard that enables Windows to recognize and configure hardware automatically

Adding a New Printer

When you add a printer to Windows 7, you are actually adding a printer *driver*, not the printer itself. A driver is a piece of software that acts as a translator between a hardware device and Windows 7. You can have more than one driver installed for the same printer, each configured with different settings, and thereby make the printer behave differently depending on which driver you print with. For example, if a printer is able to print using two different modes, you could have a driver set up for each mode. Windows 7 calls printer drivers "printers," but keep in mind that this term refers to the driver, not the printer hardware.

The best procedure for setting up a printer in Windows 7 depends on whether you have a Setup disc for that printer or not. If a Setup disc is available, it is preferable to use it. During the setup, you will be prompted to turn on and connect your USB printer to the system. Most printers come with print management software that must be installed in Windows 7 to use the printer's full capabilities. If you allow Plug and Play to detect the printer, it installs a minimal set of drivers for the printer and sometimes does not install the extra software.

If you have a driver disc for the printer but it does not contain a Setup program, you can simply connect the printer to the PC via USB interface and allow Windows 7 to prompt you for the driver disc. Or, if it is a parallel printer, you can connect the printer, and then power up the PC and use the Add Printer Wizard to set up the printer. The wizard will prompt you for the location of a driver, and, at that point, you can point it toward the driver disc. This method also works well if you do not want to install the full suite of software that came with the printer.

Tip: Most printer manufacturers maintain a library of drivers for various models and operating systems on their Web sites, free for downloading.

If you do not have any type of driver for the printer, you can try connecting the printer (USB) or using the Add Printer Wizard (parallel) anyway; Windows 7 comes with a small collection of printer drivers, and if your printer happens to be one of the included models, Windows 7 can set it up for basic printing functionality.

Tip: Multifunction devices might work as printers without any setup software, but to enable the extra functions, like copying, you will need the software designed specifically for the device. You might be able to download it from the manufacturer's Web site if you do not have the disc.

You can set up either a local or a network printer with the Add Printer Wizard. A *local printer* is one that is attached directly to your PC. A *network printer* is one that is attached to your network (wired or wireless) or shared by another PC on your network. You can also set up a Bluetooth printer, provided both the PC and the printer have compatible Bluetooth interfaces. *Bluetooth* is a type of short-range wireless interface designed to allow PCs and devices to communicate without cables.

In most cases, you do not need to use the Add Printer Wizard to set up a local printer because Windows 7 will detect the printer automatically and offer to set it up. The Add Printer Wizard is mostly for use with network printers and for local parallel printers (nearly obsolete). However, you might use the Add Printer Wizard with a USB printer for which you already have a driver installed and want to install an additional driver for (such as having both a PostScript and a non-PostScript driver installed for a dual-mode printer).

To set up a local printer:

1. Choose Start, *Control Panel*.
2. Under Hardware and Sound, click View devices and printers.
3. Click the Add a printer button.
4. Click Add a local printer.
5. Choose the port to which the printer is attached and click Next. You normally would not need to use this Wizard to set up a USB printer, though.
6. Select the printer manufacturer and model, or click Have Disk, and browse for the driver. Then click Next.
7. Type a name for the printer, or accept the default name, and click Next.
8. At the Printer Sharing screen, choose one of the following:
   • Do not share this printer
   • Share this printer so that others on your network can find and use it. Then change the share name, location, and/or comment, if you want.
9. Click Next.
10. Mark or clear the *Set as the default printer* check box, as desired.
11. (Optional) Click Print a test page.
12. Click Finish.

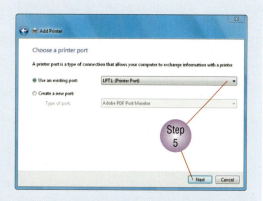

QUICK FIX

Going Back
If you need to return to a previous screen, click the left-pointing arrow button in the top-left corner of the window.

To set up a network printer:

1. Choose Start, *Control Panel*.
2. Under Hardware and Sound, click View devices and printers.
3. Click the Add a printer button.
4. Click Add a network, wireless or Bluetooth printer. A list of available printers appears.
5. Click the desired printer and then click Next.
6. Type a name for the printer and then click Next.

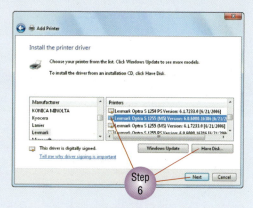

7. At the Printer Sharing screen, choose one of the following:
   - Do not share this printer
   - Share this printer so that others on your network can find and use it. Then change the share name, location, and/or comment, if you want.
8. Click Next.
9. Mark or clear the *Set as the default printer* check box.
10. (Optional) Click Print a test page.
11. Click Finish.

Tip: You can install a printer driver for a printer that you do not have, and you can even assign it to a port that does not exist on your PC. Windows 7 will see it as a valid printer; it simply will not work when you try to print to it. This is useful in situations where you need to set up someone else's PC, but you don't have his printer physically present. You can install the printer's driver and prepare the system for it, and then connect the printer later.

Figure 13.8 Choose the default printer by right-clicking a printer and clicking *Set as default printer*.

Choosing the Default Printer

When you set up a printer, as in the preceding section, you can specify whether the printer should be the default one. (Only one printer at a time can be the default, so if you choose a new one as the default, the previous setting is cleared.) You can also manually specify a different default printer at any time.

To set a printer as the default, from the Devices and Printers window (from the Control Panel), right-click the printer and choose *Set as default printer*. See Figure 13.8. The printer that is currently the default appears with a green circle and check mark.

QUICK FIX

Quick Fix: Wrong Dialog Box
If you see only two tabs, General and Hardware, you have opened the wrong dialog box. Right-click the printer's icon and choose Printer Properties, *not* Properties. This is a change from previous Windows versions.

Working with Printer Settings

Each printer has its own Printer Properties box, which you can access by right-clicking its icon and clicking *Printer Properties*. The tabs and settings in the Properties dialog box vary depending on the printer model, but generally include the ones listed in Table 13.1.

Table 13.1 Tabs in a Typical Printer's Properties Box

General	Specify the name to appear with the printer's icon, and print a test page. From here you can also click Printing Preferences to open a dialog box in which you can set paper type, resolution quality, and other appearance-based settings.
Sharing	Choose whether to share the printer with others on your network.
Ports	Choose which port the printer is connected to.
Advanced	Specify when the printer will be available (useful if sharing it, for example) and whether to use the Windows 7 print spooler. There are also buttons here for setting printing defaults and using separator pages.
Color Management	If it's a color printer, a tab appears, which contains a Color Management button that you can click to open a dialog box for syncing up the colors output by the printer to the colors on your display.
Security	You can set permissions here for who is allowed to use and control the printer.
Device Settings	A tree-style collection of many of the settings available for this individual printer. This list changes radically depending on the printer and its capabilities, and can include paper handling, font substitutions, and installable options such as duplexing and flash memory cards. Figure 13.9 shows the settings for a typical printer.
About	A screen listing the printer's driver information.

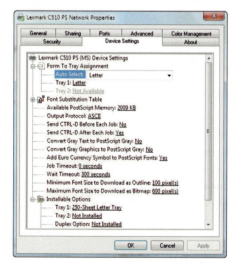

Figure 13.9 The Device Settings tab enables you to control miscellaneous settings specific to that printer.

Removing a Printer

Disconnecting a printer physically from the PC does not necessarily remove the printer's driver from Windows 7. For local USB printers, disconnecting the printer does make the printer disappear from the Printers window (in the Control Panel), but its driver remains installed, and if you reconnect the printer, it reappears automatically in the Printers window. For parallel and network interface printers, the printer's icon remains in the Printers window when the printer is disconnected.

To remove the printer's driver from Windows 7, you can delete its icon from the Printers window as you would delete any file.

Here's How ▶ To remove a printer from Windows 7:

1. Choose Start, *Control Panel*.
2. Under Hardware and Sound, click View devices and printers.
3. Right-click the printer's icon and choose Remove Device.

 ## Exercise 4

Installing and Removing a Printer Driver

1. Open the Printers window:
   a. Choose Start, *Control Panel*.
   b. Under Hardware and Sound, click View devices and printers
2. Add a LaserJet 4 driver as a local printer on LPT2:
   a. Click *Add a printer*.
   b. Click *Add a local printer*.
   c. Open the *Use an existing port* list and click *LPT2 (Printer Port)*.
   d. Click Next.
   e. On the *Manufacturer* list, click *HP*.
   f. On the Printers list, click *HP LaserJet 4*.
   g. Click Next.
   h. Click Next when prompted to change the printer's name.
   i. Click Next when prompted to enable sharing or not.
   j. Clear the *Set as the default printer* check box.
   k. Click Finish.
3. Open the Printer Properties box for the new printer and display its Device Settings tab:
   a. Right-click the *HP LaserJet 4* icon and choose Printer properties.
   b. Click the Device Settings tab.
4. Capture a screen print of the window to submit to your instructor for grading. Name the file **C13E04**. See "Capturing a Screen Picture to Complete an Assignment" in Chapter 1 for help, if needed.
5. Click OK to close the Properties box.
6. Remove the HP LaserJet 4 printer:
   a. Right-click the *HP LaserJet 4* icon and choose Remove Device.
   b. Click Yes.

Working with Hardware

Hardware: The physical components of a PC, such as the keyboard, mouse, disk drives, and CPU

Hardware refers to the physical components of a PC, such as the keyboard, the mouse, the disk drives, the CPU, and so on. Windows 7 communicates with each piece of hardware and coordinates operations between devices. The most essential pieces of hardware, such as the processor, memory, and motherboard, are automatically detected and configured in Windows 7 when you install Windows 7 itself. Other less critical devices can be installed, updated, and removed by the end user.

Device driver: A piece of software that works with Windows to send and receive instructions for a particular piece of hardware

Understanding Device Drivers and System Resources

Each piece of hardware speaks its own language. To translate between it and Windows 7, a *device driver* is required. A device driver is a piece of software that works with Windows 7 to send and receive instructions for a particular piece of hardware. In many cases, several files work together to form the device driver. You can see what files a device is using by viewing its properties.

Windows 7 comes with a large collection of device drivers for popular devices, including many display adapters, sound cards, modems, and so on. In addition, when you buy a new device, it comes with drivers on disc for various operating systems. You can also download and install new device drivers for existing devices to add capabilities or fix problems.

Each device communicates with Windows 7 via a set of *system resources*. System resources are assigned to the device to provide conduits through which the device can communicate with Windows 7 and with the CPU. The types of system resources a device uses may include:

- **Memory range**. An area of RAM set aside for the device's use.
- **I/O range**. An area of RAM set aside for transferring data to and from the device.
- **Interrupt Request (IRQ)**. A signaling line that the device uses to get the CPU's attention.
- **Direct Memory Access (DMA) channel**. A less commonly used channel that enables the device to bypass the CPU to write directly to memory.

Windows 7 automatically assigns system resources to devices via Plug and Play (PnP).

Note: *In previous Windows versions, sometimes resource assignments would conflict and users would need to manually change them. However, this is almost never necessary in Windows 7 because it handles resource assignments more smoothly.*

Windows 7 strongly prefers that drivers be *signed drivers*. A signed driver has been certified by Microsoft to work with Windows 7. Companies that make drivers must put their drivers through an approval process to receive certification. Signed drivers have a digital signature that also indicates that they have not been corrupted or altered since their signing. Driver-signing was invented to combat problems with poorly written drivers that cause tough-to-troubleshoot system problems.

You can display the Device Manager window by resource by choosing View, *Resources by Type*. That way you can see exactly what DMA channels, I/O addresses, IRQs, and memory addresses are in use.

To display a device's Properties box:

1. Click Start.
2. Right-click *Computer* and choose *Properties*.
3. Click Device Manager. The Device Manager window opens.
4. Click the arrow next to the device's category. The category expands.
5. Double-click the device to open its Properties box.

Here's How

To view device driver details:

1. Display the device's Properties box, as in the preceding steps.
2. Click the Driver tab.
3. Click Driver Details.
4. Note the driver files listed.
5. Click OK.
6. Click OK.

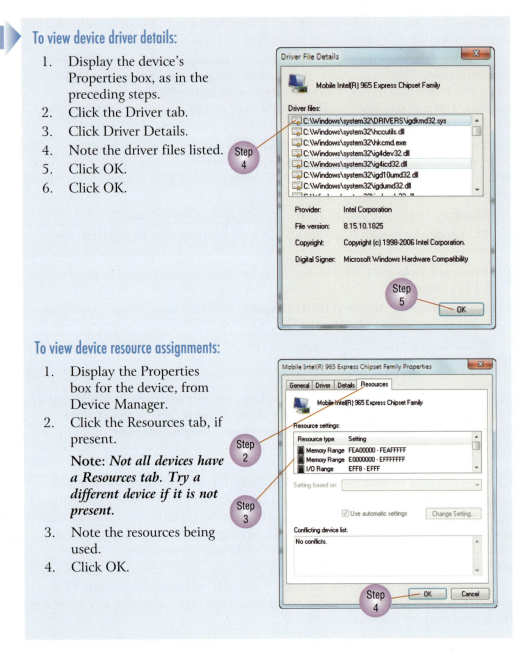

To view device resource assignments:

1. Display the Properties box for the device, from Device Manager.
2. Click the Resources tab, if present.

   Note: *Not all devices have a Resources tab. Try a different device if it is not present.*

3. Note the resources being used.
4. Click OK.

Adding a Plug and Play Device

As you learned earlier in this chapter, devices that can be connected when the PC is running are referred to as hot-pluggable. The interface type determines whether a device is hot-pluggable; USB, FireWire (IEEE 1394), and Ethernet network connectors (RJ-45) are all hot-pluggable interfaces. On the other hand, most of the older interfaces, such as legacy parallel and serial ports, and PS/2 ports are not hot-pluggable; you must shut down the PC and power off the device (if applicable) before you make those connections. You must also shut down the PC to insert expansion boards inside the PC.

Regardless of the interface type, if the device is Plug and Play compatible (and almost all devices are, since Plug and Play technology is over a decade old), Windows 7 should recognize it automatically. The device will either automatically install the driver, or it will prompt you to insert a driver disc, or prompt you to point it toward a driver on your hard disk or other disk. You can insert a driver disc if you have one, or allow Windows 7 to go online and/or search the hard disk for an appropriate driver.

The prompts vary depending on the native support Windows 7 provides for the device. For example, for a USB flash drive, an indicator appears briefly in the notification area letting you know a driver is being installed for the drive, automatically. For other devices, such as sound or display adapters, you will likely need to run a Setup utility or at least provide a driver for the device to work properly.

 Exercise 5

Viewing Device Driver Information

1. Open Device Manager and view the properties for your display adapter:
   a. Click Start, and then right-click *Computer* and choose *Properties*.
   b. Click Device Manager.
   c. Click the arrow next to Display adapters.
   d. Double-click the display adapter.
2. View the current driver information and make a note of the driver version:
   a. Click the Driver tab.
   b. Make a note of the Driver Provider, Driver Date, and Driver Version.
3. Capture a screen print of the window to submit to your instructor for grading. Name the file **C13E05**. See "Capturing a Screen Picture to Complete an Assignment" in Chapter 1 for help, if needed.
4. Close all open windows.

Understanding and Using Device Stage

As was first mentioned in Chapter 5, Device Stage is a new Windows 7 feature that provides an easy interface for working with device settings and features. A device manufacturer must provide extra setup files to enable the device to provide the Device Stage interface. Various models of printers, digital media devices, and mobile phones are compatible. After you connect and power on the device, click the Start button and then click Devices and Printers. As shown in Figure 13.10, the device shows up with an icon that looks like the device itself, rather than a generic icon.

To see the available tasks for the device in the Device Stage window as is in the example in Figure 13.11, double-click the device's icon in the Devices and Printers window, or double-click the

Figure 13.10 The icon for a Device Stage compatible device is not generic.

Figure 13.11 Device Stage shows tasks you can perform with the device.

device icon on the taskbar. The tasks that the Device Stage window shows will vary depending on the type of device connected. As you can see in Figure 13.11, for the digital media device that's connected, you can handle tasks that you otherwise couldn't in Windows, such as shopping for device accessories or updating its firmware. To perform a particular task, double-click the task in the Device Stage window.

> **Tip:** You also can right-click the device icon on the taskbar to open a Jump List with device tasks.

Two important tasks you might want to handle with a mobile phone or digital media device is to set it up for synching, and then to sync it. For example, you can set up a device to sync music or pictures automatically.

Here's How ▶ To set device sync settings in Device Stage:

1. Connect and power on the device, and open its Device Stage window using the method of your choice.
2. Double-click Set up sync.
3. Click the check box beside the type of item you want to sync.
4. Click Settings.

5. To limit the items that sync, click *Sync with music folders, playlists or songs that I select*, and then use the buttons to the right of the list to add and remove folders, playlists, and songs.
6. Click OK.
7. Click Save changes.
8. Close the Device Stage window if desired.

To sync a device manually in Device Stage:

1. Connect and power on the device, and open its Device Stage window using the method of your choice.
2. Double-click Set up sync.
3. Click Sync now.
4. Click Close.
5. Close the Device Stage window if desired.

Using Multiple Monitors

Windows 7 enables you to use more than one monitor at once. You can set all monitors to duplicate the same display, or you can extend the display across the monitors so that each one displays a different section of the desktop.

Installing the Second Monitor

A PC monitor connects to a *display adapter*, which is a circuit board (or built-in component) that translates between the PC and the monitor. The two types of connections that a PC monitor can have to the PC are:

- **Video Graphics Array (VGA)**. A 15-pin, *D*-shaped connector
- **Digital Video Interface (DVI)**. A white, rectangular connector

Many display adapters have one connector of each type. On such cards, you can connect two separate monitors. If your display adapter has only one connector, you must install a second display adapter in order to use multiple monitors.

Note: *Many notebook PCs have two separate connectors for external monitors: one VGA and one DVI. That does not necessarily mean, however, that you can have three separately configurable monitors (the built-in screen plus two others). The display adapter built into a notebook PC typically supports only one display at a time, so if you hook up an external monitor, the same image will appear on both at once; you might not be able to extend the desktop onto a second monitor.*

To connect a second monitor, shut down the PC and the monitor. Then connect it through a cable to the PC, and restart Windows 7. Windows 7 should automatically detect the new display adapter. Follow the instructions earlier in this chapter for adding new hardware.

> **Display adapter:** A circuit board or built-in component to which the monitor attaches, and which translates between the PC and the monitor

Configuring the Second Monitor

When you initially install a second monitor, the same display appears on both monitors. You can change this by adjusting the display settings, shown in Figure 13.12. Each monitor appears as a separate box there.

To determine which monitor each box represents, click Identify. The number flashes briefly on each monitor screen. Then drag the monitor boxes in the sample area around so that they represent on-screen the way they are physically oriented on your desk.

Each monitor's settings can be separately adjusted. Click the monitor's box, and then set the following for it:

- **Resolution**. The number of individual pixels (dots) that make up the display image. The higher the resolution the smaller things will appear.

Drag these boxes to represent the actual arrangement of the monitors at your desk.

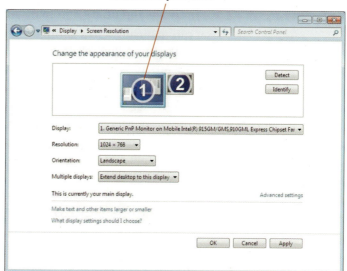

Figure 13.12 **Each monitor's display can be configured separately if you have more than one.**

- **Orientation**. The direction of the display. The default is landscape, but you might choose to stand a monitor on its side and use Portrait, for example.
- **Multiple displays**. One monitor is your main monitor; that's the one on which the taskbar appears. You can choose which is the main one from the *Multiple displays* drop-down list.

Here's How **To configure a second monitor:**

1. Right-click the desktop and choose *Personalize*.
2. Click Display.
3. Click *Change display settings*.
4. Click Identify to figure out which monitor is which.
5. Drag the sample boxes in the dialog box to match the monitors' physical locations.
6. Click the box for the new monitor.
7. Open the *Multiple displays* list and choose *Extend desktop to this display*.
8. If needed, click *Resolution*, and drag the slider to choose a different resolution.
9. If needed, click *Orientation*, and choose a different orientation.
10. Click OK.

CHAPTER Summary

- Installing software copies files to the hard disk, makes changes to the Registry, and adds a shortcut to the Start menu.
- Software on CD typically contains an Autorun file that tells Windows 7 how to start its Setup utility automatically when the disc is inserted.
- You can manually add a shortcut to the Start menu by dragging an icon onto the Start button and pausing while each level of menu opens until you see the location where you want the shortcut.
- To uninstall (remove) a program, from the Control Panel click Programs, Uninstall a program. Choose the program, click its Uninstall button, and follow the prompts.
- Compatibility Mode helps Windows 7 simulate previous versions of Windows to allow programs that were written for those previous versions to run. Right-click a program and choose *Properties*, and then click the Compatibility tab and set up compatibility options.
- To specify the default programs to use for certain file types, from the Control Panel, choose Programs, Default Programs.
- To set a program to start automatically at Windows 7 startup, place a shortcut to it in the Startup folder on the Start/All Programs menu.
- To prevent a program from starting automatically, remove its shortcut from the Startup folder. If that does not work, click Start, type **msconfig**, and press Enter; then on the Startup tab, clear the check box for that program.
- Most printers use a USB device, so they are hot-pluggable. Connect them, and Windows 7 will automatically install a driver for them or prompt you for a disc containing the driver.

- If you have a Setup disc for the printer, run the Setup program to install the printer's software, which may include not only a driver, but also helper programs. This is important, especially for multifunction devices (printer/scanner/copier/fax).

- You can also use the Add Printer Wizard. From the Control Panel, choose Hardware and Sound, View devices and printers, Add a Printer, and then follow the prompts.

- To set the default printer, right-click the printer's icon and choose *Set as default printer*.

- To set a printer's properties, right-click the printer's icon and choose *Printer Properties*.

- Each piece of hardware requires system resources and a device driver.

- Plug and Play enables devices to be automatically configured when connected to the PC (that is, set up with resources and drivers as needed).

- System resources include memory range, I/O range, an Interrupt Request (IRQ), and a Direct Memory Access (DMA) channel. Not all devices require all types of resources.

- A driver is a translation utility that relays commands between Windows 7 and the device. Windows 7 prefers signed drivers, which are drivers certified to work with Windows 7.

- A display adapter is a circuit board or built-in component to which a monitor connects. To configure the display adapter, right-click the desktop and choose *Personalize*, then click *Display, Change Display Settings*.

CONCEPTS Check

Completion: Answer the following questions on a blank sheet of paper or in a Word document.

Part

1

MULTIPLE CHOICE

1. The _____ is a configuration database where system settings are stored.
   a. task list
   b. registry
   c. storage bank
   d. Windows 7 archive

2. Which of these operating systems does Compatibility Mode *not* emulate?
   a. MS-DOS
   b. Windows NT 4
   c. Windows 95
   d. Windows Server 2003

3. To make a program load automatically at Startup, place a shortcut to it
   _____ .
   a. in the root directory (C:\) of the hard disk
   b. in the C:\Windows\System folder
   c. on the desktop
   d. on the Start menu, in the All Programs\Startup folder

4. Which of these types of programs should not be disabled from loading automatically at startup?
   a. Antivirus software
   b. Word processing software
   c. Game software
   d. Accounting software

5. Older printers use a parallel interface, also known as a(n) _____ port.
   a. COM
   b. USB
   c. LPT
   d. legacy serial

6. Which type of printer interface is hot-pluggable?
   a. USB
   b. LPT
   c. COM
   d. Legacy serial

7. A _____ printer is one that is directly connected to your PC.
   a. network
   b. remote
   c. local
   d. legacy

8. Which of these is NOT a type of system resource?
   a. USB port
   b. I/O range
   c. IRQ
   d. DMA channel

9. What is a signed driver for Windows 7?
   a. A driver written specifically for the device it's being used with
   b. A driver certified to work with Windows 7
   c. A driver written and provided by Microsoft
   d. None of the above

10. To have two monitors on a system, what hardware do you need?
    a. A display adapter with two connectors on it
    b. Two separate display adapters
    c. A built-in display adapter
    d. Either a or b

Part 2   SHORT ANSWER

11. What three things does a Setup program typically do?

    _____

12. When you remove a program, what three things are removed?

    _____

13. What is the purpose of Compatibility Mode and what problems does it solve?

    _____

14. Describe the advantages and drawbacks of having programs load automatically at startup.

   _____

15. How is a hot-pluggable device different from one that is not hot-pluggable?

   _____

16. What is Plug and Play?

   _____

17. What is the purpose of a device driver?

   _____

18. Describe how to open the Printers folder, from which you can add and remove printer drivers.

   _____

19. What distinguishes hardware from software?

   _____

20. Describe two ways to get a driver for a device.

   _____

SKILLS Check

Save all solution files to the default Documents folder, or any alternative folder specified by your instructor.

Guided Check

Assessment **INSTALL AND REMOVE SOFTWARE**

1

Your instructor will provide software for you to install for this exercise. It may be a commercial product on a disc, or instructions to download a Setup file from a Web site or a server on your LAN.

   1. Install the software on your PC.
      a. Insert the disc containing the software. If an Autoplay window appears, close it (if it came on disc).
      b. In an Explorer window, double-click the Setup file for the software.
      c. Follow the prompts to install it.
   2. Run the software and capture a screen print of it. Submit it to your instructor for grading. Name the file **C13A01**.
   3. Uninstall the software.
      a. Click Start, and then click *Control Panel*.
      b. Under Programs, click Uninstall a program.
      c. Click the program to uninstall.
      d. Click the Uninstall button or the Uninstall/Change button, whichever appears.
      e. Follow the prompts to uninstall the program.

RUNNING AN APPLICATION IN COMPATIBILITY MODE

1. Pick a third-party program installed on your PC (not one that was supplied with Windows 7), and start it and then exit it.
   a. Click Start.
   b. Click *All Programs*.
   c. Find a program that did not come with Windows 7 itself and click it.
   d. Open a few menus in the program to confirm that it works, and then exit the program (usually File, *Exit*).
2. Display the Properties box of the shortcut to that program on the Start menu.
   a. Click Start.
   b. Click *All Programs*.
   c. Right-click the shortcut to the program and choose *Properties*.
3. Set the program to operate in Compatibility Mode for Windows 98 and for 256 colors.
   a. Click the Compatibility tab.
   b. Mark the *Run this program in compatibility mode for* check box.
   c. Open the drop-down list and click *Windows 98/Windows Me*.
   d. Mark the *Run in 256 colors* check box.
   e. Click OK.
4. Run the program from its shortcut.
   a. Click Start.
   b. Click *All Programs*.
   c. Click the program's shortcut. If a Windows User Account Control dialog box appears, choose to allow the program to run.
   d. Capture a screen print of the running application. Submit it to your instructor for grading. Name the file **C13A02**.
5. Return to the Properties box and turn off Compatibility Mode for that program.
   a. Click Start.
   b. Click *All Programs*.
   c. Right-click the shortcut to the program and choose *Properties*.
   d. Click the Compatibility tab.
   e. Clear the *Run this program in Compatibility mode for* check box.
   f. Clear the *Run in 256 colors* check box.
   g. Click OK.

CONTROLLING PROGRAM STARTUP

1. Set up Internet Explorer to run at startup.
   a. Click the Start button.
   b. Drag the Internet Explorer shortcut from the top of the Start menu to the desktop.
   c. Drag the new shortcut onto the Start button and hold it there with mouse button pressed.
   d. When the Start menu opens, hover over *All Programs*.
   e. When the All Programs menu opens, hover over *Startup*.
   f. Drop the shortcut onto the Startup folder.
2. Restart the PC and make sure that Internet Explorer loads at startup.
3. Open the System Configuration utility and capture a screen print of the Startup tab showing the Internet Explorer shortcut on it. Submit it to your instructor for grading. Name the file **C13A03**.

4. In the System Configuration utility, disable Internet Explorer from starting automatically.
   a. Click the Startup tab, and then locate Windows® Internet Explorer.
   b. Clear the check box next to *Windows Internet Explorer*.
   c. Click OK.
   d. Click Restart and wait for the PC to restart.
5. Confirm that Internet Explorer did not start.
6. Run the System Configuration Utility again and re-enable the Internet Explorer item.
   a. Mark the check box next to *Windows Internet Explorer*.
   b. Click OK.
   c. Click Exit without restart.
7. Delete the Internet Explorer shortcut from the Startup folder.
   a. Click Start, *All Programs, Startup*.
   b. Right-click the Internet Explorer shortcut and choose *Delete*.
   c. Click Yes.

Assessment GET PRINTER INFORMATION

4

1. Open the Devices and Printers folder from the Control Panel.
   a. Click Start and then click *Control Panel*.
   b. Under Hardware and Sound, click View devices and printers.
2. Display the properties for the default printer and display printing preferences.
   a. Right-click the default printer and choose *Printer properties*.
   b. On the General tab, click *Preferences*.
3. Capture a screen print of the Printing Preferences dialog box. Submit it to your instructor for grading. Name the file **C13A04**.
4. Click OK to close the Printing Preferences dialog box.
5. Click the Print Test Page button on the General tab of the printer's Properties box.
6. Write your name on the printout and submit it to your instructor for grading.
7. Close all open windows.

On Your Own

Assessment INSTALL AND REMOVE SOFTWARE ON YOUR OWN

5

Your instructor will provide software for you to install for this exercise. It may be a commercial product on a disc, or instructions to download a Setup file from a Web site or a server on your LAN.

1. Install the software on your PC and document the step-by-step actions you took on a blank piece of paper.
2. Run the software and capture a screen print of it. Name the file **C13A05**. Submit it to your instructor for grading.
3. Uninstall the software.

FINDING A PRINTER DRIVER

6

On a blank piece of paper, write your name and **C13A06**, or in a Word document, type your name and save the file as **C13A06.** Write down or type your answers to the following and submit it to your instructor:

1. What is your printer's make and model, and how did you determine this?
2. What is the printer's driver version, and how did you determine this?
3. What is the URL for the Support portion of the printer manufacturer's Web site?
4. What is the most recent driver version number available for this printer?

VIEWING RESOURCE ASSIGNMENTS

7

1. Display Device Manager.
2. Display a list of resources by type. (***Hint: Use the command on the View menu.***)
3. Expand the Direct memory access (DMA) category by clicking its plus sign.
4. Capture a screen print of the Device Manager window. Submit it to your instructor for grading. Name the file **C13A07**.

WORKING WITH MULTIPLE MONITORS

8

For this exercise, you will need a PC that has two display adapters, or a single display adapter with multiple monitor ports on it, and you will need two monitors that can connect to those ports.

1. Shut down the PC, and connect the second monitor, if it is not already connected.
2. Restart the PC.
3. In the display properties, set up the new monitor to extend the desktop.
4. Capture a screen print of the Device Manager window. Submit it to your instructor for grading. Name the file **C13A08**. The screen print will contain the images from both monitors, side by side.

CHALLENGE Project

Suppose you need to add a printer and an additional monitor to your PC. Examine your PC and determine the following:

1. What types of printer interfaces can your PC accept? LPT (parallel)? USB? Bluetooth? Wireless?
2. How many more monitors (if any) can your PC accept without having to add another display adapter? What type of interface(s) are available: VGA or DVI?

Part 4

Windows® 7

Power Computing Topics

➤ Troubleshooting and Repairing Your System

➤ Securing and Monitoring Your System

➤ Sharing Information On and Off the Road

Troubleshooting and Repairing Your System

PERFORMANCE OBJECTIVES

Upon successful completion of Chapter 14, you will be able to:

- **Check a disk for errors**
- **Troubleshoot programs**
- **Use Advanced Boot Options to fix startup problems**
- **Troubleshoot printing**
- **Troubleshoot hardware problems**
- **Use Remote Assistance**

Over time, problems can develop with Windows 7, due to improper shutdowns, poorly written applications, file corruption, or other situations. You can troubleshoot and repair many of the most common problems yourself, without the help of an IT professional.

Getting Troubleshooting Help

Windows 7 includes a Troubleshooting utility in the Control Panel. This utility walks you step-by-step through some common problems and solutions. The steps are different depending on the problem type you choose. For example, if you are having a problem with the sound on your PC not working, a hardware troubleshooter would examine your system and either fix the problem itself or suggest things for you to try.

Here's How > To get troubleshooting help:

1. Click Start.
2. Click *Control Panel*.
3. Under System and Security, click Find and fix problems.

4. Click the heading that most closely matches the category of problem.

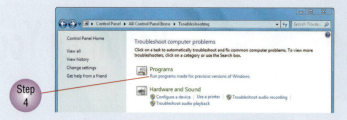

Step 4

5. If a list of topics appears, click the topic you want.

Step 5

6. Follow the prompts to run the Troubleshooting utility for the selected problem.

Exercise 1

Troubleshooting a Sound Problem

1. Mute the sound on your system. You can do this in any of these ways:
   - Click the *speaker* icon in the notification area and click the *Mute* icon at the bottom of the pop-up that appears.
   - Press the Mute button on your keyboard or laptop, if it has such a button.
   - From the Control Panel, click Hardware and Sound. Under the Sound heading, click Adjust system volume. Click the *Mute* icon under the Speakers slider.
2. Open the Control Panel and under System and Security, click Find and fix problems.
3. Click Troubleshoot audio playback. The Playing Audio troubleshooter opens.
4. Click Next.
5. Wait for the troubleshooter to identify that the speaker is muted and fix the problem.
6. Capture a screen print of the window showing the troubleshooting results, and submit it to your instructor for grading. Name the file **C14E01**. See "Capturing a Screen Picture to Complete an Assignment" in Chapter 1 for help, if needed.
7. Close all open windows.

Checking a Disk for Errors

Each disk has an internal table of contents that maps the physical locations on the disk to specific file and folder names. When Windows 7 needs to retrieve a file from the disk, it consults this table of contents to find out where to look on the disk for that file.

On a disk formatted with the NTFS file system (the default for Windows 7), this table of contents is called the *master file table (MFT)*. On a disk formatted with the FAT32 file system (the default for some previous Windows versions, such as Windows 98), the table of contents is called the *file allocation table (FAT)*.

When Windows 7 shuts down abnormally, such as from a power outage or crash, the abnormal shutdown sometimes creates *file system errors*. For example, if a file was in the process of being written to the hard drive when the power went out, the file's information may be improperly recorded on the hard drive's MFT or FAT. Such errors, if uncorrected, can potentially snowball. An error in the file system can cause a system crash, which can in turn cause more file information to be improperly recorded. File system errors can also cause the files themselves to become corrupted by writing their data to the wrong spot on the disk.

Another type of error a disk can have is a *bad sector* error. Bad sectors are physically unreadable or unwritable spots on the surface of the disk. These errors are sometimes caused by physical trauma to the PC, such as falling off a table or being kicked, but bad sector errors can also develop spontaneously as a hard disk begins to fail. Such errors can typically be detected only with a sector-by-sector check in which a utility reads and writes from each sector to confirm it is okay. Such a check may take several hours.

> **Tip:** How do you know when to take the extra time to run a check for bad sectors? Some people run such a check every few months as preventive maintenance, but it is usually necessary only if you see an error message when reading or writing to the disk that reports a "data error." Data errors are errors resulting from an inability of the disk to read or write the data to the physical surface of the disk.

The *Check Disk* utility in Windows 7 runs a logical check of the file system and, optionally, can be set to also check for bad sectors. It does not actually repair the bad sectors it finds; instead, it relocates the data (if possible) from a bad sector to a good one, and it updates the MFT or FAT to reflect the new location of the data.

Depending on the disk you are checking, Windows 7 might not be able to check the disk without restarting the computer. If you see a message that Windows 7 cannot check the disk while it is in use, click *Schedule disk check*. The disk will then be checked for errors after you restart. You can then restart immediately or wait until a more convenient time.

Master file table (MFT): The table of contents for a disk formatted with the NTFS file system

File allocation table (FAT): The table of contents for a disk formatted with the FAT32 file system

File system error: An error or discrepancy in the way the disk's file system keeps track of storage locations

Bad sector: A sector on a disk surface from which the drive cannot read, write, or read and write data

Check Disk: A Windows 7 utility that finds and corrects file system errors and, optionally, relocates data away from bad sectors

---

To check a disk for errors:

1. Click Start, and click *Computer*. The Computer window shows all available drives.
2. Right-click the drive letter and click *Properties*. The Properties dialog box opens.
3. Click the Tools tab.
4. Click Check now.

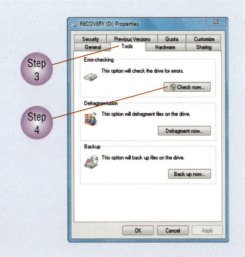

Here's How

5. (Optional) Mark or clear the *Automatically fix file system errors* check box.

6. (Optional) Mark or clear the *Scan for and attempt recovery of bad sectors* check box.

7. Click Start.

8. If a warning appears saying Windows 7 cannot check the disk while it is in use, click *Schedule disk check* and then restart the PC (Start, *Shut down, Restart*).

9. Wait for the disk check to finish, and then click OK.

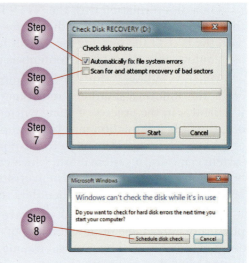

Note: *Error checking is performed in Windows 7 separately for each drive letter, so if you have multiple hard disk drives listed in the Computer window, you must repeat the process for each drive.*

Troubleshooting Application Problems

Crash: A situation in which a program ceases to operate normally

An application can have either or both of two problems: it can fail to start, or it can crash while running. The term ***crash*** is somewhat generic, referring to the program ceasing to function normally. It can involve any of the following:

• Program becomes unresponsive to keyboard, mouse input, or both

• Program operation slows to a crawl

• Program shuts down unexpectedly, sometimes losing unsaved work

• Error messages appear

• Windows 7 itself becomes unresponsive to keyboard, mouse input, or both

Program crashes can be due to any of several causes, both hardware- and software-related. To troubleshoot such a problem, first shut down the malfunctioning software if it did not terminate by itself, and then figure out the root cause of the malfunction.

Shutting Down a Malfunctioning Program with Task Manager

When a program crashes, it might terminate itself automatically, usually with an error message explaining what happened. However, in some cases, the program window stays open, and you must shut down the malfunctioning program manually.

In Windows 7, when a program stops responding to keyboard and mouse input, Windows 7 displays that program's window with a white haze over it, and a message box appears letting you know that the program has become unresponsive. From there you can choose to restart the program or return to the program to wait for it to respond. (Some programs trigger false alarms because they take longer than normal to respond to certain commands.)

Note: *When a program crashes, you might be prompted to send more information about the crash to Microsoft. This is optional and sends no personal data about you or your usage habits. It helps Microsoft track what problems occur most frequently among users, so the development team can focus its efforts on correcting those problems in future updates.*

If Windows 7 does not notice that the program has become unresponsive, you can display the Task Manager, and shut down the program manually from there.

Here's How

To shut down a program with the Task Manager:

1. Right-click the taskbar and click *Start Task Manager*. The Windows 7 Task Manager opens.
2. Click the Applications tab.
3. Click the program to shut down.
4. Click End Task.

Diagnosing the Root Cause of Program Crashes

Programs may crash for several reasons. Table 14.1 explains some of the possibilities. It can be difficult to know which problem is the root cause in a given instance, so you might need to try several fixes.

Table 14.1 Program Problems and Solutions

Problem	Possible Fixes
Setup not successfully completed OR Program files missing or corrupted	Repair or reinstall the program, as described in the next section. This is the most common fix.
Poorly written program	Download a program patch or update from the manufacturer's Web site.
Program not compatible with Windows 7	Run program in Compatibility mode, as described in Chapter 13.
File system errors OR Bad sectors	Run Check Disk, as described earlier in this chapter. You might then need to repair or reinstall the program.
Compatibility problems between program and the display adapter	Update the device driver for the display adapter, as described later in this chapter. Download an update from the program's Web site.

Repairing a Program

Repairing or reinstalling the program can fix program problems that are caused by corrupted or missing files. Repairing is often better than reinstalling because it does not require removing the program first. (If you need to remove and reinstall a program, see Chapter 13.)

Not all programs can be repaired. If a program can be repaired, an option for repairing is available via the Uninstall a program subcategory of the Control Panel.

In some cases, the Repair command silently does a repair in the background; in other cases, it reopens the application's Setup utility to perform the repairs, as in Figure 14.1.

Change your installation of Microsoft Office Enterprise 2007.

○ Add or Remove Features
○ Repair

Figure 14.1 If a program's Setup program has a Repair function, you can use it to correct problems with the program installation without having to remove and reinstall it.

Exercise 2

Practice Correcting Program Problems

1. Open WordPad (Start, *All Programs, Accessories, WordPad*).
2. End WordPad using the Task Manager:
   a. Right-click the taskbar and click *Start Task Manager*.
   b. Click the Applications tab.
   c. Locate and click WordPad in the Task List.
   d. Click End Task.
   e. Close Task Manager.
3. Check the *C* drive for errors using Check Disk:
   a. Click Start and click *Computer*.
   b. Right-click the *C* drive and click *Properties*.
   c. Click the Tools tab.
   d. Click Check Now.
   e. Click Start.
   f. If prompted that you must restart the computer to check the disk, capture a screen print of that window and submit it to your instructor for grading. Otherwise, wait for the disk check to finish, and then when a message appears that the disk check is complete, capture a screen print of the window showing that confirmation message, and submit it to your instructor for grading. Name the file **C14E02**.
   g. If the Check Disk window is still open, close it.
4. (Optional) Repair Microsoft Office, if installed:
   a. Open the Control Panel (Start, *Control Panel*).
   b. Under Programs, click Uninstall a program.
   c. Click Microsoft Office. (The exact name varies depending on your version.)
   d. Click *Change*.
   e. Choose *Repair*.
   f. Click Continue.
   g. Follow the prompts to finish repairing Office.

Using Advanced Boot Options to Fix Startup Problems

On a system that has started normally in the past, a sudden inability for Windows 7 to start up often means that the Registry has been improperly modified or that an incompatible device driver or application is attempting to load itself at startup.

None of those problems are insurmountable. You can reverse bad Registry changes using System Restore, as you learned in Chapter 12, and you can roll back or remove device drivers and remove software, as you learned in Chapter 13. However, there's a catch–22 there; you can't do any of those things if Windows 7 will not start up.

When Windows 7 does not start up properly, the next time you try to start it, the Advanced Boot Options menu appears. From here, you can select one of the boot options to help you regain access to Windows 7.

The first option to try, assuming Windows 7 has not booted successfully at all since the problem occurred, is the *Last Known Good Configuration* option. This overwrites the current version of the Registry with the last automatic backup made of it when the system last booted successfully. Try this first because it is the easiest fix.

Note: *Last Known Good Configuration relies on a backup that is updated each time Windows 7 boots successfully. This is different from a restore point in System Restore; System Restore points are made only once a day and do not depend on whether the system boots to be made or not made.*

Safe Mode Options

If *Last Known Good Configuration* does not work, restart the PC again, and this time, choose one of the Safe Mode options on the Advanced Boot Options menu. Each of these loads Windows 7 with only the essential drivers and services, so that the item causing the problem is bypassed:

- **Repair Your Computer**. Opens the Windows Recovery Environment, a utility that can help you repair your system. See "Repairing Windows 7" later in this chapter for details.
- **Safe Mode**. Bypasses all nonessential drivers and services.
- **Safe Mode with Networking**. Same as Safe Mode, but loads networking-related drivers and services.
- **Safe Mode with Command Prompt**. Same as Safe Mode, but opens a command prompt window.

In addition to the three Safe Mode options, the Advanced Boot Options menu also contains the choices shown in Table 14.2. These are not covered in this chapter in detail, but may be useful in specific troubleshooting situations.

Table 14.2   Other Advanced Boot Options

Enable Boot Logging	Creates ntbtlog.txt, which lists all drivers that load during startup, including the last file to load before a failure.
Enable Low-Resolution Video	(640 × 480) Sets or resets the display resolution. Starts Windows 7 in low-resolution display mode.
Last Known Good Configuration (Advanced)	Starts Windows 7 using settings from the last successful boot attempt.
Directory Services Restore Mode	Starts Windows 7 in Directory services repair mode (for Windows domain controllers only).
Debugging Mode	Enables the Windows 7 kernel debugger.
Disable Automatic Restart On System Failure	Prevents Windows 7 from automatically rebooting after a crash.
Disable Driver Signature Enforcement	Allows drivers containing improper signatures to be loaded.
Start Windows Normally	Aborts any special boot options and starts Windows 7 using its default settings.

When you boot into Safe Mode, Windows 7 appears different from normal in several ways. The display resolution is plain VGA, which is 640 × 480 resolution and 16 colors. The words "Safe Mode" appear in the four corners of the desktop, and a Help window appears explaining the purpose of Safe Mode. Figure 14.2 shows an example.

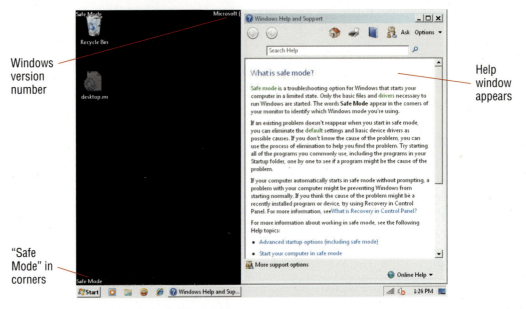

Windows version number

Help window appears

"Safe Mode" in corners

Figure 14.2 **Boot into Safe Mode to correct problems that are preventing Windows 7 from starting normally.**

Here's How

To boot into Safe Mode:

1. Restart the PC, and as soon as any text appears on the screen, start pressing and releasing the F8 key at one-second intervals until the Advanced Boot Options menu appears.

   Note: *The menu might appear automatically if Windows 7 failed to start correctly last time.*

2. Press the Down Arrow key to highlight the desired option:
   • Last Known Good Configuration (Advanced)
   • Safe Mode
   • Safe Mode with Networking
   • Safe Mode with Command Prompt
3. Press Enter.

Once you are in Safe Mode, you can go about fixing the root cause of the problem. Think about what you did right before the problem started, and then do one or more of the following:

• If you recently updated a device driver, roll back the update, as described later in this chapter in "Rolling Back a Driver."

• If you recently installed a new program, remove it, as described in Chapter 13 in "Removing a Program."

• If you think a program loading automatically at startup is causing the problem, disable that program from starting, as described in Chapter 13 in "Preventing a Program from Starting Automatically."

- If you are not sure what caused the problem, restore the system to an earlier restore point, as described in Chapter 12 in "Restoring Settings to an Earlier Time with System Restore."

Note: *Not all of your hardware may work in Safe Mode. For example, sound will not play, and unless you chose Safe Mode with Networking, you will not be able to access your local network or the Internet.*

 Exercise 3

Booting into Safe Mode with Networking

1. Restart Windows 7 (Start, *Shut down*, *Restart*).
2. As the PC begins rebooting, press F8 at one-second intervals until the Advanced Boot Options menu appears.
3. Press the Down Arrow key to highlight *Safe Mode with Networking* and press Enter.
4. When the PC finishes booting, close the Help and Support window.
5. Explore the menus, the Computer window, the Network window, and so on. Make a list of the differences you observe between regular operating mode and Safe Mode. Record your list on a piece of paper or in a Word file, title the paper or name the file **C14E03**, put your name on it, and submit it to your instructor for grading.
6. Reboot the PC normally.

Repairing Windows 7

When Windows 7 crashes frequently or fails to start properly, it may be necessary to repair Windows 7 itself. To do this, use Startup Repair, a recovery tool that fixes missing or damaged system files. This utility is installed on your hard drive automatically when Windows 7 is installed, so it is always available.

To repair Windows 7 using Startup Repair:

1. Restart Windows 7 (Start, Shut down, Restart).
2. As the PC begins booting, press F8 at one-second intervals until the Advanced Boot Options menu appears.
3. Select Repair Your Computer and press Enter.
4. Click Startup Repair.
5. Follow the prompts to complete the repair.

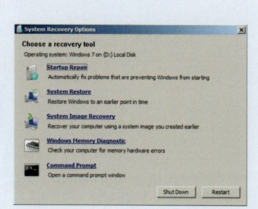

Here's How

QUICK FIX

Set the Boot Order
If the PC does not boot from the CD/DVD, you may need to go into the BIOS Setup for the PC and tell it to prefer the CD/DVD drive as a boot device.

Troubleshooting Printing Problems

Windows 7 manages the printing processes for all of the installed printers, so that each application is relieved of that responsibility. You can print from several different applications to the same printer, and Windows 7 will send each print job to the printer one by one.

Sometimes, however, problems occur and the print job does not emerge from the printer as intended. The problem can be with the printer itself, with the print queue, or with the individual print job.

Troubleshooting Physical Problems with a Printer

Often the root cause of a printer problem is the printer itself. Before assuming that Windows 7 or the printer driver is at fault, check the following:

- Is the printer plugged in and turned on? Look for a power light or message on the printer that indicates it is receiving power.
- Is the printer online? Some printers have an Online button that toggles the printer online and offline. This is different from being powered on; it controls the connection to the PC.
- Is the printer connected to the PC? This connection can be via a cable (parallel or USB), Bluetooth, wireless, or LAN.
- Does the printer have sufficient paper and ink or toner?

Tip: If all the physical aspects of the printer appear to be operational, you might try printing a test page from the printer's own controls. The instructions for doing this can be found in the printer's documentation; it usually involves pressing certain buttons on the printer in a prescribed sequence or choosing a test page from the printer's LED interface. If the printer will print a test page, then you know the problem is with Windows 7 or with the printer's connectivity.

Opening the Print Queue to View Printer Status

Assuming you have confirmed that the problem is not with the printer itself, the next step is to open the printer's queue. Windows 7 maintains a separate queue for each printer driver installed.

Here's How

To view a printer's status and queue:

1. Click Start, and then click *Control Panel*.
2. Under Hardware and Sound, click View devices and printers.
3. Double-click the printer for which you want to get information.
4. Examine the information that appears, including the number of documents in the queue.
5. If the print queue does not already appear, double-click the *See what's printing* icon. The queue for the printer appears.
6. Examine the queue. For example, here you can see that the queue has been paused and one print job is waiting.

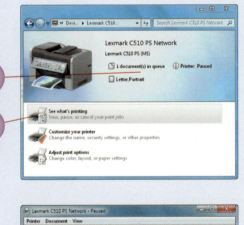

Controlling the Queue

The queue shown in the preceding steps has been paused. You might want to pause a queue to prevent a print job from completing what you sent to the printer accidentally, for example, so as not to waste the paper. You could also pause the print queue to reorder the jobs so that an important one prints before the others.

The Printer menu in the print queue (see Figure 14.3) contains commands for controlling the entire queue at once:

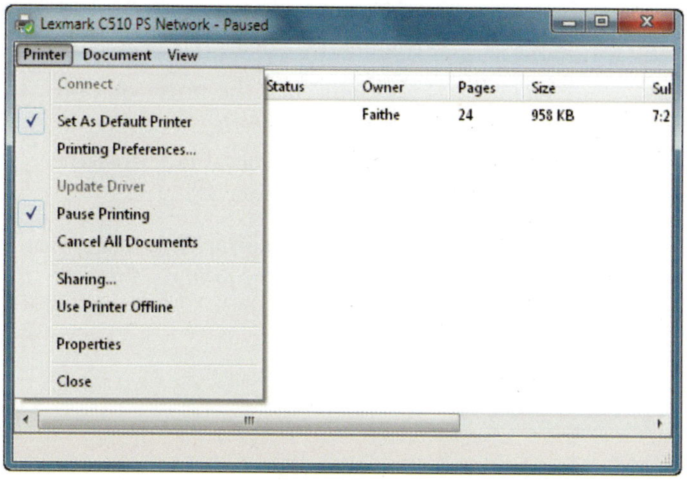

- **Printer, Pause Printing**. Pauses the entire print queue. You can select this same command again to toggle the queue back on again.

- **Printer, Cancel All Documents**. Clears the entire print queue. Any unprinted print jobs are deleted.

Figure 14.3 Control a printer's queue from the Printer menu.

Controlling an Individual Print Job

In addition to pausing, restarting, and clearing the entire queue, you can also pause, restart, and clear individual print jobs within it. For example, you could pause a print job so that other jobs could go ahead of it in the queue, or so you could get more information about it before allowing it to print.

Another way to reorder the jobs in a print queue is to change a job's priority. By default, all print jobs have the lowest priority; you can make a job rise to the top of the queue by setting its priority higher than that of the other print jobs with which it is competing.

To pause a print job:

1. Click the print job in the queue.
2. Click Document, *Pause*, or right-click the print job and click *Pause*.

To resume a paused print job:

1. Click the print job in the queue.
2. Click Document, *Resume*, or right-click the print job and click *Resume*.

To delete a print job:

1. Click the print job in the queue.
2. Click Document, *Cancel*, or right-click the print job and click *Cancel*.
3. Click Yes.

Here's How

Here's How ➤ To reprioritize a print job:

1. Right-click the print job and choose *Properties*.
2. On the General tab, drag the Priority slider.

   Note: *The priority numbers run from low (1) to high (99).*

3. Click OK.

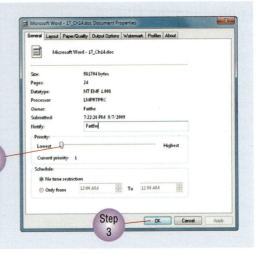

Exercise 4

Controlling a Print Queue

1. Pause the queue for the default printer:
   a. Choose Start, *Control Panel*.
   b. Click View Devices and Printers.
   c. Right-click the printer and choose *See what's printing*.
   d. Open the Printer menu and choose *Pause Printing*.

   Note: *Pausing printing may not be possible if your default printer is a network printer that another computer controls. If so, try a different printer if one is available, or ask your instructor for help.*

2. Open Notepad, type your name, and print to the default printer. Then close Notepad without saving your changes.
3. Open Paint, draw an oval, and print to the default printer. Then close Paint without saving your changes.
4. Open Internet Explorer and browse to www.emcp.com. Print to the default printer. Then close Internet Explorer.
5. Open the print queue. It contains three documents.
6. Delete the second print job (the print job from Paint):
   a. Select the second print job.
   b. Click Document, *Cancel*.
   c. Click Yes.
7. Set the priority for the Web page print job to 99:
   a. Right-click the print job and choose *Properties*.
   b. Drag the Priority slider to the highest setting.
   c. Click OK.
8. Pause the Web page print job:
   a. Select the Web page print job.
   b. Click Document, *Pause*.
9. Click Printer, *Pause Printing* to resume the print queue and allow the Notepad print job to print.
10. Resume the Web page print job and allow it to print.
11. Submit the two printouts to your instructor for grading.

Troubleshooting Hardware Problems

Most hardware problems are not actually problems with the hardware itself, but with its configuration in Windows 7. As you learned in Chapter 13, each device needs a driver and some system resources to function. If either of these is not set up correctly, the device will not function correctly.

When a device is not functioning properly, first check that Windows 7 has correctly identified the device, assigned resources to it, and loaded its driver.

- **Is the device identified correctly?** If the device appears as Unknown Device, Windows 7 was not able to identify it correctly. To solve this problem, run the Setup utility for the software that came with the device.

- **Are there any resource conflicts?** A *resource conflict* occurs when two devices both try to claim the same resources (for example, the same IRQ or I/O address). When this happens, one or both of the devices involved in the conflict does not function correctly.

- **Does the driver load?** When a device driver cannot be loaded, the device cannot function. A driver might not load because of incompatibility between it and Windows 7 (especially if it is an older driver) or because it is corrupted.

All these questions can be answered by examining the device in Device Manager. Device Manager shows a list of all the installed hardware. When you double-click a device, a Properties box opens for it, showing its status. See Figure 14.4.

Double-click the device to open its Properties box

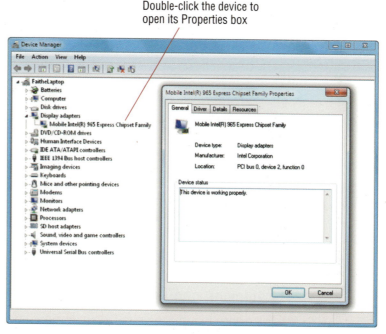

Figure 14.4 Use Device Manager to examine the properties for a device and ascertain its status.

You can find the following information in the device's Properties box:

- **General tab.** Look for a message that "This device is working properly" as shown in Figure 14.4. If the device is not working, a message explaining the problem appears here instead.

- **Resources tab.** Look for a "No conflicts" message, as in Figure 14.5. If there is a resource conflict, information about it will appear in that area instead.

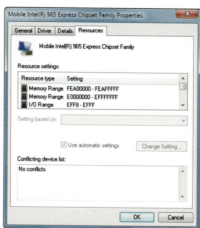

Figure 14.5 Examine the device's resource usage on the Resources tab.

To check a device's status:

1. Click Start, and then click *Control Panel*.
2. Click System and Security.
3. Under System, click Device Manager.
4. If the device's category is not expanded, click the arrow next to the category to expand it.

   Note: *In most cases, if a device has a problem, its category automatically appears expanded so the device is visible.*

5. Double-click the device to open its Properties box.
6. On the General tab, check the Device Status area for a message. If the device is working properly and its driver is installed, it looks like this:
7. Click the Resources tab, and check the Conflicting Device List area for a message. If there are no resource problems, it looks like this:
8. Click OK.

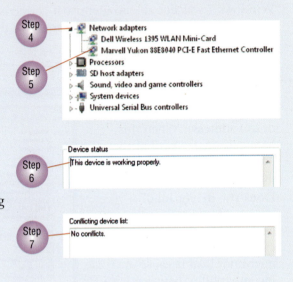

Removing and Redetecting a Device

If a device reports an error, you can sometimes correct it by removing the device and allowing Windows 7 to redetect it. Removing the device removes its hold on the resources assigned to it, so that Windows 7 can reassign new resources when it redetects the device later. This corrects most resource-related problems.

To remove and redetect a device:

1. From Device Manager, select the device.
2. Press the Delete key, or click the *Uninstall* icon on the toolbar.
3. Click OK.
4. Click *Scan for hardware changes* on the toolbar.

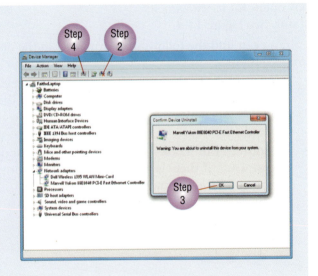

Enabling and Disabling a Device

When you remove a device, as in the preceding section, the device is redetected automatically the next time Windows 7 scans for hardware changes. It does this not only when you click the *Scan for hardware changes* icon, but also automatically at startup each time. Therefore, a device that has been removed in Windows 7, but is still physically attached or installed will usually be redetected.

If you want a device to be permanently disabled, so that it does not use any resources or load any drivers, you must either physically remove it from the PC or set it to be disabled in Windows 7. (Motherboard devices such as built-in sound or display adapters must be disabled, because they cannot be removed.)

Note: *One reason you might disable a device is that a duplicate device exists in the PC that is better than the original. For example, you might have built-in sound support on the motherboard, but also have a PCI expansion board that is an advanced sound card with better features. You could disable the onboard sound to free up its resources.*

To disable a device:

Here's How

1. From Device Manager, double-click the device.
2. Click *Disable o*n the toolbar. A warning appears.
3. Click Yes.

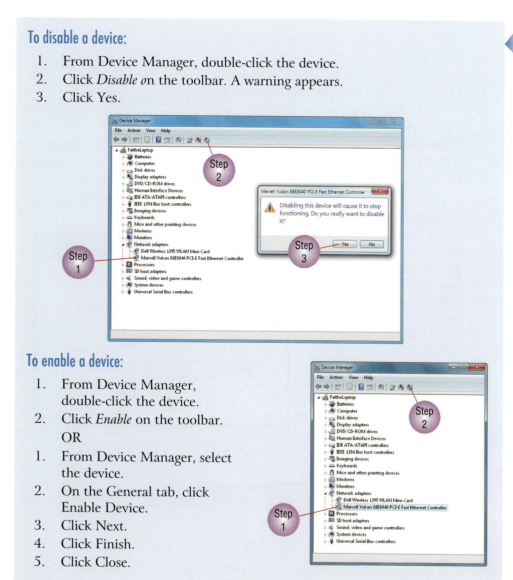

To enable a device:

1. From Device Manager, double-click the device.
2. Click *Enable* on the toolbar.
   OR
1. From Device Manager, select the device.
2. On the General tab, click Enable Device.
3. Click Next.
4. Click Finish.
5. Click Close.

Updating a Device Driver

Device manufacturers periodically release updates to their drivers that either enhance the device's capabilities or correct problems with it. For example, if you install a new game and the game crashes frequently, sometimes an update to the display adapter's device driver will correct the problem.

Driver updates are typically available from the manufacturers' Web sites. Driver updates usually come in an executable package (that is, a file with an .exe extension). You download the file and then double-click it to run it.

When you run the executable file, one of two things might happen:

- A Setup program might run that automatically installs the update (most common).
- The driver files might extract themselves to a folder on your hard disk, and then you would need to install the driver update manually (less common).

Here's How ▶

To manually install a driver update:

1. Click Start.
2. Right-click *Computer* and choose *Properties*.
3. Click Device Manager.
4. Click the arrow next to the device's category.
5. Double-click the device to open its Properties box.
6. Click the Driver tab.
7. Click Update Driver.
8. Click *Search automatically for updated driver software*. If software is found, follow the prompts to install it.

   OR

   Click *Browse my computer for driver software* and continue to Step 9.
9. If you know the location of the driver, click Browse to locate it. Otherwise enter your hard disk's letter in the *Search for driver software in this location* box, and make sure the *Include subfolders* check box is marked.
10. Click Next and follow the prompts. If Windows is unable to locate a better driver, a message appears that the best driver is already installed.
11. Click Close.

QUICK FIX

Using the Roll Back Driver Button
If a device stops working correctly after you update its driver, use the Roll Back Driver button in its Properties box (Driver tab) to restore the earlier driver.

Rolling Back a Driver

Windows 7 retains the previously used driver when you install a new one, so you can return to it later if the new one proves to be a problem. To reverse an update, use the Roll Back Driver feature.

Here's How

To roll back a driver update:

1. From Device Manager, double-click the device.
2. Click the Driver tab.
3. Click Roll Back Driver.
4. Follow the prompts to roll back the driver to the previous version.

 ## Exercise 5

Working with device drivers

1. Open Device Manager, and view the properties of your sound card, or if your PC does not have sound, of a nonessential component such as a modem:
   a. Click Start. Then right-click *Computer* and choose *Properties*.
   b. Click Device Manager.
   c. Click the arrow next to the device category.
   d. Double-click the device.
2. View the current driver information, and make a note of the driver version:
   a. Click the Driver tab.
   b. Make a note of the Driver Provider, Driver Date, and Driver Version.
   c. Capture a screen print of the window to submit to your instructor for grading. Name the file **C14E05S02**.
   d. Click OK.
3. Use the Internet to find the device manufacturer's Web site or the Web site of the PC manufacturer. Look up your device by model number, and if a driver is available that is newer (by date and version number) than the current one, download it.
4. Check with your instructor, and, if directed, install the driver update. Otherwise, simply make a note of the Web site where the driver could be downloaded.

   Note: *Depending on the update and its format, you might either run an executable setup program or use the Update Driver button in the display adapter's Properties box.*

5. Identify a nonessential device that has a Resources tab in its properties:
   a. Display the properties box for a device. (A wireless network adapter is a good choice. Ask your instructor to help identify a device to use if needed.)
   b. If it does not have a Resources tab, click Close and try another device.
6. Disable the device using Device Manager:
   a. Select the device.
   b. Click the *Disable* icon on the toolbar.
   c. Click Yes.
7. Display the Resources tab in the Properties dialog box for the device.
8. Capture a screen print of the window to submit to your instructor for grading. Name the file **C14E05S08**.
9. Reenable the device:
   a. Select the device.
   b. Click the *Enable* icon on the toolbar.
10. Close all open windows.

Using Remote Assistance

It can often be difficult for a technician to troubleshoot a computer problem over the phone or via e-mail because he or she cannot see the PC's screen and must rely on the end user to try different fixes. Remote Assistance makes remote troubleshooting much easier by enabling someone to view and take control of a PC over the Internet or a LAN.

Note: *Do not confuse Remote Assistance with Remote Desktop. The latter enables you to log into another computer remotely, exactly as if you were sitting at that computer physically. It grants the connecting user more privileges and is less controllable than Remote Assistance, so it is not the preferred connection type for troubleshooting. Remote Desktop is covered in Chapter 16.*

Configuring Remote Assistance Settings

Because the person taking control of your computer via Remote Assistance has the power to make changes to your system that can help or harm it, Windows 7 has security measures in place to prevent unauthorized access to your system, using this tool.

You can enable or disable Remote Assistance as a whole by using the System properties in Windows 7 (Remote tab). You can also configure its settings to allow only the access you prefer. For example, you can prevent the person connecting from taking control of your system, and you can specify the amount of time an invitation can remain open. You can also restrict connections to only people using Windows 7.

Here's How ▶

To enable and configure Remote Assistance:

1. Click Start, and then click *Control Panel*.
2. Click System and Security.
3. Under the System category, click Allow remote access.
4. The *Allow Remote Assistance connections to this computer* check box is checked by default.
5. Click Advanced.
6. Mark or clear the *Allow this computer to be controlled remotely* check box. If you clear this check box, people connecting to your computer will be able to watch what you are doing, but will not be able to do anything themselves.
7. Use the drop-down lists to set the maximum amount of time that an invitation can be open. The shorter the amount of time, the less likely an invitation will be intercepted by an unauthorized person, but the less time a legitimate helper will have to respond as well.
8. Mark or clear the *Create invitations that can only be used from computers running Windows Vista or later* check box.
9. Click OK.

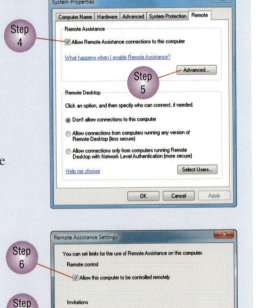

Requesting Remote Assistance

To request remote assistance, you send an invitation to someone from whom you want help. The easiest and most common way to send this invitation is via e-mail. When you work through the invitation process, Windows 7 prompts you for the e-mail address to which to send the invitation, and then generates the e-mail to be sent via your default e-mail program with the invitation as an attachment.

Here's How

To request Remote Assistance:

1. Click Start, *Help and Support*.
2. Click the *Ask* icon
3. Click Windows Remote Assistance.
4. Click Invite someone you trust to help you.
5. Click Use e-mail to send an invitation.
6. When Remote Assistance opens a new e-mail in your default e-mail program, fill in the recipient's e-mail address.
7. Click Send. A box appears with a string of letters and numbers; this is the connection password.
8. Send another e-mail to your helper (or contact him or her in some other way), to provide the connection password.

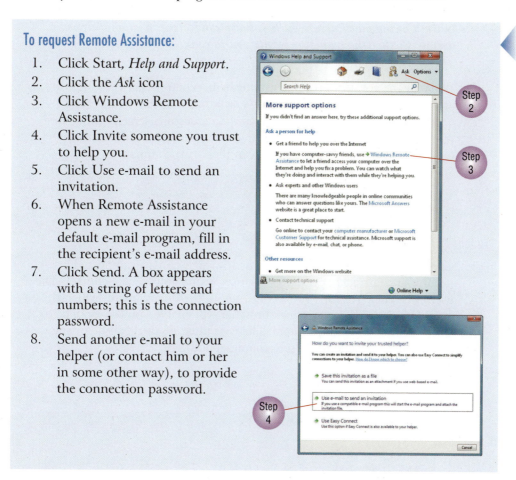

After you send a Remote Assistance request, a small Remote Assistance window appears, containing the connection password. Leave this window open as you wait for the person to respond.

Giving Remote Assistance

When you receive a Remote Assistance request via e-mail, the file attachment contains an invitation, including all the technical details needed for your computer to connect to the requestor's computer.

After the invitation has been accepted and the two PCs are connected, you can share control of the remote PC (so that your keyboard and mouse work on it). This does not take away that user's ability to continue using his or her own keyboard and mouse; it simply adds yours as additional input devices.

You can also choose to chat with the other user by opening a Chat window, and you can choose to send and receive files between you.

To give remote assistance:

1. Double-click the attachment file in the e-mail you received. When prompted to save or open it, click Open.
2. Type the connection password. If you do not know it, phone or e-mail the person who sent the invitation to find out what it is.
3. Click OK.

   Note: *On the machine to which you are connecting, a prompt appears asking whether the requestor wants you to connect. The requestor must click Yes for you to continue.*

4. Wait for the connection to be established. When it is, a Helping window appears showing you the requestor's desktop.
5. (Optional) Click *Actual size* to display the requestor's screen at the same resolution she is using, or click *Fit to screen* to see her entire desktop at once. (A single button toggles between these two commands.)

Step 5

To take control of the remote PC:

• Click *Request control*. On the machine to which you are connected, a prompt appears asking whether the user wants you to take control. The user must click Yes for you to continue. In the dialog box in which the user clicks Yes, there is a check box that will enable you to respond to User Account Control prompts. The user must mark this if he or she wants you to be able to do so (recommended).

To release control of the remote PC:

1. Click *Stop sharing*.

Step 1

To chat with the user of the remote PC:

1. Click *Chat*. A Chat panel appears to the right of the desktop display.
2. Type a message in the bottom of the chat panel and click Send or press Enter. On the machine to which you are connected, a chat window opens, and that user can chat back to you using that interface.

Step 2

CHAPTER Summary

- To troubleshoot problems, open the Control Panel, and under System and Security, click Find and fix problems.

- A disk can develop physical and/or logical errors that cause programs and Windows 7 to crash or have other problems. To fix them, from the drive's Properties box's Tools tab, click Check Now.

- To shut down a malfunctioning program, display the Task Manager by right-clicking the taskbar and choosing *Task Manager*. Then select the program on the Applications tab, and click End Task.

- The root cause of a program crash can include Setup not being completed correctly, program files missing or corrupted, a bug in the program, an incompatibility with Windows 7, errors on the disk, and incompatibility between the program and the display adapter.

- Some programs can be repaired via the Uninstall a Program subcategory of the Control Panel. Select an installed program and click the Change or Uninstall/ Change button, and if a Repair option appears, work through it. Not all programs have this feature.

- To display the Advanced Boot Options menu at startup, press F8 as the PC boots. This menu also appears automatically when rebooting after Windows 7 fails to start correctly. From here you can try Last Known Good Configuration to return to an internal backup of the Registry.

- Choose Safe Mode (with or without networking or command prompt) to boot Windows 7 in a mode with minimal driver support. This often enables you to get into Windows 7 to run repair utilities when Windows 7 will otherwise not boot.

- Printer problems are often due to the printer itself. Check that it is plugged in, online, connected to the PC, and stocked with ink and paper.

- To check a printer's status, open Devices and Printers from the Control Panel and open the queue for the printer by double-clicking the printer's icon.

- In the print queue window, use the Printer menu for operations involving the entire printer, such as pausing it or cancelling all pending print jobs.

- Use the Document menu for operations involving individual print jobs. For example, you can pause or resume a print job, delete it, or display its properties (from which you can adjust its priority).

- Most hardware problems are actually problems with the device's configuration in Windows 7. The most common problems are device driver issues and resource assignment issues.

- Use Device Manager to see a list of installed devices and check the status of each device. To see a device's status, double-click it and look on the General tab of its Properties box. Operational devices display "This device is working properly."

- Look on the Resources tab of a device's Properties box for information about its resource assignments. Operational devices display "No conflicts."

- To remove a device from Device Manager, select it and press the Delete key or click Uninstall. The device will likely be redetected either the next time you start Windows 7, or when you refresh Device Manager's listing with *Scan for hardware changes*.

- To turn off a device in Windows 7 so that it is not redetected later, disable it. Select it from Device Manager and click the *Disable* icon.

- Updating a device driver will sometimes correct a problem with it. In most cases, driver updates are executable downloads, but you might occasionally need to install a driver update manually. To do so, from Device Manager, double-click the device, click the Driver tab, and click Update Driver.

- If a driver update causes the device to malfunction, you can return to the previous driver by using Roll Back Driver. From the Device Manager, double-click the device, click the Driver tab, and click Roll Back Driver.

- Remote Assistance enables one user to connect to another user's PC in order to provide troubleshooting help.

CONCEPTS Check

Completion: Answer the following questions on a blank sheet of paper or in a Word document.

Part 1

MULTIPLE CHOICE

1. To troubleshoot problems with your computer, open the Control Panel and, under _____, click Find and fix problems.
   a. System and Security
   b. Programs
   c. Network and Internet
   d. Hardware and Sound

2. On a disk formatted with NTFS, the table of contents for the disk is stored in a _____ .
   a. registry
   b. boot sector
   c. master file table
   d. file allocation table

3. In Windows 7, what utility finds and fixes file system errors?
   a. Disk Cleanup
   b. Disk Defragmenter
   c. Scan Disk
   d. Check Disk

4. From which tab of the Task Manager should you shut down an application that is not responding?
   a. Applications
   b. Processes
   c. Services
   d. Performance

5. What key displays the Advanced Boot Options menu at startup?
   a. F1
   b. F5
   c. F8
   d. F11

6. Which option from the Advanced Boot Options menu loads a minimal set of drivers at startup?
   a. Safe Mode with Networking
   b. Last Known Good Configuration
   c. Enable Boot Logging
   d. Disable Driver Signature Enforcement

7. After booting into Safe Mode, how would you fix a problem that was caused by recently updating a device driver?
   a. Uninstall the device in Device Manager.
   b. Roll back the driver.
   c. Re-update the driver.
   d. Do a System Restore.

8. From which menu in a printer's queue would you pause the printer (all print jobs at once)?
   a. Document
   b. Printer
   c. File
   d. Edit

9. If you want to turn off a device so that Windows 7 will not try to redetect it next time it starts up, what should you do to the device in Device Manager?
   a. Uninstall
   b. Disable
   c. Remove
   d. Hibernate

10. Where in the Control Panel do you enable or disable Remote Assistance?
    a. System and Security
    b. Users
    c. Network and Internet
    d. Desktop

SHORT ANSWER

11. Name three possible causes of a file system error.

    _____

12. What are bad sector errors and what can be done about them?

    _____

13. How do you initiate a Check Disk operation on a hard disk?

    _____

14. How can you tell that a program has crashed?

    _____

15. List three causes of program crashes.

    _____

16. Suppose a program will run in Windows XP, but after you upgrade to Windows 7, it fails. How could you make the program run under Windows 7?

    _____

17. How is Last Known Good Configuration different from restoring from the most recent System Restore point?

    _____

18. What are three visual clues that would tell you that Windows 7 was running in Safe Mode?

    _____

19. List three things you can check on a printer to eliminate the printer itself as the cause of not being able to print.

    _____

20. List three things to check in Device Manager for a device that is not working correctly.

    _____

SKILLS Check

Save all solution files to the default Documents folder, or any alternate folder specified by your instructor.

Guided Check

TROUBLESHOOTING A NETWORK PROBLEM

1
1. On a blank piece of paper, write your name and C14A01, or in a Word document, type your name and save the file as **C14A01**.
2. Open the Windows Help and Support system from the Start menu.
3. Disable your network adapter from Device Manager.
   a. Click Start, right-click *Computer*, and choose *Properties*.
   b. Click Device Manager.
   c. Expand the Network Adapters category.
   d. Click your network adapter and click *Disable* on the toolbar.
   e. Click Yes to confirm.
3. Troubleshoot your network connection, allowing Windows 7 to correct the problem.
   a. Open the Control Panel, and under the System and Security category, click Find and fix problems.
   b. Click Hardware and Sound.
   c. Click Network Adapter.
   d. Click Next.
   e. If prompted to choose which adapter to troubleshoot, click All Network Adapters.
   f. Click Next.
   g. Follow the prompts that appear to complete the repair. Write on your paper the exact prompts that appeared and the choices you made. Or, if the repair was not performed successfully, explain on your paper what happened, and then make the repair manually by re-enabling the device.
4. Close all open windows and submit your results to your instructor for grading.

CHECKING A DISK FOR ERRORS

2
1. Display the Tools tab for your hard drive's properties.
   a. Click Start, *Computer*.
   b. Right-click the *C* drive and choose *Properties*.
   c. Click the Tools tab.
2. Check the *C* drive for file system errors.
   a. Click Check now.
   b. Click Start.
   c. If prompted, click Schedule disk check, and then restart the PC to commence with the check.
3. As the check is running, make notes about the messages that appear on-screen. Write your notes on a piece of paper and label it **C14A02**. Write your name on it and submit it for grading.

EXPLORING PRINTER ERROR MESSAGES

1. On a blank piece of paper, write your name and C14A03, or in a Word document, type your name and save the file as **C14A03**. Record the answers to the questions in the following steps.
2. Remove the paper from your printer.
3. Open Notepad, type your name, and print to the default printer.
   a. Click Start, *All Programs, Accessories, Notepad*.
   b. Type your name.
   c. Click File, *Print*.
   d. Click the Print button. What indicator or message appears in Windows 7, if any, alerting you that the printer is out of paper?
4. Open the printer's queue.
   a. Click Start, *Control Panel*.
   b. Under Hardware and Sound, click View Devices and Printers.
   c. Right-click the printer and choose *See what's printing*.
   d. What indicator or message appears in the print queue window indicating that the printer is out of paper? Write your answer on your paper.
5. Turn off the printer's power. What indicator or message appears in the print queue window?
6. Replace the paper in the printer.
7. Pause the print queue in Windows 7.
   • From the print queue window, click Printer, *Pause Printing*.
8. Turn the printer back on again. What indicator or message appears in the print queue window?
9. Delete the print job without printing it.
   • Select the print job and press Delete.
10. Resume the print queue.
    • From the print queue window, click Printer, *Pause Printing*.
11. Submit your paper or file to your instructor for grading.

REMOVING AND REINSTALLING A DEVICE.

1. Open Device Manager.
   • Choose Start, *Control Panel*, System and Security, Device Manager.
2. Uninstall the driver for your keyboard.
   a. Click the arrow next to Keyboards.
   b. Select your keyboard and press Delete.
   c. Click OK.
3. Reinstall the keyboard by clicking *Scan for hardware changes*.
4. View the driver information for the keyboard.
   a. Click the arrow next to Keyboards.
   b. Double-click your keyboard.
   c. Click the Driver tab.
   d. Click Driver Details.
5. Capture a screen print of this window and submit it to your instructor for grading. Name the file **C14A04**.
6. Close all open windows.

On Your Own

Assessment 5 — UPDATING AND INSTALLING A DEVICE DRIVER

1. Open Device Manager.
2. Identify a device that is made by some other manufacturer than the PC itself, such as a modem, sound card, display adapter, or network card.
3. Find that device manufacturer's Web site, and find the available driver downloads for the device.
4. View the device's current driver information in Device Manager, and compare its version number and date to that found on the Web site.
5. If the version on the Web is newer than the one installed on your PC already, download and install it.
6. Write a one-page report detailing the version numbers you found, whether you installed the update, and if so, what steps you took to do so. Name the paper or file **C14A05**. Submit it to your instructor for grading.

Assessment 6 — TEAM EXERCISE: USING REMOTE ASSISTANCE

Work in pairs for this exercise, with each person on a different PC. One person will be the Requestor and the other will be the Helper.

1. Requestor: Make sure Remote Assistance is enabled on your PC.
2. Requestor: Send a Remote Assistance invitation to your partner's e-mail address.
3. Helper: Receive the invitation and respond to it, connecting to the Requestor's PC.
4. Requestor: Respond to the prompt to enable the Helper to connect to your PC.
5. Helper: Open a Chat window and have a short chat conversation.
6. Requestor: Send a file from the Requestor's PC to the Helper's PC.
7. Helper: Receive the sent file, and store it in the Documents folder.
8. Helper: Capture a screen print of the window showing the Requestor's PC on your screen. Name the file **C14A06**. Submit it to your instructor for grading.
9. Helper: Disconnect your connection to the Requestor's PC.

Assessment 7 — CHECKING A FLOPPY DISK FOR ERRORS

Note: *If you do not have a floppy disk drive, you can use a USB flash drive for this exercise. However, a floppy is better because it is more likely to have actual errors you can fix.*

1. Insert a floppy disk in your PC.
2. Run Check Disk and include the option to fix bad sectors.
3. When the check is complete, click *Show Details* and then capture a screen print of the window showing that the check was successful. Save the file as **C14A07** and submit it for grading.

Assessment 8 — USING ADVANCED BOOT OPTIONS

1. On a blank piece of paper, write your name and C14A08, or in a Word document, type your name and save the file as **C14A08**. Record the notes you make in the following step.
2. Boot in each of the boot modes from Table 14.2, except Debug mode, and make notes about the difference you observe for each one, if any, in terms of the appearance, performance, and functionality of Windows 7. Submit your findings to your instructor for grading.

CHALLENGE Project

Suppose your friend Jennifer has asked you for help with troubleshooting a problem with her PC. She claims that ever since she installed a sound card last week, her favorite game crashes intermittently. Write a letter to her explaining what she should try to fix the problem, and in what order you recommend she try the various possible fixes you propose.

CHAPTER
15

Securing and Monitoring Your System

PERFORMANCE OBJECTIVES

Upon successful completion of Chapter 15, you will be able to:
- **View system information**
- **Use the Task Manager to track system performance**
- **Evaluate system performance**
- **Work with user accounts and passwords**
- **Use encryption to secure files**

As you become more proficient with Windows 7, you may want to explore its tools and utilities for enhancing system performance and security. You can view system information, evaluate system performance, manage permissions to log on and to perform certain activities, keep sensitive files secure between users, and more.

Viewing System Information

CPU: Central Processing Unit, also called the processor; the main microchip that serves as the brain of the PC

RAM: Random Access Memory, a type of memory used by the PC as its main temporary storage space for running programs

When evaluating your system for compatibility with new software you might want to purchase, or for possible upgrades, the first step is to gather a set of basic facts about the PC's hardware and software. This information is available via several utilities in Windows 7.

Viewing the Installed CPU and RAM

The **CPU**'s type/speed and the amount of **RAM** installed are the two most significant indicators of system performance. When you shop for new software, the system requirements listed on the box will always include a minimum value for each of those specifications. To find out the CPU (processor) and the RAM amount, look in the System section of the Control Panel, as in Figure 15.1.

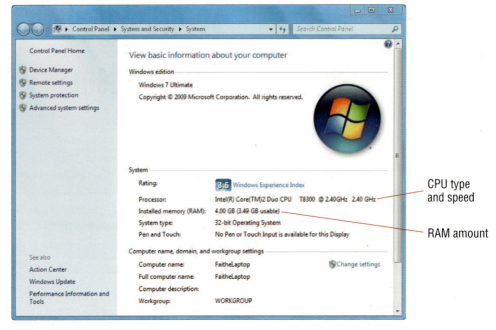

CPU type
and speed

RAM amount

Figure 15.1 Check the system's CPU and RAM configuration in the System area of the Control Panel.

Here's How

To open the System section to check CPU and RAM:

1. Click Start, *Control Panel*.
2. Click System and Security.
3. Click System, or click View amount of RAM and processor speed.

Alternate method:

1. Click Start.
2. Right-click *Computer*.
3. Click *Properties*.

Viewing Detailed System Information

Sometimes you might need more detailed system information than just the CPU and RAM specifications. For example, you might need a summary of all the installed hardware, or you might need to know the exact version of Windows you have. To gather this information, you can use the System Information utility.

Note: *Windows 7 has many versions: Home Basic, Home Premium, Business, and so on, and each has different features. In addition, when Windows 7 is updated with service packs, there are minor feature and compatibility changes too. That is why sometimes just knowing that you have Windows 7 is not enough, especially if you are gathering information for troubleshooting purposes.*

The System Information utility presents a system summary, as shown in Figure 15.2, which provides the most often needed facts about a system. This data appears when the top level of the System Summary tree is displayed. Beneath that top level are three other levels: Hardware Resources, Components, and Software

Click here for summary data

Expand/collapse categories for more specifics

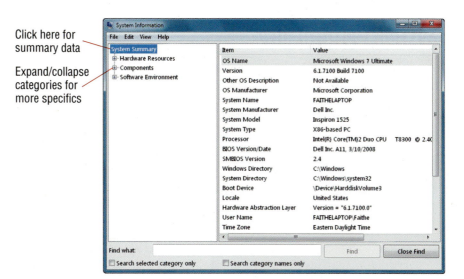

Figure 15.2 Gather more detailed information about the system from System Information.

Environment. Each of these can be selected to gather other, more specific information in those areas.

As you learned in Chapter 13 in "Working with Hardware," you can use the Device Manager to see a list of all the installed hardware. You can then view driver and resource information for each device from there.

Another way to get information about hardware is via the System Information utility's Components section. The Components section breaks down the hardware by type, and you can select a type to see very detailed information about each item of that type. See Figure 15.3, for example, which shows detailed information about a hard disk.

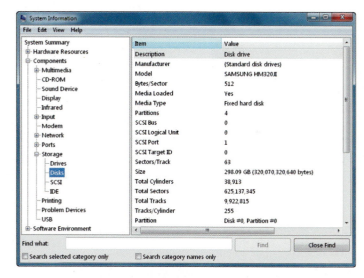

Figure 15.3 Detailed information about each piece of hardware is available in the Components section of System Information.

To open System Information:

- Click Start, and point to *All Programs*, *Accessories*, *System Tools*, and then click *System Information*.

To view detailed information about a hardware component:

1. Open System Information.
2. Click the plus sign next to Components.
3. Click the component subcategory.

Here's How

Rating System Performance

Some computer experts can quickly tell, by looking at the data in System Information, how well the PC will perform in Windows 7, but for the average user, the data can be difficult to interpret. To help simplify the process of evaluating system performance, Windows 7 provides a Performance Rating and Tools utility, shown in Figure 15.4. It reduces the complex matter of a system's performance level to a simple numeric value called the Windows Experience Index base score, and suggests ways to improve that number.

The system is evaluated on five criteria: Processor, Memory (RAM), Graphics, Gaming graphics, and Primary hard disk. Each of these is assigned a numeric value, with higher being better. The PC's overall score is determined by the lowest score in these five areas. For example, in Figure 15.4, the PC's overall score is a 3.5 because of the graphics, even though it scores significantly higher in other areas. Based on the results in Figure 15.4, a reasonable recommendation for improving this system's performance would be to install a better display adapter.

Figure 15.4 Rate your system with the Performance Information and Tools utility, available from the Control Panel.

Here's How

To rate system performance:

1. Click Start, *Control Panel*.
2. Click System and Security.
3. Under the System section, click Check the Windows Experience Index.
4. Click *View and print detailed performance and system information* to open the More details about my computer window.
5. (Optional) Scroll down for more information.
6. (Optional) Click Print this page to print the information.

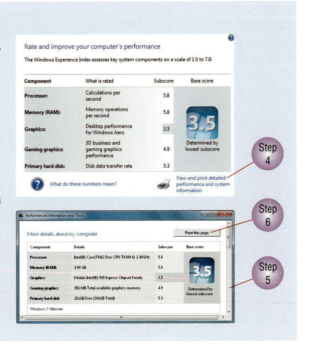

Tracking System Performance

Whereas the Performance Information and Tools utility in the preceding section predicts system performance based on its configuration, the Task Manager describes actual performance at a given moment in time.

Note: *Task Manager is a multipurpose utility, and performance data analysis is only one small part of its capability. It also displays running applications, processes, and servers; and shows which users are connected to the PC.*

To view the Task Manager, right-click the taskbar and choose *Start Task Manager*. Then click the Performance tab to see information about CPU and memory usage. See Figure 15.5.

CPU Usage shows how much of the CPU's time is being occupied by running programs. If the CPU is running at 100 percent for more than a few seconds at a time, then a program is probably malfunctioning. This is by far the most common cause of sluggish system performance caused by high CPU usage. Shut down the malfunctioning program from the Applications tab, as you learned to do in Chapter 14, in "Shutting Down a Malfunctioning Program with Task Manager."

If the CPU is consistently running at higher than 50 percent most of the time, not just when a program is malfunctioning, then you could probably get better performance from a PC with a better, faster CPU. It is normal for the CPU usage to spike and sag as the PC operates, so brief spikes to 100 percent CPU usage is not an indicator of an insufficient CPU.

Memory shows how much of the physical memory is being used. The actual number (in megabytes) is less important than the percentage of usage. If the green Memory bar consistently runs very high (that is, higher than 50 percent on an ongoing basis), your system could benefit from the addition of more RAM.

To get more detailed performance tracking information, click the Resource Monitor button, opening the Resource Monitor utility. This utility shows not only CPU and Memory information, but also disk and network performance. You can click a category bar to expand more information about that category. For example, in Figure 15.6, detailed CPU usage data is shown.

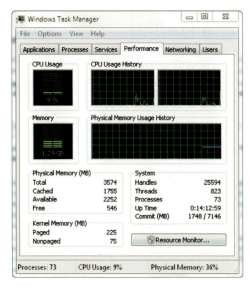

Figure 15.5 Check out CPU and memory usage on the Performance tab of the Task Manager window.

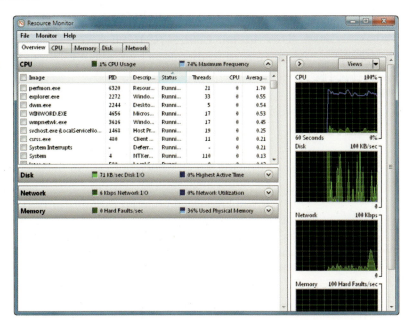

Figure 15.6 The Resource Monitor shows performance monitoring in more detail than the Task Manager can provide.

Exercise 1

Examining Your System Configuration

1. On a blank piece of paper, write your name and C15E01, or in a WordPad document, type your name and save the file as **C15E01**.
2. Using the System properties, determine your CPU type/speed and amount of RAM and record it on the paper or in the file.
3. Using System Information, determine the model and size of your primary hard disk and record it.
4. Using System Information, determine the driver version for your display adapter and record it.
5. Using Performance Information and Tools, determine your PC's Windows Experience Index base score and record it.
6. Determine which component is the limiting factor in the score and record it.
7. Display Task Manager, and on the Performance tab, click Resource Monitor.
8. In the Resource Monitor window, determine the percent used of physical memory and record it.
9. Close all open windows.
10. Submit your paper or file to your instructor for grading.

Working with User Accounts and Passwords

User account: The user name, password, settings, permissions, and restrictions that govern how Windows 7 allows a particular user to work with the system

User Account Control (UAC): A security feature that restricts certain activities based on the permission level of the logged-on user

Security at the local PC level is handled via *user accounts*, which are secured by passwords. Depending on the user logged on, certain activities are either allowed or disallowed, such as configuring system settings, adding and removing programs, and accessing certain files and folders. The feature that regulates these permissions is called User Account Control.

Understanding User Account Control (UAC)

User Account Control (UAC) is a security feature in Windows 7. It provides an easy way to restrict users from making system changes that will affect other users or the system itself.

Windows 7 users can be configured for either of two levels of permission:

- **Administrator**. Has full rights to do anything to the system, including changing security settings.
- **Standard**. Has full rights to do anything that affects only that user, such as changing screen colors, but cannot make changes that affect other users, and cannot change security settings.

If you are logged on as an Administrator (that is, if your user account is part of the Administrator group), then whenever you do something that requires UAC permission, a box appears asking you to confirm that it is really "you" doing it intentionally. This prevents applications from making such changes without your knowledge.

If you are logged on as a Standard user, Windows 7 prevents you from performing the operation altogether, or asks you to enter an Administrator-level user's name and password as an override.

Throughout the Windows 7 interface, activities that require Administrator-level UAC permission are shown with a multicolored shield symbol next to their links, as in Figure 15.7.

— *Shield* icon

Figure 15.7 A *Shield* icon means that Administrator-level permission is required.

Setting the UAC Notification Level

In Windows 7, you can customize the level of security that UAC provides by choosing one of four UAC notification levels:

- **Always notify**. The strongest setting. Provides UAC notification when a program installs software, makes changes to software, or changes your Windows 7 settings.

- **Notify me only when programs try to make changes to my computer**. This is the default setting. UAC messages appear with program changes, but not with changes to Windows 7 settings.

- **Notify me only when programs try to make changes to my computer (do not dim my desktop)**. This is the same as the above setting except the Windows 7 desktop does not become dimmed and unusable when the messages appear; you can respond to them at your leisure.

- **Never notify**. UAC notifications are turned off entirely.

Microsoft recommends leaving UAC set to its default, and recommends that you run Windows 7 as a Standard user most of the time, for the greatest security against unwanted system changes. However, on your home system, you might decide that UAC is too intrusive, and you might want to use a more lenient setting than the default.

Here's How ➤ **To adjust the User Account Control level:**

1. Click Start, *Control Panel*.
2. Click User Accounts and Family Safety.
3. Click User Accounts.
4. Click Change User Account Control settings.
5. Drag the slider to the desired setting.
6. Click OK.

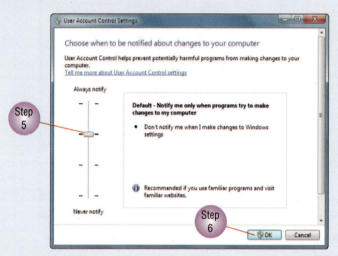

7. If a UAC box appears, click Yes.
8. If prompted to restart, click Restart Now.

You can fine-tune the behavior of User Account Control through the Local Security Policy utility. By default, for example, Standard users cannot perform any system activities, and you cannot override that by entering the credentials of an Administrator account. However, you can change that behavior and enable Windows 7 to prompt you for Administrator credentials when needed, by changing the security policy.

Here's How ➤ **To open the Security Policy configuration for User Account Control:**

1. Click Start.
2. Type **secpol.msc** and press Enter. If prompted to confirm, click Continue.
3. Double-click Local Policies.
4. Double-click Security Options.
5. Scroll down to the User Account Control entries.

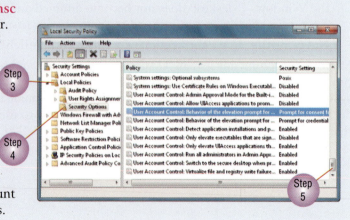

Adding a User Account

Windows 7 starts out with a single user account, based on the name you entered when you installed Windows 7. (There is also a Guest account, which you will learn about later in this chapter, but it is turned off by default.)

You can create as many new accounts as you like. Each will have its own Windows 7 settings, libraries, Recycle Bin, and visual preferences. You can choose at startup which account you want to log on to, in order to use different settings. You can switch user accounts at any time by logging off and then logging on as someone else. Each account can be set as either a Standard or an Administrator account and can have its own password. (You assign the password to a new account as a separate step, covered later in this chapter.)

> **Tip:** If you have only one user account, and if the Guest account is turned off, Windows 7 will not prompt you to select an account when you start up. Otherwise, a list of user accounts appears at startup and you click the one you want.

You can create a new user account in two ways. The Control Panel method is simple and easy, but lacks some of the administrator options available with the Local Users and Groups method. For example, the Local Users and Groups method enables you to require that the new user change his or her password at first logon, and enables you to create an account that is initially disabled.

To create a user account (Control Panel method):

◀ **Here's How**

1. Make sure you log on using an Administrator account.
2. Click Start, *Control Panel*.
3. Under User Accounts and Family Safety, click Add or remove user accounts.
4. Click Create a new account.
5. Type the name for the new account.
6. Click *Standard user* or *Administrator*.
7. Click Create Account.

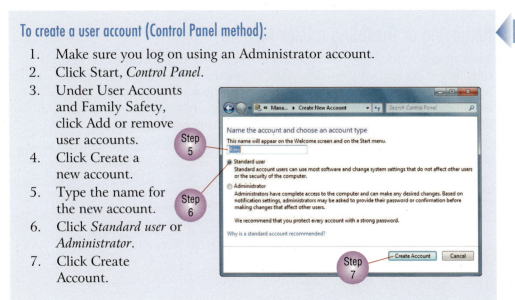

To create a user account (Local Users and Groups method):

1. Click Start.
2. Right-click *Computer* and click *Manage*.
3. Double-click Local Users and Groups.
4. Double-click Users.
5. Click More Actions.
6. Click *New User*.

7. Type a user name.
8. (Optional) Type a full name.
9. (Optional) Type a description.
10. (Optional) Type and confirm a password.
11. (Optional) Mark or clear the *User must change password at next logon* check box.
12. Click Create.

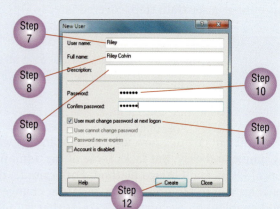

Removing or Disabling a User Account

You can either delete or disable a user account. Deleting it removes it entirely. Disabling it prevents it from appearing at Windows 7 startup as one of the choices, but retains its settings and documents in case you want to use them later. In the preceding steps, you saw how you can create a new account that starts out disabled; you can then enable it later, when you are ready to use it.

If you delete a user account, you are prompted to choose whether you want to keep its files or not. If you decide to keep its files, they are moved to a folder on your desktop.

To delete a user account:

1. Make sure you log on using an Administrator account.
2. Click Start, *Control Panel*.
3. Under User Accounts and Family Safety, click Add or remove user accounts.

4. Click the account to delete.
5. Click Delete the account.
6. Click Delete Files to remove the account's files, or click Keep Files to retain them.
7. Click Delete Account.

To disable a user account without deleting it:

1. Click Start.
2. Right-click *Computer* and click *Manage*.
3. Double-click Local Users and Groups.
4. Double-click Users.
5. Double-click the user to disable.
6. Mark the *Account is disabled* check box.
7. Click OK.

To reenable a disabled user account:

1. Click Start.
2. Right-click *Computer* and click *Manage*.
3. Double-click Local Users and Groups.
4. Double-click Users.
5. Double-click the user to enable.
6. Clear the *Account is disabled* check box.
7. Click OK.

There is a special account with the user name of Administrator that all Windows 7 systems have; it is not used for normal operations, but only for special administrative tasks such as repairing a Windows 7 installation. By default it is disabled. You can access it from the Local Users and Groups window, though, and you can enable it the same way you enable any other disabled account.

Setting, Resetting, or Changing an Account Password

A new account has no password by default. Microsoft recommends, however, that you assign a password to each Administrator account, to prevent unauthorized changes to the system settings.

Tip: For the best security, use strong passwords. A *strong password* is one that is difficult to guess. That means it has sufficient length (usually six characters or more), is not a word from the dictionary, includes both capital and lowercase letters, and includes both numbers and letters.

Strong password:
A password that is difficult to guess. Strong passwords have at least six characters, use numbers and letters, and use both capital and lowercase letters.

To set a password for the currently logged-on user (if one is not already set):

Here's How

1. Click Start, *Control Panel*.
2. Click User Accounts and Family Safety.
3. Click Change your Windows password.
4. Click Create a password for your account.

5. Type the desired password.
6. Repeat the password.
7. (Optional) Type a password hint.
8. Click Create Password.

To change the password for the currently logged-on user:

1. Click Start, *Control Panel*.
2. Click User Accounts and Family Safety.
3. Click Change your Windows password.
4. Click Change your password.
5. Type the current password.
6. Type the new password.
7. Repeat the new password.
8. (Optional) Type a password hint.
9. Click Change Password.

To remove the password for the currently logged-on user:

1. Click Start, *Control Panel*.
2. Click User Accounts and Family Safety.
3. Click User Accounts.
4. Click Remove your password.
5. Type the current password.
6. Click Remove Password.

To change the password for some other user account:

1. Log on as an Administrator.
2. Click Start, *Control Panel*.
3. Click User Accounts and Family Safety.
4. Click User Accounts.
5. Click Manage another account.
6. Click the account to change.
7. Click Change the password.
8. Type the current password.
9. Type the new password.
10. Repeat the new password.
11. (Optional) Type a password hint.
12. Click Change Password.

To remove the password for some other user account:

1. Log on as an Administrator.
2. Click Start, *Control Panel*.
3. Click User Accounts and Family Safety.
4. Click User Accounts.
5. Click Manage another account.
6. Click the account for which you want to remove the password.
7. Click Remove the password.
8. Type the current password.
9. Click Remove Password.

To force password change at next logon:

1. Click Start.
2. Right-click *Computer* and click *Manage*.
3. Double-click Local Users and Groups.
4. Double-click Users.
5. Double-click the user who requires a password change.
6. Mark the *User must change password at next logon* check box.
7. Click OK.

Creating a Password Reset Disk

You must know an account's password in order to change it, so if you forget a password, you may be out of luck for accessing that account. However, Windows 7 enables you to create a password reset disk using either a floppy disk or a USB flash drive. A password reset disk enables you to reset passwords to restore access to accounts that you are locked out of because you don't know their passwords.

You need to create a password reset disk only once for the logged-on account. Then no matter how many times you change the passwords after that point, you will still be able to reset them as long as you have the disk (or flash drive). That's because the password reset disk does not store the actual passwords; it just stores a code that grants permission to reset them.

Note: *A password reset disk is only for the currently logged-on account; if you want to be able to recover passwords for all accounts, you must repeat the process while logged onto each user account on your system.*

To create a password reset disk:

Here's How

1. Connect a USB flash drive or insert a blank floppy disk.
2. Click Start, *Control Panel*.
3. Click User Accounts and Family Safety.
4. Click User Accounts.
5. Click Create a password reset disk. The Forgotten Password Wizard opens.
6. Click Next.
7. From the drop-down list, choose the drive on which to create the password reset disk.

8. Click Next.
9. Type the current password for the logged-on account, or leave the box blank if there is currently no password.
10. Click Next.
11. Wait for the Wizard to finish, and then click Next.
12. Click Finish.

To use a password reset disk:

1. Restart Windows 7, so you see the logon screen where you are prompted to select a user and enter a password.
2. Connect the USB flash drive or insert the floppy disk containing the password reset data.
3. Leave the password box blank and click the arrow button to attempt a logon. A message appears that the user name or password is incorrect.
4. Click OK. A Reset password link appears below the logon box.
5. Click Reset password. The Password Reset Wizard runs.
6. Click Next.
7. Choose the drive on which the password reset data is stored and click Next.
8. Type the new password and then type it again to confirm.
9. (Optional) Type a password hint.
10. Click Next.
11. Click Finish.

Turning the Guest Account On or Off

A **guest account** enables visitors to your PC to use it without knowing the password for any of the user accounts. It is by nature a limited account; users logged on as Guest cannot make system changes.

The guest account is disabled by default, meaning that it does not appear on the Welcome screen when the PC starts up.

Guest account: A limited-access user account designed to be used by anonymous users who do not have a regular account on the PC

Here's How

To enable the Guest account:

1. Click Start, *Control Panel*.
2. Click User Accounts and Family Safety.
3. Click User Accounts.
4. Click Manage another account.
5. Click Guest.
6. Click Turn On.

To disable the Guest account:

1. Click Start, *Control Panel*.
2. Click User Accounts and Family Safety.
3. Click User Accounts.
4. Click Manage another account.
5. Click Guest.
6. Click Turn off the guest account.

Exercise 2

1. On a blank piece of paper, write your name and C15E02, or in a WordPad document, type your name and save the file as **C15E02**.
2. Log on using an Administrator account, if you are not already logged on that way.
3. Turn the Guest account on.
4. Create a new Standard user account called *Test*. Do not assign a password to it.
5. Set the Test account so the user is forced to change the password at first logon.
6. Log off, and log back on as the Test user. Set the account password to *Test*. Record the exact wording of the password prompt on your paper or in your file.
7. Try making changes to any Control Panel option that has a *Shield* icon on it. Note what happens, and record it.
8. Log off, and log back on as *Guest*.
9. Try making changes to any Control Panel option that has a *Shield* icon on it. Note what happens, and record it.
10. Log off, and log back on with the original account you used in Step 2 or the account you usually use (if different).
11. Submit your paper or file to your instructor for grading.

Using Encryption to Secure Files

By default, Windows 7 uses **NTFS** as its *file system*. Windows 7 also supports some older file systems for backward compatibility, such as **FAT16** and **FAT32**, but if you use NTFS you get some additional benefits in file management. One of these benefits is the ability to encrypt files.

Understanding Encryption

When multiple users share a PC, each user account has its own private file storage areas, including its libraries. Users cannot browse each other's libraries. However, when a user stores a file in a folder that all users can access, that file is unprotected and anyone may work with it.

Encrypting provides some security for a file that is stored in one of those public areas. When a user encrypts a file or folder, it becomes the private property of that user, and it can be accessed only when the user that created it is logged on. This is true regardless of its storage location, as long as it is stored on a drive that uses NTFS.

Encryption is based on the user account, not on a password (except in the sense that the user account itself has a password for logging on). As long as you are logged on as the user who encrypted the file, the encryption is invisible. The only indication that a file or folder is encrypted is that its name appears in green. You can encrypt either a folder or an individual file. When you encrypt a folder, everything inside that folder is also encrypted, but if you move any of those items outside the folder, they lose their encryption. On the other hand, when you encrypt an individual file, it remains encrypted as long as it is on an NTFS drive. (If you move it to a drive that uses some other file system, it becomes unencrypted.) Microsoft recommends encrypting folders rather than files whenever feasible because it is easier to keep track of what is encrypted that way.

NTFS: New Technology File System, a 32-bit file system for Windows 2000, Windows XP, Windows Vista, and Windows 7, offering improvements over older file systems

File System: A set of rules for how the operating system stores and retrieves files on a disk

FAT16: A 16-bit file system, now mostly obsolete, used with MS-DOS and Windows 95

FAT32: A 32-bit file system, now mostly obsolete, used with Windows 98 and Windows Me

Here's How

To encrypt a folder:

1. Right-click the folder and click *Properties*.
2. On the General tab, click Advanced.
3. Mark the *Encrypt contents to secure data* check box.
4. Click OK.
5. Click OK to close the Properties box.
6. Click *Apply changes to this folder, subfolders and files*.
7. Click OK.

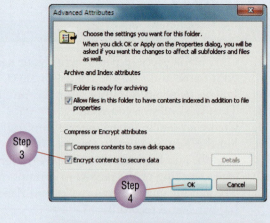

Step 3

Step 4

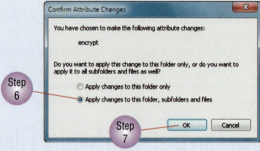

Step 6

Step 7

To encrypt an individual file:

1. Right-click the file and click *Properties*.
2. On the General tab, click Advanced.
3. Mark the *Encrypt contents to secure data* check box.
4. Click OK.
5. Click OK to close the Properties box.
6. Click *Encrypt the file only*.
7. Click OK.

To decrypt a folder or file:

1. Right-click the file and click *Properties*.
2. On the General tab, click Advanced.
3. Clear the *Encrypt contents to secure data* check box.
4. Click OK.
5. Click OK to close the Properties box.

QUICK FIX

Creating Another User
If there are no other users, you will need to create one first, as explained previously in this chapter.

Exercise 3

Encrypting and Decrypting Files

1. On a blank piece of paper, write your name and C15E03, or in a WordPad document, type your name and save the file as **C15E03**.
2. Open the Chapter 15 data folder.
3. Encrypt the file **EncryptMe.doc**. Encrypt only the individual file, not the folder.

   Note: *If prompted to back up your encryption certificate and key, click Back Up later.*

4. Log off, and log on as a different user.

5. Try to open **EncryptMe.doc**. Record the error message that appears, on your paper or in your file.
6. Log off, and log on using your original user account.
7. Copy the file **EncryptMe.doc** to the desktop. Is it still encrypted? Record the answer and explain how you determined this.
8. Decrypt the original **EncryptMe.doc**.
9. Encrypt the entire Chapter 15 data folder and all its contents.
10. Log off, and log on as a different user.
11. Try to open the Chapter 15 data folder. Record the error message that appears.
12. Log off, and log on using your original user account.
13. Copy the file **EncryptMe.doc** from the Chapter 15 folder to the desktop. Is it still encrypted? Record the answer and explain how you determined this.
14. Decrypt the Chapter 15 data folder.
15. Drag all copies you made on the desktop to the Recycle Bin.
16. Submit your paper or file to your instructor for grading.
17. Delete the new user account named Test.
18. [Optional] Disable the Guest user account.

CHAPTER Summary

- To view system information, from the Control Panel click System and Security, and then click System. You can also click Start and then right-click *Computer* and choose *Properties*.

- For more detailed information, choose Start, *All Programs*, *Accessories*, *System Tools*, *System Information*.

- To rate your system's performance, from the Control Panel choose System and Maintenance, Check your computer's Windows Experience Index base score.

- To view CPU and memory usage, display the Task Manager by right-clicking the taskbar and choosing *Task Manager*. Then click the Performance tab.

- Windows 7 security is handled via user accounts, which are secured by passwords.

- User Account Control (UAC) is a security feature that restricts certain activities based on the permission level of the logged-on user. Users can have either Administrator (full) or Standard (partial) permission level.

- To adjust the UAC level, from the Control Panel choose User Accounts and Family Safety, User Accounts, Change User Account Control settings.

- To create a user account, from the Control Panel choose User Accounts and Family Safety, Add or remove user accounts, Create a new account.

- To remove a user account, from the Control Panel choose User Accounts and Family Safety, Add or remove user accounts. Click the account, and then click Delete the account.

- A strong password is one that is difficult to guess.

- To change an account's password, from User Accounts and Family Safety, click Change your Windows password and follow the prompts.

- To enable or disable the Guest account on the system, from User Accounts and Family Safety, click User Accounts, Manage another account, Guest.

- The Windows 7 file system, NTFS (New Technology File System), enables users to encrypt files so that other people logged on to the same computer cannot view them.
- To encrypt a file or folder, right-click it and choose *Properties*, and on the General tab, click Advanced. Click *Encrypt contents to secure data*, and then click OK.

CONCEPTS Check

Completion: Answer the following questions on a blank sheet of paper or in a Word document.

Part

1

MULTIPLE CHOICE

1. Which piece of information is *not* available from the System section of the Control Panel?
   a. CPU speed
   b. CPU type
   c. Amount of RAM
   d. Display adapter

2. How do you find out the PC's Windows Experience Index score?
   a. Start, *All Programs*, *Accessories*, *System Tools*, *System Information*
   b. Start, *All Programs*, *Accessories*, *Performance*
   c. From Control Panel, in the System and Security section
   d. From the Control Panel, in the Advanced Tools section

3. Suppose a system has different subscores for each of the five performance areas. What is the PC's overall Windows Experience Index base score?
   a. The average of those numbers
   b. The lowest of those numbers
   c. The highest of those numbers
   d. None of the above

4. What two factors are measured on the Performance tab of the Task Manager?
   a. Hard disk access and CPU usage
   b. CPU usage and display adapter frames per second
   c. CPU usage and memory usage
   d. Number of applications running and number of services

5. If your system suddenly starts running sluggishly and your CPU usage is at 100 percent, what is probably the problem?
   a. Inadequate CPU
   b. Not enough RAM
   c. Malfunctioning application
   d. Bad device driver

6. The primary purpose of User Access Control (UAC) is to _____ .
   a. prevent users from reading each other's documents
   c. prevent virus infection
   b. enhance the effectiveness of the Windows Firewall
   d. prevent one user from making system changes that will affect other users

7. Which type of user is blocked from performing certain system activities via UAC?
   a. Remote
   b. Standard
   c. Administrator
   d. Roaming

8. What is the name of the built-in user account that is designed to allow people to use the PC who do not have their own individual user account on it?
   a. Standard
   b. Open
   c. Visitor
   d. Guest

9. When a file is encrypted, in what color does its file name appear?
   a. Black
   b. Red
   c. Green
   d. Blue

10. What happens when you copy a file (not individually encrypted) from an encrypted folder to an unencrypted one?
    a. The file stays encrypted.
    b. The file becomes unencrypted.
    c. An error message appears and the file does not copy.
    d. A shortcut rather than a true copy is created.

Part 2

SHORT ANSWER

11. What can you find out from System Information that you cannot glean from the System section of the Control Panel? List at least three things.

    _____

12. How is the Windows Experience Index base score determined?

    _____

13. What is the primary difference between the Windows Experience Index score and the performance information you can gather from the Task Manager's Performance tab?

    _____

14. What four factors can you monitor from the Resource Monitor?

    _____

15. What does a *Shield* symbol mean when it appears next to a link in the Control Panel?

    _____

16. Why does Microsoft recommend that you run Windows 7 as a Standard user rather than as an Administrator on a day-to-day basis?

    _____

17. Describe the two ways of creating a new user account, and explain the ways in which one of them is more powerful than the other.

_____

18. Why would you disable a user account rather than remove it?

_____

19. Describe the qualities of a strong password and give an example.

_____

20. Why would you typically not need to encrypt the Documents folder?

_____

SKILLS Check

Save all solution files to the default Documents folder, or any alternate folder specified by your instructor.

Guided Check

Assessment COLLECTING SYSTEM INFORMATION

1

1. Determine the model and speed of your PC's CPU and the amount of RAM it has.
   a. Click Start.
   b. Right-click *Computer* and click *Properties*.
   c. View the Processor and Memory (RAM) information in the System area.
   Processor model: _____
   RAM speed: _____
2. Determine the exact version of Windows 7 you have from System Information.
   a. Click Start, *All Programs, Accessories, System Tools, System Information*.
   b. Read the Version number from the System Summary.
   Windows version: _____
3. Determine the display adapter model from System Information.
   a. Double-click Components.
   b. Click Display.
   c. Read the display name on the top line of the right pane.
   Display adapter model: _____
4. Record your name, **C15A01**, and the information you gathered on a piece of paper or WordPad document, and submit it to your instructor for grading.

RATING SYSTEM PERFORMANCE

2

1. View your system's Windows Experience Index base score and determine which subsystem has the lowest score.
   a. Click Start, *Control Panel*.
   b. Click System and Security.
   c. Click Check the Windows Experience Index.
   d. Examine the information about the scores of each subsystem.
   Your system's overall score: _____
   Subsystem with lowest score: _____
2. Open the Resource Monitor.
   a. Right-click the taskbar.
   b. Click *Start Task Manager*.
   c. Click the Performance tab.
   d. Click Resource Monitor.
3. In the Resource Monitor window, make notes of the following information as you open and close several applications.
   Average usage level when using a small application such as Calculator:
   _____

   Average usage level when using a large application:
   Application: _____
   CPU usage: _____
   Highest usage percentage observed at any point: _____
4. Record your name, **C15A02**, and the information you gathered on a piece of paper or in a WordPad document, and submit it to your instructor for grading.

Assessment **CREATING AND DELETING USER ACCOUNTS**

3

1. Create a Standard user account (unless one already exists to which you have access).
   a. Make sure you log on using an Administrator account.
   b. Click Start, *Control Panel*.
   c. Under User Accounts and Family Safety, click Add or remove user accounts.
   d. Click Create a new account.
   e. Type Standard Student.
   f. Click *Standard User*.
   g. Click Create Account.
2. Set a password for Standard Student.
   a. Click the Standard Student account you just created.
   b. Click Create a password.
   c. Type student in the *New password* box.
   d. Type student in the *Confirm new password* box.
   e. Click Create password.
3. Capture a screen shot of the Manage Accounts window showing icons for each user account on the system at this point. Name the file **C15A03S03** and submit it for grading.
4. Log off, and log on as Standard Student.
   a. Click Start.
   b. Click the right-pointing arrow in the bottom-right corner of the Start menu.
   c. Click Log off.
   d. Click Standard Student.
   e. Type student and press Enter.

5. Open the Control Panel and attempt to create another user account.
   a. Click Start, *Control Panel*.
   b. Under User Accounts and Family Safety, click Add or remove user accounts.
   c. Note the error that appears.
6. Remove the password from the Standard Student account.
   a. Click Start, *Control Panel*.
   b. Click User Accounts and Family Safety.
   c. Click Remove your password.
   d. Type student in the *Current password* box.
   e. Click Remove Password.
   f. Close the User Accounts window.
7. Log off and log on as the user you were originally logged on as.
   a. Click Start.
   b. Click the right-pointing arrow in the bottom-right corner of the Start menu.
   c. Click Log off.
   d. Click your user account.
   e. If prompted for a password, type it and press Enter.
8. Delete the Standard Student account.
   a. Make sure you logged on using an Administrator account.
   b. Click Start, *Control Panel*.
   c. Under User Accounts and Family Safety, click Add or remove user accounts.
   d. Click Standard Student.
   e. Click Delete the account.
   f. Click Delete Files.
   g. Click Delete Account.
9. Enable the Guest account.
   a. Click Guest.
   b. Click Turn On.
10. Capture a screen shot of the Manage Accounts window at this point, showing that the Standard Student account has been deleted and the Guest account enabled. Name the file **C15A03S10** and submit it for grading.
11. Disable the Guest account.
    a. Click Guest.
    b. Click Turn off the Guest account.

Assessment ENCRYPT FILES

4

1. Encrypt the entire Paradigm Windows 7 folder on your hard disk.
   a. Right-click the Paradigm Windows 7 folder and click *Properties*.
   b. On the General tab, click Advanced.
   c. Click *Encrypt contents to secure data*.
   d. Click OK.
   e. Click OK to close the Properties box.
   f. Click *Apply changes to this folder, subfolders and files*.
   g. Click OK.
2. Copy the Chapter 15 data folder to a USB flash drive.
   a. Double-click the Paradigm Windows 7 folder.
   b. Select the Chapter 15 data folder and press Ctrl+C.
   c. Display the USB flash drive contents.
   d. Press Ctrl+V.

3. Log on as a different user. Create a new user account if needed.
   a. Click Start.
   b. Click the right-pointing arrow in the bottom-right corner of the Start menu.
   c. Click Log off.
   d. Click a different user account than you used previously.
   e. If prompted for a password, type it and press Enter.
4. Attempt to access the Chapter 15 data folder both on the hard disk and on the USB flash drive.
5. Write a brief explanation of what happened when you tried each. Name it **C15A04** and submit it to your instructor for grading.
6. Log back on using the original user account you started out with.
7. Remove encryption from the Paradigm Windows 7 folder.
   a. Right-click the Paradigm Windows 7 folder and click *Properties*.
   b. On the General tab, click Advanced.
   c. Clear the *Encrypt contents to secure data* check box.
   d. Click OK.
   e. Click OK to close the Properties box.

On Your Own

Assessment COMPARING INFORMATION FROM DIFFERENT UTILITIES

5

1. Open the System Information utility.
2. Open Device Manager. (Device Manager was covered in Chapter 14.)
3. In Device Manager, choose View, *Resources by type*.
4. Compare the information presented in the Hardware Resources section of System Information to the information shown in Device Manager.
5. Write a report summarizing the major differences and similarities, and describe situations where one or the other might be more useful. Name it **C15A05S05**.
6. Open the System Configuration utility (MSCONFIG).
7. Click Start, type msconfig, and press Enter. (This utility was covered in Chapter 13.)
8. On the System Configuration window, click the Startup tab.
9. In the System Information window, open the Software Environment category and click Startup Programs.
10. Compare the information presented in the two windows.
11. Write a report summarizing the major differences and similarities, and describe situations where one or the other might be more useful. Name it **C15A05S11**.
12. Submit your reports to your instructor for grading.
13. Close all open windows.

Assessment PLANNING SYSTEM IMPROVEMENTS

6

1. Complete Assessment 1 to get a snapshot of your system's performance and bottleneck areas.
2. Formulate a plan for improving the system's Windows Experience Index base score, which might include buying new hardware, finding new drivers, or other activities.
3. Research online the prices and availability of the solution you propose.
4. Write a report explaining your plan, its benefits, and its estimated cost. Name it **C15A06** and submit it to your instructor for grading.

Assessment

7

EXPERIMENTING WITH USER ACCESS CONTROL

1. Click Start, type **secpol.msc**, and press Enter.
2. Open Local Policies/Security Options.
3. Make sure that User Account Control: Behavior of the elevation prompt for standard users is set to *Prompt for credentials*.
4. Log off, and log on as a Standard user. (Create a standard account first if none exists.)
5. Try to access something in the Control Panel that a standard user would not normally be able to access. Record the exact wording of the message or prompt that appears on a piece of paper or in a Notepad or WordPad file. Name it **C15A07**.
6. Log off, and log on with an Administrator-level user account.
7. Open the Local Security Policy utility (**secpol.msc**).
8. Open Local Policies/Security Options.
9. Set User Account Control: Behavior of the elevation prompt for standard users to *Automatically deny elevation requests*.
10. Log off, and log on as a Standard user.
11. Try to access something in the Control Panel that a standard user would not normally be able to access. Record the exact wording of the message or prompt that appears.
12. Log off, and log on with an Administrator-level user account.
13. Turn User Access Control off altogether and restart the PC.
14. When the PC reboots, log on as a Standard user.
15. Try to access something in the Control Panel that a standard user would not normally be able to access. Observe what happens.
16. Write a report explaining what happened at Steps 5, 11, and 15 in your **C15A07** paper or file, and submit it to your instructor for grading.
17. Reset User Access Control to its default (restart your computer afterward, if necessary).

Assessment

8

EXPERIMENTING WITH ENCRYPTION

1. Encrypt an individual file (any file from the Windows 7 folder).
2. Make copies of that file in as many of these locations as you have access to:
   - In a different folder on the same hard disk
   - On a different hard disk that also uses the NTFS file system
   - On a hard disk that uses the FAT16 or FAT32 file system
   - On the Windows 7 desktop
   - On a USB flash drive
   - On a floppy disk
   - On a writable CD or DVD disc
3. Log off, and log on as a different user.
4. Try to access each of those copies. Write a report listing which ones you could access and which ones you could not. Try to determine on what basis some copies were available and others were not, and include your hypothesis as to why this is so in your report. Name the report **C15A08** and submit it for grading.

CHALLENGE Project

Your company is considering purchasing a new 3-D graphics application. The product has the following minimum requirements:

- Windows Vista or higher
- 2 GHz or faster CPU
- 2 GB of RAM
- CD or DVD drive
- Display adapter with at least 128 MB video RAM
- Hard disk drive with at least 2 GB of free space

1. Gather information about your system, and determine whether it meets these requirements in every area.
2. Write a brief report explaining how you gathered the needed information and comparing the system's actual specifications to the required ones. Name the report **C15A09**.
3. Given that often the minimum specifications for a program are just that—minimums—and often insufficient for that program's top performance, how likely is it that this program will run at its top performance on your current PC? Explain your answer.

CHAPTER 16

Sharing Information On and Off the Road

PERFORMANCE OBJECTIVES

Upon successful completion of Chapter 16, you will be able to:

- Synchronize folders and PCs
- Fix syncing problems
- Set up your system to use offline folders
- Set an offline folder and work offline
- View Web content offline
- Enable Remote Desktop connections and specify allowed users
- Make a Remote Desktop connection
- Prepare to collaborate with other users
- Use Windows Mobility Center to manage battery power and more
- Use Presentation features
- Conserve battery power on a Mobile PC

Today's mobile computers and devices facilitate a "work anywhere" environment like never before. Windows 7 includes a number of features to help you work more effectively with mobile computers in the business environment. This chapter shows you how to use the mobile computing and networking functions offered in Windows 7.

Syncing Files between Computers

Synchronization (a.k.a. sync) is the process of keeping multiple copies of the same file matched with each other. For example, if you have the same document on your desktop PC and your notebook PC, the Sync feature can make sure that every time the two computers connect with one another, they compare notes about who has the more recent version, and the PC containing the older copy updates itself from the newer copy.

Windows 7 syncing is handled via the Sync Center, shown in Figure 16.1. It helps you keep files synced between mobile devices such as phones, music players, and cameras and your PC, and with network locations.

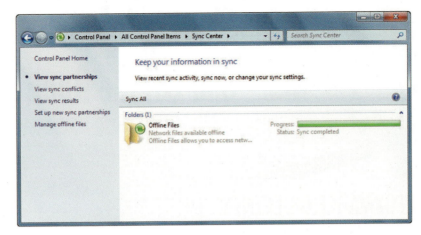

Figure 16.1 The Sync Center manages synchronization settings; access it from the Start menu.

Here's How ▶ To open the Sync Center:

Click Start, click *All Programs*, click *Accessories*, and then click *Sync Center*.

OR

1. Click Start, *Control Panel*.
2. Click *View by*, and then click *Large icons*.
3. Click Sync Center.

Note: *Syncing with network locations is not supported in the Starter or Home Premium versions of Windows 7.*

When you issue a command to perform synchronization, the Sync Center compares the versions in each location. If they are already identical, it does nothing. If they are different, it determines which version to keep and which to replace. If it finds a new file in one place, it copies it to the other; if it finds that you have deleted a file, it deletes it from the other. (You set up rules to tell it which location should be the ruling one when locations differ in their content.)

Before you can use the Sync Center, you must have something to synchronize. The next section explains how to set up offline files for this purpose.

Making Files Available Offline

Offline files: Network files that are locally cached (saved) on your hard disk so that a copy will always be available even when the network is not functioning; also refers generically to the copies of the network files stored on your local computer

When important files are stored on a network, and then the network becomes unavailable for a period of time, anyone who needs to use those files is out of luck. Depending on the nature of the files, this can be a significant inconvenience. *Offline files* help with this problem by storing copies of those network files locally on your own hard disk. That way if the network copy is unavailable, you can still use the local copy.

You can set an individual file or an entire folder to be available offline. The only criteria are that the location must exist on some other PC than your own and that both locations are on the same network. You can synchronize between a desktop PC and a notebook, between two notebooks, or any other combination.

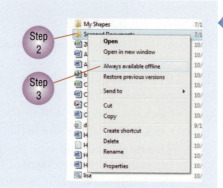
To set a file or folder for offline use:

1. Using the Computer window (Start, *Computer, Network*), browse to the folder or file on the network.
2. Right-click the folder or file.
3. Click *Always available offline*.

Viewing Synchronization Status

Once you have set up at least one file or folder to be available offline, synchronization occurs automatically in the background. A *Sync Center* icon appears among the hidden icons, visible by clicking the Show hidden icons button in the notification area (see Figure 16.2); you can click this icon to display the Sync Center.

In the Sync Center, you can check the synchronization status by clicking the View sync results choice in the list at the left. If there are any errors, they appear in the Sync Results; otherwise, messages appear here showing the sync started and completed normally, as in Figure 16.3. When a sync runs, a progress bar appears. After the sync finishes, if there are any errors, a link identifying the number of errors appears. Clicking that link is another method of viewing errors. Click View sync partnerships in the list at the left side of Sync Center to return to the starting point for syncing.

Sync Center icon

Figure 16.2 The *Sync Center* icon appears in the notification area after the first Synchronization.

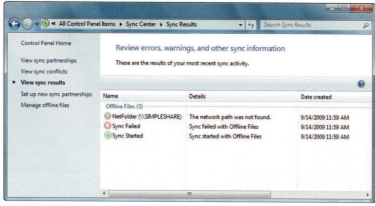

Figure 16.3 Display information about the most recent sync activity.

Setting Up a Sync Partnership

If you have a portable device such as a digital music player, PDA, or compatible mobile phone with which you want to sync information, you also can accomplish that through Sync Center if you prefer to use it rather than Device Stage.

QUICK FIX

No Offline Files Feature Is Available

If you are not able to take files offline, then your system probably has a consumer version of Windows 7 that does not support this feature. If you are a mobile worker and this feature is of interest, then you will need to upgrade to one of the more fully functional Windows 7 versions that supports it, such as the Professional or Ultimate version. Or, you may not have the Offline Files feature that works with Sync Center enabled. See the section "Working with Network Information Offline" to learn more.

To create a sync partnership:

1. With Sync Center open, attach the device to your system and power it on.
2. In the Tasks list at the left side of Sync Center, click *Set up new sync partnerships*. Sync Center lists available devices to sync.
3. Click the device to add in the list.
4. Click Set up above the list.
5. This establishes the sync partnership and performs the first sync, such as launching Windows Media Player to sync song files. A dialog box from that application might prompt you to specify what information to sync. Make your choices and click Finish.
6. Click View sync partnerships, and then you can see the newly listed sync partnership for the device.
7. Click the item in the list.
8. Click the Sync button to perform the first sync. (The button changes to a Stop button so that you can stop the sync, if desired.)

To remove a sync partnership, right-click it and click *Delete*.

Tip: Double-click the Offline Files choice in Sync Center to view the individual synced locations. Click an individual location to select it for manual syncing, change its settings, or delete the sync partnership. Click View sync partnerships in the list at left to return to the highest-level items.

Scheduling Synchronization

Synchronization occurs automatically by default, but you may want to adjust its frequency and set up a certain time at which files should be synchronized. For example, you might want synchronization to occur in the middle of the night, when network load is at its lowest point.

To schedule synchronization, click the Schedule button in the Sync Center, and then follow the prompts to set up a specific time and interval.

To schedule synchronization:

1. Open the Sync Center (Start, *All Programs, Accessories, Sync Center*).
2. Select the item to sync, such as Offline Files or a specific folder within Offline Files.
3. Click the Schedule button.
4. Mark or clear check boxes for the items to sync. The items listed here are the remote folders/files you have previously set up to be available offline.
5. Click Next.
6. Select the way the sync will be triggered:
   - At a scheduled time
   - On an event or action

7. If you chose *At a scheduled time* in Step 6, specify a start date and time and how often the sync should repeat. Or if you chose *On an event or action* in Step 6, mark the check boxes for the events that should trigger the sync.

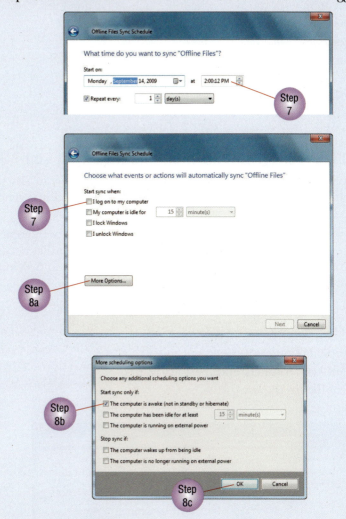

8. (Optional) Set additional options as follows:
    a. Click More Options.
    b. Mark or clear check boxes as desired to fine-tune the scheduling.
    c. Click OK.
9. Click Next.
10. Type a name for the sync schedule.
11. Click Save schedule.

To edit an existing sync schedule:

1. Open the Sync Center (Start, *All Programs, Accessories, Sync Center*).
2. Select the item with the sync schedule, such as Offline Files.
3. Click the Schedule button.
4. Click *View or edit an existing sync schedule*.
5. Click the sync schedule you want to change.
6. Click Next.
7. Complete Steps 4–11 of the preceding procedure.

To delete a sync schedule:

1. Open the Sync Center (Start, *All Programs, Accessories, Sync Center*).
2. Select the item with the sync schedule, such as Offline Files.
3. Click the Schedule button.
4. Click *Delete an existing sync schedule*.
5. Click the sync schedule to delete.
6. Click Delete.
7. Click OK.

Performing a Manual Synchronization and Resolving Conflicts

In addition to following a synchronization schedule, Windows 7 can also perform manual synchronization any time you request it. To initiate a manual sync, click the item to sync in the Sync Center, and then click the Sync button.

When a network connection is temporarily unavailable and both copies are edited in the interim, the next time you try to synchronize, a conflict occurs. That is because both the local and the network version have changed, and Windows 7 is not sure which changes should prevail.

To resolve a sync conflict:

1. Open the Sync Center, if needed.
2. Click View sync conflicts in the list at the left.
3. Click a conflict in the list.
4. Click Resolve.

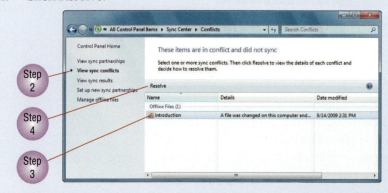

5. Select the version you want to keep, or choose to keep both versions.

 ## Exercise 1

1. Click Start, *Computer, Network*.
2. Use the navigation pane to browse to a network location that contains one or more documents. Your instructor may provide a path to a network location to use for this exercise. If not, you can use any folder on any shared drive, either on a file server or on another user's PC. To keep it simple, try a document in plain text or RTF format.
3. Make one or more network documents or folders always available offline from your PC:
   a. Right-click the document.
   b. Click *Always available offline*.
4. Allow the sync to complete, and then close the window.
5. Disconnect your network connection. You can open the Network and Sharing Center and disable the wireless connection from there. If it is a wired connection, unplug the network cable from the back of your PC.
6. Open Sync Center (Start, *All Programs, Accessories, Sync Center*).
7. Click Manage offline files in the list at the left.
8. Click the View your offline files button.
9. In the window that appears, browse again to that network document. (You may have to start from the *Computers* icon.) Ordinarily you would not be able to do this, but because Offline Files are active by default, you will be able to browse the local copies of the files in that location. You will see Offline Files Folder in the path in the Address bar, and the folder icon on the taskbar will have a sync symbol on it.
10. Capture a screen print of the file window, showing the *Offline Files* icon next to each of the files or folders. Name the file **C16E01S10**.
11. Open an offline document file in that location (look for the sync symbol in the lower left corner of the file's icon) and make a minor change to it; then save and close it.
12. Reconnect the network connection.
13. Sync the files:
    a. Open the Sync Center.
    b. Click Offline Files.
    c. Click the Sync button.
14. If any conflicts occurred (which may happen if other students also opened and modified the same file and then synchronized their changes), choose to keep the copy on your own local hard disk.
15. Submit the screen shot via e-mail or USB flash drive to your instructor, as required.

Working with Network Information Offline

Many business mobile computer users use their computers in two ways—standalone systems and connected to a company or organization network. There are cases where some files that the user needs to work with need to be stored in a network folder—as a safety measure to ensure a backup copy is available, or so that those files are available to other users of the network. This creates a problem when the mobile computer user is away from or otherwise not connected to the network and needs to work on the files.

The solution for this feature is the Offline Files feature in Windows 7. When offline files is enabled (the default setting), you can mark a folder or file on the network to make it ***available offline***, as you've already learned. This creates a copy of the folder and files to a special location on your computer's hard disk, also called a local hard disk in this instance. When you are away from the network, or if

Available offline: A folder identified to be synchronized via the offline files feature

you, for some reason, lose your network connection, you can work on those offline files as you normally would. When you later reconnect to the network, the Offline Files features works with the Sync Center to synchronize the offline and network copies of the files automatically.

Enabling Offline Folder and File Use

Although offline files works with the Sync Center that you learned about already in this chapter, you can enable and disable this feature as needed. This process requires rebooting the system, so make sure that you have saved and closed any files with new work before turning Offline Files on or off.

Here's How **To enable or disable Offline Files**

1. Click Start, *All Programs, Accessories, Sync Center*.
2. Click Manage offline files in the list at the left.
3. In the Offline Files dialog box, click the Enable offline files button on the General tab. If Online Files is already running and you need to disable it, the button reads Disable offline files, so click it.
4. If a User Account Control dialog box appears, enter the administrator password, and click Yes.
5. Click OK.
6. In the Offline Files dialog box that appears and asks whether to restart your computer, click Yes. The system restarts, and Offline Files is active when it does so.

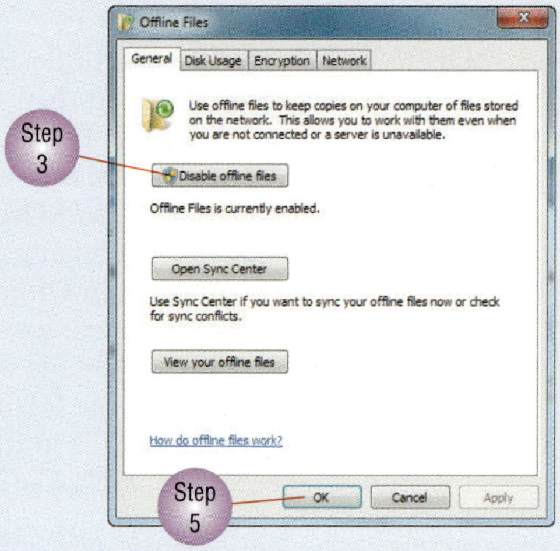

Making a File or Folder Available Offline

Once you have enabled offline files you can quickly set up a file or folder to make it available offline. To do so, navigate to the location that holds the folder or file you want to make available offline. Right-click the folder or file icon, and click *Always available offline*.

The first time you set up a folder for offline uses, you should wait a few minutes to ensure that Windows 7 synchronizes the files properly. This process may appear to take place immediately, but it may take some minutes behind the scenes.

You can identify a folder or file marked for offline uses by looking closely at it in an Explorer window. The folder or file icon will include an added Sync Center logo, like the example shown in Figure 16.4.

To unmark a file or folder for offline use, right-click it and click the *Always available offline* choice to remove the check beside it.

Figure 16.4 **The logo in the lower-left corner of the icon identifies that the folder or file is set up for offline use.**

Viewing Your Offline Folders and Files

The process of "switching" between online (on the network) and offline is seamless to the user. Once you have marked a network folder to be available for offline use, if your system disconnects from the network because you have left the office, or, for some reason, have lost the network connection, you can use the Sync Center to access your files.

To go to the Offline Files folder window, choose Start, *All Programs*, *Accessories*, *Sync Center*. Click Manage offline files in the list at the left. In the Offline Files dialog box, click the View your offline files button. The window that then appears looks like any other Explorer window, but shows the contents of the Offline Files Folder on your system (Figure 16.5). From there, you should be able to navigate to and open the offline folders and files. In some cases, you will need to start by selecting the *Computers* icon.

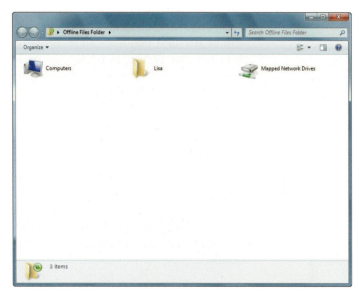

Figure 16.5 **You can access copies of your offline files by clicking the View your offline files button in the Offline Files dialog box to display this window.**

> **Tip:** Exercise 1 includes steps for viewing offline files. If you skipped that exercise, you can go back to it now to practice this skill.

Work offline: Disconnect from the network or Internet and instead use offline files or offline Web information

Occasionally, while you are working via your network connection (not in your Offline Files folder), the connection may make working with a particular file or folder slow. If you have already marked the file or folder for offline use, you can disconnect from the location on the network manually to **work offline**. To disconnect and go offline, click the Work offline button that appears on the command bar (Figure 16.6) when you browse to a location that is marked for offline use. After you click the button, it changes to the Work online button, which you can click to go back online.

Note that you can sync offline files manually at any time by clicking the Sync button that appears on the command bar (refer to Figure 16.6), and then clicking *Sync offline files in this folder if it appears* when you browse to the location marked for offline use. You also can use the Sync Center to sync offline files.

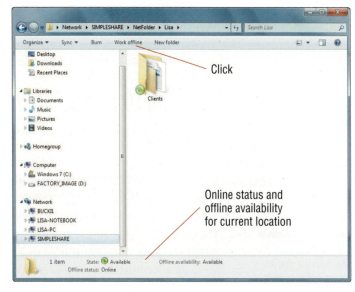

Figure 16.6 **Use the Work offline button to go offline manually.**

Viewing Web Content Offline

You also can switch to offline viewing when browsing the Web in Internet Explorer (IE). This can be useful if you have an insecure or pricey Internet connection, as when you are browsing via a "free" dialup plan where your usage minutes are limited. You can browse to a page, wait until it fully loads, go offline, read the contents, and then go back online when you are ready to move to the next page.

Figure 16.7 **You also can go offline and back online in Internet Explorer.**

To go offline after you have viewed a Web page, click Tools on the IE toolbar, and click *Work Offline*, as shown in Figure 16.7. *[Working Offline]* appears to the right of the Web site or page name in the IE title bar. To resume working online, click Tools, *Work Offline* again to remove the check beside it.

Exercise 2

Going Offline While Browsing

1. Click the Internet Explorer button on the taskbar to launch Internet Explorer.
2. Browse to the www.emcp.com Web site.
3. Click the Paradigm image at left on the home page, and then click the Visit Site button at the bottom.
4. In the navigation bar at the left, click *Company Info*, and then click the *Our Commitment to Service* link in the box at the top of the page that appears.
5. After the page loads, click Tools, and then click *Work Offline*.
6. Click the Back button. A Webpage unavailable while offline message box appears.
7. Capture a screen shot, paste it into Paint, and save the file as **C16E02S07**.
8. Click *Stay Offline*.
9. Click Tools, and then click *Work Offline* again.
10. Click Back. The prior EMC/Paradigm Web page viewed should reappear.
11. Click the window Close (X) button to close IE.
12. Submit the screen shot via e-mail or USB flash drive to your instructor, as required.

Connecting to a System with Remote Desktop

The Remote Desktop capability goes beyond giving you the simple ability to work with copies of files offline. With a Remote Desktop connection, you can connect to another computer over the local network or the Internet. Not only can you access files on the computer, but you also can use the programs installed on that computer and possibly other resources, such as printers, if the network permits.

Making a Remote Desktop connection works like this:

Host: The computer that holds the files, programs, and resources to be used during a Remote Desktop connection

- The computer that holds the files, programs, and other resources to access is called the *host*. This computer must use a Windows version that enables it to serve as a Remote Desktop host. Window XP Professional, and the Business, Enterprise, and Ultimate Editions of Windows Vista and Windows 7 enable a computer to serve as a host. The host computer must be set up to allow

Remote Desktop connections, and the host computer must be turned on. The host computer might be your desktop computer at work that has the working files and programs you need to complete a project.

- The computer that you will use to access the host from a remote location is called the **client**. This computer can be running any version of Windows 7 or Vista, as well as either version of Windows XP, as long as the Remote Desktop client software has been downloaded from Microsoft and installed, if needed. The client computer might be your mobile computer for work, with which you are accessing the Internet wirelessly or over the company network, for example.

- Both computers must be connected directly to the company network or connected remotely to the company network via the Internet and on the same workgroup. The network must allow permission for this type of connection. Windows Firewall also has to be set on both computers to allow Remote Desktop as an Exception. Also, if authentication is not required, then that security feature must be turned off on the host computer.

Client: The remote computer accessing the host resources during a Remote Desktop connection

If your office desktop computer is set up to serve as the host and is connected to the company network, you could connect to your desktop over the company's network with your mobile computer while in a colleague's office to demonstrate a new piece of software, for example. Or, if you live quite a distance from work and need to do some work at home, you could leave the office system on and connected to the Internet just in case you need to log on and transfer some files or access a program not installed on your mobile computer, such as a corporate accounting program.

Enabling Your Computer for Remote Desktop Connections

Enabling your Windows 7 computer to serve as the host for Remote Desktop connections might sound intimidating, but you turn the feature on easily through Control Panel.

To enable Remote Desktop connections to your computer (the host):

1. Click Start, and then click *Control Panel*.
2. Click System and Security.
3. Click the Allow remote access link in the System category. If a User Account Control dialog box appears, enter the administrator password, and click Yes. The System Properties dialog box appears with the Remote tab selected. (Click the tab if it isn't selected.)

Here's How

4. Click one of the following two options:
   - *Allow connections from computers running any version of Remote Desktop (less secure).* This choice enables you to connect to a computer over a connection with less security.
   - *Allow connections only from computers running Remote Desktop with Network Level Authentication (more secure).* Use this choice to log on to networks that require logon authentication. When this method is enabled, Remote Desktop will be required to complete an additional authentication logon to make the connection.

Trouble Going Remote?
Please note that these procedures cover working with Remote Desktop Connection on a Windows 7 system only. Consult Help on these procedures if you are using an earlier Windows version.

5. If a Remote Desktop message box warns you about the system being set for sleep and hibernate, click OK.

6. Click OK.

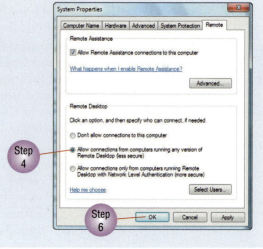

Specifying Who Can Connect via Remote Desktop

For security reasons, the ability to connect to a host system via Remote Desktop works by inclusion. On the host system, you have to identify each user who is allowed to connect. Generally speaking, you should add yourself (because you might be signing on to your own system from another system to fix it) or any other users who have a user account on the host system).

To add yourself or another user to the list of users who can log on to the host system:

1. On the host system, click Start, and then click *Control Panel*.

2. Click System and Security.

3. Click the Allow remote access link in the System category. If a User Account Control dialog box appears, enter the administrator password, and click Yes. The System Properties dialog box appears with the Remote tab selected. (Click the tab if it isn't selected.)

4. Click Select Users.

5. Click Add in the Remote Desktop Users dialog box.

6. Type the user's name in the *Enter the object names to select* box of the Select Users dialog box.

7. Click OK.

8. Click OK three times, and close Control Panel.

Can't Log On

To connect to a host system with Remote Desktop, you must use a user account that has a password. If your user account on the host system does not have a password, edit the account to include one.

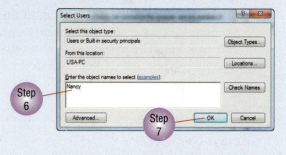

Making a Remote Desktop Connection

To connect remotely to another PC, your PC and the remote one must both be connected to a common network and both must be powered up. You can then start Remote Desktop and make the connection.

To connect to a host computer via Remote Desktop:

1. On the client computer, choose Start, *All Programs, Accessories, Remote Desktop Connection*. (The command is Start, *Programs, Accessories, Communication, Remote Desktop Connection* if you are connecting to a Windows 7 host from a computer with XP.)

2. In the Remote Desktop Connection dialog box, type the name of the computer to connect to on the network in the Computer text box. (Or, if you click the drop-down list arrow, you can click a listed computer or browse for another, depending on the version of Windows that you are using and how the network is set up.) For some networks, you may need to type the host system's IP address. For connecting over the Internet, you need to include both the domain name and computer name.

3. Click Connect.

4. Type your user name (the one you added to the host system) in the top *User name* text box.

5. Type your password in the bottom *Password* text box.

6. Click OK.

7. If a message informs you that Remote Desktop cannot verify the host computer's identity, click Yes.

8. If your remote system is on a network that requires authentication, you will be prompted to enter that information. Do so at the prompt and click OK or Connect to continue.

9. If you see a message that another user is logged on to the host and your logon will cause that user to be logged off, click Yes.

Here's How

QUICK FIX

Need to Use Another User Name

Note that if you have previously logged on to the host, the Windows Security dialog box will already display your user name, so you can skip this step; to try another user name in this case, click the *Use another account* or *Log on as a another user* choice and use the new *User name* and *Password* text boxes that appear.

Step 2

Step 3

Step 4

Step 5

Step 6

Note: *Some Remote Desktop connections require a Terminal Services Gateway (TS Gateway) for connecting to a corporate network and may require the assistance of your network administrator. You can click Options in the Remote Desktop Connection dialog box, click the Advanced tab, and then click the Settings button to change TS Gateway settings as advised by your system administrator.*

When the remote desktop appears, at first it will be maximized on the desktop. Click the Restore Down button on the control bar at the top to reduce it to a window (Figure 16.8). With the window, you can start programs, view folders and files, and perform other needed activities using the resources of the

Figure 16.8 **Running a Windows Vista machine on the Windows 7 desktop with Remote Desktop.**

host computer. To close the connection, close the window. In the Remote Desktop Connection dialog box that prompts you to confirm the disconnect, click OK.

Logging On to People Near Me

Collaboration programs like Microsoft Office Groove enable people on nearby computers to connect to one another to collaborate in working with applications. "Nearby" is a relative term, but generally refers to computers that are on the same workgroup as you or on the same wireless access point or subnet.

There are two parts to setting up a connection with another computer user: enabling the People Near Me feature and then starting up the collaboration (or peer-to-peer) program. People Near Me is part of Windows 7, so it will be covered here. The collaboration software must be selected and installed by the user's organization, and therefore is outside the scope of this book.

People Near Me is a networking session that enables other computer users to invite you to online collaboration meetings and to participate in other sharing activities through other software, as well.

To make your PC available for such connections, you can sign in to People Near Me via the Control Panel.

Here's How

To sign in to People Near Me:

1. Click Start, *Control Panel*.
2. Type **People** in the *search* box.
3. Click *Sign in or out of People Near Me*.
4. Click the *Sign in to People Near Me* option button.
5. Click the Settings tab.
6. (Optional) Change the user name if desired.
7. (Optional) Mark or clear the check box in the Options section for automatic sign-in.
8. Click OK.

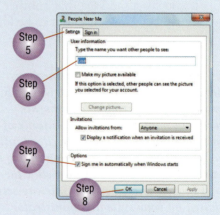

To sign out of People Near Me:

1. Click Start, *Control Panel*.
2. Type **People** in the *search* box.
3. Click *Sign in or out of People Near Me*.
4. Click *Sign out of People Near Me*.
5. Click OK.

 **Exercise 3**

Make a Remote Desktop Connection

Note: *This exercise requires you to have access to two PCs that are both running Windows 7 and are on the same network. One person can do this with two PCs, or two people can do the exercise together each on his or her own PC. One PC will be arbitrarily designated "A" and the other one "B." Your instructor will provide an administrator password. Both users should be logged on to an account with a password.*

1. Enable Remote Desktop Connection on both PCs:
    a. Choose Start, *Control Panel*, System and Security.
    b. Click the Allow remote access link in the System category. If a User Account Control dialog box appears, enter the administrator password, and click Yes. The System Properties dialog box appears with the Remote tab selected. (Click the tab if it isn't selected.)
    c. Click *Allow connections from computers running any version of Remote Desktop (less secure)*.
    d. If a Remote Desktop message box warns you about the system being set for sleep and hibernate, click OK.
    e. Click OK.
2. On PC A, start Remote Desktop Connection (if the connection isn't successful, specify users who can connect using the steps shown previously in this chapter):
    a. Click Start, *All Programs, Accessories, Remote Desktop Connection*.
    b. Enter the name of PC B in the *Computer* text box. (This is its name in the system properties, accessed by clicking Start, right-clicking *Computer* in the Start menu, and then clicking *Properties*.)
    c. Click Connect.
    d. Enter or select the user name.
    e. Enter the password.
    f. Click OK, and then click Yes if prompted that the identity of the remote system can't be verified.
3. On PC A, open Control Panel in the Remote Desktop session:
    a. Click Start, *Control Panel*.
    b. If the Remote Desktop Connection window appears maximize, click the Restore Down button on the control bar at the top middle area of the screen.
    c. The user of PC A should take a screen shot of the desktop, paste it into Paint, and name it **C16E03S03**.
4. On PC A, stop the Remote Desktop Connection:
    a. Click the connection window Close (X) button.
    b. Click OK when prompted to finish disconnecting.
5. Reverse roles, and repeat Steps 2–4 above to connect to PC A from PC B. The user of PC B should take a screen shot as instructed from his or her own computer, so that each user has a screen shot of the connection that they made.
6. Submit the screen shots via e-mail or USB flash drive to your instructor, as required.

Improving Notebook Performance

Windows 7 collects a variety of system settings useful to road warriors in a new section of Control Panel called Windows Mobility Center. Mobility Center provides the settings you need for activities such as choosing another power management method, syncing, and working with settings for presentations.

Using the Windows Mobility Center

You can open Windows Mobility Center via Control Panel.

Here's How

To start Windows Mobility Center:

1. Click Start, and then click *Control Panel*.
2. Click Hardware and Sound.
3. Click Windows Mobility Center.

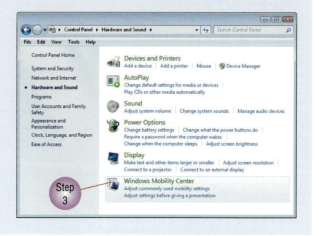

Figure 16.9 **Use Windows Mobility Center to access settings you will work with often for your mobile PC.**

As shown in Figure 16.9, Windows Mobility Center collects settings for Volume, Battery Status, Wireless Network, External Display, Sync Center, and Presentation Settings.

If you have not yet set up sync partnerships, you can click Sync Settings to do so. If sync partnerships are already in place, a Sync button appears; you can click that to sync files immediately. Use the button in the *Wireless Network* section to turn wireless networking on and off, a feature you might use for security reasons. You can also adjust the display brightness here and connect to an external display. When you finish using Windows Mobility Center, you can click its window Close (X) button to close it; then close Control Panel, as well.

Viewing and Managing Battery Power

One important factor to manage for a mobile PC is its power consumption when it is not plugged in to a power outlet. Battery charge life has not improved by leaps and bounds in recent years as have other aspects of computer efficiency, so it pays to make sure the system has the right power settings if you know you will be away from a power source for some time.

Figure 16.10 **Check your mobile PC's battery level frequently in the notification area.**

When you are using your mobile computer on battery power alone, get in the habit of moving the mouse pointer over the *Battery Meter* icon in the system notification area. When you do so, information about the current battery level (or battery levels, if your mobile PC has two batteries) pops up, as shown in Figure 16.10. If the battery gets low, a battery alarm will appear to prompt you to plug in fast.

You can choose another power plan to help conserve battery power or not, depending on what you are currently doing with your mobile PC. The power plans that Windows 7 offers by default generally work by adjusting system (CPU) performance. These plans are:

• **Balanced**. Adjusts the CPU speed based on the programs you are using. This setting works in general-purpose circumstances.

• **Power saver**. Reduces system performance to conserve power. You might use this setting if you will be away from power for some time and are performing less intense activities like typing a letter or working on a spreadsheet. This setting is not available on the *Battery Meter* icon's menu.

• **High performance**. This setting consumes the most power, but allows maximum system performance in situations where you need it. For example, you might use this setting if you are delivering a presentation that includes animations and video, which consume a lot of power.

Windows 7 enables you to use one of a couple of methods to change to another power plan on your mobile PC.

Here's How

To change power plans on a mobile PC:

1a. Click the *Battery Meter* icon, then click the desired power level, and click the desktop.
    OR

1b. Choose Start, *Control Panel*, Hardware and Sound, Windows Mobility Center. Open the drop-down list in the Battery Status section, and click the desired plan.
    OR

1c. Choose Start, *Control Panel*, Hardware and Sound, Power Options. Click the desired power plan.

If the Power Saver option does not appear, click the down-pointing arrow next to Show Additional Plans.

Certain parts of the mobile computer hardware can be power hogs. For example, on many mobile computers, the display consumes more power than other parts such as the hard disk or CPU. You can edit plan settings and create custom power plans that manage how long the system can be idle before the display shuts off or the computer goes to sleep. Chapter 12 presented the details about creating and managing power plans. As a reminder, you can find power plan settings by choosing Start, *Control Panel*, System and Security, Change Battery Settings (under Power Options), Change Plan Settings (under the plan to change). Another way to get there is to choose *Start, Control Panel*, Hardware and Sound, Change Battery Settings (under Power Options), Change Plan Settings (under the plan to change).

Note: *The exercises in the remainder of the chapter assume that you have access to a mobile computer, either your own or one provided by your instructor for class use.*

 Exercise 4

1. Unplug the mobile PC so that it is running on battery power.
2. Wait a few minutes, and then move the mouse pointer over the *Battery Meter* icon in the notification area.
3. Capture a screen shot of the battery level, paste it into Paint, and save the file as **C16E04S03**.
4. Click the *Battery Meter* icon in the notification area.
5. Click *High Performance*.
6. Capture a screen shot with the power plan selections still on-screen, paste it into Paint, and save the file as **C16E04S06**.
7. Click the desktop.
8. Change back to the prior power plan.
9. Submit the screen shots via e-mail or USB flash drive to your instructor, as required. If you plan to continue using the computer, plug it back in.

Conducting a Presentation

Sharing information over a network or the Internet works for many purposes. But sometimes, you need to deliver your message in person. Mobile computers enable you to carry your on-screen presentation with you and deliver it to the people who need to see it, whether you are trying to land a new client, report results at the home office, or train a group of colleagues about a new procedure. This section presents the mobile computing features that will help you present more effectively on the road.

Setting Up the System to Present

As noted earlier, a key time when you do not want the monitor powering down or other such interruptions is when you are delivering a live presentation. Windows 7 enables you to tell the system that you are delivering a presentation. When you do so, the system will not sleep or shut down, and no pop-up notifications will appear in the notifications area. You also can turn off any screen saver in use, change volume, and display an alternate background for the desktop.

Here's How ➤ ### To turn on presentation settings:

1. Choose Start, *Control Panel*, Hardware and Sound, Windows Mobility Center.
2. In the Presentation Settings area, click Turn on.

To turn on and adjust presentation settings:

1. Choose Start, *Control Panel*, Hardware and Sound, Adjust settings before giving a presentation (under Windows Mobility Center).
2. Mark the *I am currently giving a presentation* check box.
3. Adjust other settings as desired.
4. Click OK.

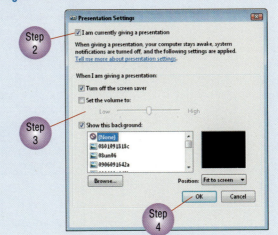

After you turn on presentation settings, an icon for presentation settings appears in the notification area. You can double-click that icon to reopen the Presentation Settings dialog box to make changes. You also can right-click the icon and click *Stop Presentation* to turn off presentation settings.

The Windows Mobility Center (Figure 16.9) also includes settings you might want to use when presenting, and using it is a good option because you can minimize and maximize it easily to change settings. You can drag the Volume slider to change system volume. If you already made changes in the Presentation Settings dialog box and merely want to turn those presentation settings on and off, you can click the Turn on/Turn off button in the *Presentation Settings* section.

Displaying a Presentation on a Projector or Other External Device

When you deliver a presentation, it is increasingly common to need to connect to a larger external monitor or projector to deliver the presentation at a size that is more visible to audience members. Windows 7 offers functionality to ensure that an external display is connected and functioning in the manner that you need.

To work with an external display:

Here's How

1. Connect the display to the external display port on the mobile PC, and power on the display, if needed.
2. Click Start, *Control Panel*, Appearance and Personalization. Under Display, click Connect to an external display.
3. Open the *Multiple displays* drop-down list and choose one of the following:
   a. Choose *Duplicate these displays* in normal circumstances, when you want to deliver the presentation normally.
   b. Choose *Extend these displays* when you want to display different information on your desktop and the external display. For example, you would click this option to use PowerPoint's Presenter view.
   c. Choose *Show desktop only on 1* or *Show desktop only on 2* when you want the presentation to appear on the external display and want to shut off the mobile PC display to conserve power. (Click Identify if you need help determining which monitor is 1 and which is 2.)

4. Click OK.

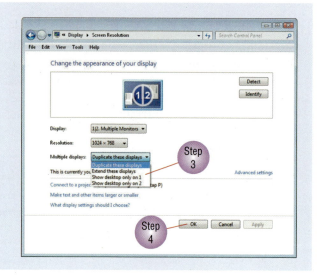

Note: *Depending on the nature of the display you connect, Windows 7 may automatically change the color scheme or other display settings.*

If you choose to show the presentation on an external display only, you can press the fn key plus the display key (one of the function or F keys with an external display icon on it in the same color as the label on the fn key button) on the mobile computer to toggle between showing the presentation externally, on the mobile PC display, or both.

When Windows 7 does not automatically detect an external display, you can click the Connect display button in the *External Display* section of Windows Mobility Center (Start, *Control Panel*, Hardware and Sound, Windows Mobility Center) to detect and connect to the monitor. When you do so, a panel of options appears from which to select the display mode (Computer Only, Duplicate, Extend, or Projector Only). Or, you can choose Start, *All Programs, Accessories, Connect to a Network Projector*, and follow the prompts that appear to search for and connect to a projector, as described in the next section.

Connecting to a Projector on the Network

Some external projector models now can be networked. If such a projector is connected to a network and you can connect wirelessly to that network, it means that you can deliver your presentation on the projector without physically connecting to the projector. To do so, however, you need to set up a connection to the network projector under Windows 7.

To start this process, choose Start, *All Programs, Accessories, Connect to a Network Projector*. In the Connect to a Network Projector dialog box that appears (Figure 16.11), you can click *Search for a projector (recommended)* to have Windows 7 look on the network for you and then display a list of available projectors. Click the projector to which you want to connect in the list, and then click Connect. If a password prompt appears, enter the password and click Connect again.

Figure 16.11 Choose whether to search for or enter the address for a network projector.

If you instead click *Enter the projector network address*, the next dialog box prompts you to enter the *Network address* and *Projector password*. Type in those two items (see the projector address examples in the dialog box), and click Connect.

Once the system connects to the projector, you can access controls for working with the projector in the Network Presentation dialog box that minimizes to the taskbar. In particular, use its *Disconnect* choice to disconnect when you finish the presentation so that another user can access the network projector.

 Exercise 5

Work with Presentation Settings

1. Choose Start, *Control Panel*, Hardware and Sound, Adjust settings before giving a presentation (under Windows Mobility Center).
2. Mark the *I am currently giving a presentation* check box.
3. Click the *Set the volume to* check box, and drag the slider to the right to set the volume to 70 or so, according to the pop-up tip that appears.
4. Capture a screen shot, paste it into Paint, and save the file as **C16E05S04**.
5. Click OK.
6. Click the window Close (X) button to close Control Panel.
7. Right-click the presentation settings icon in the notification area.
8. Capture a screen shot with the icon menu choices open, paste it into Paint, and save the file as **C16E05S08**.
9. Right-click the presentation settings icon in the notification area again, if needed, and click *Stop Presentation*.
10. Submit the screen shots via e-mail or USB flash drive to your instructor, as required.

Working with Power Conservation Options on a Mobile Computer

Chapter 1 explained that the sleep and hibernate modes help conserve power while preserving information for when you are ready to resume work. These features are worth a second mention for mobile computer users, because power conservation becomes critical when using the system on the road. These modes reduce the mobile system's power consumption to 1–2 percent of the norm.

Using Sleep Mode

When you put the system to sleep, Windows 7 saves your files and information about which programs are opened both in system memory and on the computer's hard disk (or just system memory for a mobile computer); then it puts the computer in a lower-power state. (It does not shut the computer down.) When you wake the system up, your programs and files reappear on the desktop after a brief time, as little as several seconds.

Your work remains secure when the system is asleep because if your account is password-protected, you must enter the password when you wake up the system. Unauthorized users therefore cannot wake up your computer and pry. You also can set up the system to go to sleep after a particular timeframe. If you then leave the computer unattended, it will save and secure your work automatically, plus save power.

To put a computer to sleep, click Start, and then click the Power button, which resembles the physical (hardware) power button on the computer. On many mobile computer models, you can use the hardware power button to put the system to sleep, as well. Press the power button partially down and hold it for a few seconds. When you use the hardware power button in this way, Windows 7 calls it the sleep button.

When the computer goes to sleep, the computer's power and disk lights may remain on, and the hardware power button might blink slowly. To wake the computer back up, press the hardware power button quickly. If a logon screen prompts you to enter your account password, type your password in the *Password* text box, and then press Enter or click the blue right-pointing arrow button to the right of the *Password* text box.

Hibernating the System

Mobile computers by default also offer the hibernate state. Hibernate saves the current work session, but shuts down the computer. Restarting opens your files and programs back on the desktop; however, this process works more slowly than waking up a sleeping computer. To hibernate the system, click Start, then point to the right-pointing arrow button that is on the Start menu to the right of the Power and Lock buttons, and click *Hibernate* in the pop-up menu that appears. Restart with the hardware power button to resume work.

Note: *Sleep and hibernate settings work with power plans in Windows 7. The BIOS (basic input/output system) for the computer must support sleep or hibernate for those modes to be available.*

Note: *If hibernate is not available, that means that hybrid sleep is enabled. To turn if off so you can hibernate the system, choose Start, Control Panel, System and Security. Click Power Options, click Change when the computer sleeps, and then click Change advanced power settings. In the list that appears in the Power Options dialog box, expand the sleep item, and then change the setting for Allow hybrid sleep to Off.*

Adjusting Sleep and Hibernate Settings

By default on a mobile computer, if you leave the system in sleep mode for three hours and the battery power gets too low, sleep mode will make sure all your work is saved to the hard disk and then will shut down the system. Also, by default you can put the system to sleep by shutting the computer's lid. Open the lid to wake it back up as usual.

You can change this functionality to suit how you use your mobile computer. For example, it makes more sense to have the computer hibernate when you shut the mobile PC lid, because that typically means you will not be resuming work for a while. You can change how the power button and lid work with sleep and hibernate using Control Panel.

1. Choose Start, *Control Panel*, Change battery settings (under Mobile PC).
2. Click either Choose what the power buttons do or Choose what closing the lid does in the list of tasks at the left side of Control Panel. (Either choice leads to the same location.)
3. Choose the desired mode from each drop-down list as needed.
4. Click Save changes.
5. Click the window Close (X) button to close Control Panel.

 ## Exercise 6

Sleep and Hibernate the Mobile System

1. Shut the lid of the mobile system. Or, press the hardware power button halfway down until the system begins to sleep.
2. Open the lid of the mobile system, if needed.
3. Press the hardware power button quickly to wake up the system.
4. Type your password, and press Enter at the logon screen.
5. Click Start, *Control Panel* and leave the window open.
6. Click Start, click the right-pointing arrow to the right of the Lock button, and click Hibernate. Wait 10–15 seconds for the system to put itself into hibernate mode.
7. Press the hardware power button all the way down to turn the system back on.
8. Type your password, and press Enter at the logon screen. The Control Panel window should appear on the desktop.
9. Click the window Close (X) button to close Control Panel.

CHAPTER Summary

- Synchronization (or sync) is the process of keeping multiple copies of the same file (on different computers) matched with each other. In Windows 7, syncing is handled via the Sync Center.

- Choose Start, *All Programs*, *Accessories*, *Sync Center* to start Sync Center.

- To sync, a folder or file must be marked as available for offline use. To mark a folder or file as such, right-click the folder or file, and then click *Always available offline*. (If the command is unavailable, the Offline Files feature needs to be enabled, as described in the section "Making Files Available Offline.")

- You can sync a portable device such as a digital music player, PDA, or compatible mobile phone with Sync Center. With Sync Center open, attach the device to your system and power it on. In the Tasks list at the left side of Sync Center, click Set up new sync partnerships, click the device to add in the list that appears, and then click Set up above the list. This establishes the sync partnership and performs the first sync.

- To schedule synchronization, select the item to schedule, click the Schedule button in the Sync Center, and then follow the prompts to set up a specific time and interval.

- To initiate a manual sync, select the item to sync and click the Sync button in the Sync Center.

- To resolve a sync conflict, open the Sync Center, click View sync conflicts in the Tasks list, click a conflict on the list, and then click Resolve. Select the version you want to keep, or choose to keep both versions.

- Although Offline Files works with the Sync Center, you can enable and disable this feature as needed. Choose Start, *All Programs*, *Accessories*, *Sync Center*. In the Offline Files dialog box, click Enable offline files on the General tab. (If Online Files is already running and you need to disable it, the button reads Disable offline files, so click it.) Click OK, and then follow the prompts to restart the system.

- To view files when working offline, click Start, *All Programs*, *Accessories*, *Sync Center*. Click Manage offline files in the list at the left. In the Offline Files dialog box, click the View your offline files button.

- You can disconnect from the location on the network manually to work offline. To disconnect and go offline, click the Work offline button that appears on the command bar when you are browsing to a location that is marked for offline use. After you click the button, it changes to the Work online button, which you can click to go back online.

- You also can switch to online viewing when browsing the Web in Internet Explorer (IE). To go offline after you have viewed a Web page, click Tools on the IE toolbar, and click *Work Offline*. To resume working online, click Tools, *Work Offline* again.

- With a Remote Desktop connection, you can connect to another computer over the local network or the Internet. Not only can you access files on the computer, but you also can use the programs installed on that computer and possibly other resources, such as printers, if the network permits.

- The computer that holds the files, programs, and other resources to access is called the *host*. The computer that you will use to access the host from a remote location is called the *client*.

- For a Remote Desktop connection to work, both computers must be connected directly to the company network or connected remotely to the company network, the Internet, and on the same workgroup. The network must allow permission for this type of connection. Windows Firewall also has to be set on both computers to allow Remote Desktop as an Exception. Also, if authentication is not required, then that security feature must be turned off on the host computer.

- Click Start, *Control Panel*, System and Security, Allow remote access (under System) to set up your computer to enable Remote Desktop connections.

- You can specify which users are allowed to connect to your system remotely.

- To connect to the host via Remote Desktop Connection, choose Start, *All Programs*, *Accessories*, *Remote Desktop Connection*. In the Remote Desktop Connection dialog box, type the name of the computer to connect to on the network. Click Connect, and then enter your user name and password when prompted.

- To sign in to People Near Me in order to work with collaboration programs, choose Start, *Control Panel*, and type People in the *search* box. Under People Near Me, click Sign in or out of People Near Me, click the *Sign in to People Near Me* option button, specify settings, and click OK.

- Windows Mobility Center provides the settings you need for mobile computer activities such as choosing another power management method, syncing, and working with settings for presentations.

- To start Windows Mobility Center, choose Start, *Control Panel*, Hardware and Sound, Windows Mobility Center.

- When you are using your mobile computer on battery power alone, get in the habit of moving the mouse pointer over the *Battery Meter* icon in the system notification area to see remaining battery power.

- You can choose another power plan to help conserve battery power or not, depending on what you are currently doing with your mobile PC. To change power plans, click the *Battery Meter* icon, then click the desired power level, and click the desktop.

- Windows 7 enables you to tell the system that you are delivering a presentation so that the system will not sleep or shut down and no pop-up notifications will appear in the notifications area. You also can turn off any screen saver in use, change volume, and display an alternate background for the desktop.

- To turn on presentation settings, choose Start, *Control Panel*, Hardware and Sound, Adjust settings before giving a presentation (under Windows Mobility Center). Mark the *I am currently giving a presentation* check box. Adjust other settings, as desired, and then click OK.

- When Windows 7 does not automatically detect an external display, or after you have set one up with the New Display Detected dialog box, you can choose Start, *All Programs*, *Accessories*, *Connect to a Projector* and then make a choice to connect to the monitor.

- The sleep and hibernate modes help conserve power while preserving information for when you are ready to resume work.

- To put a computer to sleep, click Start, and then point to the right-pointing arrow to the right of the Shut down button, and click *Sleep*. To wake up the computer, press the hardware power button quickly. If a logon screen prompts you to enter your account password, type your password in the *password* text box, and then press Enter.

- To hibernate the system, click Start, then point to the right-pointing arrow button to the right of the Shut down button, and click *Hibernate*. Restart with the hardware power button to resume work.

CONCEPTS Check

Completion: Answer the following questions on a blank sheet of paper or in a Word document.

Part 1

MULTIPLE CHOICE

1. From where is it easiest to access the Sync Center?
   a. Control Panel
   b. Personal folder
   c. Documents library
   d. Start menu, under *All Programs*, *Accessories*

2. Where do you go to enable and disable offline files?
   a. Windows Meeting Space
   b. Sync Center
   c. Offline Files dialog box
   d. People Near Me

3. You must _____ the system when you enable or disable offline files.
   a. sleep
   b. hibernate
   c. backup
   d. restart

4. What do you have to create when you want to use Sync Center to sync a portable device?
   a. People Near Me
   b. Contacts sharing
   c. Sync partnership
   d. Offline Files

5. When you want to sync a location automatically at a later time, what can you do?
   a. Create a synchronization schedule.
   b. Create a task.
   c. Both A and B.
   d. None of the above.

6. The _____ enables you to change common Mobile PC settings.
   a. Sync Center
   b. Network and Sharing Center
   c. People Near Me
   d. Windows Mobility Center

7. Changing the _____ adjusts the rate at which the mobile PC depletes the battery.
   a. battery monitor
   b. power plan
   c. battery setting
   d. screen saver

8. Enable _____ to reduce on-screen interruptions during a presentation.
   a. ratings
   b. captions
   c. presentation settings
   d. presentation pointers

9. Attach a _____ to a mobile PC to give a presentation.
   a. external monitor
   b. digital camera
   c. projector
   d. Either a or c

10. Use the _____ button to wake a sleeping system.
    a. Start menu
    b. Start menu power
    c. hardware power
    d. Close (X)

SHORT ANSWER

11. Explain briefly how offline files work.

_____

12. Explain how to make a file always available offline.

_____

13. Suppose you have a file set up to be always available offline, and the network is down. Where can you go to see your files?

_____

14. What causes a synchronization conflict to occur?

_____

15. What is Remote Desktop Connection for?

_____

16. What is People Near Me for?

_____

17. Explain one way to check battery power status.

_____

18. Explain how to display Windows Mobility Center.

_____

19. Name the command used to start the process for connecting to a network projector.

_____

20. Name at least two reasons to hibernate a mobile PC.

_____

SKILLS Check

Save all solution files to the default Documents folder, or any alternate folder specified by your instructor.

Guided Check

SET UP OFFLINE FOLDERS AND SYNC

1. Set up a folder for viewing offline.
   a. Click Start.
   b. Click *Computer*.
   c. Navigate to the folder on the network.
   d. Right-click the folder.
   e. Click *Always available offline*.

2. Take a screen shot.
   a. Right-click the synched folder again.
   b. Capture a screen print of the window, and save it as **C16A01** in Paint.
3. Close the window by clicking the window Close (X) button.
4. Submit the screen shot via e-mail or USB flash drive to your instructor, as required.

Assessment 2 — MANAGE THE SYNCHRONIZATION SCHEDULE

1. Start Sync Center.
   a. Click Start.
   b. Click *All Programs*.
   c. Click *Accessories*.
   d. Click *Sync Center*.
2. Click Offline Files.
3. Click Schedule.
4. Mark all the check boxes if they are not already marked, and click Next.
5. Click *At a scheduled time*.
6. Select today's date, and select a time 15 minutes from now.
7. Clear the *Repeat every* check box.
8. Capture a screen print of the window, and save it as **C16A02S08**.
9. Click More Options.
10. Mark the *The computer is no longer running on external power* check box.
11. Click OK.
12. Click Next.
13. In the *Name* box, type your name and today's date.

    Tip: You cannot use / signs in the date; use dashes to separate the parts of the date instead.

14. Capture a screen print of the window, and save it as **C16A02S14**.
15. Click Save schedule.
16. Submit the screen shots via e-mail or USB flash drive to your instructor, as required.
17. Wait for 15 minutes, and watch for sync activity on the system.
18. If required by your instructor, delete the sync schedule.

Assessment 3 — DISABLE AND ENABLE OFFLINE FILES

1. Click Start, *All Programs, Accessories, Sync Center*.
2. Click Manage offline files.
3. Click Disable offline files.
4. Enter an administrator password in the User Account Control dialog box, if it appears, and click Yes.
5. Take a screen shot, paste the shot into Paint, and save it as **C16A03S05**.
6. Click OK.
7. Click Yes to restart the system.
8. Click Start, *Control Panel*, Network and Internet, Offline Files.
9. Click Enable Offline Files.
10. Enter an administrator password in the User Account Control dialog box, and click Yes.
11. Take a screen shot, paste the shot into Paint, and save it as **C16A03S11**.
12. Click Yes to restart the system.
13. Submit the screen shots via e-mail or USB flash drive to your instructor, as required.

Assessment ## CHOOSING ANOTHER POWER SCHEME IN MOBILITY CENTER

4

1. Start Windows Mobility Center.
   a. Click Start.
   b. Click *Control Panel*.
   c. Click Hardware and Sound.
   d. Click Windows Mobility Center.
2. Change to the Power saver power plan.
   a. Open the drop-down list in the *Battery Status* area.
   b. Click *Power saver*.
   c. Take a screen shot, paste the shot into Paint, and save it as **C16A04**.
3. Click the window Close (X) button to close Windows Mobility Center.
4. Click the window Close (X) button to close Control Panel.
5. Submit the screen shot via e-mail or USB flash drive to your instructor, as required.

On Your Own

Assessment ## SYNCHRONIZING FILES FOR A TRIP

5

Suppose you are going on a trip and taking your notebook computer with you. You need to make sure that all the data files for this course have up-to-date copies on the notebook computer's hard disk. Describe step-by-step how you would do the following:

- Make the data files from the desktop PC available offline to the notebook PC.
- Manually synchronize the files just before you leave on your trip.

Write down the detailed steps to make these things happen, and submit them to your instructor as **C16A05** for grading.

Assessment ## VIEW THE OFFLINE FILES

6

Now assume you are on your trip and need to look at the files you synced in the prior assessment. Write down the detailed steps to do so, and submit them to your instructor as **C16A06** for grading.

Assessment ## SHOW MOBILE COMPUTER CONTENT ON ANOTHER DISPLAY

7

This exercise requires a mobile computer and an external monitor or projector. If you do not have access to a mobile PC and external monitor, your instructor may provide them, and you can work in teams to complete this project.

1. Start Windows Mobility Center on the mobile PC.
2. Power on the external monitor or projector.
3. Connect the monitor or projector to the display port on the mobile PC.
4. Open the Screen Resolution section of the Control Panel (Start, *Control Panel*, and click Adjust Screen Resolution under Appearance and Personalization.)
5. Open the *Multiple Displays* drop-down list and choose *Extend these displays*. Take a screen shot, paste the shot into Paint, and save it as **C16A07**.
6. Close the Windows Mobility Center and the Control Panel.
7. Display the contents of the \Public\Public Pictures\Sample Pictures folder as an on-screen slide show. If the slide show does not appear on the external display, use the Fn+display (F key) key combination on the mobile PC keyboard to toggle to the right mode.
8. When the slide show finishes, close the folder window.

9. Go back to the Screen Resolution dialog box and set the *Multiple Displays* setting to *Duplicate these displays*.
10. Disconnect the external display and turn it off.
11. Submit the screen shot via e-mail or USB flash drive to your instructor, as required.

Assessment ## CHANGE HIBERNATE SETTINGS, HIBERNATE, AND RESTART

This assessment requires a mobile PC.

8

1. Choose Start, *Control Panel*, Hardware and Sound, Change battery settings (under Power Options).
2. Click Choose what closing the lid does in the list of tasks.
3. In both the On battery and Plugged in columns, open the *When I close the lid* drop-down list, and click *Hibernate*.
4. Take a screen shot, paste the shot into Paint, and save it as **C16A08**.
5. Click Save changes, but leave the Control Panel window open.
6. Close the lid of the mobile PC.
7. After a few moments, open the lid, and then press the hardware power button to turn the system back on.
8. If prompted, type your password and press Enter.
9. Submit the screen shot via e-mail or USB flash drive to your instructor, as required.
10. Change the *When I close the lid* setting back to its original setting, and close the window.

CHALLENGE Project

You are working at home and have the ability to connect to your office computer with a Remote Desktop connection. In WordPad, describe the overall process for setting up and making a Remote Desktop connection, and list at least two reasons why you would do so. Save the file as **C16A09S01** and submit it to your instructor, as required.

If you and a classmate can connect over a network and make a Remote Desktop connection to each other's computer, do that procedure, capture a screen shot, save it as **C16A09S02**, and submit it to your instructor, as required.

Glossary

Accelerators A new feature in IE 8 that enables you to perform tasks with selected content, such as mapping or blogging about a selected location

Account In Windows Live Mail, a collection of settings that enables the program to send and receive e-mail via your ISP's mail servers (or to work with newsgroup messages)

Active (current) window The working window on-screen, where you can make selections and perform other actions

Active content Online content that is interactive or animated, also loosely including pop-ups and certain downloads that may be required to run such content

Adware A type of malware that pops up ads or redirects your Web browser

Aero desktop experience The new default appearance for Windows 7 on fully compatible systems, featuring a transparency feature called glass

Aero Peek thumbnail A thumbnail image of a file that pops up when you point to the minimized file's taskbar button

Align icons to grid A feature that snaps an icon into an alignment with a desktop grid when you move the icon

Allocation unit size The size of the storage units on the disk used for storing data

Application (program) A set of instructions for performing a particular task or set of tasks, such as word processing or drawing a picture

Arranging Summarizing the items in a library into stacks based on a property

Attributes On/off flags set for a file, such as read-only

Auto arrange icons A feature that arranges desktop icons to fill the desktop grid slots in order

Auto-hide A feature that hides the taskbar unless the mouse pointer is over the taskbar location

Auto run.inf An instruction file that tells Windows 7 what to do (for example, run a Setup utility) when the disc is inserted

Available offline A folder identified to be synchronized via the Offline Files feature

Binary A numbering system consisting of only 1 and 0

Bing The latest Internet search engine from Microsoft

Bit A single binary digit

Blu-ray A high-capacity type of DVD disc that stores 25 GB of data per layer

Bluetooth A type of short-range wireless interface designed to allow PCs and devices to communicate without cables

Browsing Displaying and reading Web pages in whatever order suits you

Byte A group of eight bits forming a single character of information

CD Compact Disc, a removable, optical disc that stores about 700 MB of data

Check Disk A Windows 7 utility that finds and corrects file system errors and, optionally, relocates data away from bad sectors

Client An end-user PC in a network

Client The remote computer accessing the host resources during a Remote Desktop connection

Client/server A type of network in which one or more servers administers the network, providing services to the client PCs

Close To remove a file from the program window and working memory

Color scheme The combination of colors and settings applied to on-screen elements

Command prompt A line of text displayed by an operating system to indicate that it is prepared for you to type in commands

Command An action that you tell a program to perform

Compatibility View A view in Internet Explorer that enables it to better display sites and pages designed for older browser versions

Compression algorithm A mathematical formula used to remove wasted space in a file so it takes up less space on the disk

Compression Using an algorithm that reduces file size

Contact A listing with e-mail address and other contact information for a person entered into the Contacts feature in Windows Live Mail

Control Panel The central location where you can change system preferences and settings, from the desktop appearance to programs installed

Controls The various types of selection mechanisms in a dialog box

Cookies Small plain text files that store your settings for certain Web sites

CPU Central Processing Unit, also called the processor; the main microchip that serves as the brain of the PC

Crash A situation in which a program ceases to operate normally

Default gateway The IP address of the port that leads out of your local subnet and into the larger network or the Internet

Defragment To reorganize the file storage on a disk drive so that as many files as possible are stored contiguously

Desktop The starting point for activities in Windows 7, where you also can view and organize information

Details Click this button for more detailed information about the connection

Device driver A piece of software that works with Windows to send and receive instructions for a particular piece of hardware

Dialog box launcher A button found in the lower-right corner of a group on a Ribbon tab that you click to open a dialog box

Digital camera A device that captures pictures and stores them on digital storage media

Digital picture An image or picture saved in digital format for use in computer documents and Web pages

Disk compression A means of decreasing the amount of space that files occupy on a disk by storing them more compactly

Disk drive A mechanical device that reads and writes disks

Display adapter A circuit board or built-in component to which the monitor attaches, and which translates between the PC and the monitor

Domain A client/server network running Windows Server software on the server

DOS Disk Operating System, an operating system that predates Windows, now obsolete

Driver A piece of software that acts as a translator between a hardware device and Windows 7

Dual-layer disc A type of DVD that stores data in two layers, enabling it to approximately double its capacity (to 8.5GB)

Duration This shows how long the connection has been up-and-running; when you restart the PC, it resets the counter

DVD Digital Versatile Disc (or Digital Video Disc), a removable, optical disc that stores about 4.7 GB of data per layer

E-mail account In Windows Live Mail, a collection of settings that enables the program to send and receive e-mail via your ISP's mail servers (or to work with newsgroup messages)

E-mail address The identifier that specifies where an e-mail address should be delivered, including a name, an @ symbol, and the ISP domain. For example, *janet22@emcp.com* (pronounced "janet 22 at emcp dot com") could be the e-mail address for a user signed up with an ISP that has the *emcp.com* domain

E-mail Short for "electronic mail," e-mail provides the ability to send and receive messages via a wired or wireless network, or more broadly, the Internet

Event A time period for which you have scheduled a particular activity in Windows Live Mail Calendar

Exiting or shutting down Closing a program to remove its instructions and open files from RAM

Extended partition A secondary partition, in addition to the primary partition(s)

Fast User Switching Changing between user accounts without shutting down files or programs for any logged on user

FAT16 A 16-bit file system, now mostly obsolete, used with MS-DOS and Windows 95

FAT32 A 32-bit file system, now mostly obsolete, used with Windows 98 and Windows Me

Favorite page A frequently visited Web site or page that is saved in the list in the Favorites Center for easy access

File or document Digital information that you create and save with a name for later retrieval; a file may include programming instructions, an image, text, or any other type of content

File attachment A file created in a program other than your e-mail software that you designate to be sent along with an e-mail message

File list The area in a folder or library window that shows the files and folders in the folder or library

File name extension A period and additional letters appended to the file name to identify the file format

File properties Information about a file or information attached to a file

File System A set of rules for how the operating system stores and retrieves files on a disk

Filtering Displaying only certain items based on a property

Firewall Software or hardware that prevents unauthorized access to ports

First-party cookie A cookie placed on your hard disk by the Web site you are visiting

Flag Identifies received messages that might require further attention by applying a flag icon

Flash card reader An internal or USB drive that reads and writes removable flash RAM cards

Flash RAM A static type of memory used as an alternative to disk storage

Floppy disk A flexible plastic disk encased in a hard square plastic shell, holding 1.44 MB of data

Folder An organizing unit for storing related files together in groups, also known as a location

Font A typeface, a style of lettering, appearing either on the screen or in print

Fragmented file A file that is stored in multiple noncontiguous clusters on a hard disk

Gadgets The mini-programs that deliver information and tools on the desktop

Gallery The images that Windows Live Photo Gallery tracks (displays) because you have either imported the images or added the folder holding the images

Graphics tablet An external input device, which generally connects to the computer via a USB port, and with which you can select commands, give user input, and draw images using a stylus (pen)

Group A named set of individual users to which the same permissions should be assigned

Grouping Arranging items into grouped sections of a list based on a property

Guest account A limited-access user account designed to be used by anonymous users who do not have a regular account on the PC

Hang When the computer appears to freeze up and stop working during a particular operation

Hard disk drive A sealed drive unit that contains a set of metal disks

Hard reboot or **restart** Restarting the system by powering it off and back on

Hardware Physical computer parts

Hardware The physical components of a PC, such as the keyboard, mouse, disk drives, and CPU

Hibernate A more advanced shutdown state that saves your work and shuts the system down; your in-process work reappears on the desktop when you restart your system

History An IE feature that tracks Web sites and pages you have visited within a recent time period—by default the previous 20 days

Homegroup A connected group of Windows 7 computers in a home (P2P) network

Host The computer that holds the files, programs, and resources to be used during a Remote Desktop connection

Hot-pluggable Able to be connected or disconnected while the PC is up and running

Hybrid Sleep A power-saving mode for a desktop computer where open documents and programs are saved to the hard disk before the computer enters the low-power state

Hyperlink An item on a Web page that you can click to display another Web page or to download information

Hypertext A document format or system in which the document contains links to other content

Icon A small picture that represents an item (object) or choice in Windows 7 and Windows programs

Inbox The Windows Live Mail folder that holds e-mail messages you have received

Indexing A process that creates an index, an internal information set about a location, used to enable faster searching

Internet Protocol (IP) address A numeric address that uniquely describes the address of a PC or other network-aware component on a network or on the Internet

Internet time server A Web site that provides highly precise times

Intranet A private network, usually within a company or organization, using the same types of content and the same protocols as the Internet

Jump List A menu of frequently used documents and commands that you can access for a program via the taskbar or Start menu

Junk e-mail filter A Windows Live Mail feature that automatically moves likely junk e-mail messages to the Junk E-mail folder

Junk e-mail or **spam** Like paper junk mail, these are commercial e-mail messages sent to you without request

Library A location for working with a particular type of file; each library may monitor a number of storage locations to identify and track a particular type of file such as a digital picture

Library pane The area above the file list in a library window that shows the library's name and how many locations it monitors, as well as presenting a menu for arranging the library contents

Live File System A type of CD and DVD file system that enables discs to be written to multiple times

Local area network (LAN) A network in which the computers are nearby one another, such as in the same building

Local file permission The permission to access a file belonging to another user on the same PC

Local printer A printer attached directly to your PC

Lock A state that hides the desktop without shutting down the system or changing its power consumption

Log off To exit your user account and desktop without shutting down the system

Magnetic disk A disk platter that stores data in patterns of magnetic polarity

Mail server A computer with software that enables it to manage e-mail sending, receiving, and storage

Malware A generic term meaning software designed to harm your computer in some way

Mastered A type of CD and DVD file system that requires files to be written to the disc all at once

MathML An XML-based standard for describing mathematical expressions in programs, published by the W3C Math Working Group (www.w3.org/Math)

Maximize To increase a window to full-screen size

Menu A list of commands

Message body The text for an e-mail message, entered or viewed in the message window

Message header Also called the e-mail header, this is the information that appears at the head (top) of the message, including date sent, sender, recipient(s), and subject

Message list The pane that lists the e-mail messages in the currently selected folder of the Folder pane

Message window (or composition window) The window where you compose and address an e-mail message in Windows Live Mail; also refers to the window where you read and respond to a received message

Metadata Information attached to a file that provides descriptive data such as the author's name

Minimize Reduce a window to a taskbar icon to clear it from the desktop temporarily

Mirror To copy the complete contents of a drive to another drive

Modem Short for modulator/demodulator, a device that converts between digital computer data and analog, sound wave data and can be transmitted via telephone lines

Mouse A device that you roll and then press buttons on to control a desktop or notebook computer

Mouse pointer The on-screen graphical indicator whose movement corresponds with your movement of the mouse so that you can select objects

Multifunction device (MFD) A printer that also has other functions, such as scanner, copier, and fax machine

Multitask The ability of Windows 7 to have multiple activities underway at the same time, such as having multiple programs running and printing simultaneously

Network addressable storage (NAS) An external hard disk that is accessed through a network interface rather than locally through the Computer window

Network interface card (NIC) A circuit board, or a built-in component on a motherboard, that provides network connectivity for a PC

Network printer A printer attached to your network or shared by another PC on your network

Network sharing permission Permission to access a file stored on a different PC

Network A group of connected computers

Network-aware printer A printer with a built-in network interface card, capable of connecting directly to the network without going through a PC

Newsgroup An online message forum where users can read and post discussion topics, questions, and responses

Nonvolatile A type of storage that does not lose its data when not powered

Notification A message that pops up in the notification area to warn you about a situation that may require action or a settings change

NTFS New Technology File System, a 32-bit file system for Windows 2000, Windows XP, Windows Vista, and Windows 7 offering improvements over older file systems

Offline files Network files that are locally cached (saved) on your hard disk so that a copy will always be available even when the network is not functioning; also refers generically to the copies of the network files stored on your local computer

Open To load a file into the program window and working memory

Operating system (OS) The interface software that enables a user to work with system hardware and other software installed on the computer system

Operating system files Files that the operating system (Windows 7) needs to start the system and keep it running

Optical disc A disc platter that stores data in patterns of reflectivity

Outbox The Windows Live Mail folder that holds e-mail messages you have composed but not sent

Parent The location immediately above the current one in the drive hierarchy

Partition To logically divide up the space on a physical hard disk into one or more logical drives

Password A secret series of characters that must be entered to access an account or make changes

Password reset disk Data stored on a floppy disk or USB or other flash drive that enables you to reset your user account password if you forget it

Patch A program update intended to fix a problem with the original version of the program

Path The complete location of a file, including its disk letter and the folders in which it is located

Peer to peer (P2P) A network consisting only of client PCs

Persistent cookie A cookie that remains on your hard disk indefinitely

Personal folder The parent folder holding folders for a user's account

Phishing Using a fake Web site or e-mail to steal username and password information

Photo e-mail message A message where the Add photos button has been used to include a photo, making special formatting options such as adding a photo caption, available

Pin Designating an item such as a program or file to appear in the left column of the Start menu, for easy access

Plain text (.txt) A file format for document files that does not allow for or save any text formatting information

Player Library The collection of songs and other media items added into Windows Media Player

Playlist A list that specifies a group of songs for Media Player to play and the order in which it should play them

Plug and Play A standard that enables Windows to recognize and configure hardware automatically

Pop-up An extra widow that appears automatically as a result of a certain Web page being displayed

Port A numbered software channel that directs network input and output

Post A message submitted to a newsgroup

Primary partition A bootable partition; a disk drive must have at least one primary partition

Print to a file A method of converting a file to a more easily shared format

Printer driver The printer control file that interprets print information from an application

Quick Tabs A feature that displays a thumbnail of each open Web page (tab) from which you can select the tab to open

RAM (random access memory) The working menu that holds programs and unsaved work

RAM Random Access Memory, a type of memory used by the PC as its main temporary storage space for running programs

Rating Assigning a certain number of stars to a file to identify how much you like it or how important it is

Recipient A person to whom you are sending an e-mail message

Refresh rate The rate at which the display redraws the image on the screen

Registry The configuration database containing the settings Windows 7 needs to recognize your installed hardware and software, and to recall your user interface preferences

Reminder An on-screen message about an upcoming appointment

Resolution The dimensions of the current display size setting, expressed in pixels (dots) wide by pixels tall

Restore To return a window to its size before it was maximized

Ribbon An enhanced tabbed toolbar, where each tab offers commands for a particular overall activity and groups commands for more specific activities

Rich Text Format (.rtf) A basic document file format that preserves some text formatting

Rip Copy music from an audio CD and convert the songs to digital format

RJ-45 connector A plug, like a telephone plug but slightly wider, used to connect a PC to a network

Root directory The top level of a disk, outside of any of its folders

Router A type of switch that is able to direct traffic between different segments of a network

RSS (Really Simple Syndication) feeds Regularly updated Web site information such as news or pictures, which a user can visit or subscribe to; also called XML feeds, syndicated content, and Web feeds

Save Preserve a file's information on disk

Save location The folder where a library will physically store any file or folder created or copied to the library

Scanner A device that optically reads a hard copy of a picture to create a digital copy

Search engine A Web site/service that uses an index method to track and retrieve Web documents matching specified terms

Search Suggestions A feature that enables Bing to suggest searches that are more specific based on the search term you enter

Secure site A Web site that uses a secure protocol, https://, rather than the usual http:// to ensure that the communication is not intercepted or hacked

Server A computer dedicated to administering the network

Session cookie A cookie that is automatically deleted when the browser window is closed

Shake A feature that enables you to minimize several open windows at once by dragging the title bar for the window you want to keep open side to side at a rapid pace

Shortcut A pointer icon to the original file that it represents

Sig Short for *signature block*, this is identifying text that Windows Live Mail adds to the bottom of every e-mail message

Signal Quality These bars, shown only for wireless networks, indicate the signal strength between the PC and the wireless access point

Signed driver A driver that has been certified to work under a certain Windows version

Sleep A power-saving state that preserves your work in memory and on the hard disk so that you can resume working quickly

Slide show A feature that automatically displays each picture from a folder on-screen in sequence

Snail mail Slang term for postal mail, derived from the fact that postal mail is very slow relative to e-mail

Snap A feature that enables you to maximize or resize a window automatically by dragging the window to the edges of the screen

Soft font A font that is stored as a file on a PC rather than stored internally in the printer

Soft reboot or **restart** Using a menu command, keyboard combination, or reset button to restart the system

Software A computer program that typically performs a specific activity

Sorting Arranging items in a particular order based on a property

Speed This states the speed of the network in megabytes per second (Mbps); for a wireless network, this is typically 11 Mbps or 100 Mbps; for a wired network it is usually either 100.0 Mbps or 1000 Mbps

Spyware A type of malware that spies on your computer usage

SSID The identifier for the wireless access point or router

Stationery A set of background, font, and color selections applied to an e-mail message

Stream To play back music from another computer or digital media receiver on your network

Strong password A password that is difficult to guess; strong passwords have at least six characters, use numbers and letters, and use both capital and lowercase letters

Subnet mask A numeric code tat indicates hat part of the IP address represents the subnet and what part represents the individual address of the PC

Subnet A group of computers that share a common top-level identifier, similar to the telephone numbers in a certain area code

Subscribe To indicate that you want to download and receive messages from a particular newsgroup in Windows Live Mail

Switch A box into which PCs connect that directs network traffic among the PCs

Switch A forward slash and a letter or phrase code that specify a further aspect of how a command line command should run

Sync To make sure a connected device or mobile computer has the same up-to-date files as your main computer

System resources Areas of memory, interrupts, and/or DMA channels that are assigned to devices so they can communicate with the system

System Restore A utility that returns the Registry to an earlier version to correct problems caused by its modification

Tablet PC A type of laptop computer on which you can select commands and give other user input using a stylus (tablet pen) or sometimes a finger

Tag A file property that you assign to identify a folder or file in more detail so you can find information more easily

Task A work item you must complete

Taskbar A bar at the bottom of the desktop that you use to manage active tasks

Template A file with formatting and possible starter content that becomes the basis for a new file

Terminal adapter A communication device that sends and receives all-digital networking data, such as for a cable or DSL Internet connection

Theme A named collection of appearance settings you can apply to the Windows 7 desktop

Third-party cookie A cookie placed on your hard disk by an advertisement on a Web site you are visiting

Title bar The bar at the top of a window that lists the program name, as well as the name of any open file, and has controls for working with the window

Toggle A command or feature that can remain in an "on" (toggled on) or "off" (toggled off) state

Touchpad A built-in control device on a mobile computer or notebook computer that you can use instead of a mouse

URL (Uniform Resource Locator) The address of a Web page

USB flash drive A USB drive with a flash RAM chip permanently embedded

User Account Control (UAC) A security feature that restricts certain activities based on the permission level of the logged-in user

User Account Control (UAC) The overall Windows 7 security component that works with user accounts to prevent unauthorized system changes

User Account The user name, password, settings, permissions, and restrictions that govern how Windows 7 allows a particular user to work with the system

User input devices Devices such as the mouse and keyboard that enable you to give commands to and enter information into a computer

Viewer application An application that can read files printed or converted to a particular type of file format

Virtual folder A temporary logical grouping of files, such as the files resulting from filtering or searching

Virtual private network (VPN) A secure software tunnel that runs from one computer to another using the Internet as its conduit

Virus A self-replicating malicious program that spreads from one executable file to another

Visual suggestions Enhanced search functionality provided by a search partner that enables the Search Suggestions list to include images and information

Volume label A text description stored on the disk and displayed in the disk's properties in Windows

Web browser A program that enables you to view and retrieve information from the World Wide Web

Web mail A service that enables you to access your e-mail through a Web browser rather than a standalone e-mail program

Web page An HTML file (Web document) stored in a particular location

Web Slice A form of favorite that enables you to subscribe to updating content from a particular Web site

Wide area network (WAN) A network in which the computers are physically separated, such as in different buildings or cities

Wi-Fi The popular name for the 802.11 wireless RF standard, encompassing variants including 802.11b, 802.11g, and 802.11n

Window An independent frame that holds a program, document, or folder contents

Windows Explorer The main file management interface in Windows 7

Windows Media Audio (wma) The default file format to which Windows Media Player converts and saves song files

Windows Update A free service from Microsoft that downloads the latest patches, fixes, and updates from Microsoft's servers for Windows 7 and other Microsoft products

Wireless access point A switch for wireless networking

Wireless Properties Available only for wireless connections; click this button for a Properties box in which you can determine whether the connection should be established automatically and whether security should be enabled

Work offline Disconnect from the network or Internet and instead use offline files or offline Web information

Workgroup A peer-to-peer Windows-based network

World Wide Web A structure of linked documents stored on Web server computers connected to the Internet

Worm A self-replicating malicious program that spreads from one PC to another, infecting the PC itself rather than any individual file

Write-protect To make a floppy disk read-only by opening the read-only slider tab on the corner of the disk

XPS (XML Paper Specification) A portable document format from Microsoft that enables you to create an XPS (.xps) document from any program by printing to the Microsoft XPS Document Writer

INDEX